CONCRETE CANVAS

How street art is changing the way our cities look

Lee Bofkin

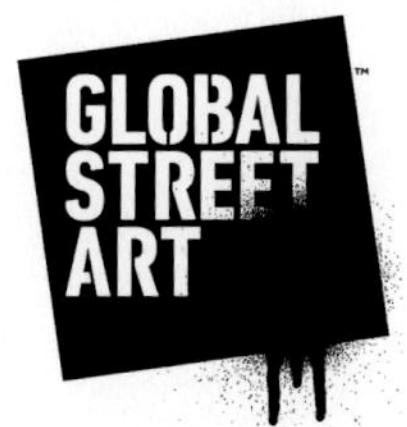

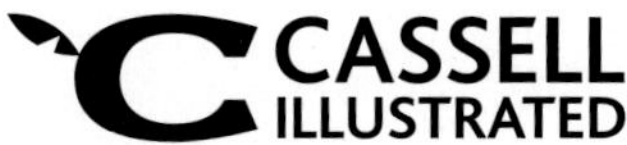

An Hachette UK Company
www.hachette.co.uk

First published in Great Britain in 2014 by
Cassell, a division of Octopus Publishing Group Ltd,
Endeavour House, 189 Shaftesbury Avenue,
London, WC2H 8JY
www.octopusbooks.co.uk

ISBN 978-1-84403-782-7

A CIP catalogue record for this book is available
from the British Library

Printed and bound in China

10 9 8 7 6 5 4 3 2 1

Commissioning Editor: Hannah Knowles
Editor: Pauline Bache
Production Manager: Peter Hunt

CONTENTS

To all the artists

Imagine a city
where graffiti
wasn't illegal,
a city where
everybody
could draw
wherever
they liked
Banksy

FOREWORD

The beauty of street art is that it teaches you to look at spaces not for what they are but for what they could be. Every day thousands of artists around the world make their art in spaces designed for altogether different purposes: an abandoned factory in the outskirts of Lisbon becomes a hidden gallery visited by only a handful of people each week; a New York fence, designed to exclude the public, becomes an ideal support for lengths of yarn, strung into elegant letters; the outside of a passenger train in Rome turns into a rolling canvas for those who are daring enough to paint it.

In the past 50 years, society has moved from regarding graffiti as a public nuisance and a menace to embracing elements of the scene, with street art and graffiti festivals celebrated around the globe, and some municipalities waking up to the possibility that these new types of muralism can beautify their cities.

In this book I look at how street art can be seen all over the world; the historical reasons behind street art developing as a distinct form – separate to gallery-based art – and how this should affect our perception of street art; the current trends in its production; and the curation of public space and the impact this is having. It's no exaggeration to say that cities which support street artists, or react less

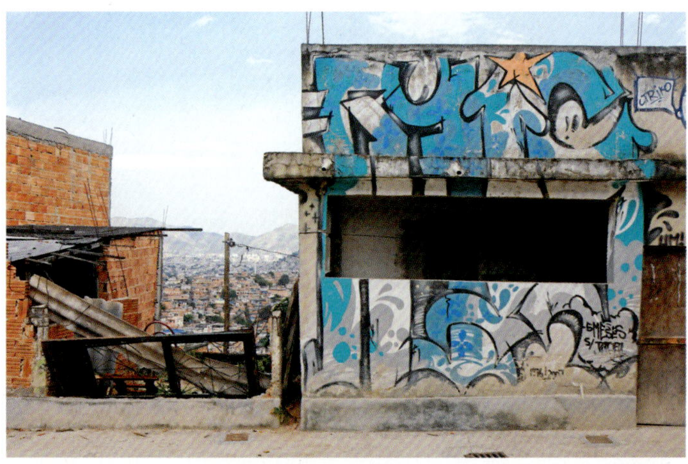

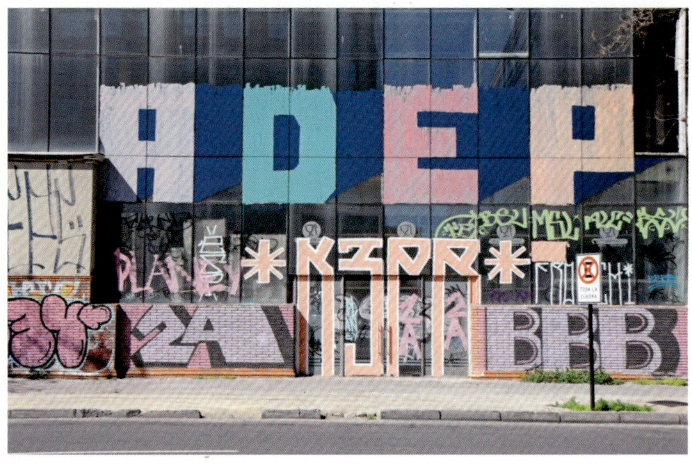

PAGE 5:
The quote is by Banksy but the stencil is a fake (it was on a popular legal wall in London).

FROM TOP:
At the top of a *favela* in Rio/Various artists in Santiago, Chile.

RIGHT:
A dilapidated house in Granada, Spain.

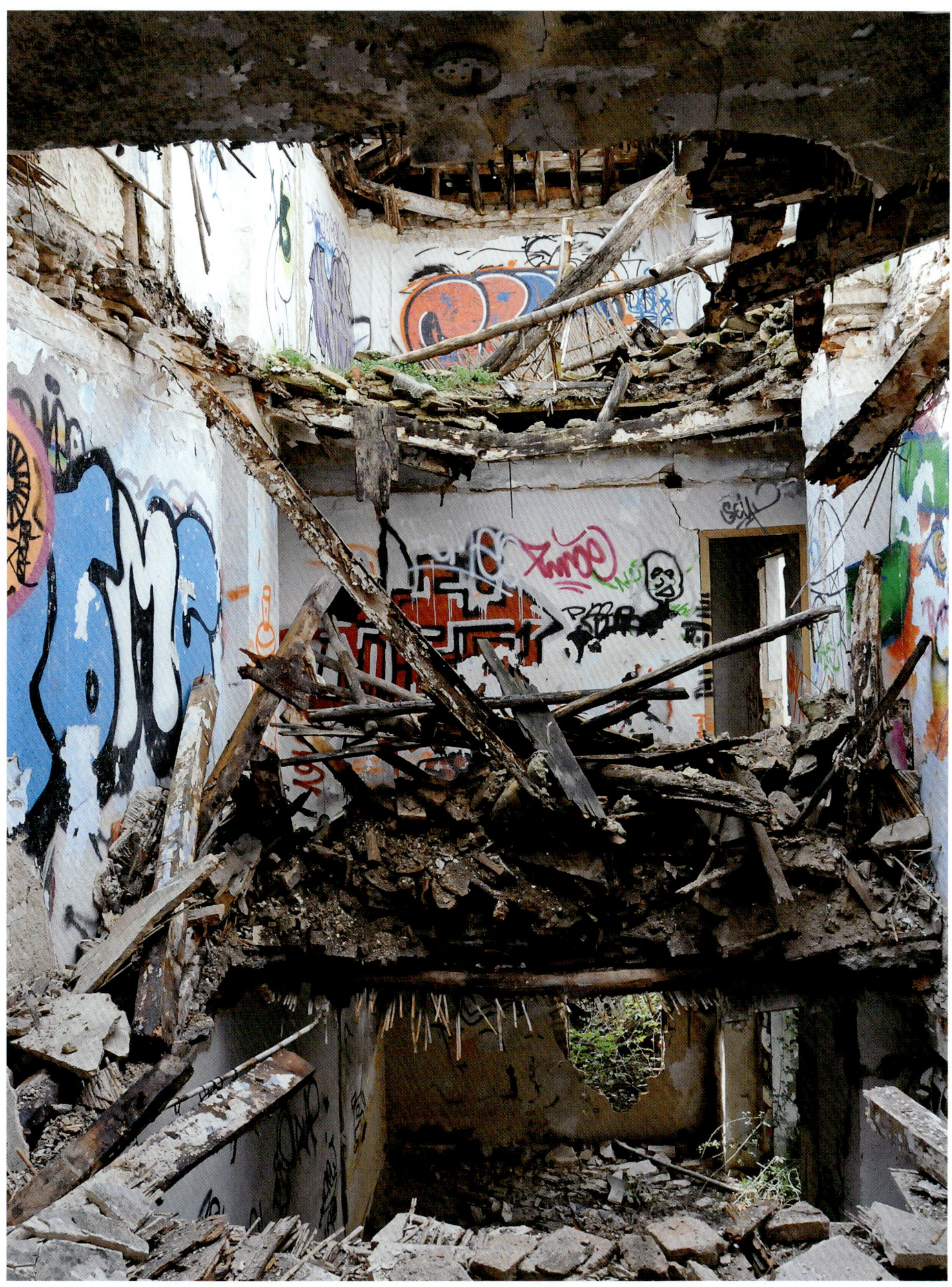

punitively against their actions, will have better opportunities for developing city identities, and engaging local communities and tourists alike.

Street art and graffiti have intermingled with and influenced each other, and will continue to do so in the future. Artists who are now recognized as street art pioneers often have backgrounds as graffiti writers or were influenced by graffiti, if only through a desire to do something different. The breaking of rules and cultural constraints was what originally led to the growth of graffiti; today, it is the breaking of *artistic* constraints that prevents creative stagnation. Narrow definitions of street art and graffiti do not constrain the artists' work and neither do they constrain the position of this book.

In the following pages there are examples of both street art and graffiti; some of the best art is produced when different ideas combine and street art and graffiti are both powerful forces for changing the appearance of our cities.

Some of the artists featured in this book think of themselves as street artists, graffiti artists or graffiti writers; others choose to be 'artists' without further qualification. There is no single terminology to cover all perspectives. What I will say is simply that all the artists featured in this book produce great work that is often *outside*: outside of the studio, outside of the commercial gallery system, and sometimes outside of the law.

There are so many artists active today that I would estimate that

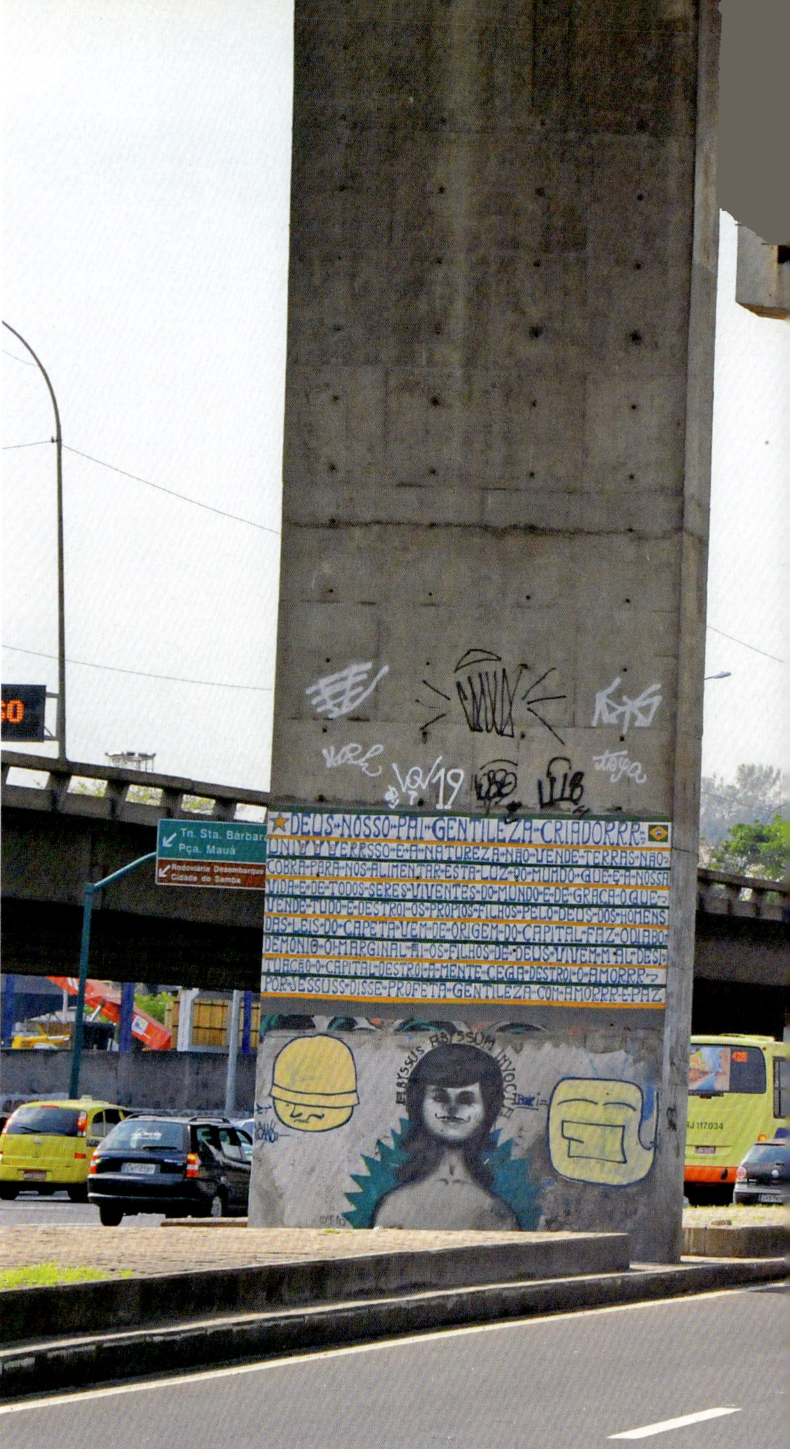

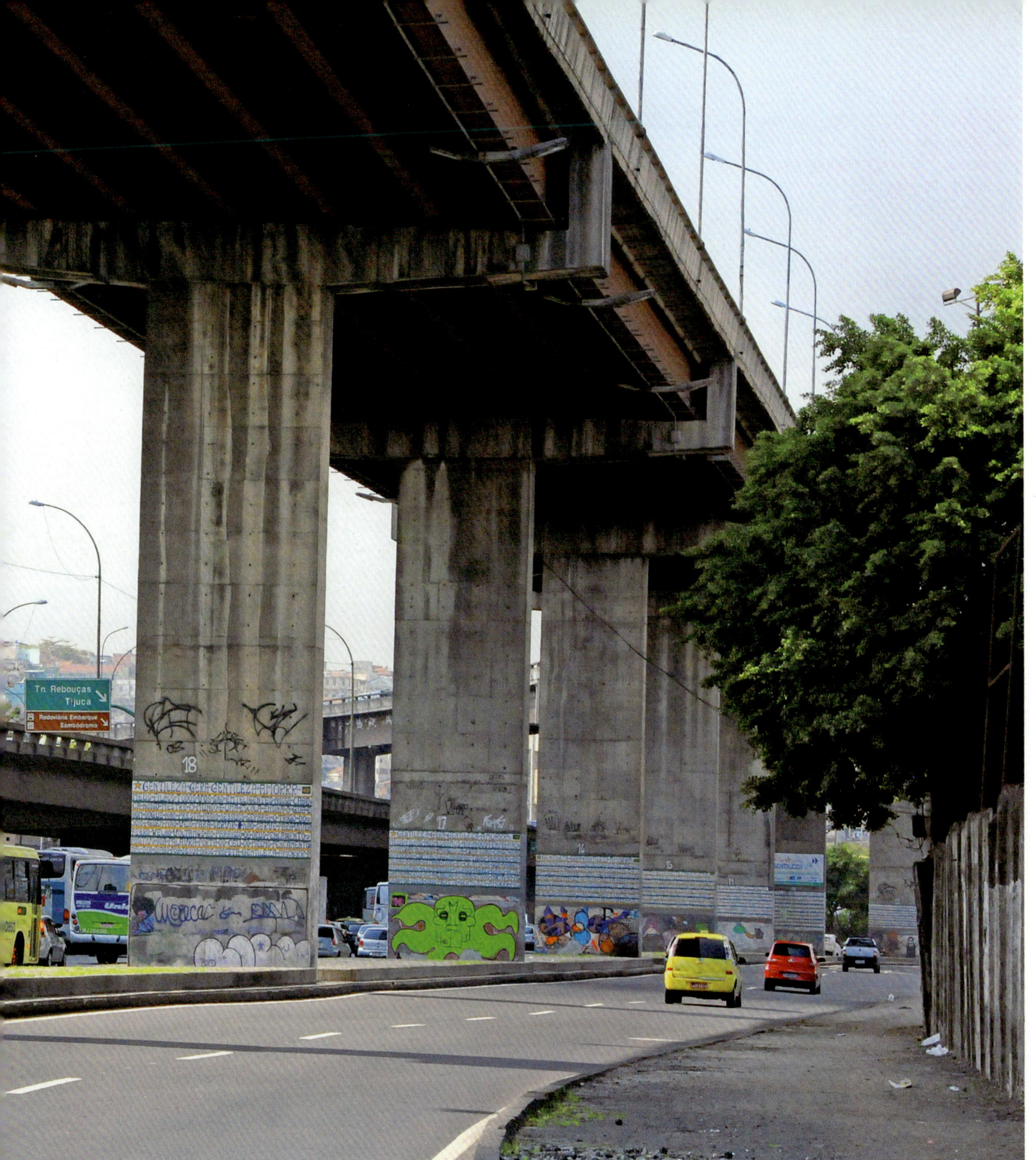

One of the main roads
through Rio in 2011.
The text on each
column with the white
background was painted
by Gentileza (which
means kindness in
Portuguese), a well-
known prophetic figure
in Brazil who passed
away in 1996, aged 79.

the amount of street art and graffiti produced around the world each weekend could fill all commercial galleries at least once over, and then again the following weekend.

This book was written and compiled to honour the thousands of artists who paint our cities around the world. It is not a complete guide to the most fashionable street artists or the most commercially successful; it is, however, a selection of stunning contemporary street art from across the globe, showing the breadth of artistic diversity through relevant work.

Curating this book has been an exhausting pleasure. I started the process by selecting one thousand favourite photographs from Global Street Art's own 70,000-photo archive spanning 25 countries (I took most of those pictures). I then added some of the best photographs shared on our blog and tried to contact every artist whose work was featured in the photos. I trawled through Facebook, Flickr, Twitter, website contact forms, paint shops, blogs and friends, working in seven or eight different languages and using translation programs to track the artists down and make sure they were happy to be featured. The results are visible in the following pages and I am tremendously grateful to the more than 300 artists who agreed to have their work represented in the book.

When I travelled around the world taking photos for this book I made friends with many artists and didn't get killed: two things that make me very happy. This book is quite academic because I'm a geek and I really believe in painted cities. To add some levity there are stories about wild dogs, train tunnels and massive freaking guns.

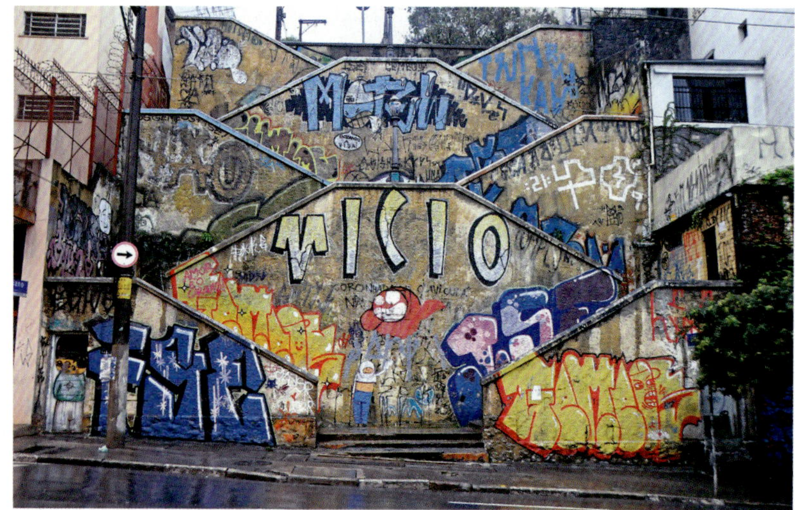

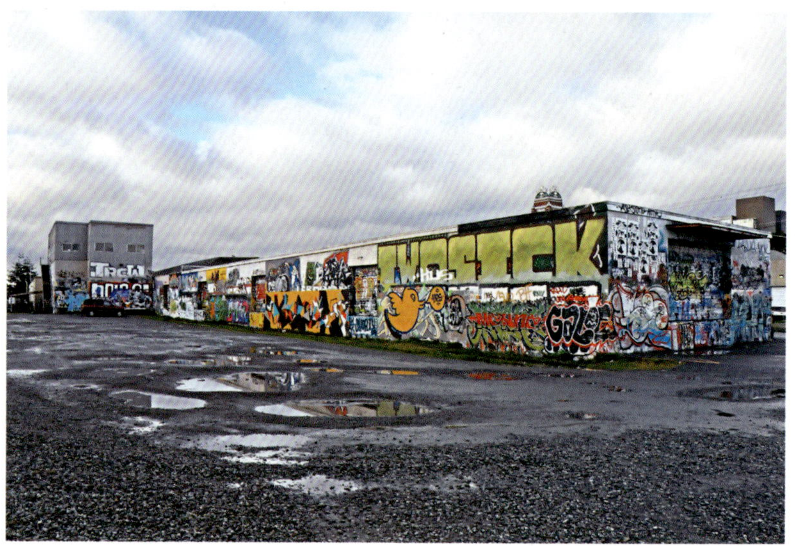

A VERY BRIEF HISTORY OF GRAFFITI & STREET ART

There have been many different types of graffiti throughout the ages. In this book, graffiti refers to 'writing' — a youth subculture that had its origins in mid-1960s Philadelphia and grew explosively after reaching New York in the late 1960s. Philadelphia and New York are rightly viewed as key locations in the history of modern writing, but other graffiti cultures have emerged independently in cities such as Los Angeles and São Paulo, displaying some features in common with the New York writing. Today, these different cultures have become somewhat intermingled, as travel and the internet become the bearers of graphic styles and influences from all over the world.

1960s New York: Right Time, Right Place

New York underwent a number of deeply influential social changes before the late 1960s, including urban renewal projects that replaced a lot of cheap working-class housing with publicly financed middle-class housing. Poor (largely ethnic minority) communities were frequently dispersed, and interstate highways were built through densely populated urban areas, which disrupted communities and further supported the migration of (mainly white) middle-class and affluent populations away from the city centre.

These road-building and urban renewal programmes shifted manufacturing jobs away from their inner-city locations. Job opportunities for poor and unskilled workers that had previously been available to new immigrants and those below the poverty line declined dramatically in New York City. The shortage of working-class jobs available in city centres resulted in a widespread surplus of cheap adult labour. The youth suffered disproportionately high unemployment, which chiefly affected African Americans and Latinos.

Against this backdrop of social destabilization, urban riots occurred throughout America in the 1960s, including in New York in 1964. Radical political movements such as the Black Panthers fostered a 'people power' spirit in young adults and school programmes brought adolescents together in a situation ripe for resisting authority. With the modern school system, age-based social networks allowed young people to learn skills and knowledge from each other that would become important in the spread of the graffiti subculture (including shoplifting, modifying painting tools, painting techniques).

It is also worth noting that New York in the 1960s was the global home of commercial signs: huge embellished names punctuated the city's skyline. Given that the written language had become an everyday and expected part of the urban landscape – and nowhere more so than in New York – we can understand why someone would write their own name on a wall, or the side of a train. All advertising asks is for the viewer to remember a name; graffiti does the same thing but emphasizes the embellishment and removes the product.

These factors not only explain the societal pre-conditions for graffiti but also help us to make sense of why the media reacted largely negatively to graffiti. Media attention at the time focused on topics such as urban decay, youth delinquency and the poor state of New York's subway infrastructure, the repair of which had been neglected from infrastructure budgets.

Early Writers

Writing your name on a wall was common in New York before 1967 but names were confined within neighbourhoods to identify the writer as a member of a given street gang. Early graffiti writers were innovative because they started writing their names way beyond their local neighbourhoods; they typically began with more familiar locations, then took trips to other parts of the city to spread their exposure, travelling around and 'tagging' the insides of subway cars. Lower-class kids from New York suddenly found opportunities for recognition outside of their own neighbourhood in a way that their parents had never had.

There was no expectation of any economic reward by writing; writers were simply looking for a form of recognition. Graffiti provided a way of finding an identity among peers. Fame was (and still is) the ultimate achievement in writing. The most significant always came from hard work and persistence. A writer who managed to 'get up' more than anyone else on a particular line or in a particular area was, and still is, declared a king.

Writers would choose names that often had little resemblance to their given name, although typically there would be some relevance for the writer (e.g. Hispanic writers would often choose names with a Spanish origin). Names were chosen because they looked good when written, usually with no more than five letters so they could be written quickly. The convention for name length persists although some modern writers choose to stand out by having longer names, but writers with longer names often have shorter versions too. A lot of a writer's identity is in their name.

Numbers were often added to the name to identify the street where the writer lived but this soon changed because writers didn't want to help the police identify them. Similarly, writers frequently used more than one name or derivations of the same name, to help them develop different styles and to avoid trouble if one name became 'hot', attracting too much police attention. Through this practice, writers would build up the profiles of their new alter-egos.

Early graffiti writers didn't start out with a self-conscious notion that they were artists; this idea developed over time. Thus, graffiti is qualitatively different from other public art movements like the Mexican muralists and the Soviet avant-garde. The professional career-based notion that underlies what it means to be an 'artist' (a person who makes art as a profession) excludes most youth from seeing themselves as artists, as it did with early writers. Some writers use the term 'vandals' but this is inappropriate too – sticks and bricks would after all be far more effective tools of vandalism than paint. Writers using the term vandals often do so in a romanticized way, implying a creative resistance to authority.

Competition & Respect

Competition increased as the number of writers swelled, making them seek new ways to stand out from their peers. The main method was to be prolific, writing your name as much as possible, to really 'get up'. Furthermore, writers became more interested in the way their name looked, making style increasingly important; but if your pieces aren't seen, then other writers won't know you have style, so getting up remains at the core of winning attention. The competitive aspects of the culture have driven a vast amount of innovation, which continues today.

Getting up was well established by summer 1971. There was no commercial element to writing so there was no risk of over-exposure: the more you got up, the more fame you achieved. In the summer of 1971 the *New York Times* published a now famous article on graffiti, '"Taki 183" Spawns Pen Pals'. Where writers had previously used only shared public space to gain recognition, there were now new opportunities through media exposure. Writers would deliberately write in locations that they thought were likely to be photographed. They began to take on a notion of being artists based on the impact competition had on garnering respect and, to some extent, on early articles in the media that described writers as artists. Writers who saw themselves as artists were driven to innovate further, which in turn encouraged more and more writers to view themselves as artists too.

Despite its illegality, graffiti culture quickly institutionalized values such as hard work and creativity, which were necessary for any writer to receive acclaim. Dedication was also a crucial factor because at any time one's status in the community could change. Writers had to get up over an increasingly broad area. Furthermore, getting up in inaccessible or dangerous places contributed to a writer's fame and prestige.

Within just a few years a solid community of writers had formed, already establishing traditions and unwritten rules. Given the need to stand out, writers would choose unique names and would not overwrite another's name, to avoid fights. Because the culture was built around fame among peers and not economic rewards or public recognition, it became self-sustaining.

Most early writers came from the poorer areas of New York and were largely Latino and African American. Throughout the 1970s, however, more whites and middle-class youths became involved in graffiti. In terms of gender, writing has always been male-dominated and remains so to this day.

Many of the norms set in the early days of graffiti remain today and some of them are equally relevant for street artists as well as graffiti writers, such as an emphasis on finding one's own style and the requirement to be unique and often prolific in order to stand out.

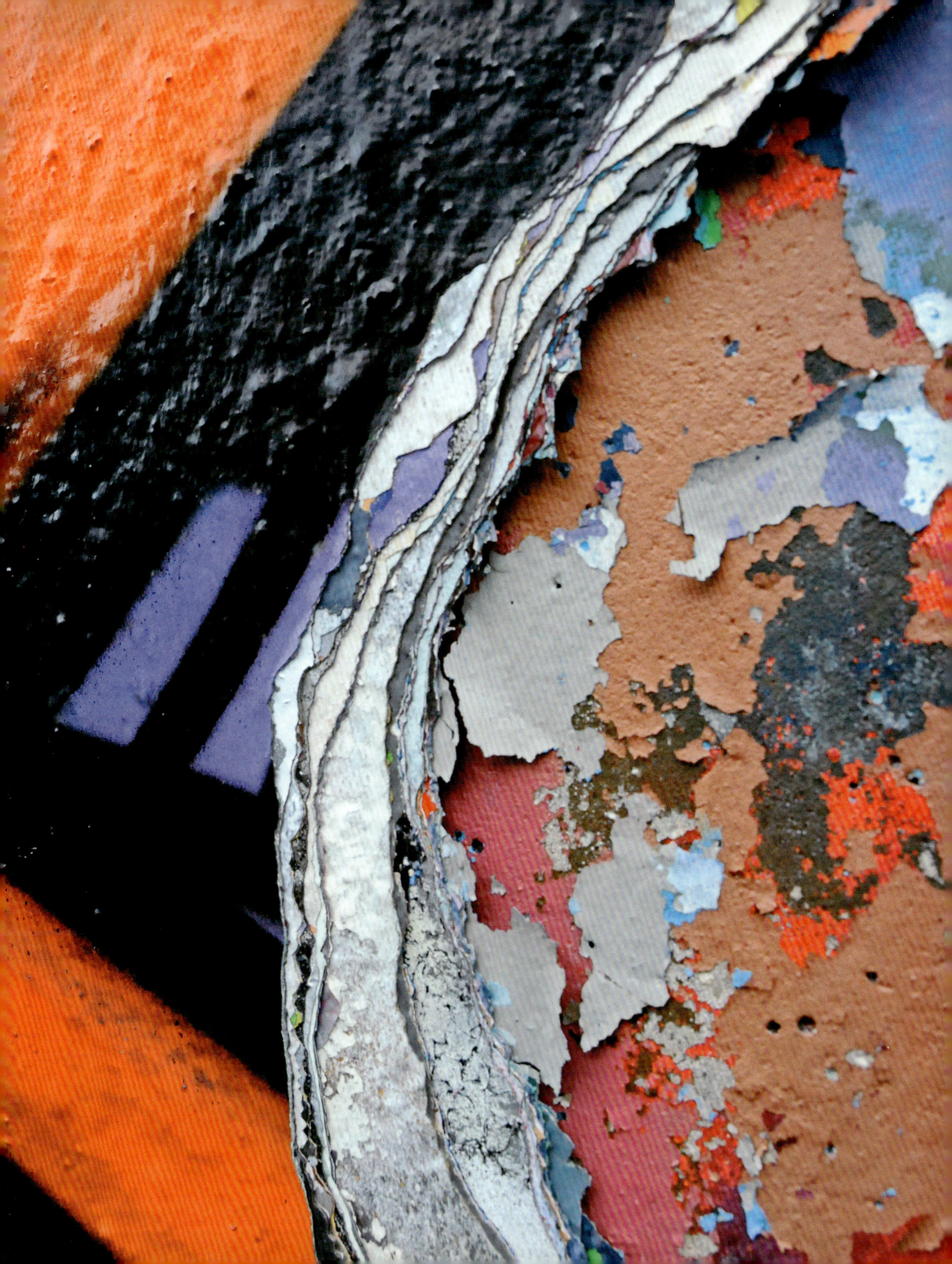

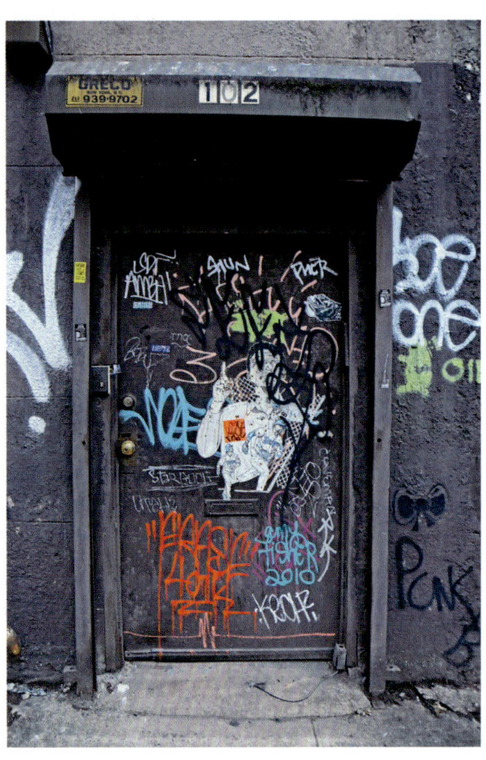

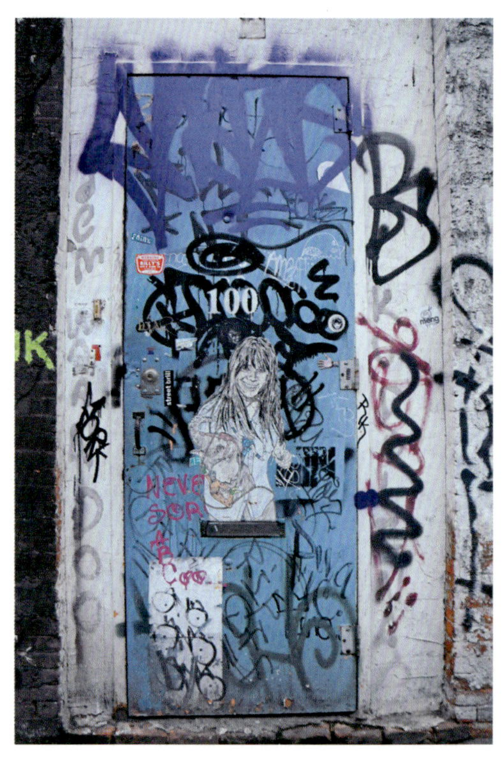

<u>ABOVE AND BELOW:</u>
Heavily tagged New York doors
photographed in 2011.

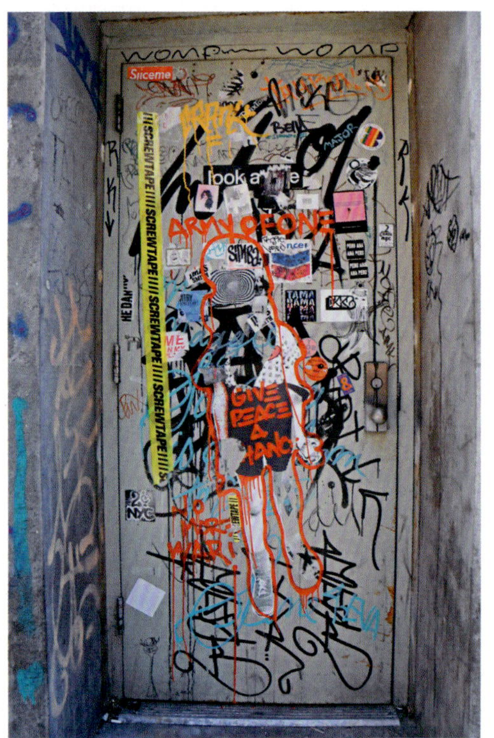

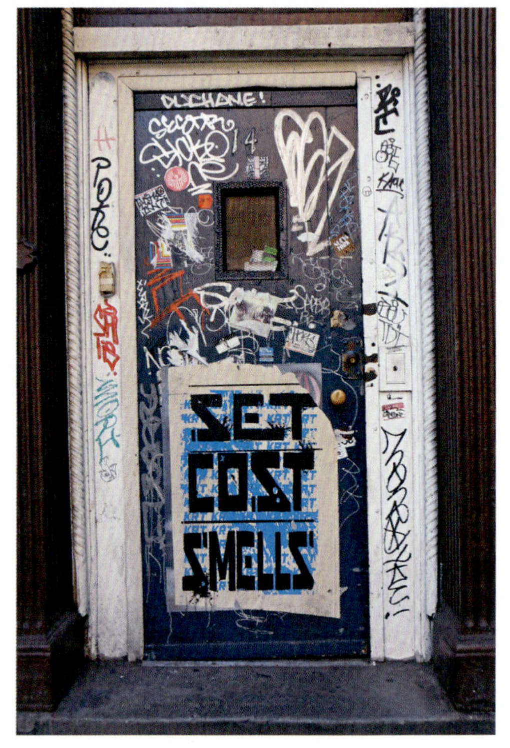

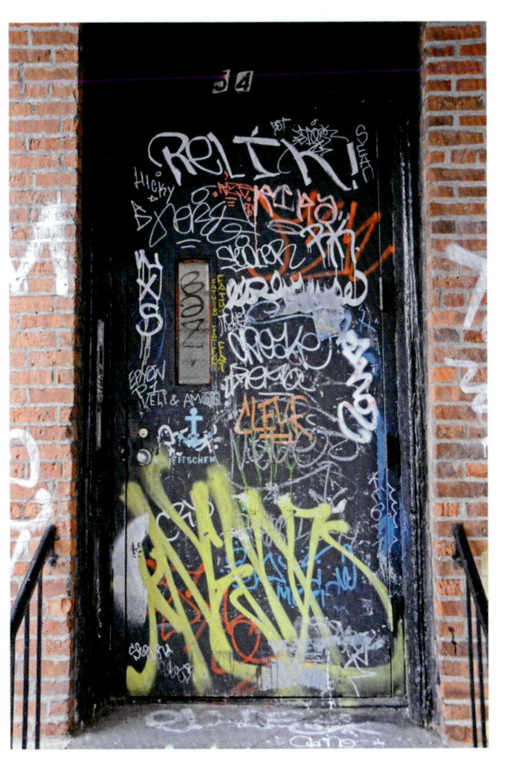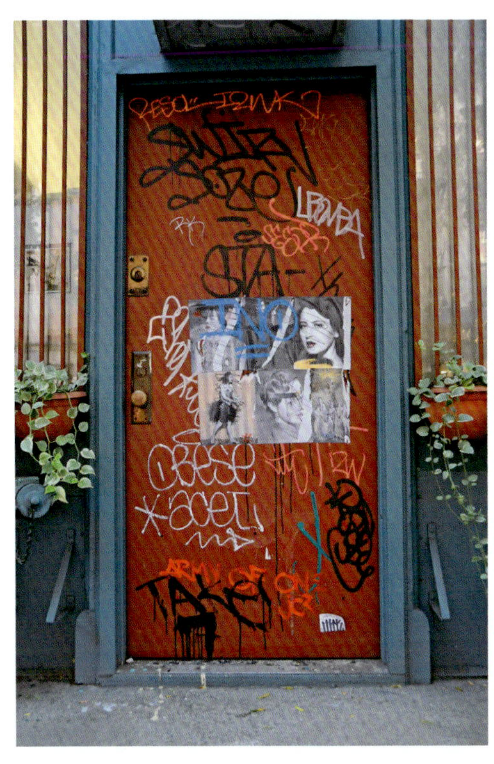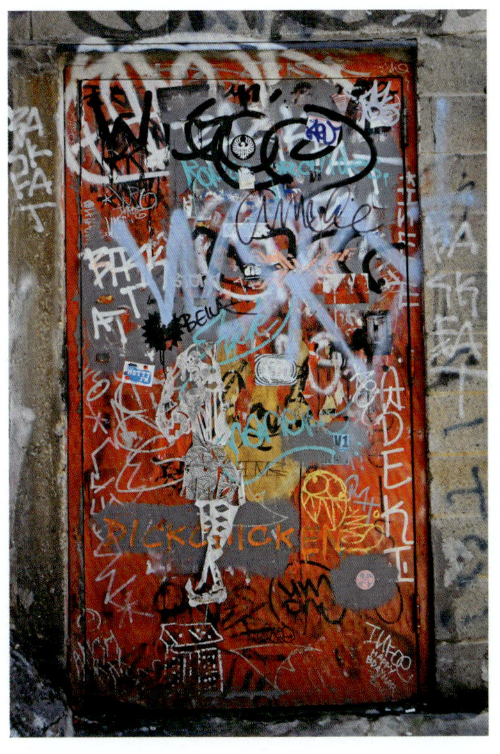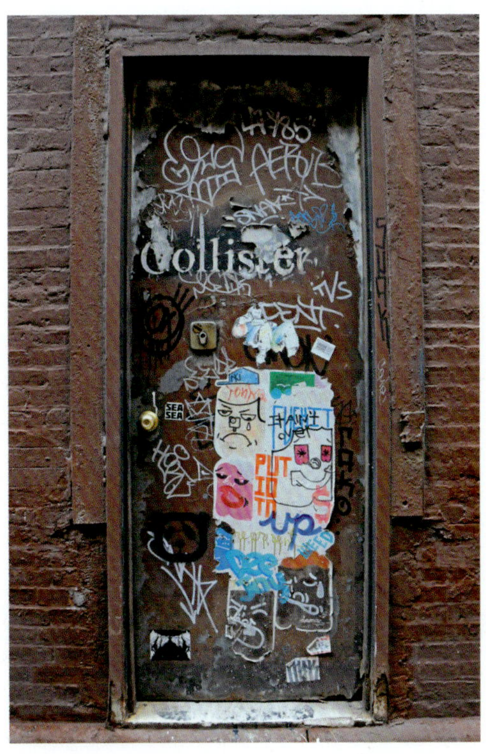

Painting Trains

By 1971 different groups of writers had discovered the train yards and lay-ups (where trains park) across New York City. Writing on the outside of trains offered new possibilities for respect and recognition, with trains transporting writers' names all across the city. The size of trains, and the distance from which the 'canvas' could be viewed, quickly led to important innovations in graffiti. During summer 1971 writers started creating letter outlines and the spaces within letters would be filled in with another colour. Writers then began to embellish their pieces with arrows, stars and other motifs. Thus, 'pieces' (short for 'masterpieces') were born. Painting pieces became the next step for serious writers after tagging (the most basic and least challenging form of graffiti). The increase in the size of pieces and the numerous artistic innovations made style all the more important in a writer gaining fame amongst their peers. Writers continued to compete to create larger, more conspicuous works.

Writing on the outside of trains served one of the key functions the internet supports today: the graffiti images travelled directly to the viewer, as opposed to the viewer needing to travel to a particular place to see the graffiti. Trains circulated pieces throughout the city so innovations in one neighbourhood of New York could quickly be seen and copied, then further developed, in another part of the city. Trains, much like the internet, allowed different writers to critique others' work across the city. Benches, where writers would meet, were places where the status of different writers was discussed and confirmed, and the internet often serves a similar function to the classic writers' benches today.

Both now and historically, new writers are introduced to the culture through friends. The excitement of writing together with your friends helps to keep new recruits involved in the culture. Although there were early graffiti gangs in New York in the 1970s, born in neighbourhoods where there were criminal street gangs, graffiti gangs often had to defend themselves against more aggressive and better armed gangs and so the notion of a graffiti gang wasn't really viable.

Graffiti crews began to form, which were associations of small groups of friends who shared a passion for writing. Crews have several functions: they are goal-orientated (i.e. they exist because the members write graffiti), protective and they are places where writers can learn from each other. Crews are distinct from gangs, who are typically confined to limited territories – the antithesis of getting up. For many early writers, graffiti writing was commonly a better alternative to gang membership and in some places this remains so today.

RIGHT, FROM TOP:
Some of the trains running on Rome's B-line today are as painted as New York's trains in the early 1970s. Trains really are the holy grail for graffiti photographers and when I was last in Rome I struggled to get good photos. I had been thrown out of two stations, chased out of one yard and been up and down the lines. Finally, with only a few hours left before my flight home, I found a university that backed onto the tracks. To date, those are the best train photos I've taken – pieces, end-to-ends and whole cars too!

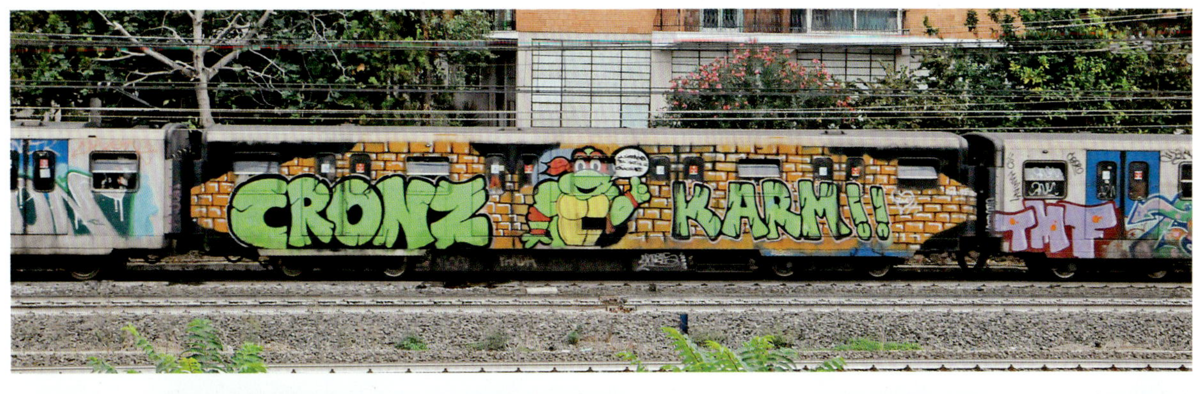
CRONZ
KARM!!
TMF

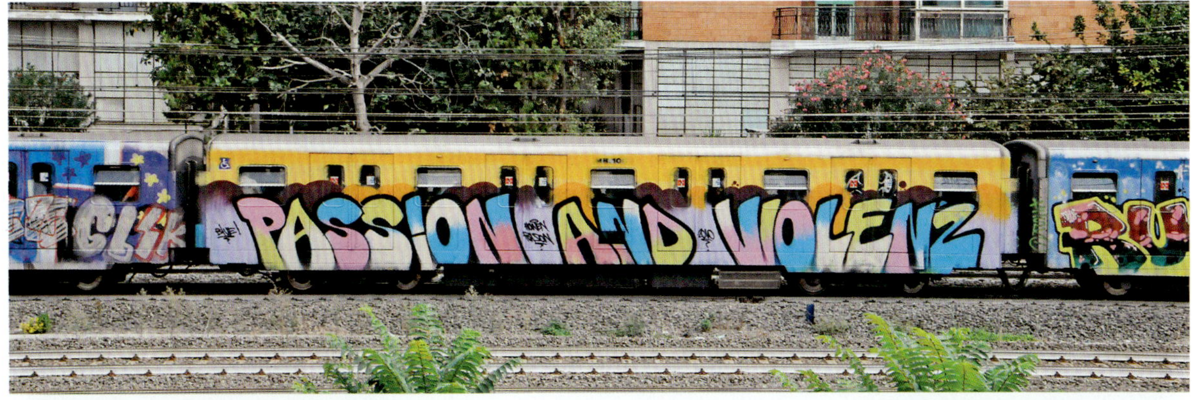
CLIK
PASSION AND VIOLENZ
MB.10

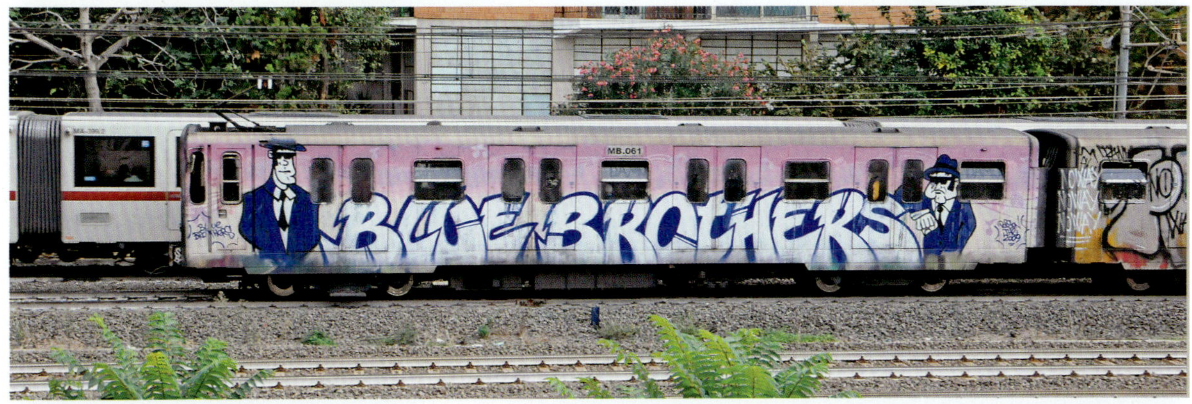
MB.061
BLUE BROTHERS

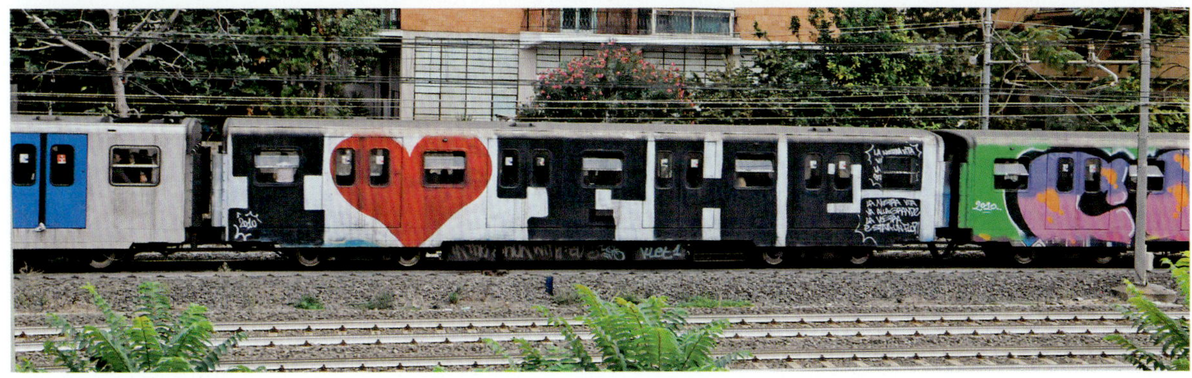

New York Subway Art

The media mostly framed graffiti as a symbol of urban decay, portraying the youth as out-of-control criminals. The New York Metro Transit Authority (MTA) held that it needed to be purged to foster a feeling of safety on the subway. The prevailing view from transit and city institutions was that graffiti removal would lead to a fall in other crimes. A prevention project in 1973 made proposals along four themes, which are still commonly discussed today: technological improvements (using special paints, solvents and coatings); security measures; psychological measures aimed at inhibiting vandalism or diverting vandals elsewhere; and control of graffiti instruments.

From 1970 to 1974 subway cars were cleaned by hand, with solvents designed to remove only dirt and grime, not paint. In 1976 MTA started using a new paint for train carriages that was resistant to the strong graffiti-removing solvents. By October 1977 MTA had developed a solvent that would remove graffiti and could be used in MTA's new train-wash machines, although this led to toxic graffiti solvents being dumped daily into the city's waterways by the authorities through connections with the storm sewer system. The Transit Authority also founded the 'vandal squad' enforcement units. In 1981 the city trialled the use of fences and attack dogs; the dogs proved too expensive but, over time, and especially after 1985, new approaches such as train-repainting programmes and the introduction of security fences

with razor wire made writing on trains much more difficult in New York. On 12 May 1989 the MTA held a press conference declaring the subway graffiti-free. If any new graffiti was found on a train, the car was taken out of service, cleaned and then returned.

Graffiti, of course, persisted, but these measures encouraged writers to move away from painting the outsides of trains to once again tagging on the insides of trains. After the exciting period in the late 1970s and early 1980s when graffiti seemed to explode across the city, New York graffiti entered an era in which innovation slowed (in a subculture with fewer writers). Meanwhile other graffiti scenes, such as LA and London, were innovating rapidly. This period in New York lasted roughly until the mid-1990s, when New York writers Cost and Revs started writing big tags with rollers and sticking up lots of mini-posters, enabling them to get up faster and in a bigger way.

As painting trains became more fraught with difficulties and stiff legal penalties, the number of graffiti writers who painted trains decreased. More writers today choose softer targets and only a dedicated hardcore group continue to paint trains in cities such as New York and London. As security measures increase, graffiti shifts forms and new canvases are being chosen, be they commuter trains in different countries or cities, or softer targets within the same cities.

It is interesting to note that the clean trains that resulted from New York's 'war on graffiti' did not lead to a decrease in crime on

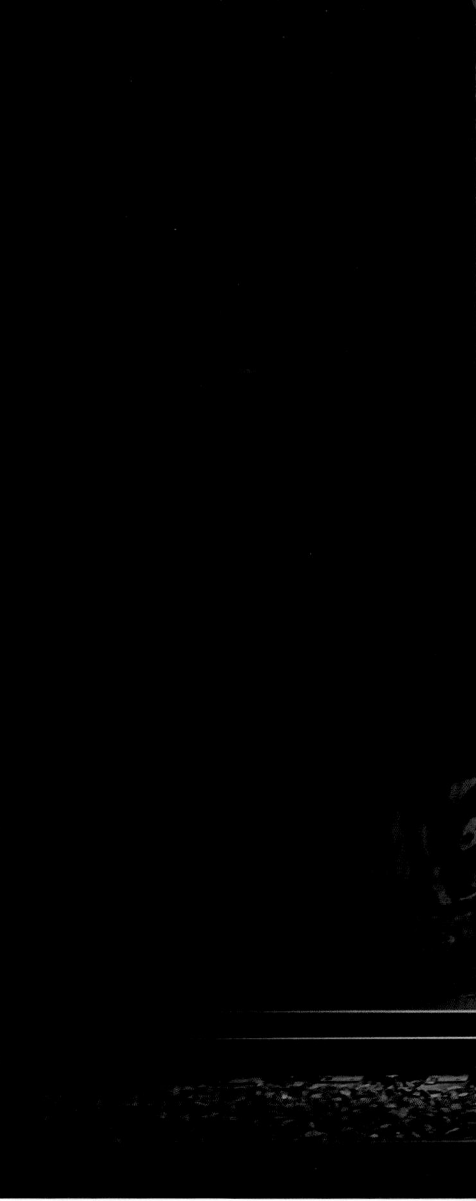

the subway, which hit an all-time high within a year of the subways becoming graffiti-free, due to a deepening recession. Fear on the subway remained high because of large numbers of homeless people on the subway system, the removal of whom became a priority only after 1989.

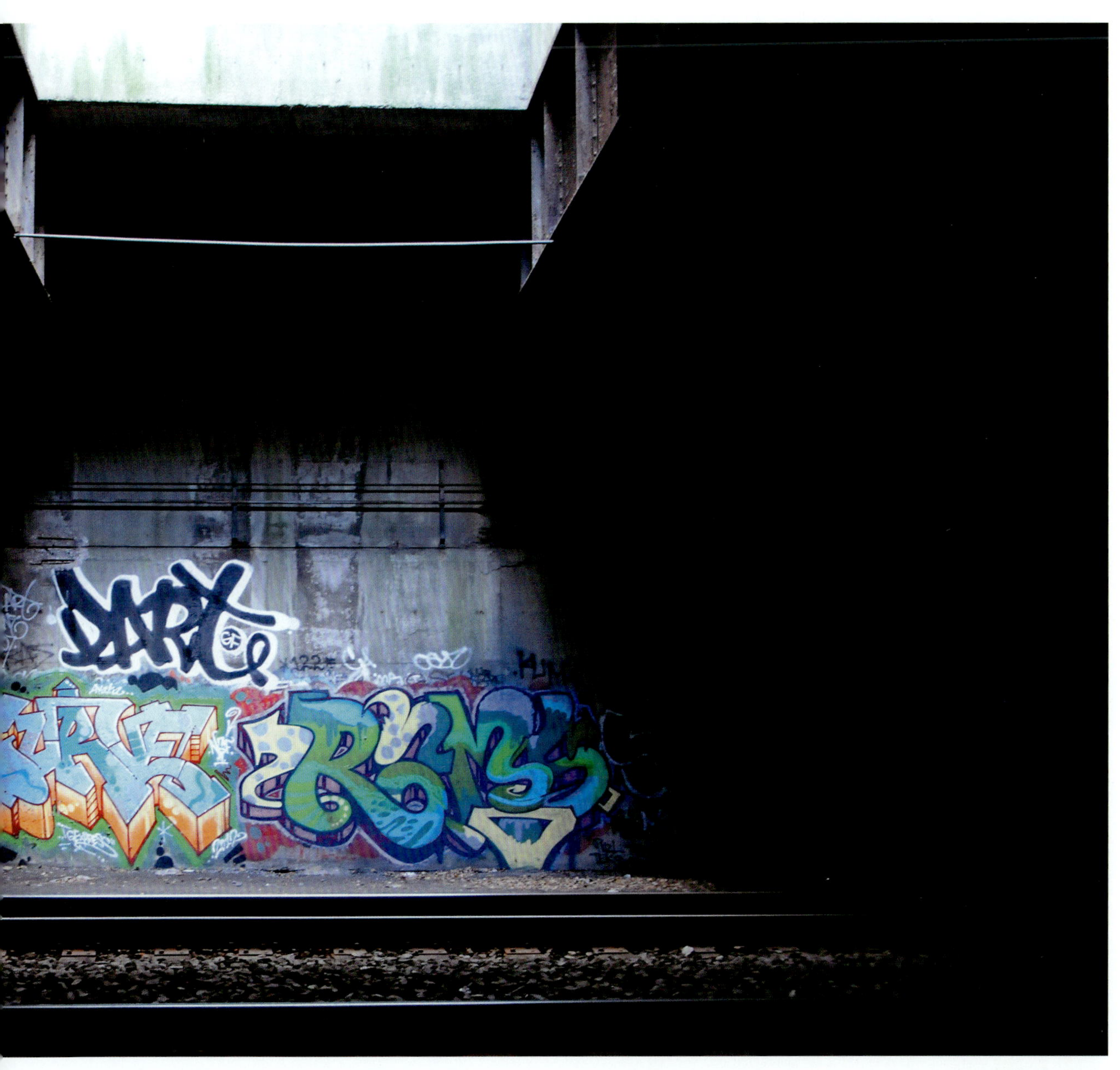

ABOVE:
New York's Freedom
Tunnels running under
Manhattan. I don't
recommend visiting when
the trains are running.

PAGES 22-3, FROM TOP:
I shot this about 20
blocks into the Freedom
Tunnels (apologies for
the blur on the right-
hand side - it was hard
to stop my hand shaking
and it's not the place
for a tripod)/A secret
trackside location in
contemporary New York.

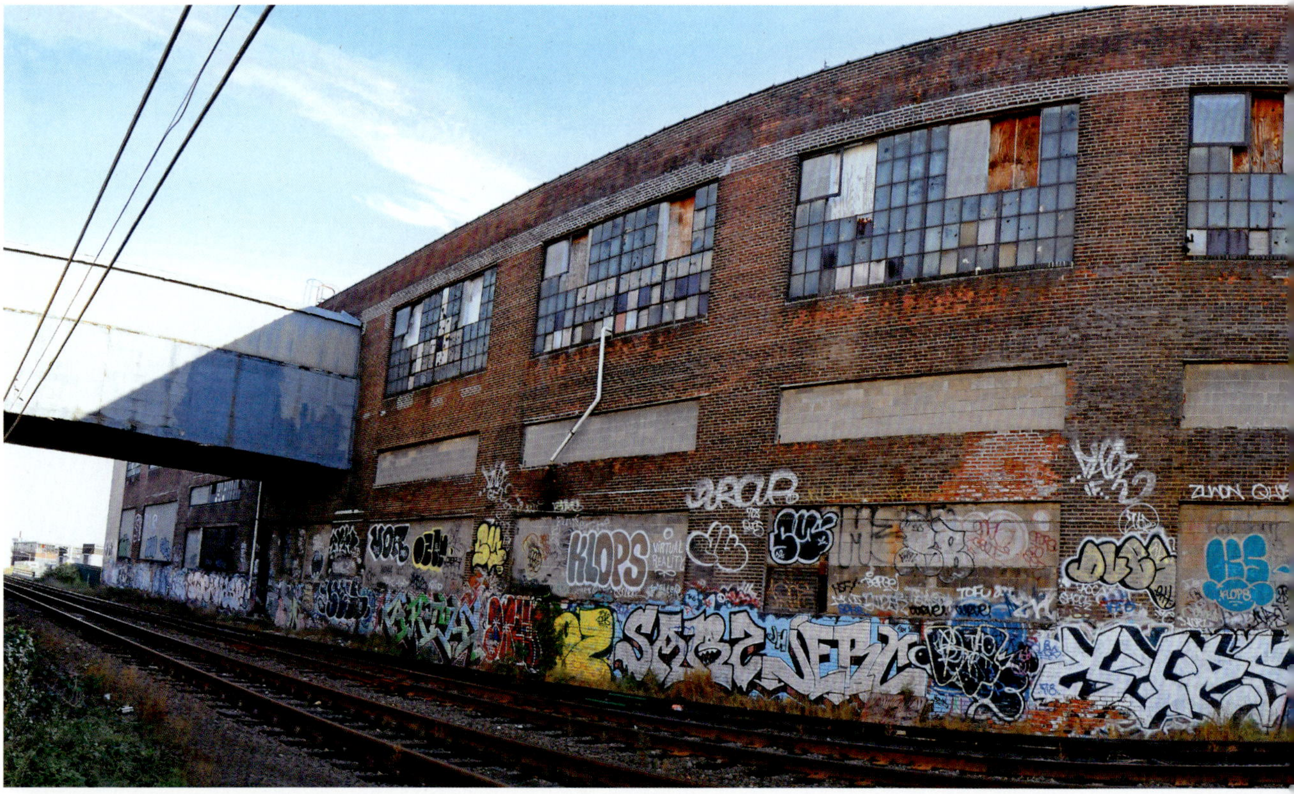

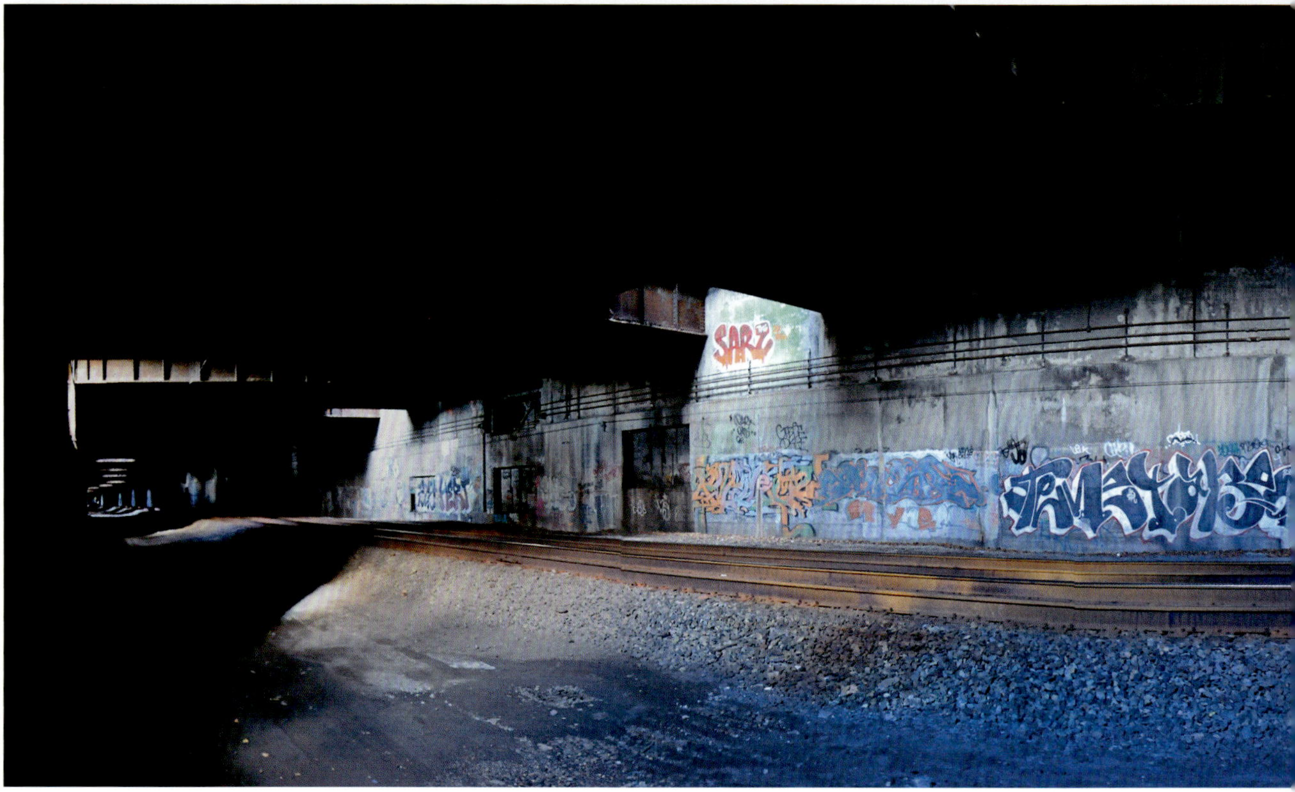

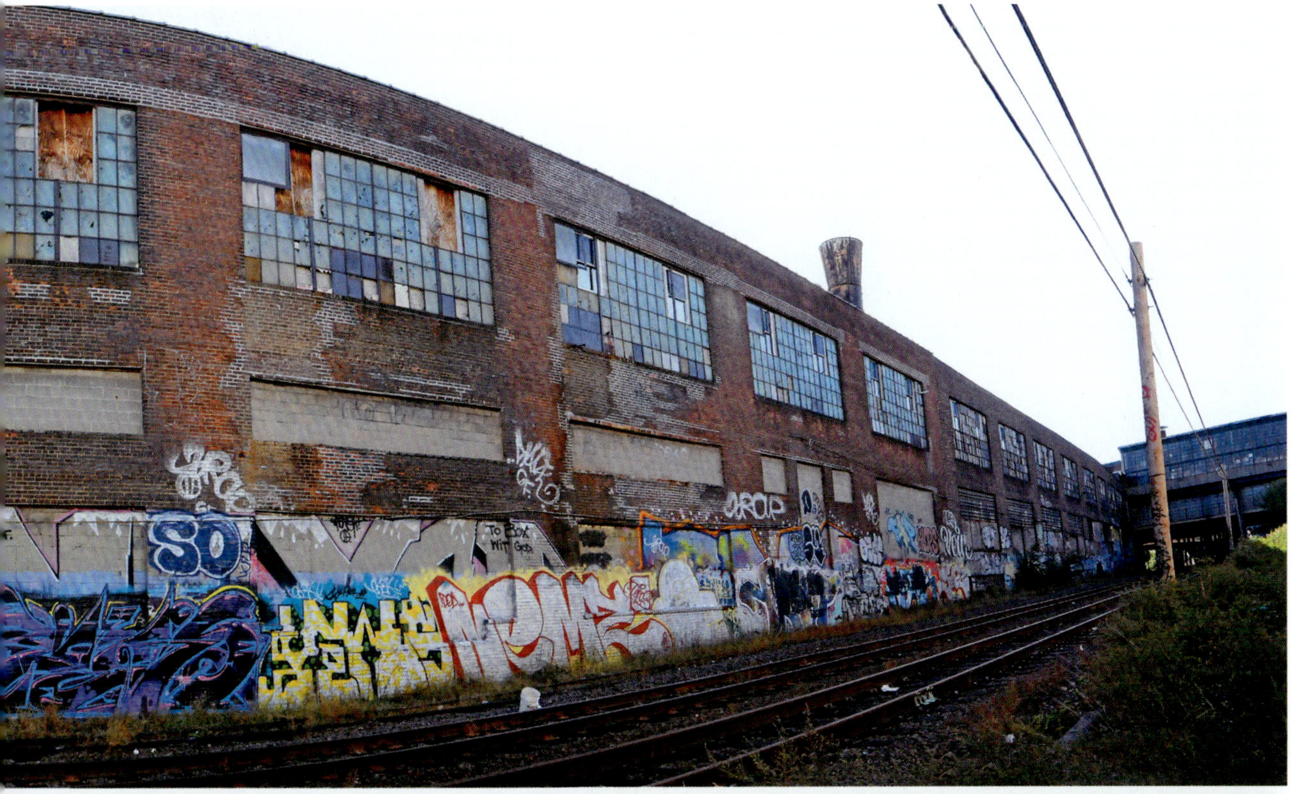

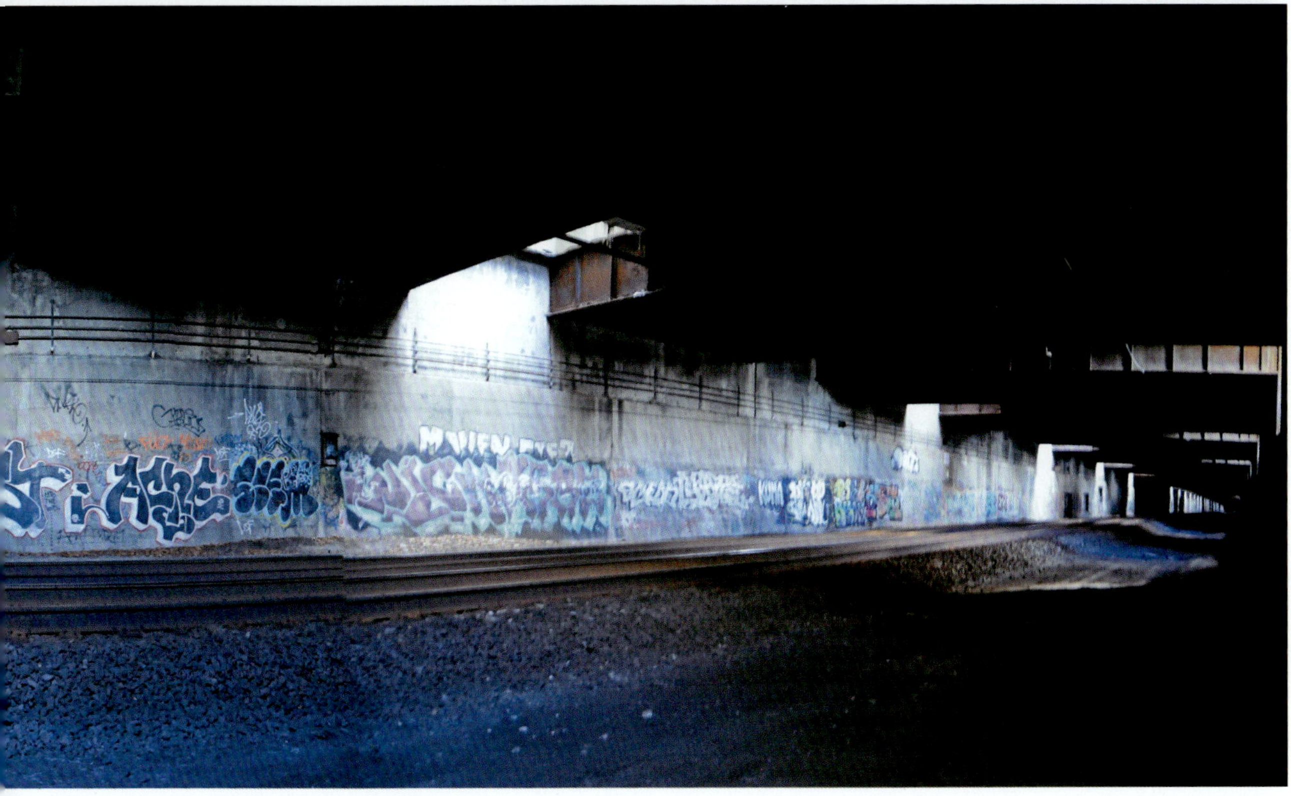

Street Art History & Pioneers

The idea of producing art outdoors is, of course, nothing new. Even before the modern street art movement there were a number of 'guerrilla muralists' and artists who chose to work outside without any official permission, including John Fekner (in New York from the late 1960s) and Walter Kershaw (who famously painted murals on the sides of houses in mill towns in the North of England in the 1970s). The notion of street art was most likely 'in the air' around the same time as the origins of graffiti.

Most street art pioneers, like graffiti pioneers, had little expectation of financial reward for their efforts. Furthermore, early street artists would often choose pseudonyms and would act anonymously, not least because of the illegality of their work. It is worth noting that street art pioneers were only referred to as 'street artists' long after they began producing art on the streets because the naming of the movement postdates the origins of the movement itself.

Techniques associated with street art, such as stencilling and postering, all existed for other functions before they were appropriated for art. Some of the techniques we think of as belonging to the domain of street art were appropriated by graffiti writers in order to get up quicker or more prolifically, perhaps reducing some of the risks behind getting up and ensuring more 'quality control' (e.g. stencils or posters).

Indeed, differences in pre-existing local cultures often explain why certain techniques are more commonly used for street art in one place than in another. For example, posters have been used for political campaigns in Italy for many years and stencils have been used for political protests in Argentina before street art became popular in either country. Today, Italy is home to some of the most progressive poster-based street artists and, likewise, Argentina has a flourishing stencil art scene.

People commonly credit the French artist Blek le Rat as being one of the first artists associated with street art as a specific movement. Blek visited New York in 1971 and was influenced by the graffiti which he saw there. A decade later, in 1981, he began stencilling rats on walls in Paris, feeling that stencils suited the architecture of his own city better than graffiti. Other early stencil pioneers include Jef Aerosol from France (stencilling from 1982) and Nick Walker, who started stencilling in Bristol in the early 1980s.

Many of the world's most famous and/or influential street artists began their careers around the 1990s. American artist Shepard Fairey, known most famously for his 'Obey' posters featuring an image derived from a picture of Andre the Giant, began producing 'Andre the Giant has a Posse' stickers in 1989. Fairey's prolific repetition of a single image, varying in size and method of application, was instrumental in his development as a recognized street artist.

Other pioneers, such as Revs and Cost from New York, have more traditional graffiti

RIGHT, FROM TOP:
John Fekner's
Industrial Fossil from
1978 in Queens, New
York/John Fekner's *The
Gasolinic Era* from 1983
in Queens, New York.

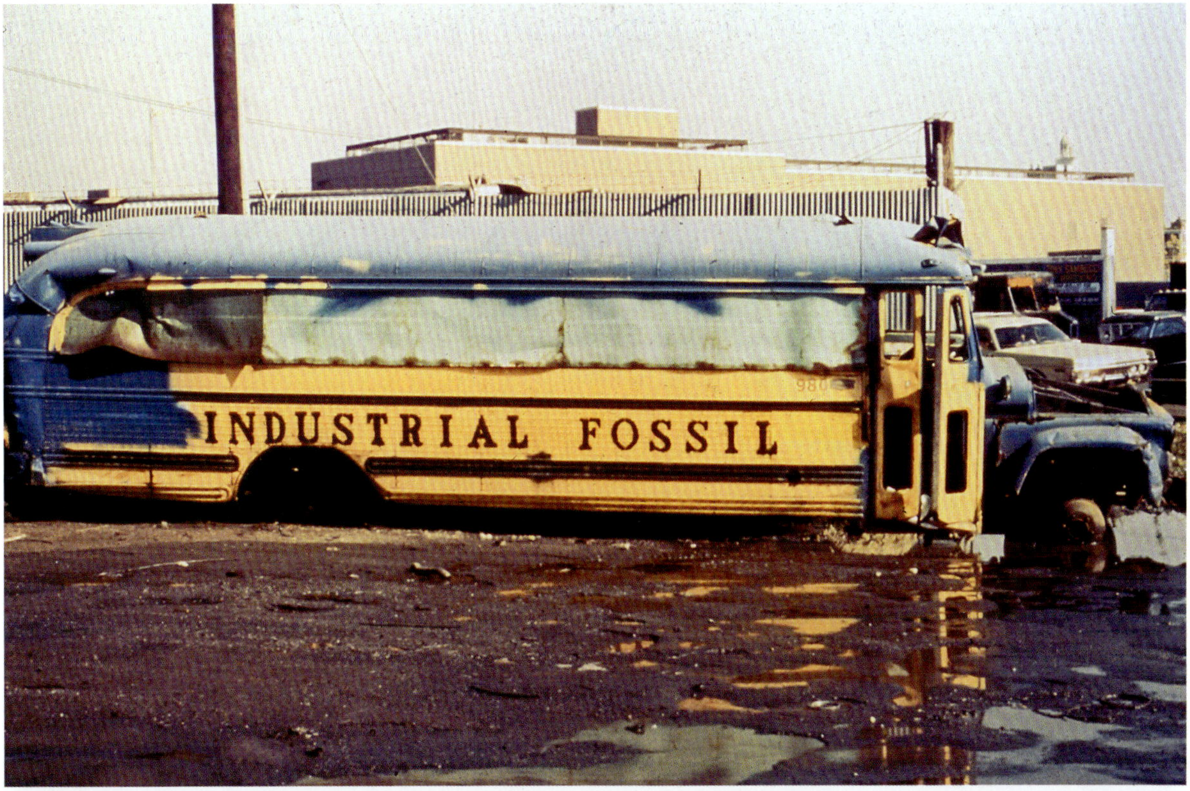

INDUSTRIAL FOSSIL

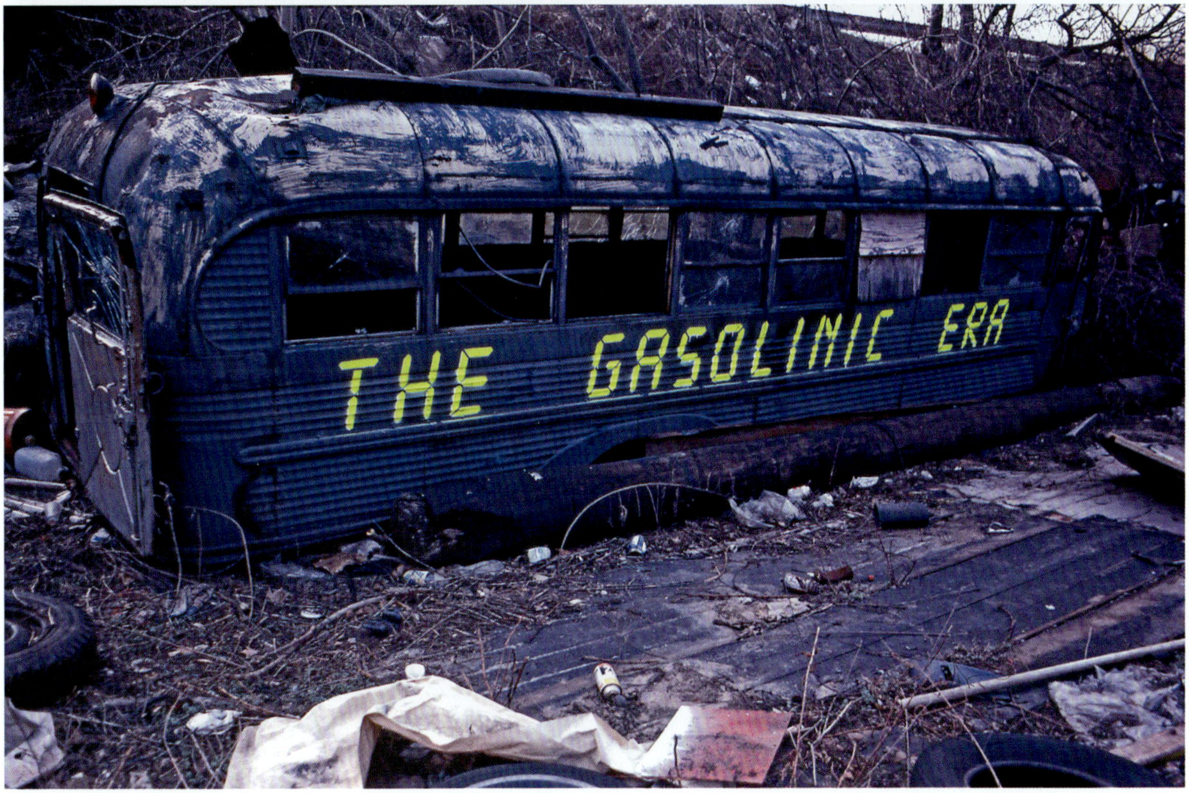

THE GASOLINIC ERA

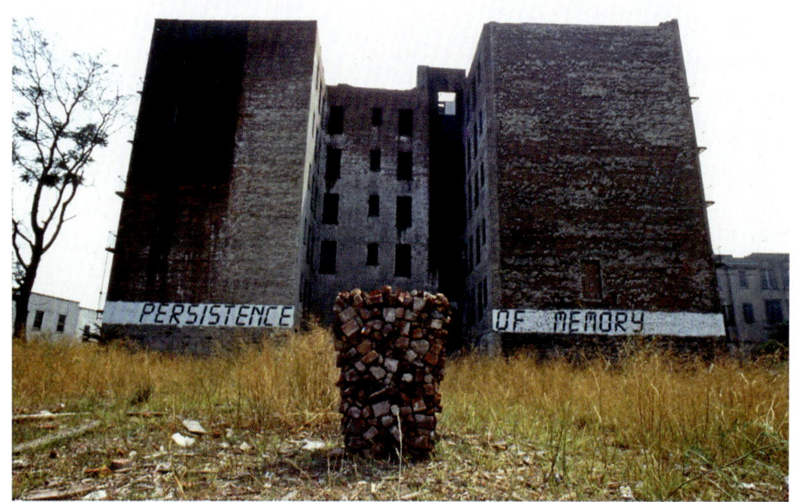

backgrounds. Revs and Cost were both active graffiti writers who began working together in the early 1990s. They pasted up posters prolifically across Manhattan with their names and short phrases. Cost and Revs likely viewed their different techniques simply as new ways to get up beyond traditional spraypaint and markers; their attitude (and the text-based subject of their posters) was rooted more in the world of graffiti than in what we might recognize as street art.

Many successful contemporary street artists began making street art around the turn of the century. For example, the French street artist Invader, who fixes tile mosaics to walls based on characters from the 1970s video game Space Invaders, started doing so around 1998. US artist Swoon started putting up her iconic paste-ups around 1999, the same year the Brooklyn-based artist collective Faile began wheatpasting and stencilling around New York and the Italian artist Blu started painting on the streets. The French artist JR began pasting photocopies of his photographs of graffiti writers on walls around 2000. Although Banksy began writing traditional graffiti in the early 1990s, he began stencilling around 2000 too.

The number of practising artists that have been later labelled as 'Street Artists' (in terms of belonging to a singular artistic movement) increased considerably. Media attention and commercial success followed rapidly. By the time Banksy painted on the West Bank wall in 2005 he was already well known. Banksy's original pieces were selling for tens of thousands of pounds by 2006 (a set of six silk-screen-print Kate Moss paintings sold at Sotheby's for over £50,000 that October). By April 2007 another piece by Banksy sold at Bonhams auction house for almost £300,000. Auction prices for other street artists also rose significantly around that time.

In the small number of years that have followed there has continued to be an elevated interest in street art and Banksy in particular, unsurprising given his very successful solo show at Bristol Museum in 2009 and 2010 movie *Exit Through the Gift Shop*. Commercial success and important exhibitions, such as *Street Art* at Tate Modern, London in May 2008 and *Art in the Streets* at MOCA, Los Angeles in April 2011, have encouraged an increasing number of institutions to accept graffiti and street art as important artistic movements. The press has kept a watchful eye on street art in recent years as it is often easily documented, sometimes comments on current events and the media is increasingly keen for image-led reporting.

GLOBAL BREAKDOWN

Although there are hundreds of images, the following pages only skim the surface of artists practicing today. A collection such as this can never be complete and there's inevitably a bias towards places with which I'm more familiar. What follows is not meant to be an accurate representation nor is it necessarily the very best work from each location but simply a collection of stunning art from that location. There are numerous countries where our own knowledge and coverage will develop over time and a lack of current photographs is not reflective of the scene there. Street art is truly global and the harder you look the more stunning examples you can see from every corner of the Globe. Many countries, indeed even cities, could furnish a stunning book twice this size in their own right. Finally, many artists travel to paint in other countries, a fact often reflected in the photographs presented here.

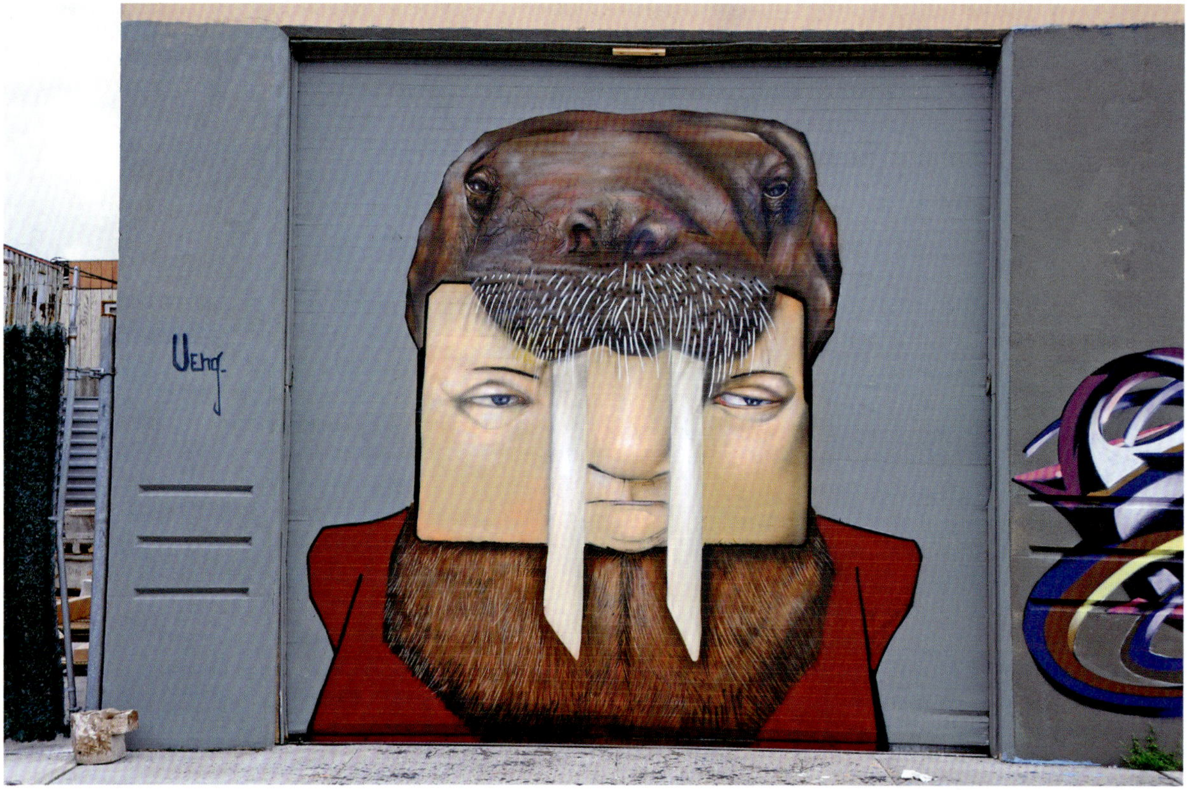

Uehg

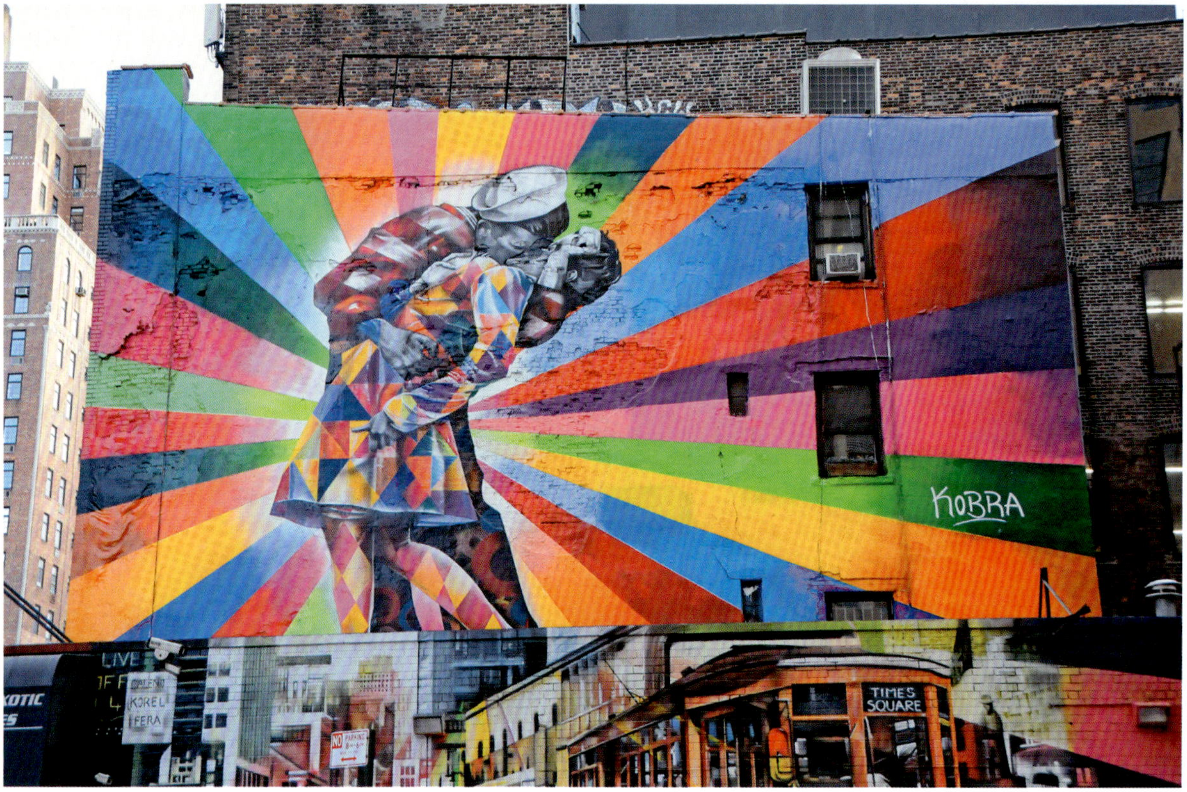

KOBRA
LIVE
KOREL
FERA
XOTIC
ES
TIMES
SQUARE

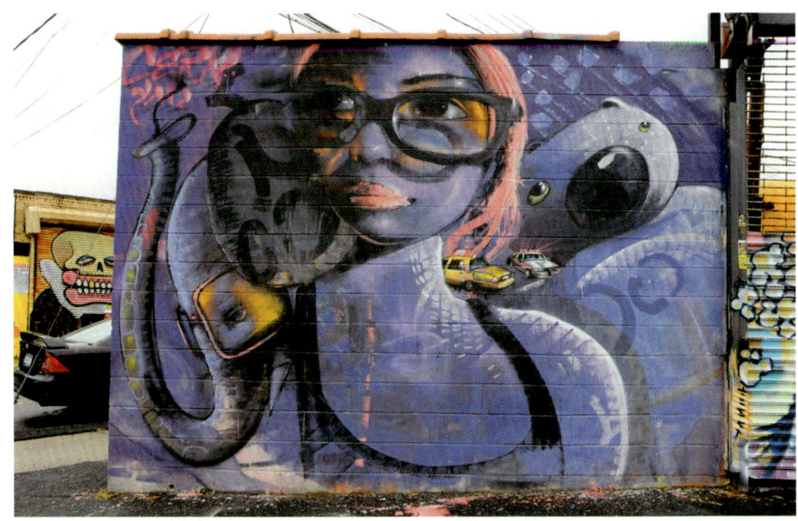

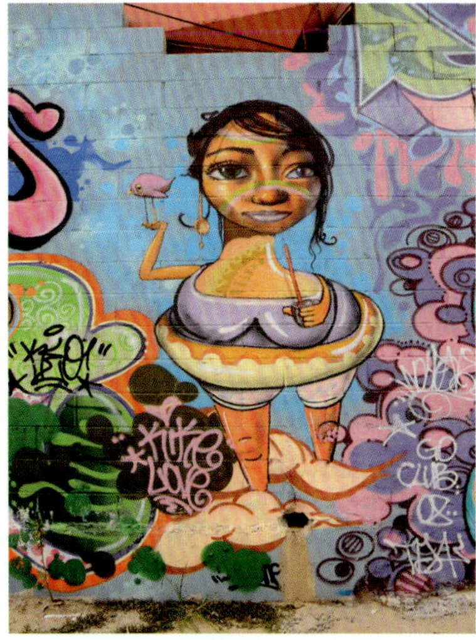

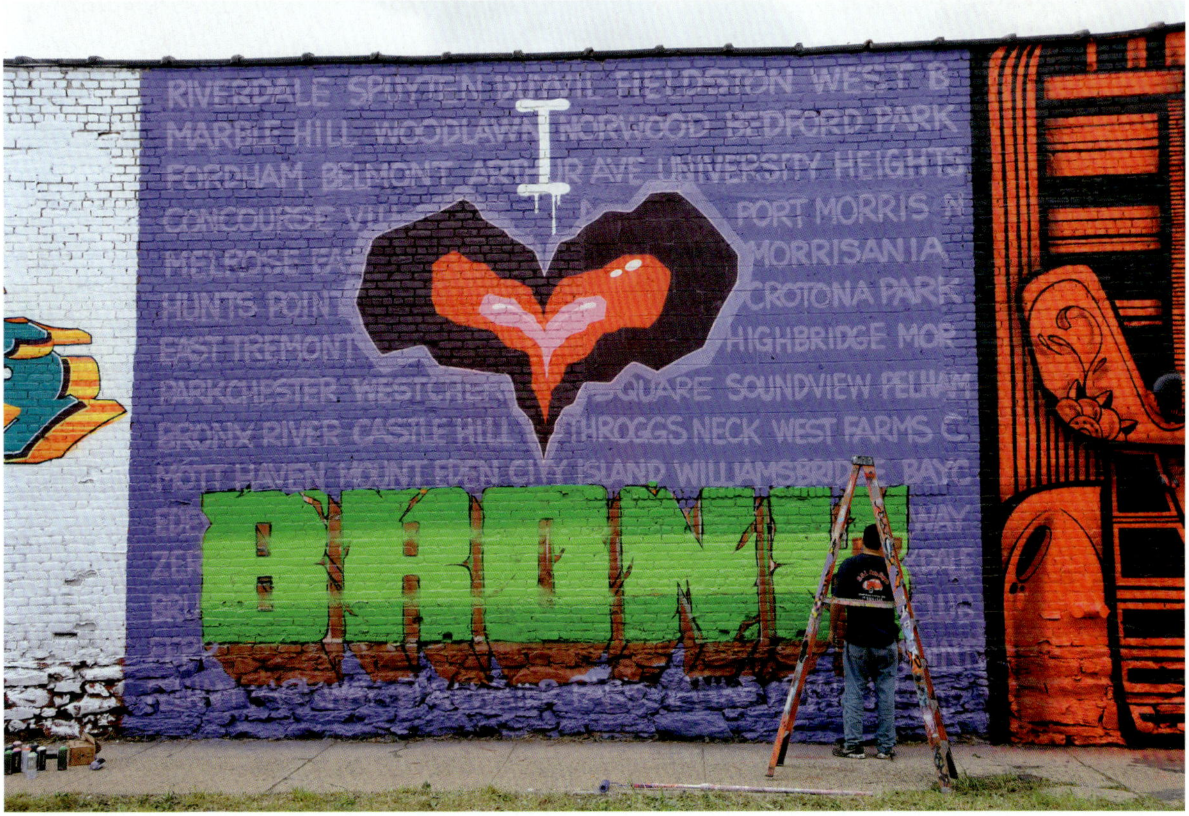

I ♥ BRONX
RIVERDALE SPUYTEN DUYVIL FIELDSTON WEST B
MARBLE HILL WOODLAWN NORWOOD BEDFORD PARK
FORDHAM BELMONT ARTHUR AVE UNIVERSITY HEIGHTS
CONCOURSE VIL
MELROSE
HUNTS POINT
EAST TREMONT
PORT MORRIS N
MORRISANIA
CROTONA PARK
HIGHBRIDGE MOR
PARKCHESTER WESTCHE SQUARE SOUNDVIEW PELHAM
BRONX RIVER CASTLE HILL THROGGS NECK WEST FARMS C
MOTT HAVEN MOUNT EDEN CITY ISLAND WILLIAMSBRIDGE BAYC

CLOCKWISE FROM TOP
LEFT:
Veng from USA's Robots
Will Kill/USA's Cern/
Cern/Bio from New
York's Tats Cru/São
Paulo's Eduardo Kobra,
near the High Line.

FOLLOWING PAGES 30-
31, CLOCKWISE FROM
TOP LEFT:
USA's Never/Germany's
Hendrik Beikirch, also
known as ECB/Hendrik
Beikirch/Never.

PAGES 32-3, FROM TOP
An abandoned building
known as The Batcave/
An abandoned military
base in Fort Tilden,
New York.

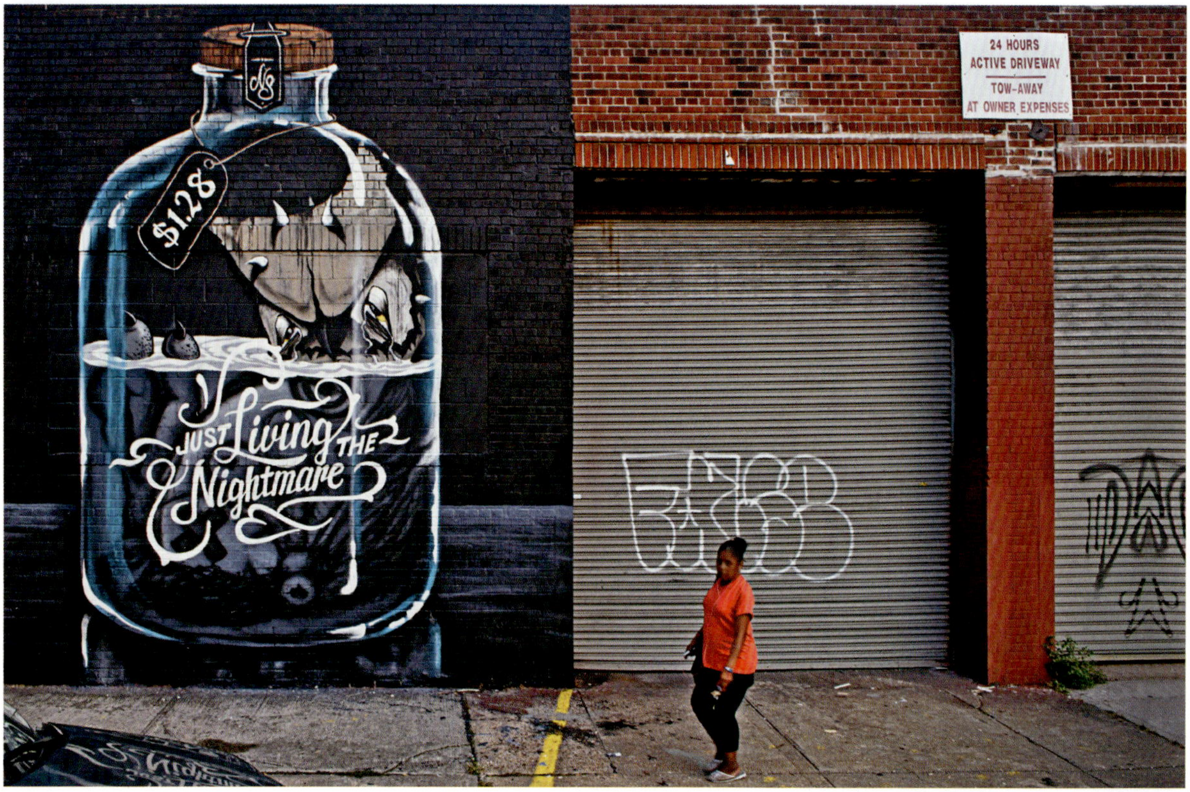

$1.28
Just Living The Nightmare

24 HOURS
ACTIVE DRIVEWAY
TOW-AWAY
AT OWNER EXPENSES

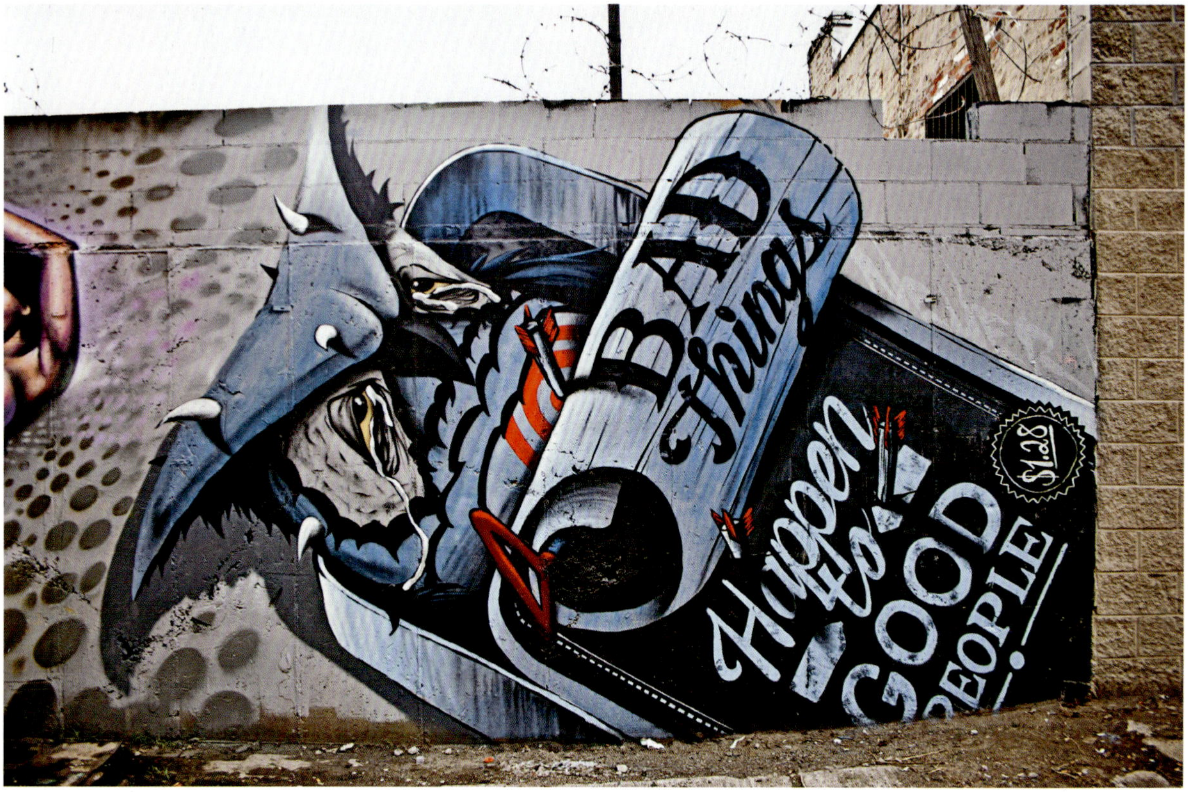

BAD Things
Happen to GOOD PEOPLE
$1.28

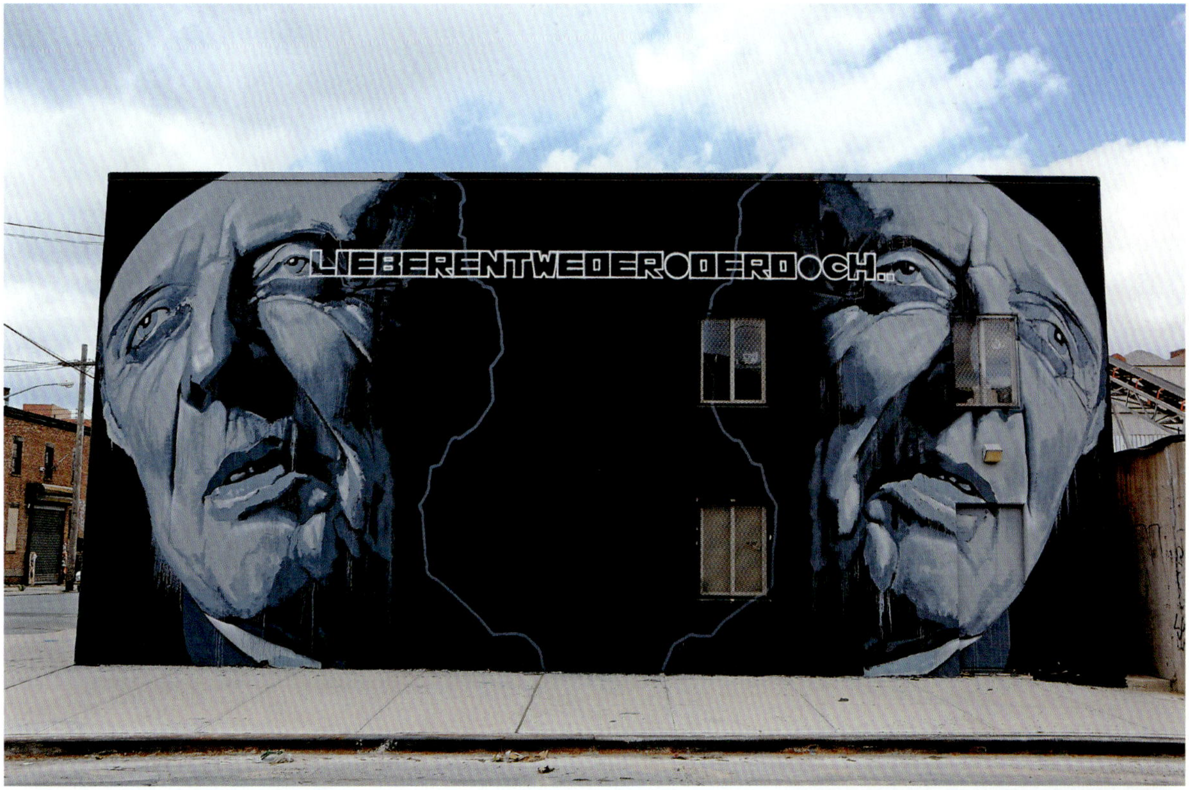

LIEBERENTWEDERODERDOCH..

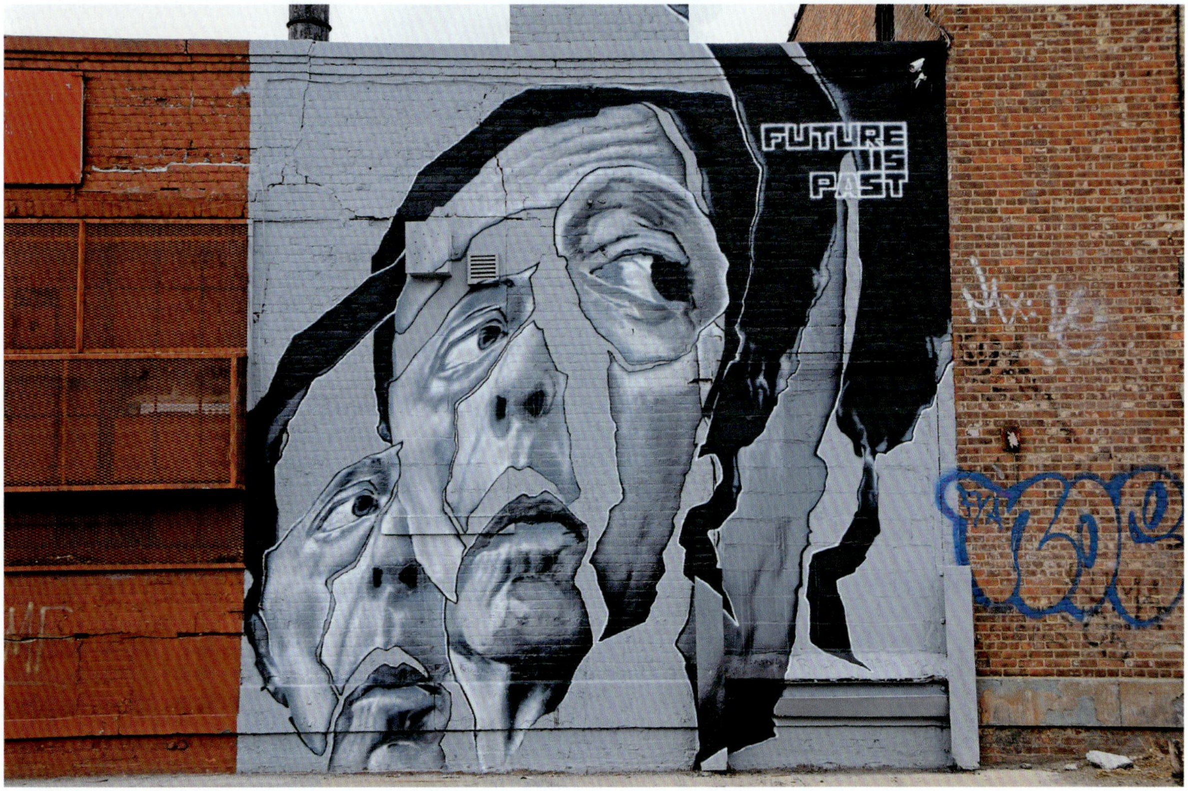

FUTURE
IS
PAST

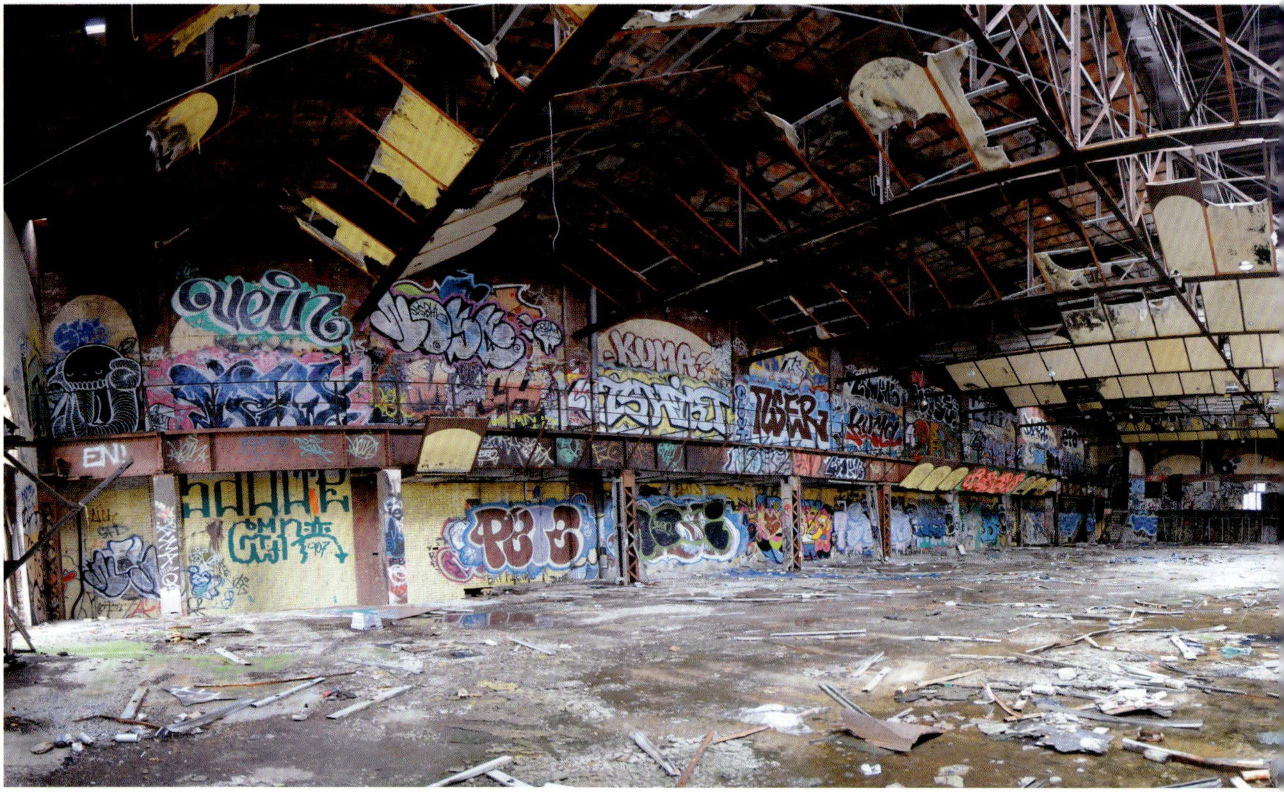

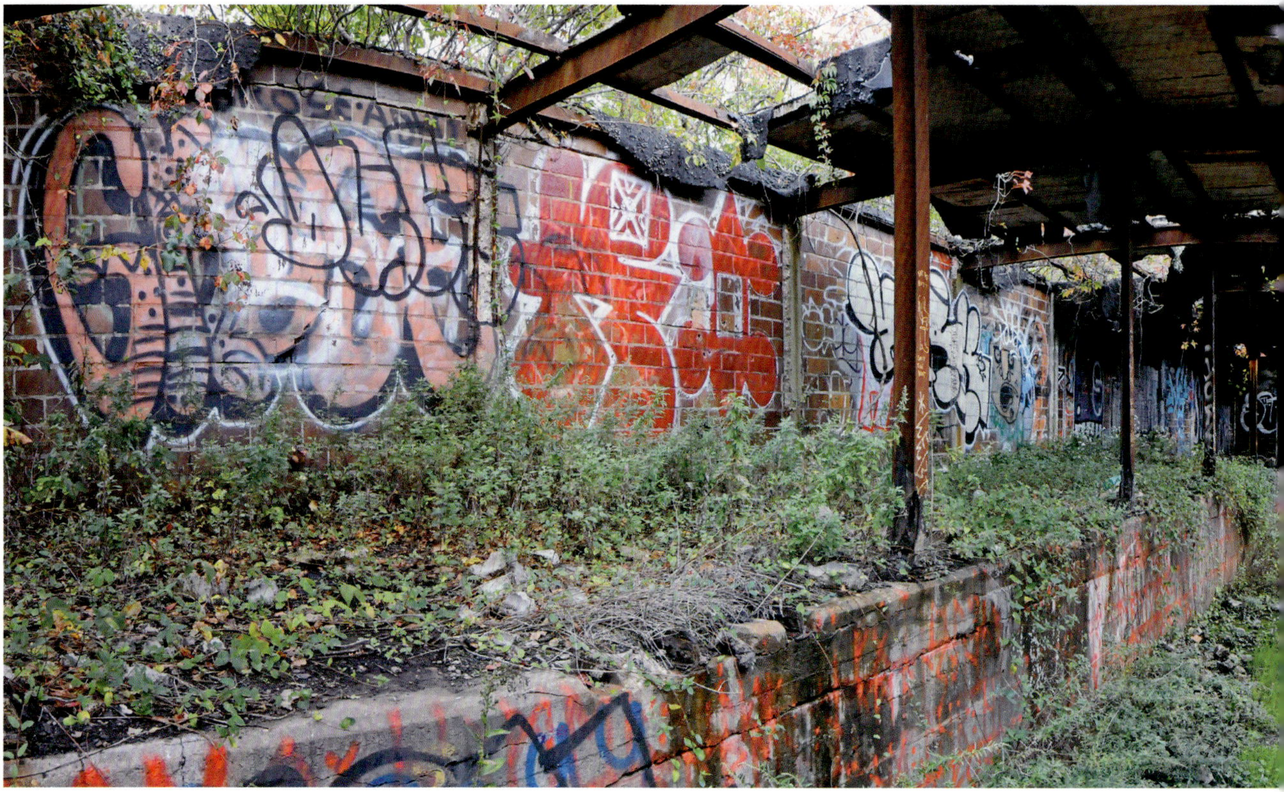

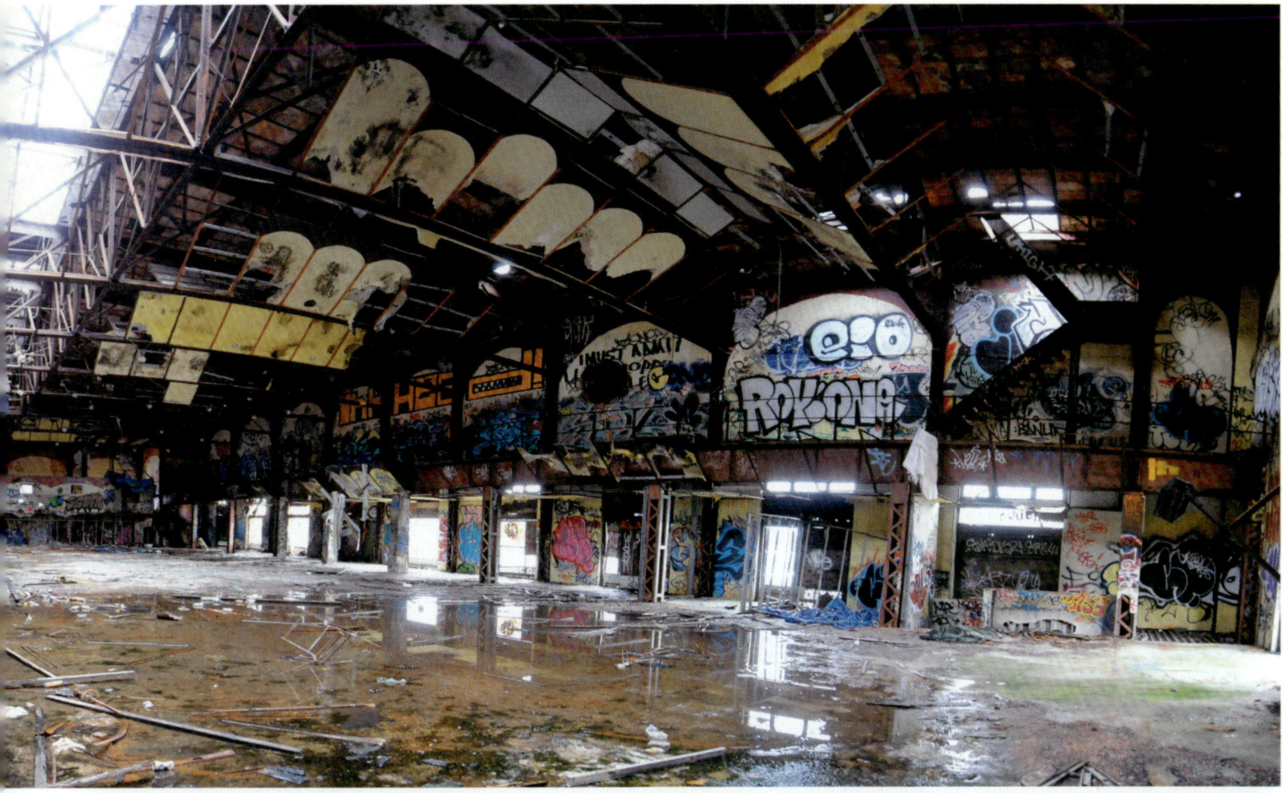

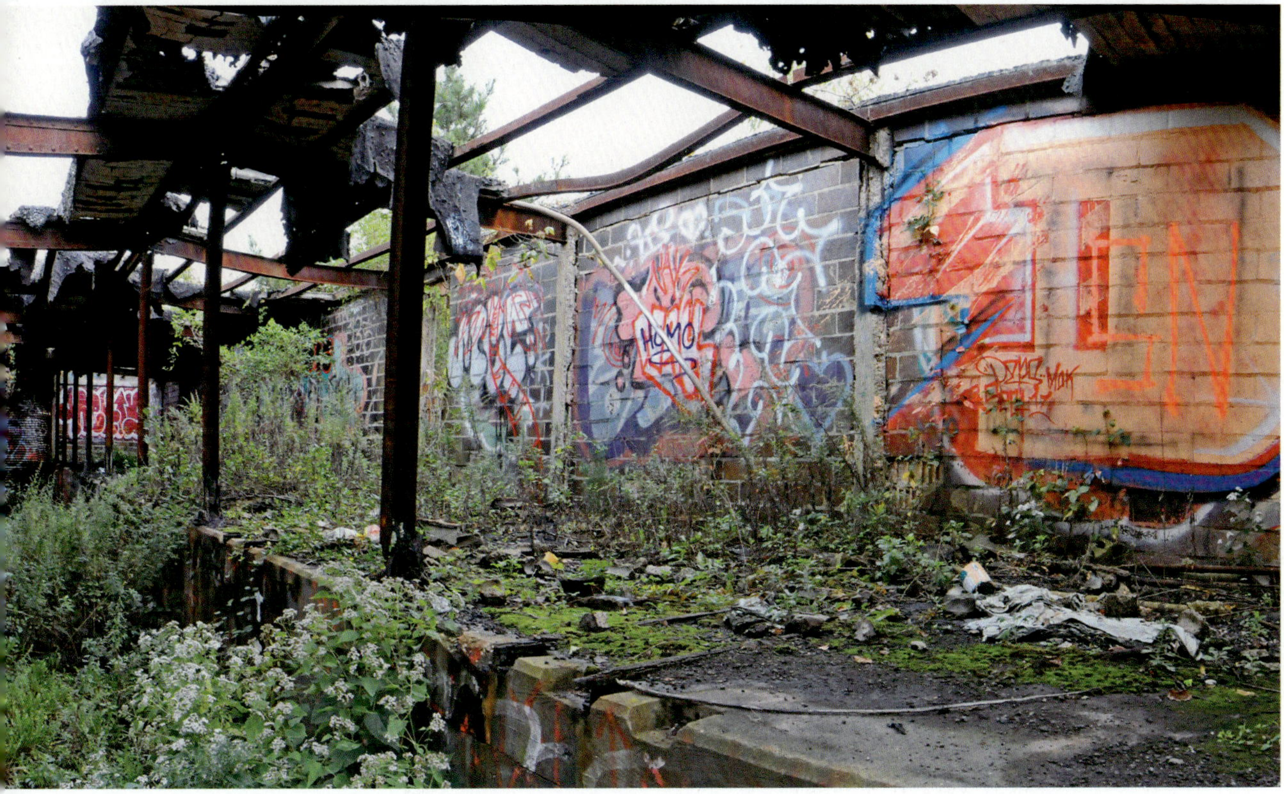

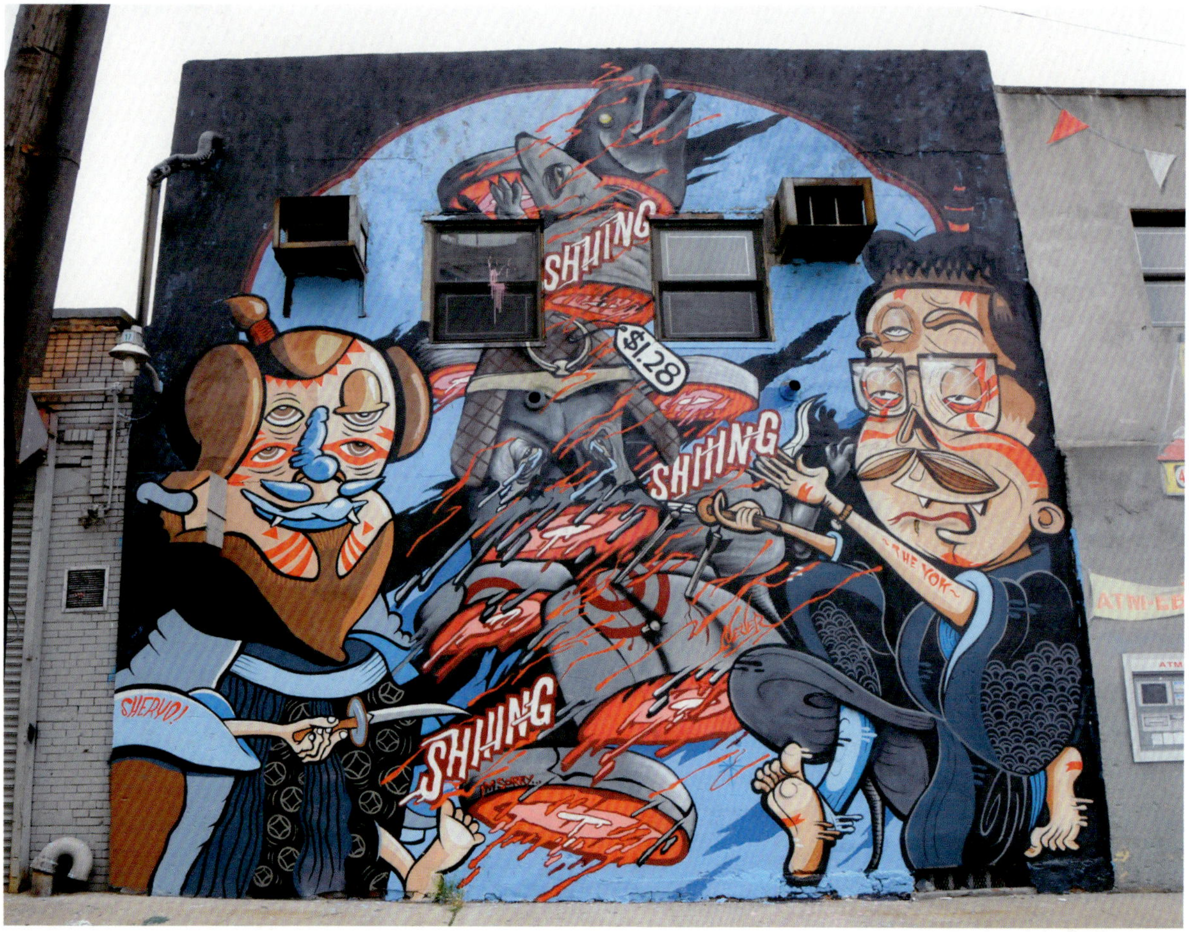

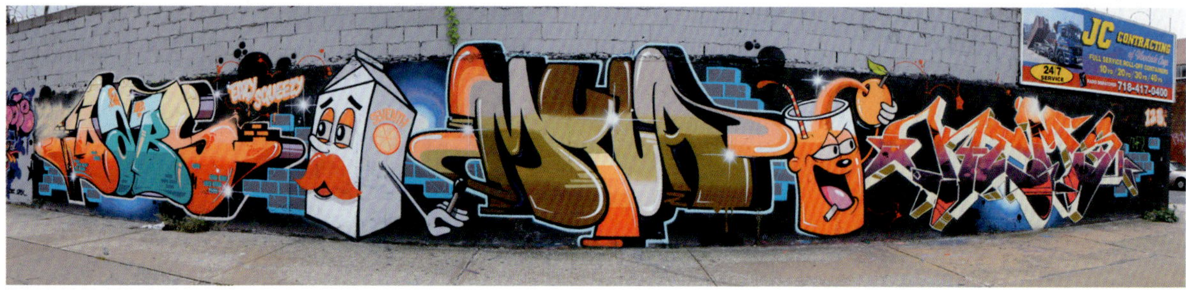

CLOCKWISE FROM TOP:
Australia's Yok,
Singapore's Sheryo and
USA's Never/Spain's
Kram/Dabs & Myla (both
Australia) and Kems
(USA).

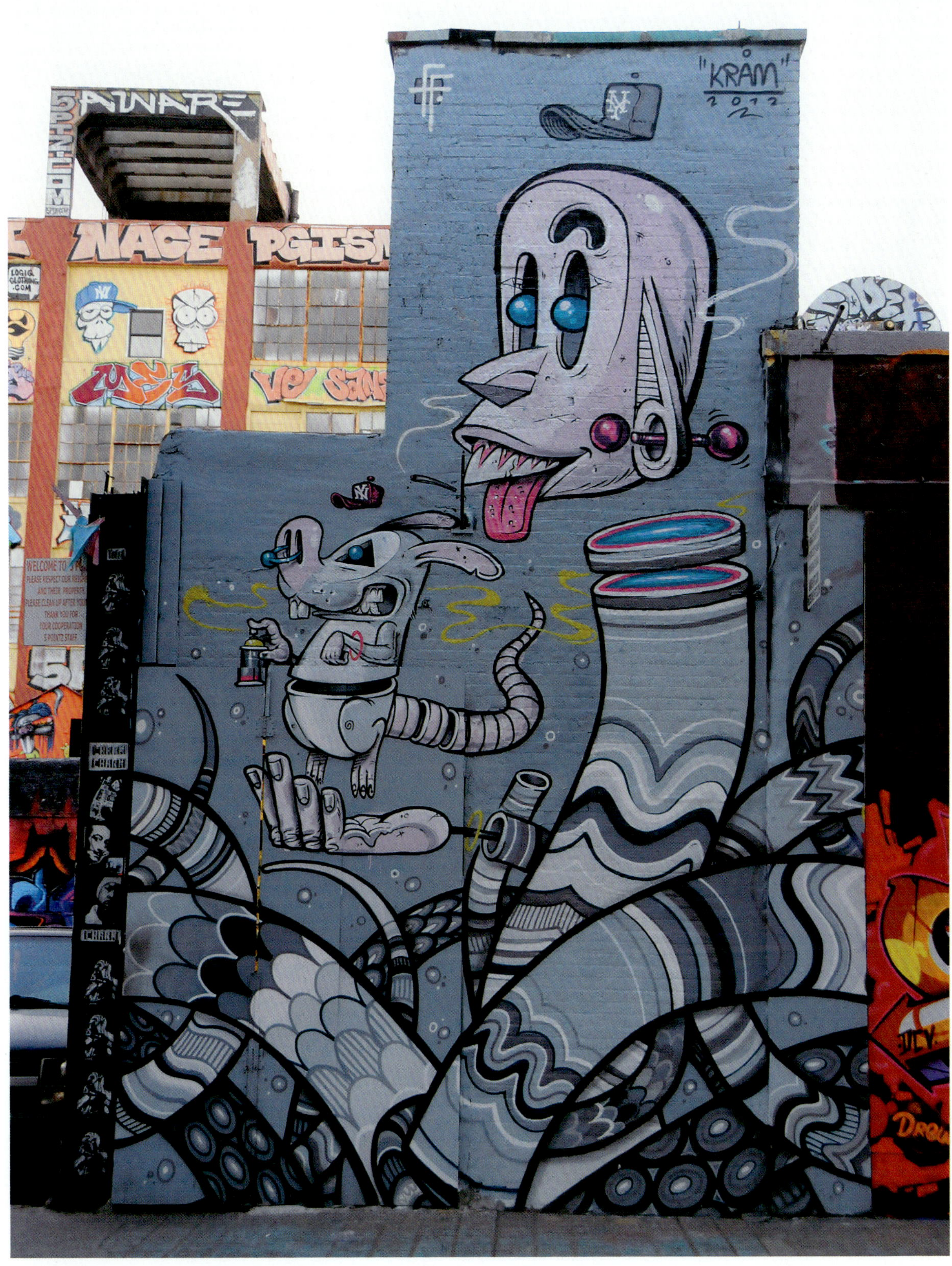
"KRAM"
2012

Los Angeles & The West Coast

Outside of the East Coast, Los Angeles was the next city to 'receive' New York's graffiti culture in 1982. However, it met with pre-existing local concepts of graffiti that had developed among Mexican-American youth and gangs. The first gang-related graffiti in LA dates back perhaps as early as the 1940s after the infamous 'zoot suit' riots, when American servicemen attacked young Mexican-Americans. 'Cholo' gangs (youth of Mexican descent but born in the United States) formed and their territorial gang-related graffiti developed particularly from the 1960s, based on fonts that were seen as prestigious, such as the Old English font.

One early graffiti pioneer in LA was Chaz Bojórquez, who built on the legacy of cholo gang graffiti in the Highland Park neighbourhood in East LA. Bojórquez famously created the Señor Suerte character (a skull wearing pimp's clothing), which he produced as a stencil as early as 1969. This is one of the first examples of image-based stencils (i.e. not text) used for graffiti. The Señor Suerte character has since been adopted by gangs as a protective icon (commonly used as a tattoo), meant to prevent the victim of a gunshot wound from dying.

The artist Risk (AWR, MSK) on the LA scene:
'Because of our local traditions, when NY graffiti arrived in 1982 there were differences in different parts of the city. The Westside of LA was more influenced by hip-hop but the Eastside had the gang tradition. That said, at the start most kids wanted to emulate New York – it took time for LA's style to really emerge as its own.

In the early days there was a healthy writer community base that used to meet in places like the Radiotron club, which held battles. The competition made writers work hard to get better and that competitive spirit has always been a part of the LA scene. Maybe because of the competition, maybe because of the bright LA sunshine, but our use of colour was distinct from NY. LA writers used brighter, more vibrant colours. That tradition persists today.'

Unlike New York, LA didn't have a ubiquitous mass transit metro system. Consequently, early taggers often targeted buses. In 1989, LA's graffiti scene developed a strategy of painting the overpass signs on freeways, which came to be known as 'heaven spots'.

Risk (AWR, MSK) again:
'There were different phases in LA graffiti – the first generation was roughly 1982–88 but then we started painting "heaven spots" in 1989 and that changed everything. Heaven spots are freeway signs; everyone here has a car and travels on the freeways. So if you really wanted to get up, you had to paint the heaven spots. Unlike train yards, everyone sees heaven spots, not just other writers that go to yards! LA is also a huge city so the idea of going all-city is a lot harder than in New York – you have to paint harder for longer to get up everywhere in LA but writers do – it's competitive. Our local influences have always made LA's graffiti different. I pay homage to the NY scene but I think LA's pushed the boundaries. I think LA is on top and really took graffiti to another level.'

I lived in LA for two years during a brief mistake working in finance. It was there I started taking photos of graffiti, and there I learned that writing graffiti was not for me. The first time I held a spraycan was at a party in downtown LA, where a girl had bought spraypaint, pens and various other artistic tools for people to write birthday messages for her on a big whiteboard. I don't quite remember the middle part but I do remember my friend Derf (not his real name) and myself sitting in the car park writing 'Lee' (my actual name) in big bubble letters on a wall. If it's not obvious from this, I'll spell it out – we were drunk. Around my name we wrote words like 'London', 'overseas', etc. I was the only British guy at the party and it was so obvious I was involved I should have just stapled my passport to the wall.

The next day, Derf's cousin Ives called me and said he couldn't get hold of Derf but the police were too busy to care about this – the cops had spoken with the girl whose party it was and she'd brokered that if we cleared up our own mess we'd be OK. I forgot to mention – we wrote on a federal building. Shit! Ives and I drove back to the car park and this may be the first time in history a (wannabe) graffiti writer has buffed himself. I still remember going into the paint shop and asking for federal-building-coloured paint. That was when I decided I was better behind a camera!

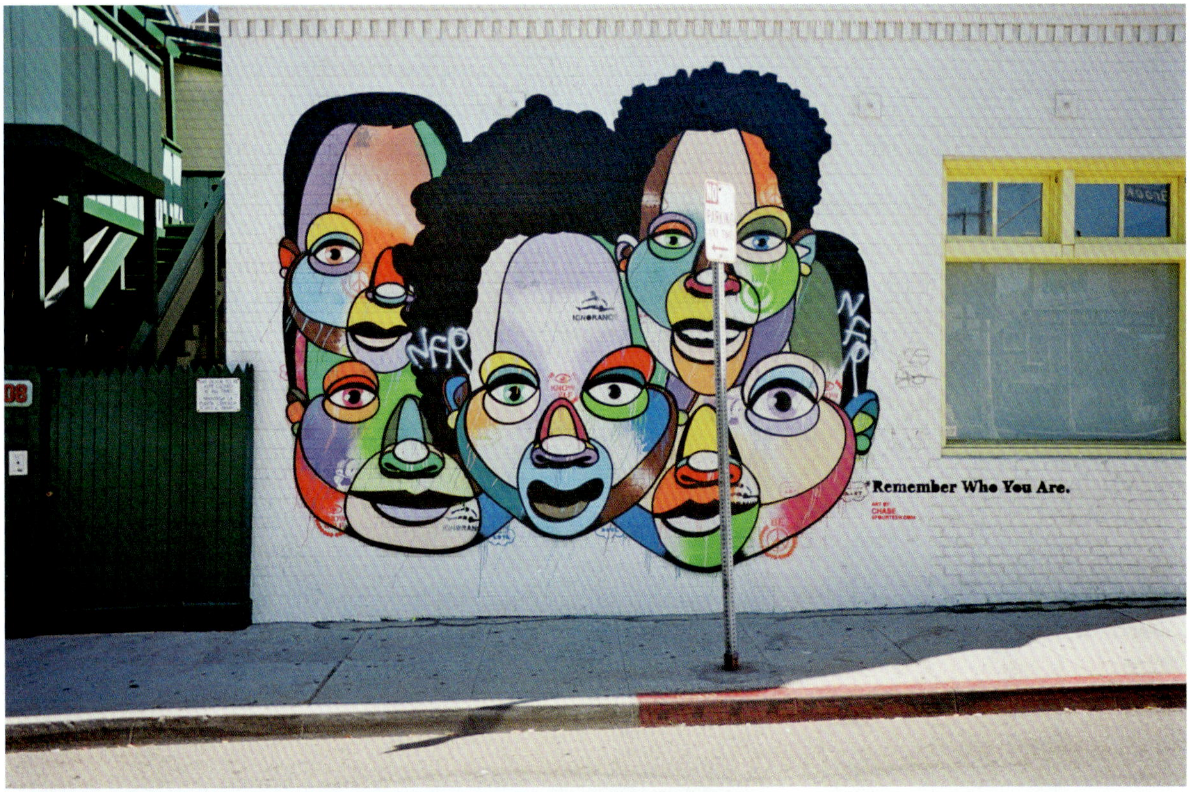

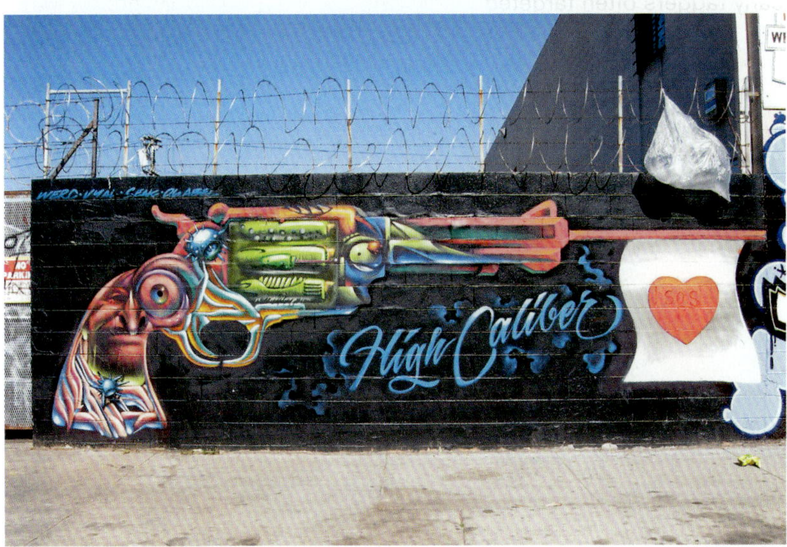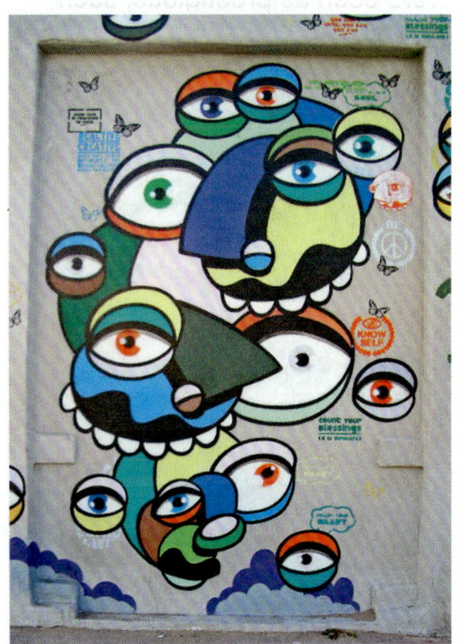

CLOCKWISE FROM TOP:
Chase (from Belgium,
but a long-term USA
resident)/Chase/Various
USA artists, including
OG Abel, Werc and Vyal,
plus Seak (Germany).

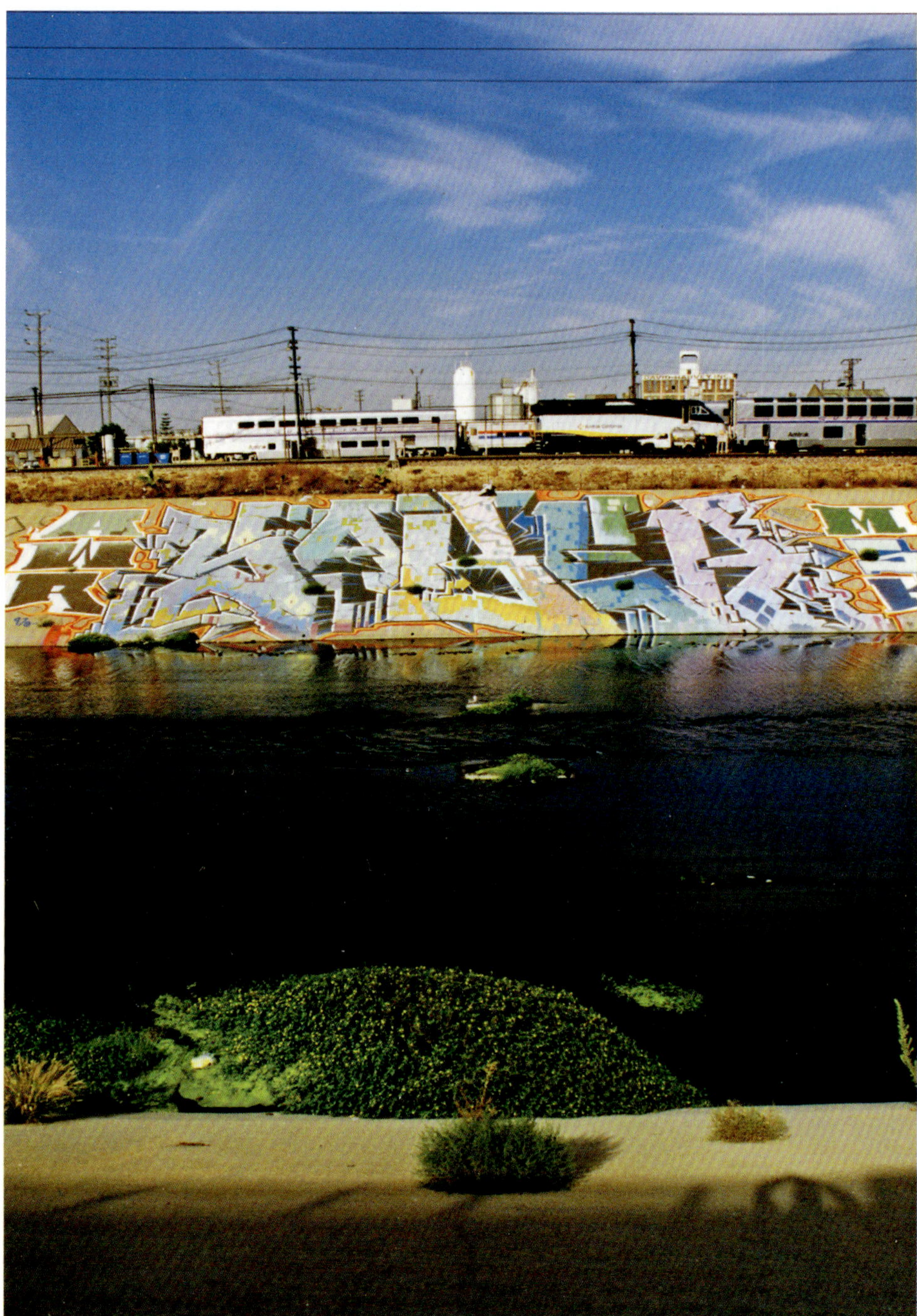

CLOCKWISE FROM
LEFT:
A legendary piece on
the LA river by MSK
Crew's Saber. This
is one of the oldest
pieces in the book,
dating back to 1997/
The Dalai Lama by
LA's Mear-One (CBS
Crew)/*Humanity vs The
Machine* by LA's Mear-
One (CBS Crew).

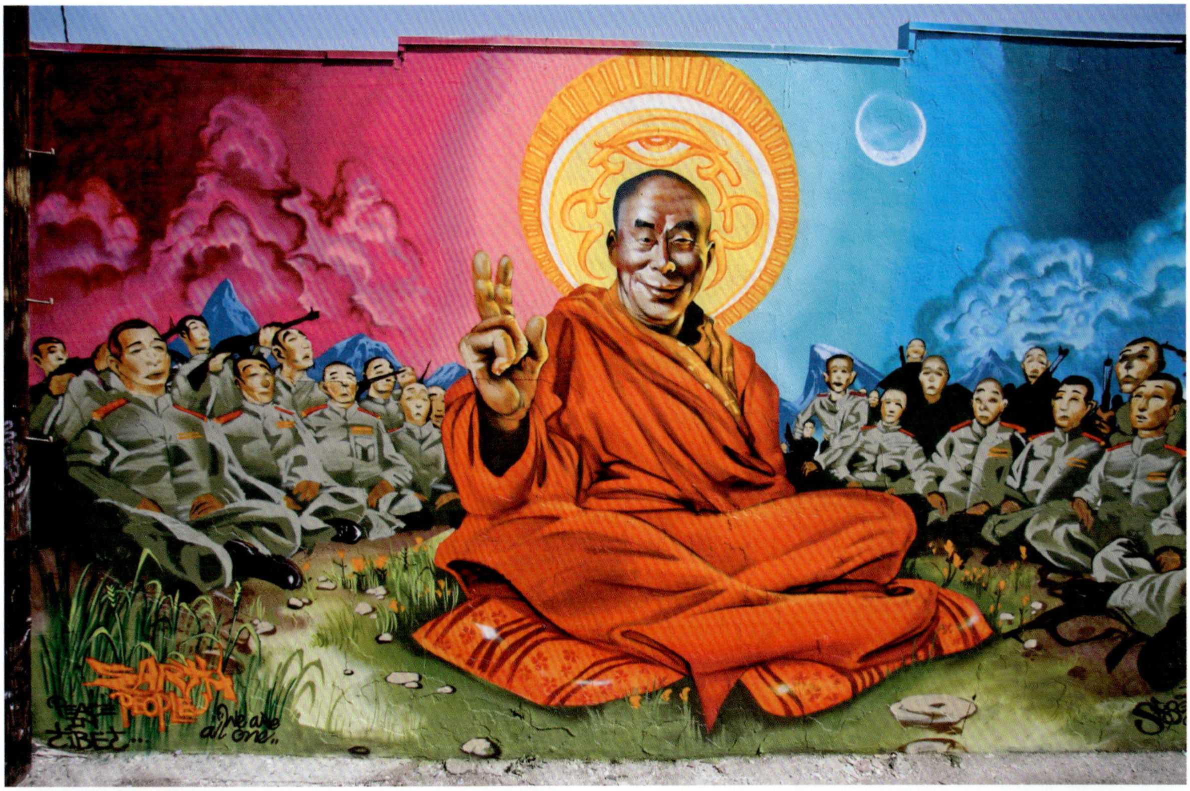

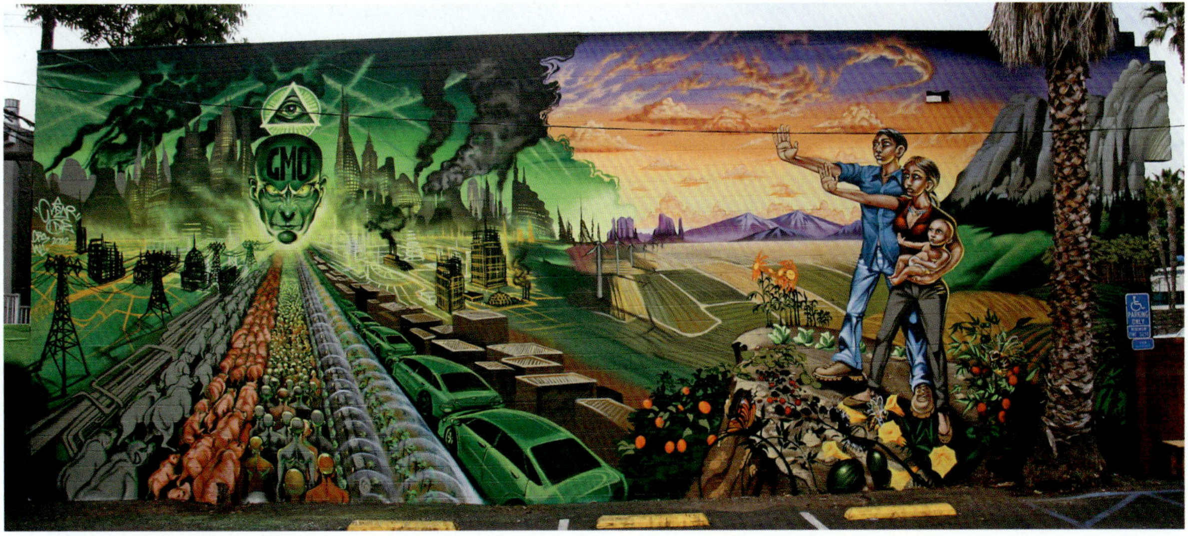

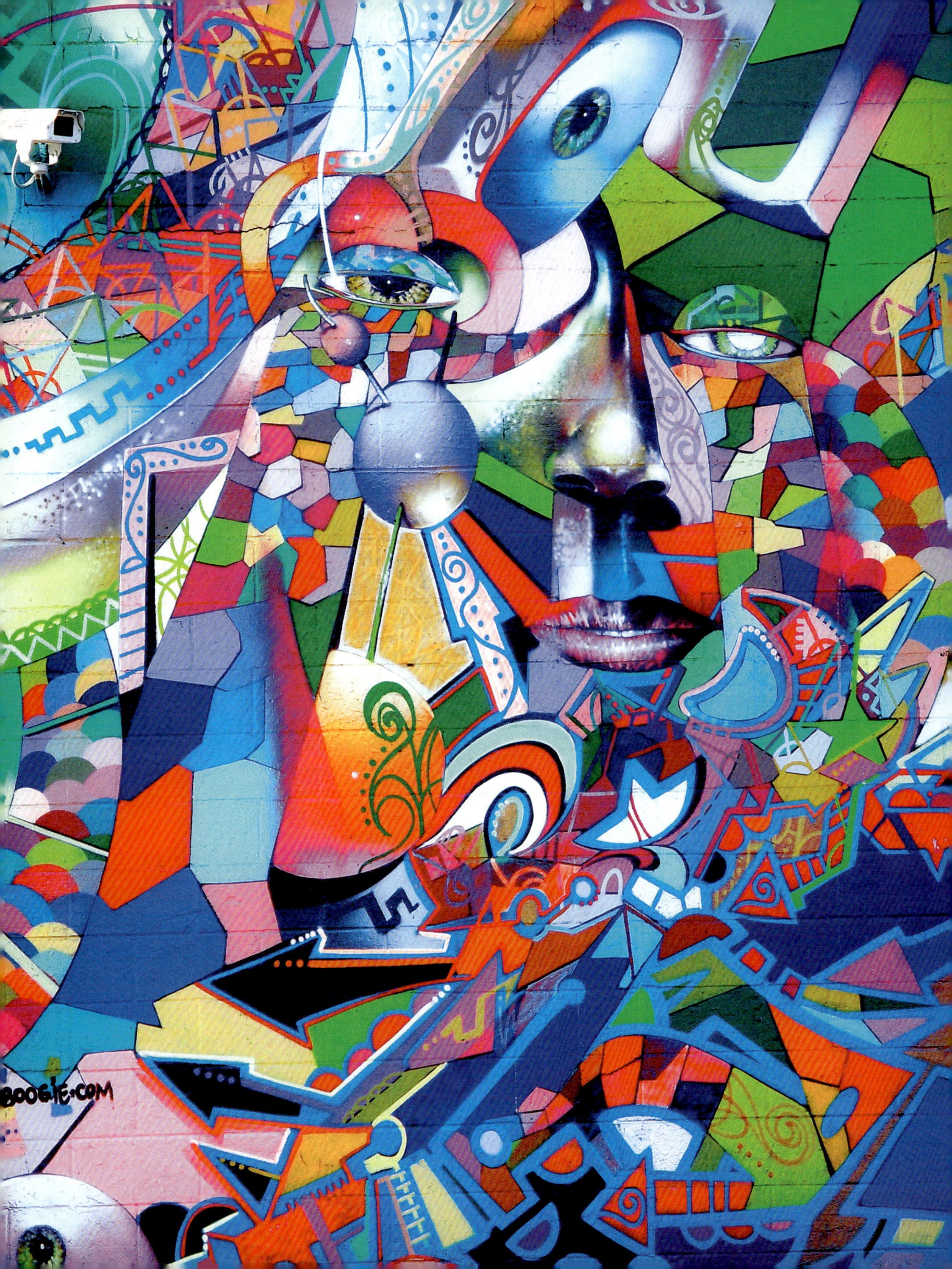

BOOGIE.COM

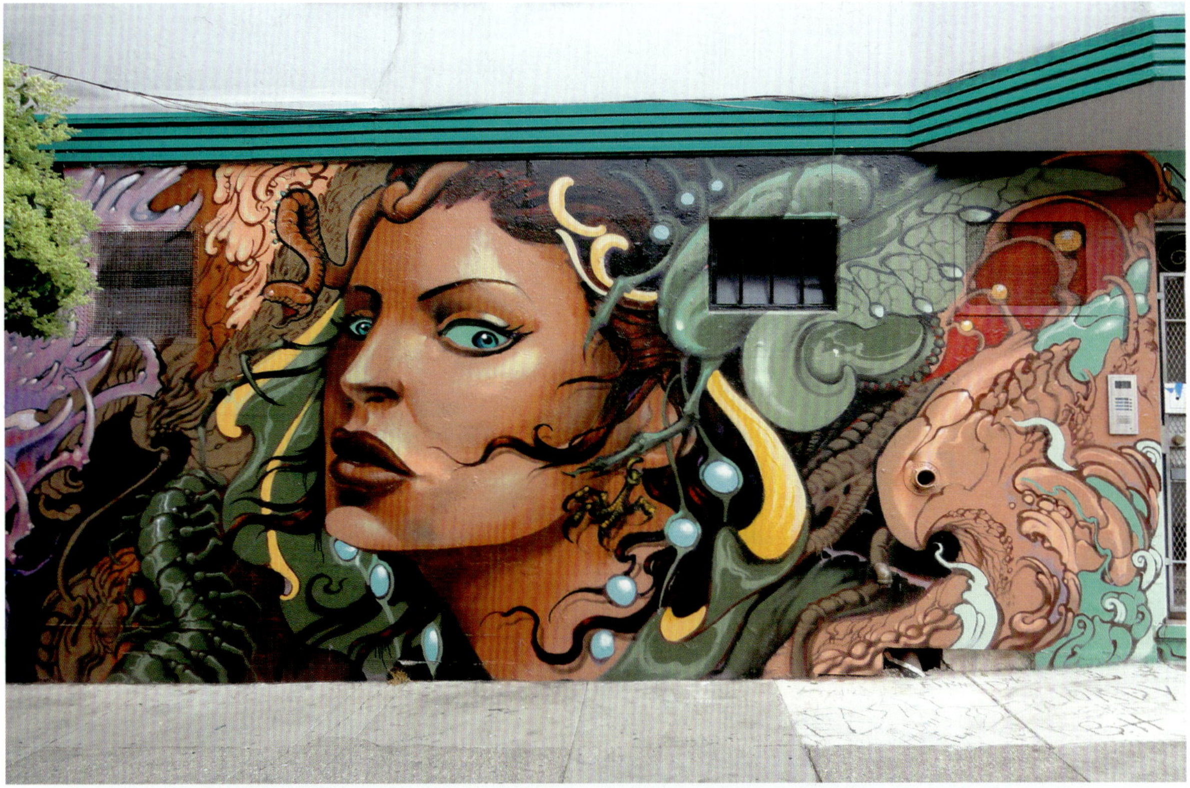

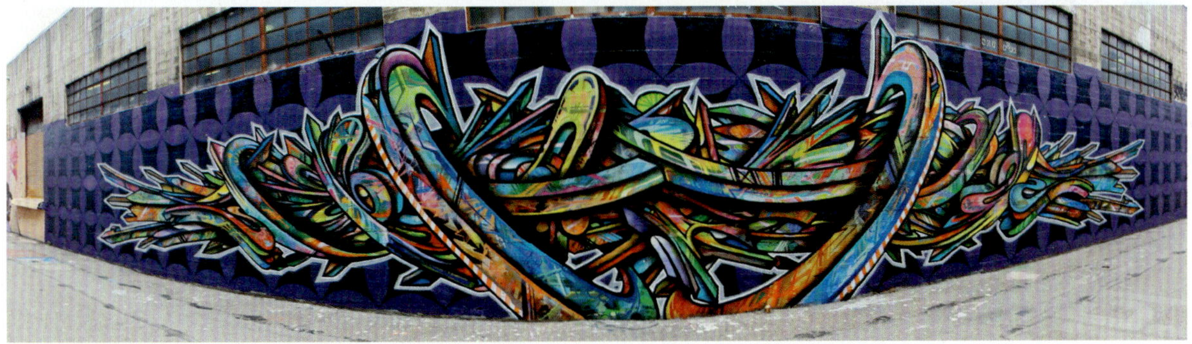

CLOCKWISE FROM LEFT: A detail from an amazing piece by San Francisco's Chor Boogie. Chor wanted me to note that his style is modern hieroglyphics, not street art. It makes sense given the very heavy symbolism/Lango Oliveira (also an amazing tattoo artist)/Apex-One.

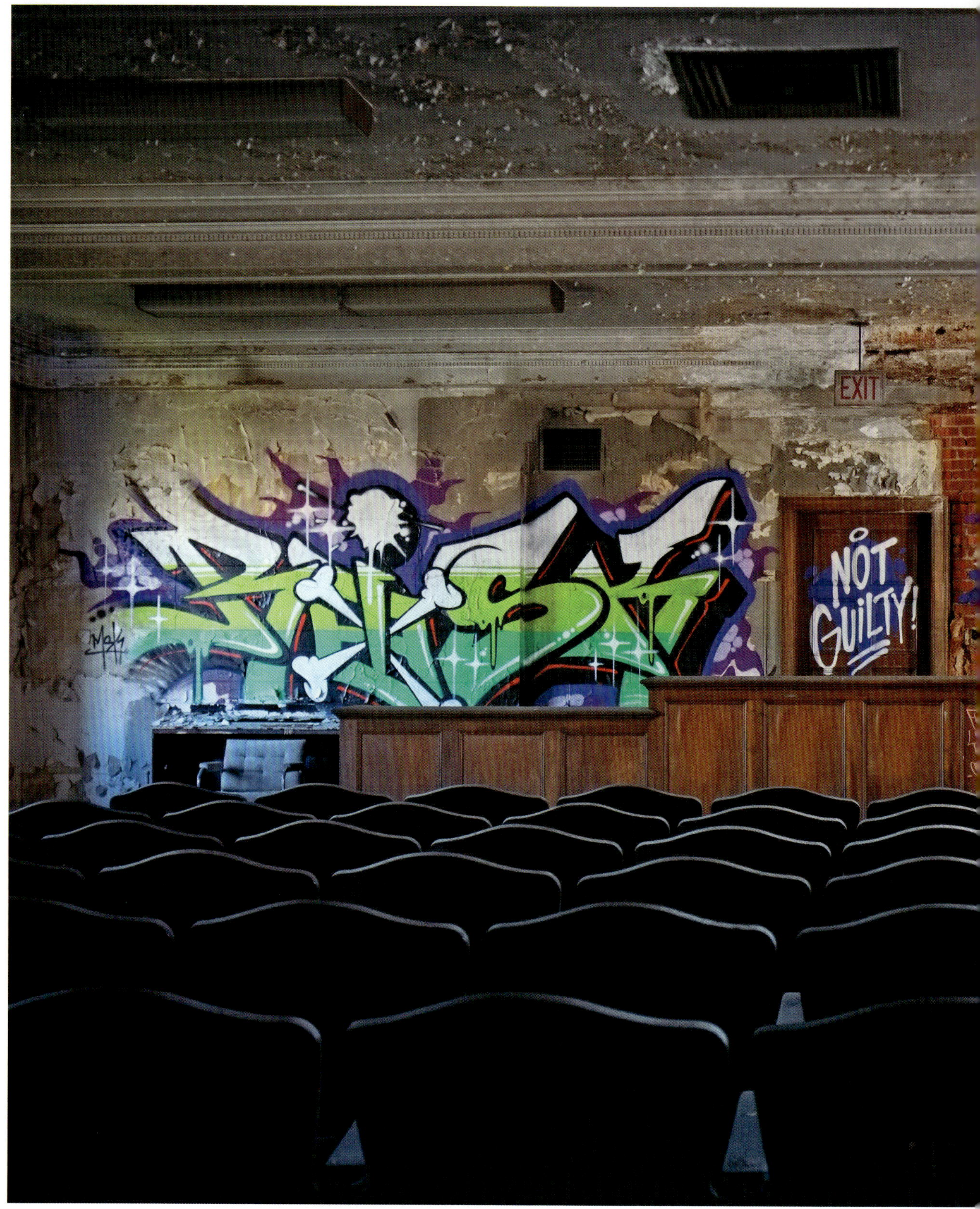

EXIT
NOT GUILTY!

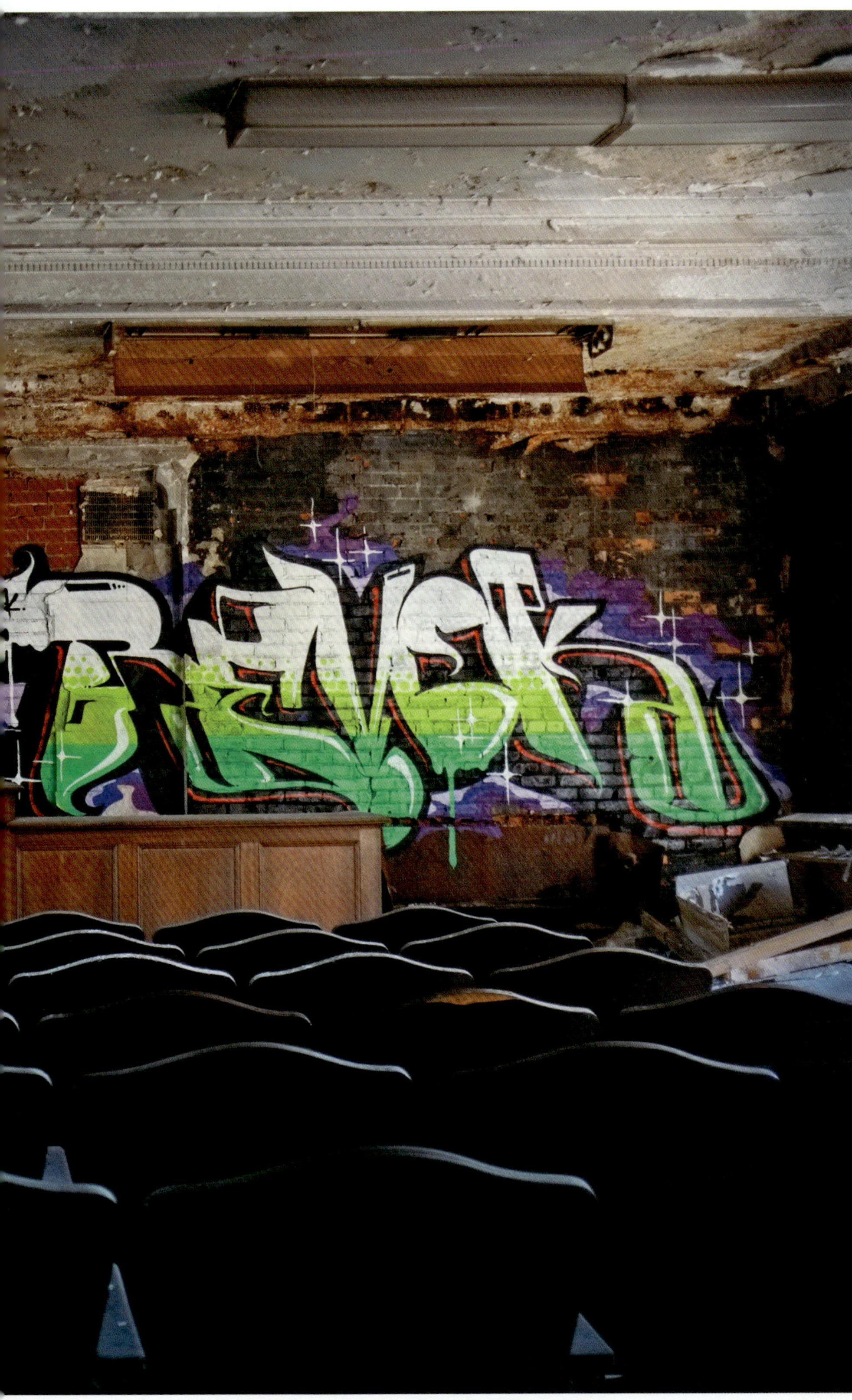

THESE PAGES:
Risk and Revok in an
abandoned courtroom.
This piece dates to
2008.

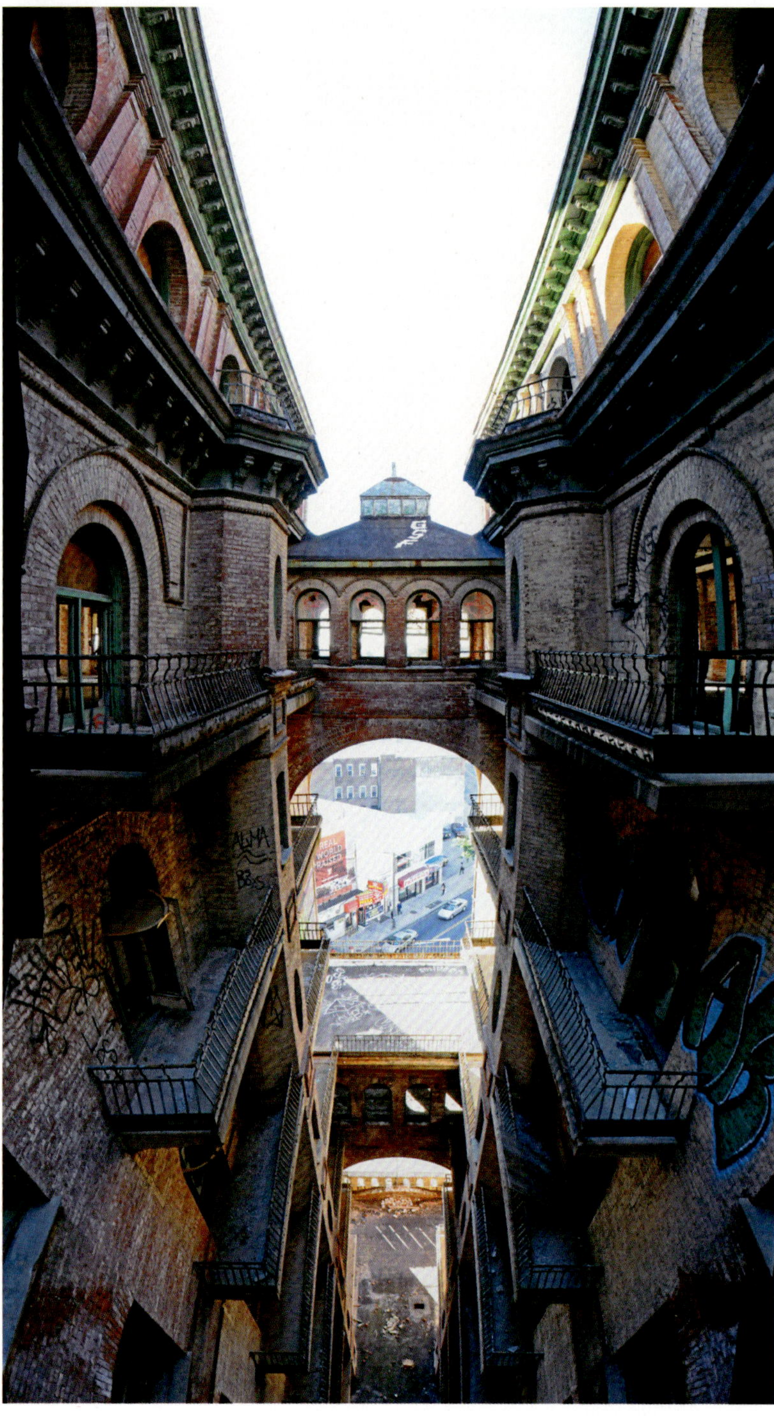

CLOCKWISE FROM LEFT:
Leaning out of a broken
window at the empty
Divine Lorraine Hotel
in Philadelphia/Vyal
in Las Vegas/Canada's
Labrona/New Zealand's
Askew in Hawaii.

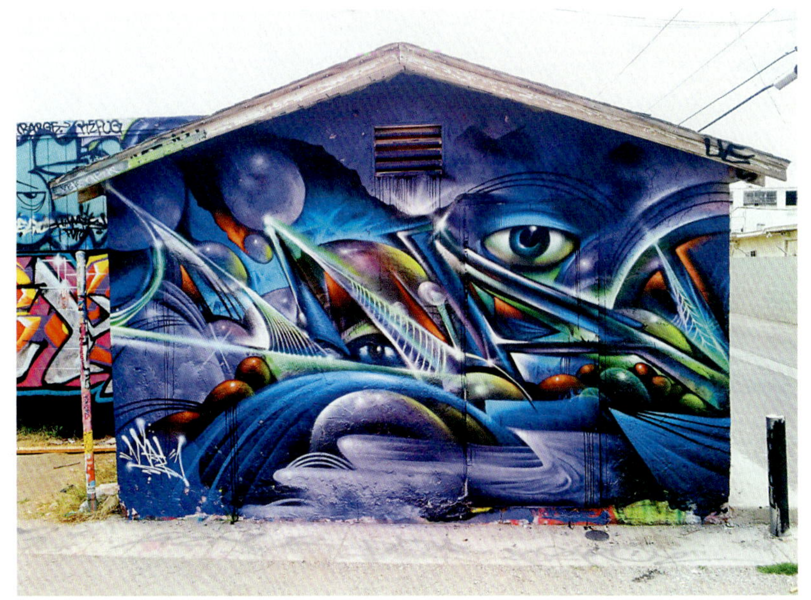
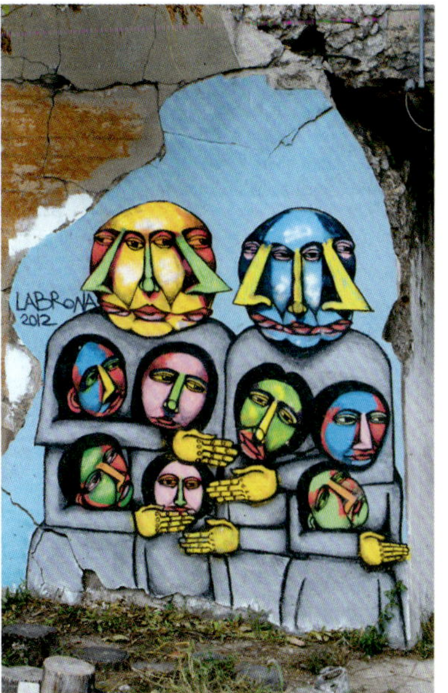
LABRONA
2012

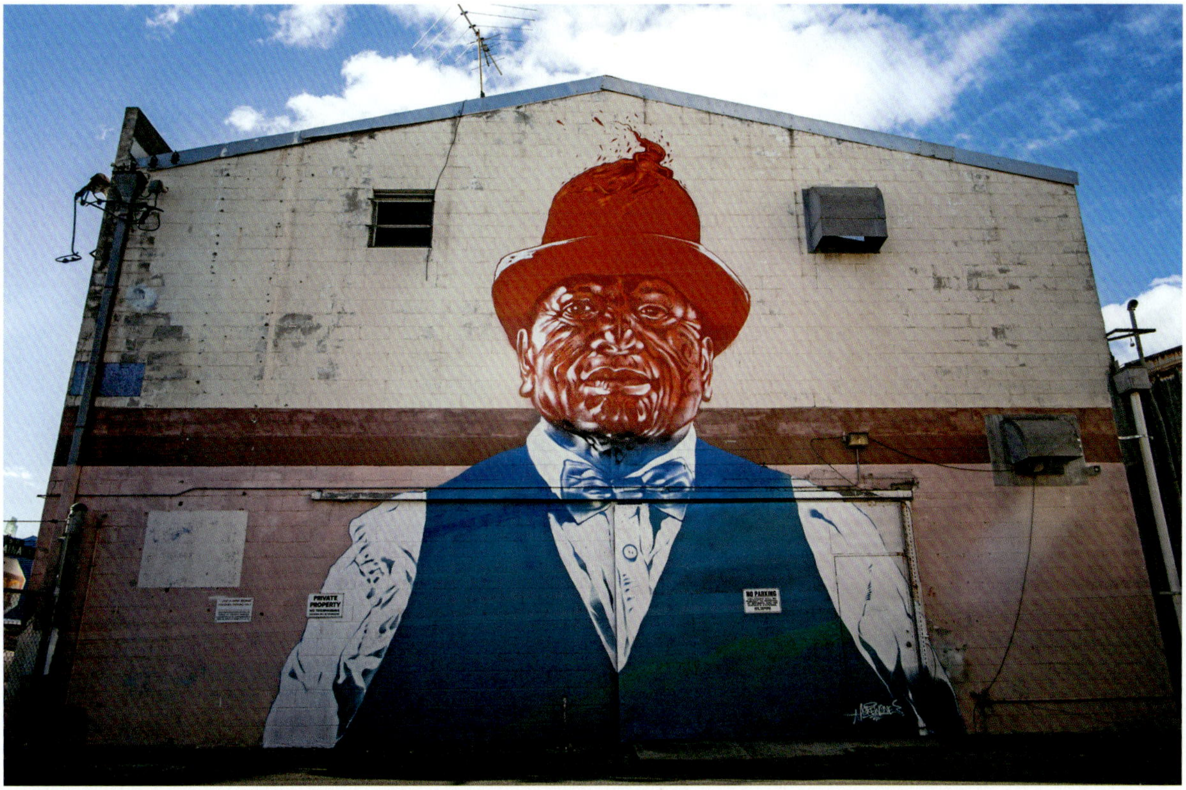

The Spread to Europe

Through its films, television and music, America has been a powerful cultural exporter for much of the 20th century. During the 1970s, hip-hop culture started to emerge in New York City and, despite its wildly different origins, graffiti became incorporated into it as one of the 'four elements', alongside DJing, MCing and b-boying (or breakdancing). The notion that graffiti has always been a part of hip-hop in America is a myth because the separate elements evolved independently. However, when graffiti reached Europe in the early 1980s it did so as a part of the 'package' of hip-hop culture.

Prior to the 1980s, the spread of graffiti outside America was largely due to US writers travelling abroad and non-Americans going to New York and finding inspiration there. Of course, many countries already had local forms of graffiti but these were more political than artistic (most early 1980s London graffiti was related to either the IRA or anarchic punk bands).

A number of high-profile movies, such as *Wildstyle* and *Style Wars* (both 1983), celebrating hip-hop culture were released, which exported graffiti *en masse* into Europe. Martha Cooper, a newspaper photographer, met graffiti writer Dondi in 1979; he introduced her to the graffiti scene. Cooper went on to document many iconic graffiti works, often featuring the writers at work. The famous 1984 book *Subway Art*, a collection of stunning photographs of New York subway train graffiti and graffiti writers taken by Martha Cooper and Henry Chalfant (an

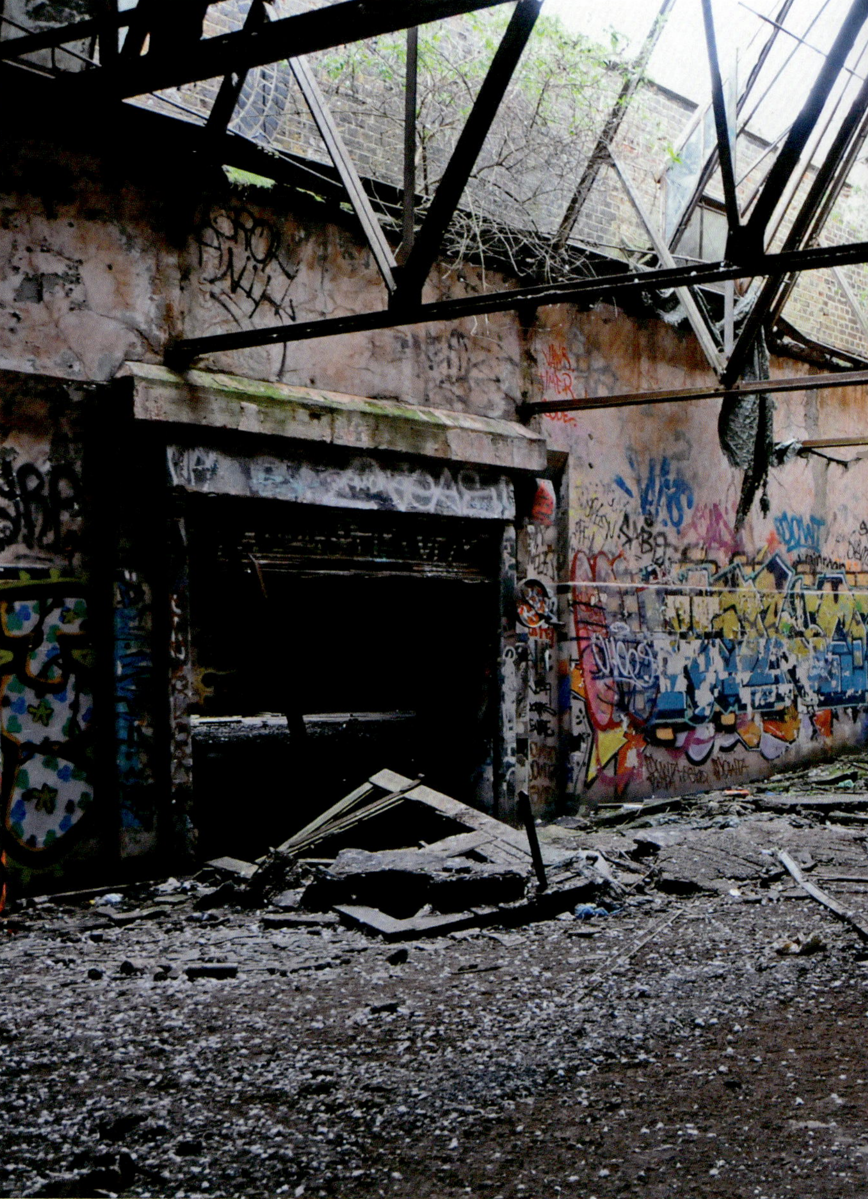

equally iconic photographer and co-producer of *Style Wars*), led to a huge increase in the number of writers around the world. Much of the European evolution of graffiti mirrored the early days in New York. In London, for example, writers rapidly took to painting on the outside of trains.

Hip-hop culture waned after the late 1980s in New York and London as rave culture and electronic music became increasingly popular. By this time closely associated with hip-hop, graffiti's popularity undoubtedly waned alongside it. However, graffiti continued to spread to different countries, growing in popularity in different parts of the world at different times. Each country has its own pioneers and stories, all of which we cannot hope to cover here. The key point is that the graffiti subculture persisted and further innovations

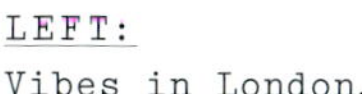

were then made possible, although much of the art today is largely separated from hip-hop and traditional graffiti.

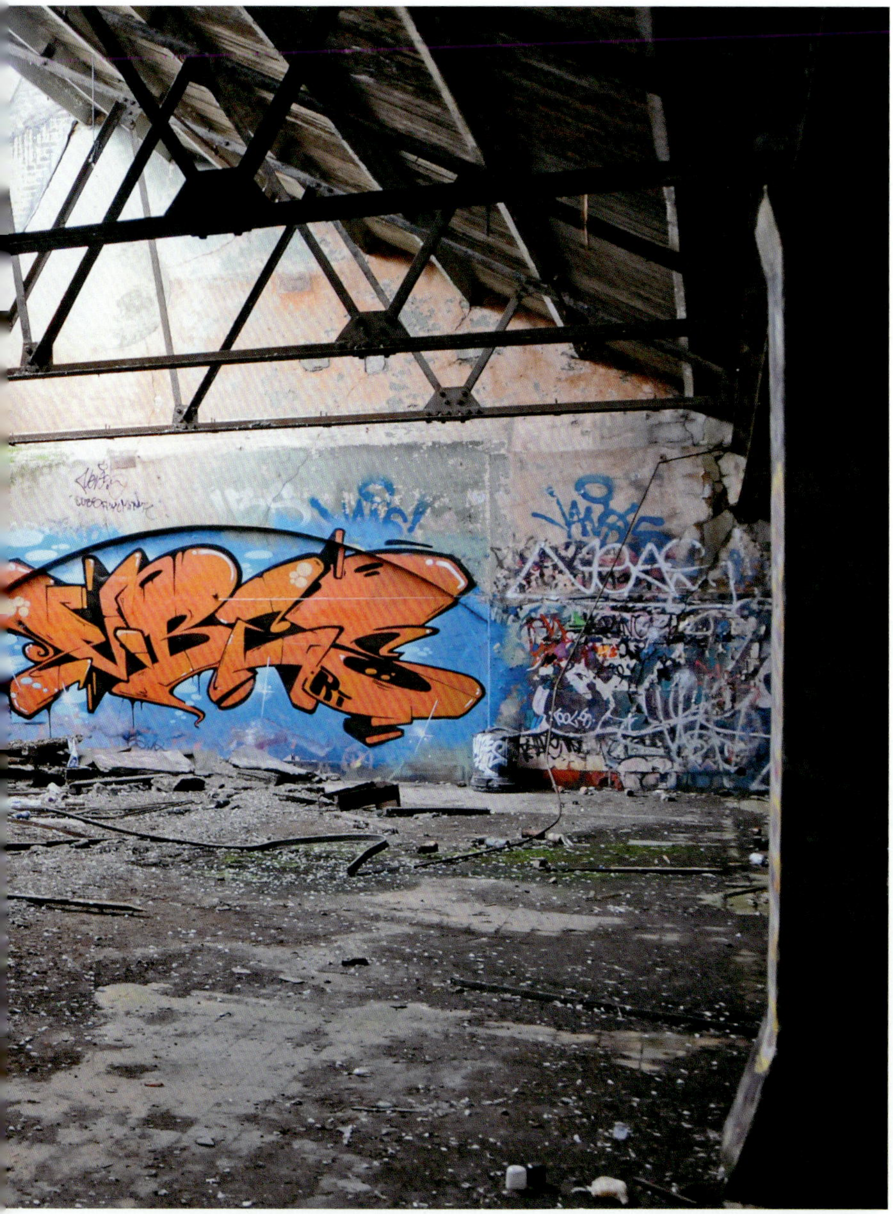

The photos in this section are all from Europe, starting with London because it has the longest history as a major graffiti centre outside of the USA. There are many talented artists in London, and the industry around the art – printmakers, galleries, tours, publications and mural-painting services – is well developed and competitive but Bristol, Brighton, Sheffield and other municipalities also have strong local graffiti and/or street art scenes.

I then move through different countries, focusing on the places where I have the most experience, but I also want to show artists from countries where I've travelled less who I think are great.

Aside from being my home city, London is a thriving centre for street art. The famous Brick Lane area has been a hotbed for street art since the early 2000s and remains a place to be seen for artists because of the high number of tourists and photographers that roam the area. However, painting in East London is something many artists struggle with because alongside the attention their artwork attracts they have to deal with an endless throng of street art tours standing behind them and commenting as they paint. How times have changed!

These photographs may represent a golden era for street art in London, specifically in East London. Today, it feels as if much of the art is being edged out; an increase in the number of high-rise buildings and modern developments is leaving fewer available surfaces for street art, and it's not yet clear whether the changing demographics of the area might also have an impact, with new residents and shop owners potentially being less open to street art than their predecessors.

CLOCKWISE FROM RIGHT:
David Walker/David Walker/Mobstr.

PAGES 50-1, CLOCKWISE FROM TOP LEFT:
Israel's Broken Fingaz Crew/Austria's Nychos/Colombia's Bastardilla making a comment on the mining industry/Broken Fingaz Crew.

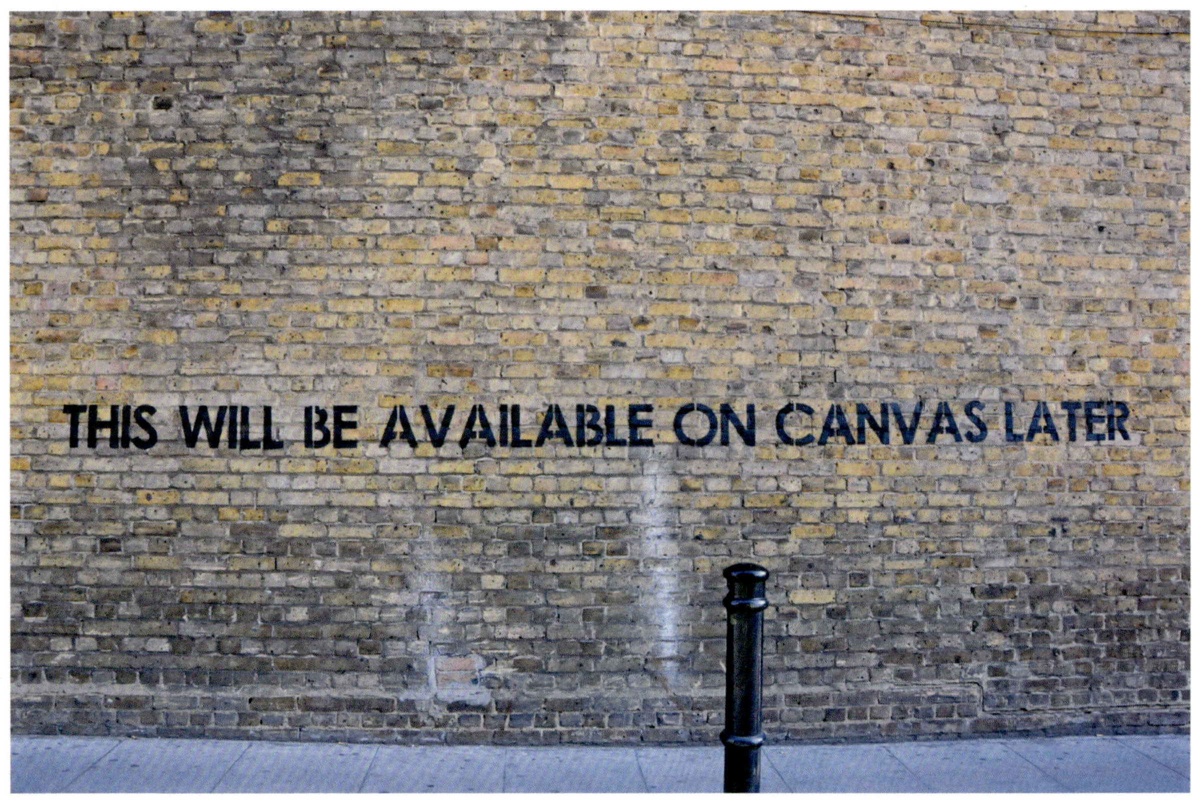

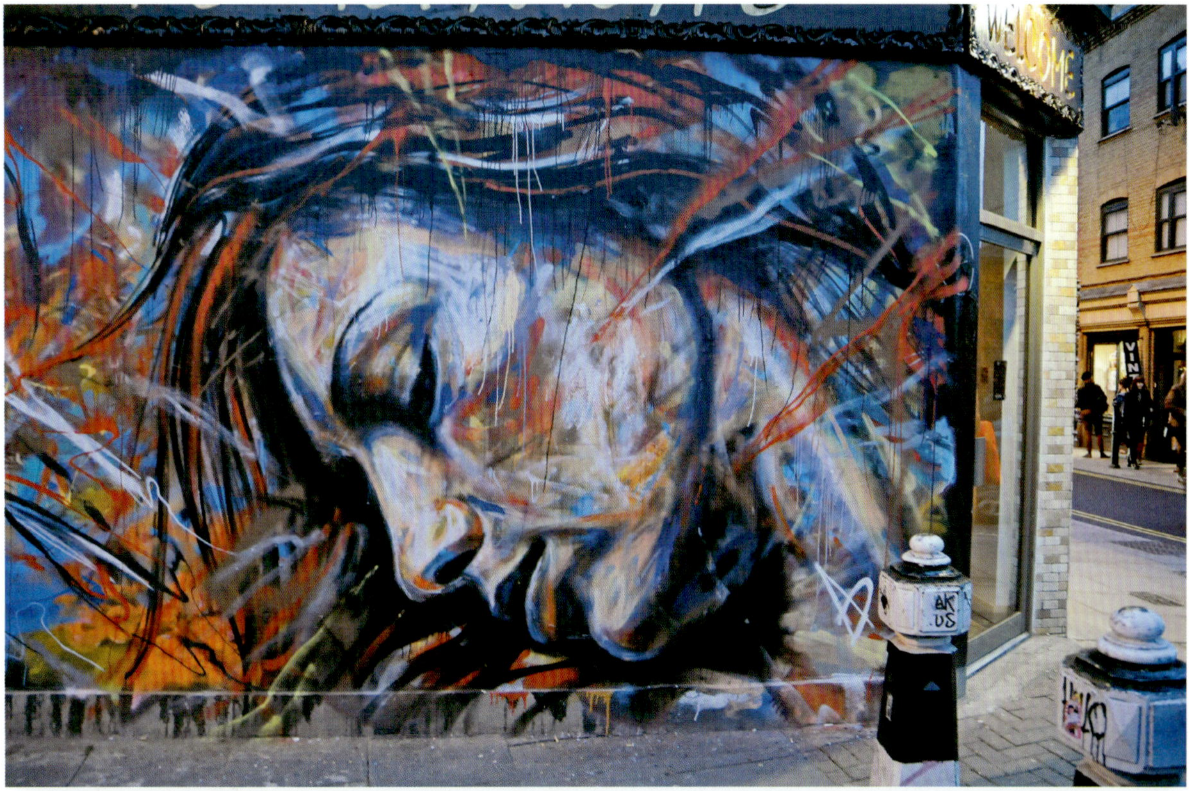

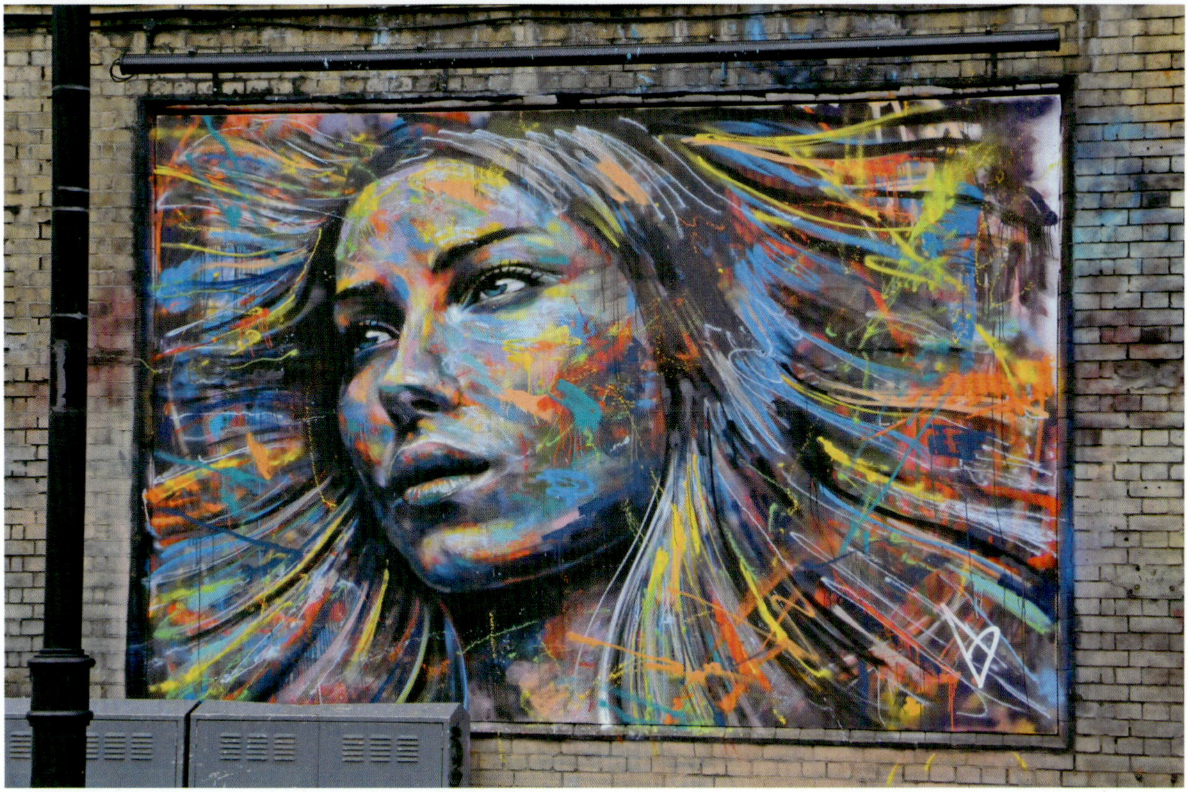

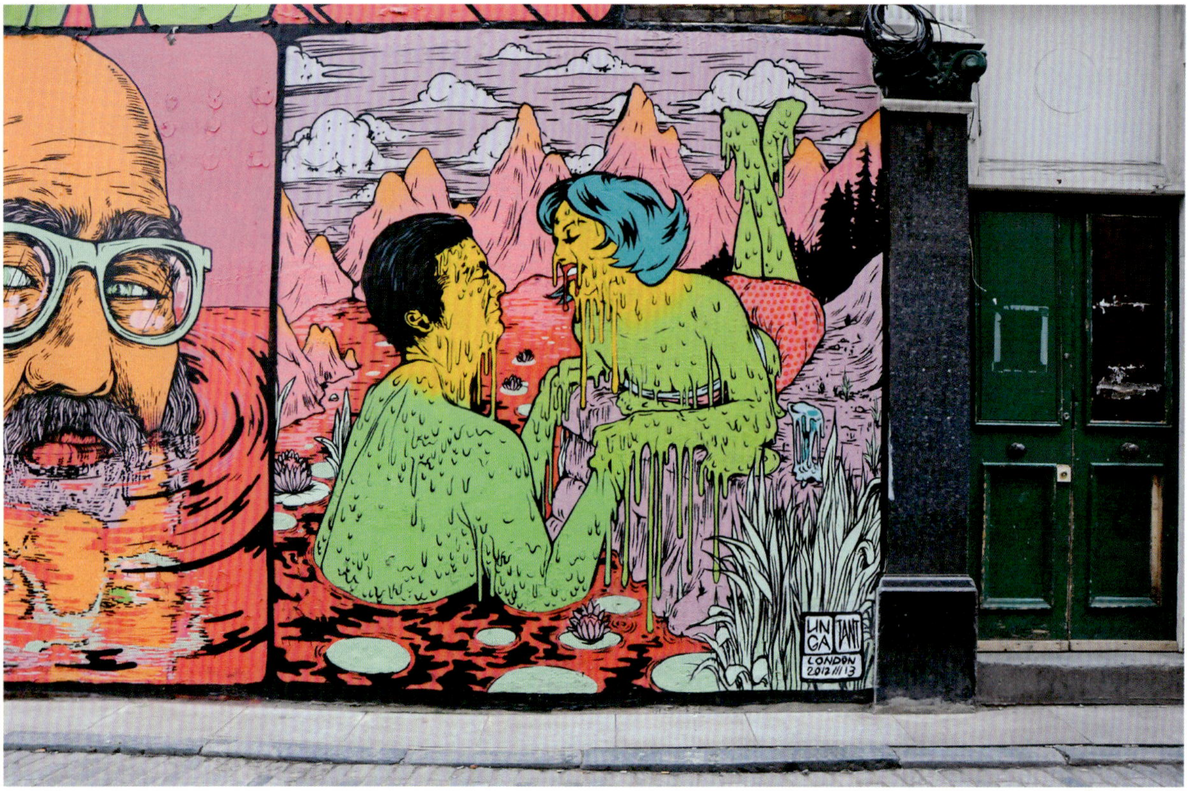
LIN
GA
TANT
LONDON
2012 III 13

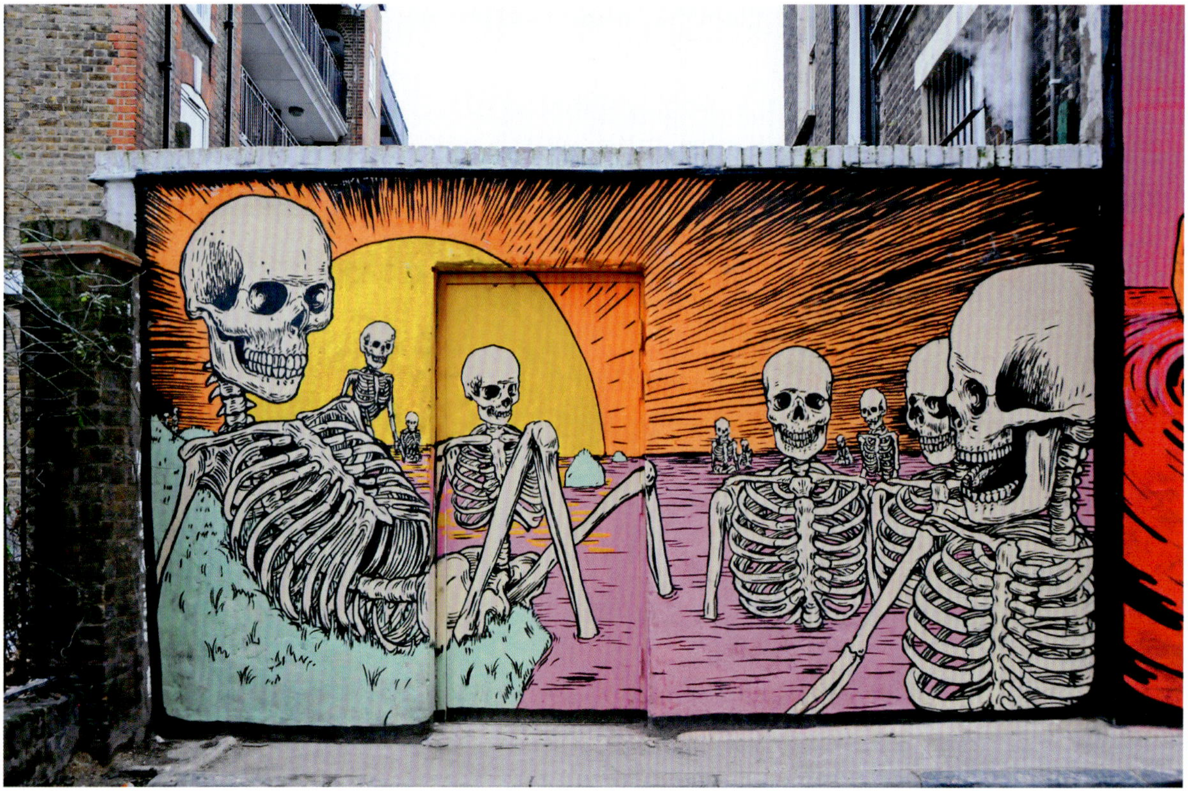

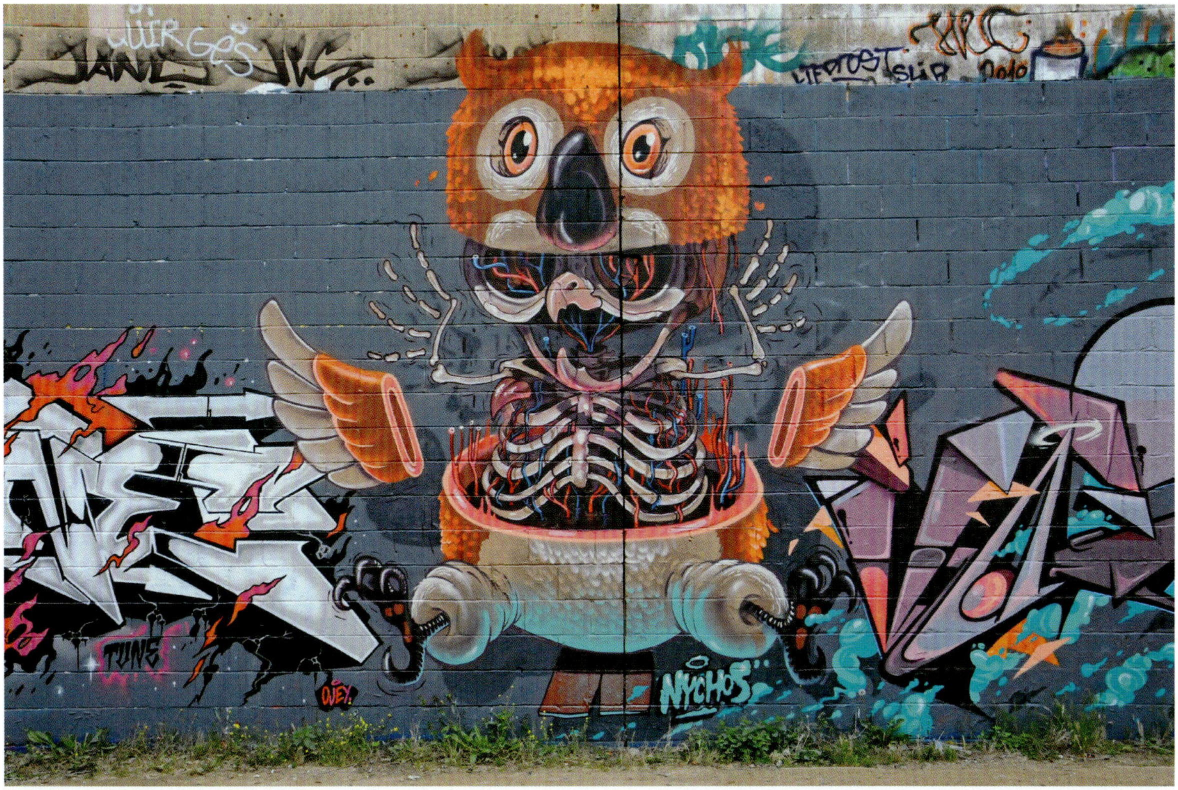

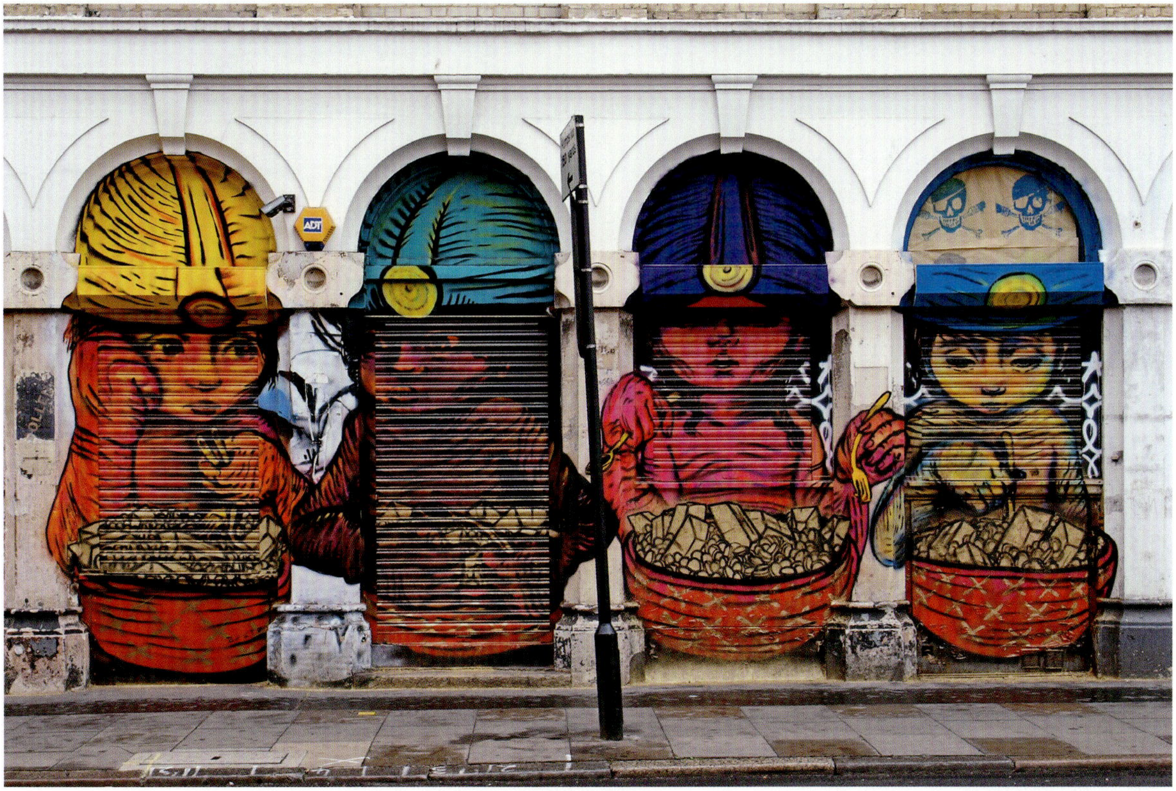

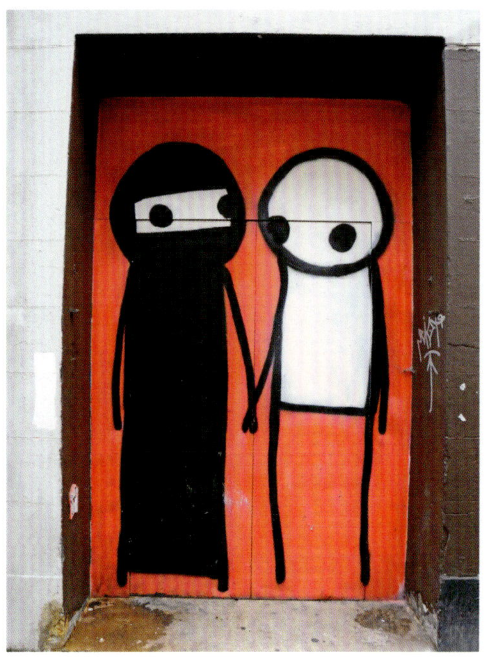

CLOCKWISE FROM LEFT:
Stik, who paints stick
men - this piece is
near Brick Lane, which
has a large Bangladeshi
community/Ireland's
Conor Harrington/
USA's Shepard Fairey
at the ill-fated London
Pleasure Gardens.

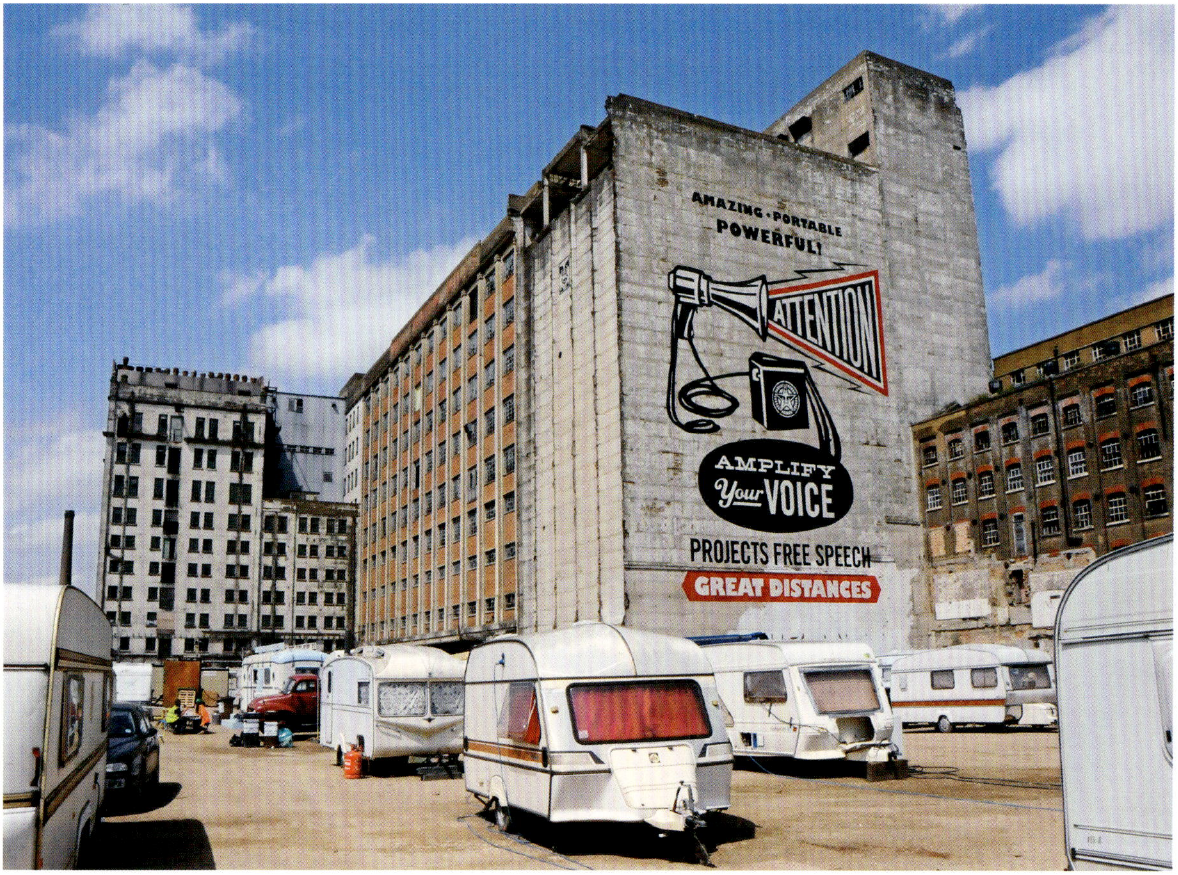

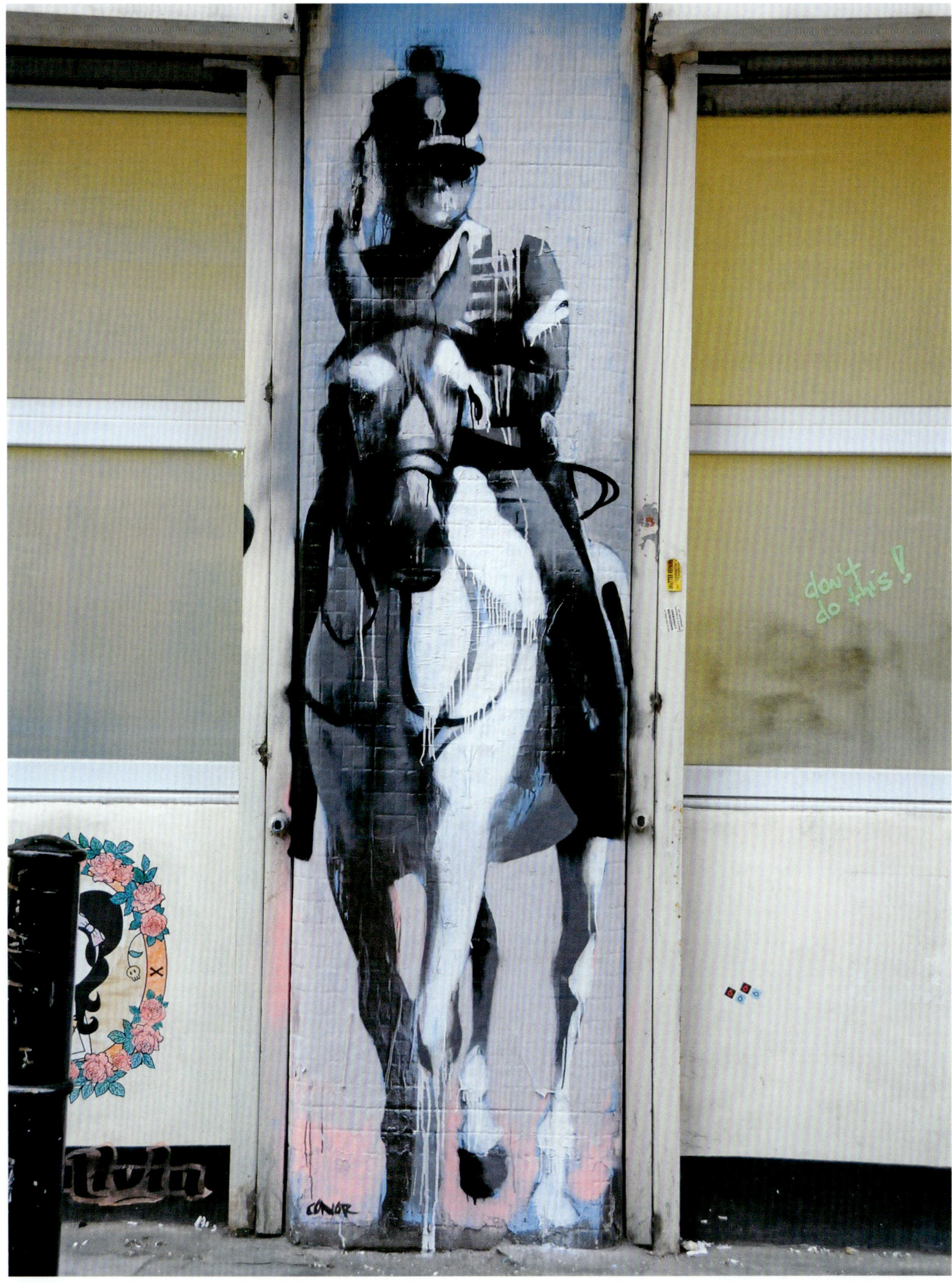
don't
do this!
CONOR

Bristol is often thought of as the UK's number two city for street art, but that's a London-centric view and unlikely to sit well with Bristolians. Considering the culture and talent prevalent in the city, together with the size of its artistic community and the success of its street art festivals, one could certainly argue that Bristol is now the leading centre of street art in the UK. Bristol is a great city with a great artistic culture and a lot of damn good street art.

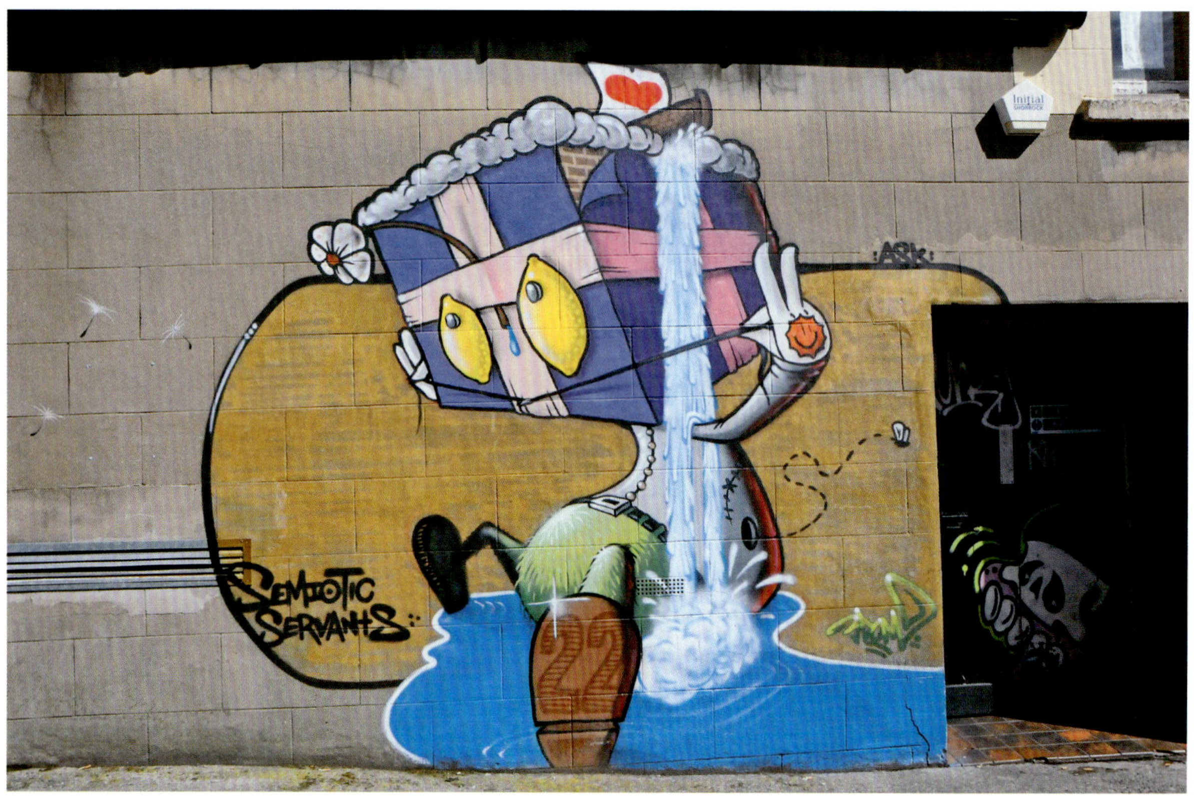

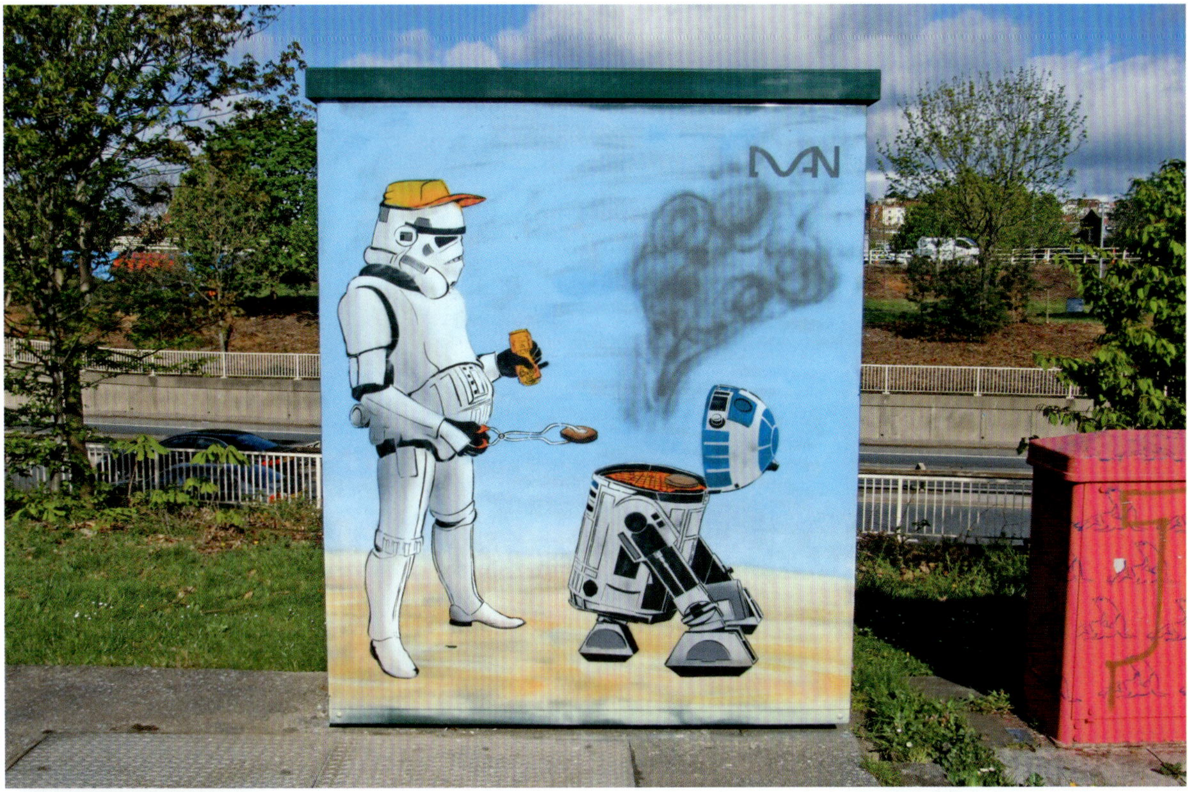

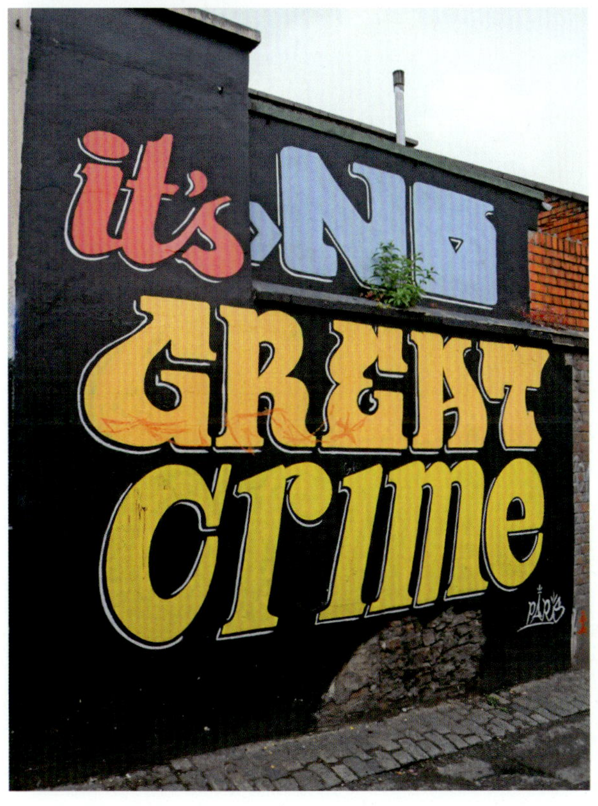
it's NO
GREAT
CrIme

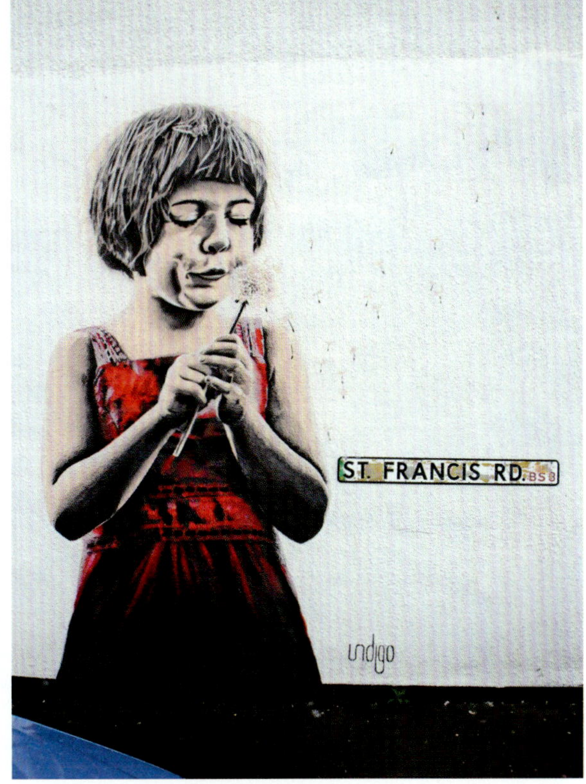
ST. FRANCIS RD.
indigo

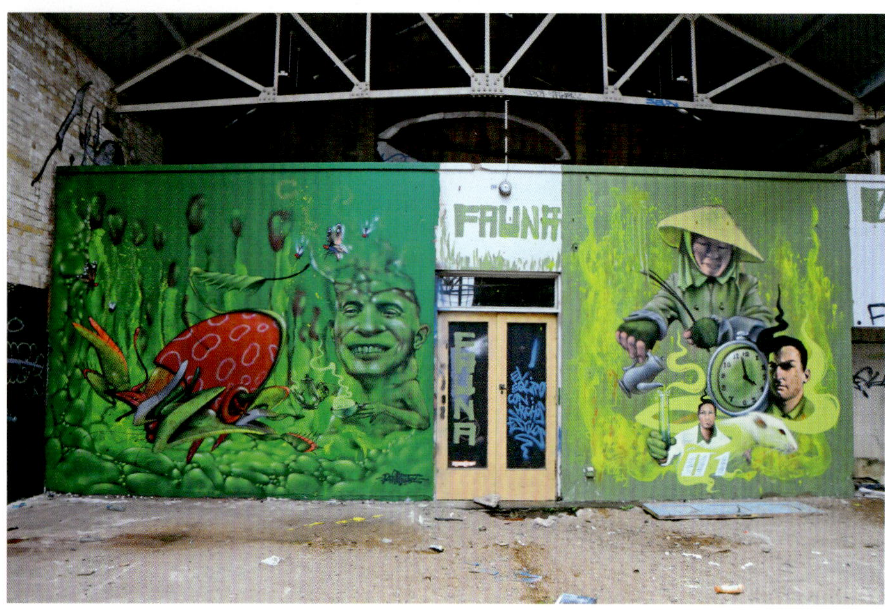

CLOCKWISE FROM LEFT:
UK's Rocket01 and
Faunagraphic/UK's
Phlegm/Phlegm/France's
EMA.

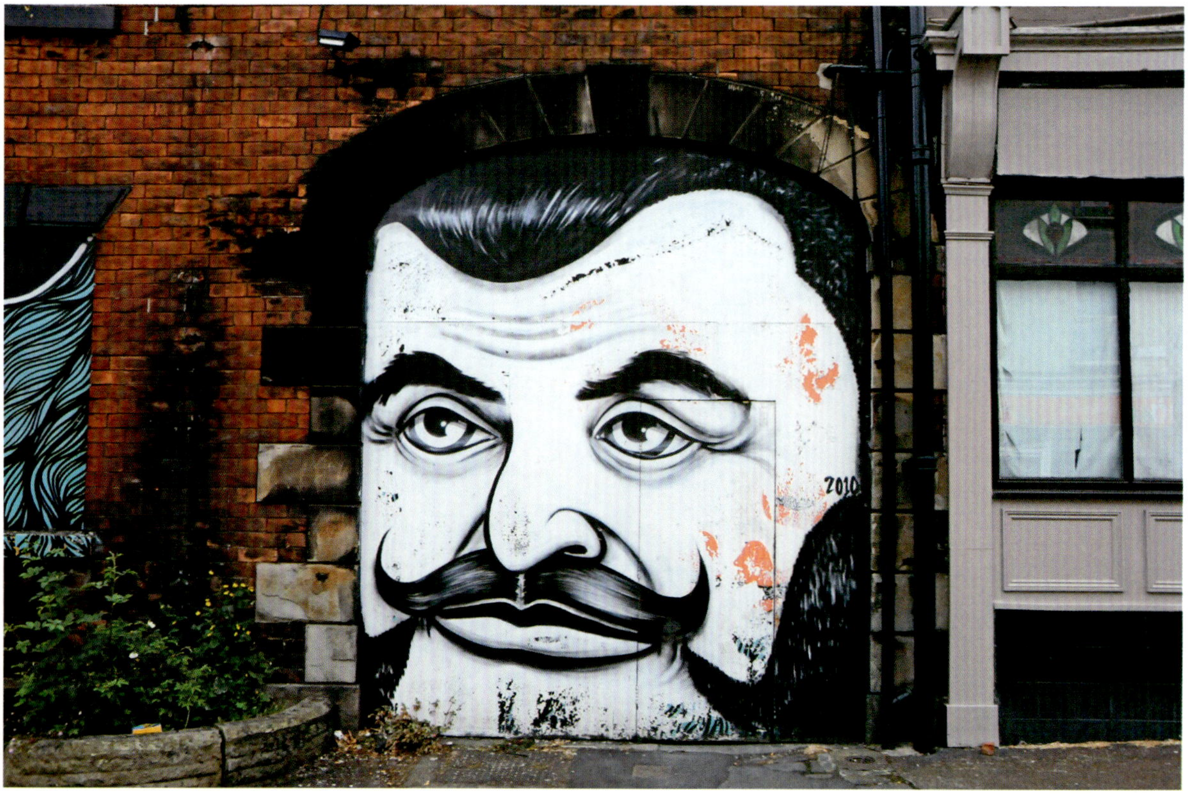

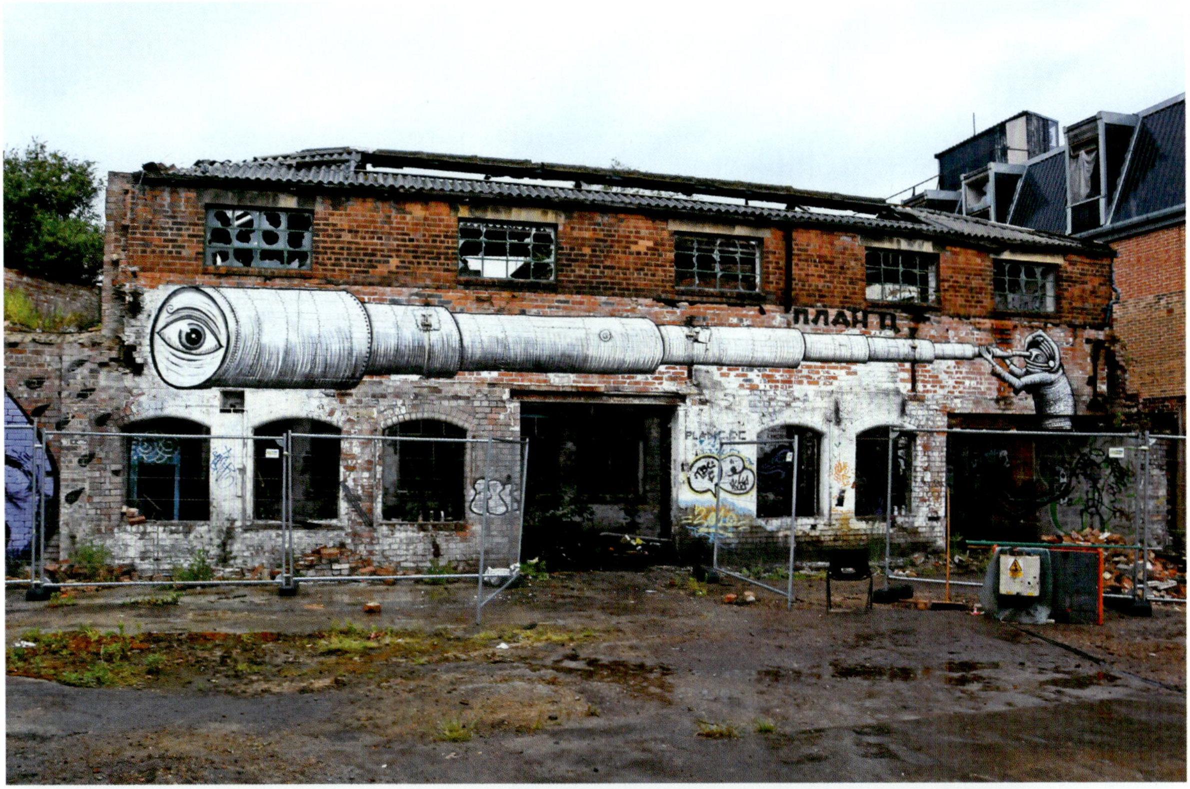

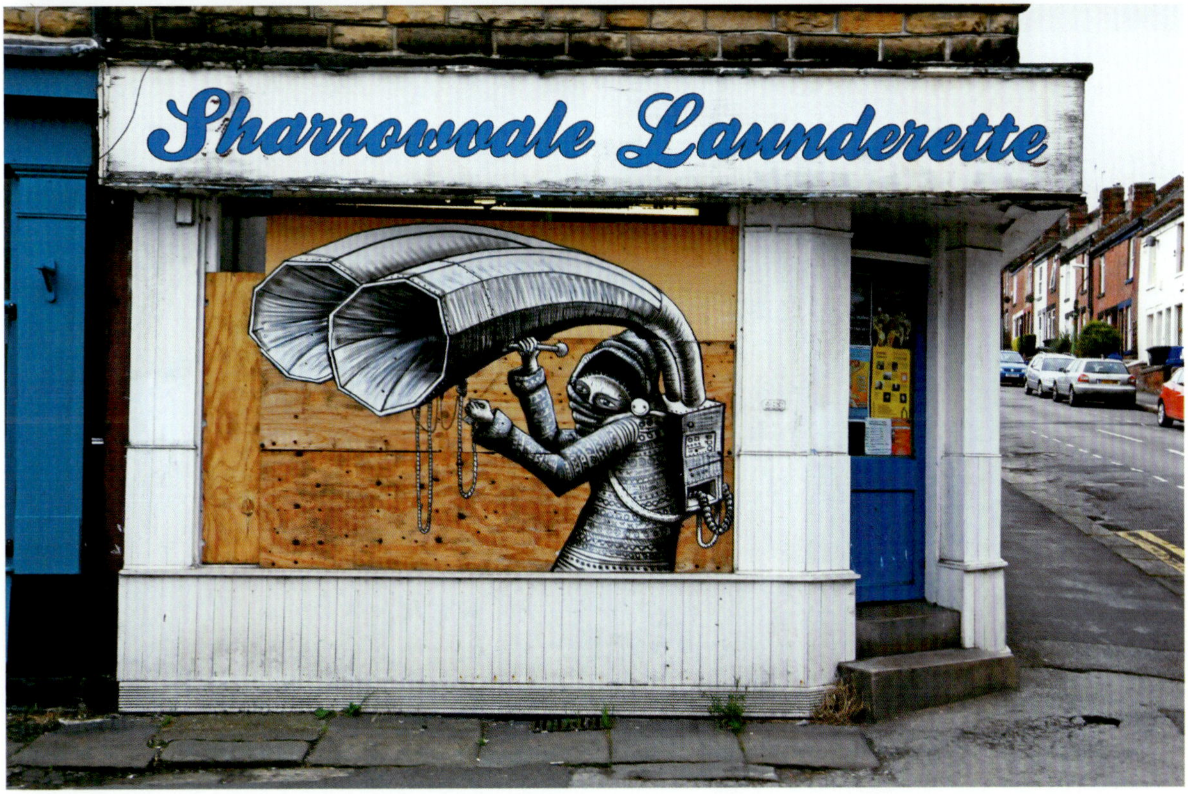

Sharrowvale Launderette

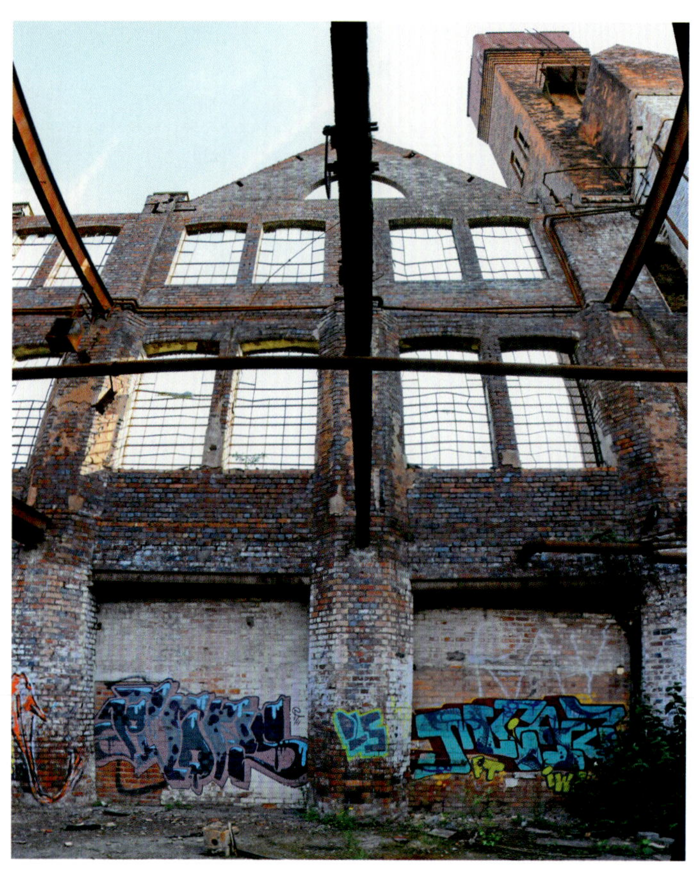

CLOCKWISE FROM LEFT: An abandoned building in the Bordesley area of Birmingham/Victor at the Copperworks site in Walsall/Many artists at an abandoned quarry, including a huge blockbuster by Kem & Mef.

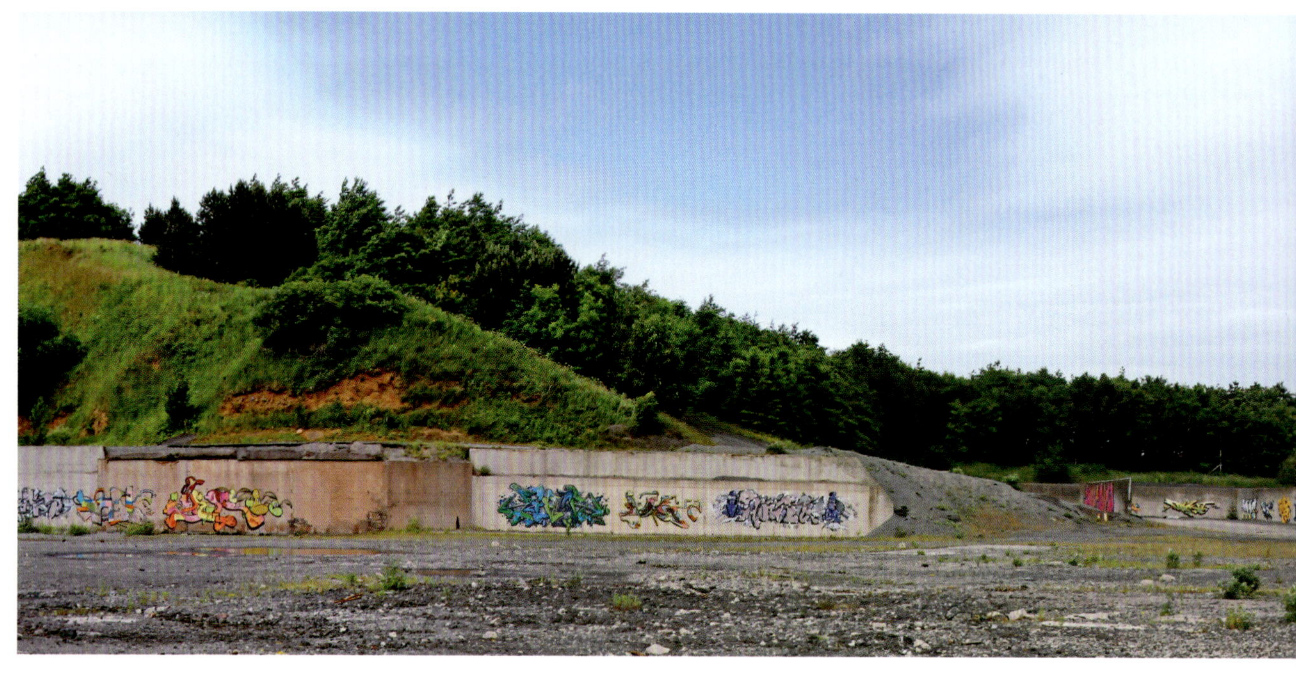

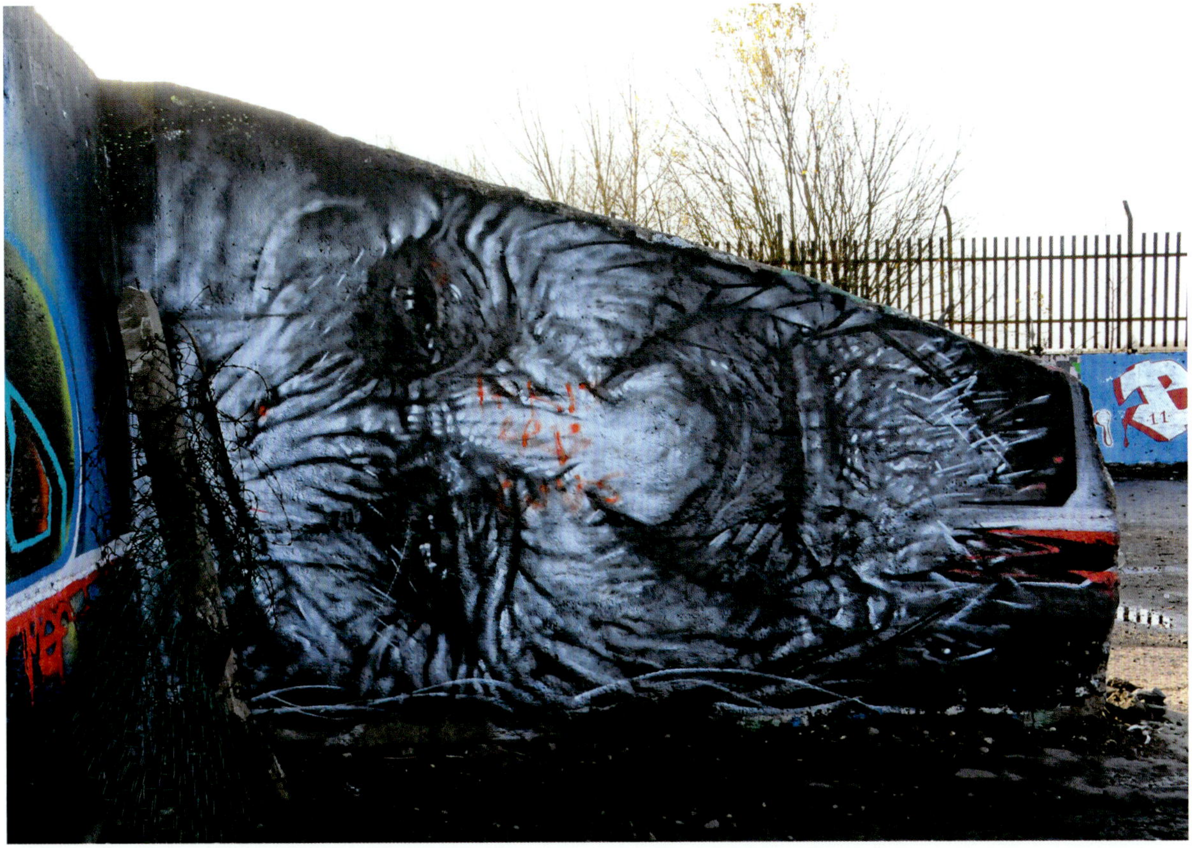

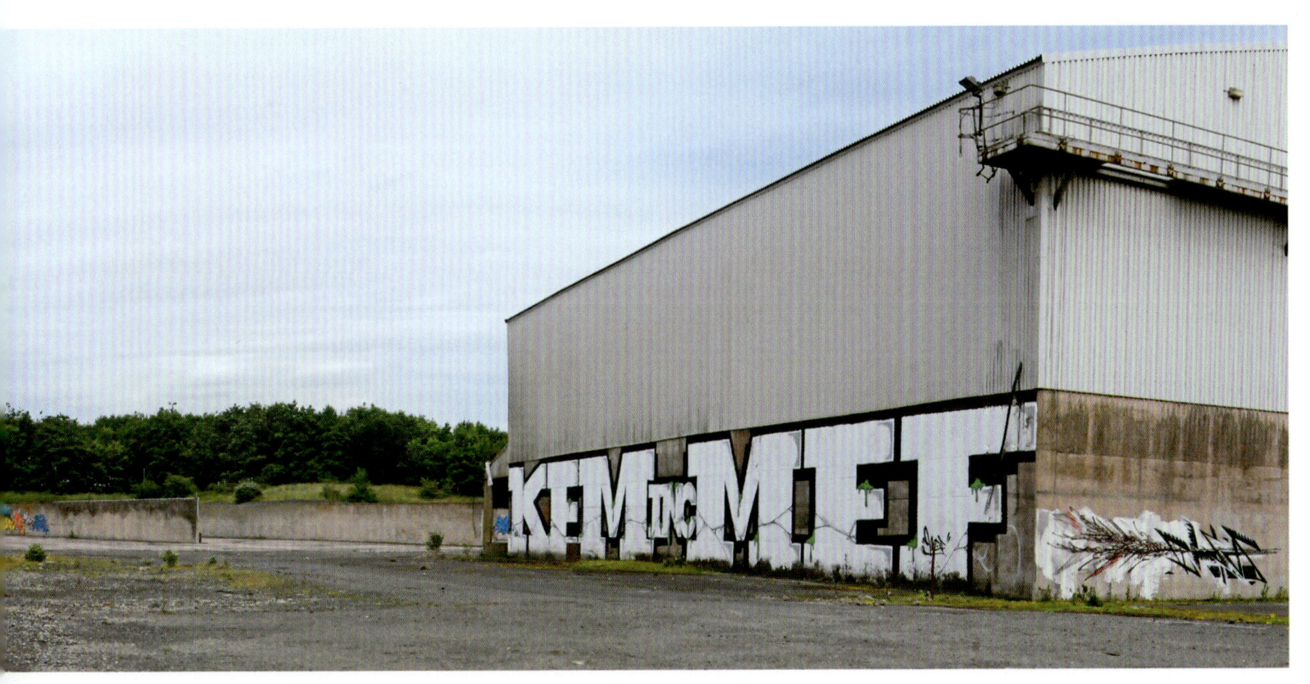

KEM INC MEF

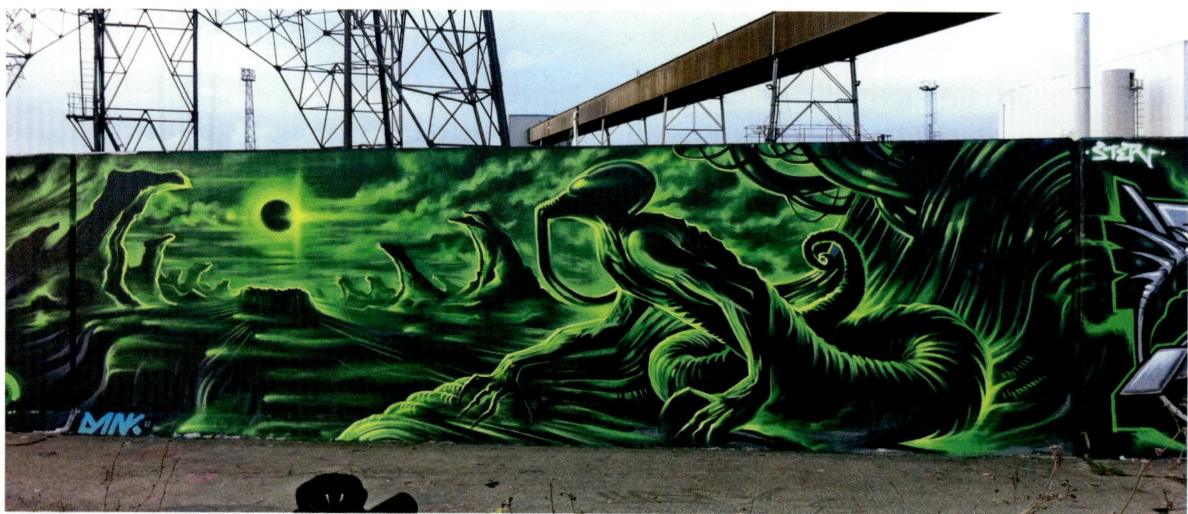

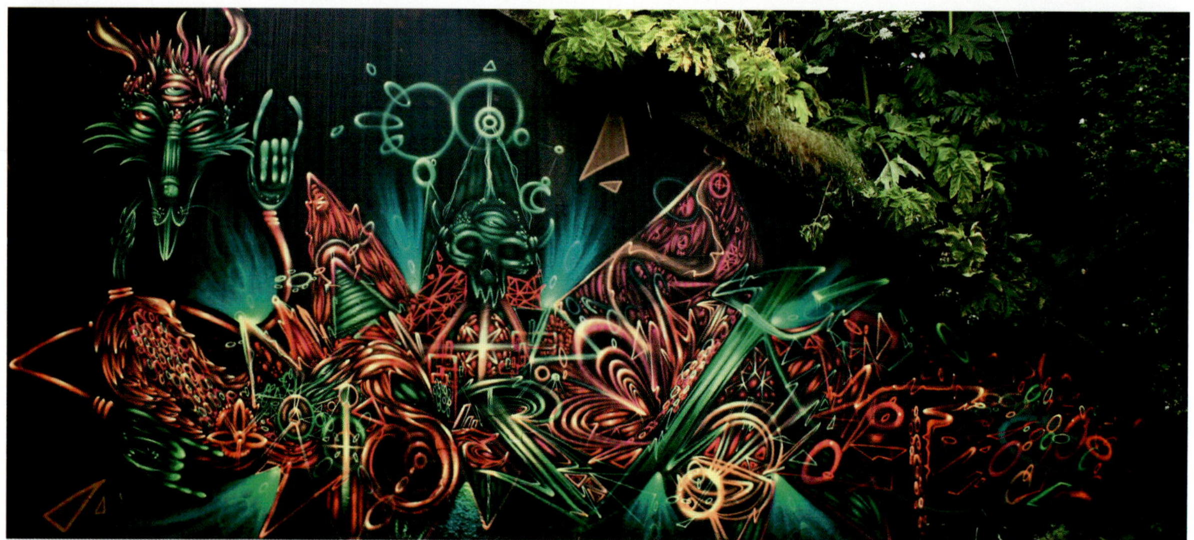

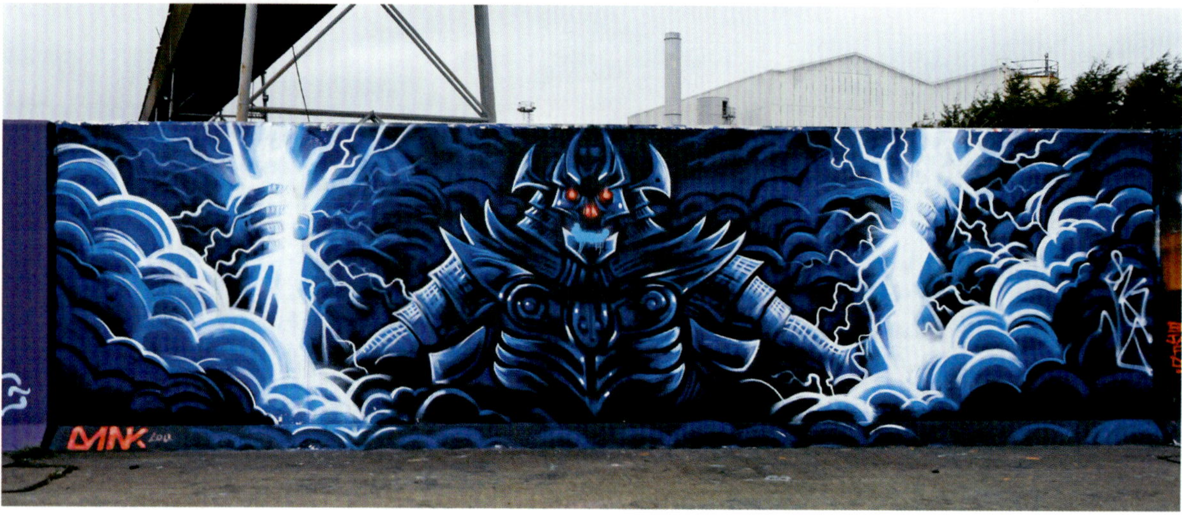

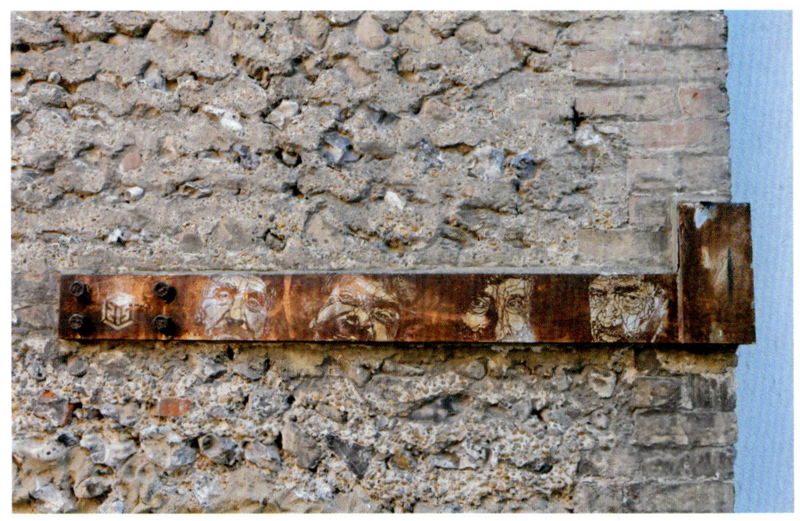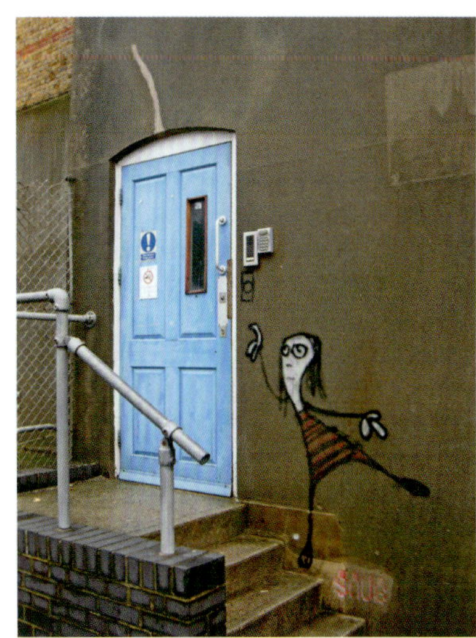

CLOCKWISE FROM TOP
LEFT:
Dan Kitchener aka Dank
in Essex/France's C215
in Brighton/Snub 23 in
Brighton/MSK Crew's Aroe
in Brighton/Dank in
Essex/Spore in Glasgow.

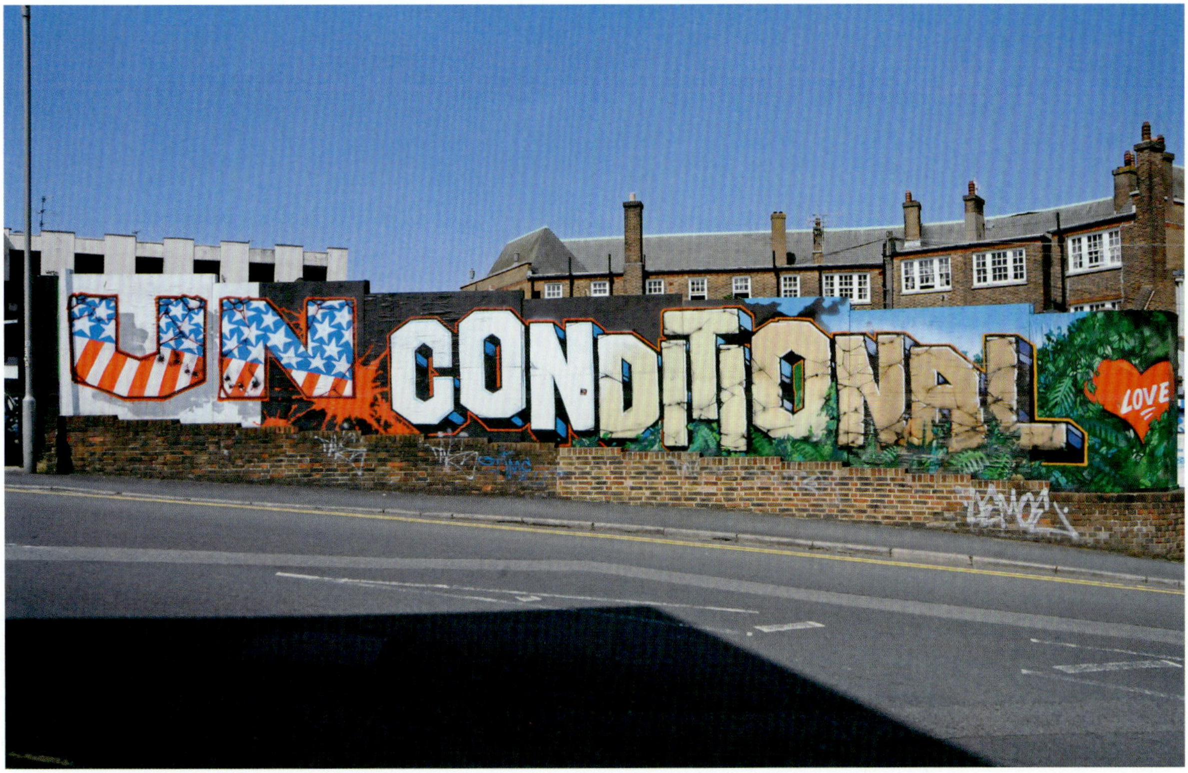

I had heard great things about the German graffiti scene and I have friends there, so I travelled around Germany for a month in 2011. I planned the trip meticulously and made maps for every city I wanted to visit, each with graffiti wall locations marked; I found out where the walls were situated from a range of websites, photographers, artists and paint shops. Starting in Berlin and ending up in Zurich, Switzerland, I visited 76 different German cities in 26 days, plus another 15 cities in Holland and Switzerland. Averaging over three cities a day, I took nearly 10,000 photos that month. I was up before sunrise and kept taking pictures until I lost the light (it was summer, so thankfully the days were long).

I covered much of the country but I still want to go back to cover more of East Germany. When I meet German people they tell me I've seen more of Germany than they have.

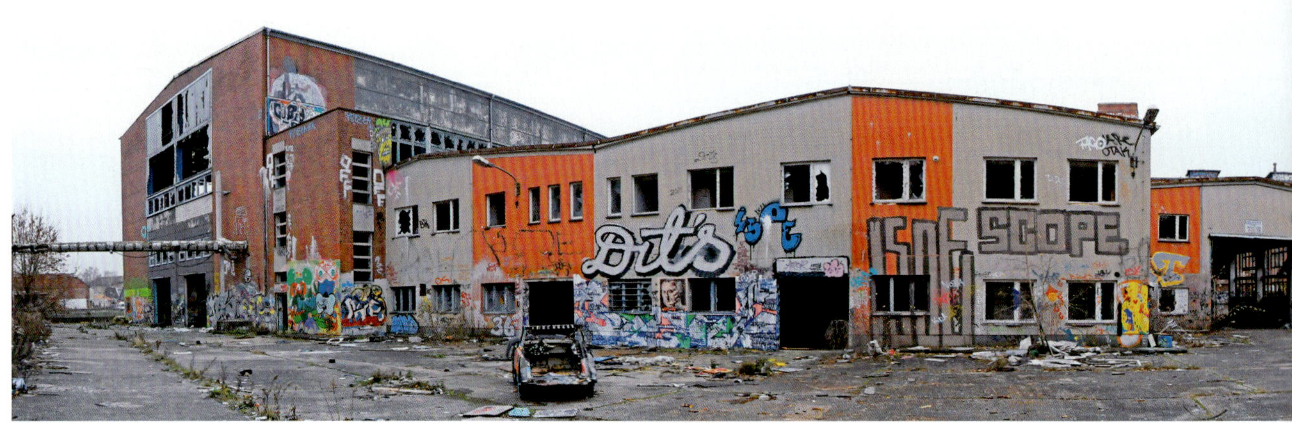

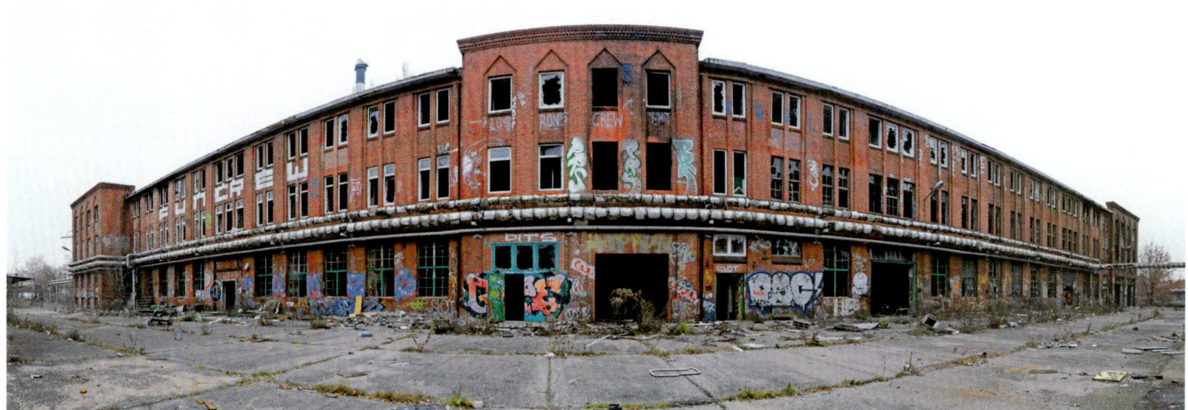

CLOCKWISE FROM
BELOW:
An abandoned factory
in Berlin/An abandoned
factory in Halle/An
abandoned factory in
Berlin.

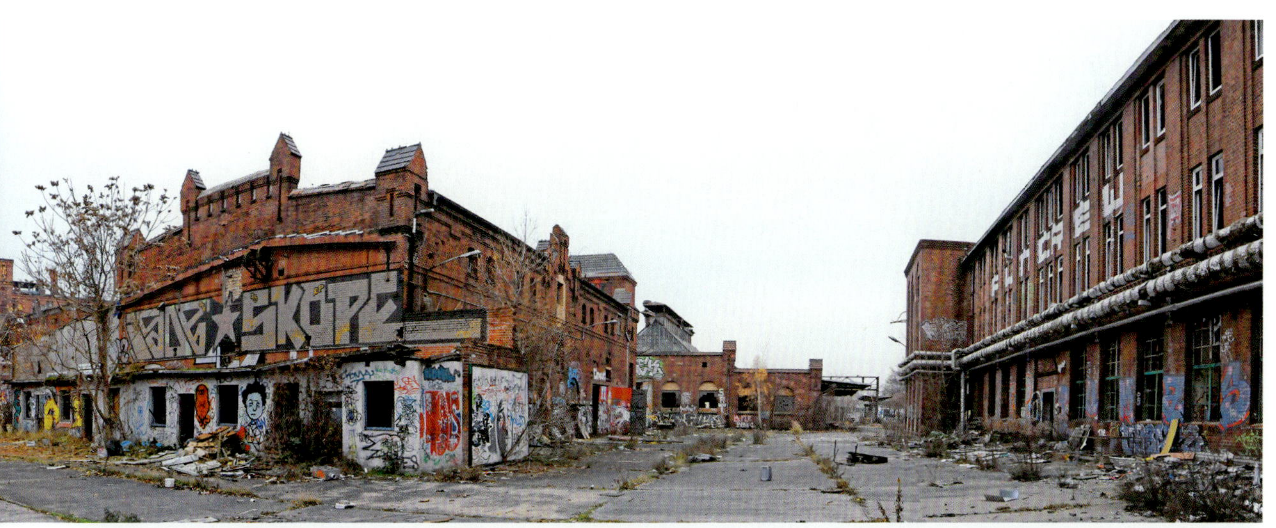

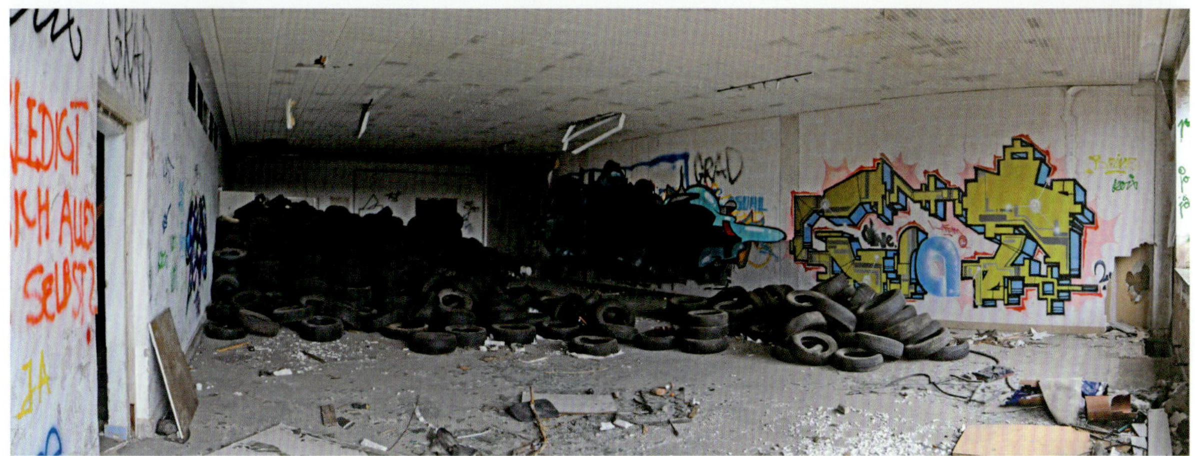

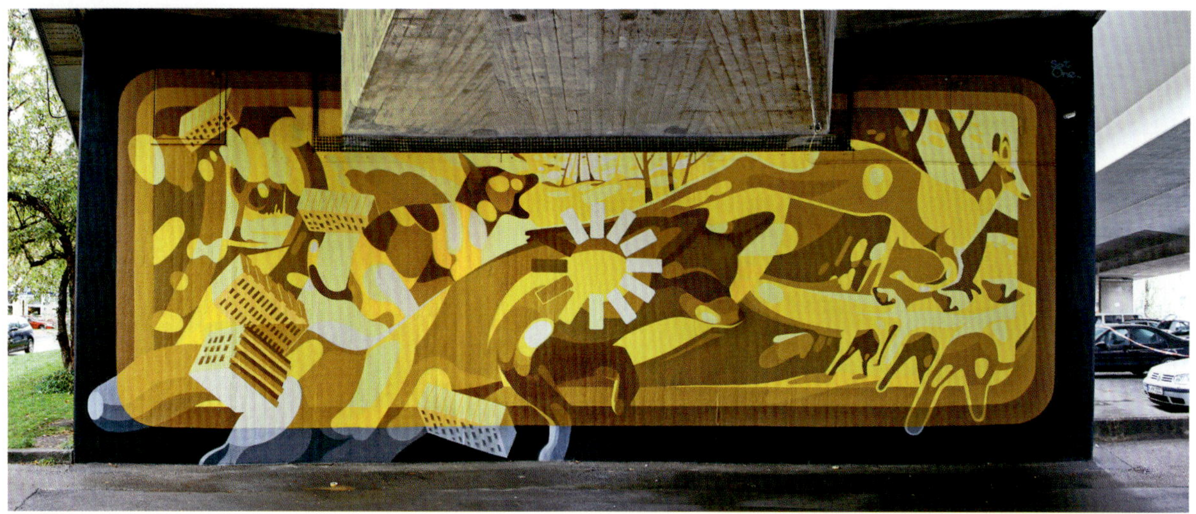

CLOCKWISE FROM ABOVE:
Sat-One/Dust in Bochum/
German duo Herakut in
Luneberg, I still can't
believe I drove past
this piece - it couldn't
have been down a more
obscure road/Herakut in
Bad Vilbel.

PAGES 66-7, CLOCKWISE
FROM LEFT:
Sdkaroe in Pfaffenhofen
an der Ilm, a tiny town
with very talented
artists/Nychos and
DXTR in Koln (Cologne)
/Law-One in Munich - I
couldn't agree more.

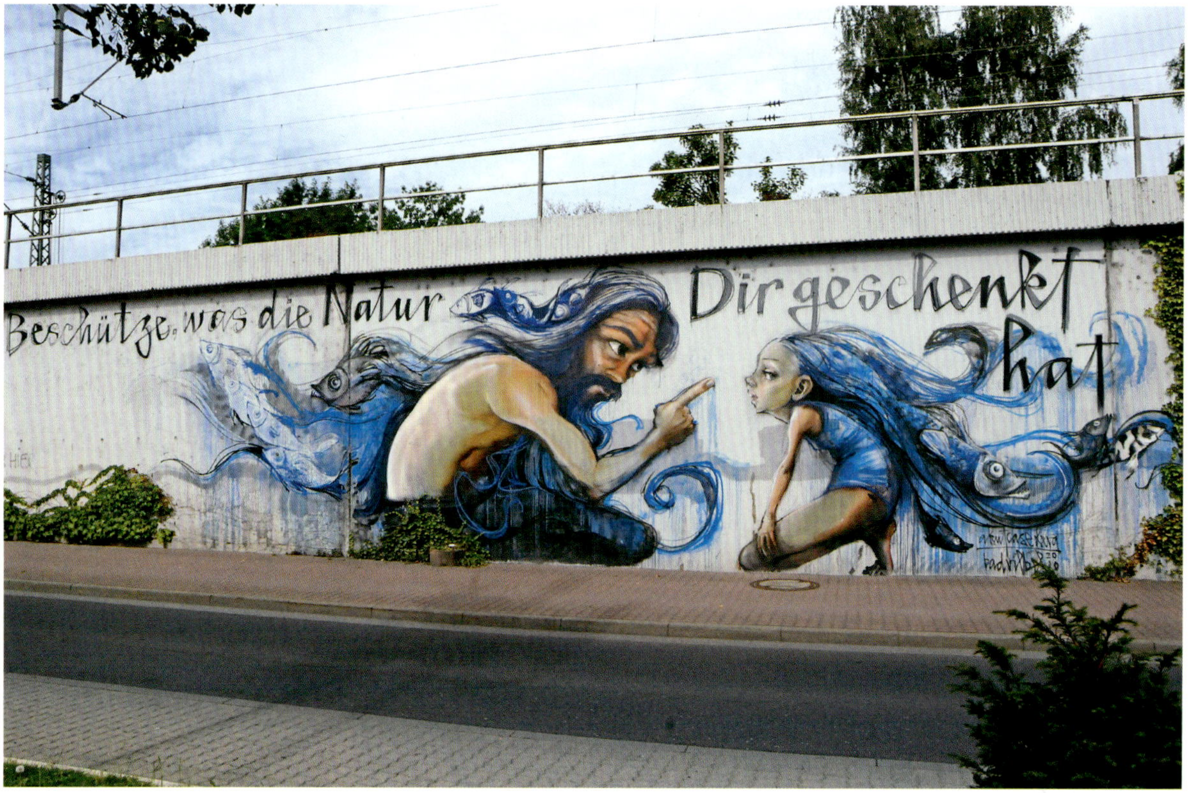

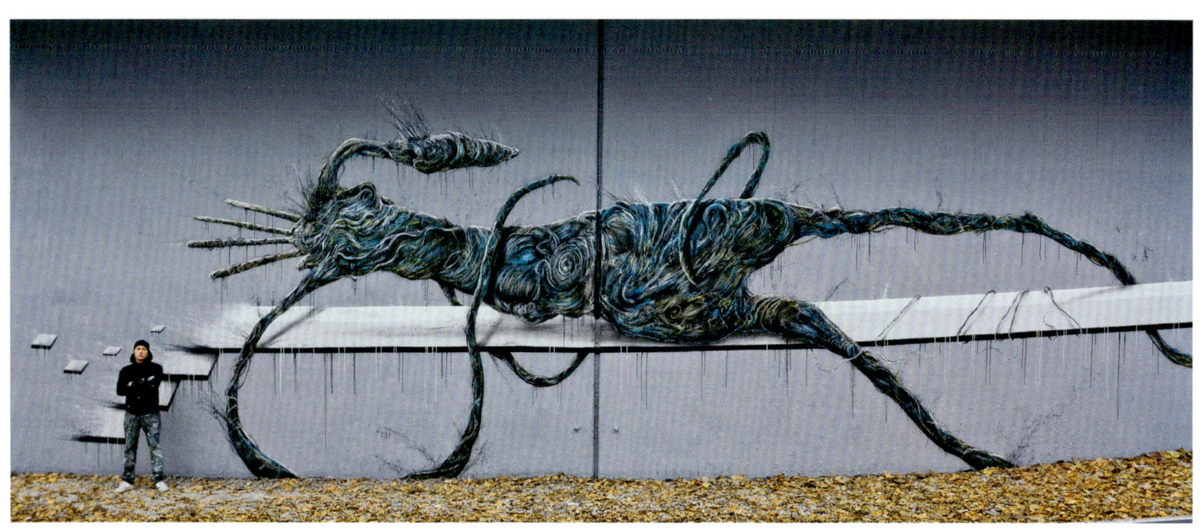

PAGES 68-9,
CLOCKWISE FROM LEFT:
Rallito X in Berlin/
Amsterdam-based Skount
in Germany/MüCke32 in
Leipzig.

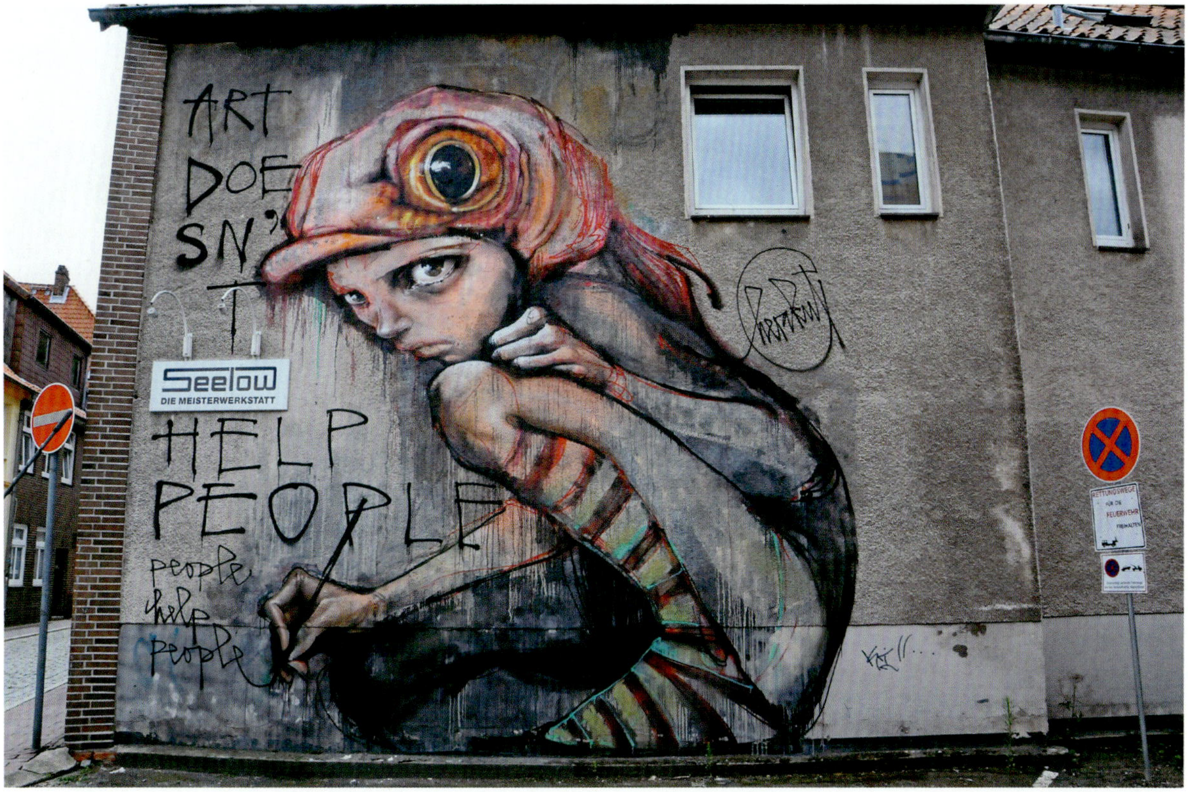

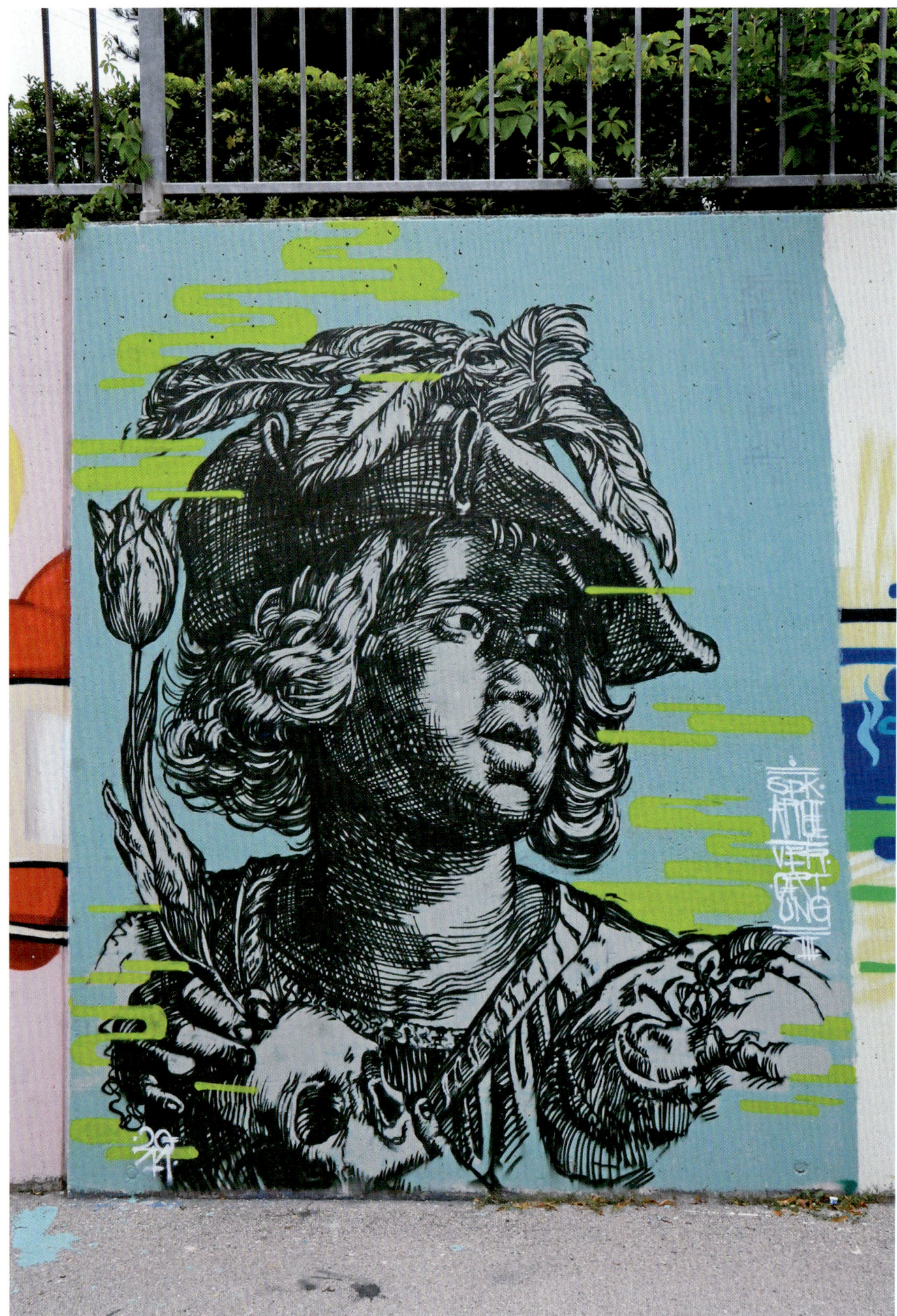

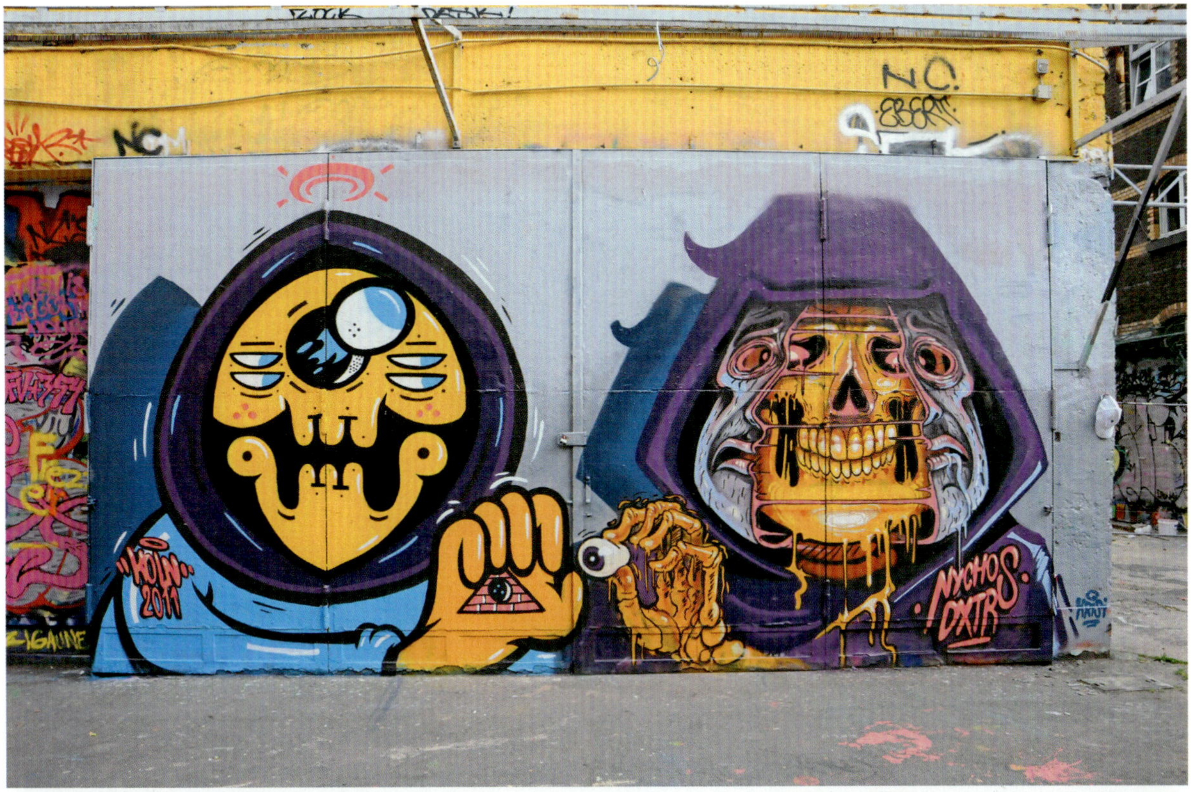

KÖLN
2011
NYCHOS
DXTR

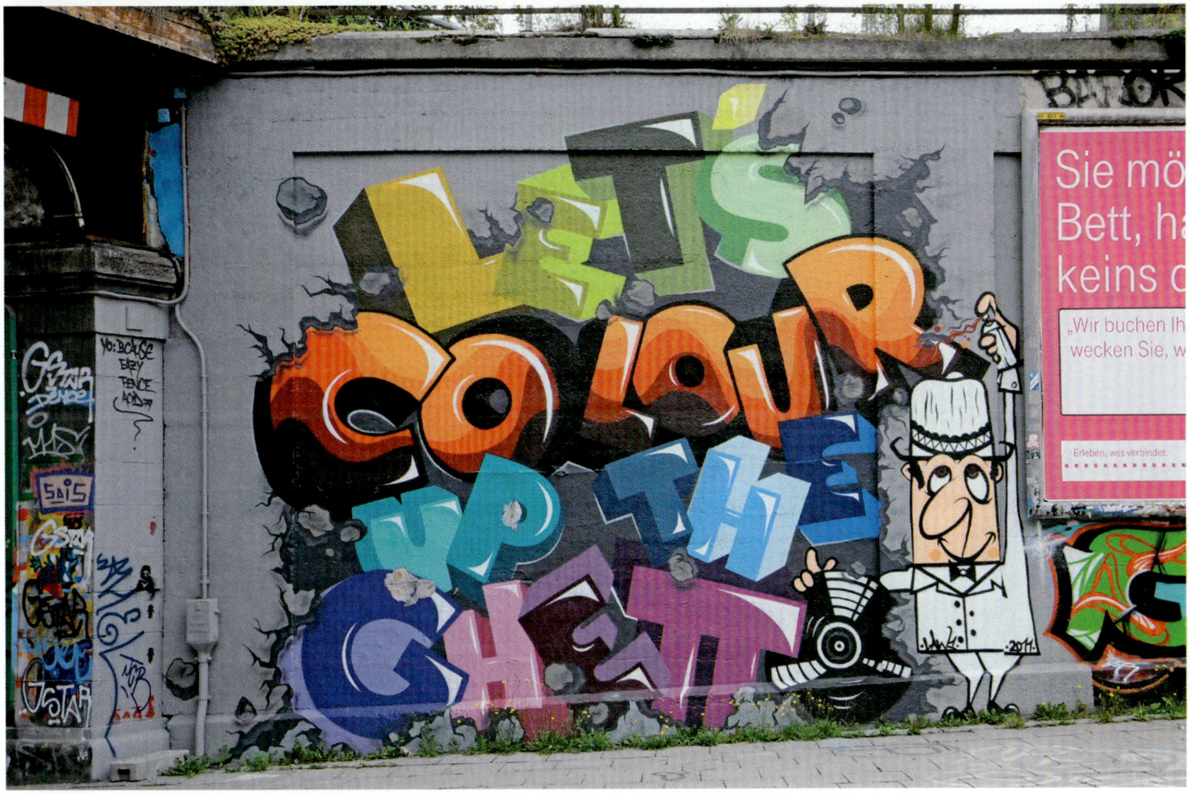

LET'S
COLOUR
UP THE
GHETT
Sie mö
Bett, ha
keins
"Wir buchen Ih
wecken Sie, w
Erleben, was verbindet.

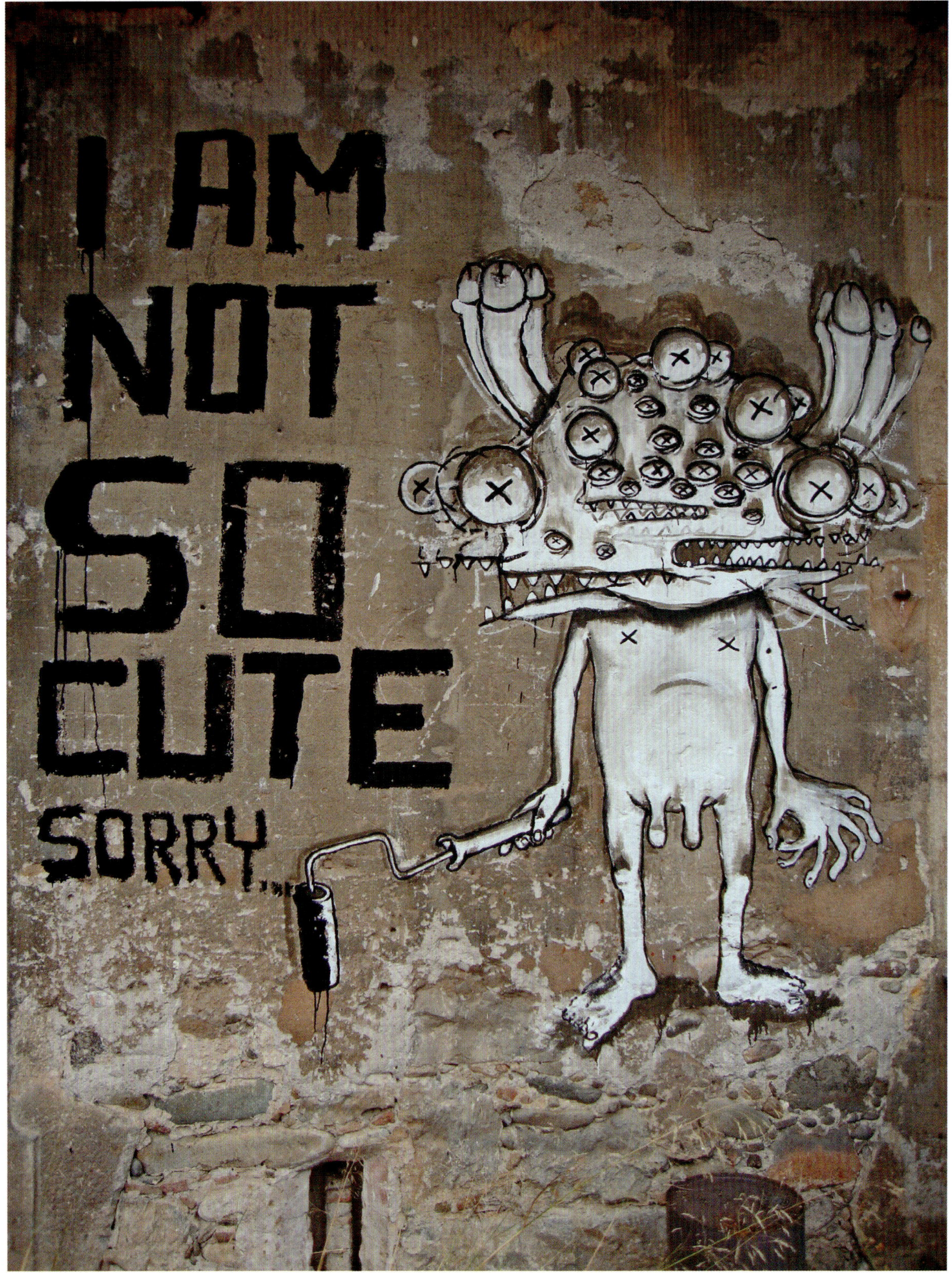
I AM
NOT
SO
CUTE
SORRY...

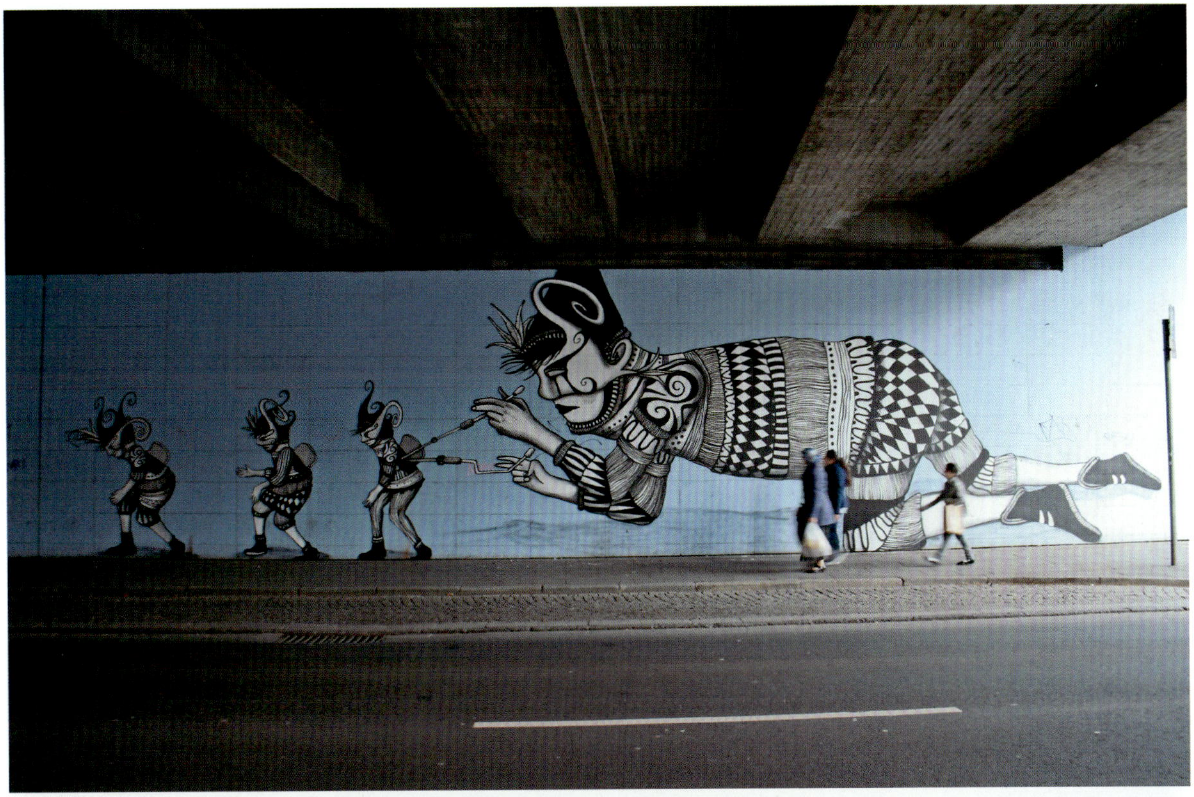

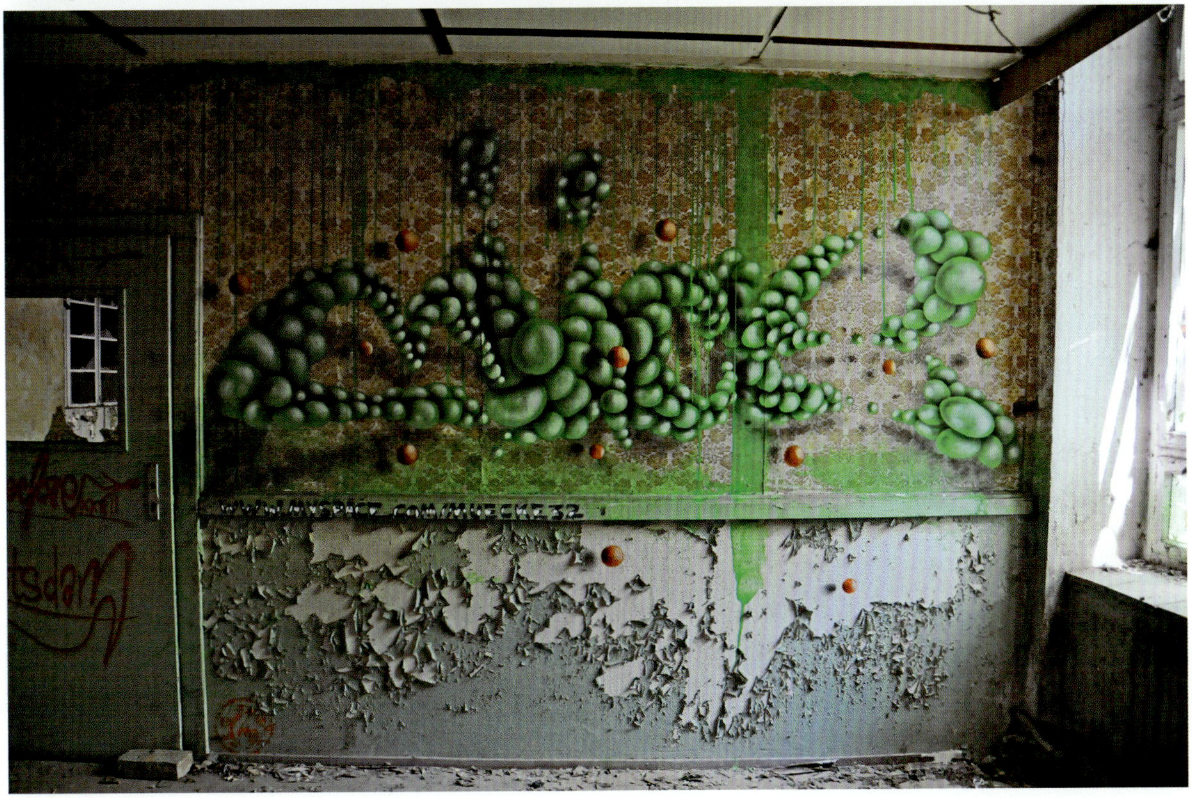
WWW.MYSPACE.COM/MUECKE32

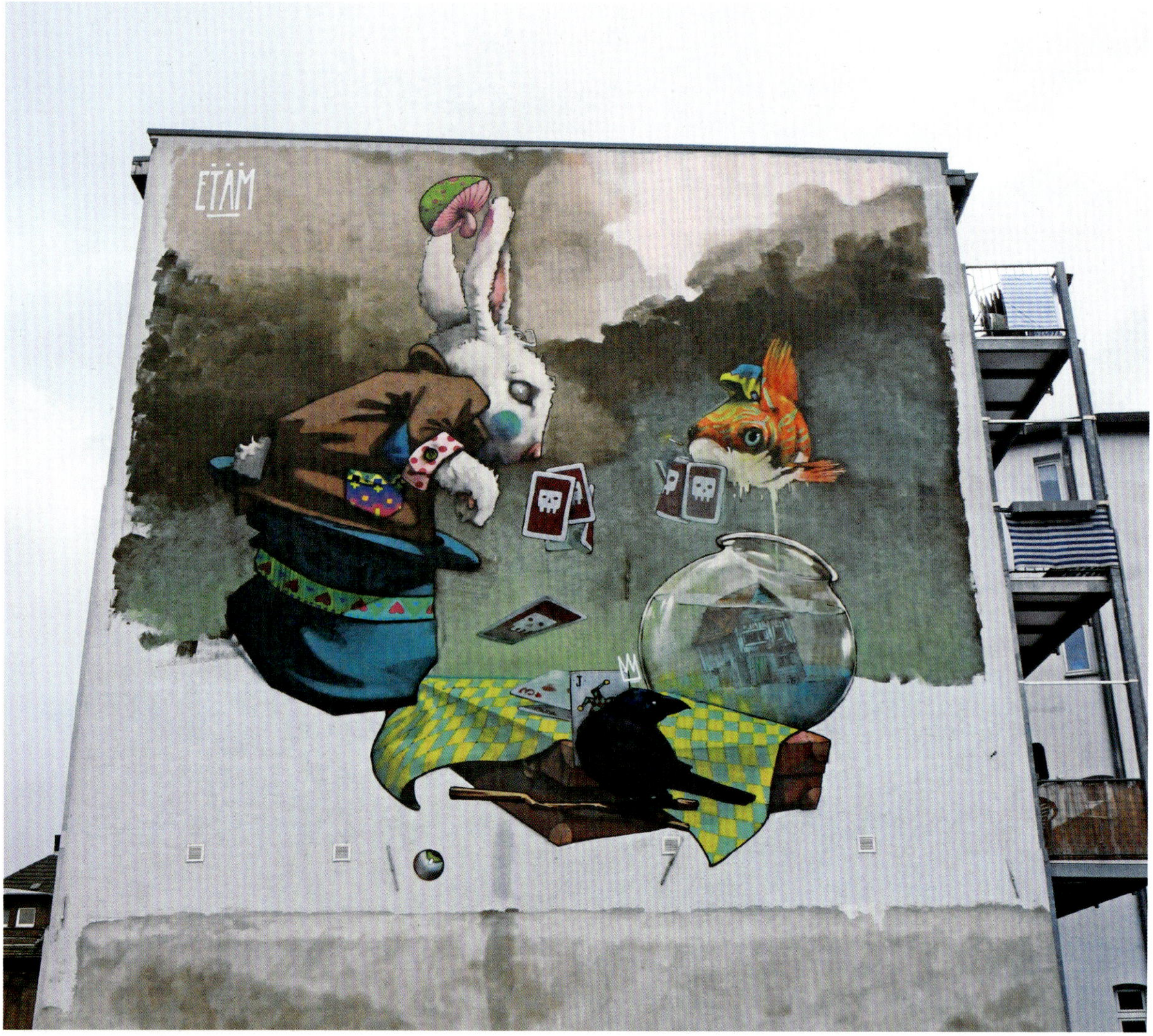

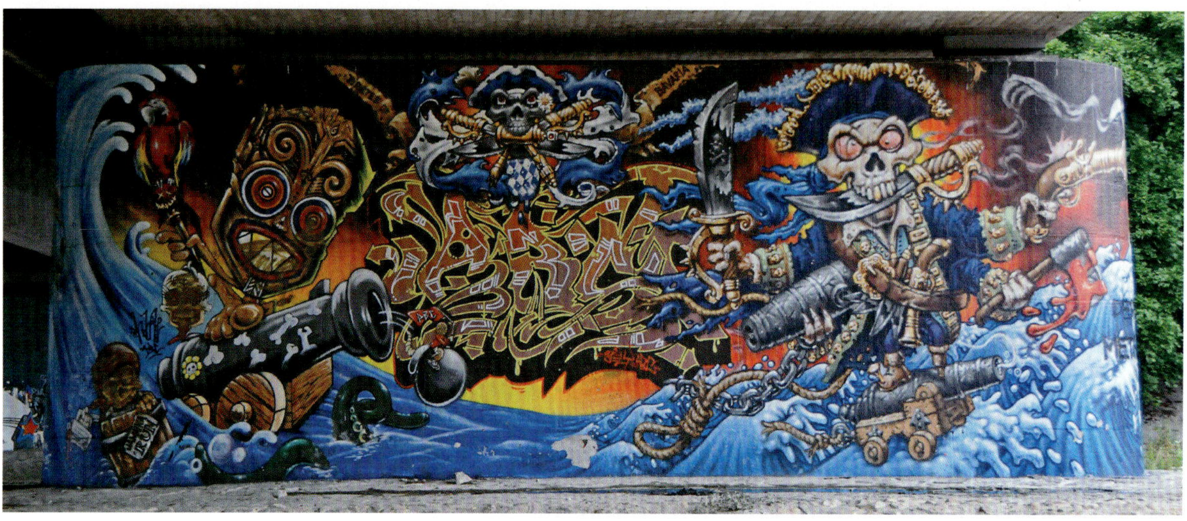

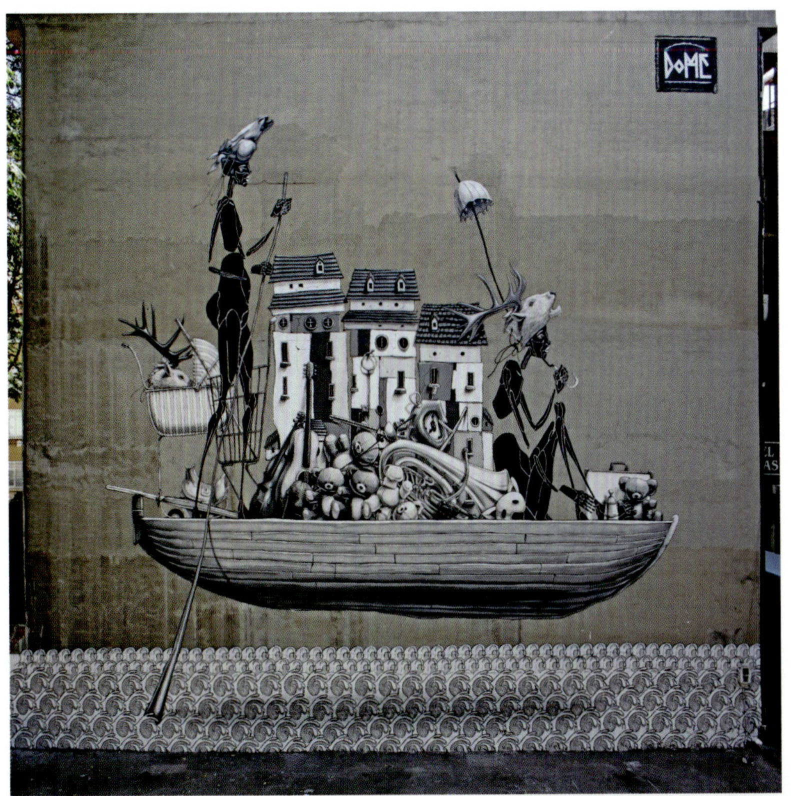

DoMe

CLOCKWISE FROM FAR
LEFT:
Karlsruhe-based Dome/
Dome/Won ABC in Munich/
Poland's ETAM Cru in
Halle as part of the
All You Can Paint
Festival.

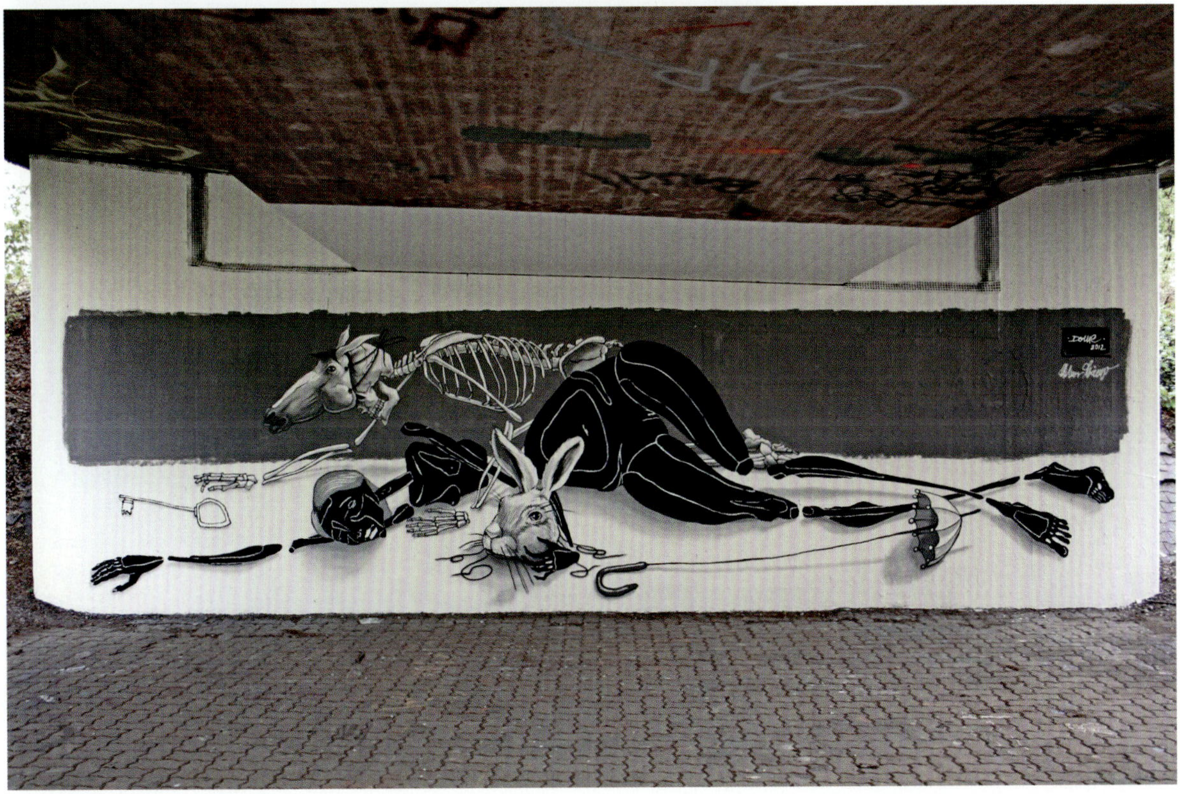

Through a different job I had the chance to live in Spain for three months. Spain is covered in graffiti! Based in south-west Spain, I tried to visit a major new city almost every weekend, covering most places except the northern tip of the country. The very modern roads in Spain make long-distance driving easy and there are a lot of abandoned buildings by the side of the roads – you can easily stumble upon different graffiti spots unintentionally.

The largest Hall of Fame I've ever seen is in southern Spain: I took 1,000 photographs in one location alone – a city river with concrete-lined walls, which stretches for two to three miles. I doubt anyone has bothered to walk the whole river before because it is dirty, smelly and slippery underfoot in parts. For some distances the river runs dry but then it suddenly reappears. I drove right into the side of it, looking for somewhere else, and knew I had to jump in. I parked my car and jumped down, walking and taking pictures as I went. There were parts of the river where the walls were so high I had no chance of getting out and I'd walked too far to turn back; the river was also curved so I had no idea where it ended or if and when I would be able to get out. The only impulse I had was to keep going, sliding along the slimy floor with my trashed trainers. Eventually, of course, I did get out of the river – thankfully with my camera intact.

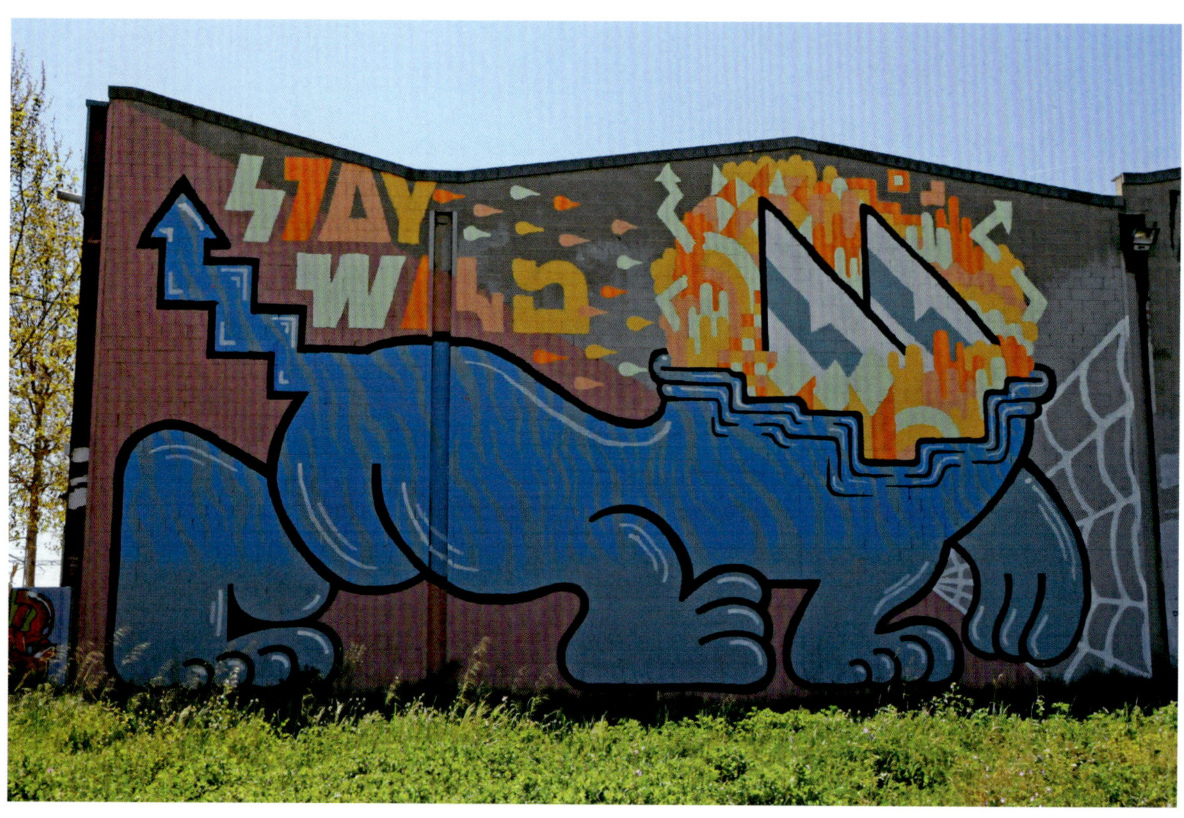

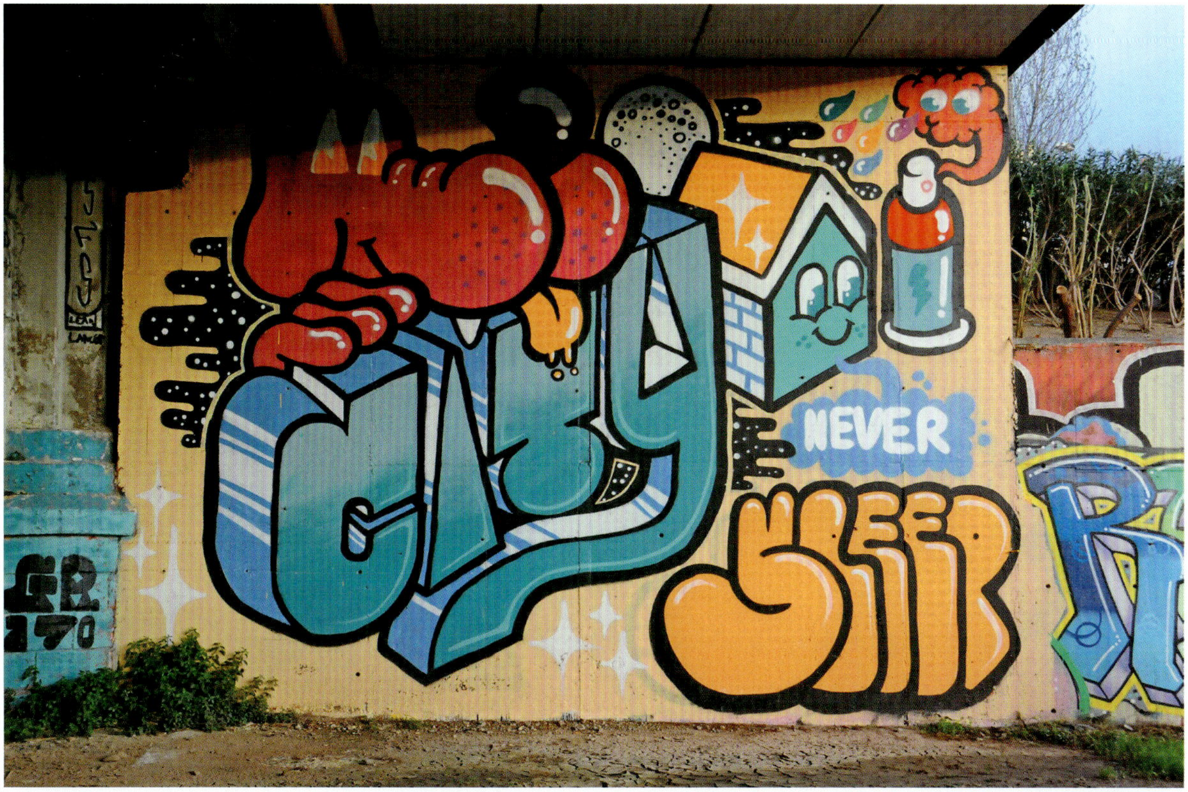

NEVER
city
JFK
CLEAN
LAMB
GR
270

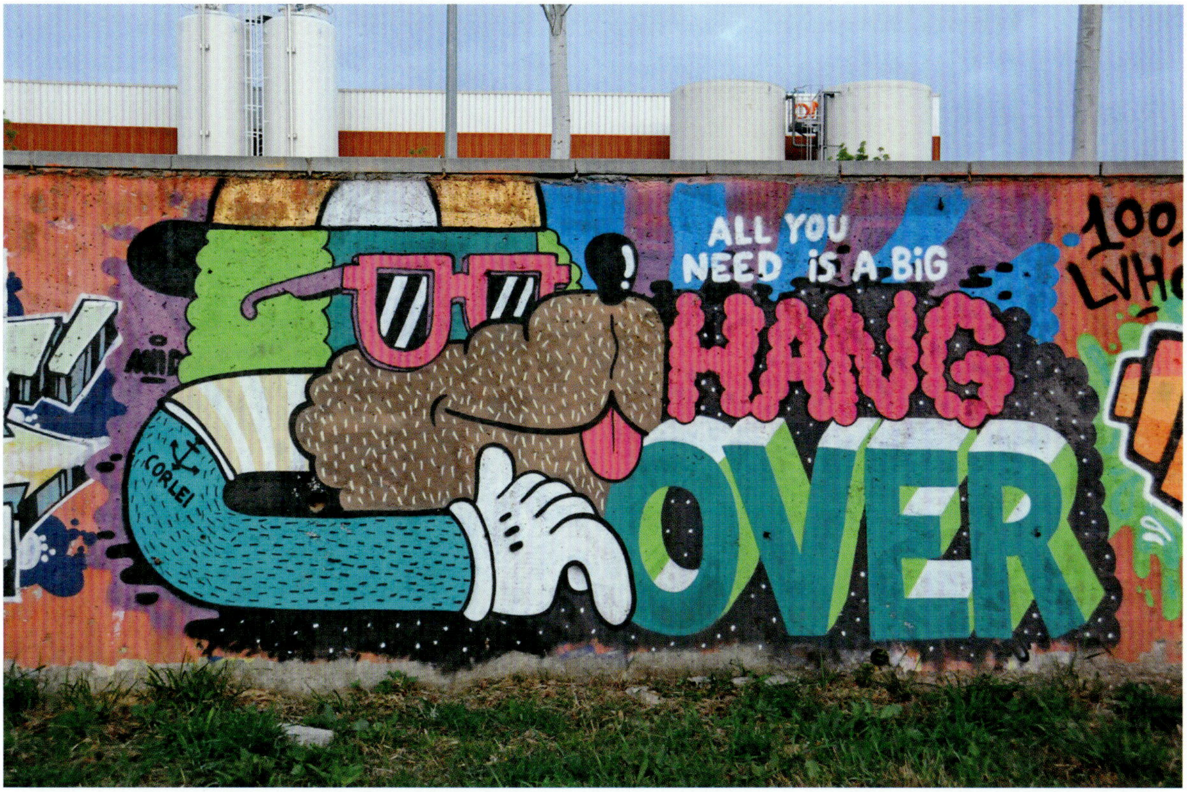

ALL YOU
NEED IS A BIG
HANG
OVER
100
LVH
CORLEI

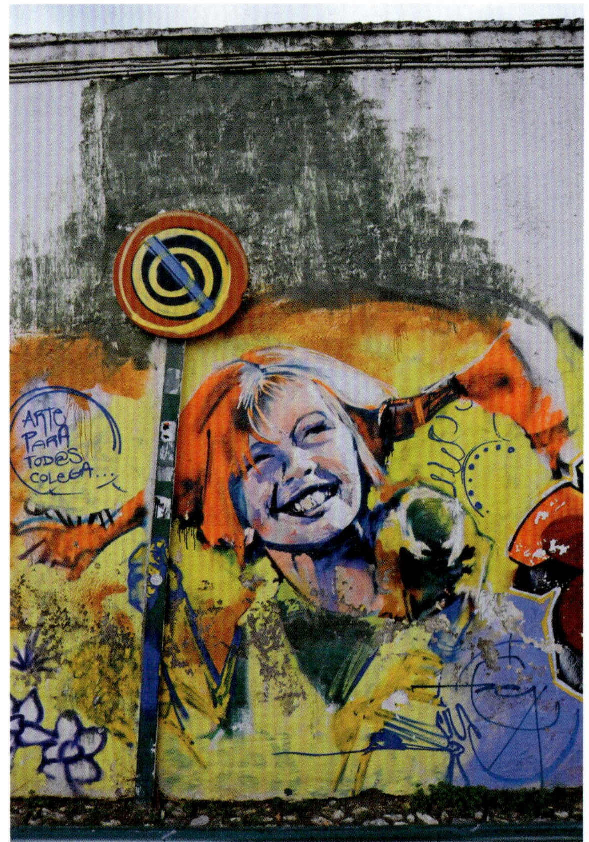

CLOCKWISE FROM LEFT:
All works by El Niño de
las Pinturas aka Sex in
Granada, Granada and
Seville (the main bus
station).

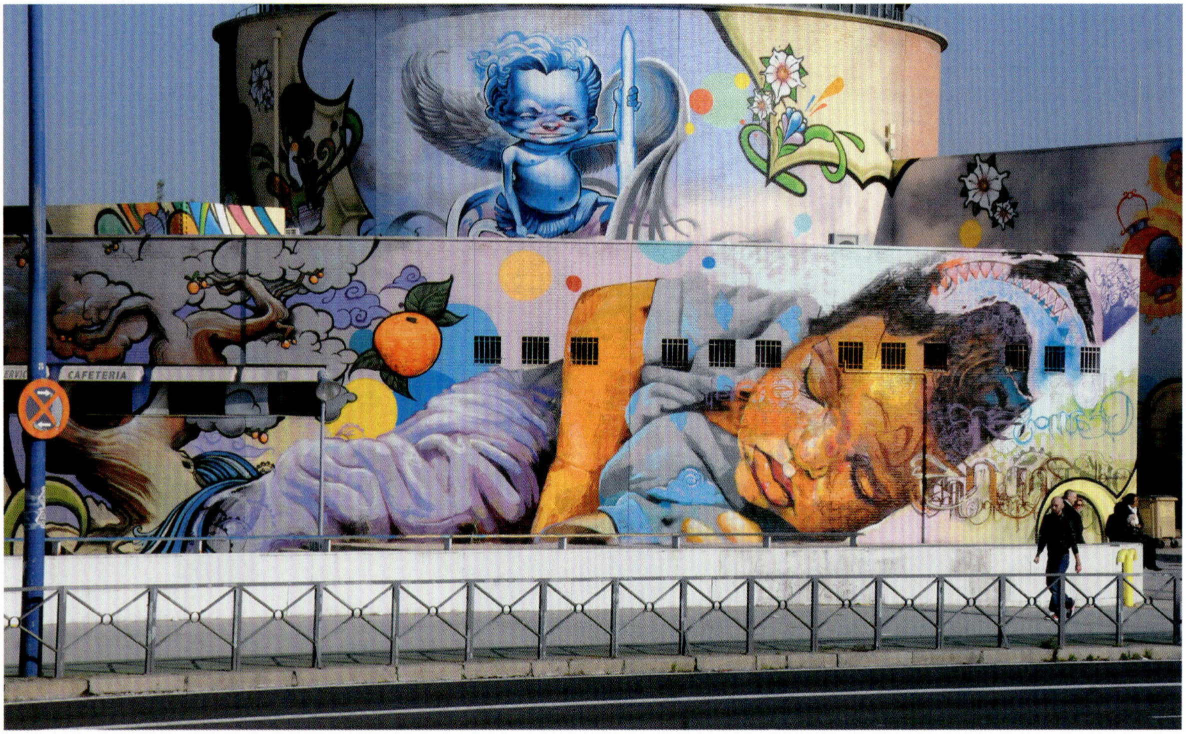

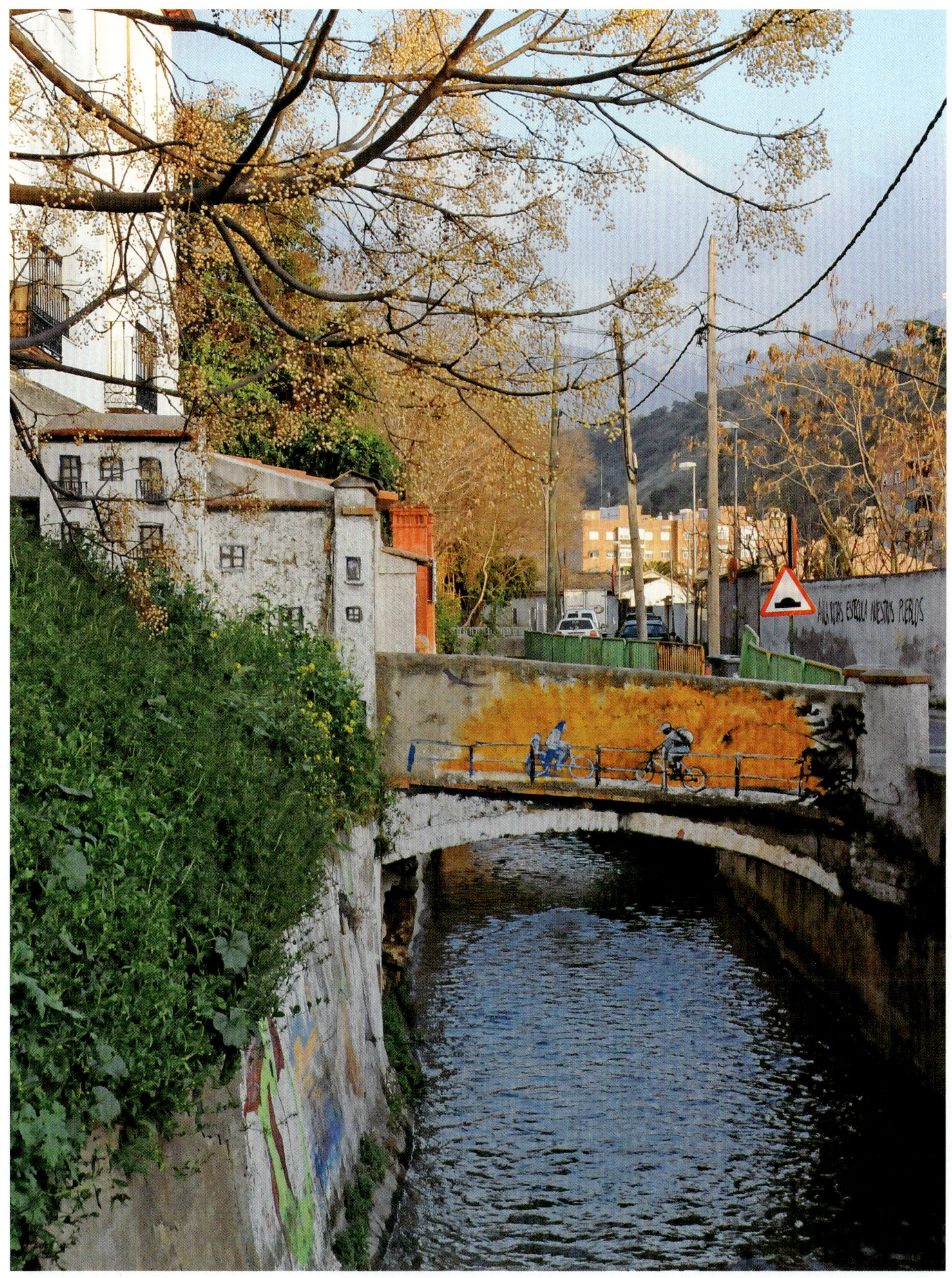
ESTRELLA NUESTROS PUEBLOS

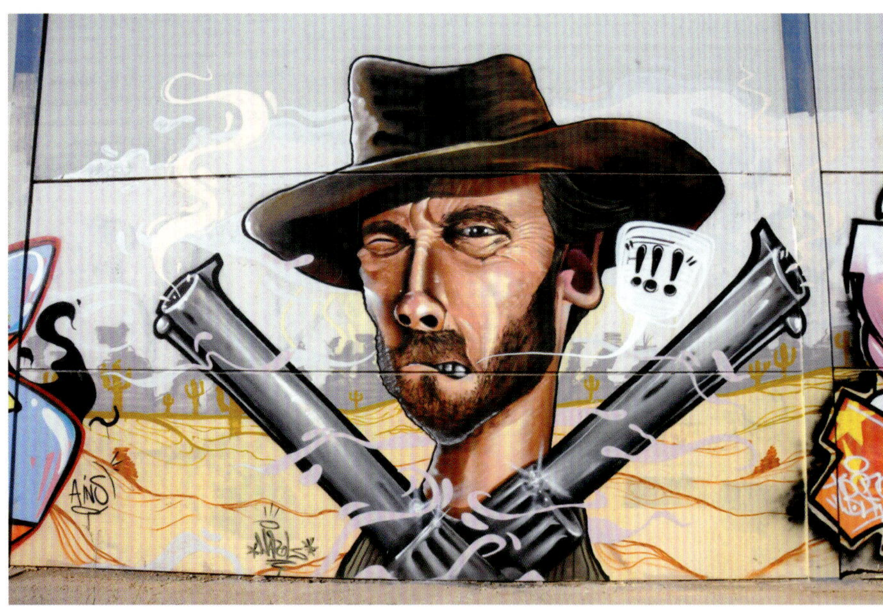

THESE PAGES:
All works by Napol
on the outskirts of
Valencia.

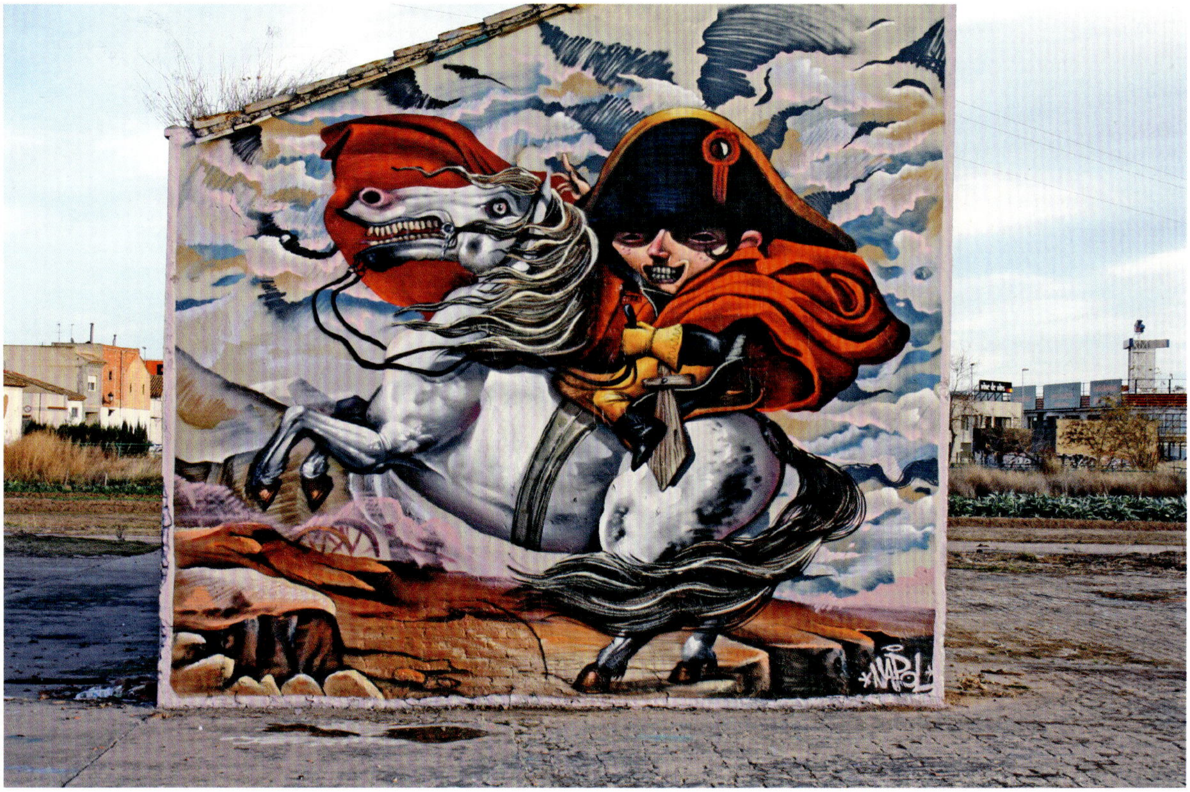

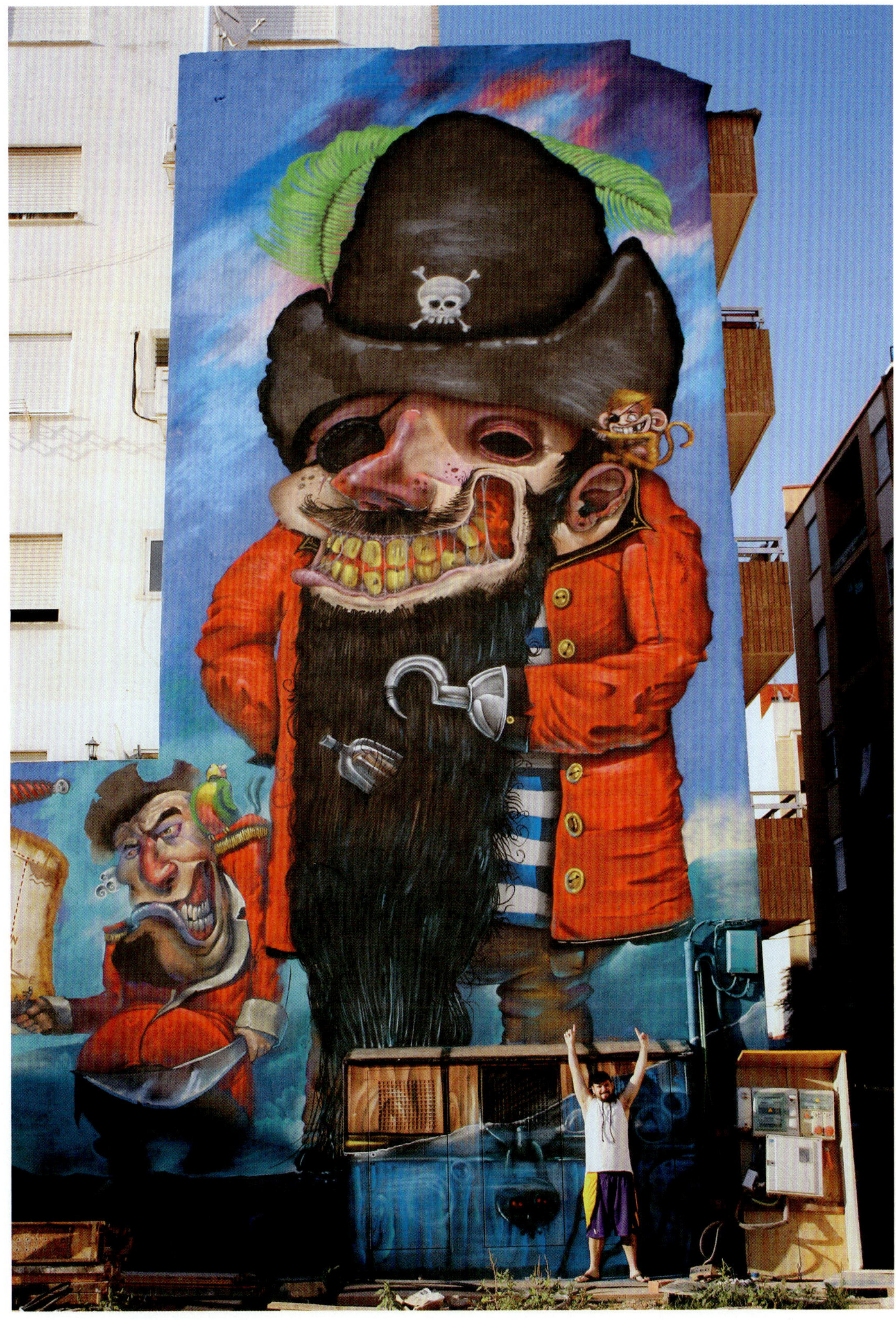

CLOCKWISE FROM
RIGHT:
Cere in Valencia/Cere
in Valencia/Chapu in
Cádiz.

PAGES 80-1,
CLOCKWISE FROM LEFT:
Malakkai in Málaga.
To date this is the
longest graffiti site
I've ever visited. It
was well worth wet feet
and wrecking a pair of
trainers/Looking down
the river in Málaga/
Lal-One (left), Sceno-
One (centre) and Kalama
(right), and yes, I'm
standing in the river!

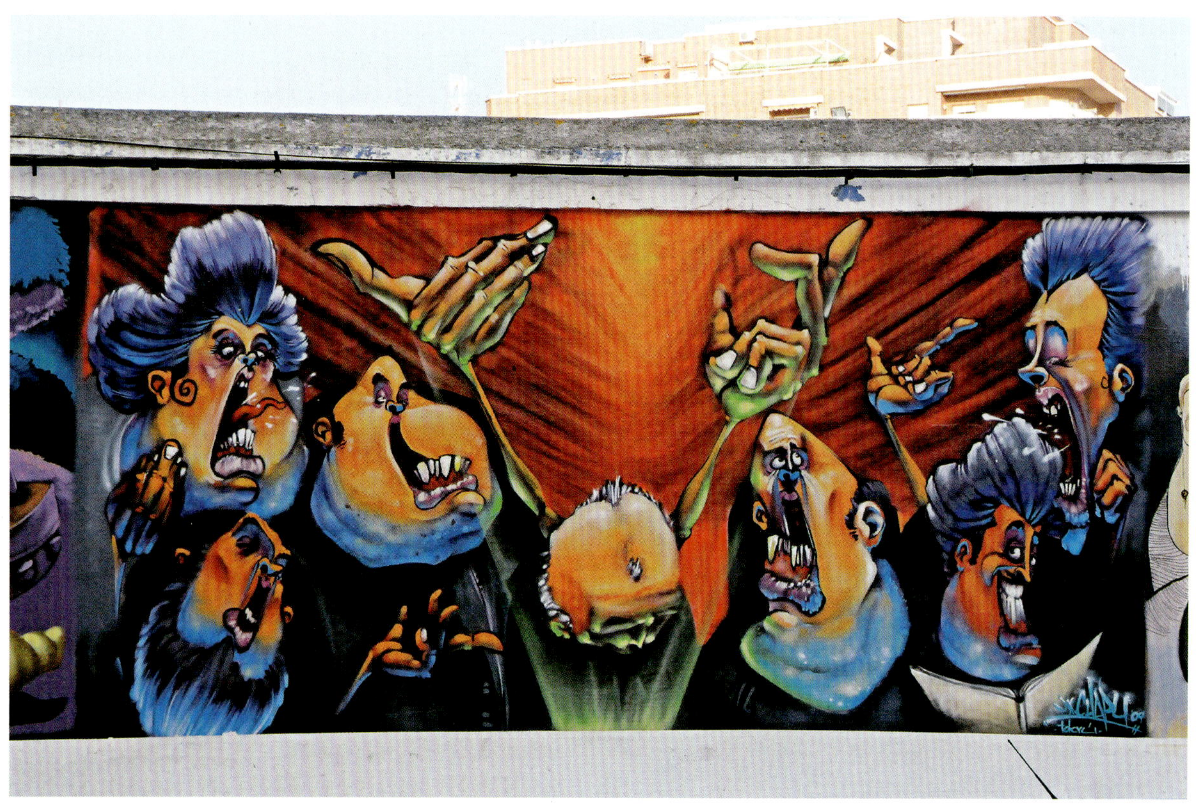

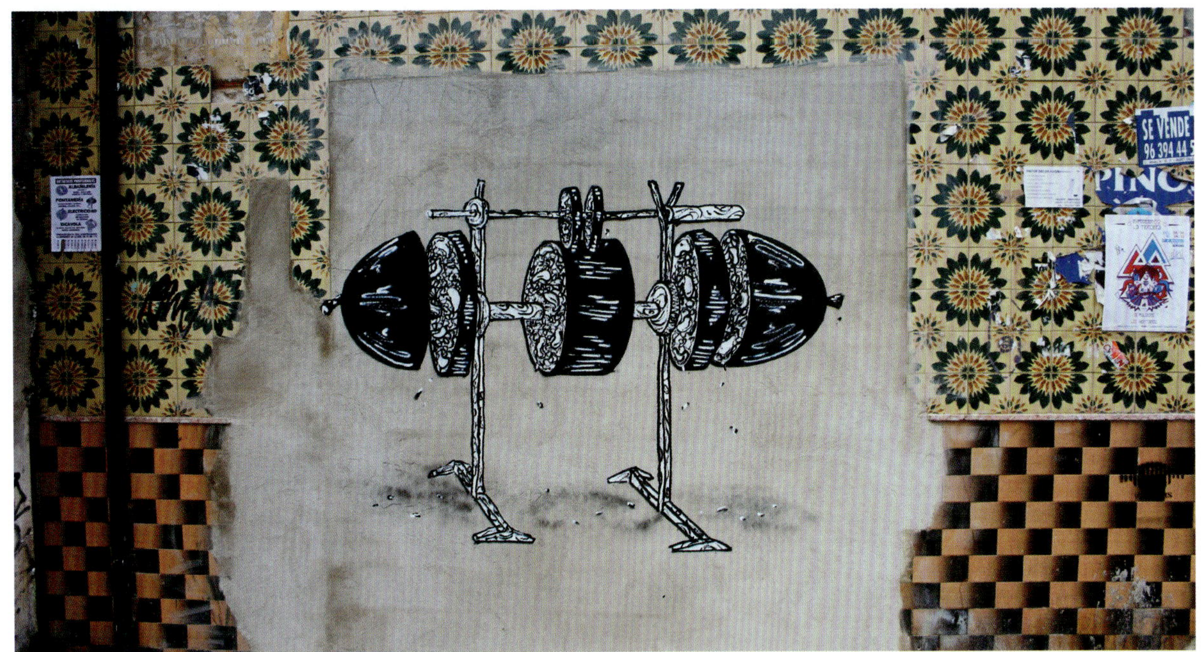

SE VENDE
96 394 44 5
PINO

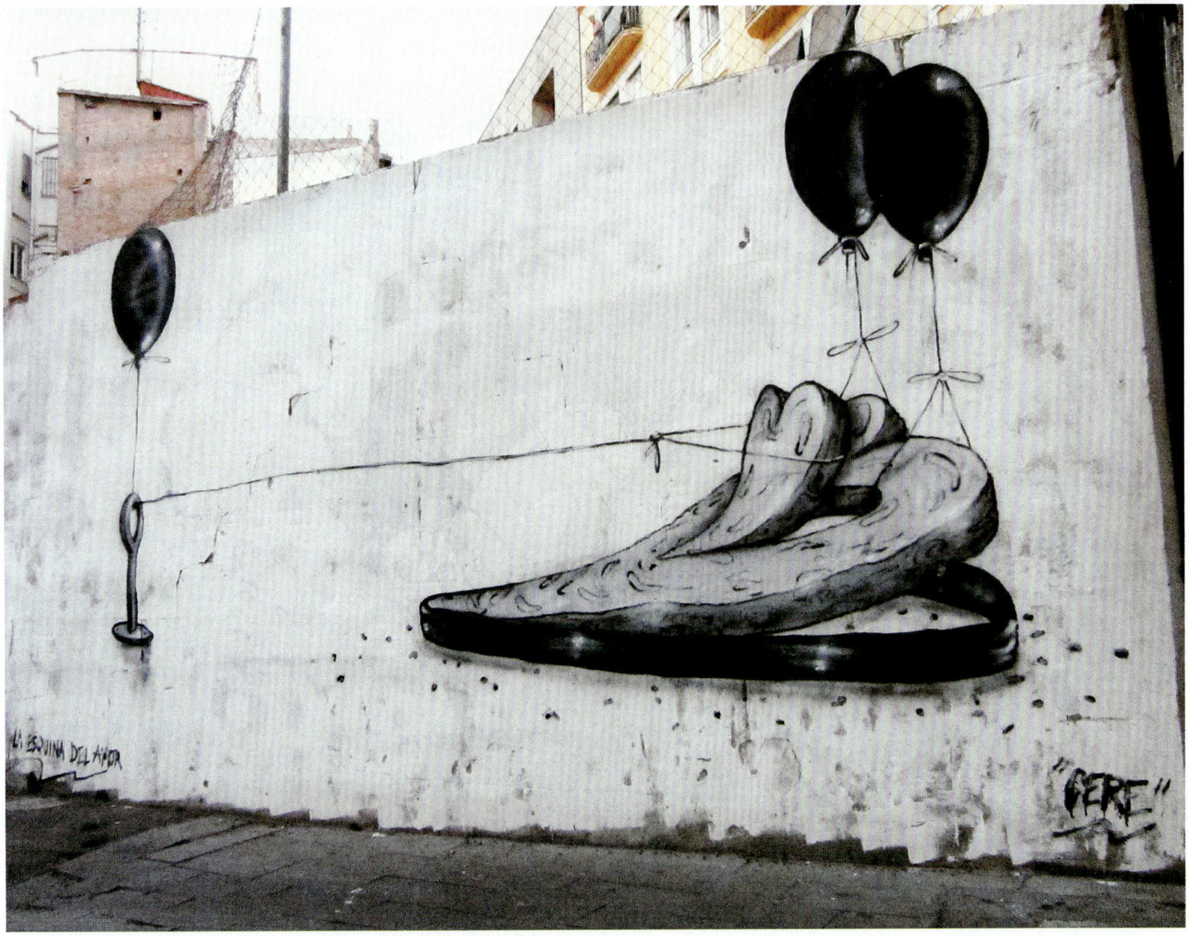

LA ESQUINA DEL AMOR
"GERE"

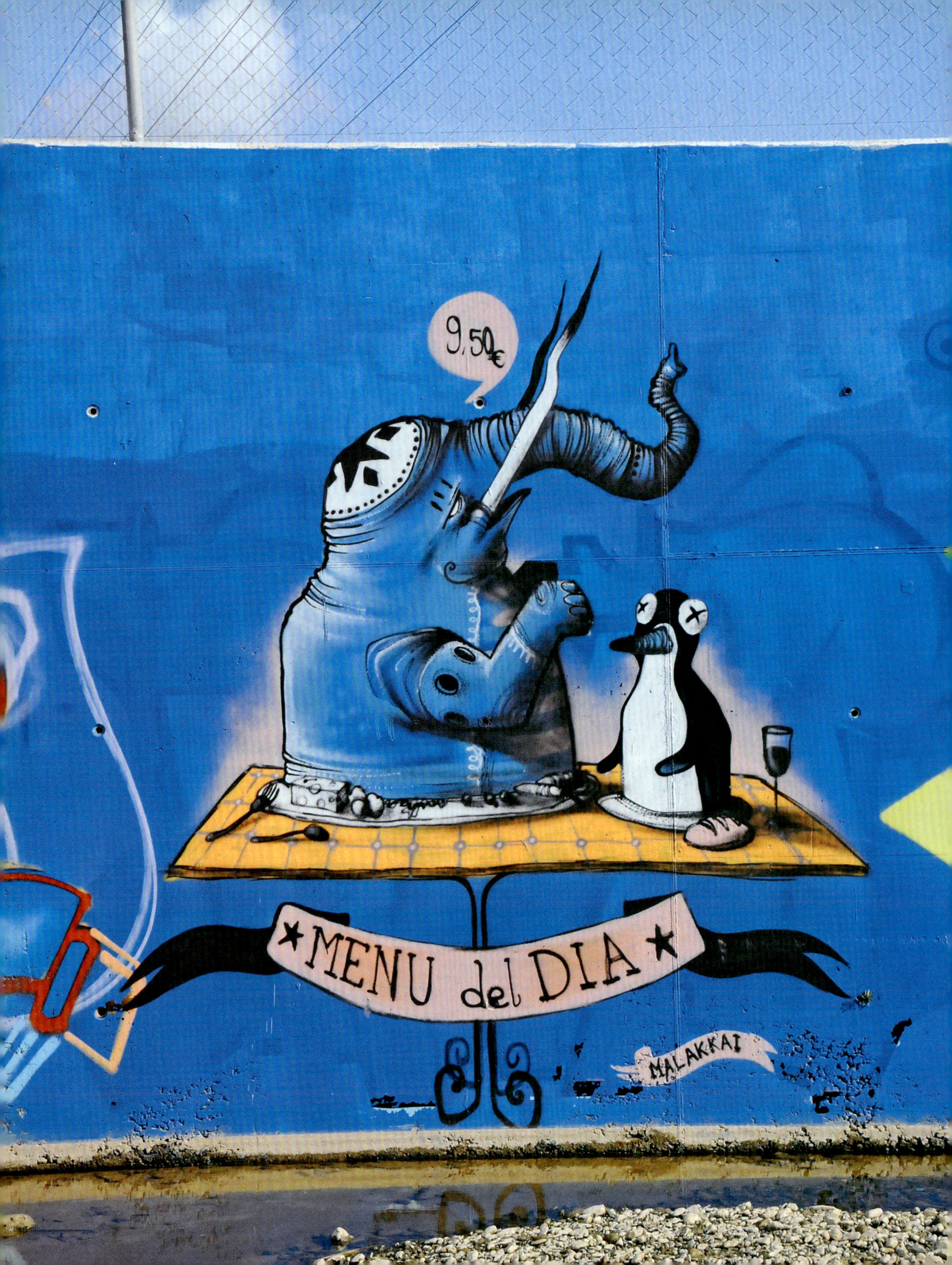

9,50€
MENU del DIA
MALAKKAI

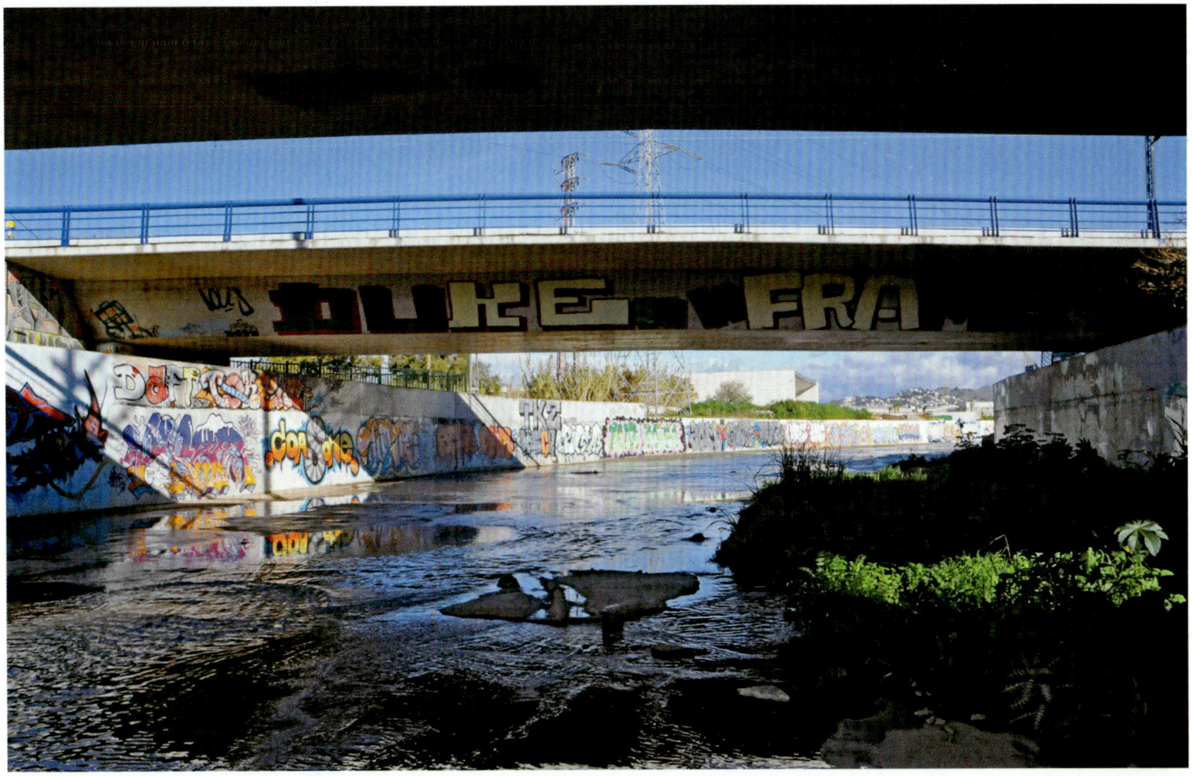

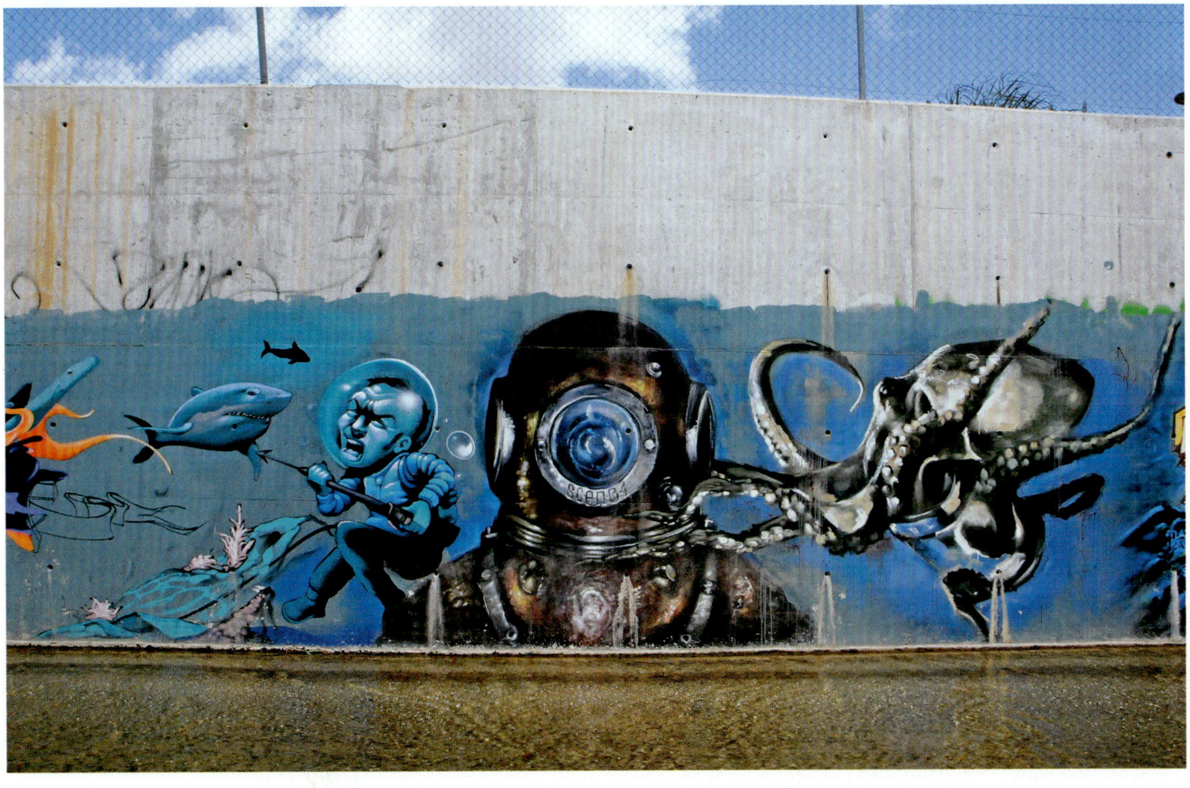

BELOW LEFT TO RIGHT:
Sokram/Dulk.

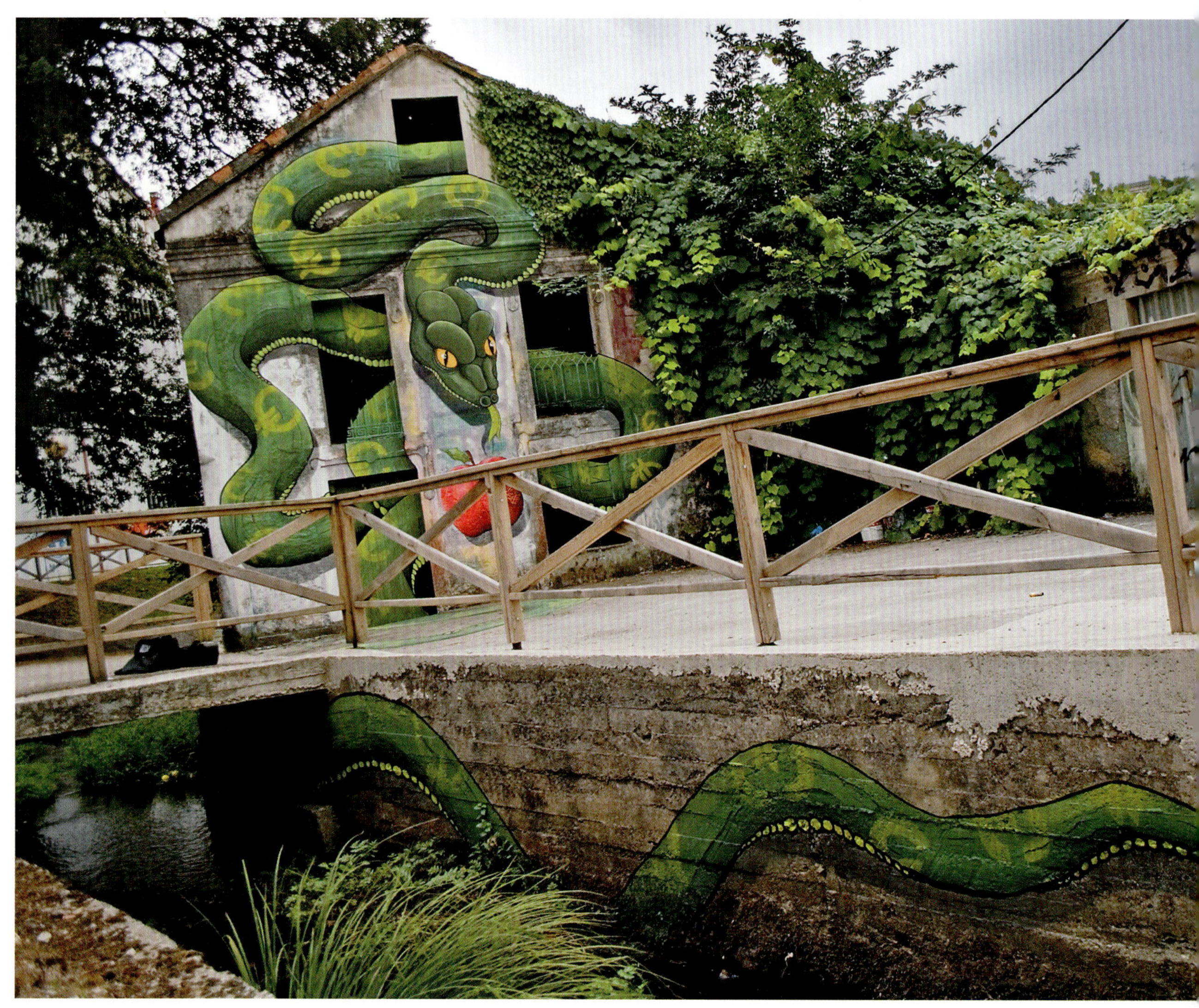

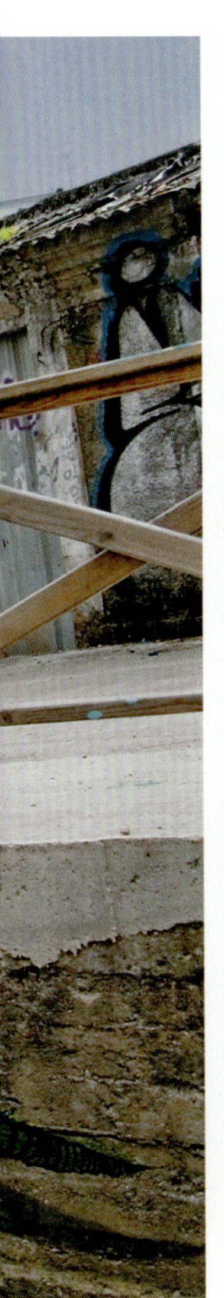

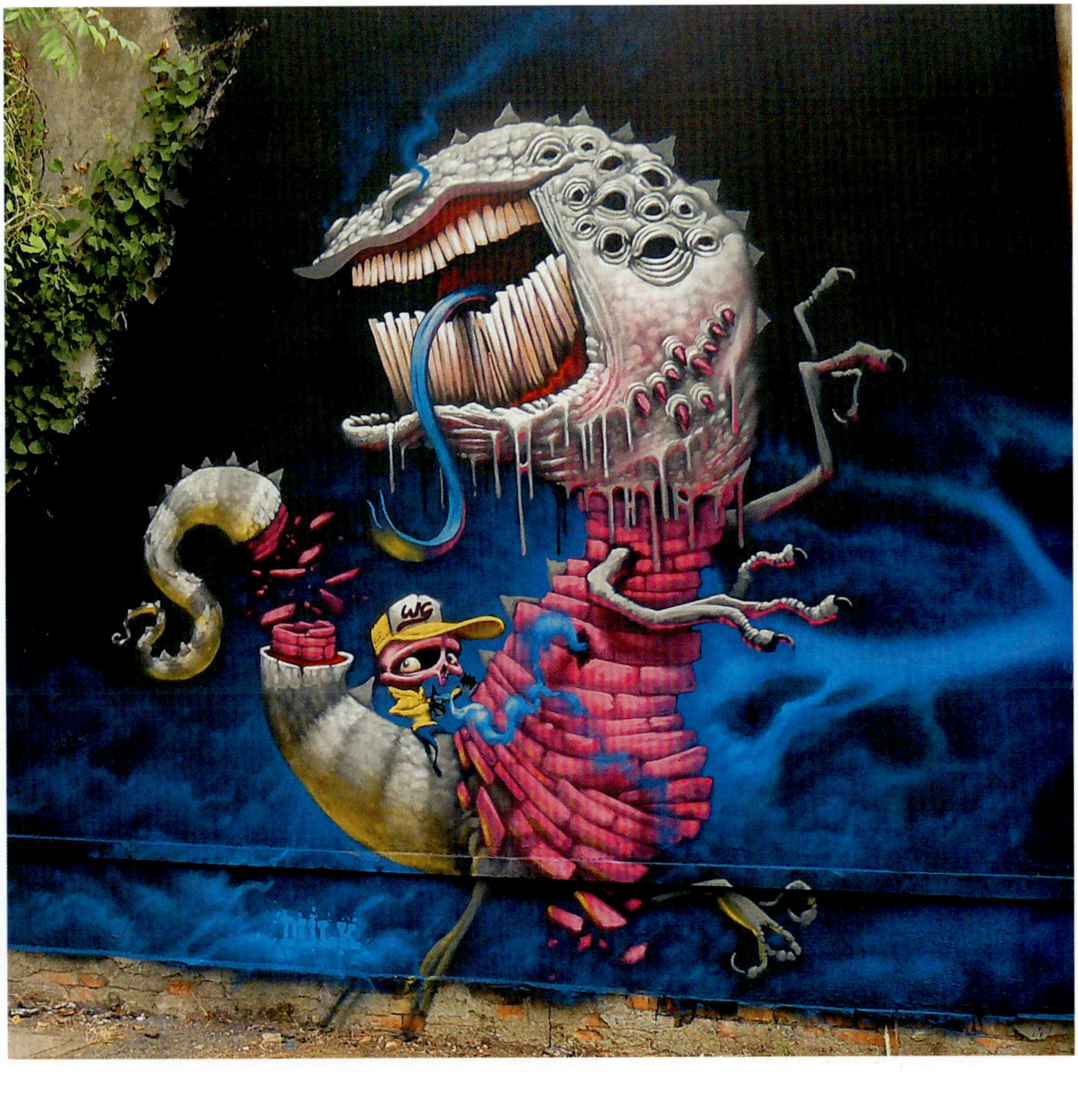

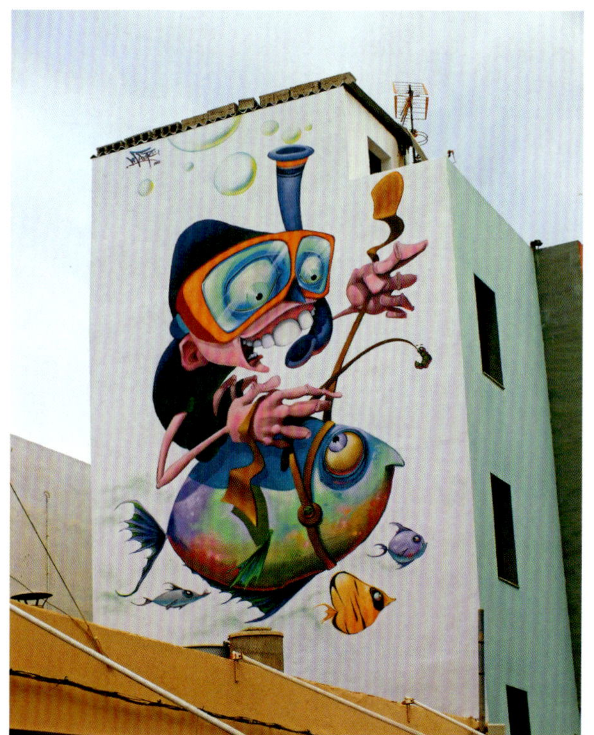

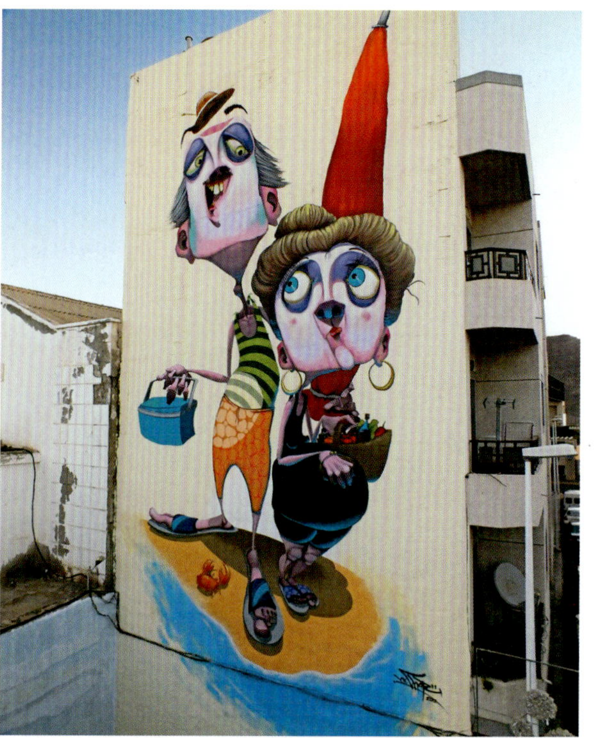

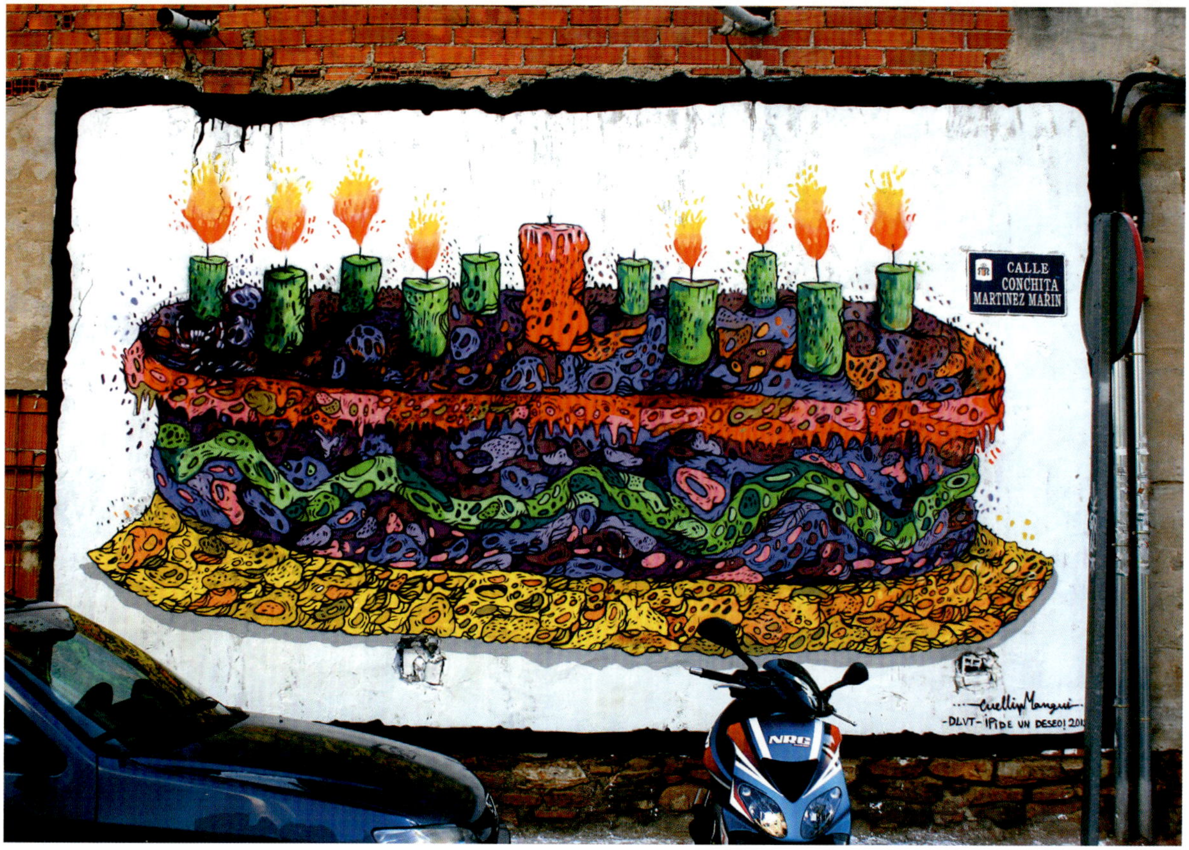

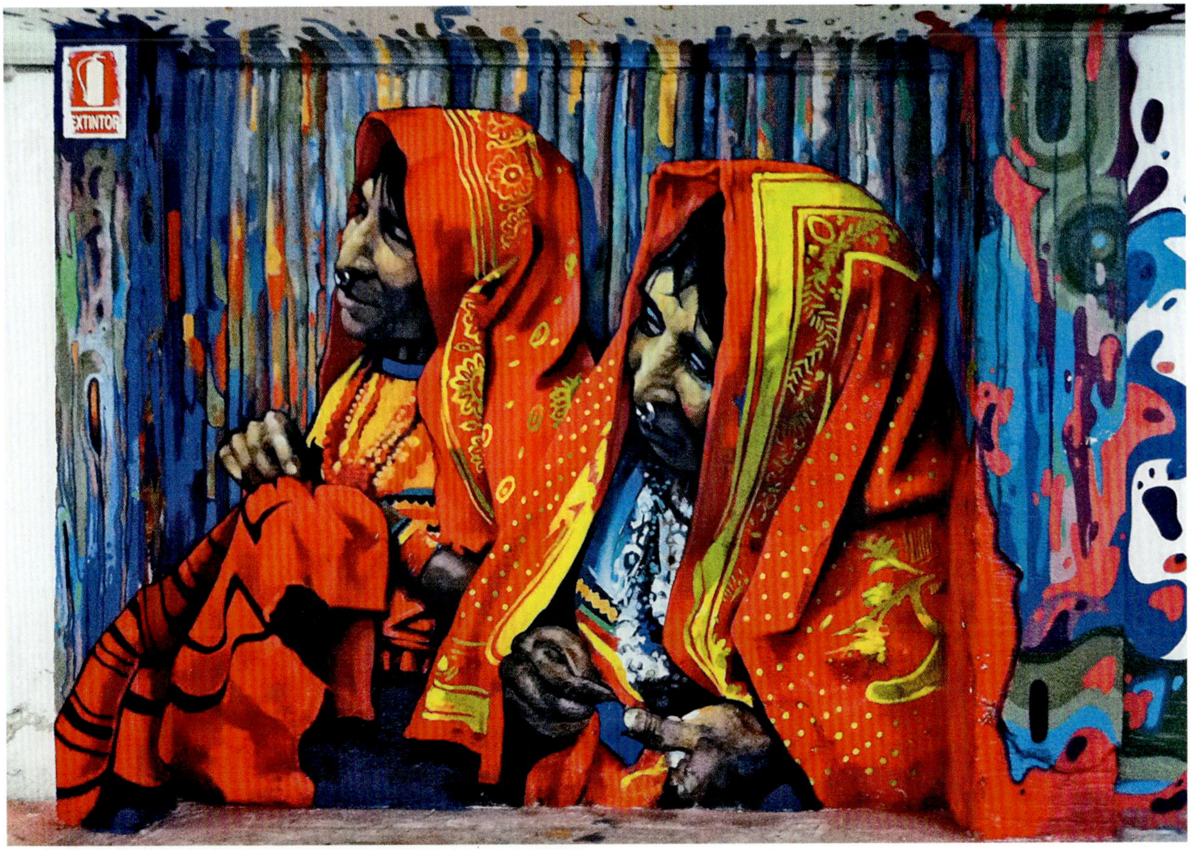

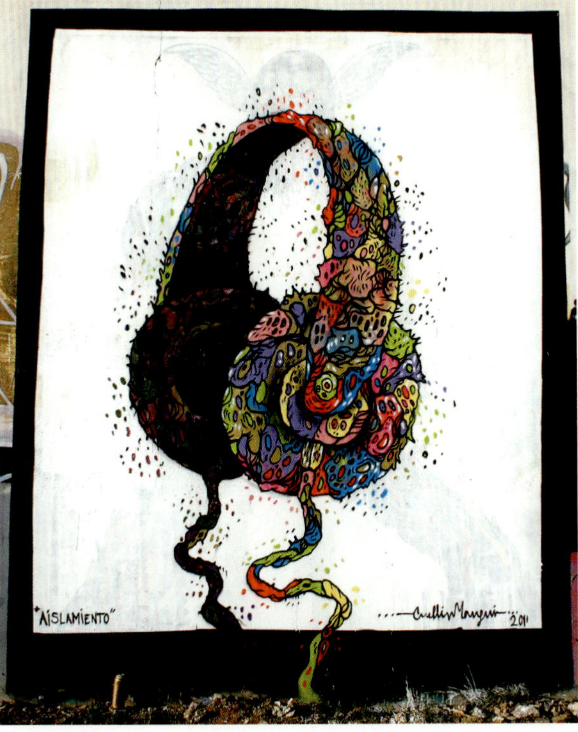

CLOCKWISE FROM TOP
LEFT:
Chapu/Chapu/A portrait
of Peru's Kuna
people by Cristian
Blanxer/Cuellimangui/
Cuellimangui.

I haven't travelled too extensively in Portugal, but I did get to spend time in Lisbon when I was living in Spain. Like many cities in neighbouring Spain, much of Lisbon is painted. I met Odeith – one of my favourite artists – and, alongside Ivan from the Dedicated paint store, he helped me find a lot of places to take pictures. There was one abandoned building in Lisbon that Odeith warned me about: 'If you see anyone, run!' The area had been used as a squat by junkies, and I was almost certain to find trouble if I came across anyone. Nevertheless, in I went, camera at the ready. I had almost finished taking photos, without a person in sight, when two huge stray dogs ran at me from the other side of a filthy room. The dogs were massive and bounding across the room, barking as they went. I didn't have any time to think and, instinctively, I barked back, louder and more aggressively than the dogs, which turned and ran. Dogs have chased me several times now and that's definitely my advice – bark back!

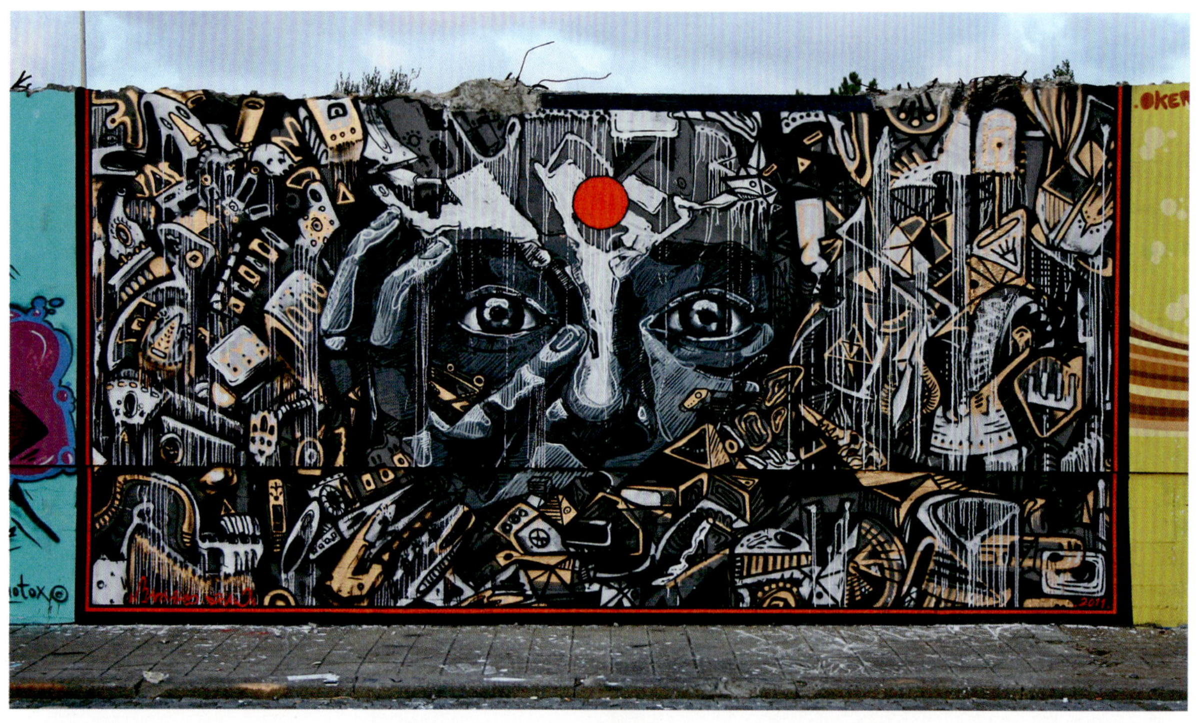

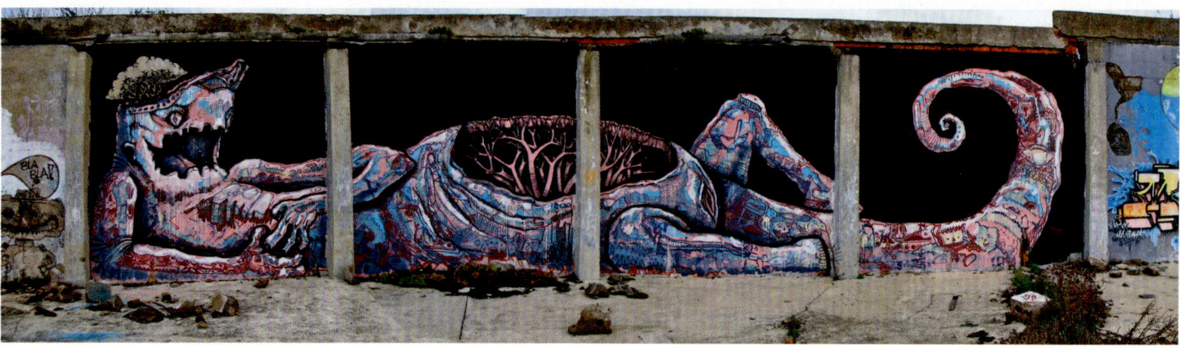

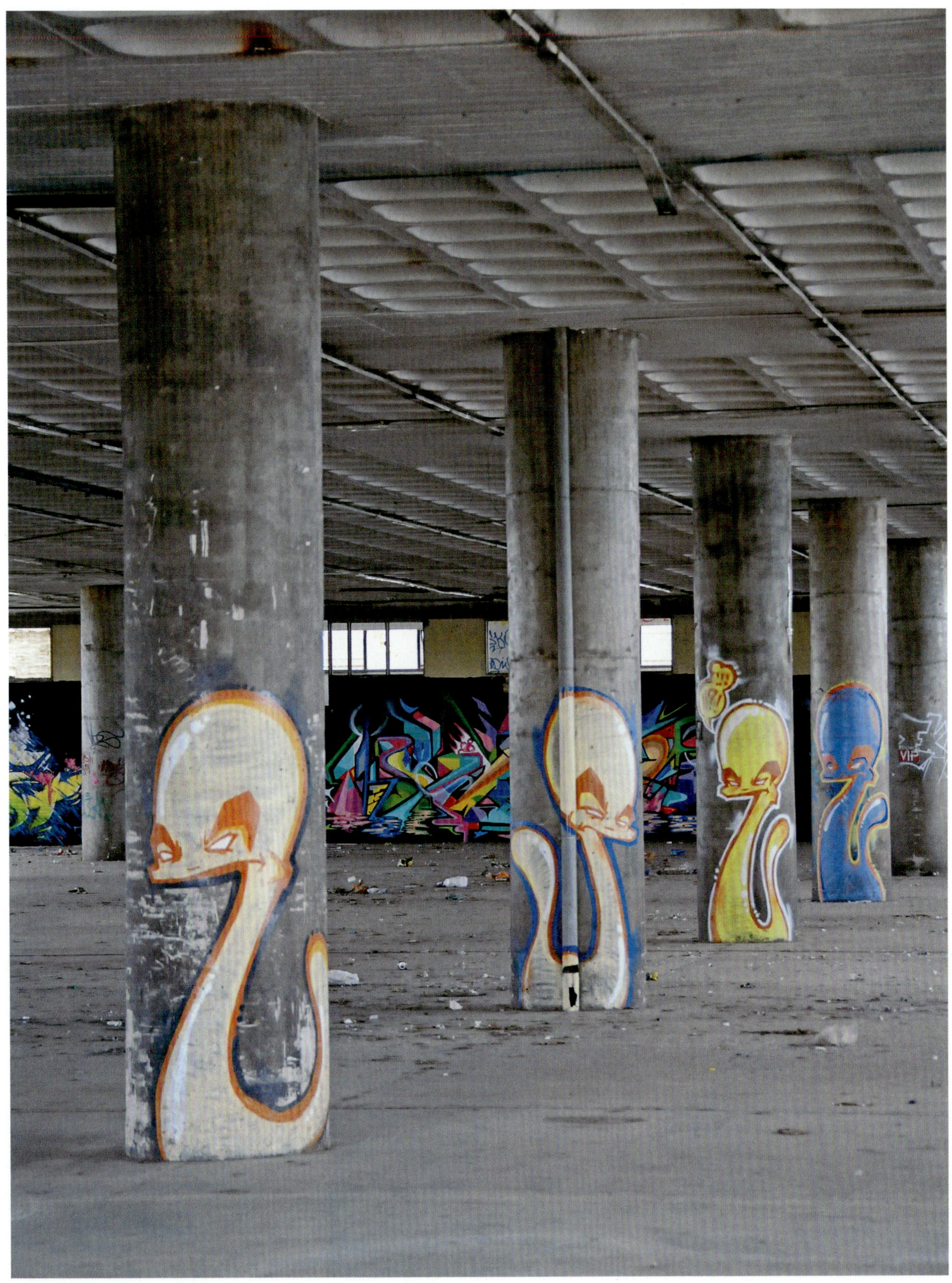

I haven't spent nearly enough time in France; I'm long overdue an extended visit. Despite that, and thanks to the proximity between France and the UK, plus the ubiquity of the internet, I still know plenty of amazing French artists, many of whom have visited London in recent years.

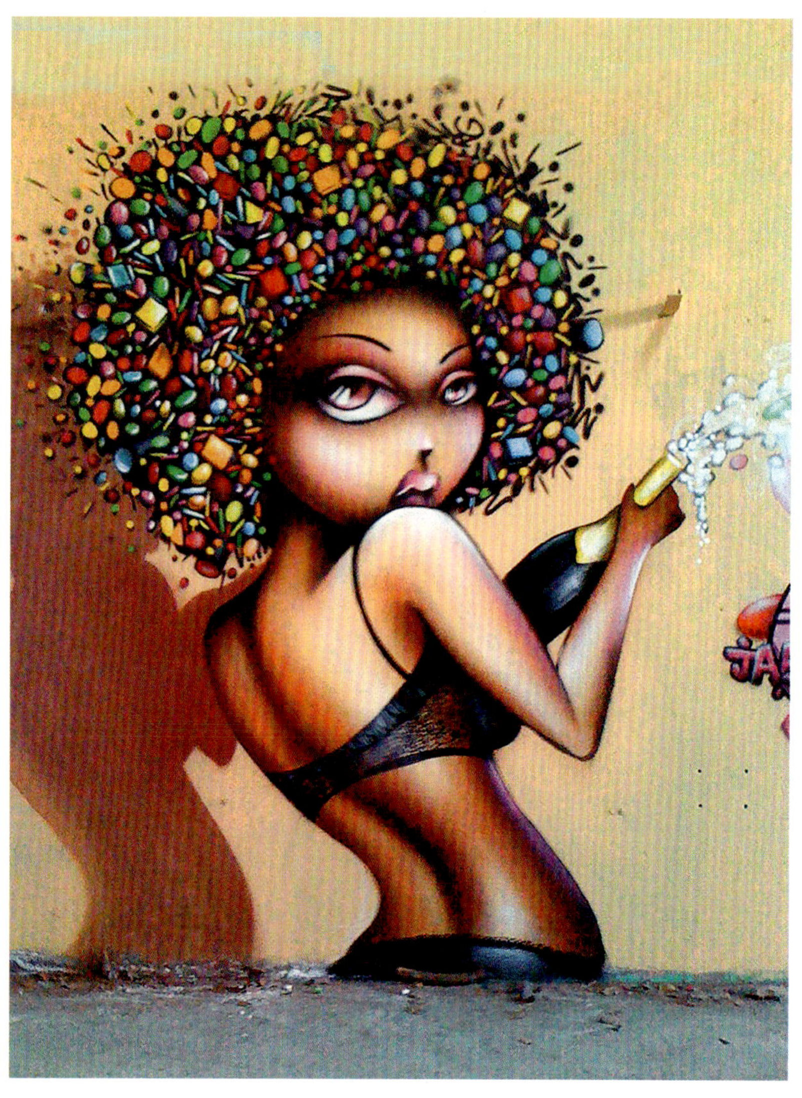

CLOCKWISE FROM LEFT:
Vinie/Ador/Yosh in
Paris.

PAGES 90-1:
MTO in an abandoned
door factory.

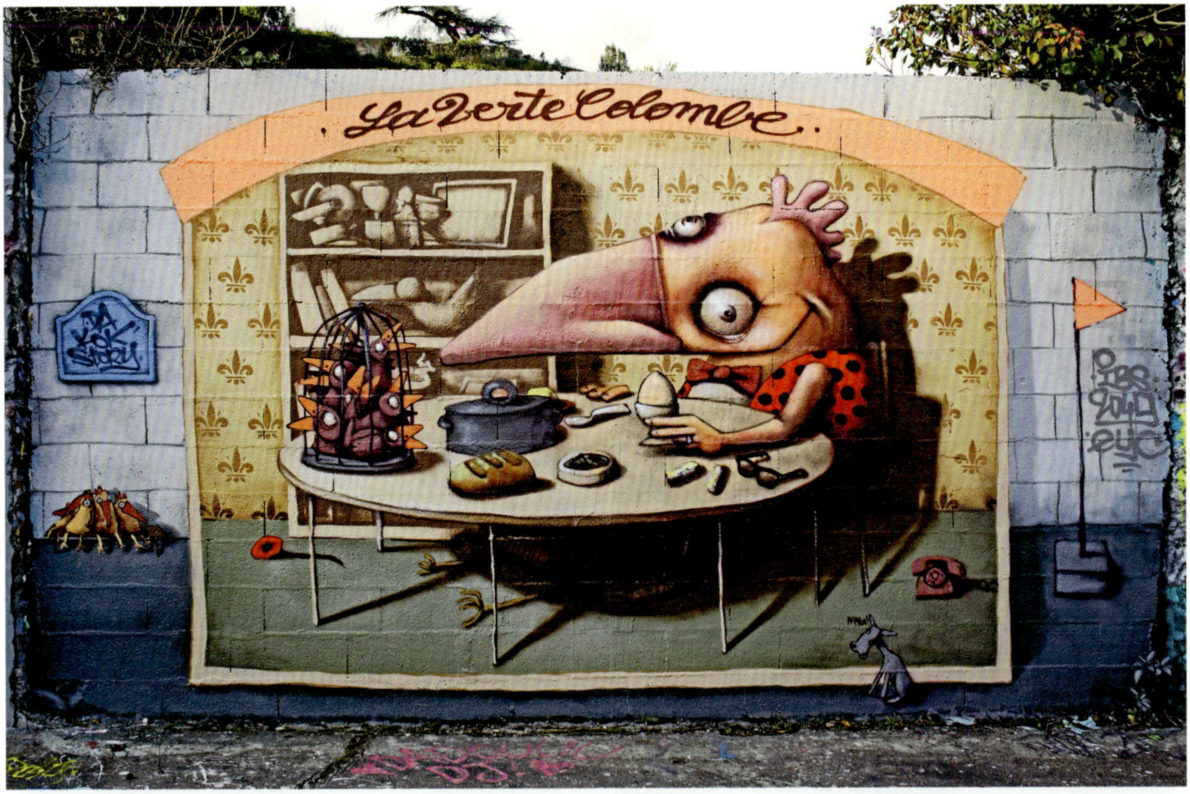
La Verte Colombe

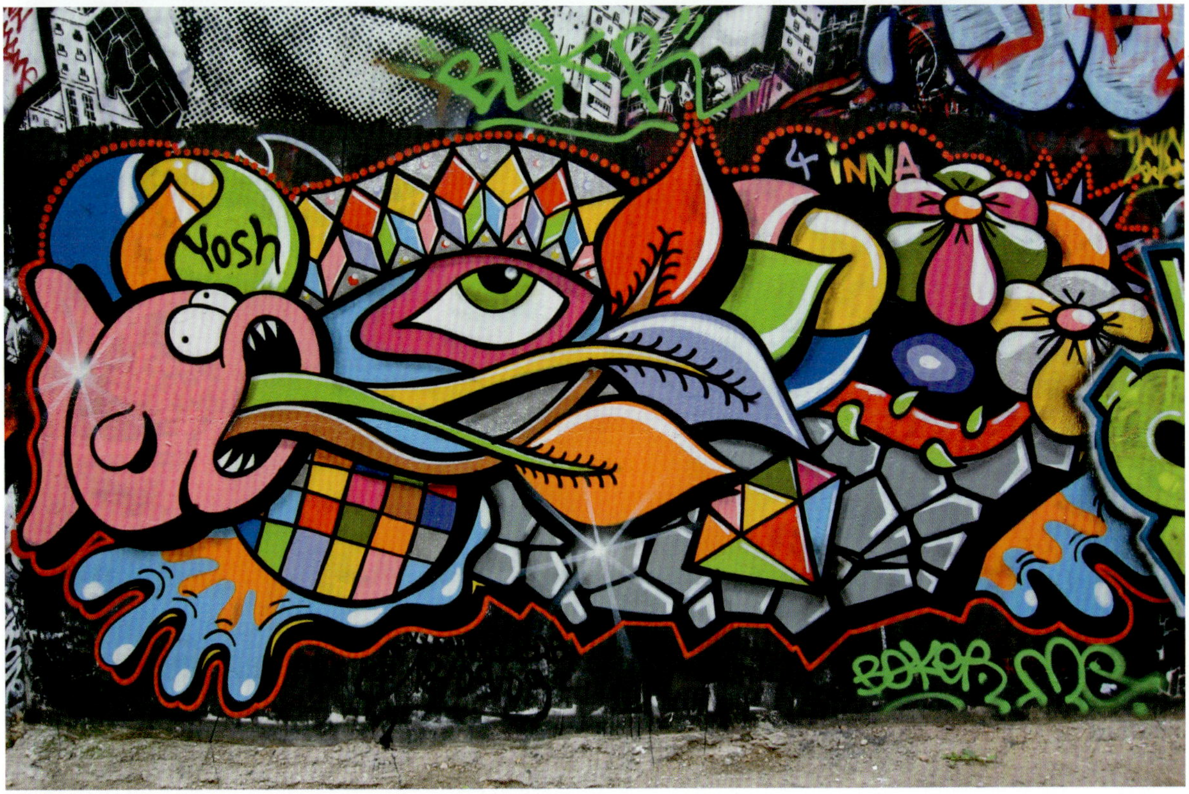
Yosh
4 INNA

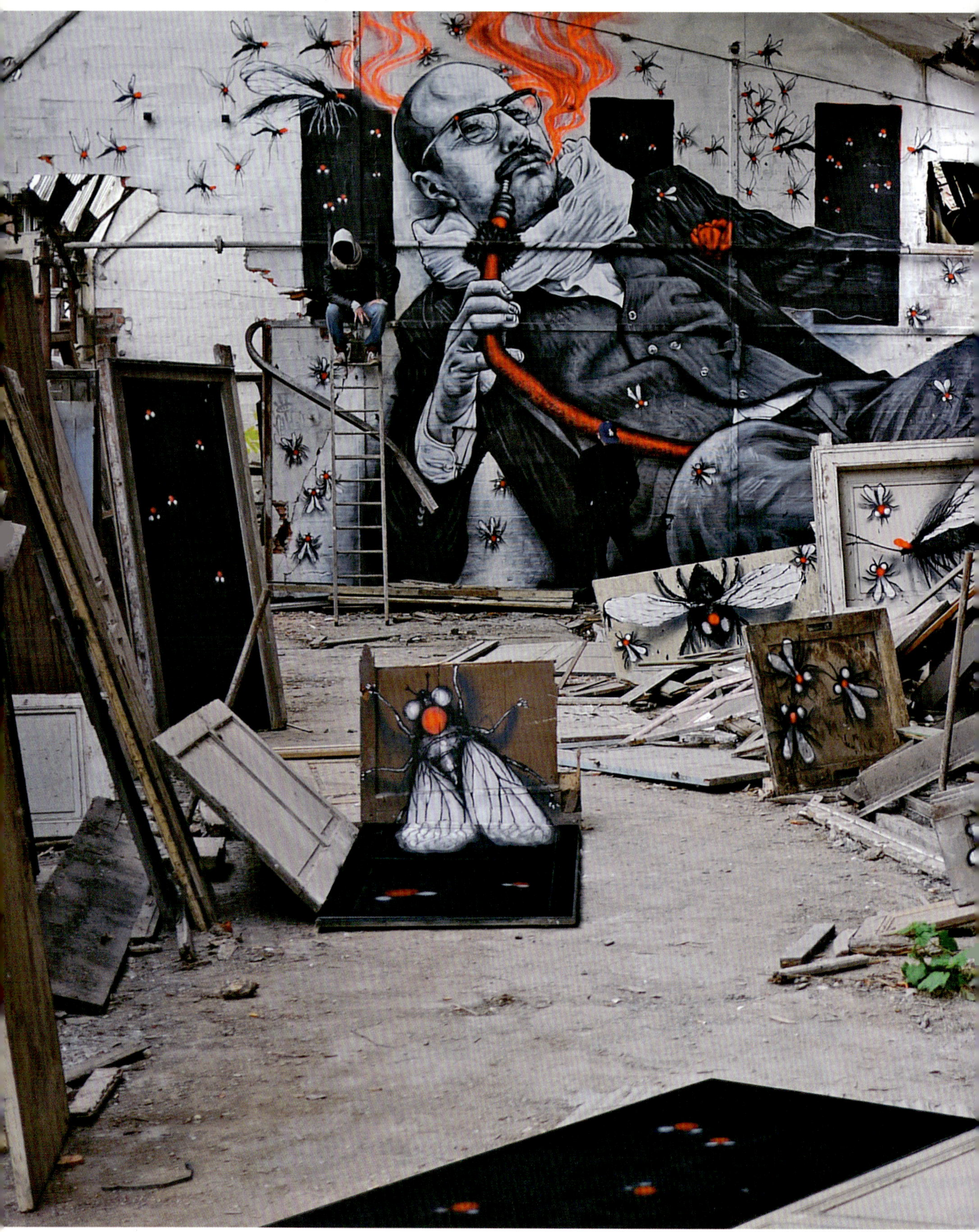

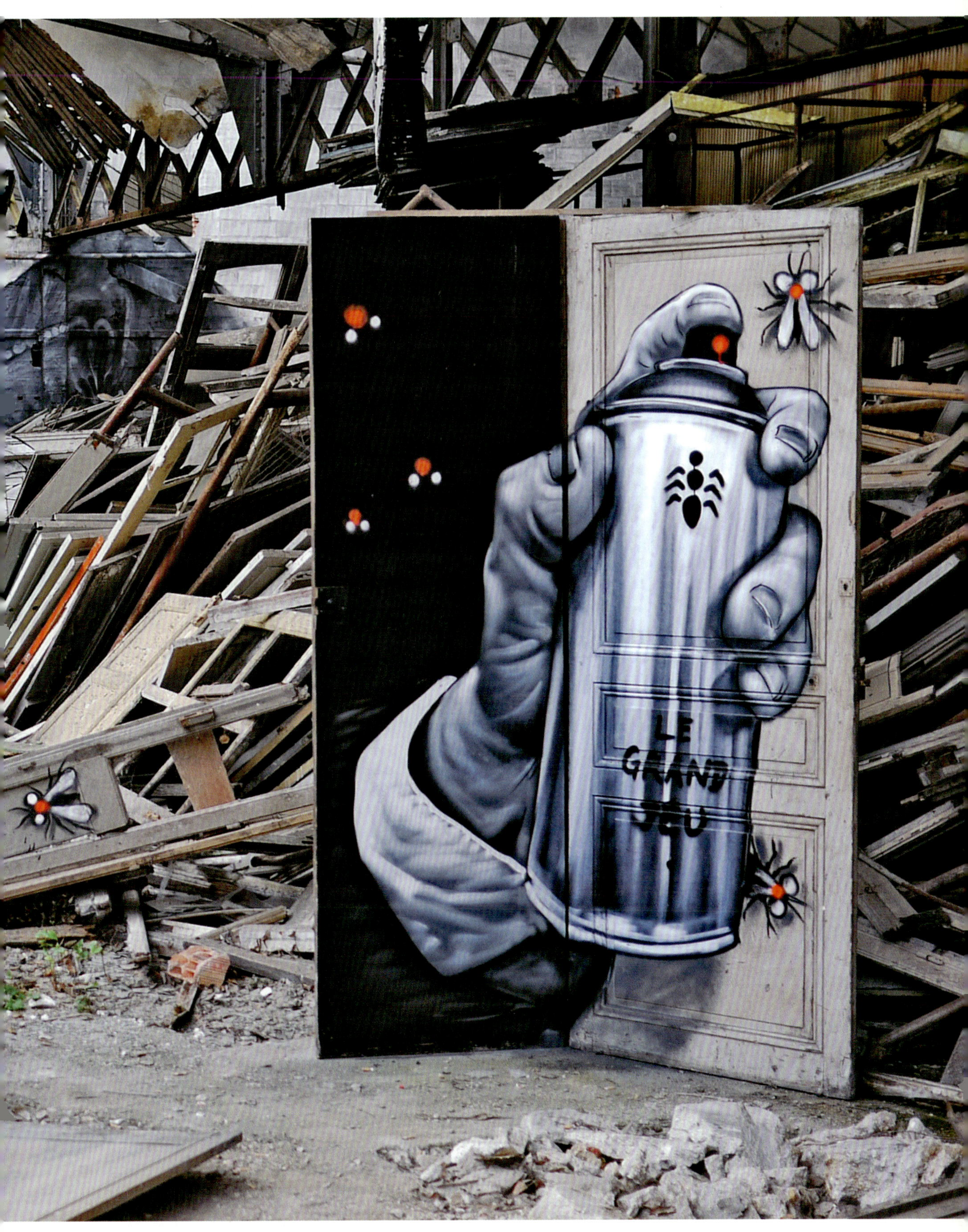

LE
GRAND
JEU

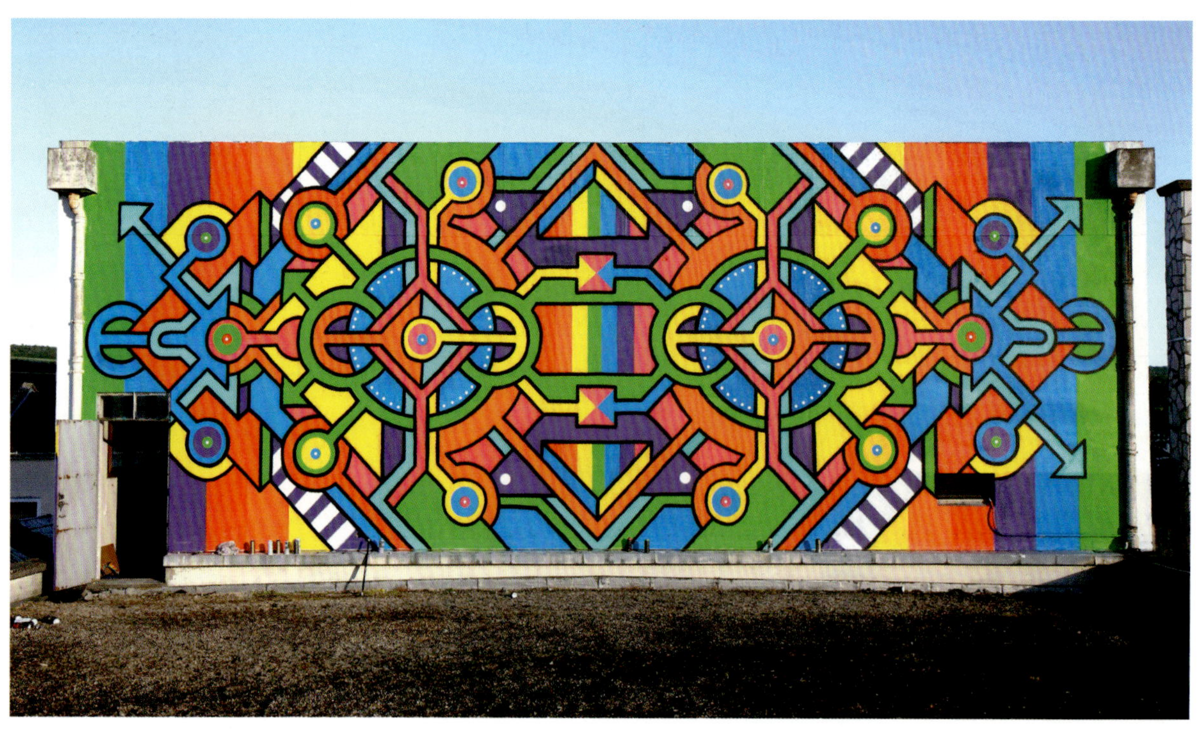

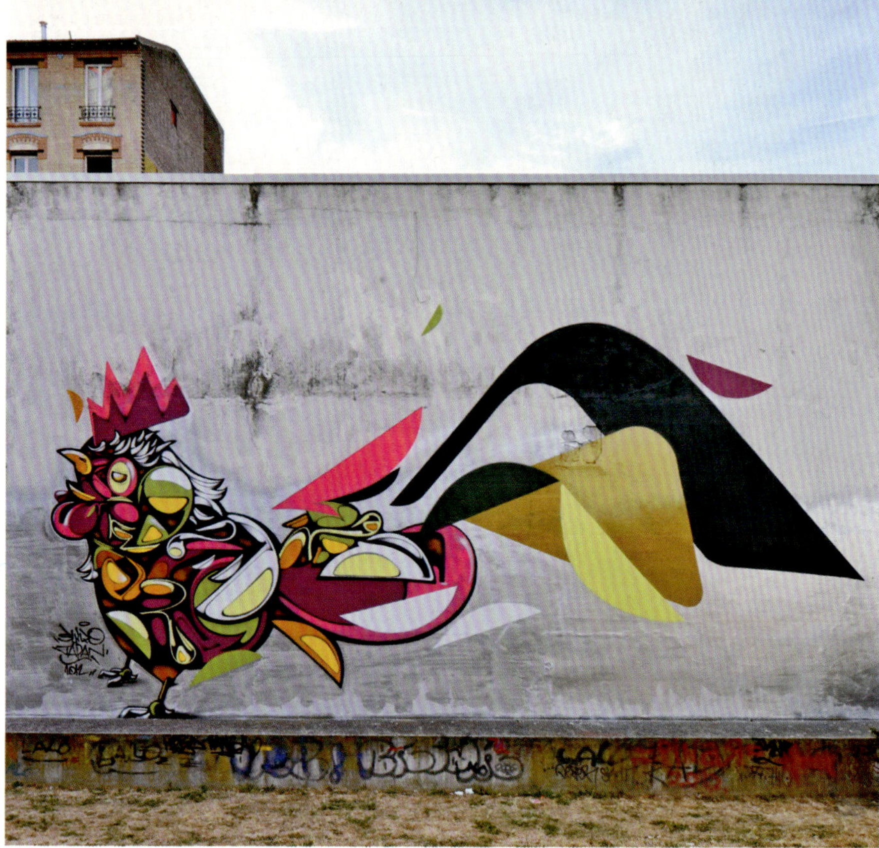

CLOCKWISE FROM LEFT: Japan's Suiko (the cockerel is an unofficial national symbol of France)/Seize aka Happy Wallmaker/Kashink/Kashink (note how these two are rare examples of street art that actively support gay marriage).

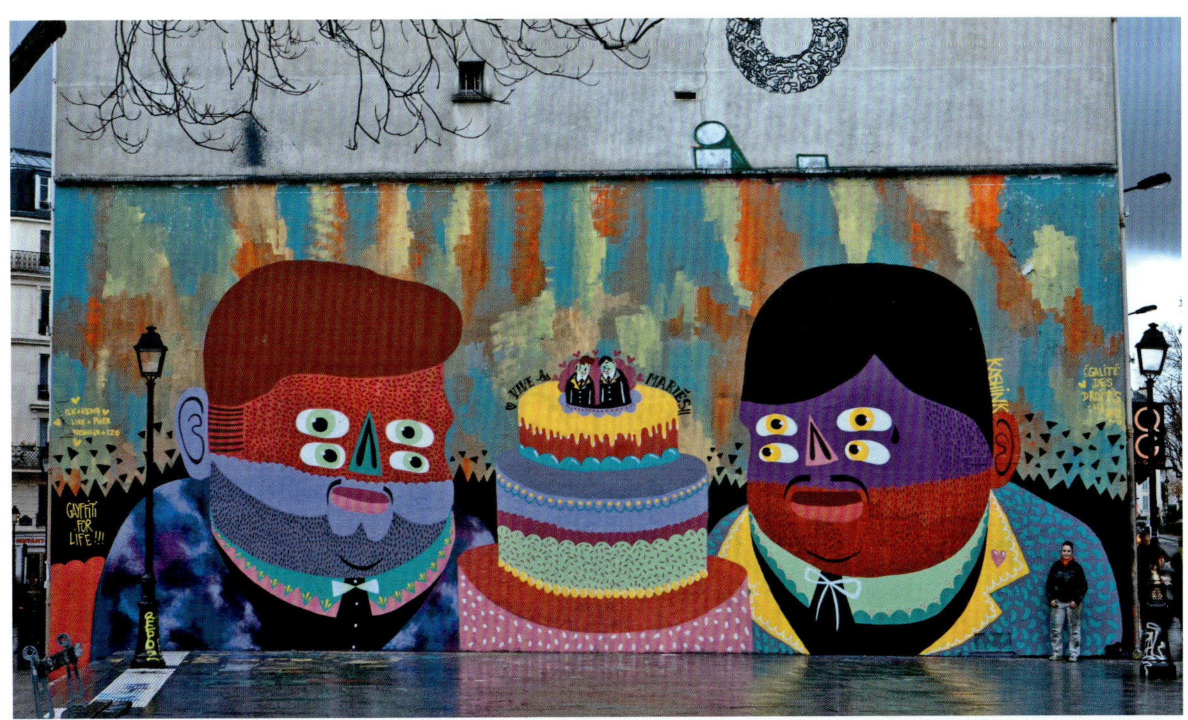

VIVE les MARIÉS!
ÉGALITÉ DES DROITS
KASHINK
GRAFFITI FOR LIFE!!!

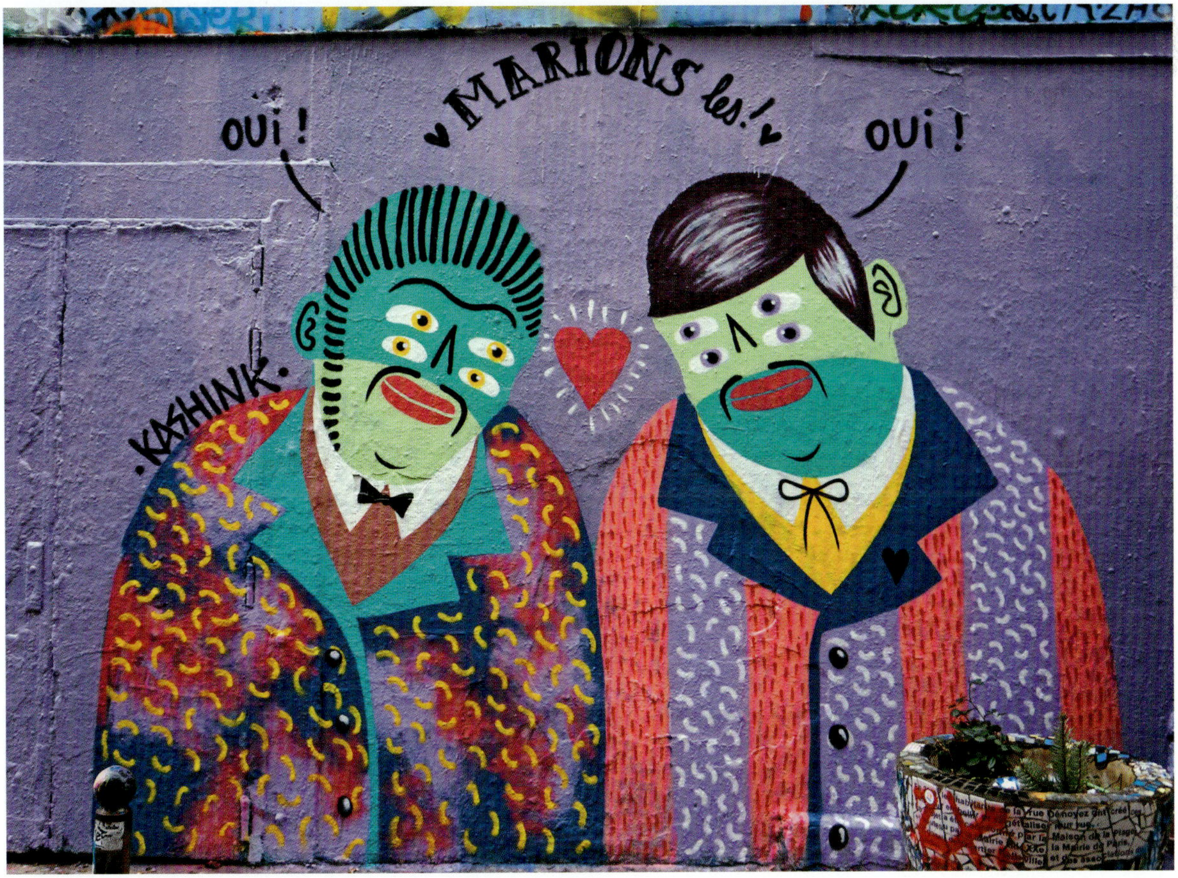

OUI !
MARIONS les !
OUI !
KASHINK

THESE PAGES:
Large-scale works by
Rensone (note how there
are letters inside each
character).

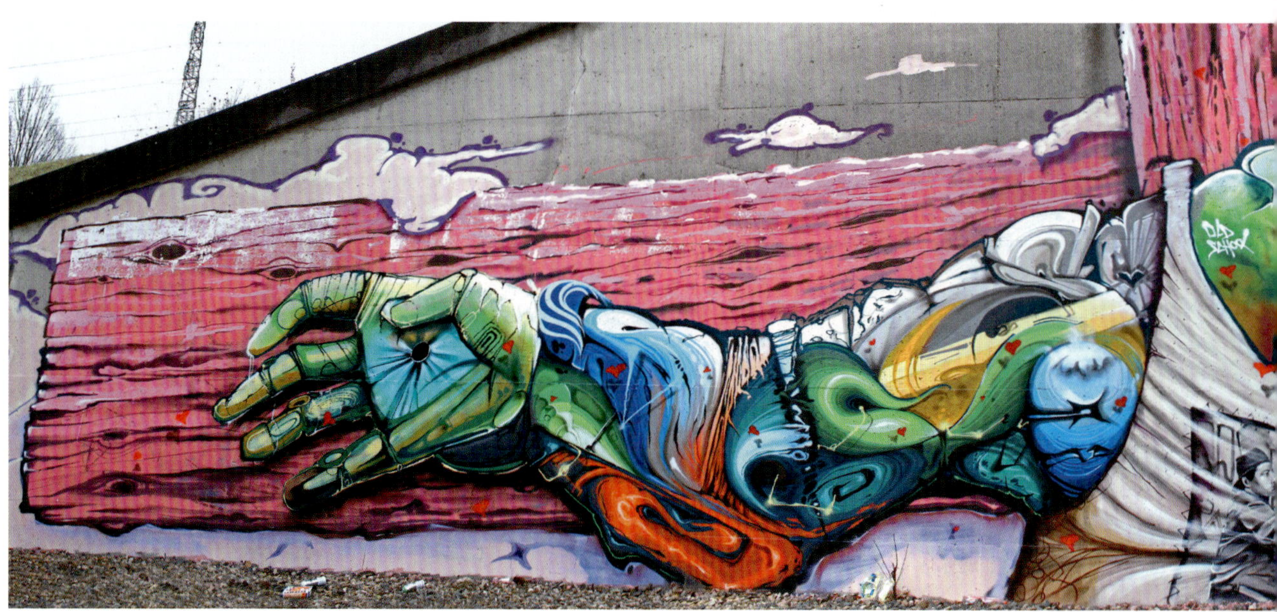

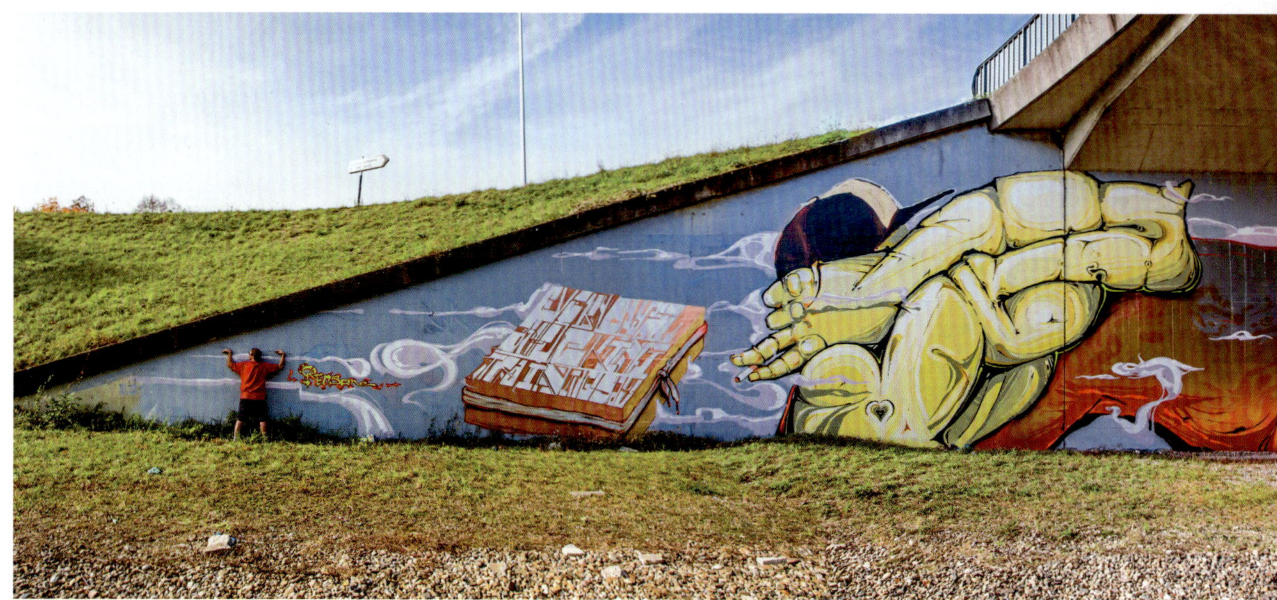

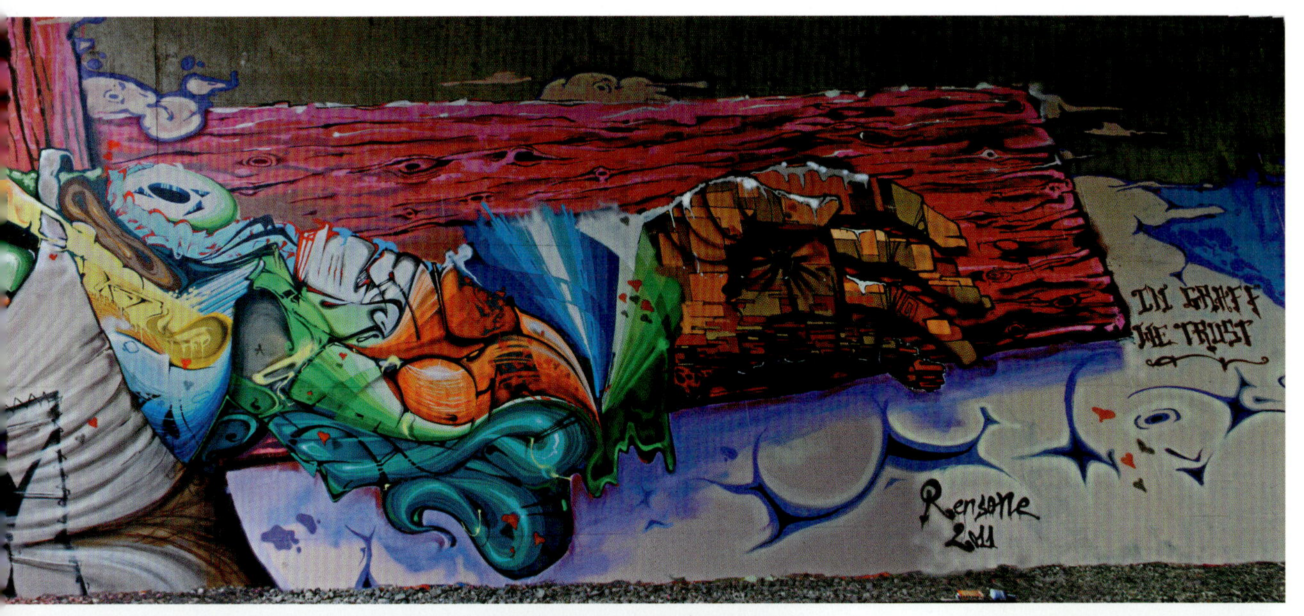

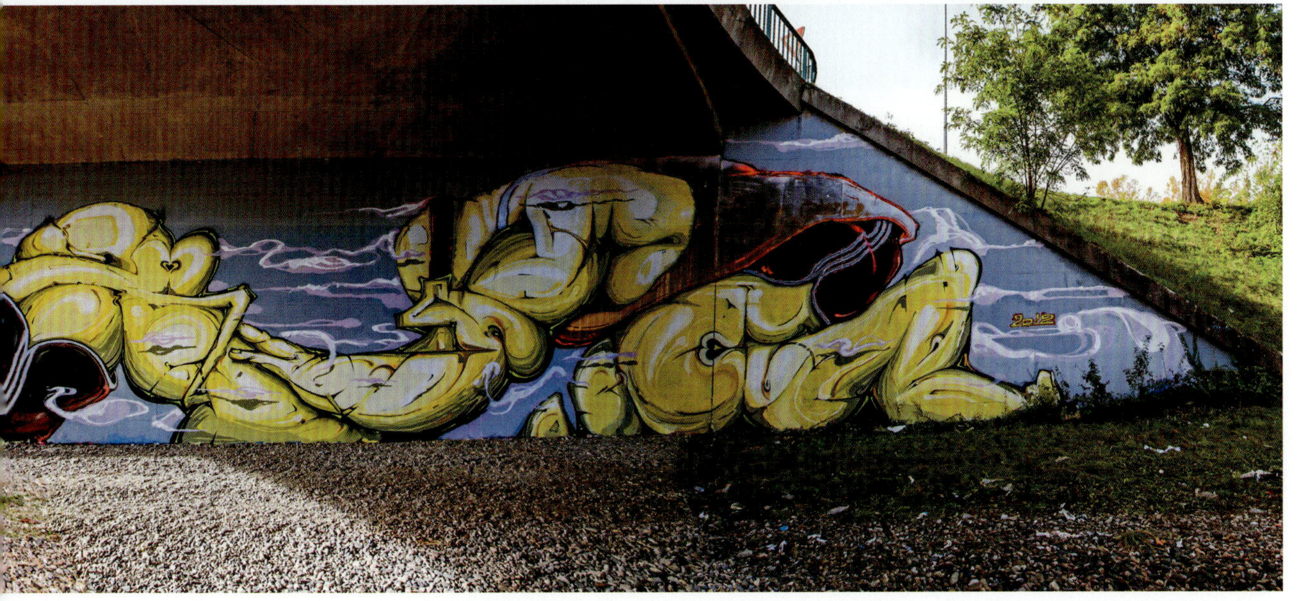

Belgium is a good country for graffiti and street art, and I've been lucky enough to visit Brussels and Antwerp. While I was in Antwerp I popped over to Doel, a tiny town of some eight streets that was cleared for a planned expansion of the port of Antwerp, a project that was shelved after the credit crunch. Some of Belgium's best street artists, plus artists from Holland and other countries, painted Doel from top to bottom. When I went there I saw almost nobody, except for the workers from the local power plant, who were eating lunch in the local pub (which I recommend). That was some years ago; the last I heard the town is still there but much of the original art has been dogged and ruined. Hopefully Doel will become a great place for art again at some point in the future, unless the houses are torn down first.

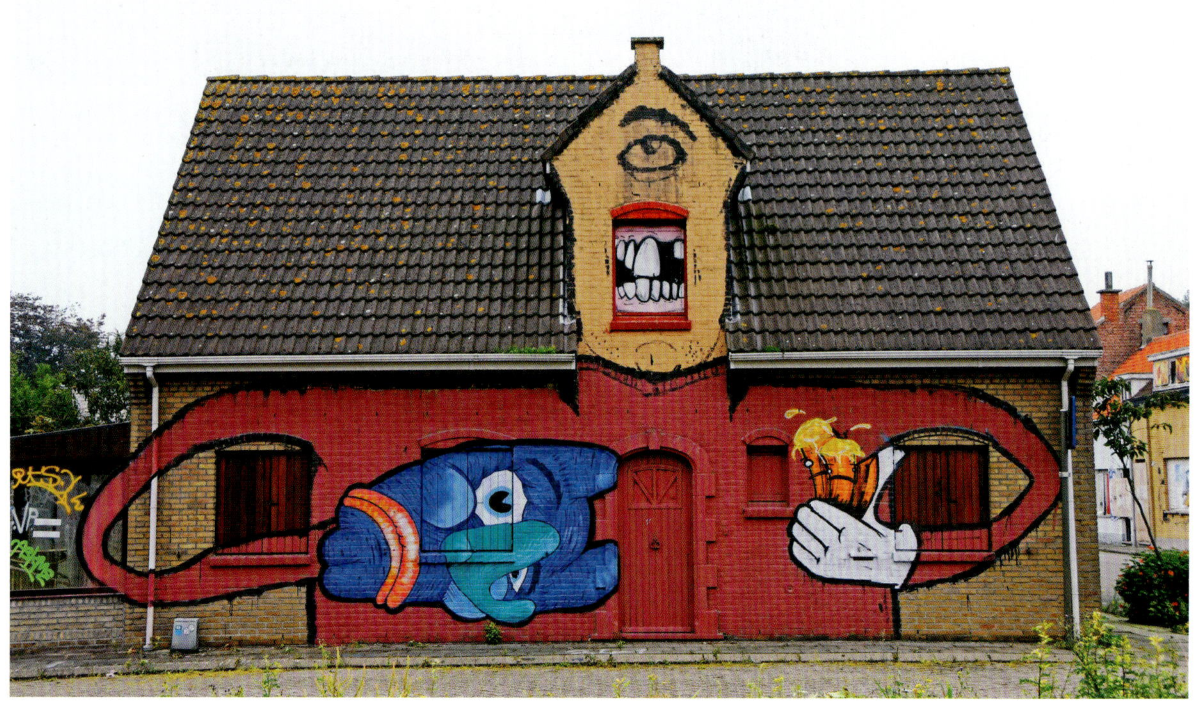

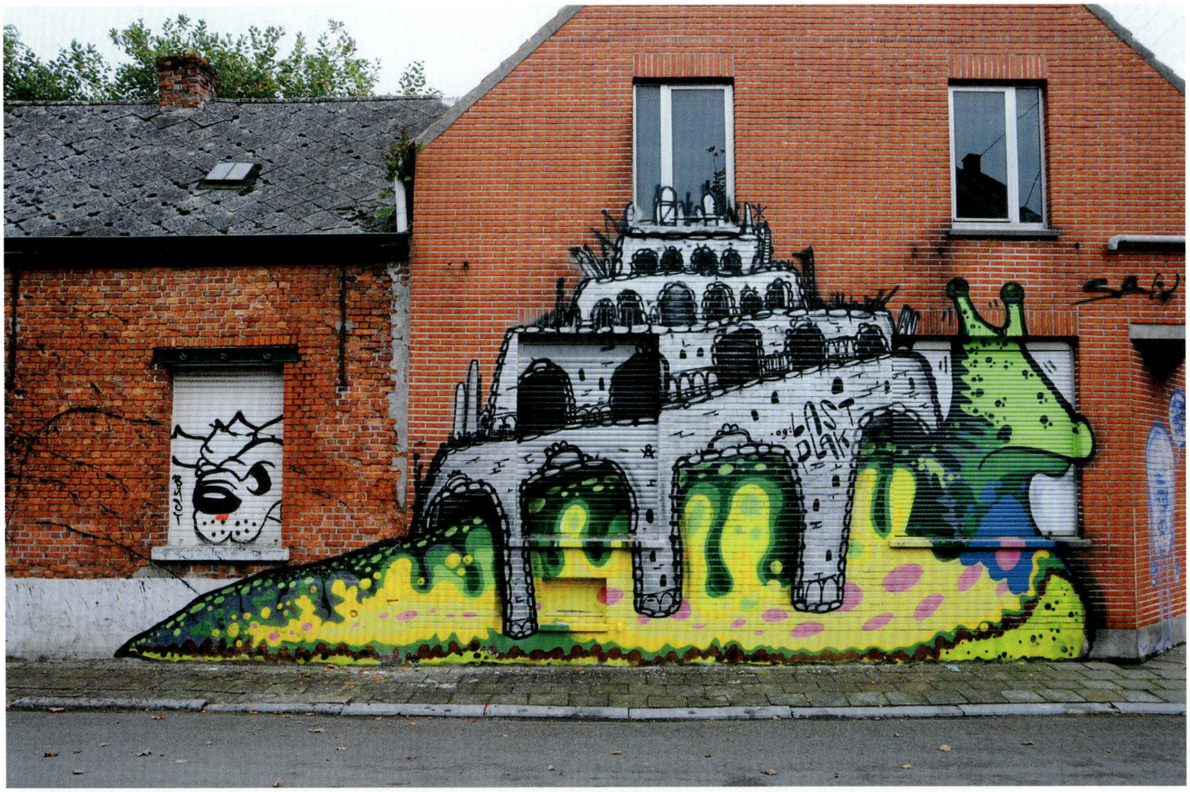

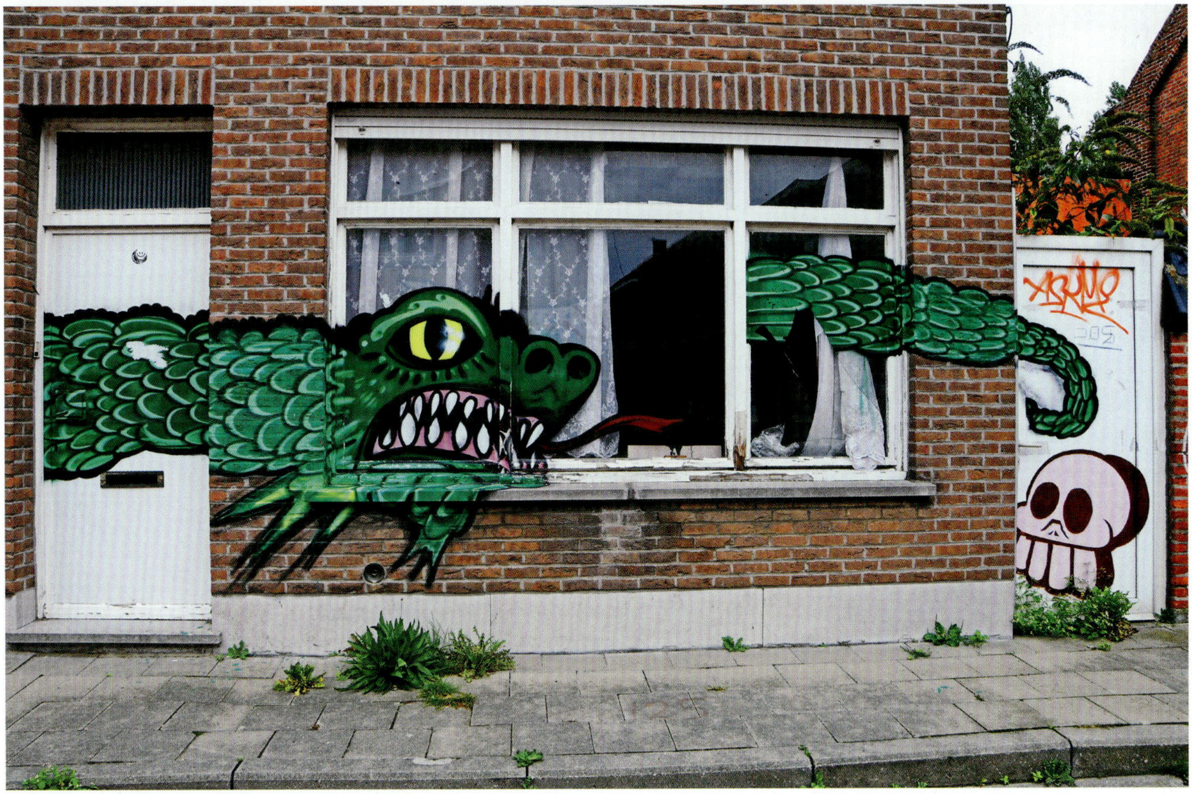

Everything shuts on a Sunday in Switzerland and, on the surface, everything appears a little dull. But spend just a few minutes walking parallel to the train tracks in Basel and the graffiti you see there will convince you that the boredom is just a veneer. There are a lot of very talented Swiss street artists.

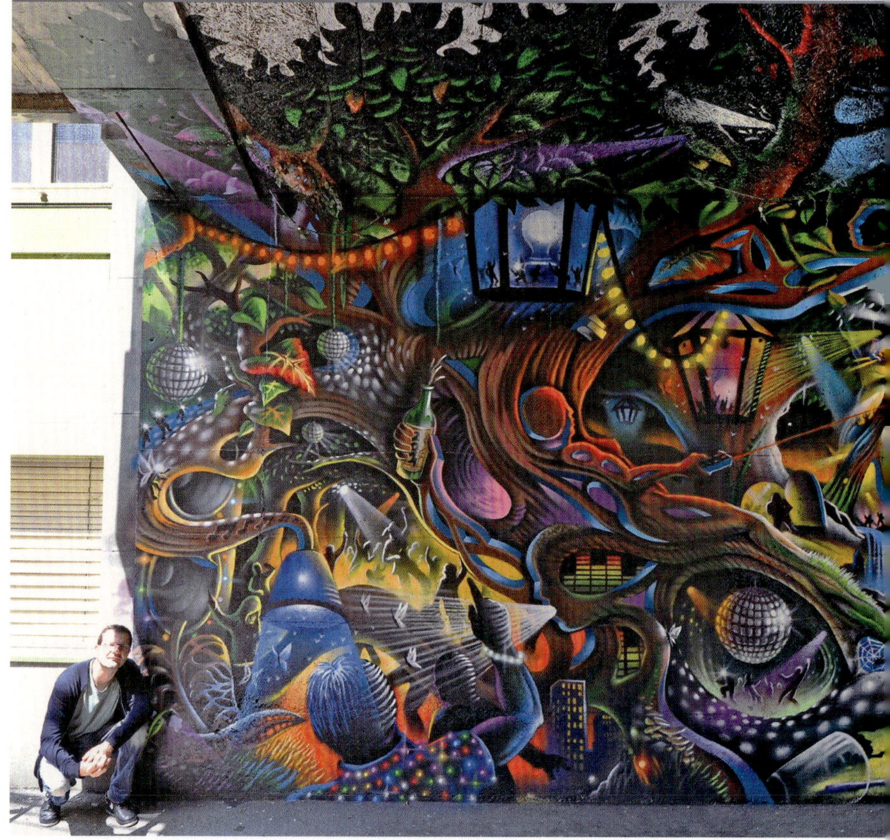

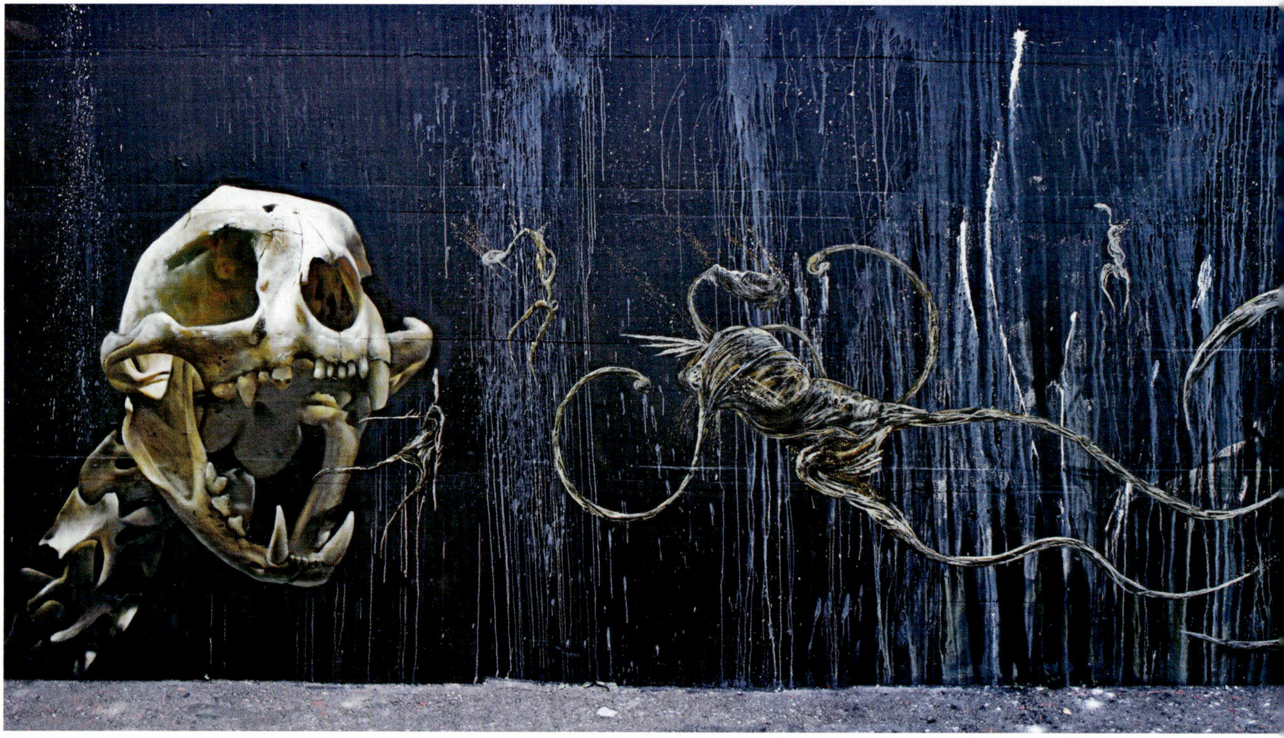

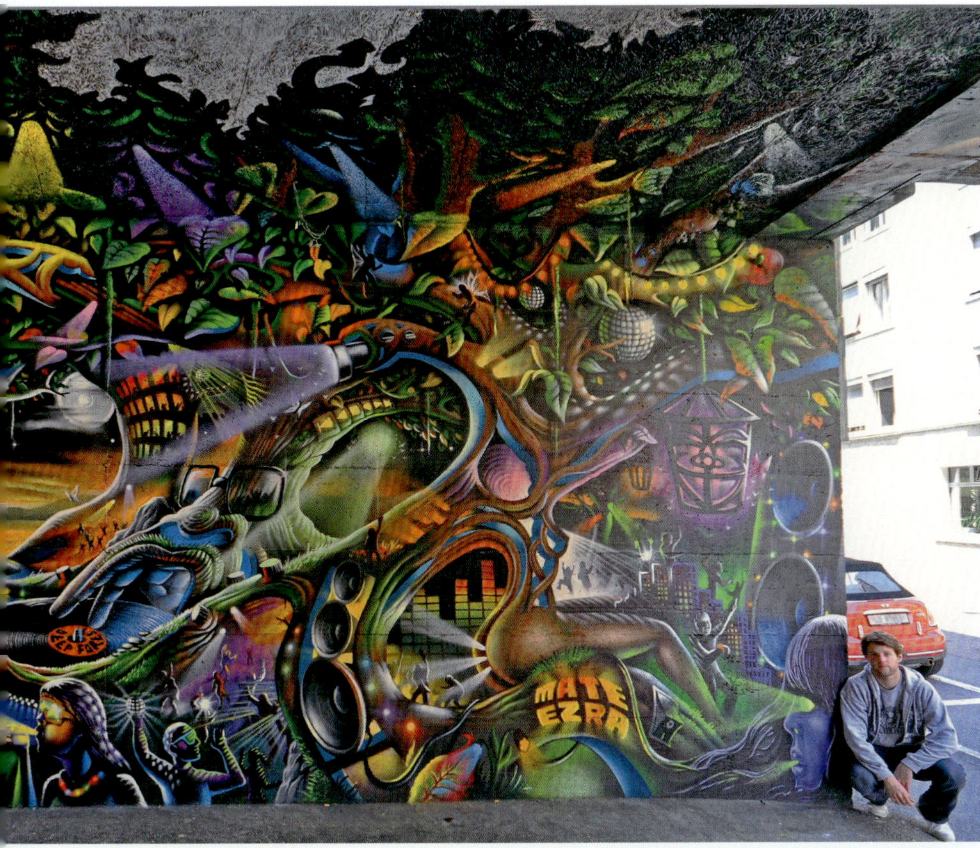

MATE
EZRA

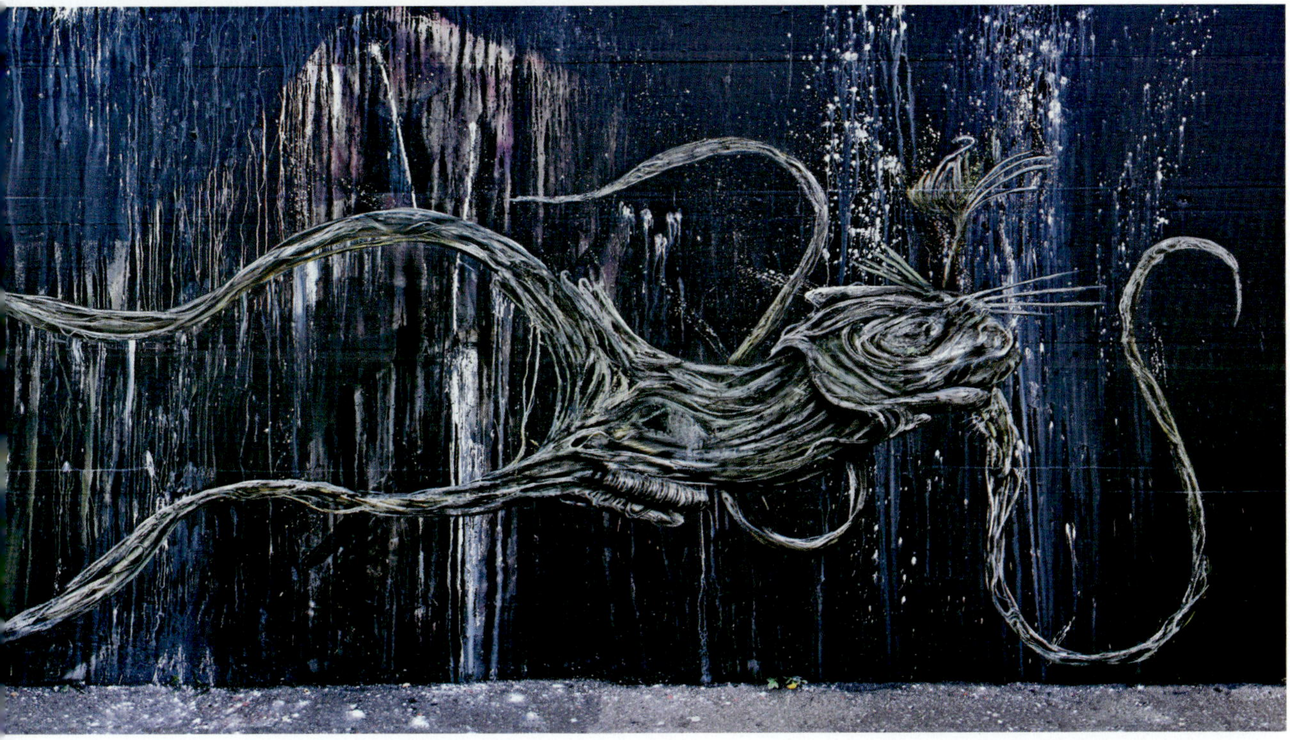

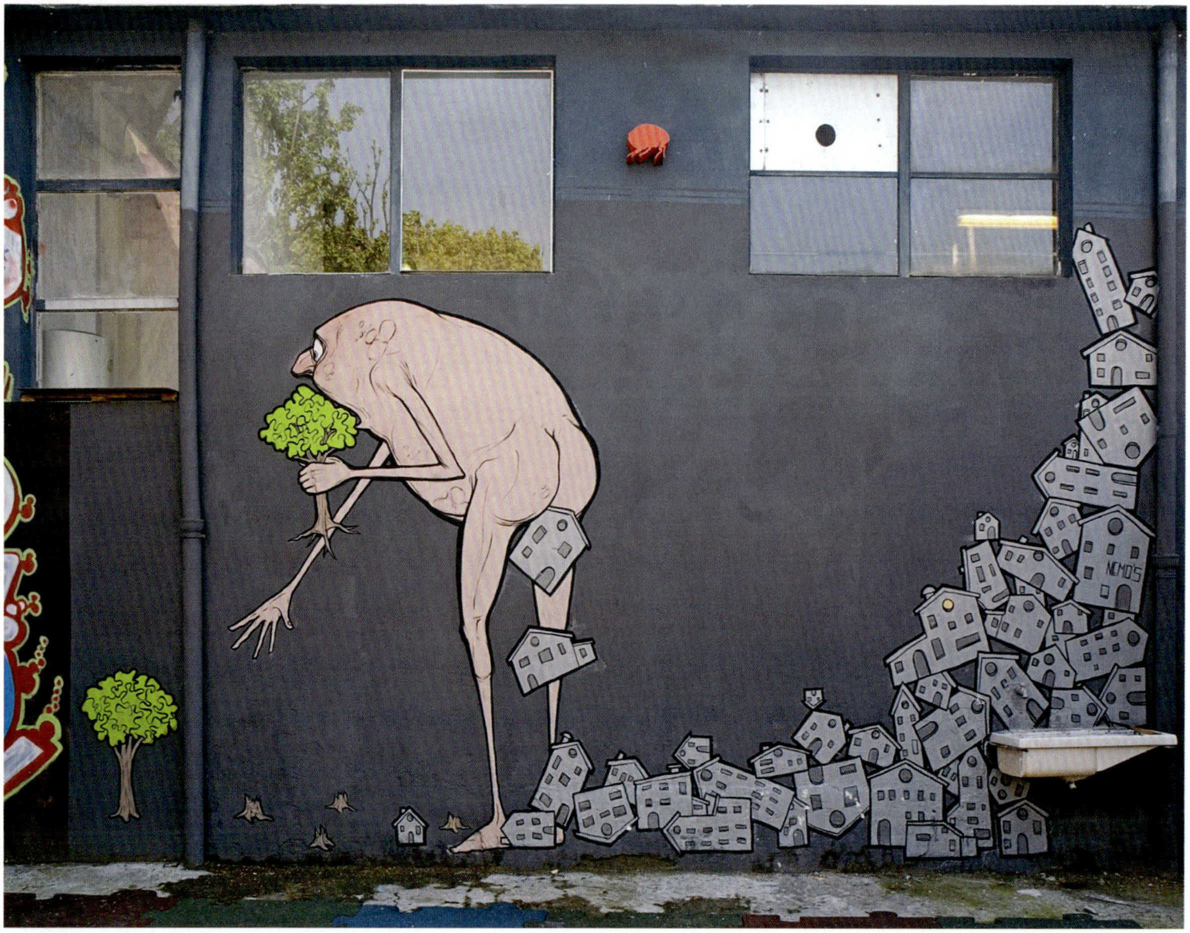

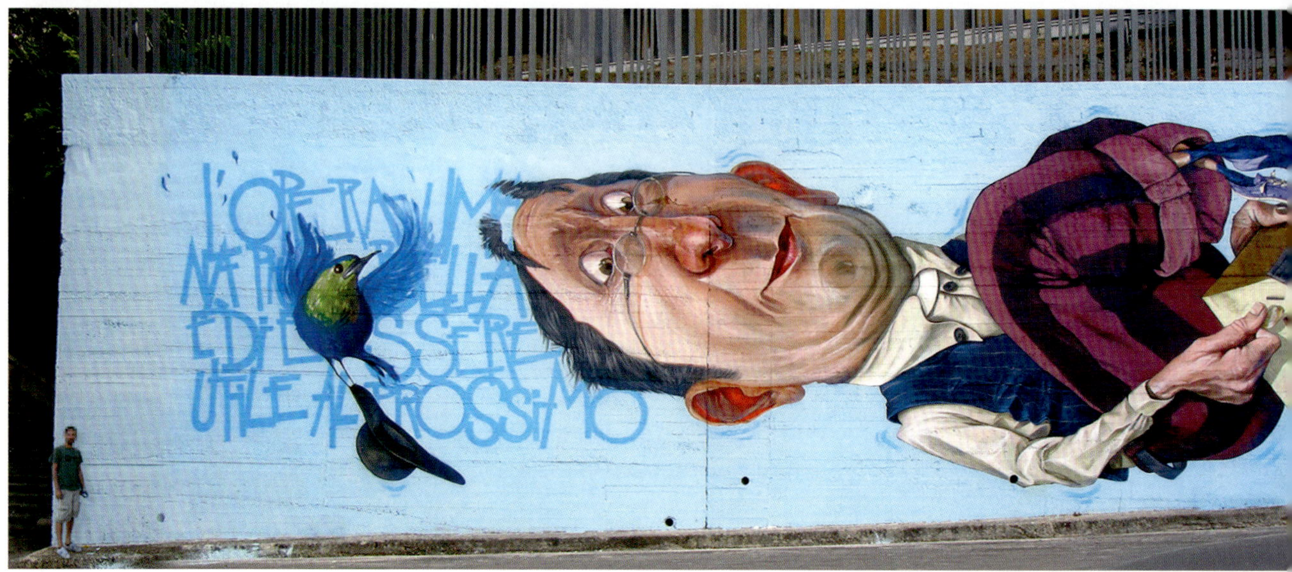
L'OTTIMISMO
NA... LLA
E DI ...SSERE
UTILE AL PROSSIMO

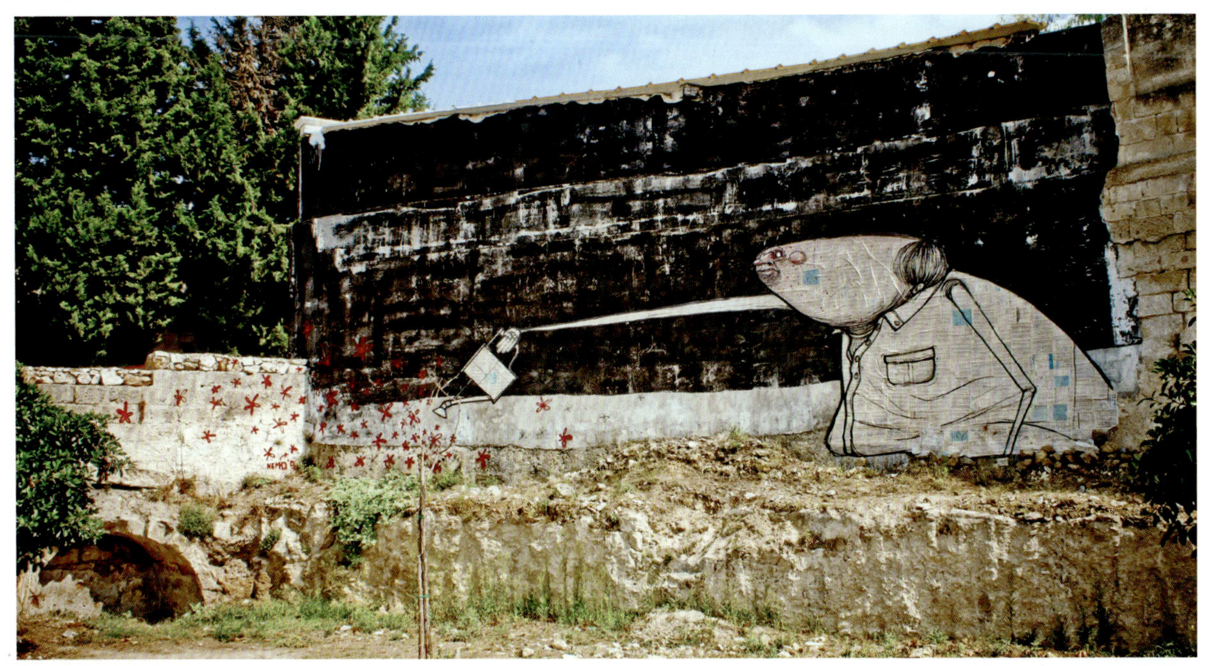

CLOCKWISE FROM LEFT:
Nemos/Nemos/Macs and
Etnik (for a sense of
scale note the artists
standing at the sides!)

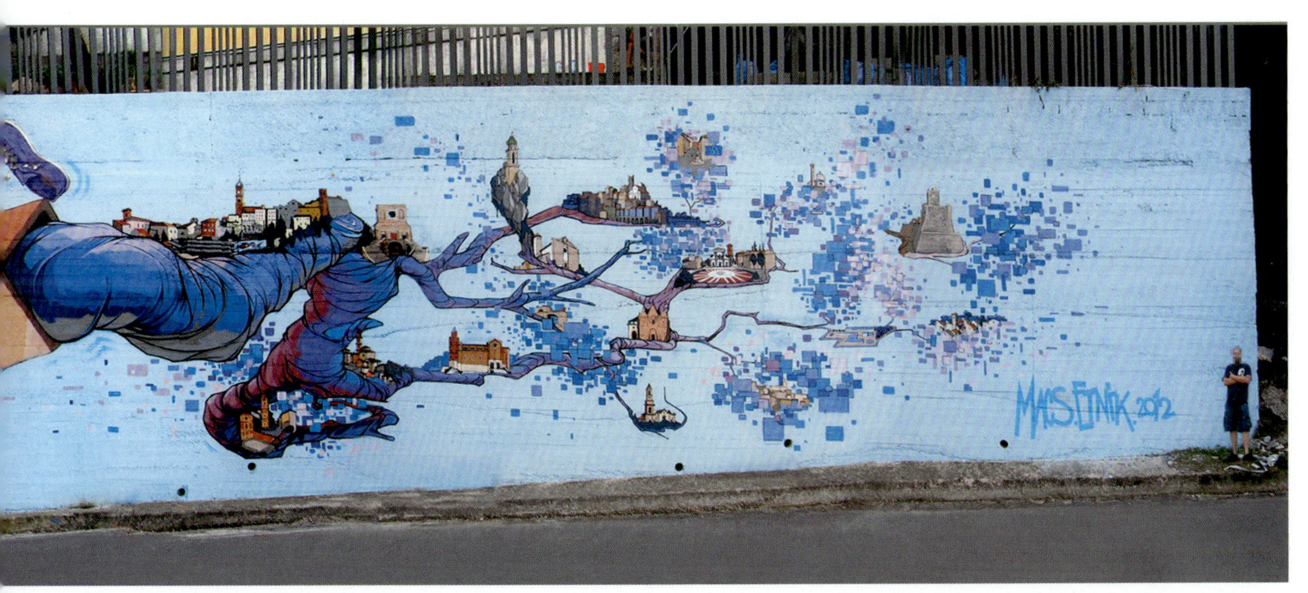

Although I have yet to visit Eastern Europe and Russia, I know from my experience as a b-boy that they have extremely strong hip-hop scenes in these countries. The same is reflected in their graffiti scenes. These pages focus on figurative street art pieces, specifically because of the clear influence of local cultural traditions.

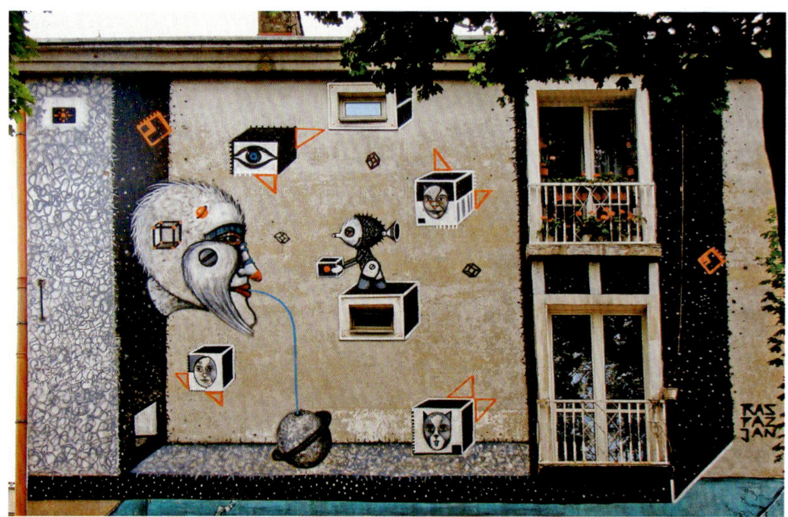

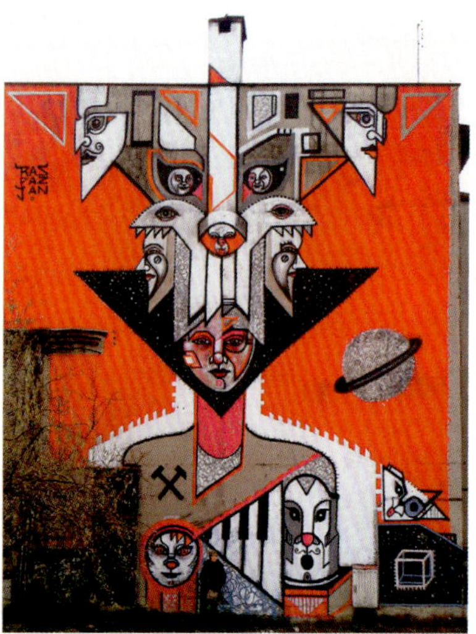

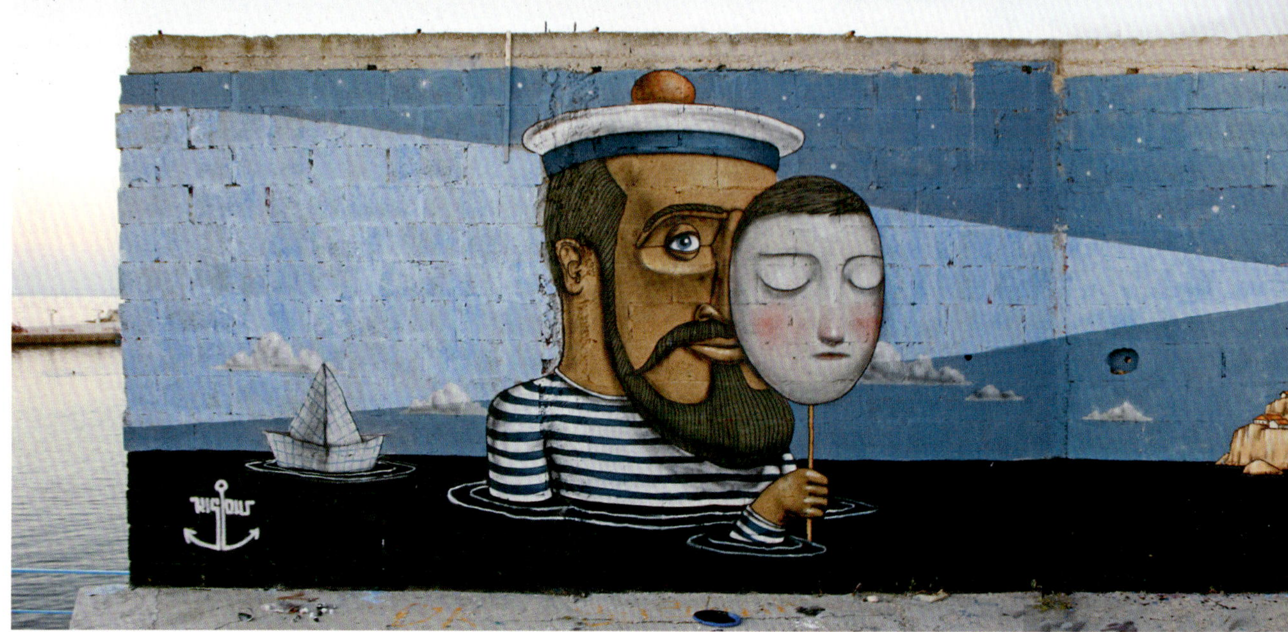

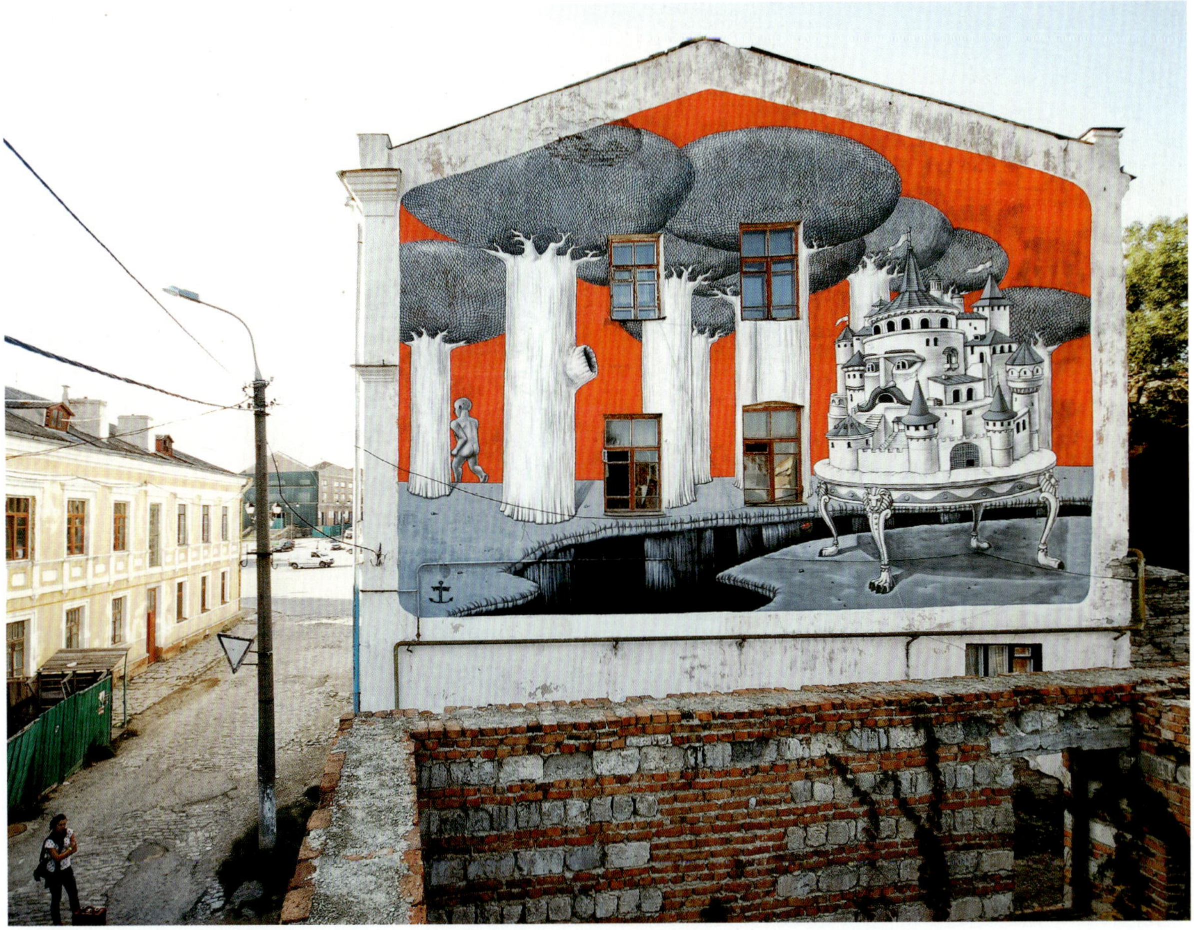

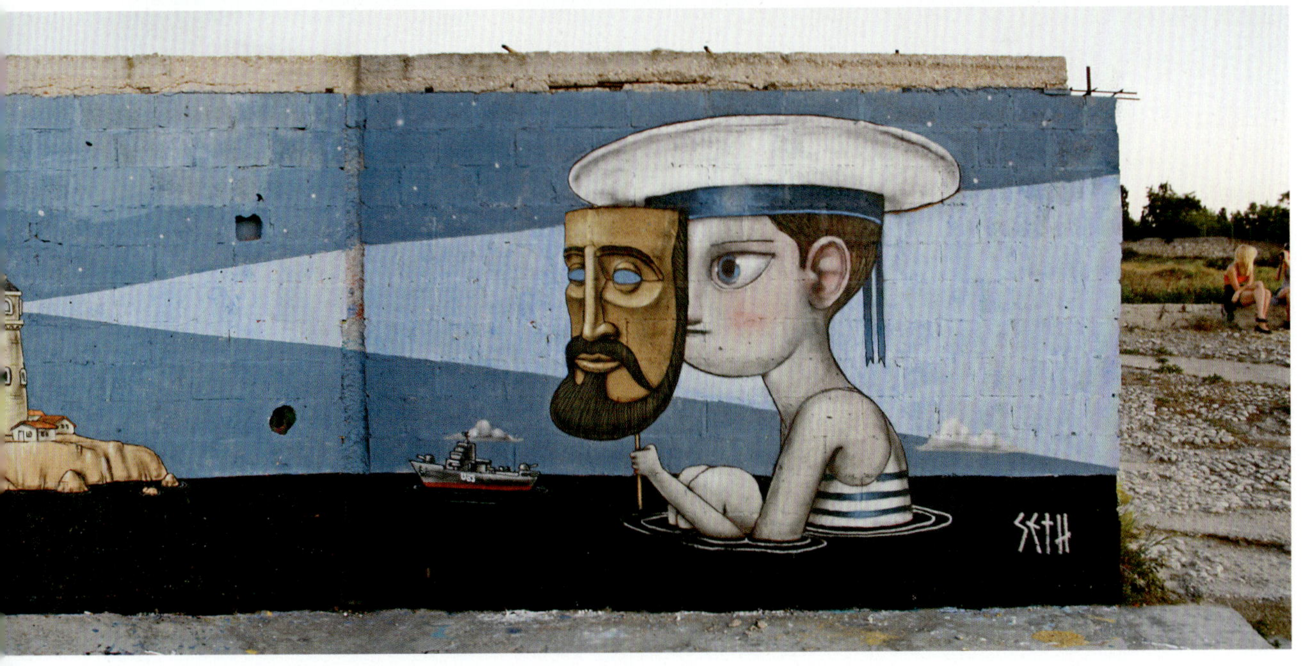

SETH

FROM TOP:
Moscow's Vitae Viazi Crew
(which means 'water of
life')/Moscow's Vitae
Viazi Crew.

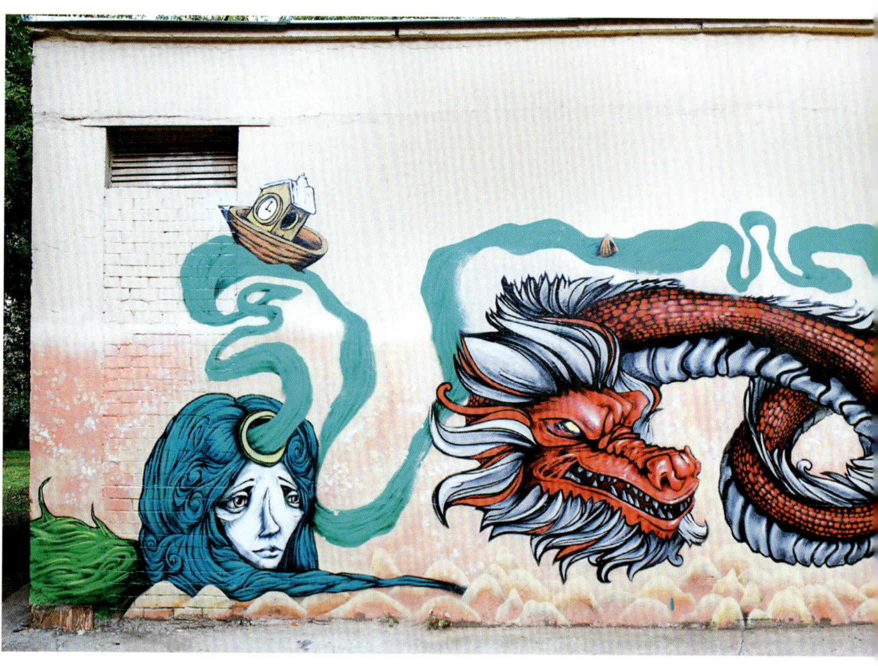

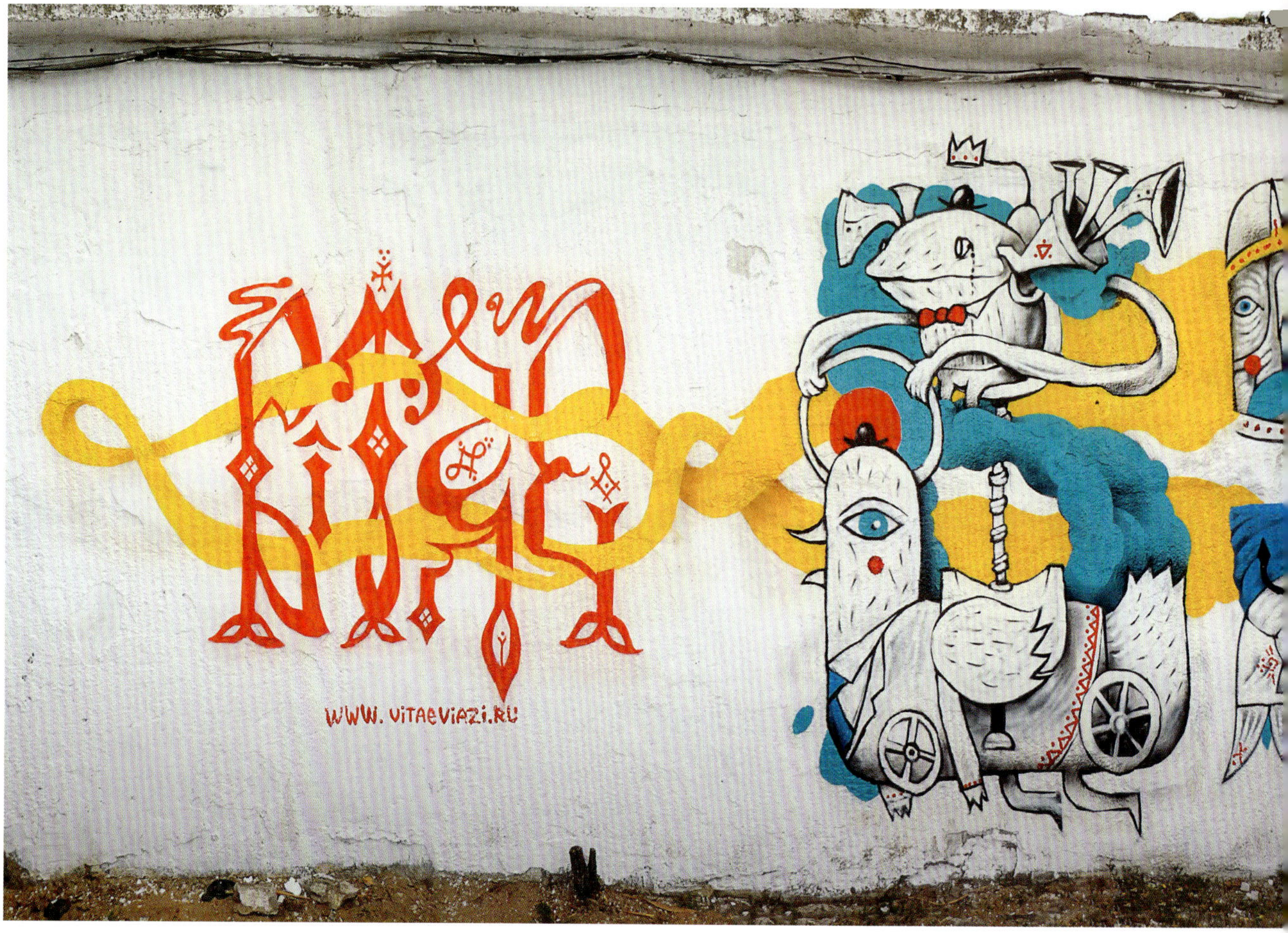

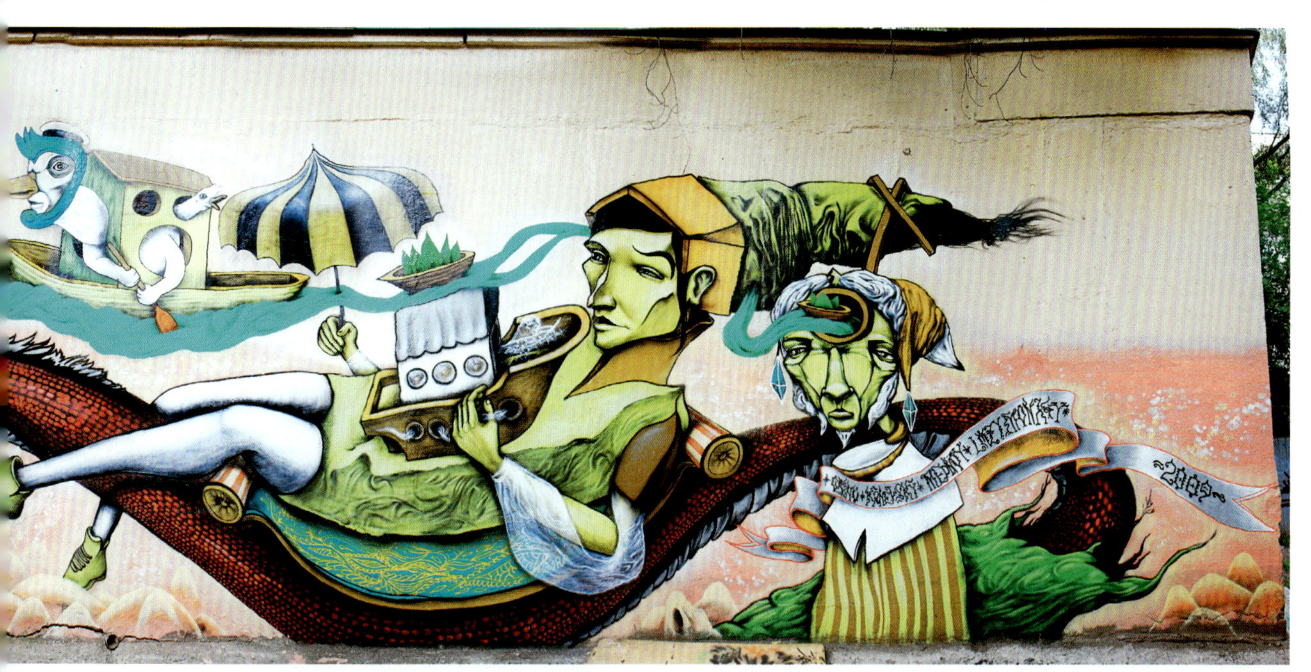

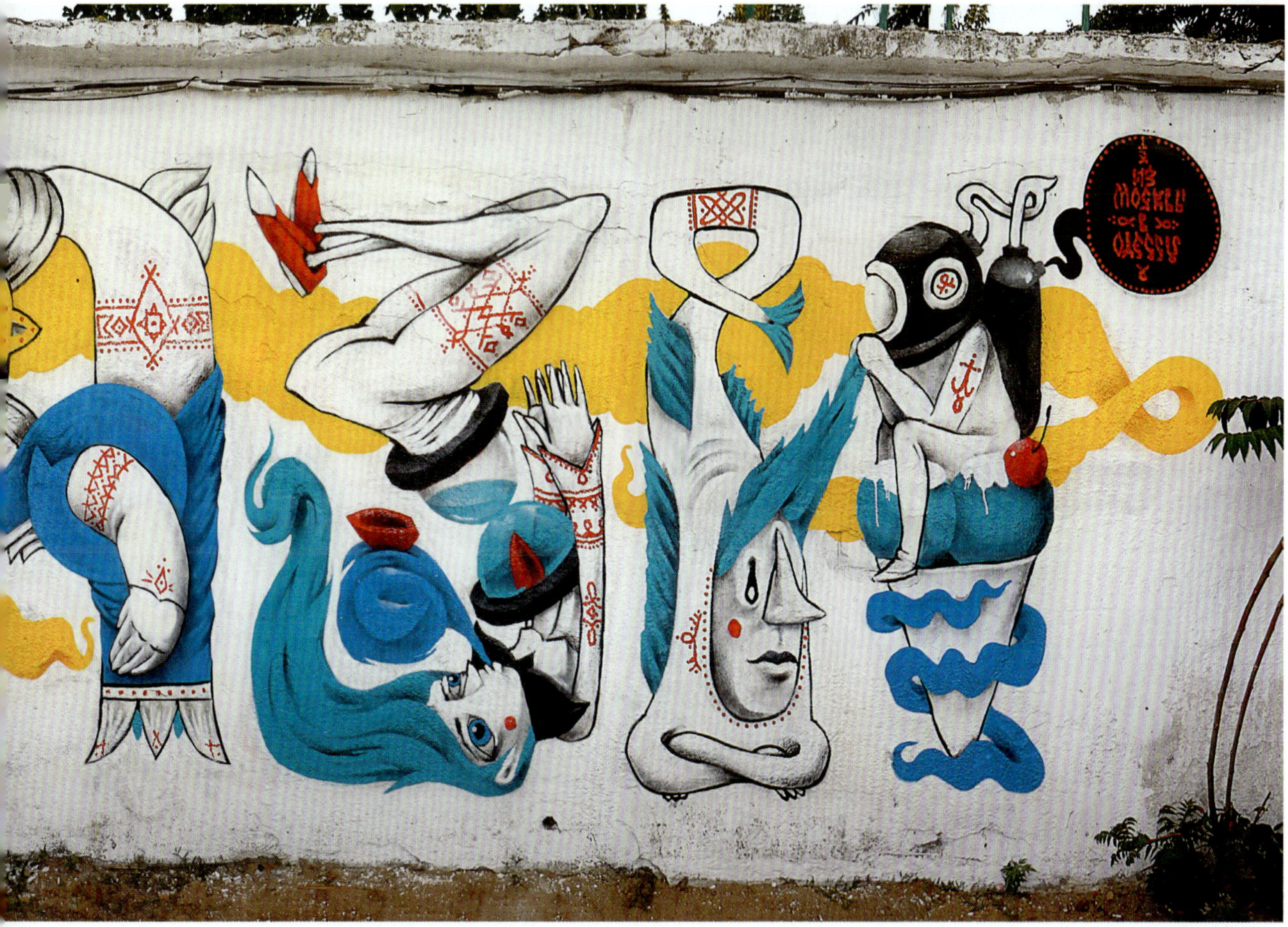

South America

South America is a hotbed of artistic talent, combining local cultures boasting strong artistic traditions with large present-day communities of street artists and relatively permissive authorities.

In my many travels I have found São Paulo in Brazil to be the global capital of contemporary street art and graffiti. The city is vast, and within it there is a staggering amount of quality graffiti and street art. Like many other countries, Brazil had a pre-existing local graffiti culture before the arrival of New York-style graffiti. São Paulo has a style of graffiti called *pixação* (see page 108), which is uniquely Brazilian, and emerged completely independently of any New York influence in 1982.

The lettering in *pixação* was influenced by heavy metal fonts; heavy metal music was (and still is) popular among Brazilian youth. Gangs used *pixação* lettering to mark their territories in *favelas* and the lettering developed from there; this had parallels to New York's graffiti origins, where tagging's initial function was to mark territory, but it was then appropriated by those who did not necessarily have any interests in writing other than simply 'getting up'.

Beyond *pixação*, there is no shortage of local influences and styles that distinguish South American graffiti and street art from that in the USA and Europe. In the following pages you will notice plenty of colourful Brazilian 'funk', strong Argentinian portraiture and the charming influence of folk art in Chile.

My own photos from South America come from a three-week trip running between Brazil, Argentina and Chile. You can't make too many maps of graffiti spots in advance as you would for Europe – there just isn't the same information online. Working with local artists is the best way to take the best pictures.

São Paulo is more painted than any other city I've seen, so being prolific is no way to stand out: unless you have style you have little chance of gaining recognition.

In Rio I'd booked into a hostel that was high up in one of the *favelas*; friends had recommended the place and I liked the idea of staying in the hills for a few days. When I arrived at the start of the *favela* there were ten or so police moving from house to house with assault rifles. I'm not a big fan of being accidentally shot in crossfire, so I put my bag down and grabbed a soda. I couldn't figure out why the locals were so calm. It turned out that my *favela* was where the SWAT headquarters were located, and they were only practising. There was probably no safer place in Rio!

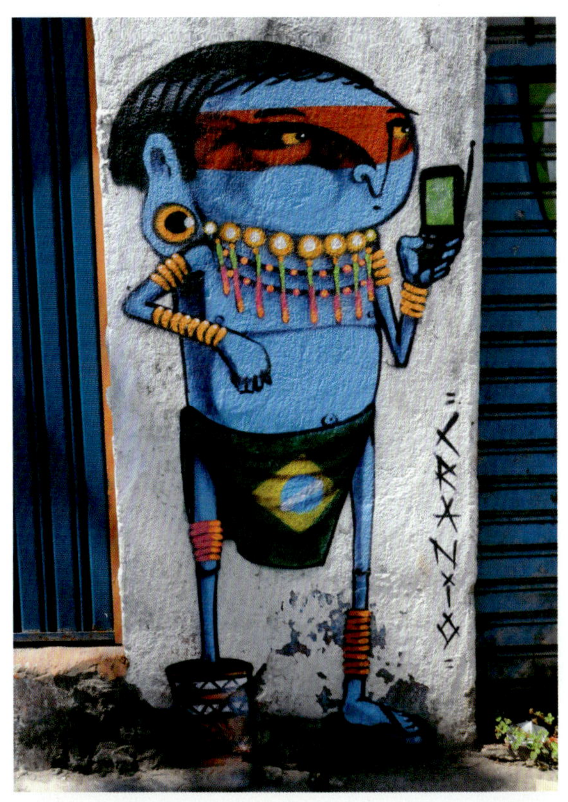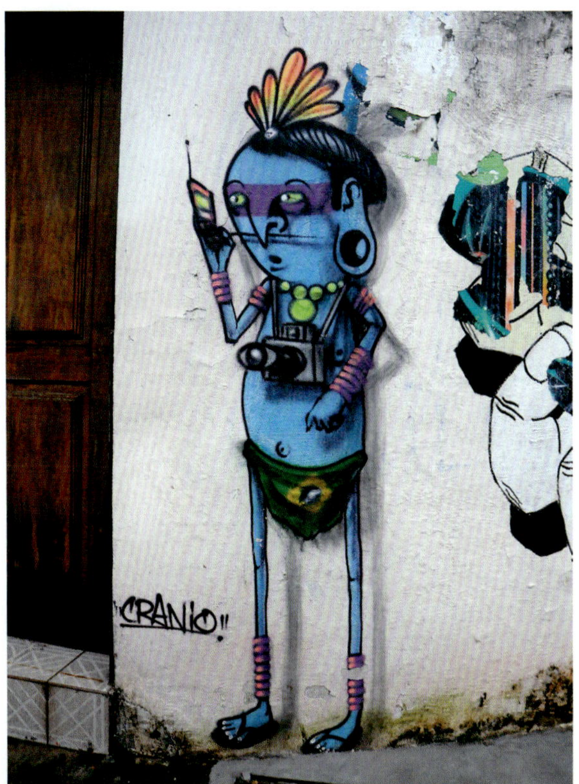

CRANIO

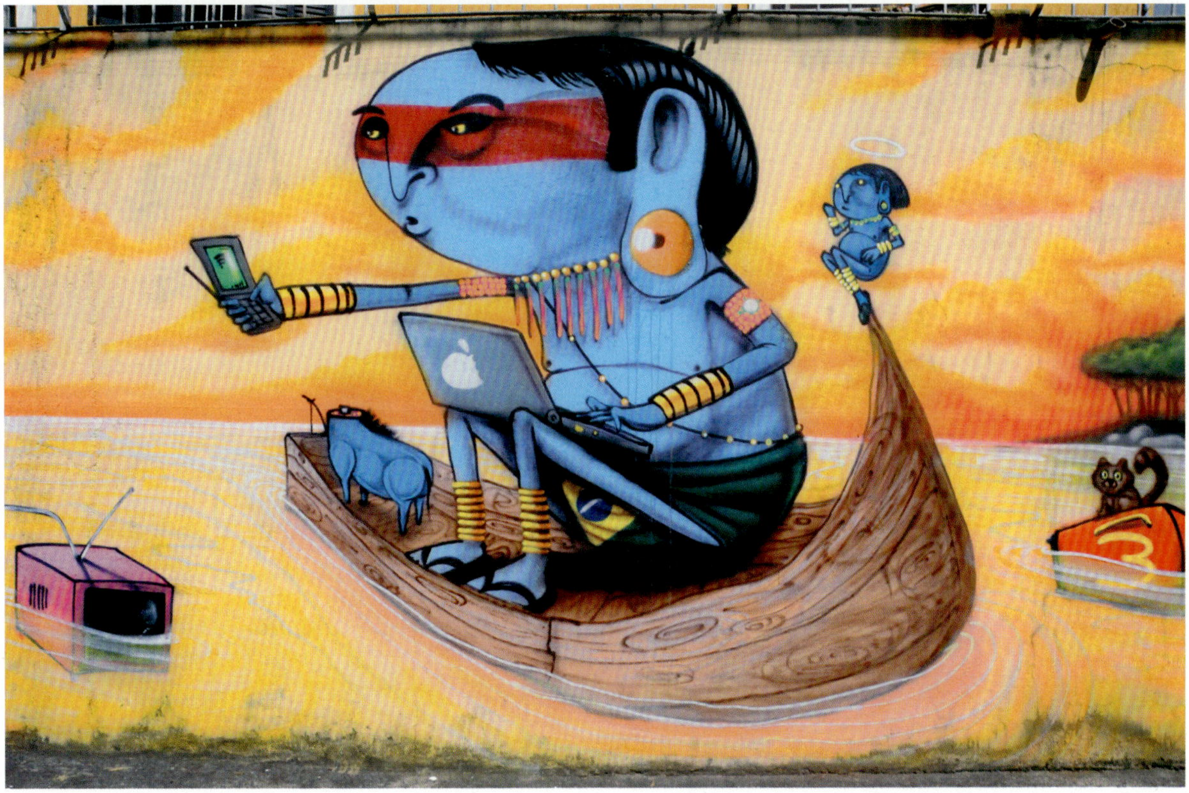

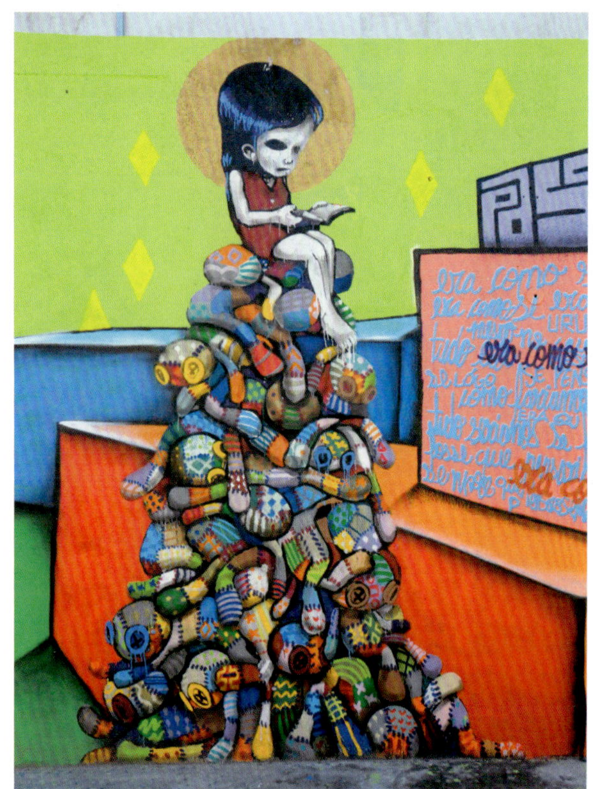

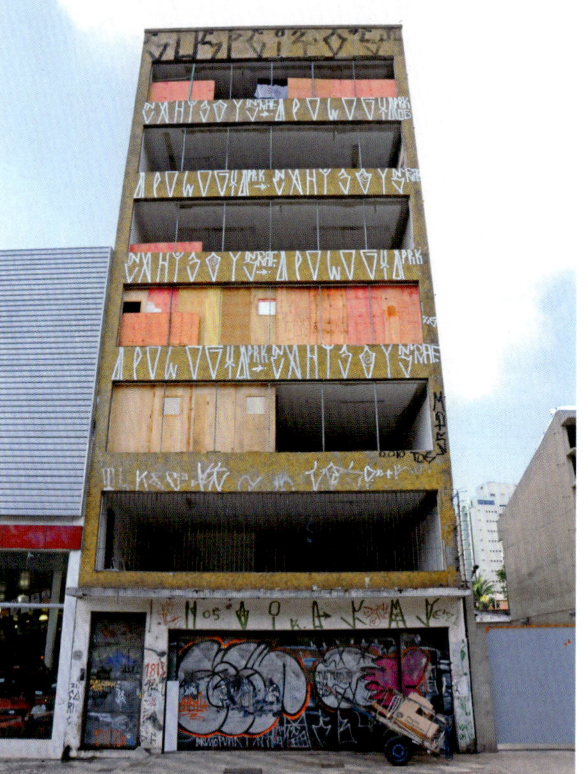

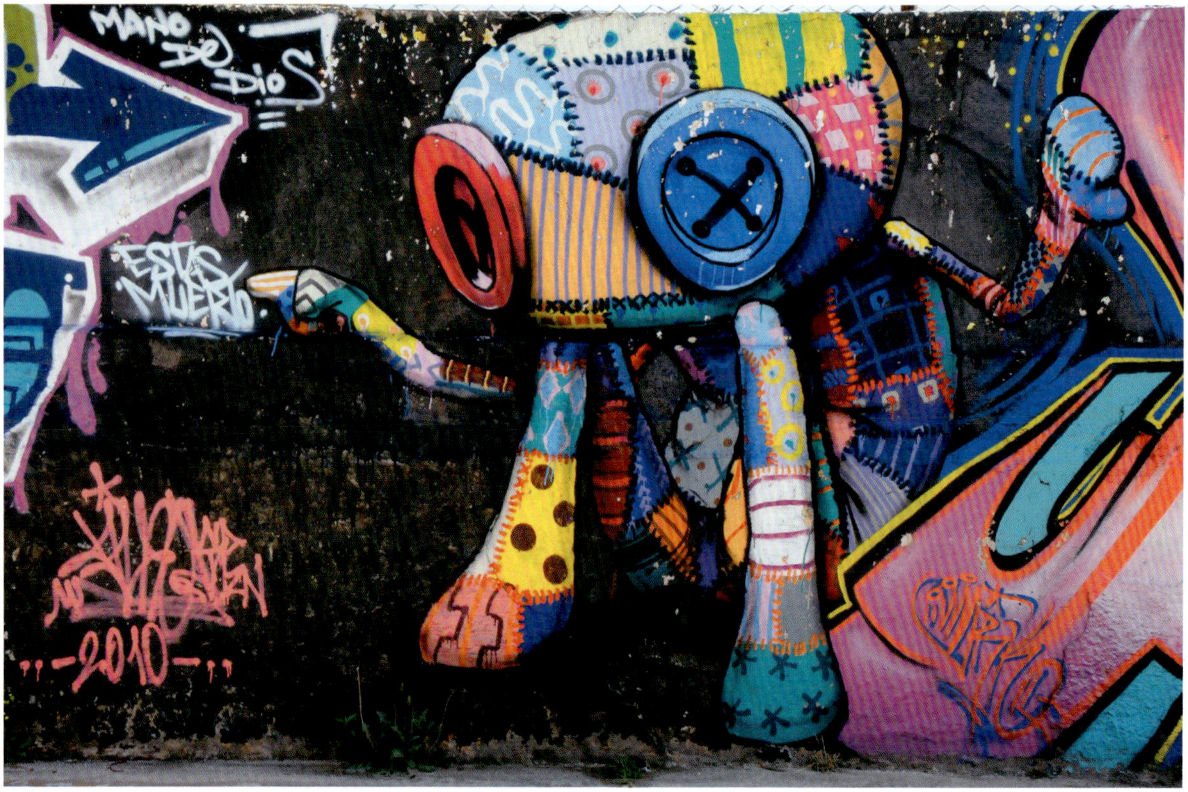

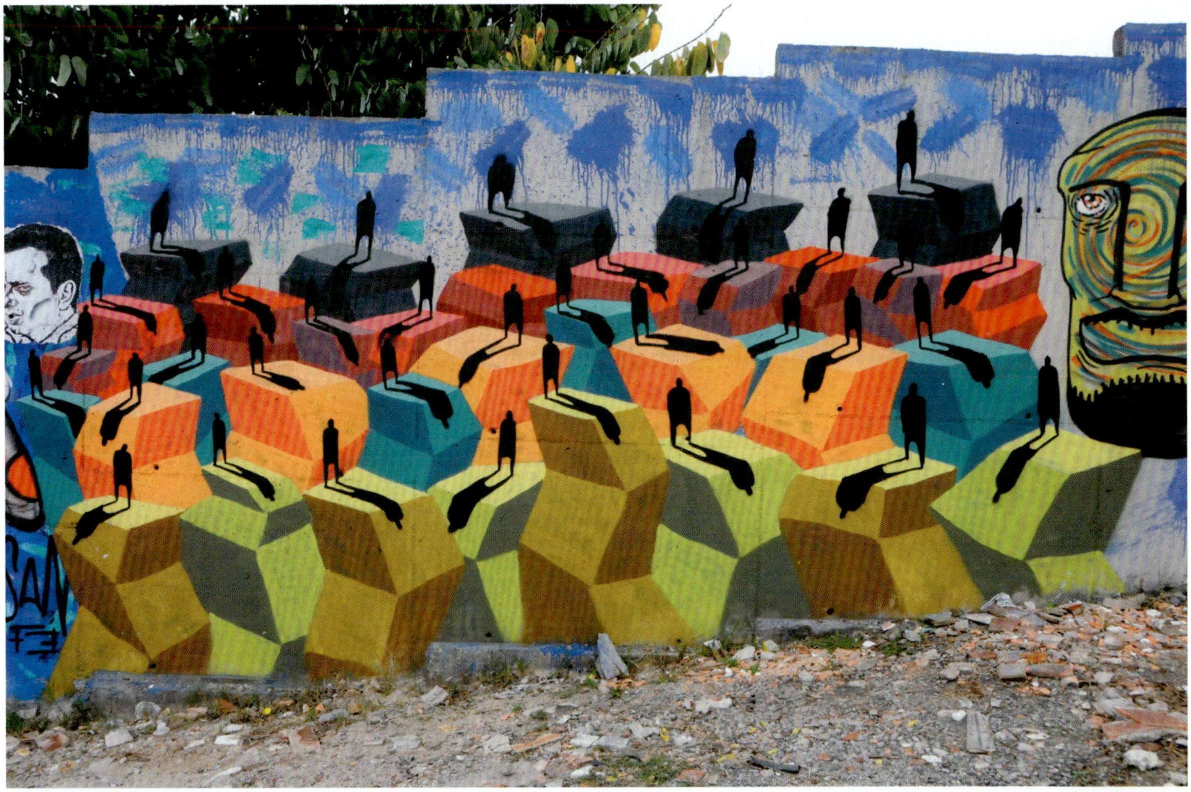

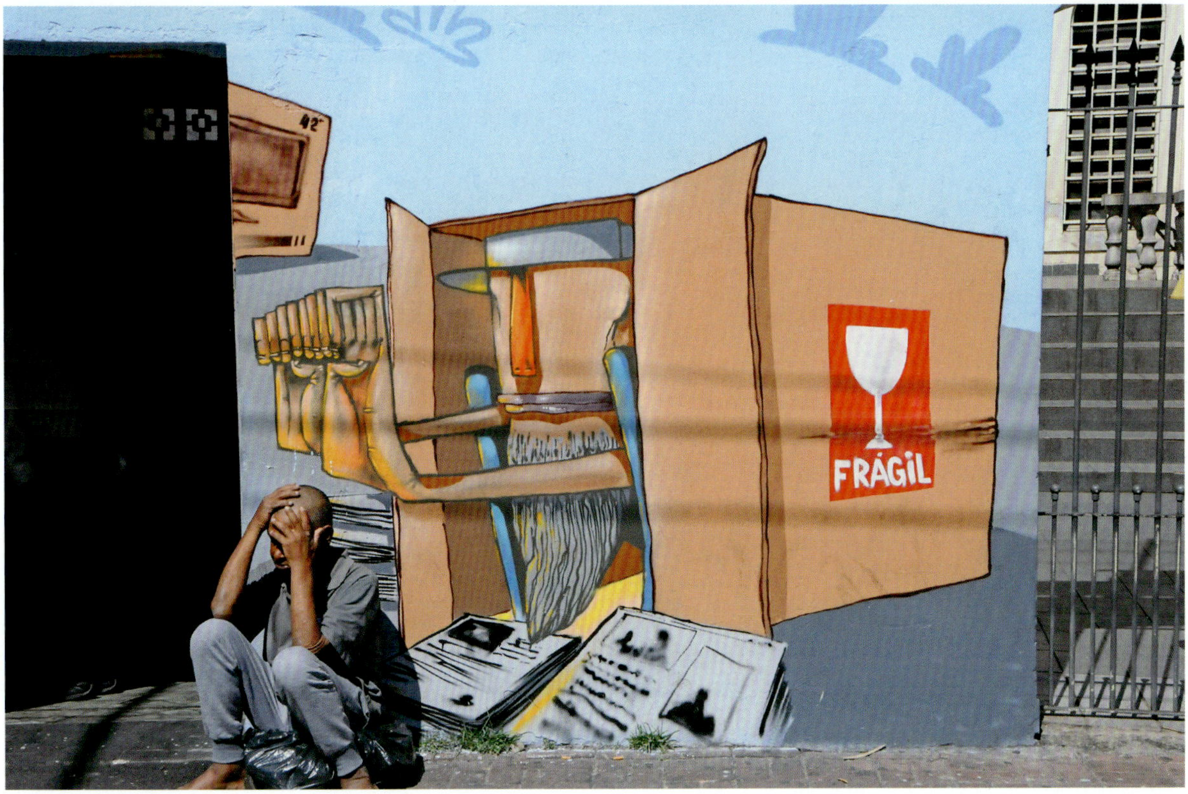

FRÁGIL

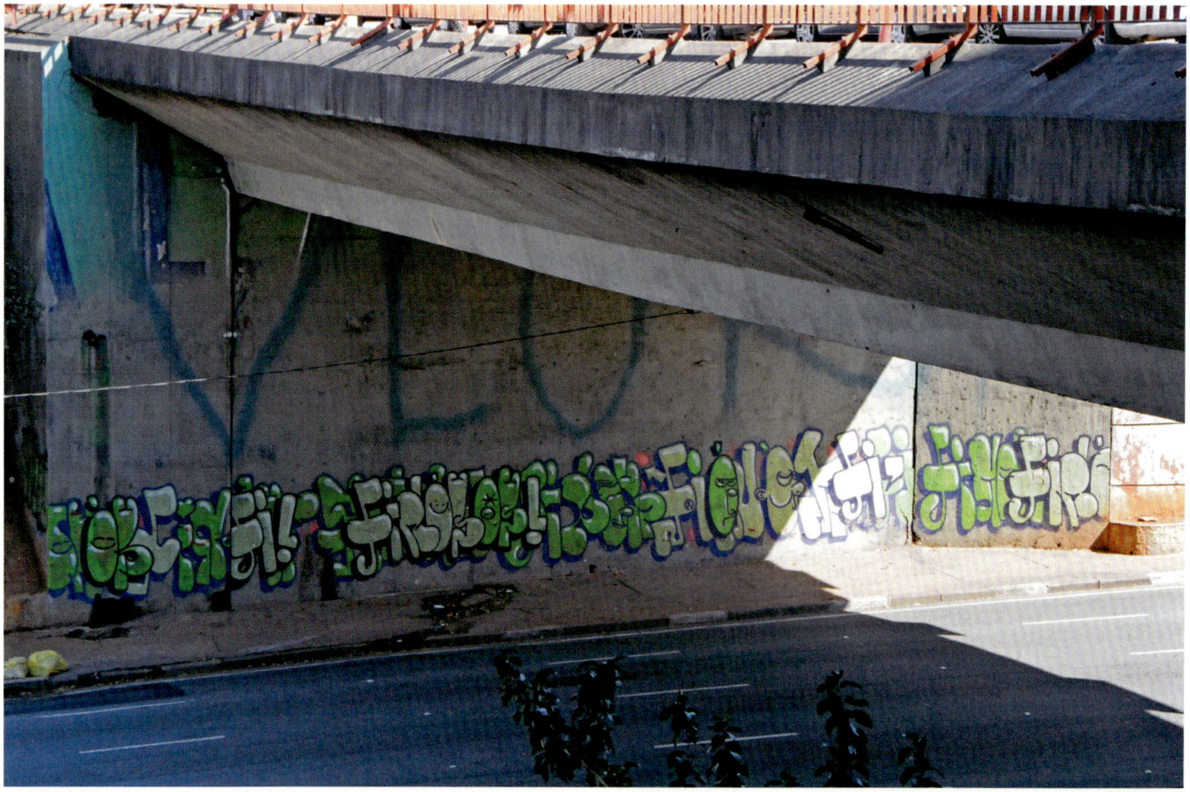

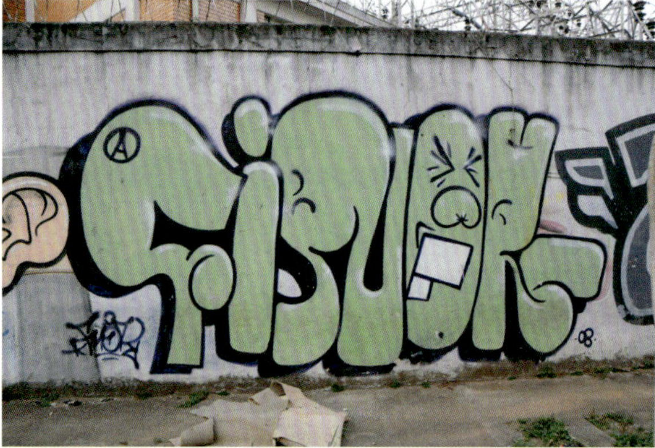

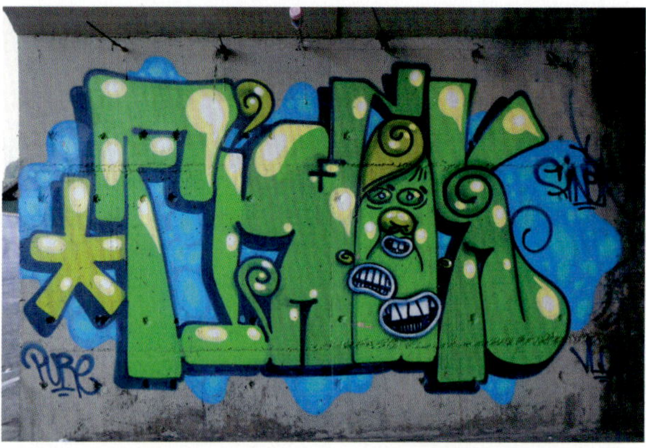

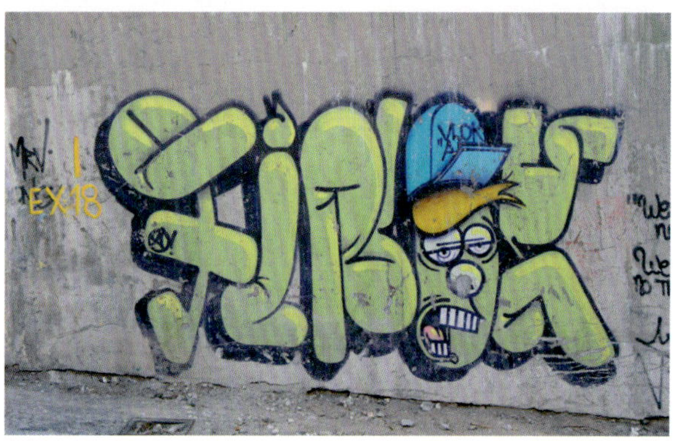

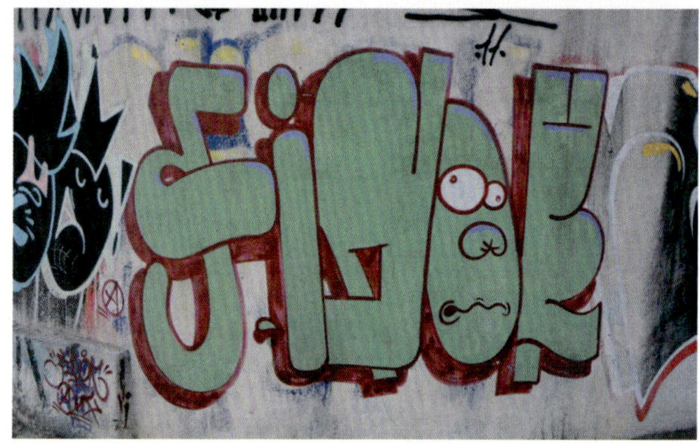

THESE PAGES:
A selection of Finok's
awesome street bombs.

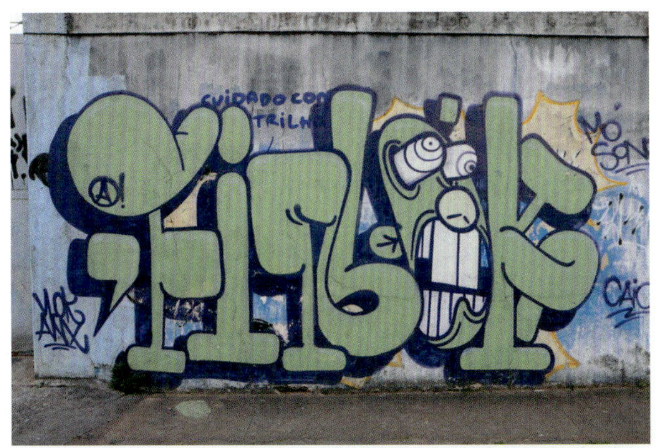

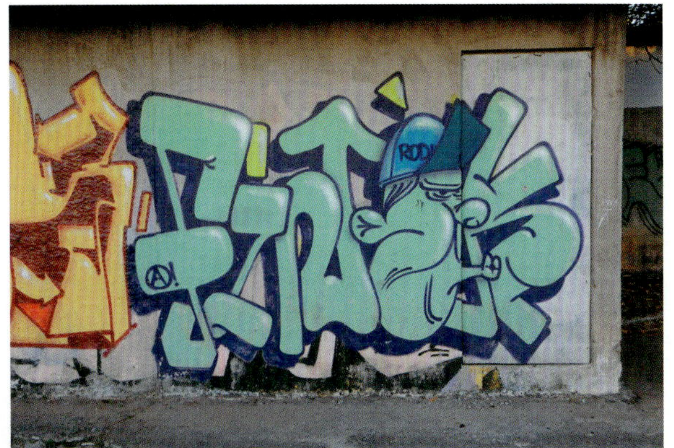

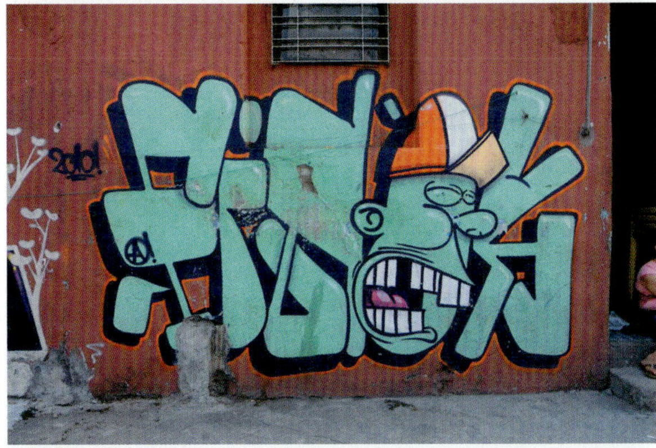

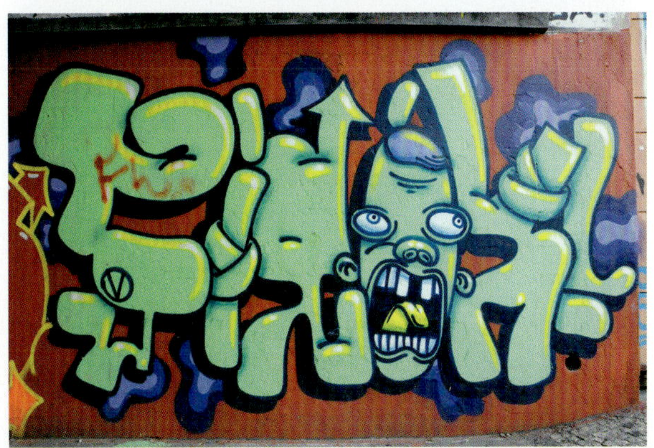

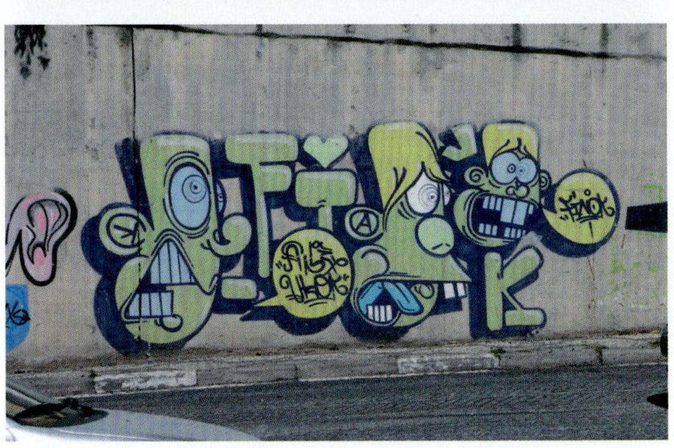

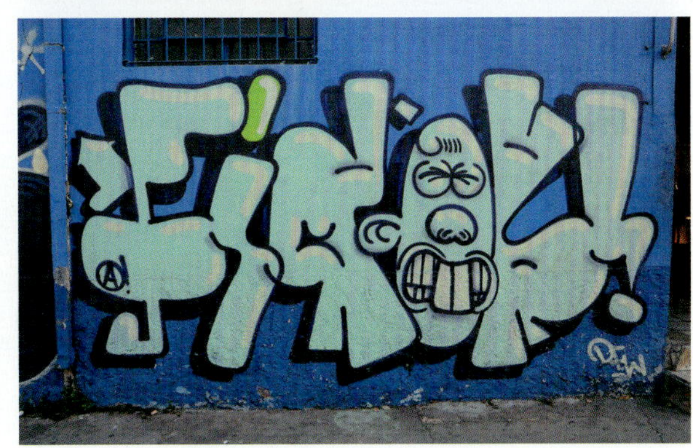

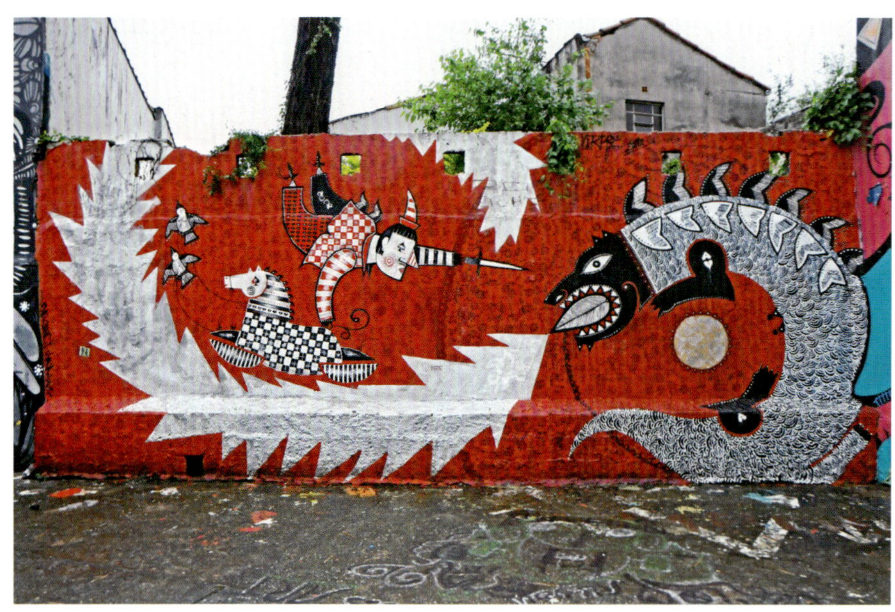

CLOCKWISE FROM LEFT:
Vitché/Claudio Ethos/
Ninguém Dorme (which
means Never Sleep)/
Vitché.

PAGES 114–15,
CLOCKWISE FROM
RIGHT:
Italy's Etnik/Binho
(the fish) and Feik
(the insect on the
left)/Feik.

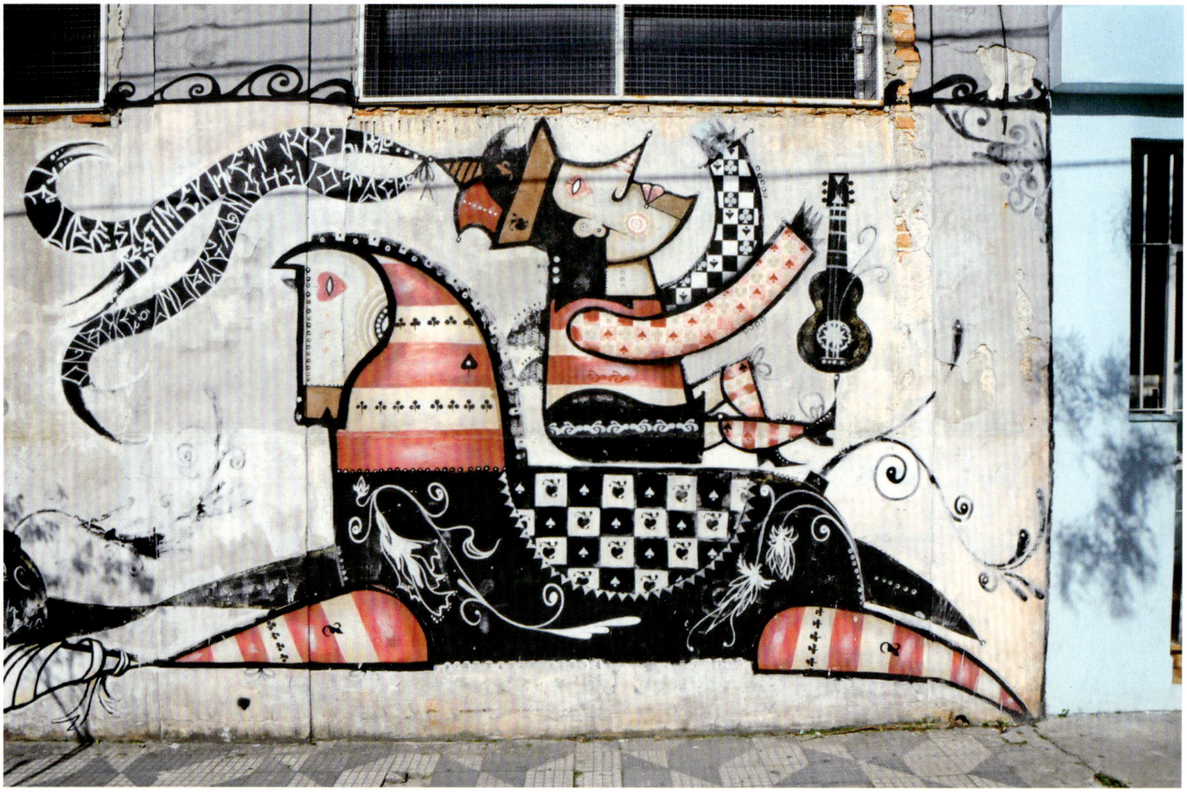

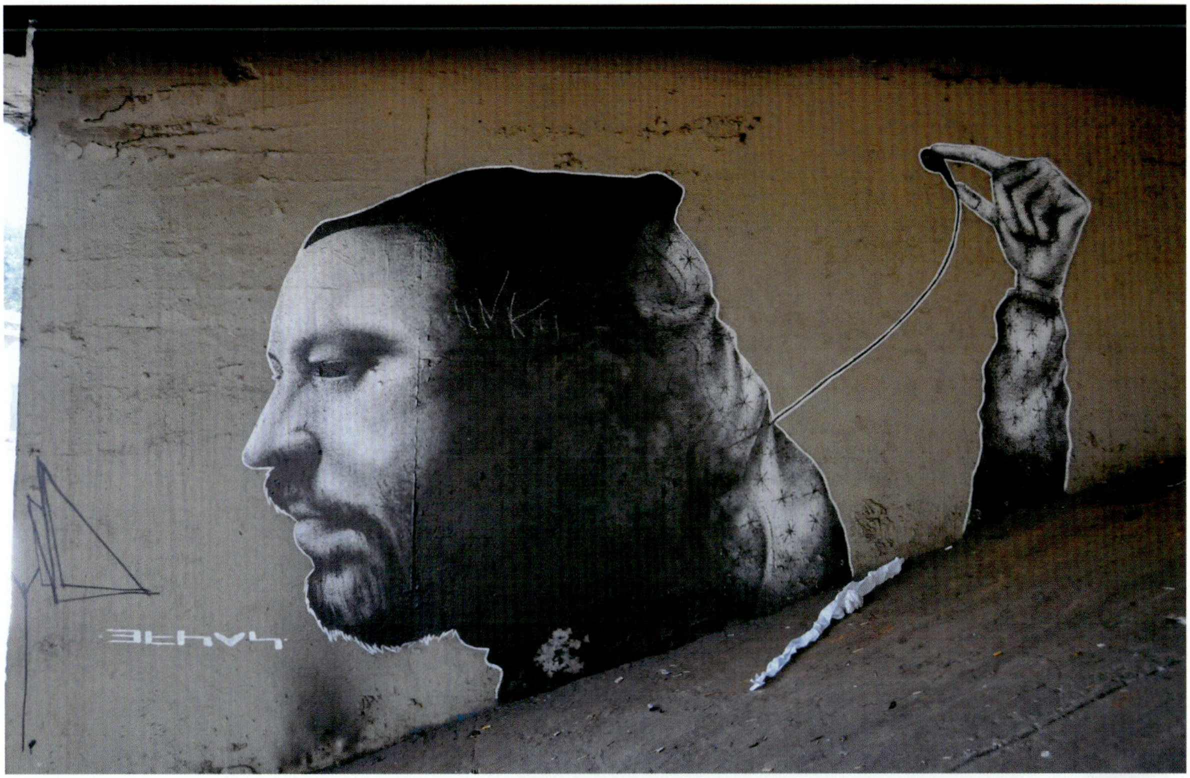

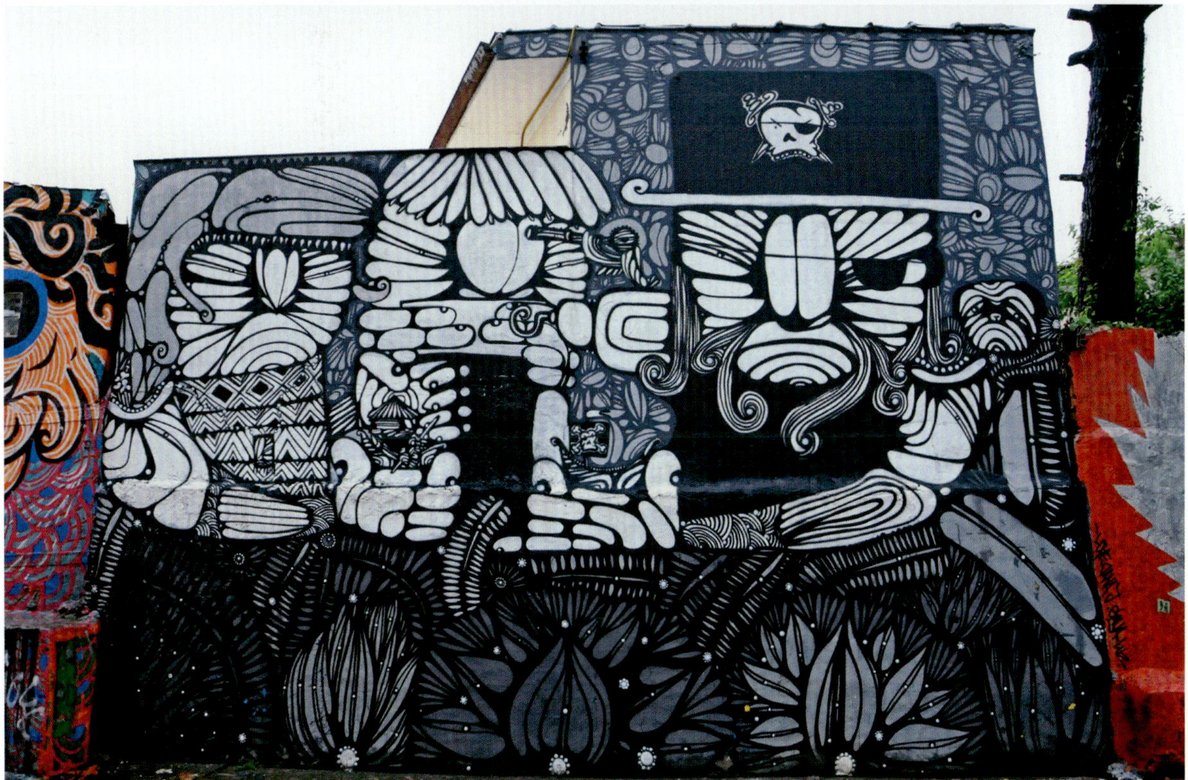

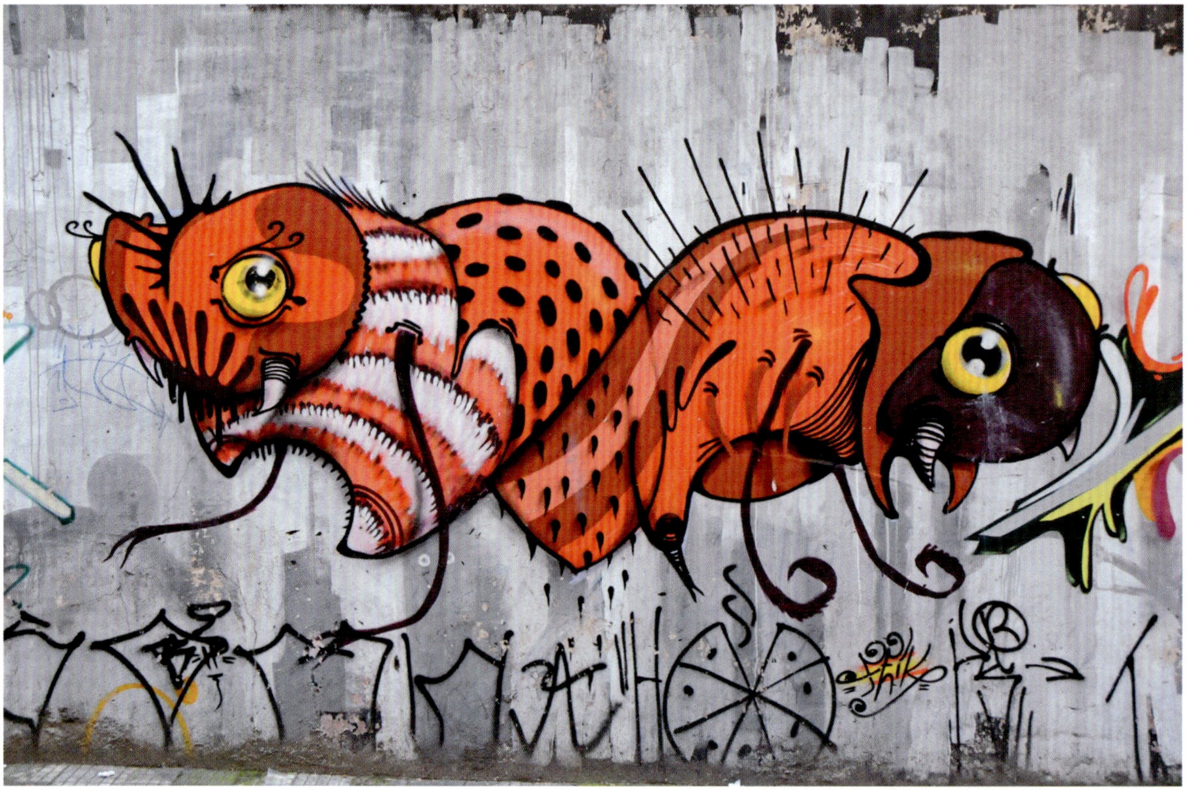

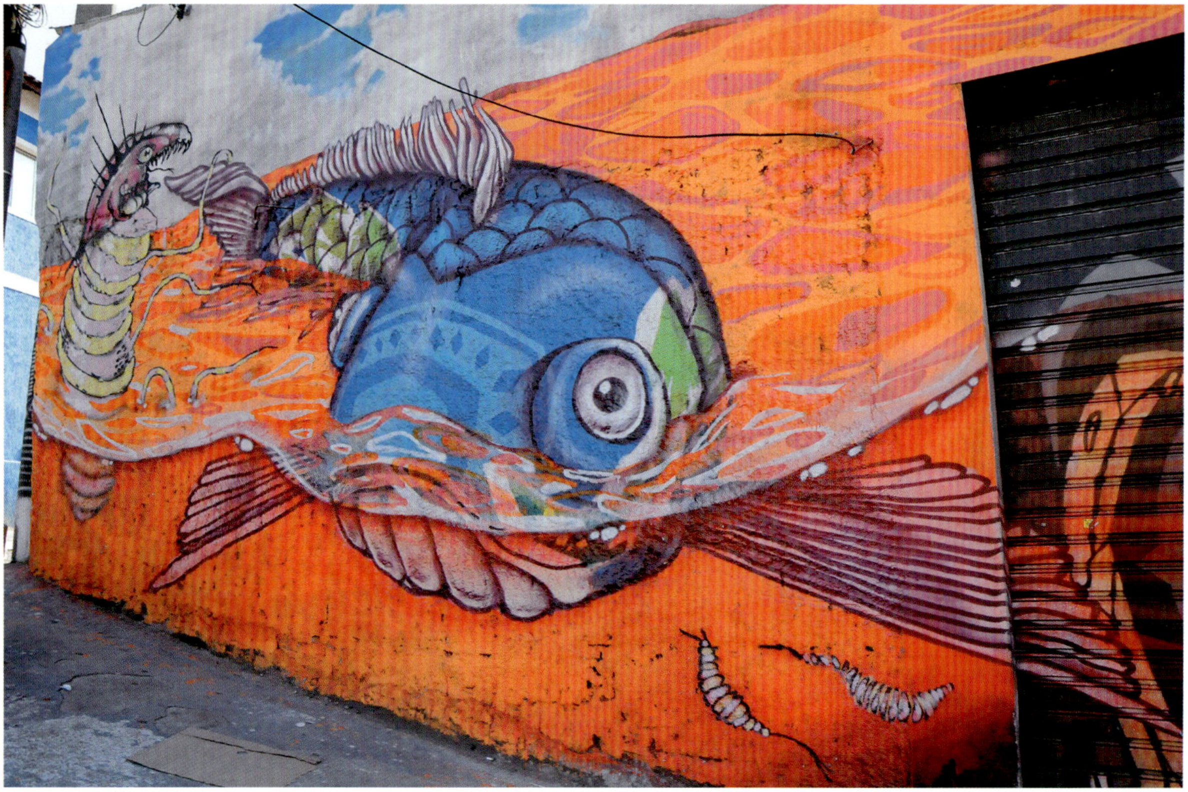

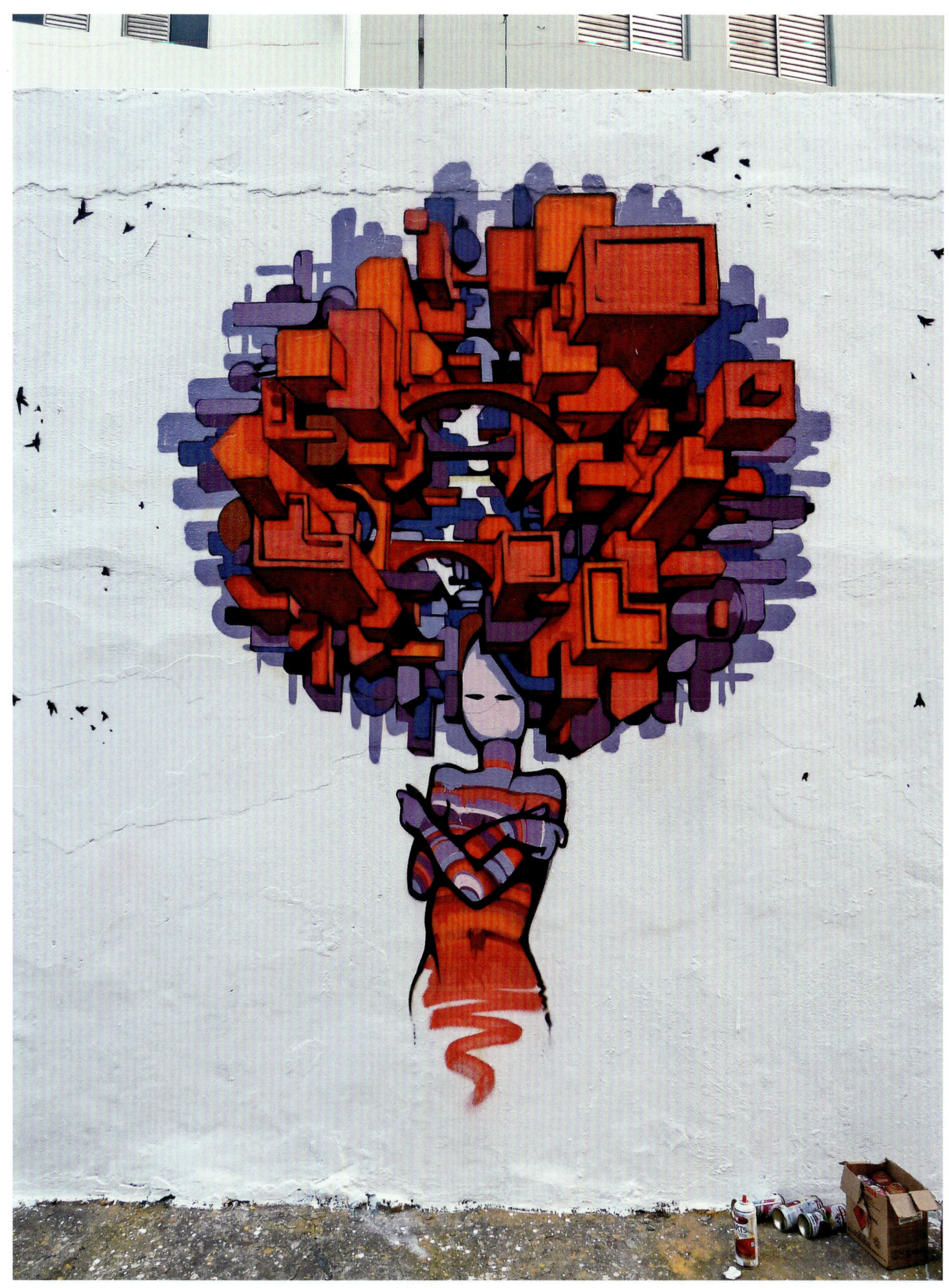

CLOCKWISE FROM
BELOW:
Zezao. I'm not going
to tell you how hard
it was to get to the
middle of the motorway
to take this photo, but
it was certainly not as
hard as it would have
been to paint!/Ato/
Graphis/Hamilton Yokota
aka Titifreak.

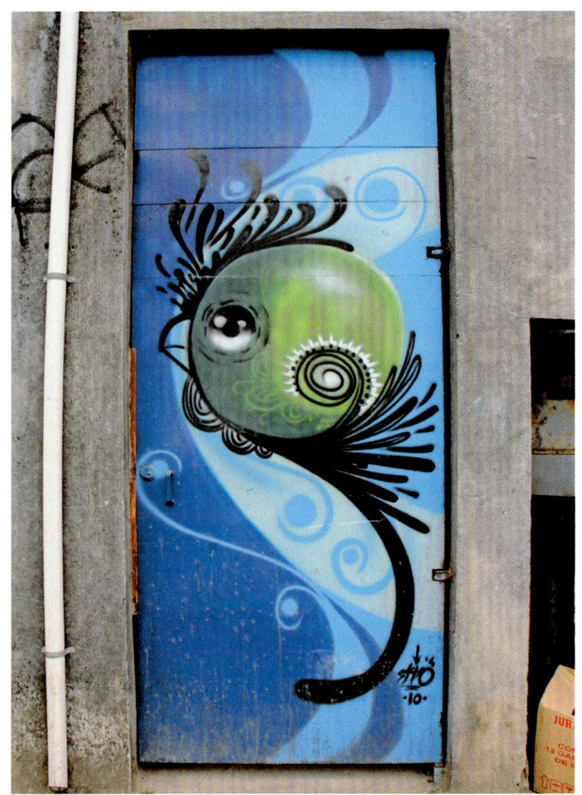

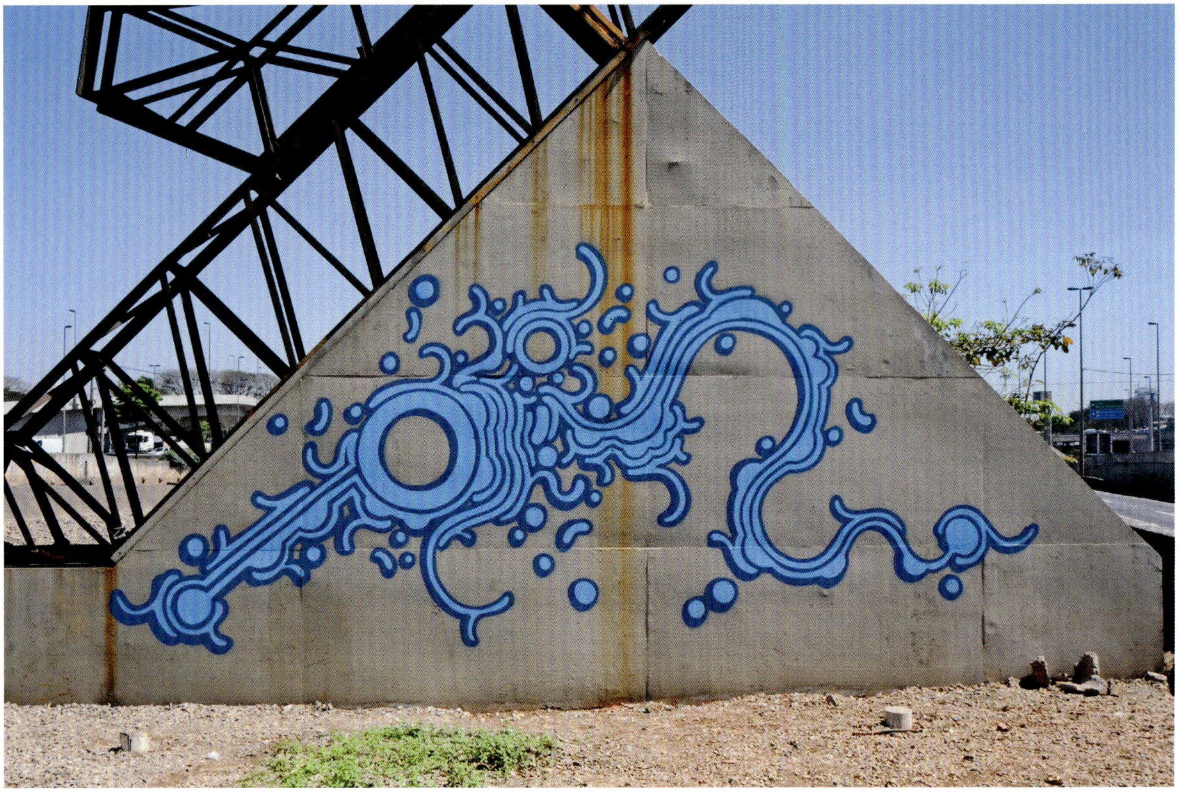

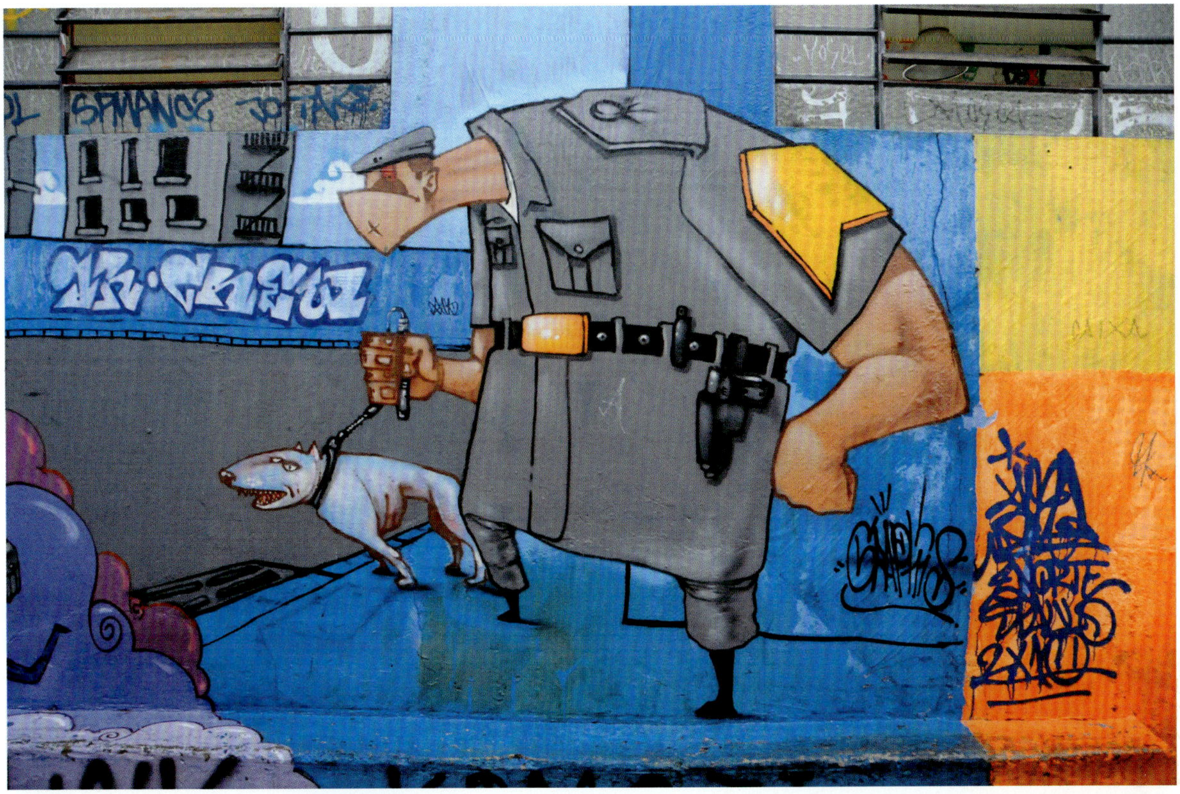

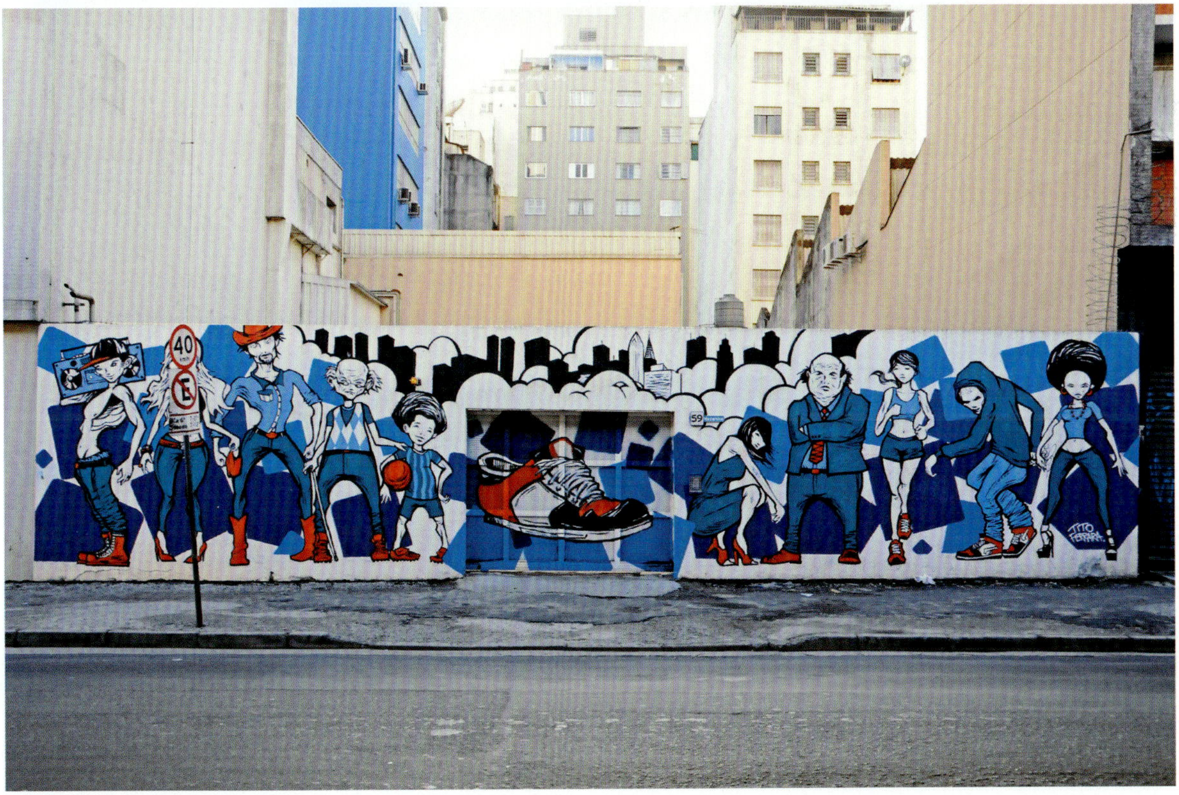

CLOCKWISE FROM
BELOW:
Rio's Big Bruno/Prozak
in São Paulo/Germany's
Lake in São Paulo.

PAGES 120-1,
CLOCKWISE FROM LEFT:
Portugal's Maniaks Crew
in Rio/Rio-based Lelo
and Swiss-born Tika
in Rio/New York's
Cern in Rio.

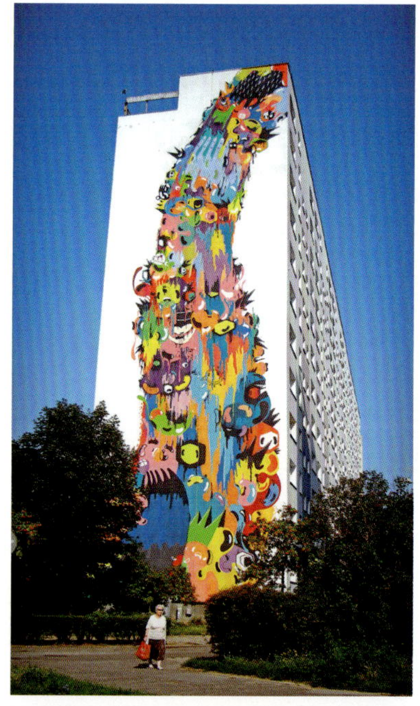

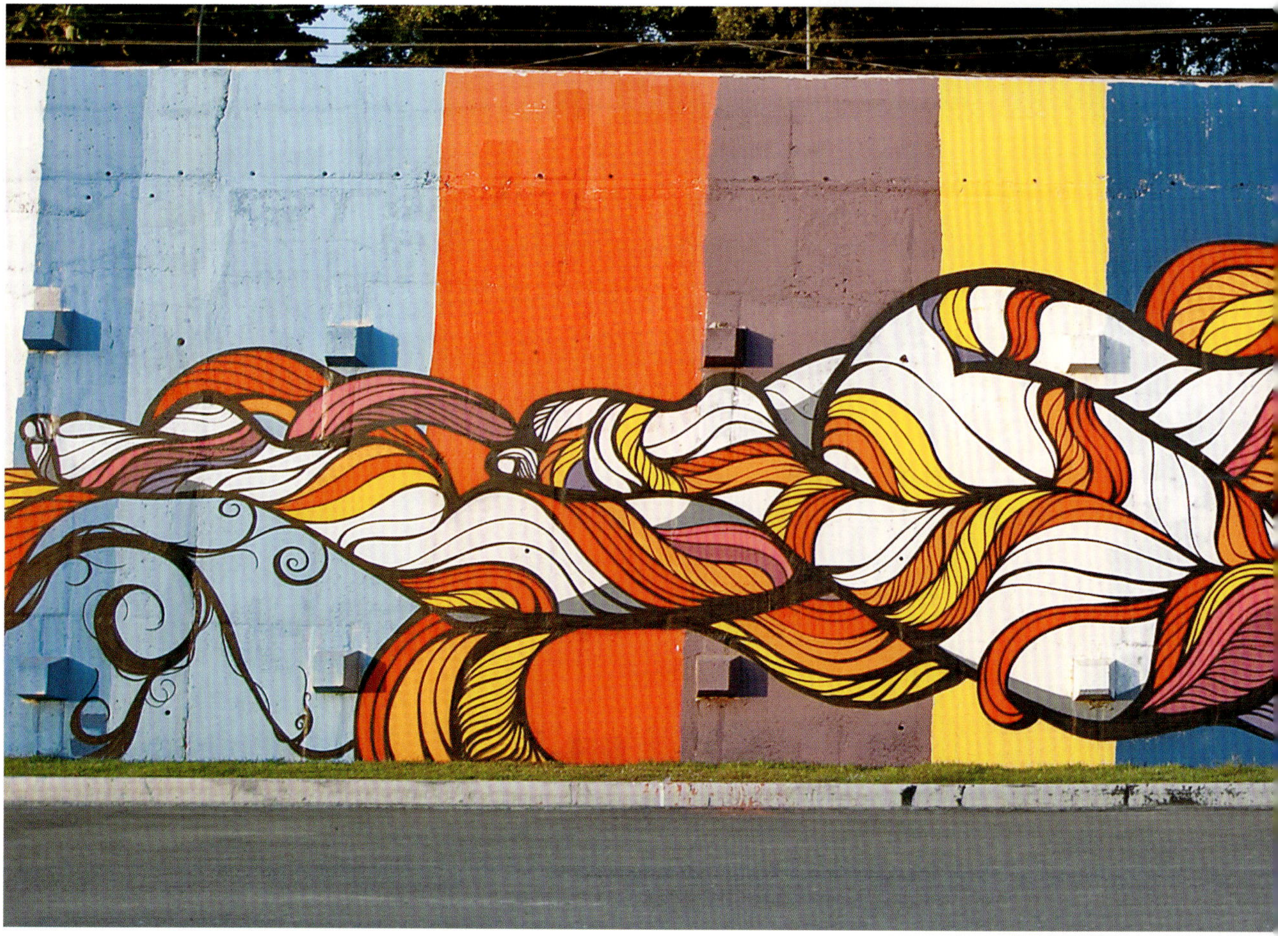

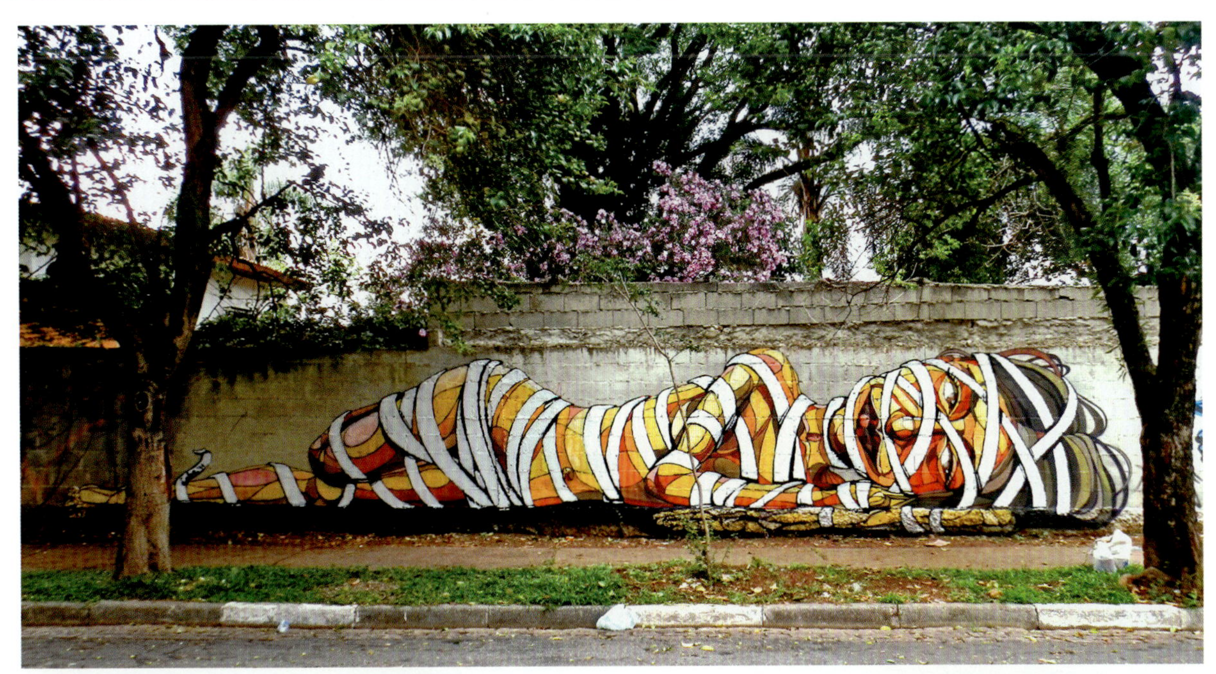

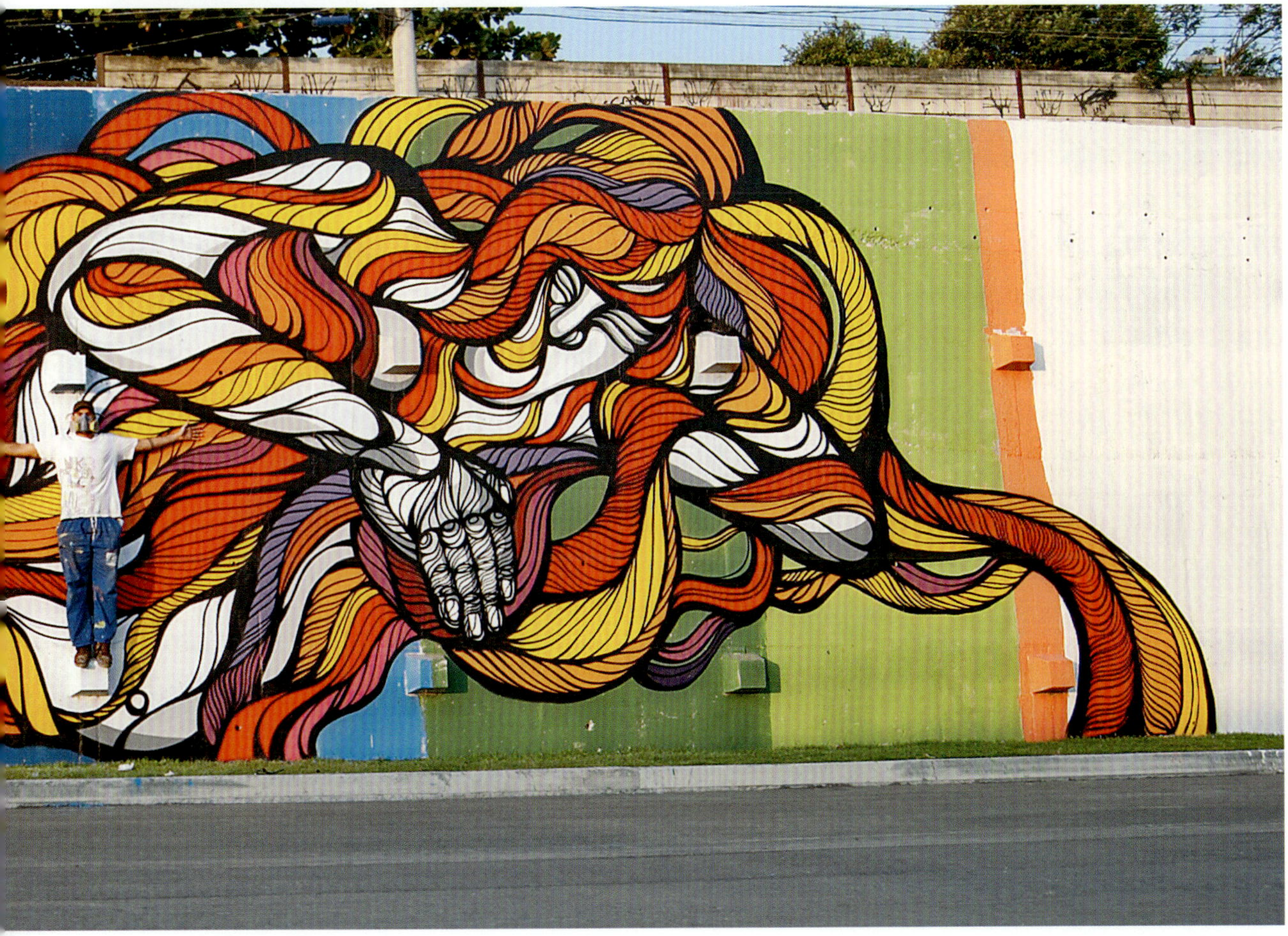

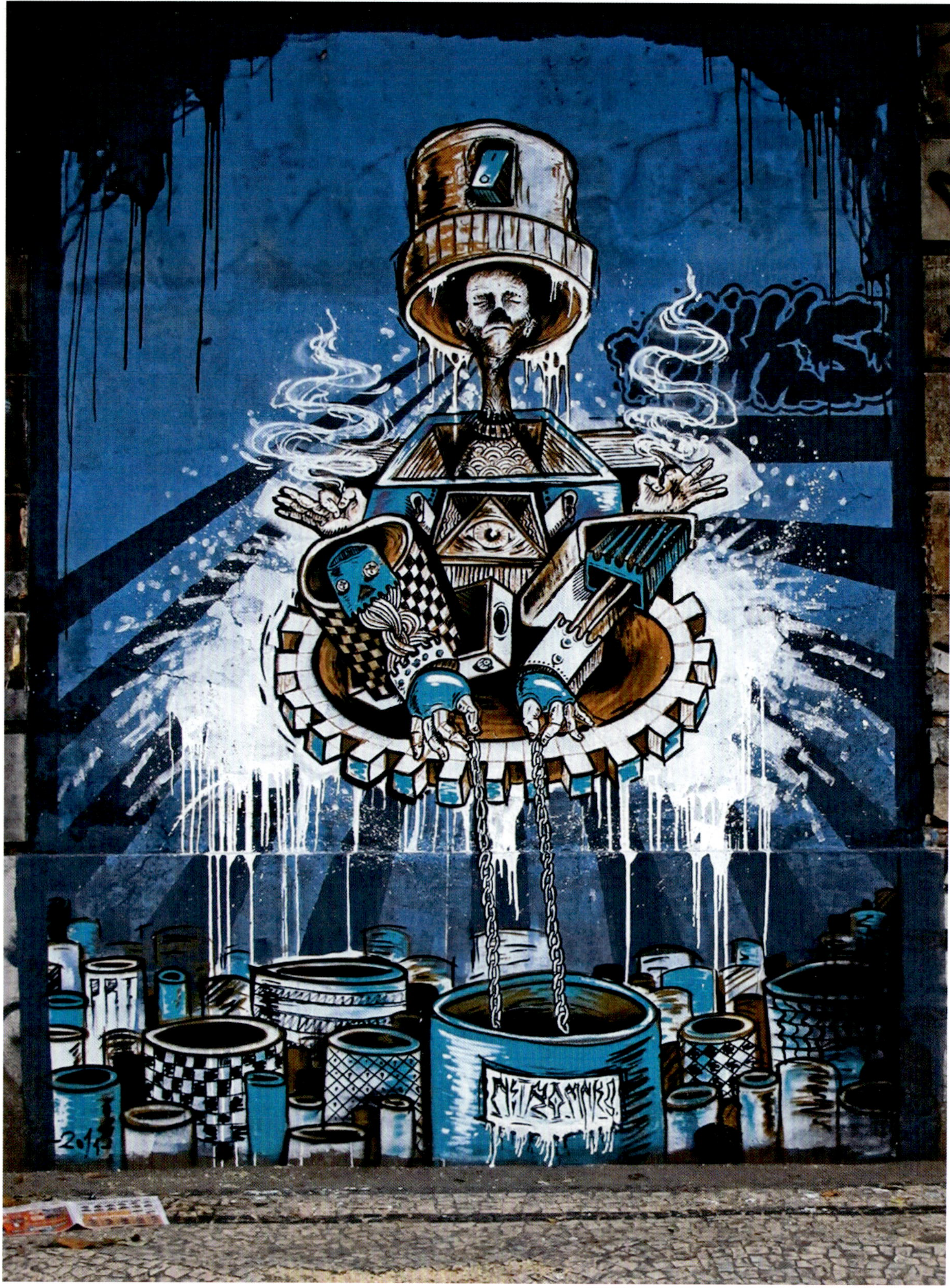

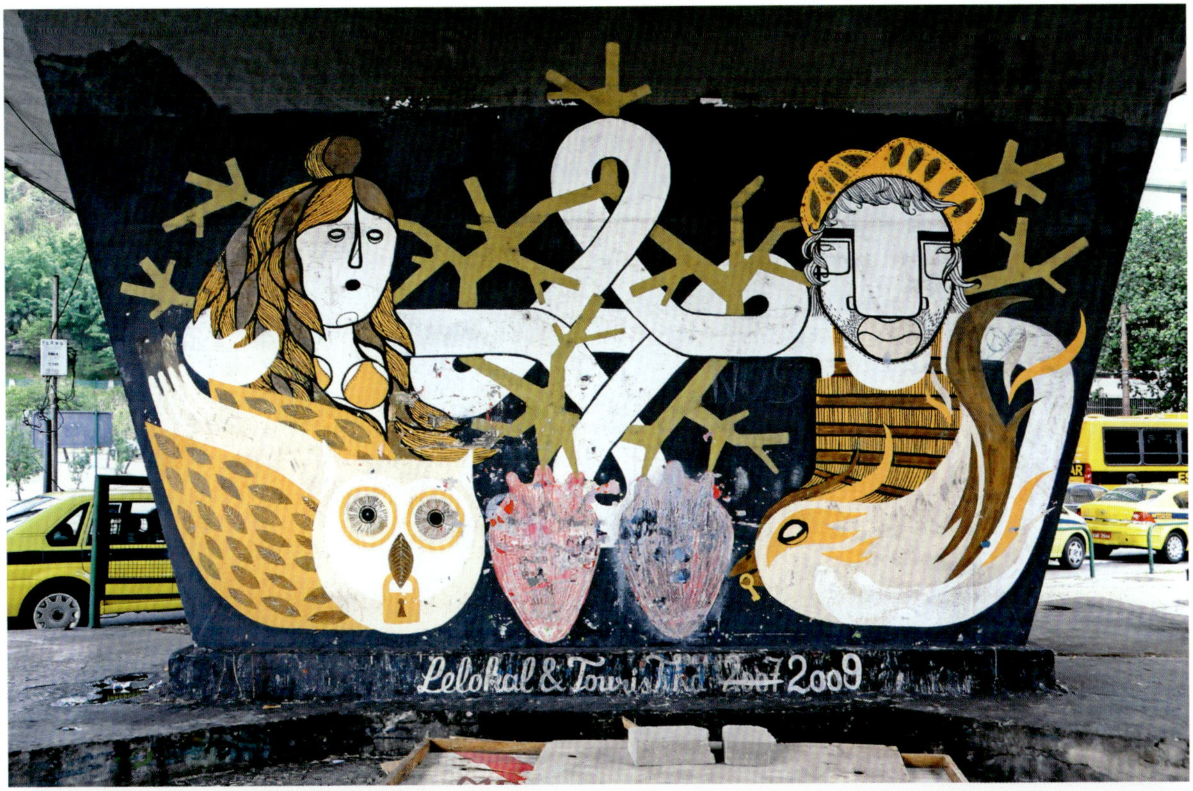

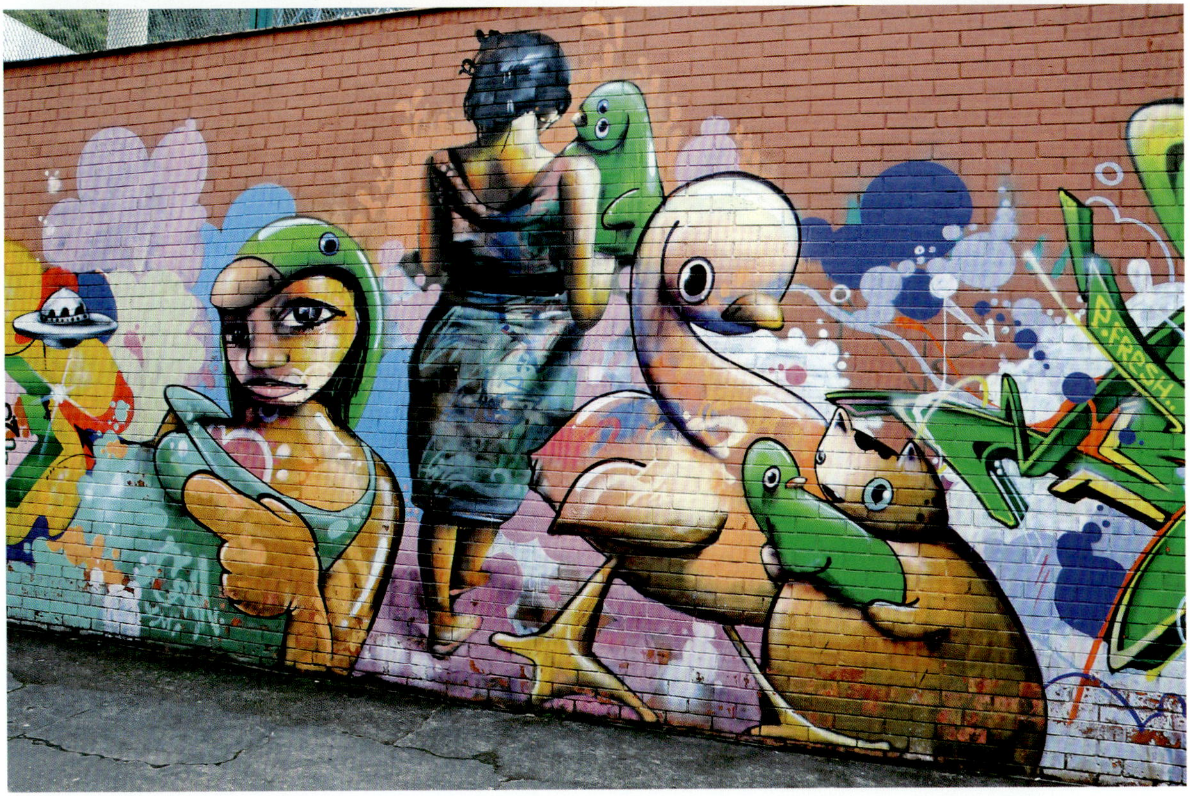

Lelokal & Touris ltd 2007 2009

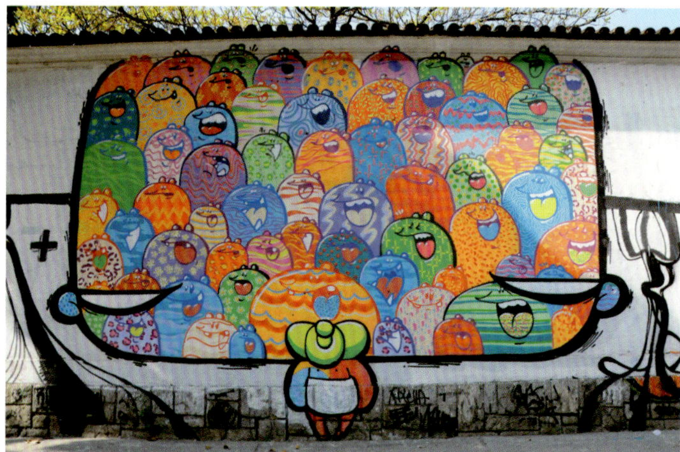

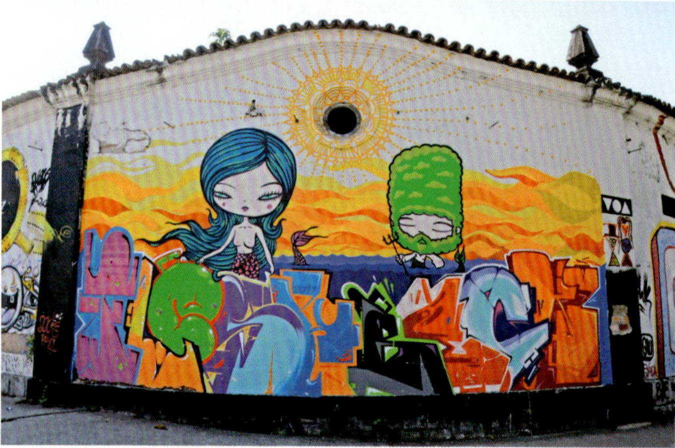

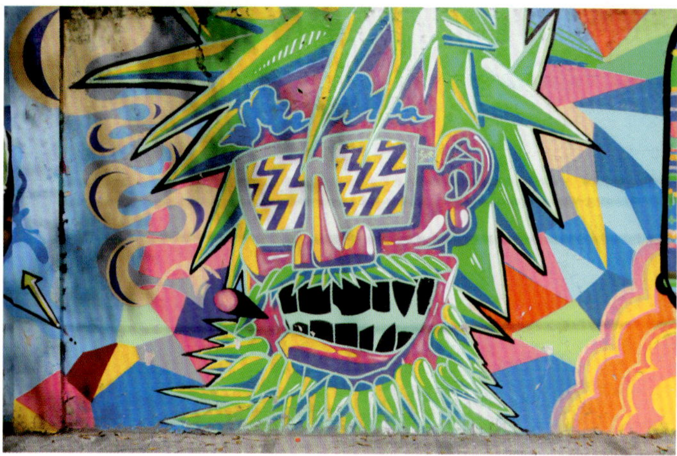

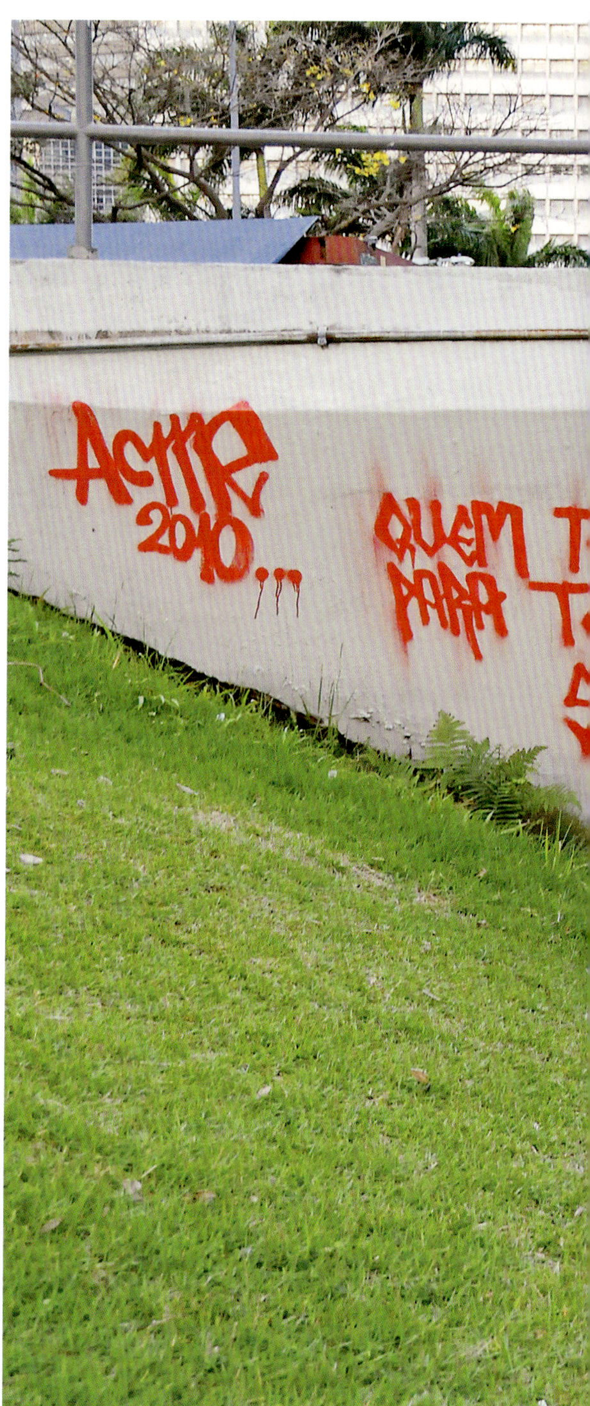

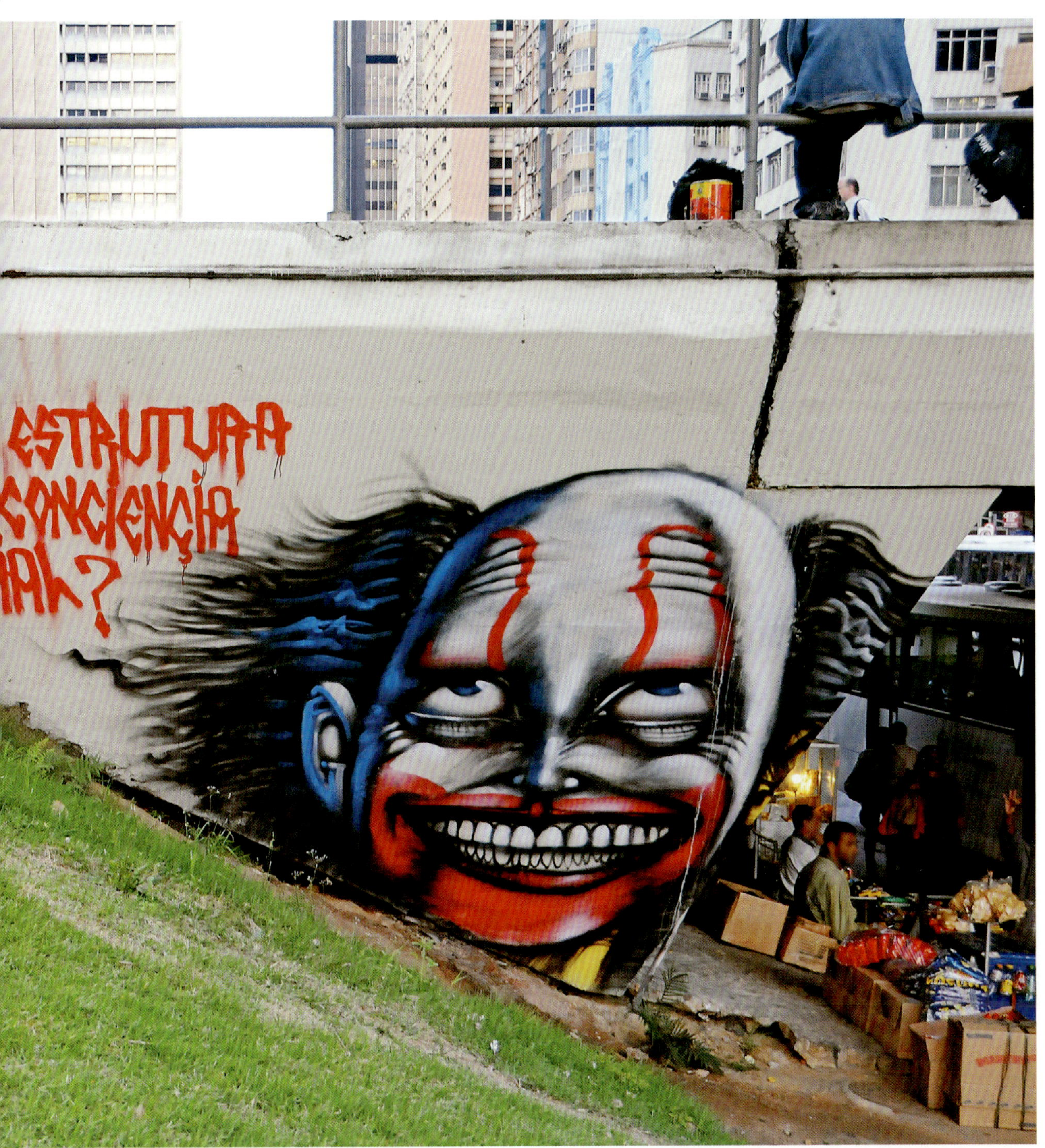

CLOCKWISE FROM ABOVE:
Acme/Members of Rio-locals Flesh Beck Crew (all three works).

PAGES 124-5, CLOCKWISE FROM TOP LEFT:
Mone and Celo in Belo Horizonte/Madruga and Nitcho in Rio/Kaja Man in Rio/Eco in Rio/Marcelo Ment in Rio.

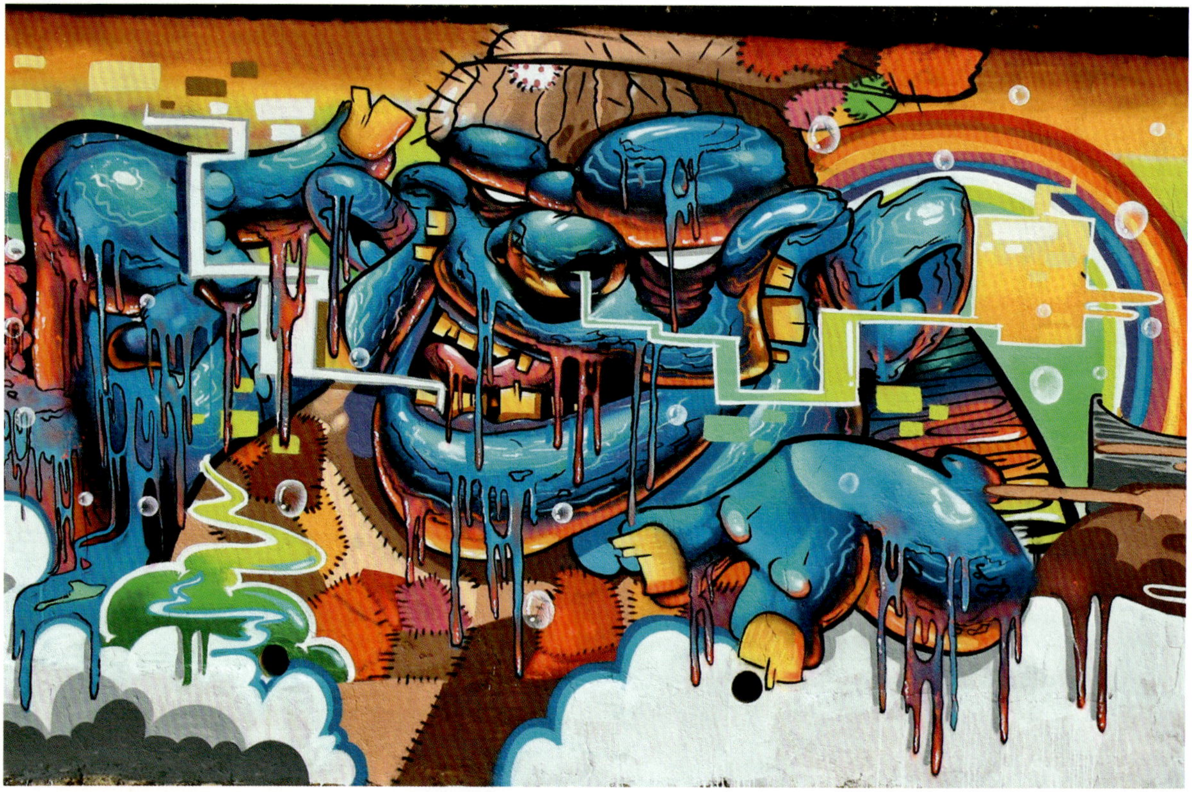

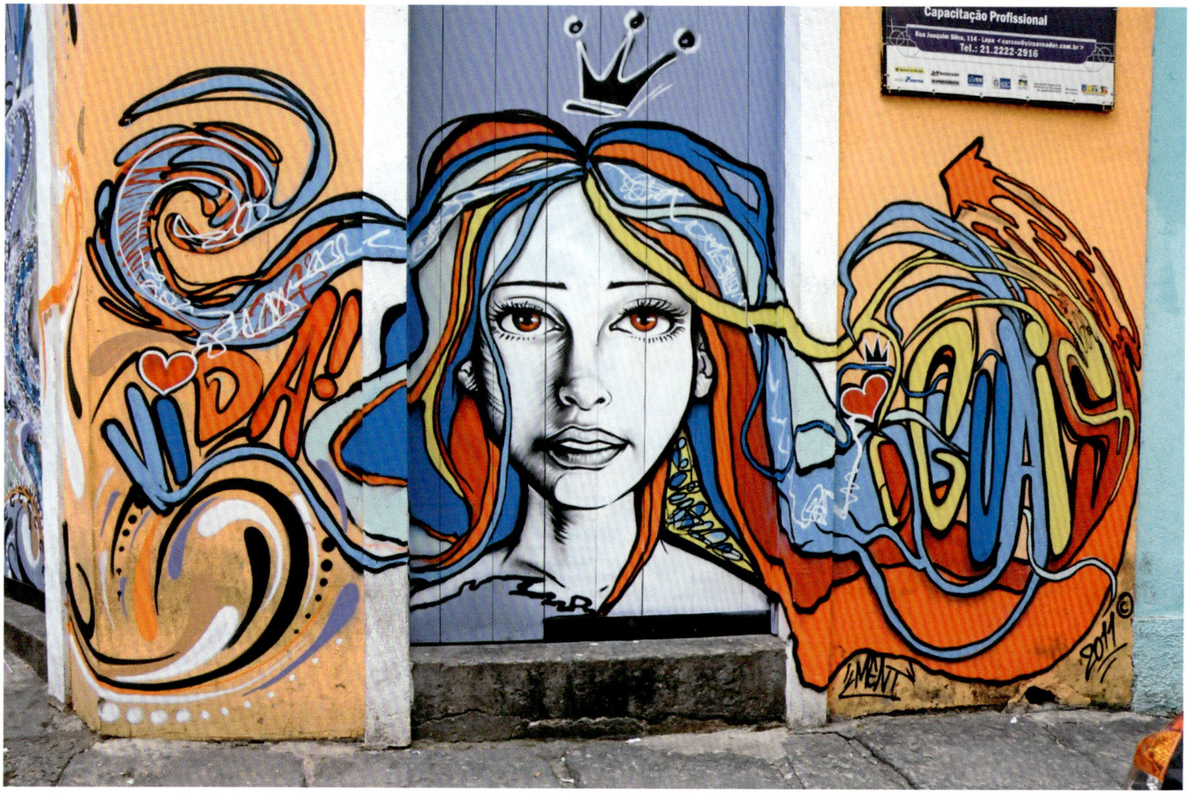

Capacitação Profissional
Rua Joaquim Silva, 154 - Lapa
Tel.: 21.2222-2916
VIDA!
GOAIS
2011

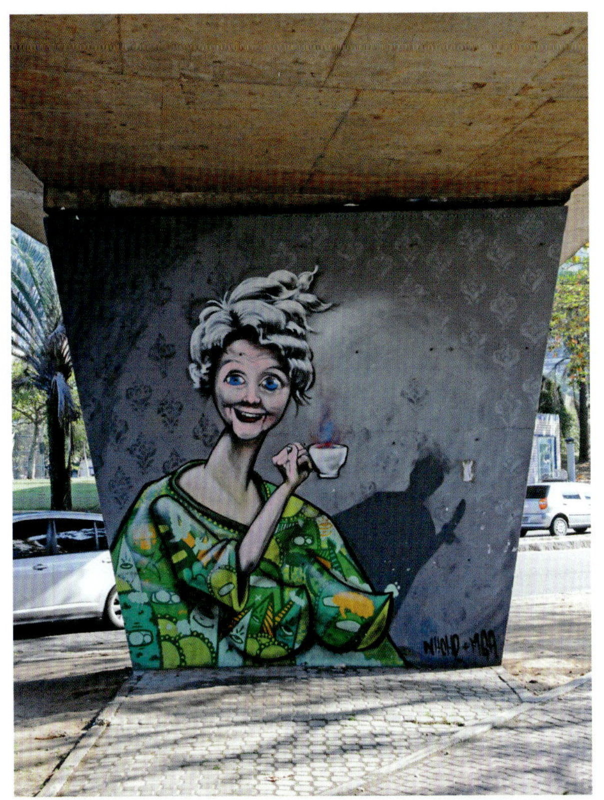

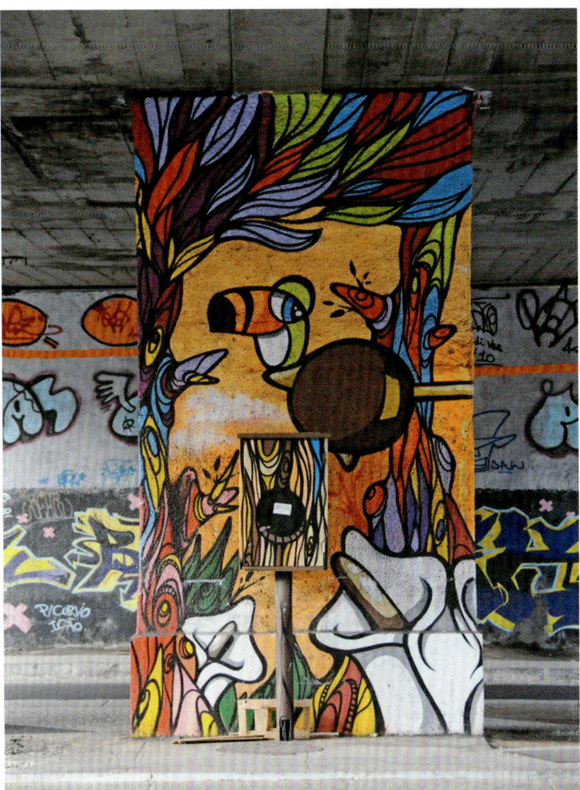

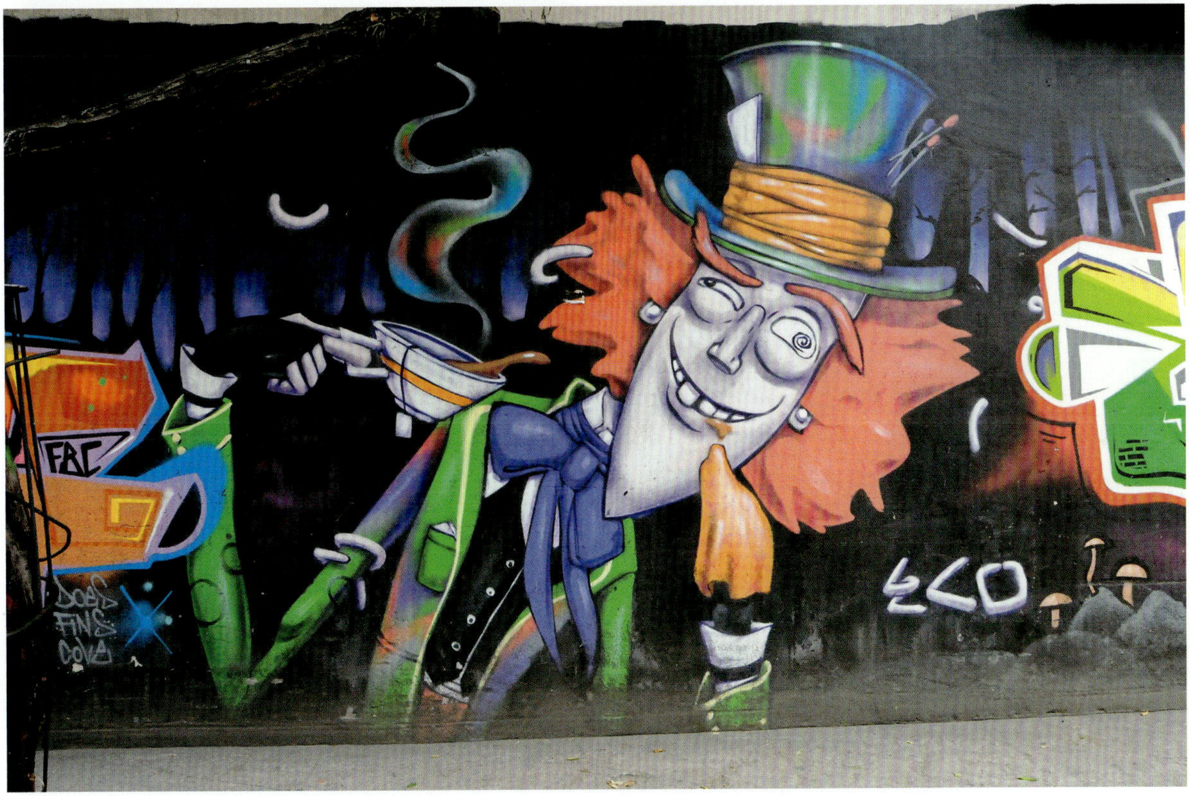

When I visited Argentina I found that the street art there was very different to the graffiti in Brazil. Argentina had less letter-based graffiti than São Paulo and was instead focused more on characters and portraiture. There were a number of artists, such as Ever and Jaz, who seemed to gravitate towards characters painted with rich tones. I was told that the brown tones in Jaz's work were because he painted mostly with mixtures of tar and petrol. A lack of available materials or the need to paint on a shoestring budget is no reason not to paint.

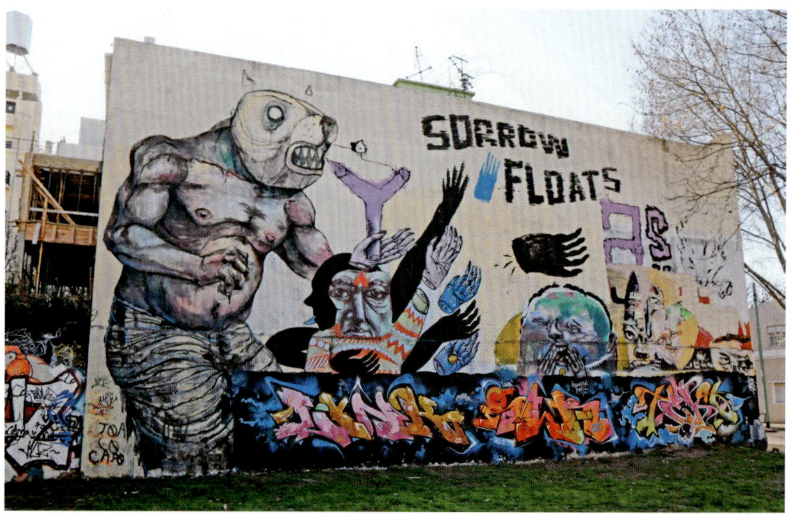

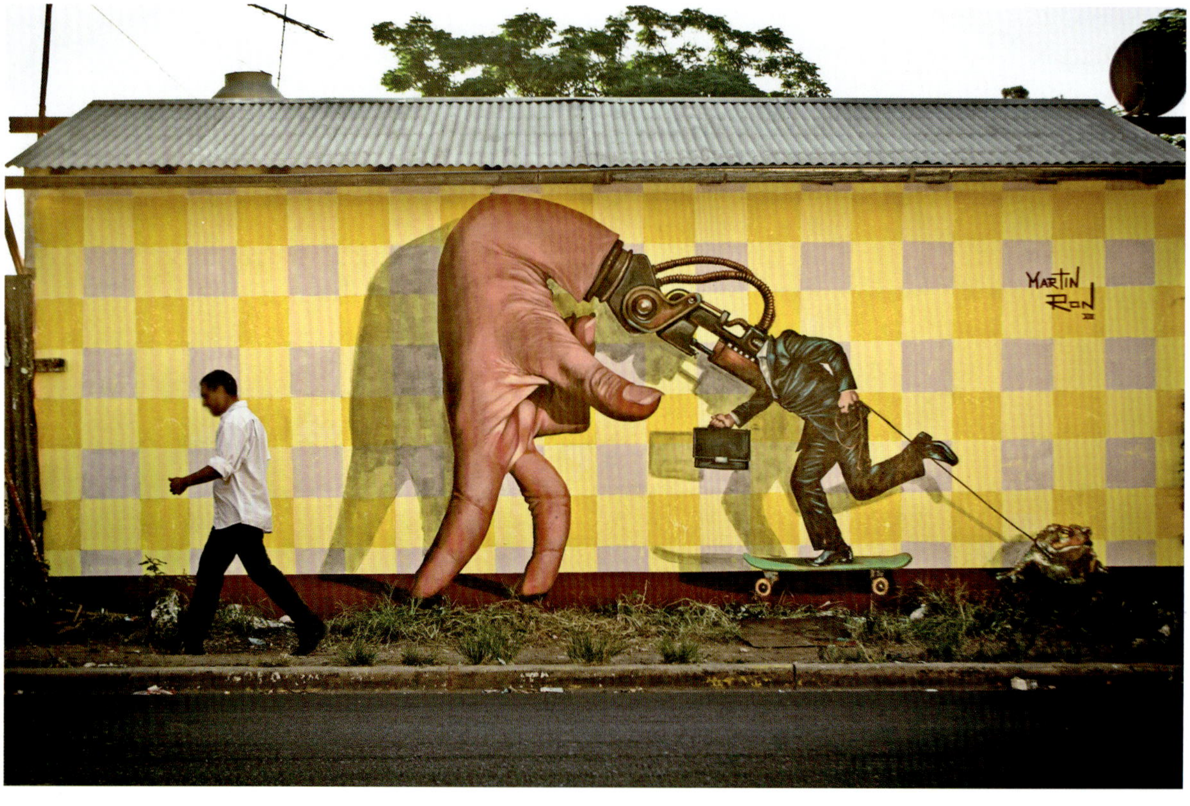

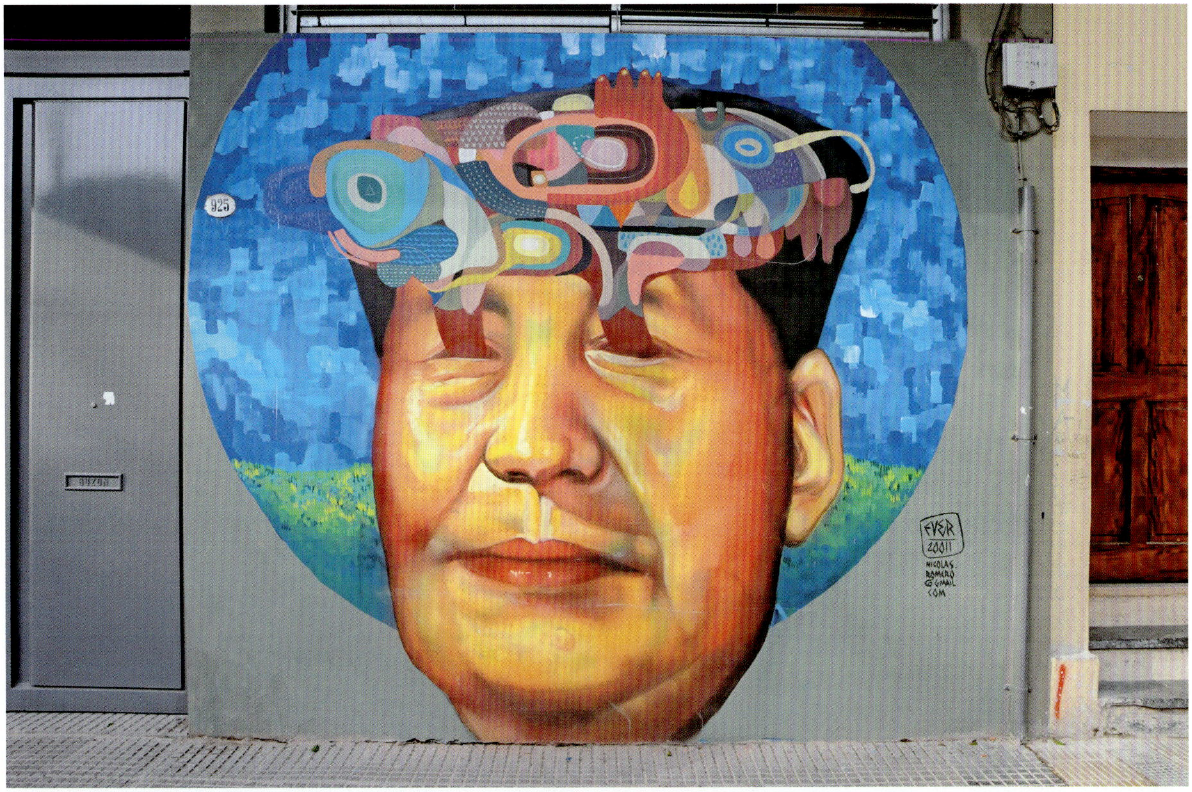

925
EVER
20011
NICOLAS.
ROMERO
@GMAIL
.COM

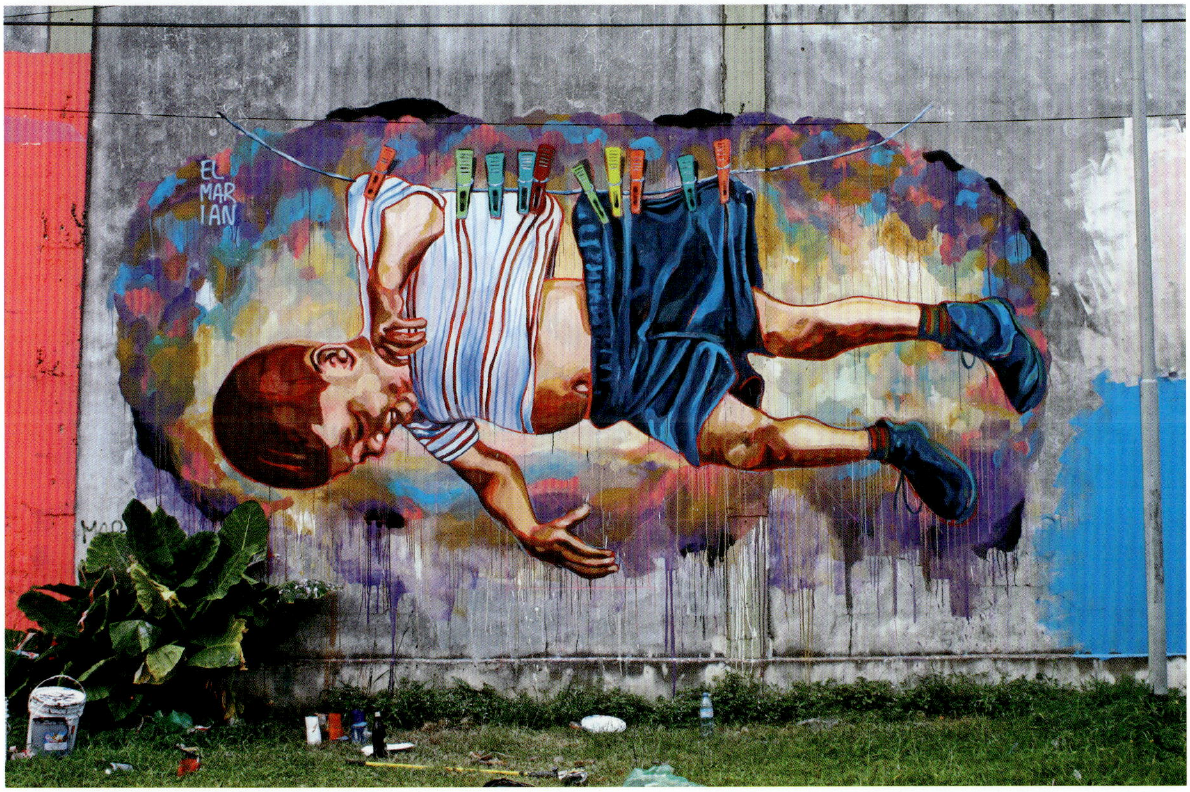

EL
MAR
IAN

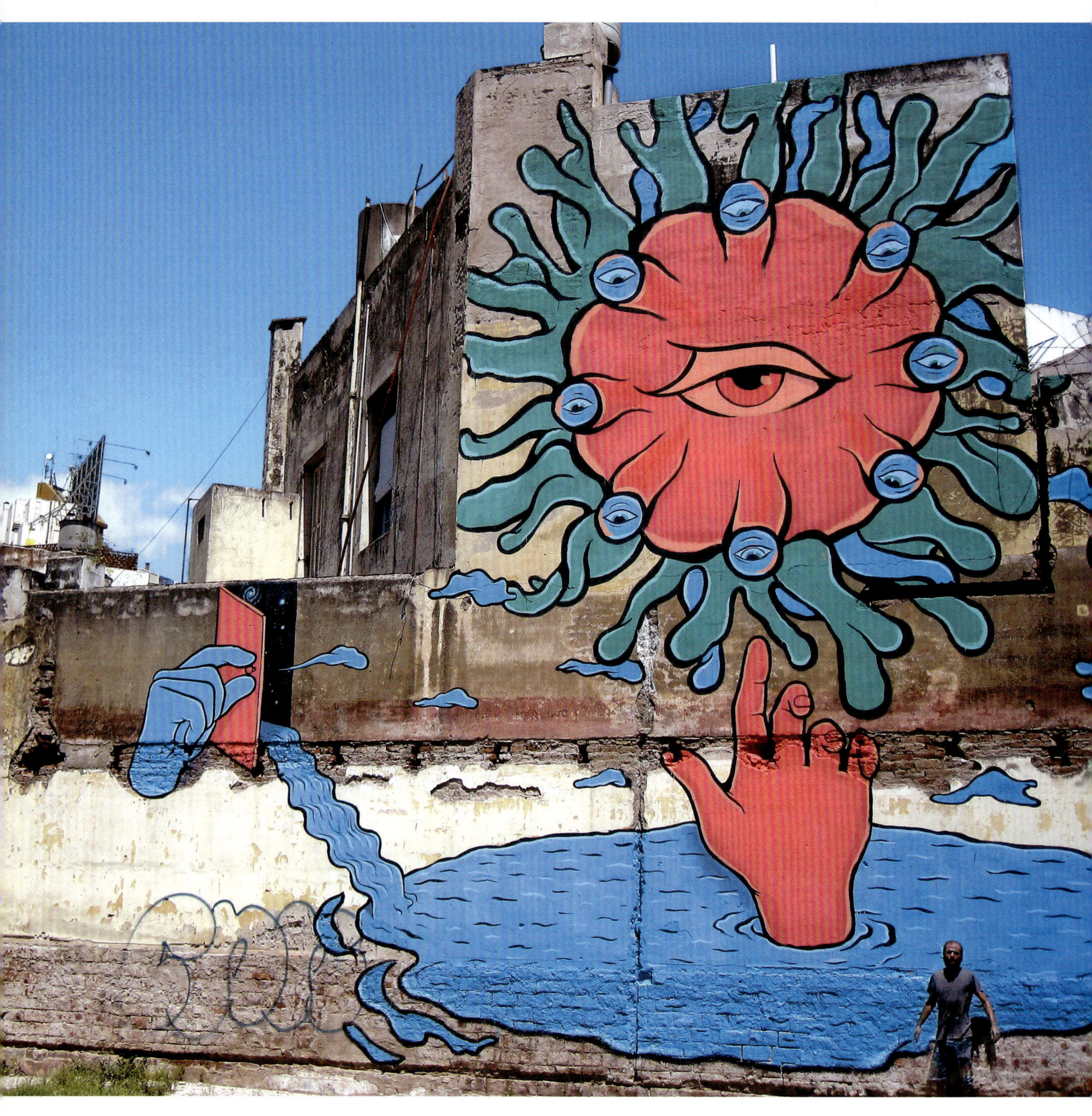

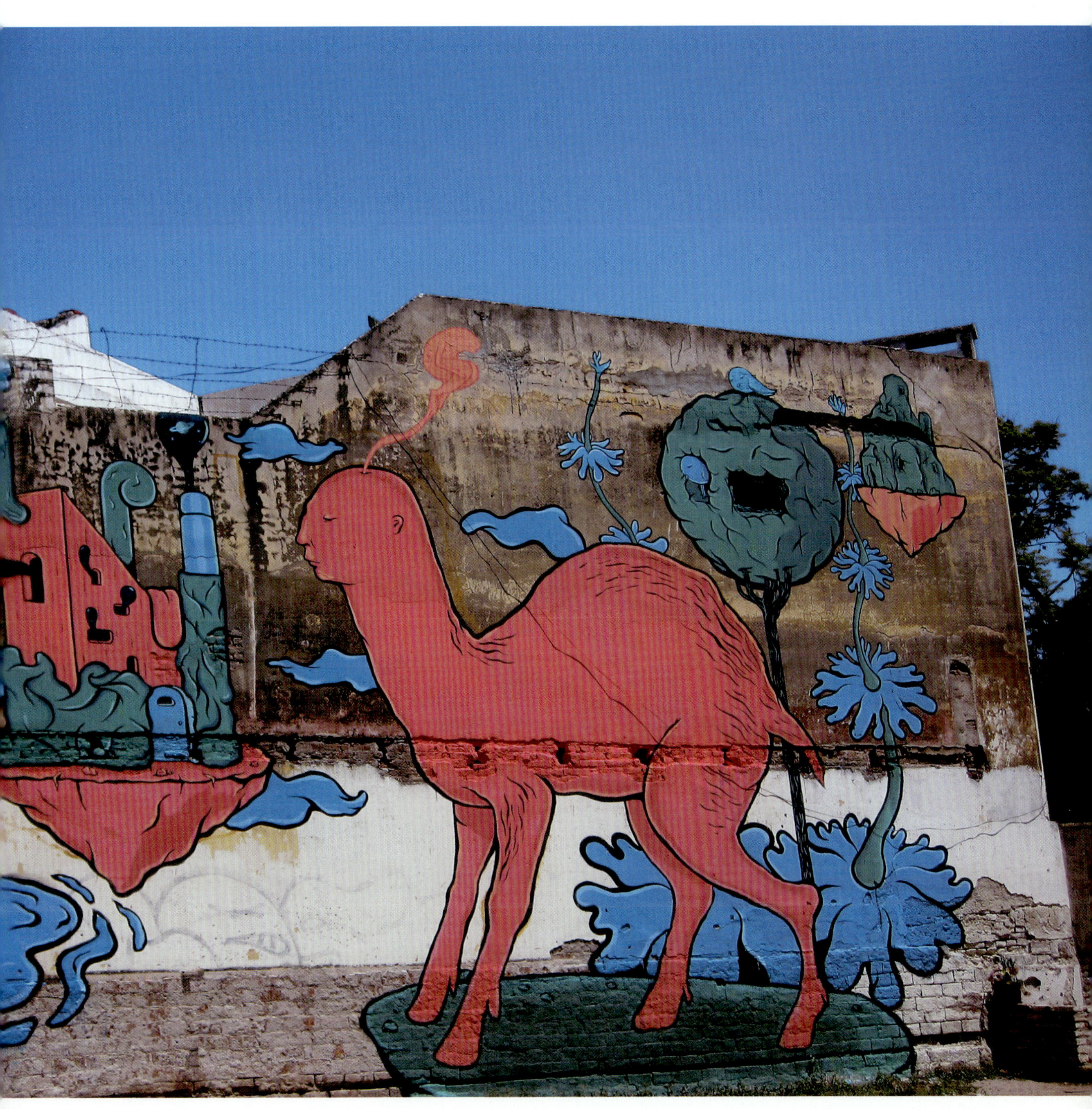

At the end of my trip to Brazil and Argentina I planned three days in Chile. I had little time for research beforehand, and the only connections I had were Mario from OKFS Crew, who runs a paint store in Santiago, and a local guide. Mario had kindly offered to pick me up from the airport – he said the taxis were dodgy and it was easier that way. I called him from Buenos Aires and explained I was going to try to get as much done as possible in three days, and cover two cities – Santiago and Valparaíso. I could have spent a week in Santiago and not found all of the art the place held, so three days for two cities was very tight.

Within a ten-minute phone call, Mario had understood how little time I had and decided to help where he could. I cancelled my hostel and stayed with him instead. The evening I arrived we went straight to the bar to meet local artists, who offered to help; we got back from the bar at 4am and were up and off to Valparaíso at 6am. In those three days, Mario and others helped me take more than two thousand photos in the two cities. It was a great way to end a trip and I can't wait to get back to see my friends and this amazing, dynamic art scene again.

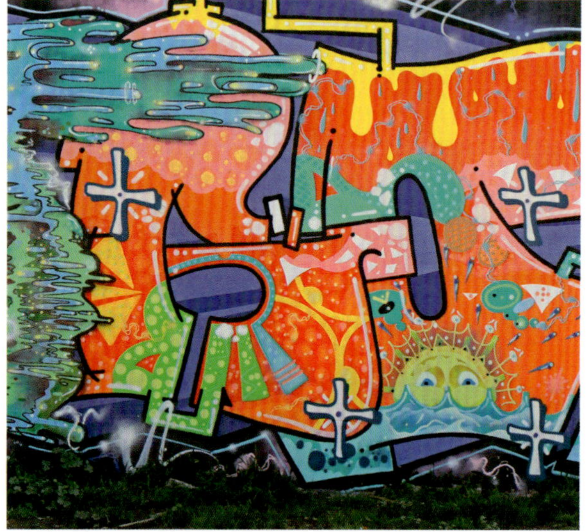

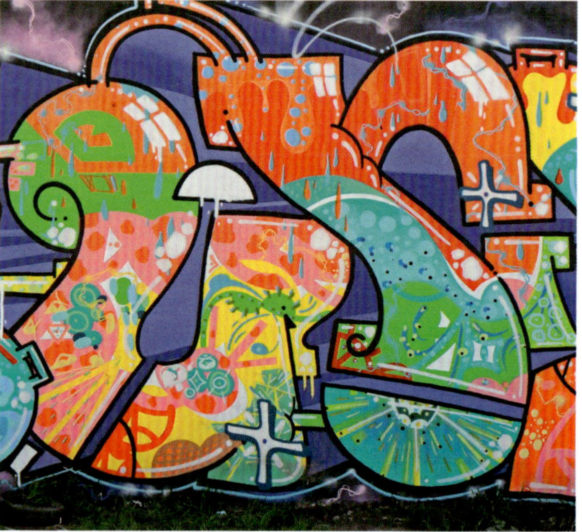

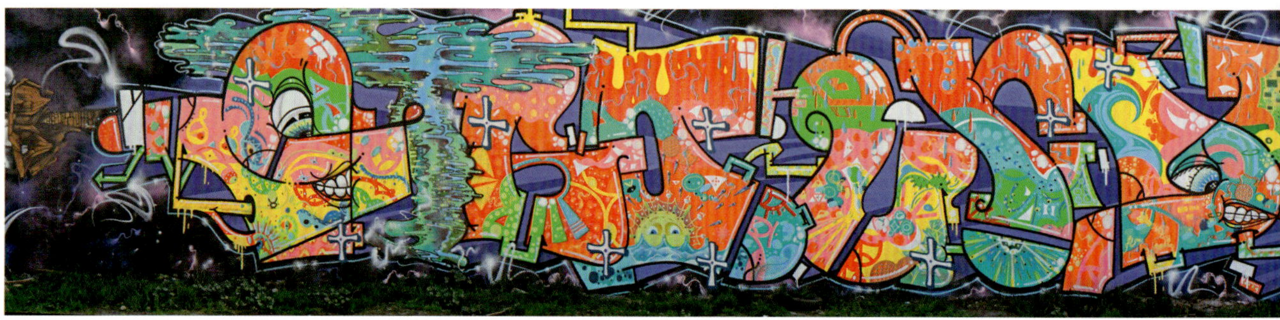

PAGES 126-7, CLOCKWISE
FROM TOP LEFT:
Jaz and others/Ever/El
Marian/Martin Ron.

PAGES 128-9:
Gualicho in Córdoba.

THESE PAGES:
Aislap (note the
phenomenal detail used
to fill in the letters).

PAGES 132-3, CLOCKWISE
FROM LEFT:
Brigada Negotropica/
Agotok/Agotok/Piguan.

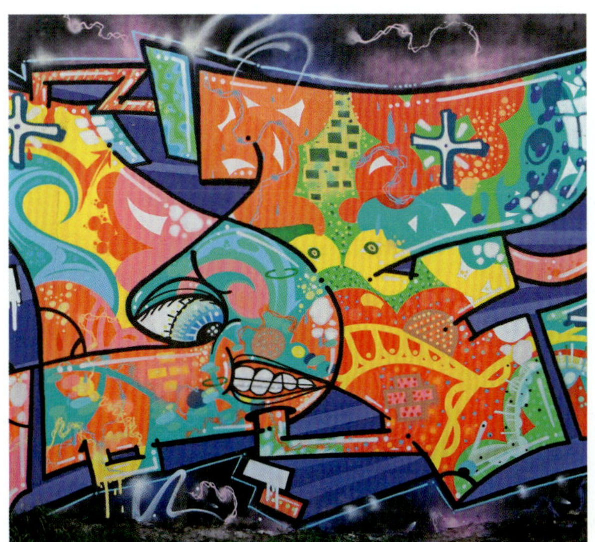

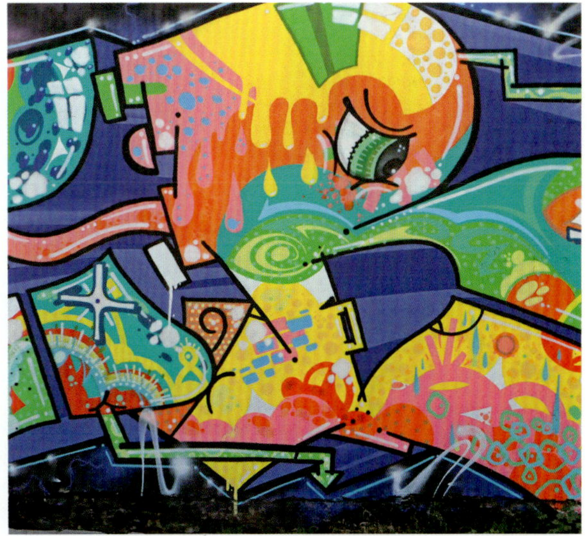

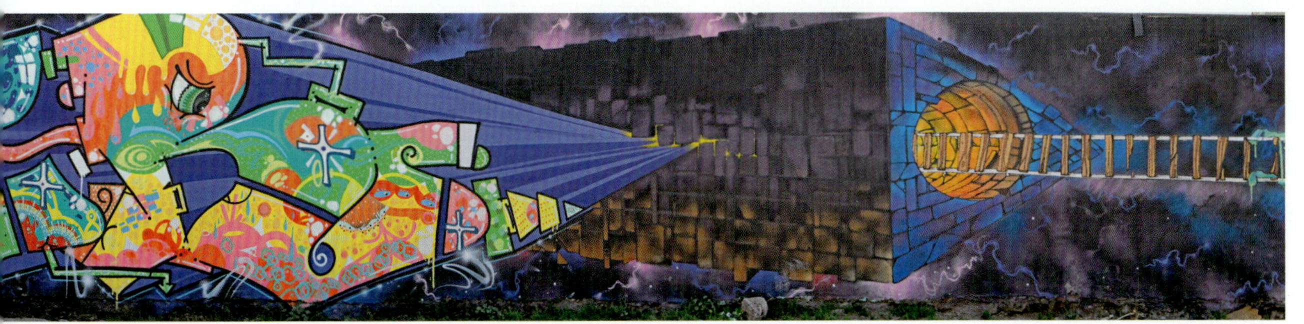

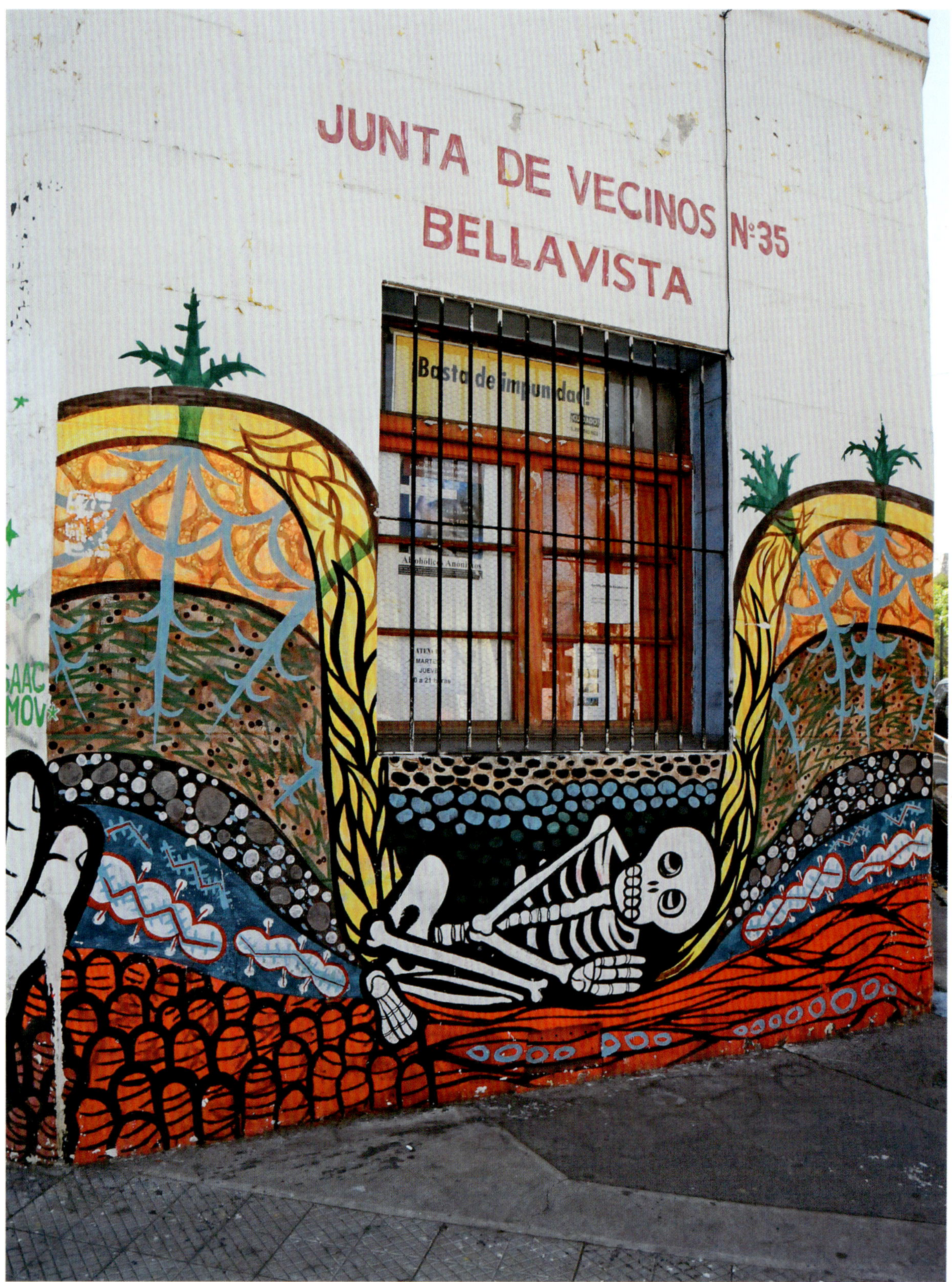
JUNTA DE VECINOS N°35
BELLAVISTA
¡Basta de impunidad!

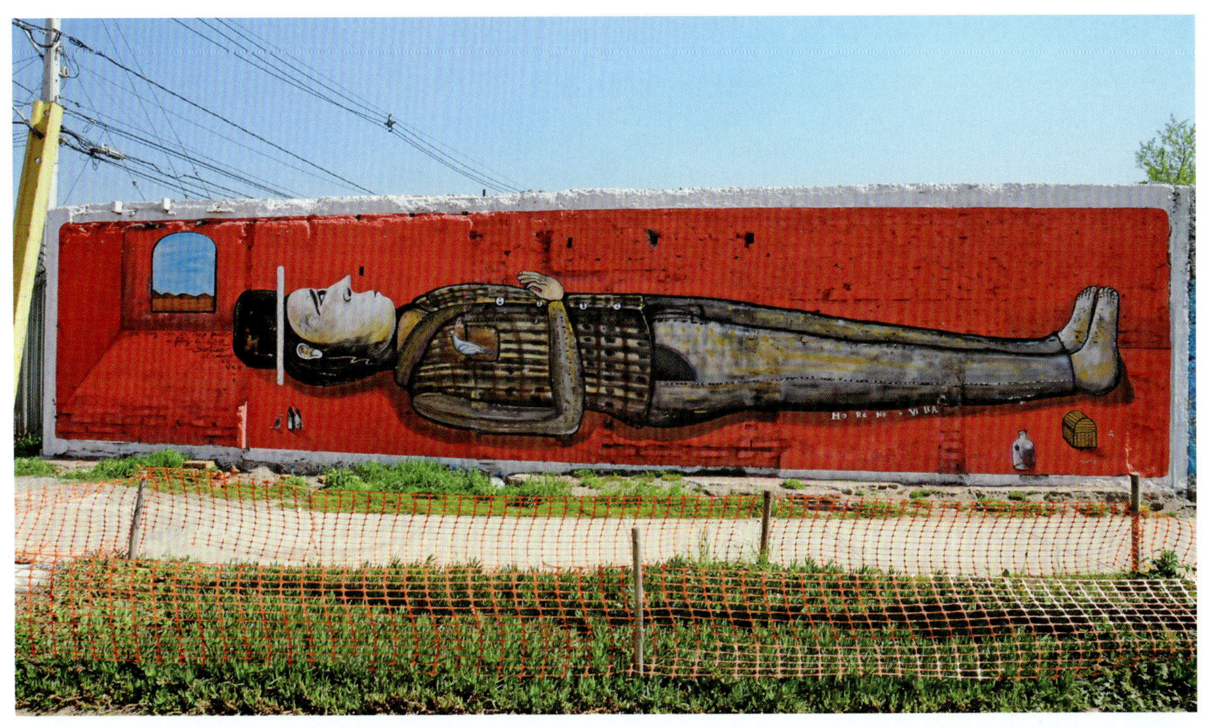

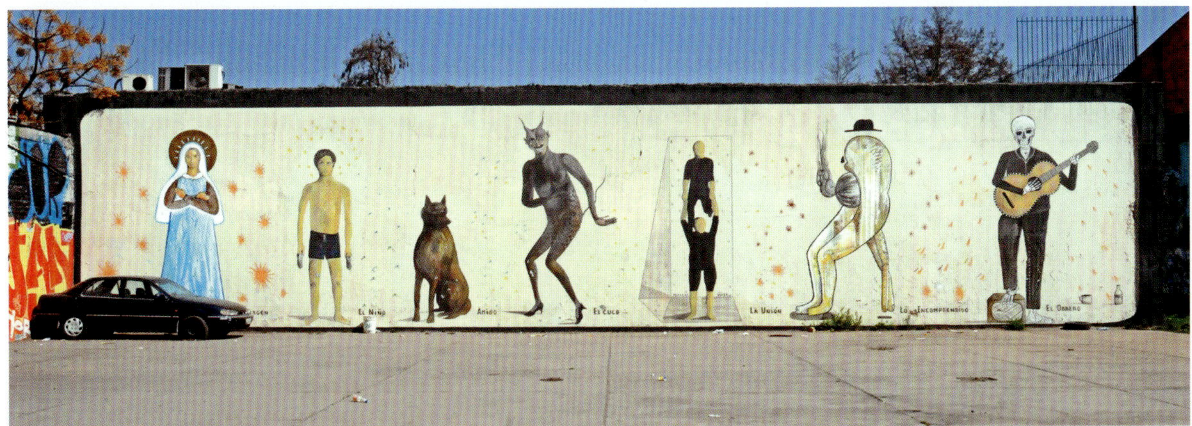
Virgen
El Niño
Amigo
El Coco
La Unión
Lo Incomprendido
El Donero

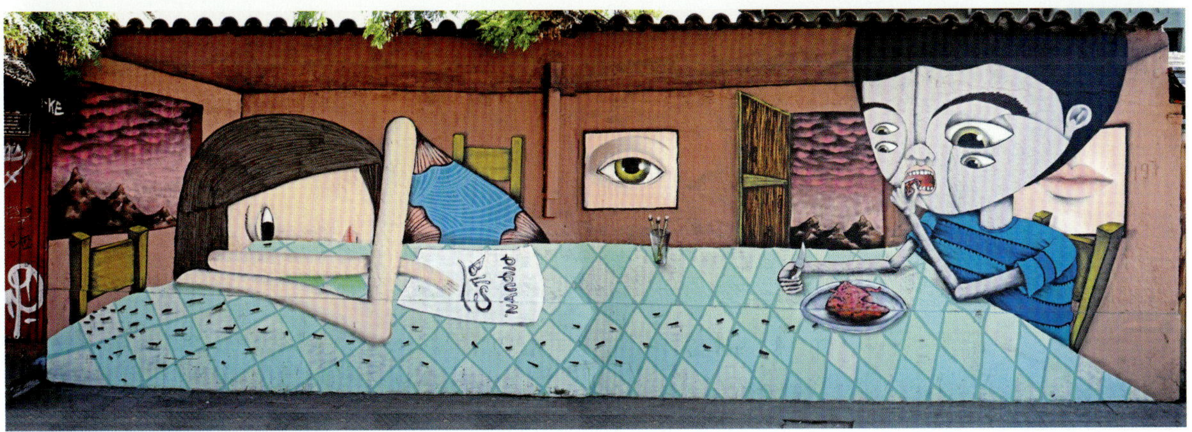

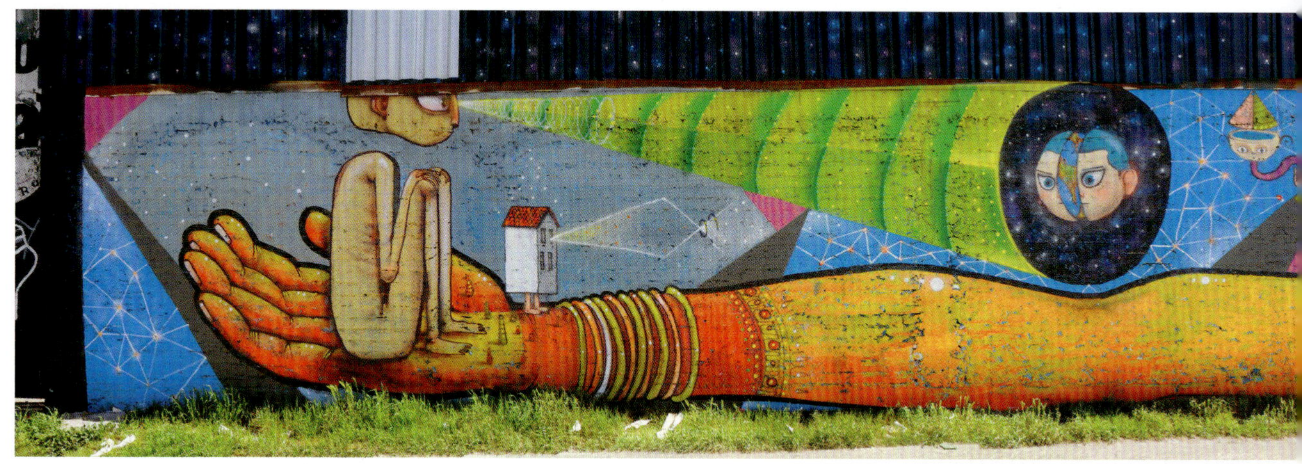

ABOVE AND BELOW:
Aislap.

PAGES 136-7, CLOCKWISE
FROM TOP LEFT:
Inti in Valparaíso (this
was his old style)/
Nicolina in Valparaíso.
I had to wait for the
cablecars to cross to
get this shot!/Inti in
Valparaíso on the same
wall years later.

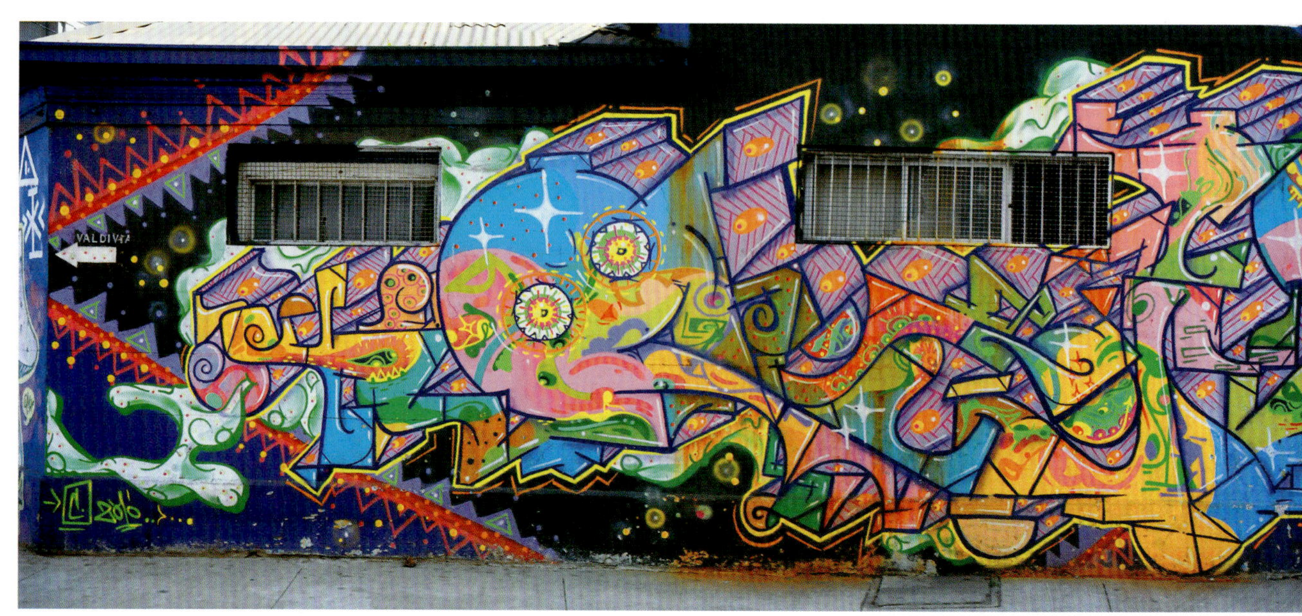

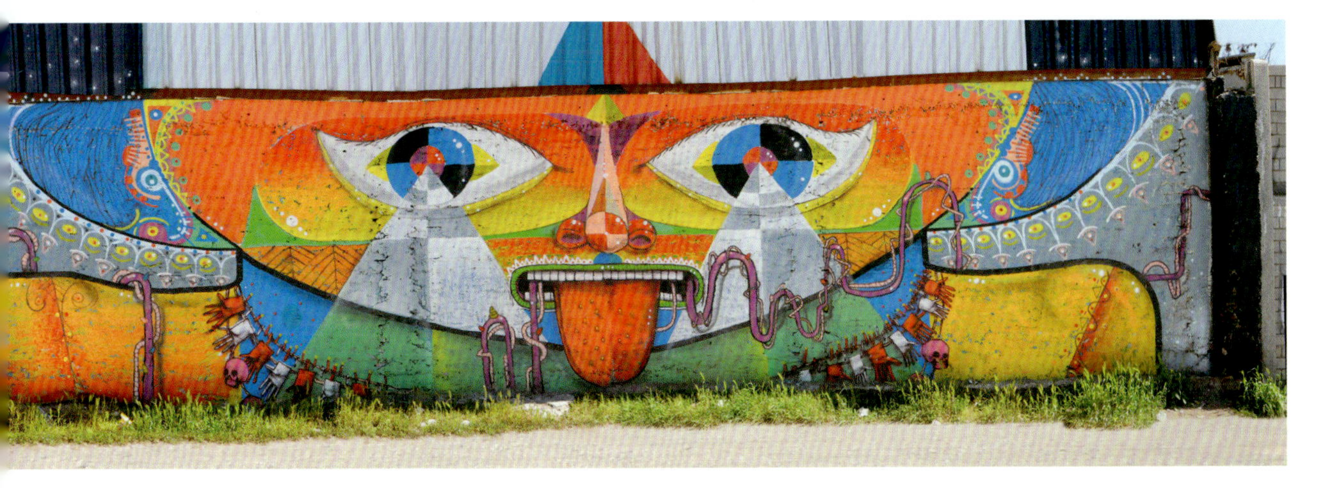

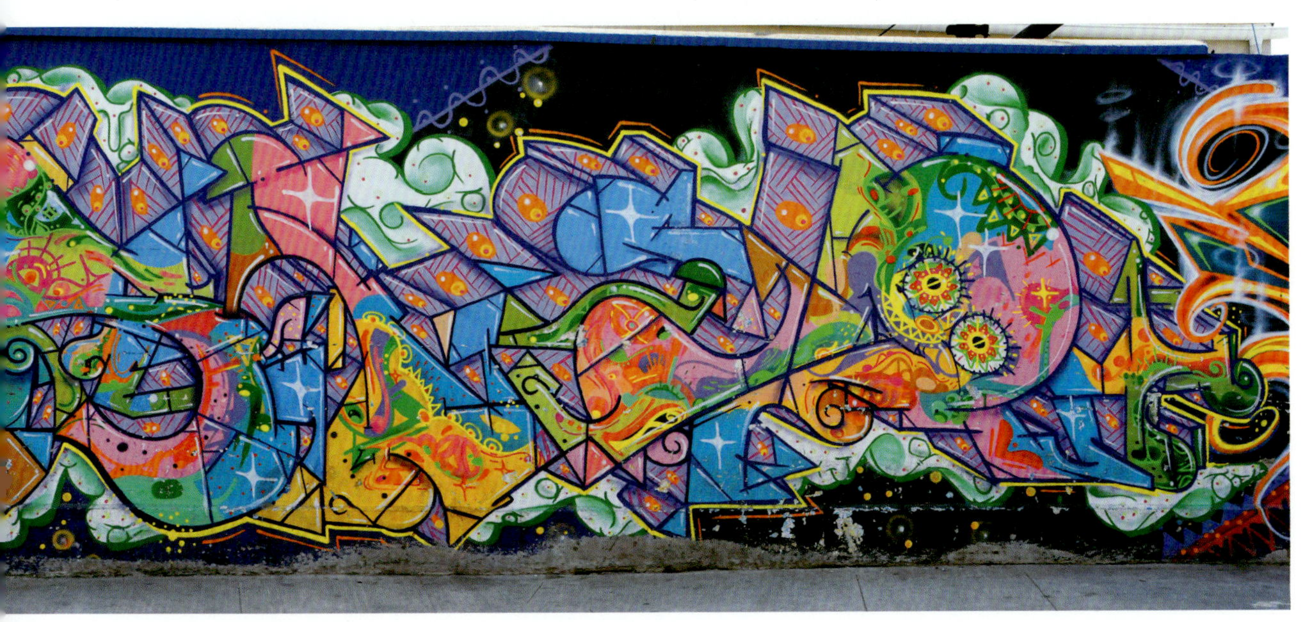

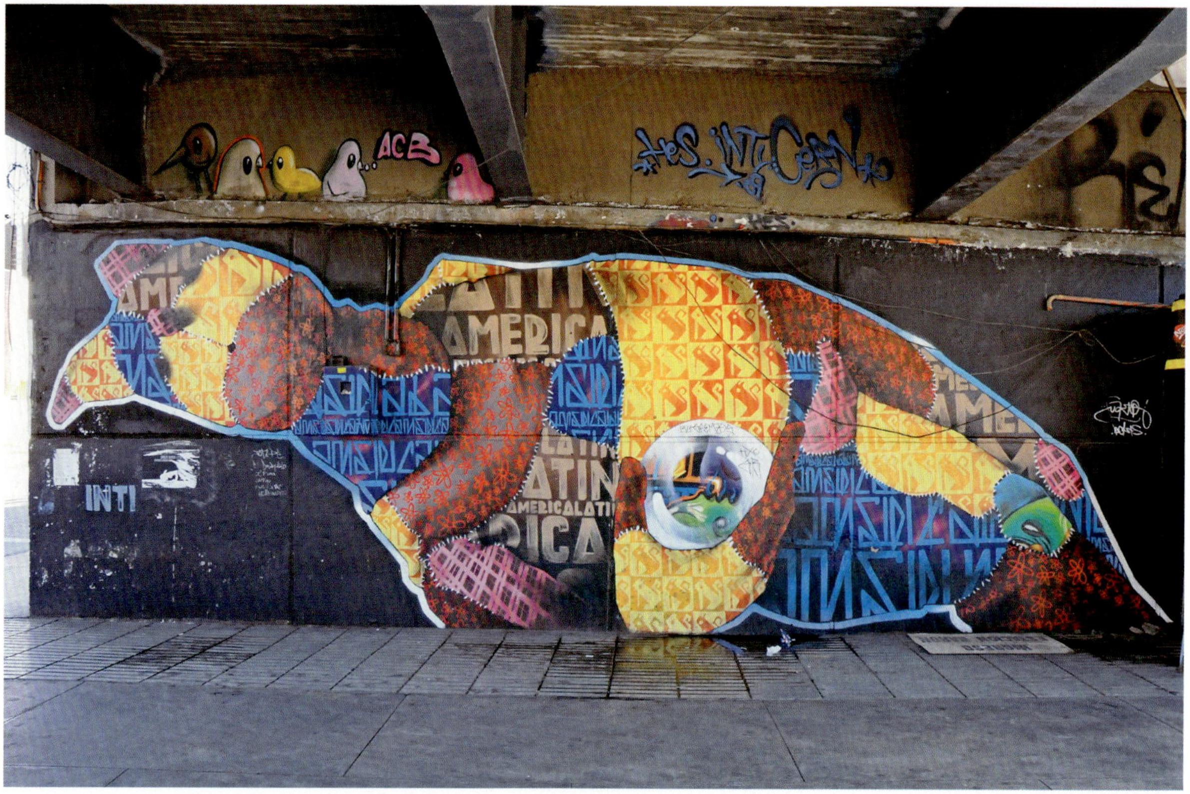
ACB
AMERICA
LATIN
INTI

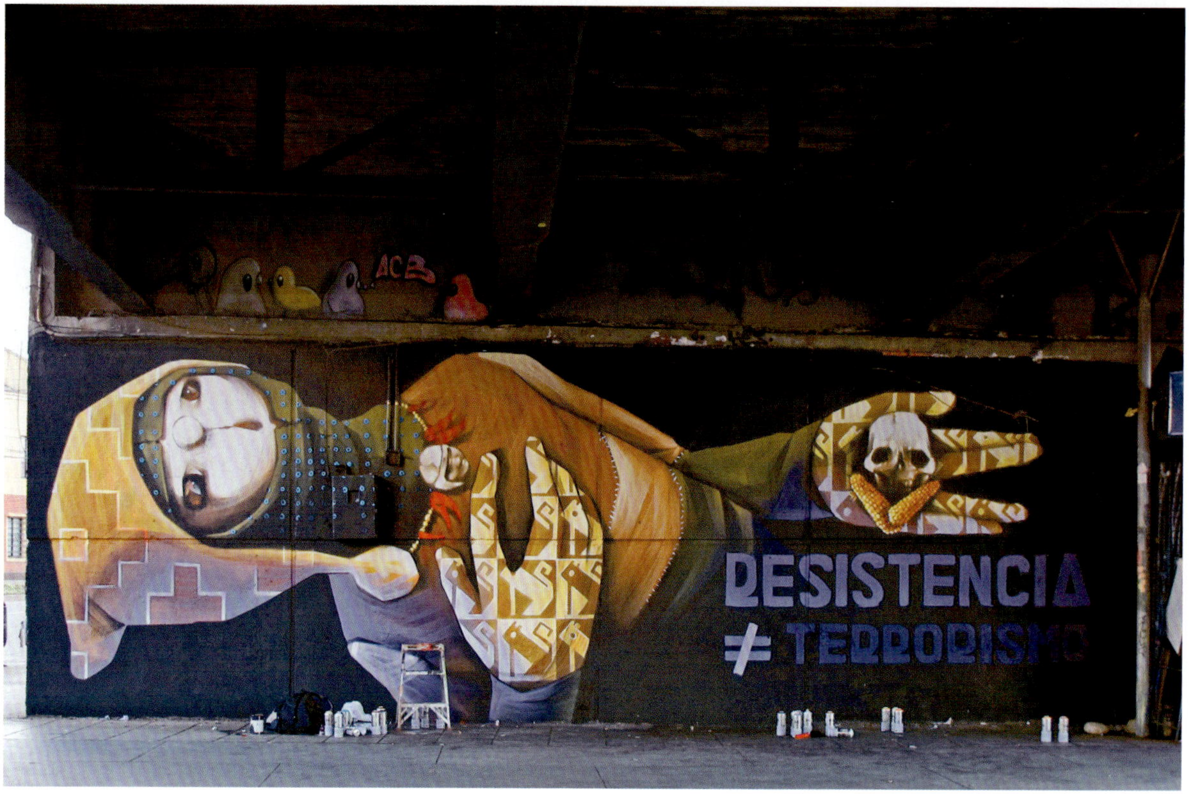
ACB
DESISTENCIA
≠ TERRORISMO

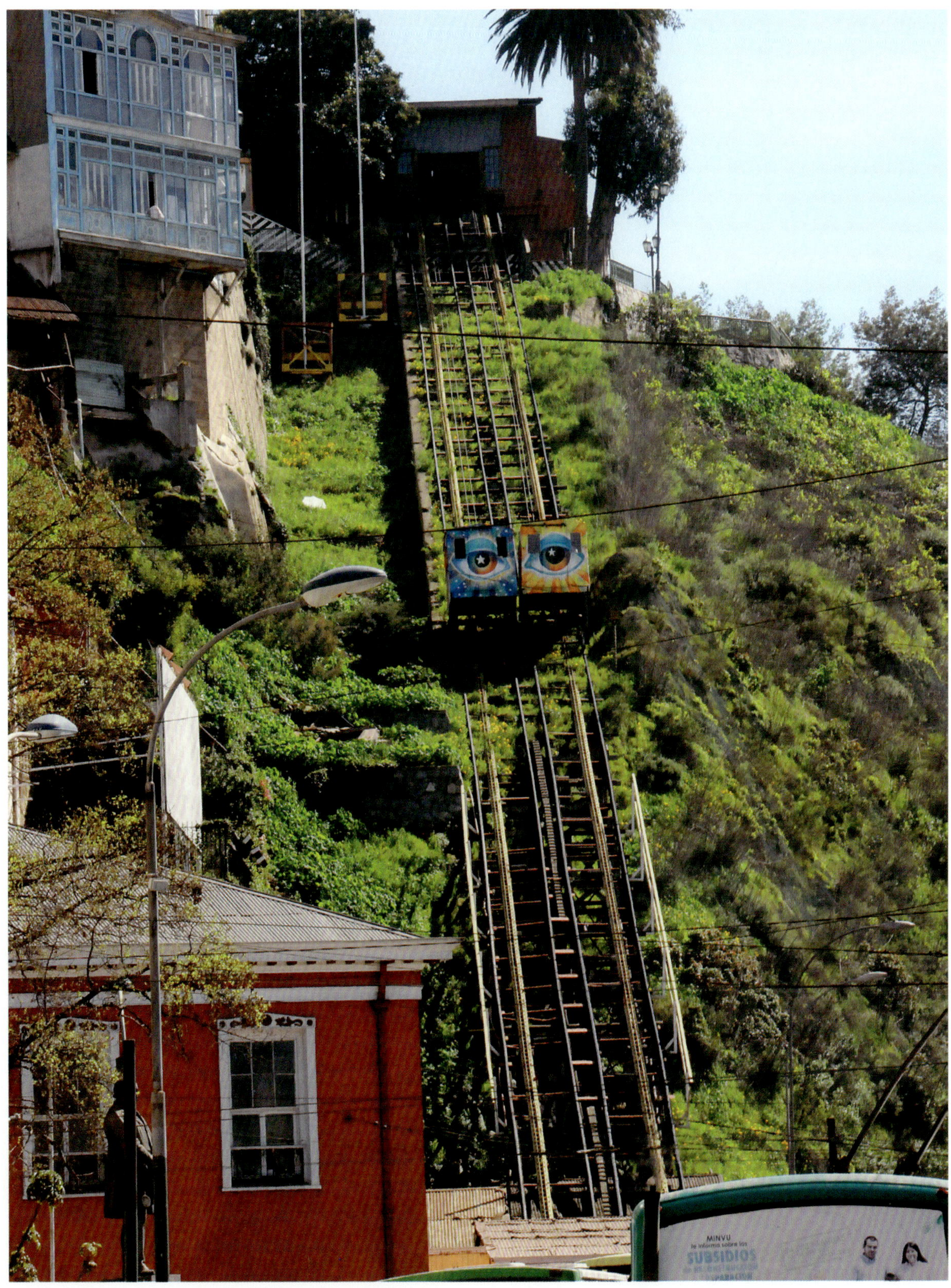
MINVU
SUBSIDIOS

RIGHT:
Irish artist Fin
DAC (Dragon Armoury
Creative).

PAGES 140-1,
CLOCKWISE FROM TOP
LEFT:
Spaik in Mexico/Seher-
One in Mexico City/
Ink Crew in Colombia
(artists include Gris
One, Ospen, Dexs,
Skore, Skida and Kops)/
Gris-One in Colombia.

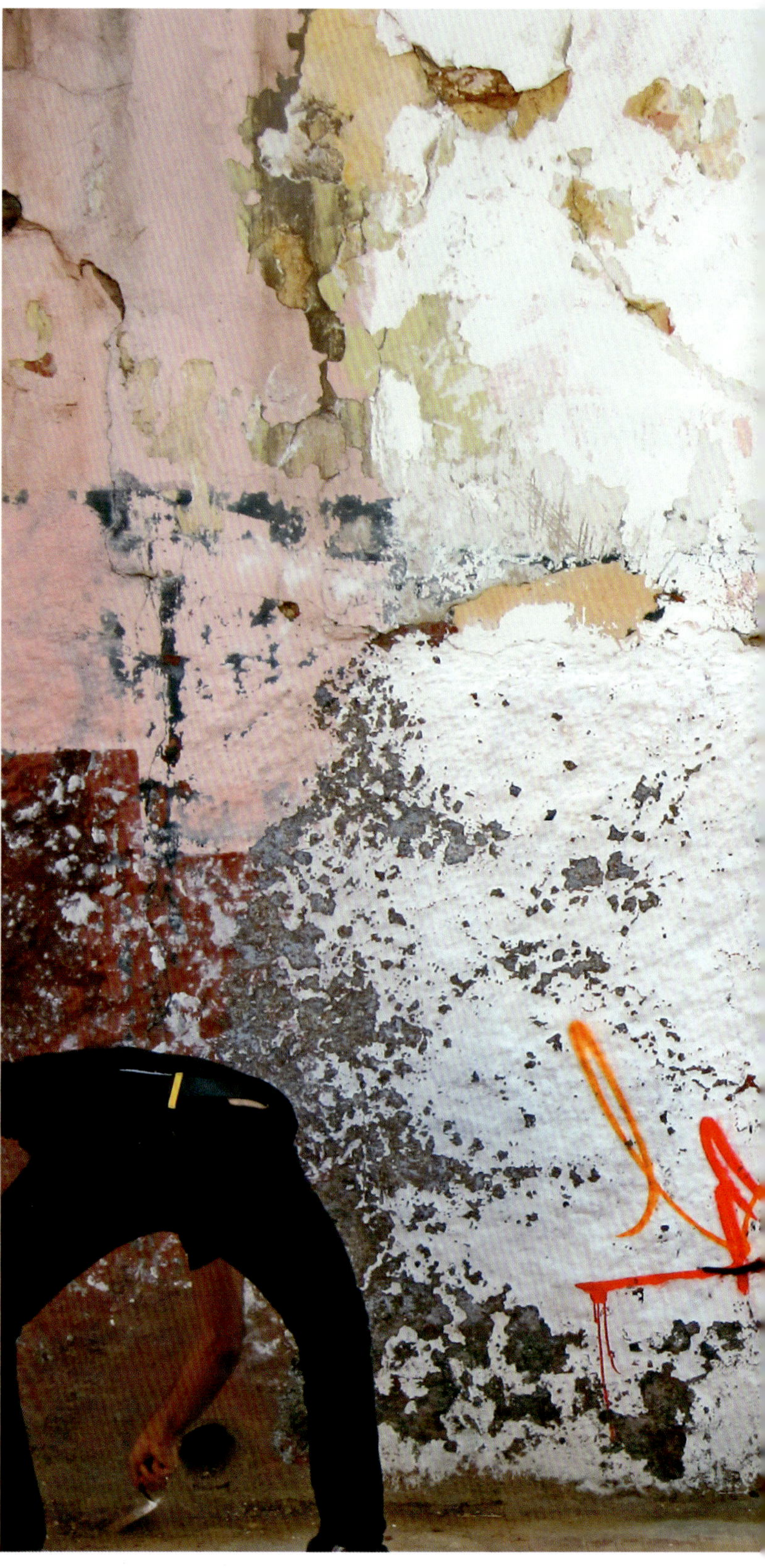

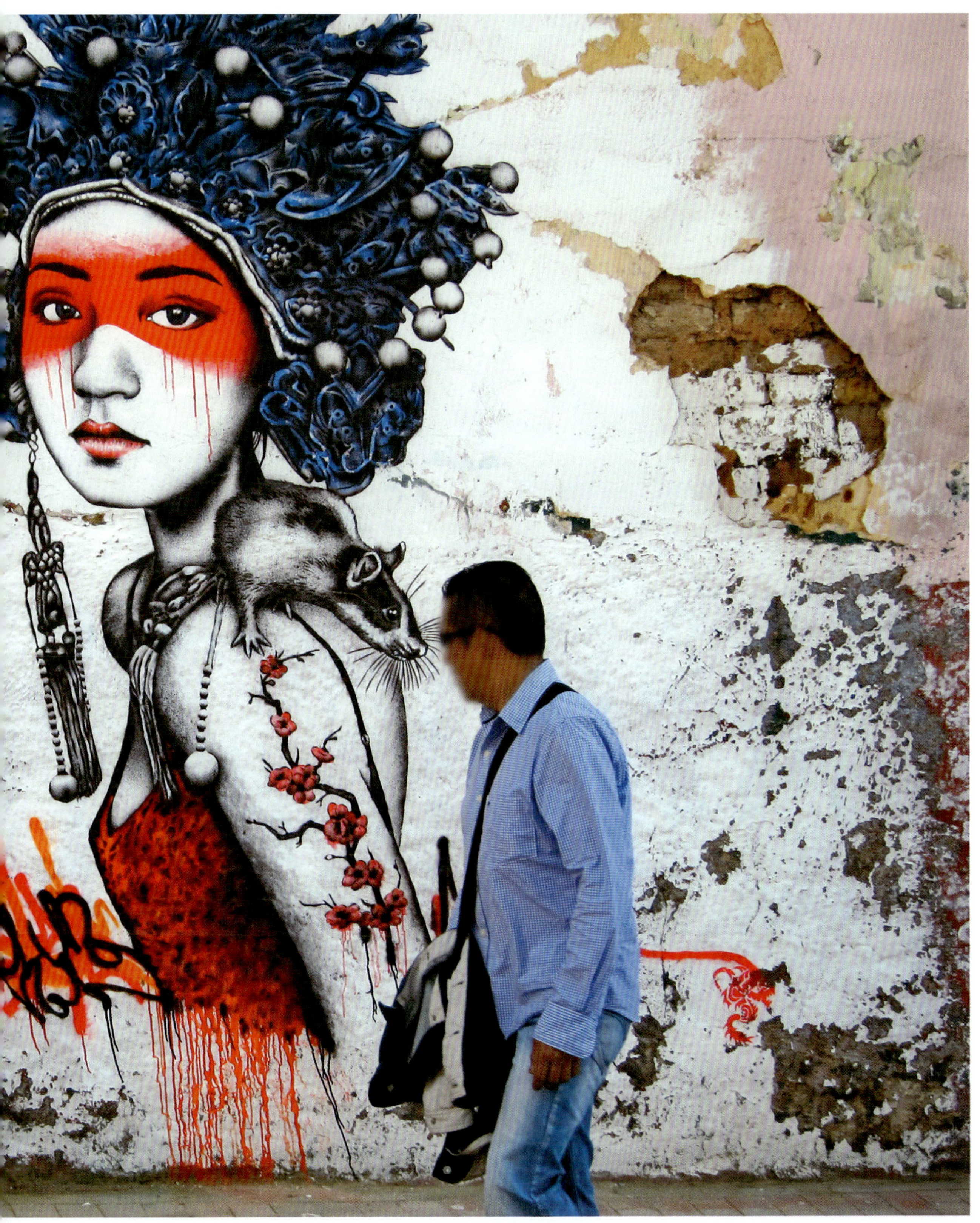

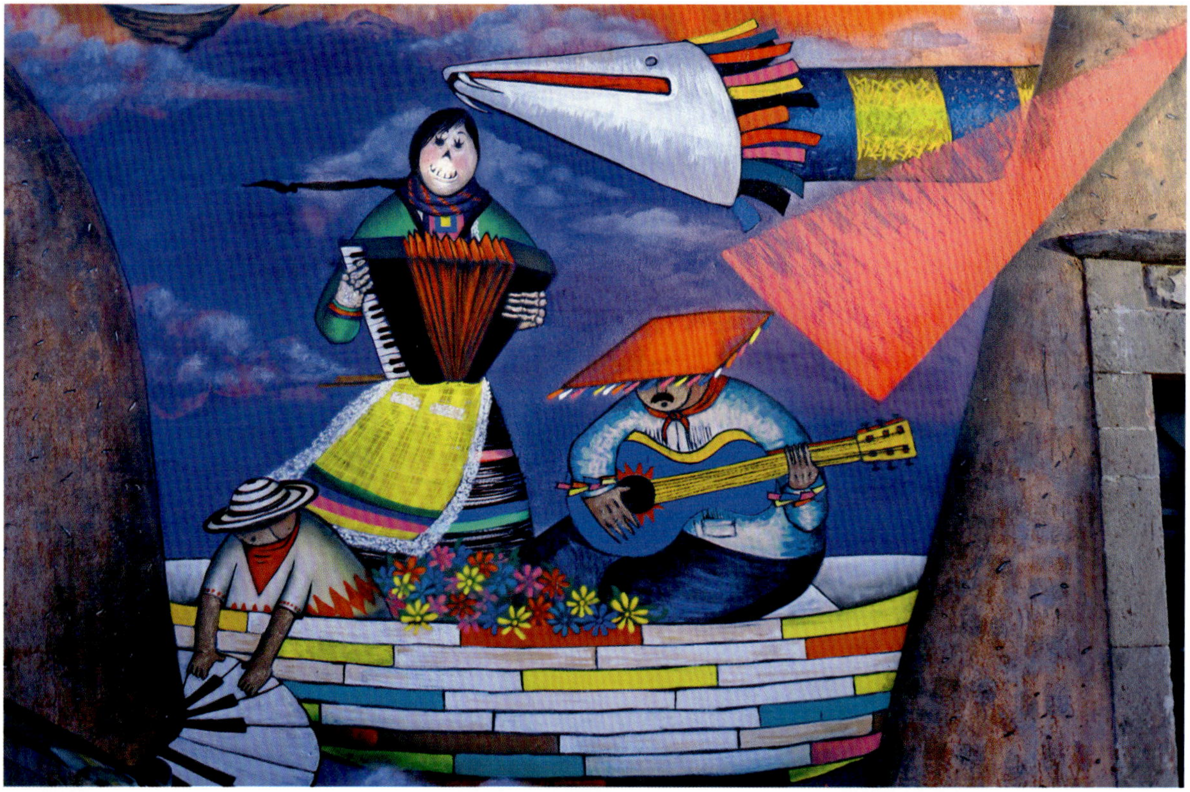

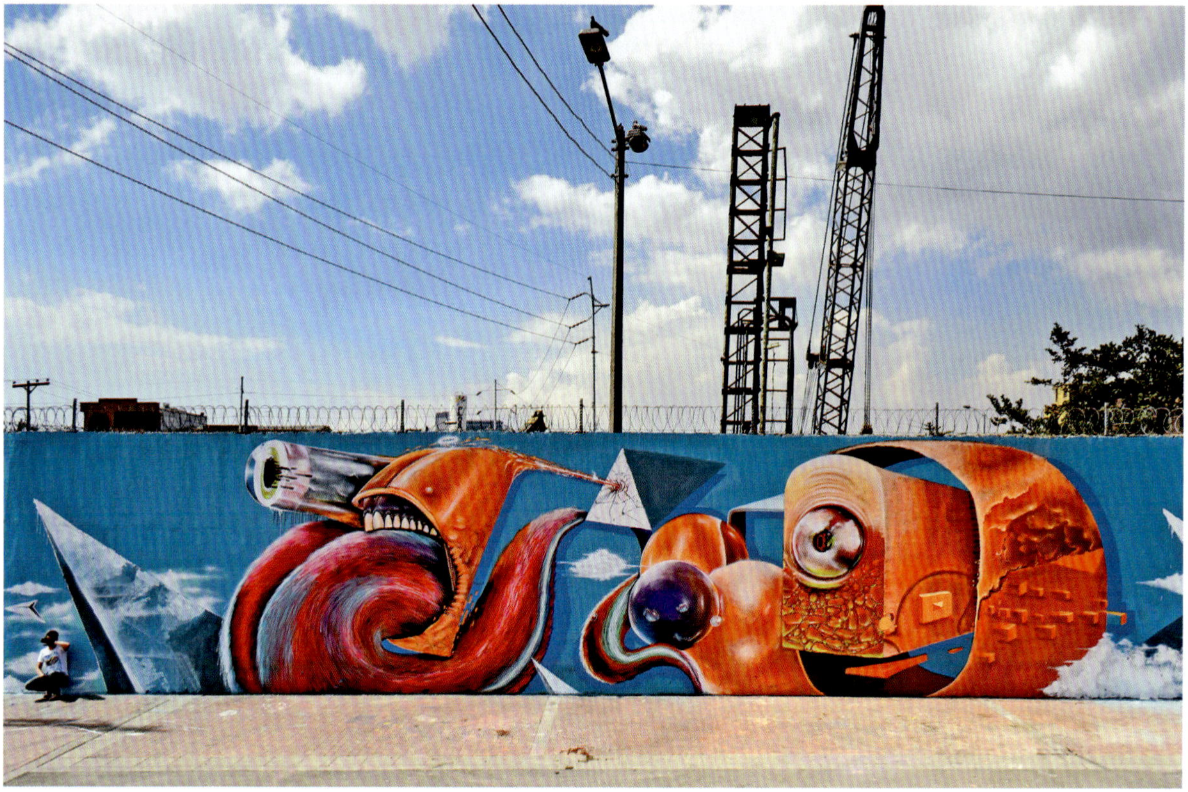

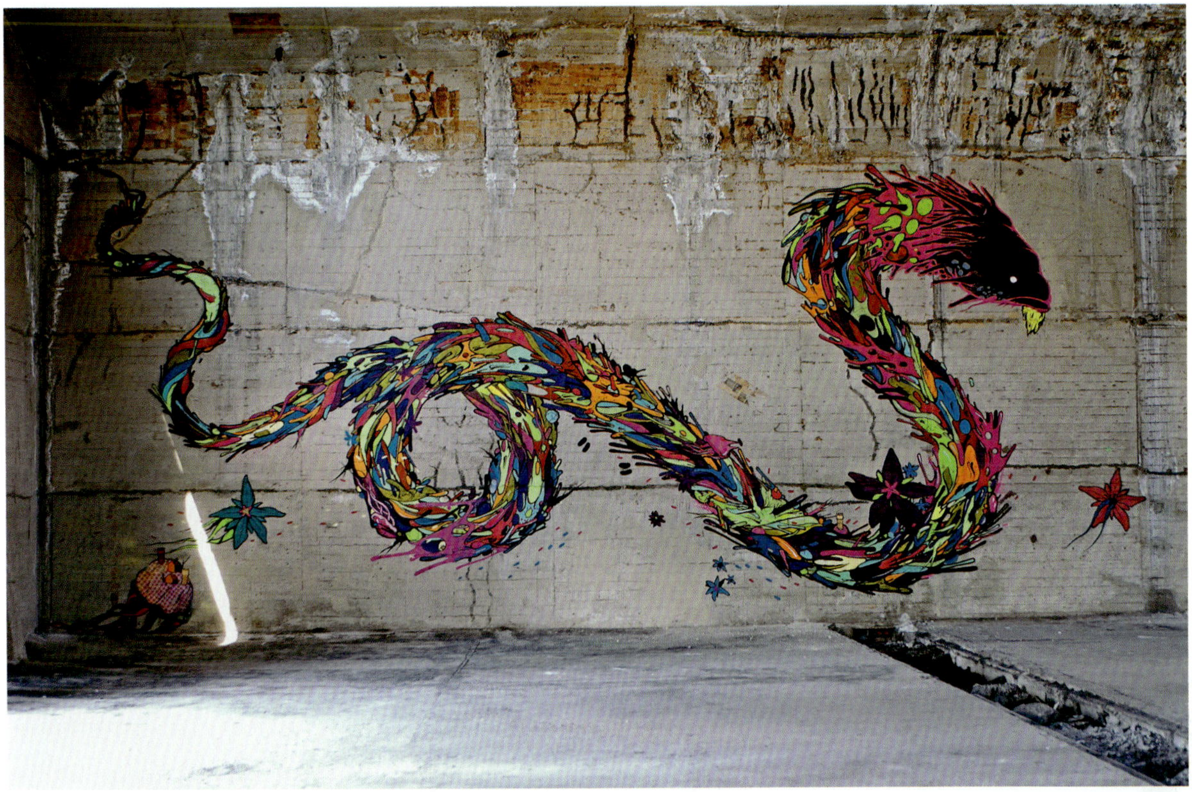

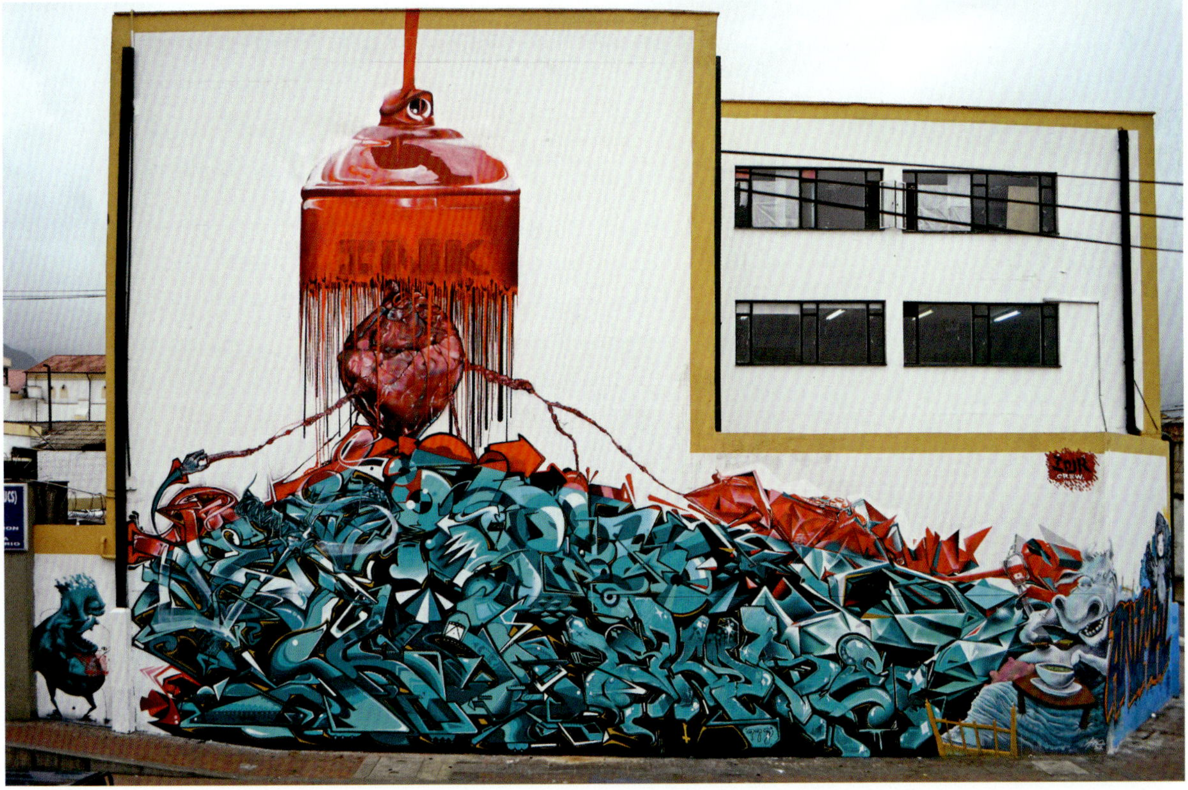

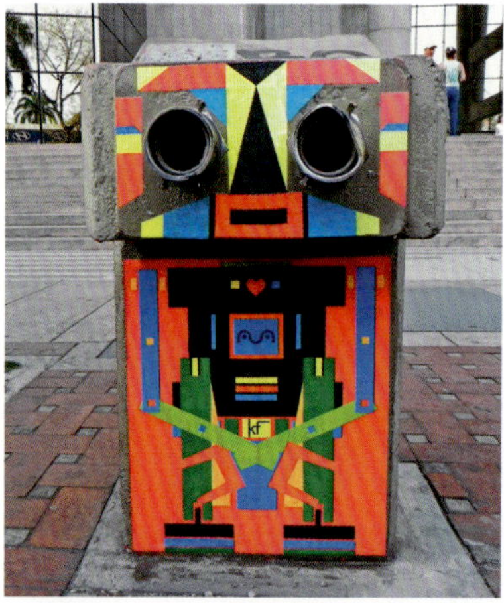

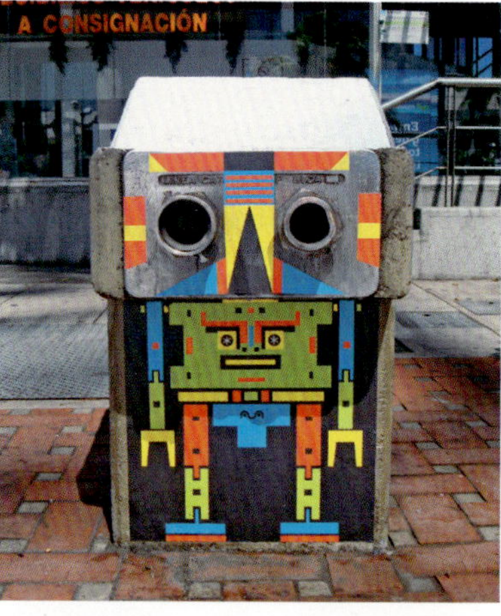

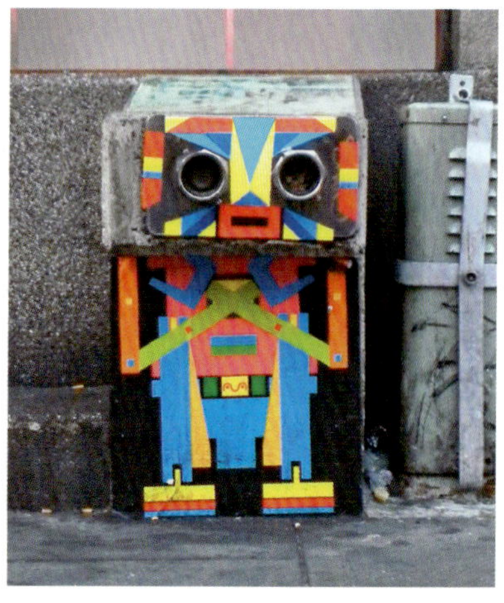

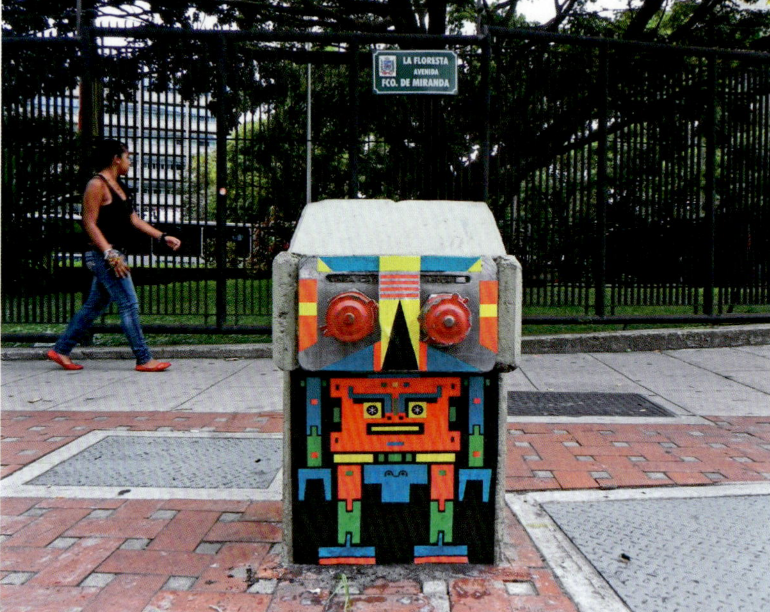

THESE PAGES:
Fire hydrants by Flix
Robotico.

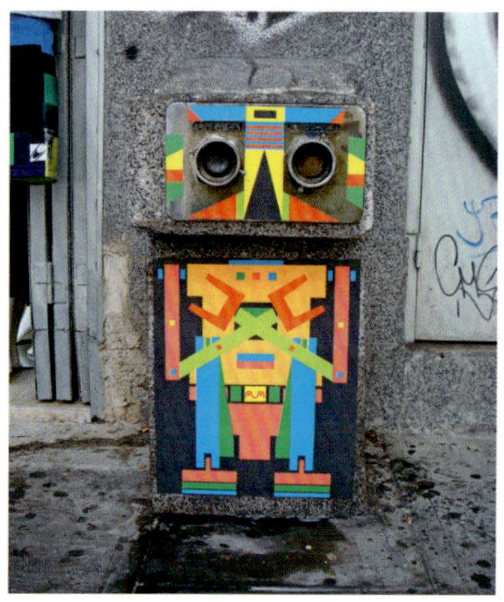

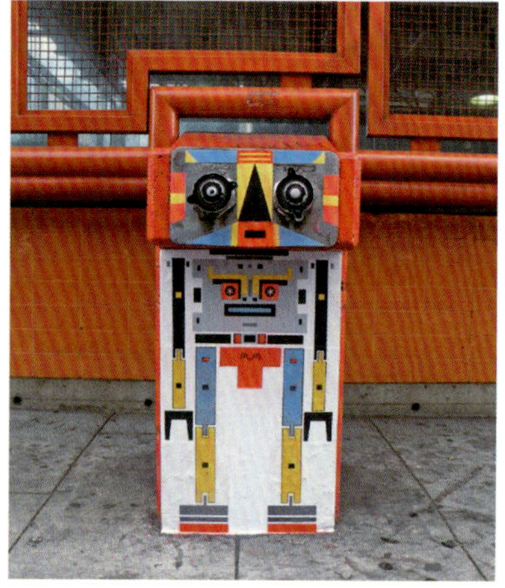

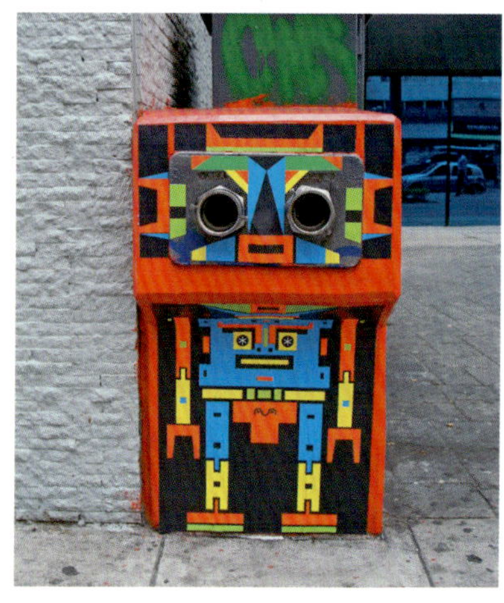

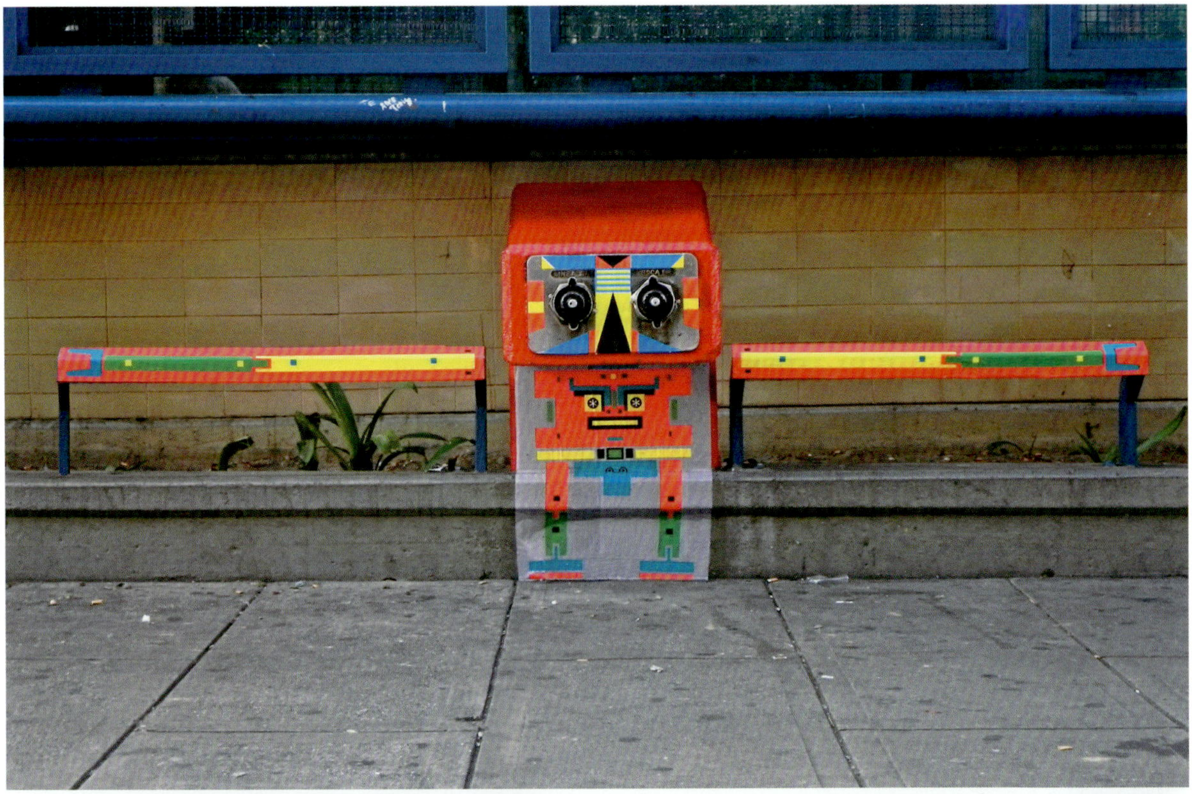

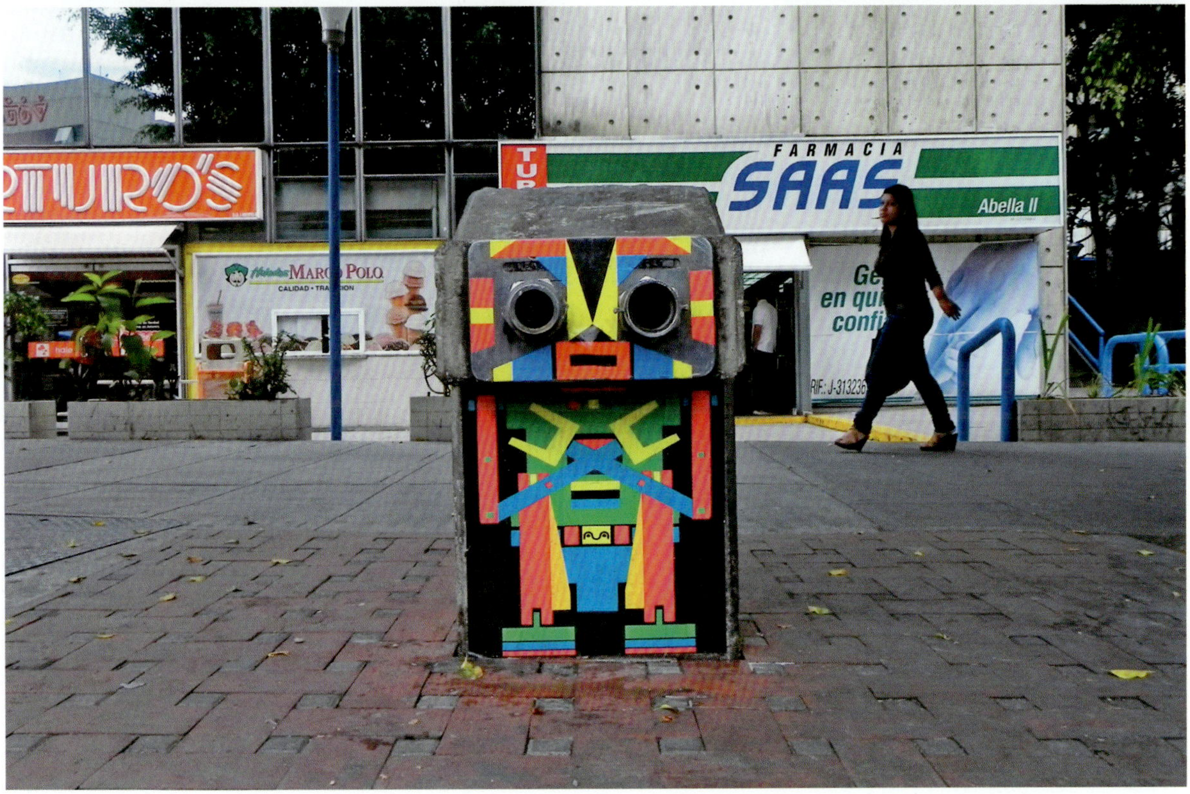

TURO'S
Helados MARCO POLO
CALIDAD · TRADICIÓN
TU
FARMACIA
SAAS
Abella II
Ge
en qu
confi
RIF.: J-31323

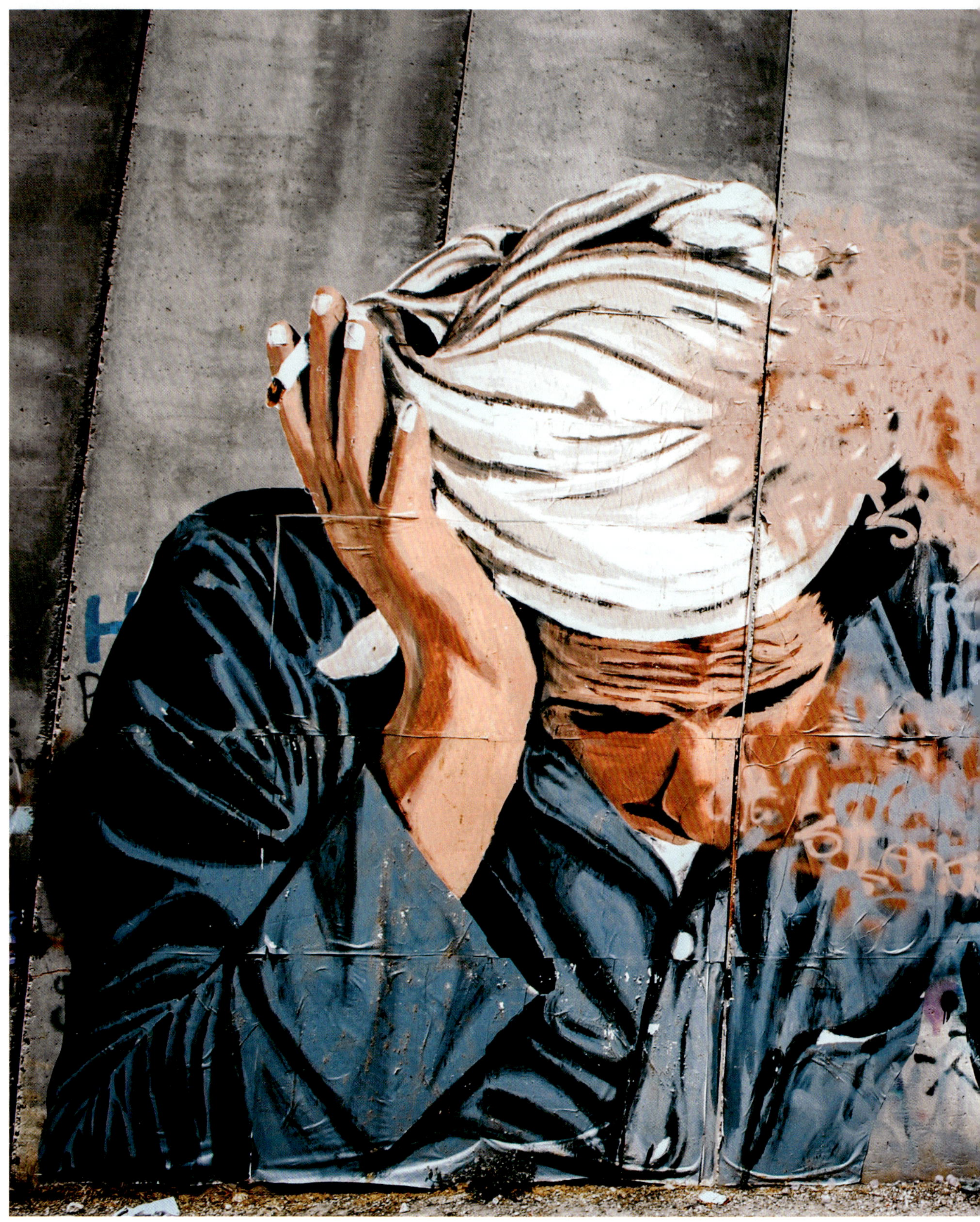

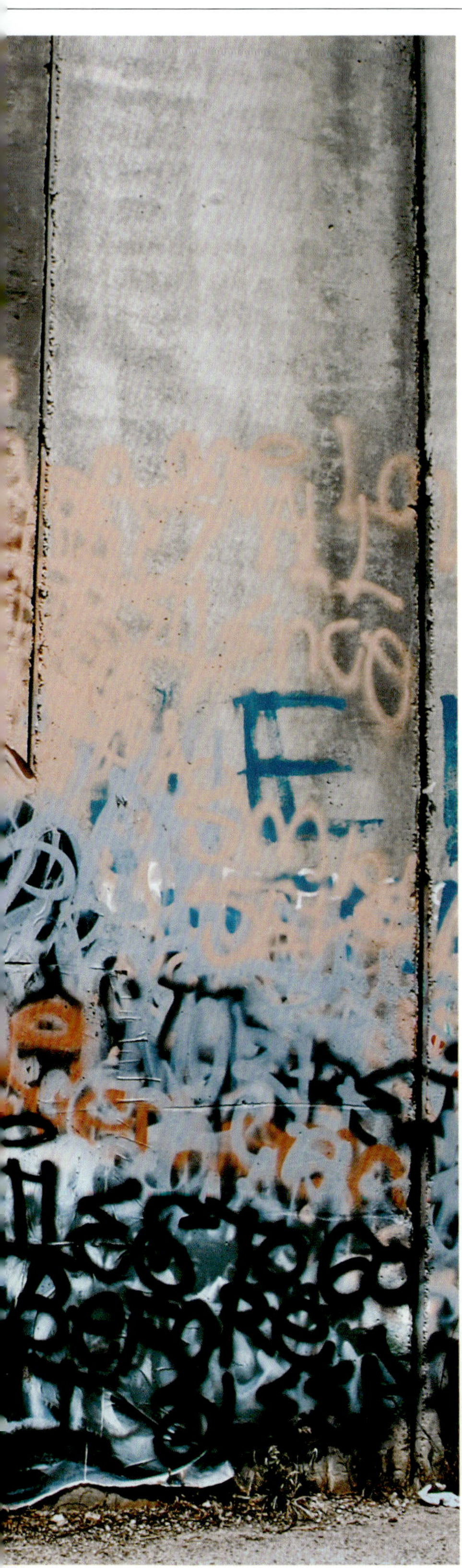

FROM LEFT:
Shai Dahan on the West
Bank/Jack from TML
(Three Meaningless
Letters) in Jerusalem.

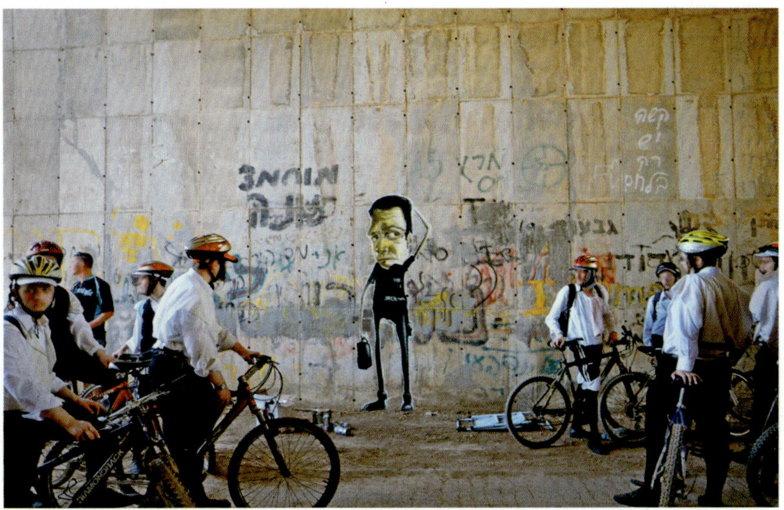

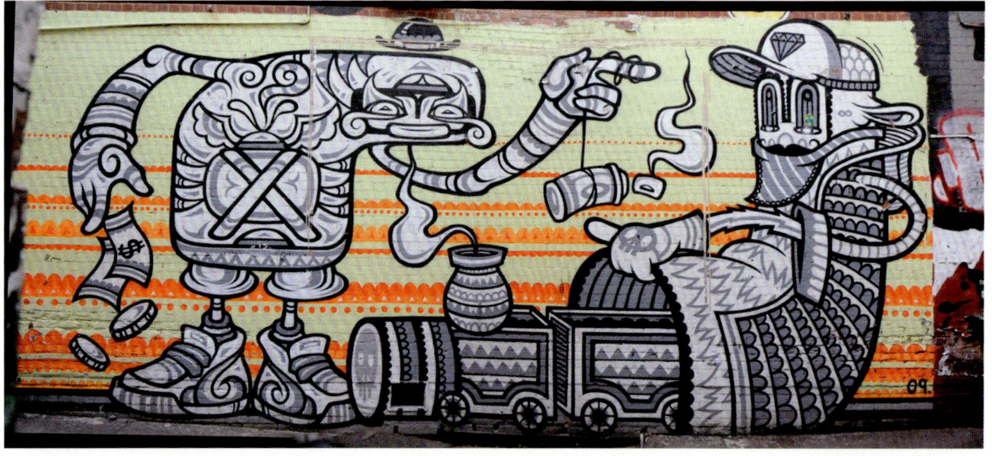

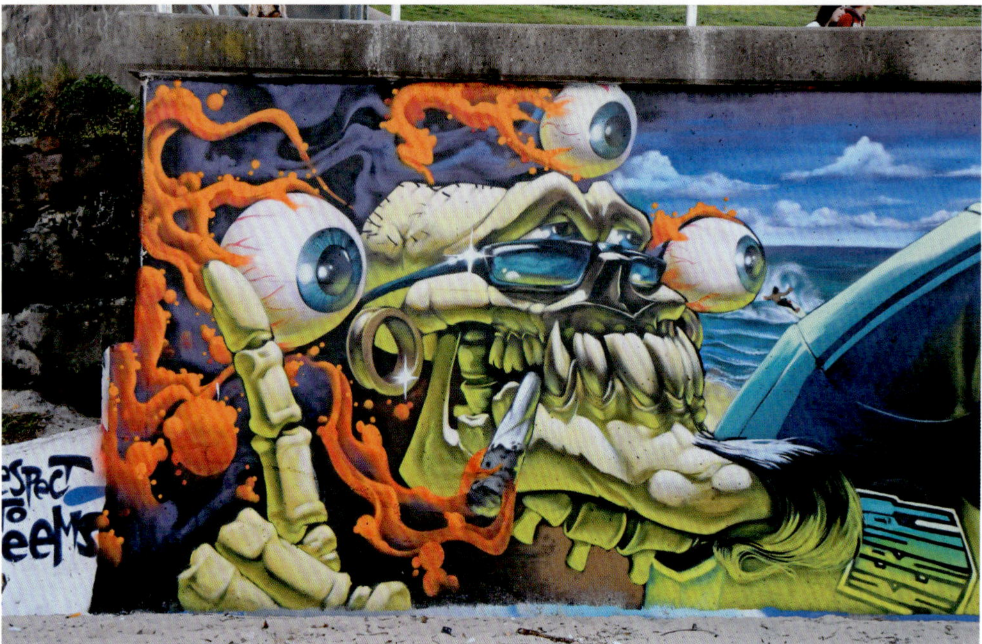

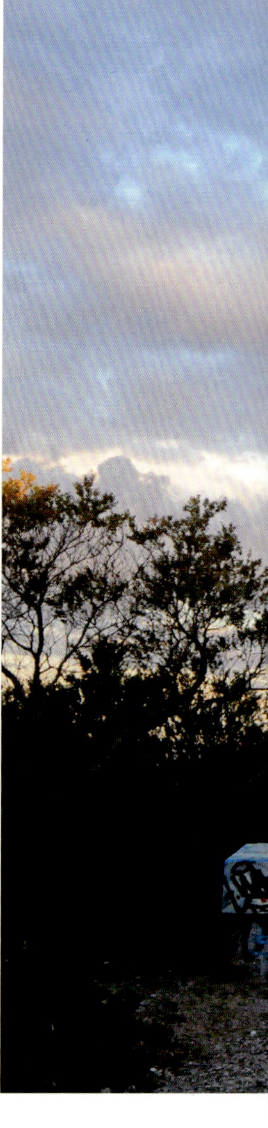

know Australia well and I've seen and photographed many great pieces on my trips to Sydney and Melbourne. Melbourne was the first city I ever visited (before São Paulo) where I felt the art had 'won'. Usually, I can cover most of the art in a major city in just a few days. After six days in Melbourne I was still running flat out with new places to photograph. Melbourne – I'll be back!

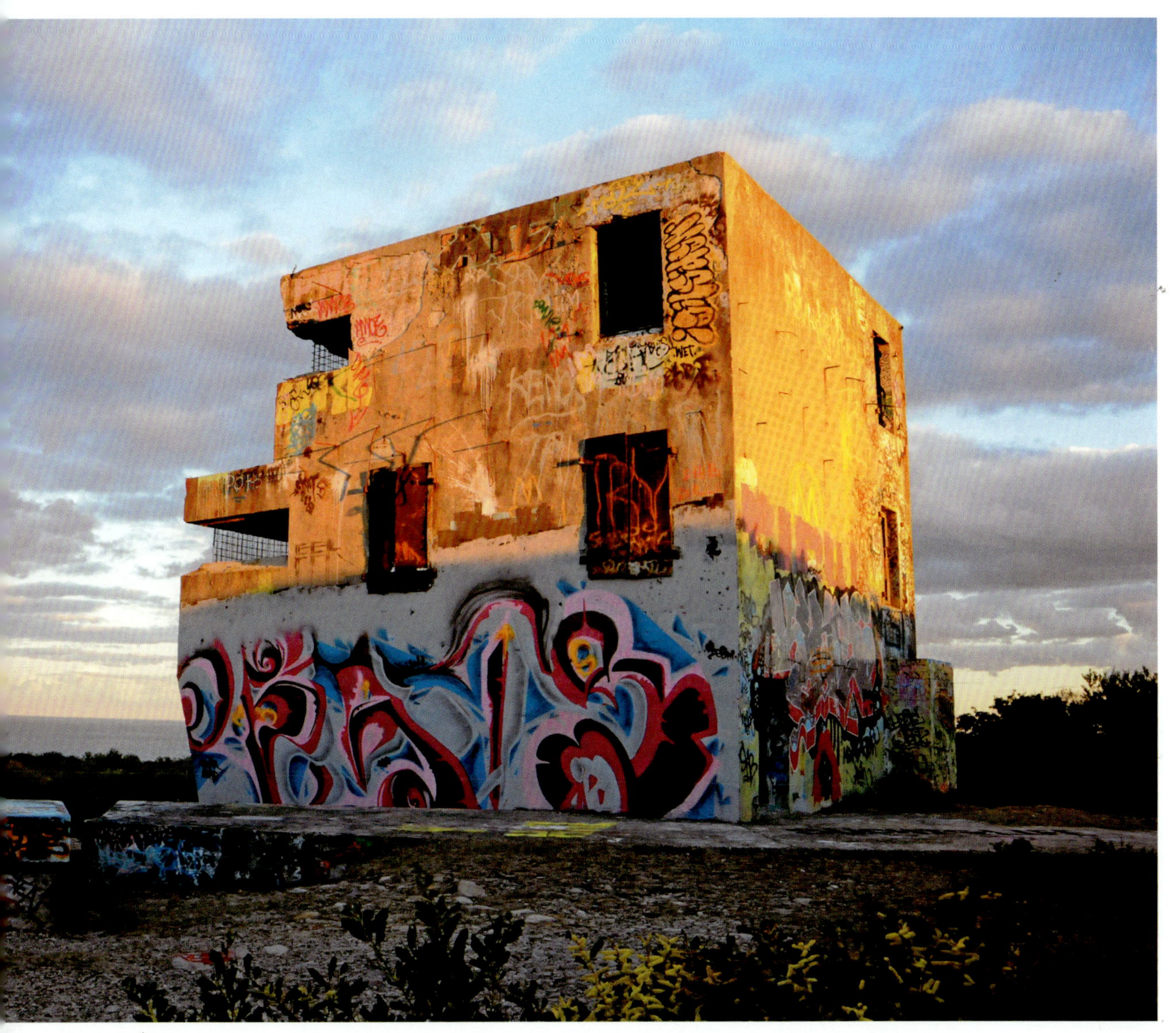

CLOCKWISE FROM TOP
LEFT:
Phibs in Melbourne/
Unknown artist at
the empty military
buildings, Malabar
Battery in Sydney/
Mexico's Peque from
VRS Crew in Sydney.

PAGES 148-9:
An abandoned factory
in Sydney. (The light
is natural! A hailstorm
had punched holes in
the rusty roof years
earlier and by the
time I visited the floor
was wet because of the
recent rain, making it
reflective.)

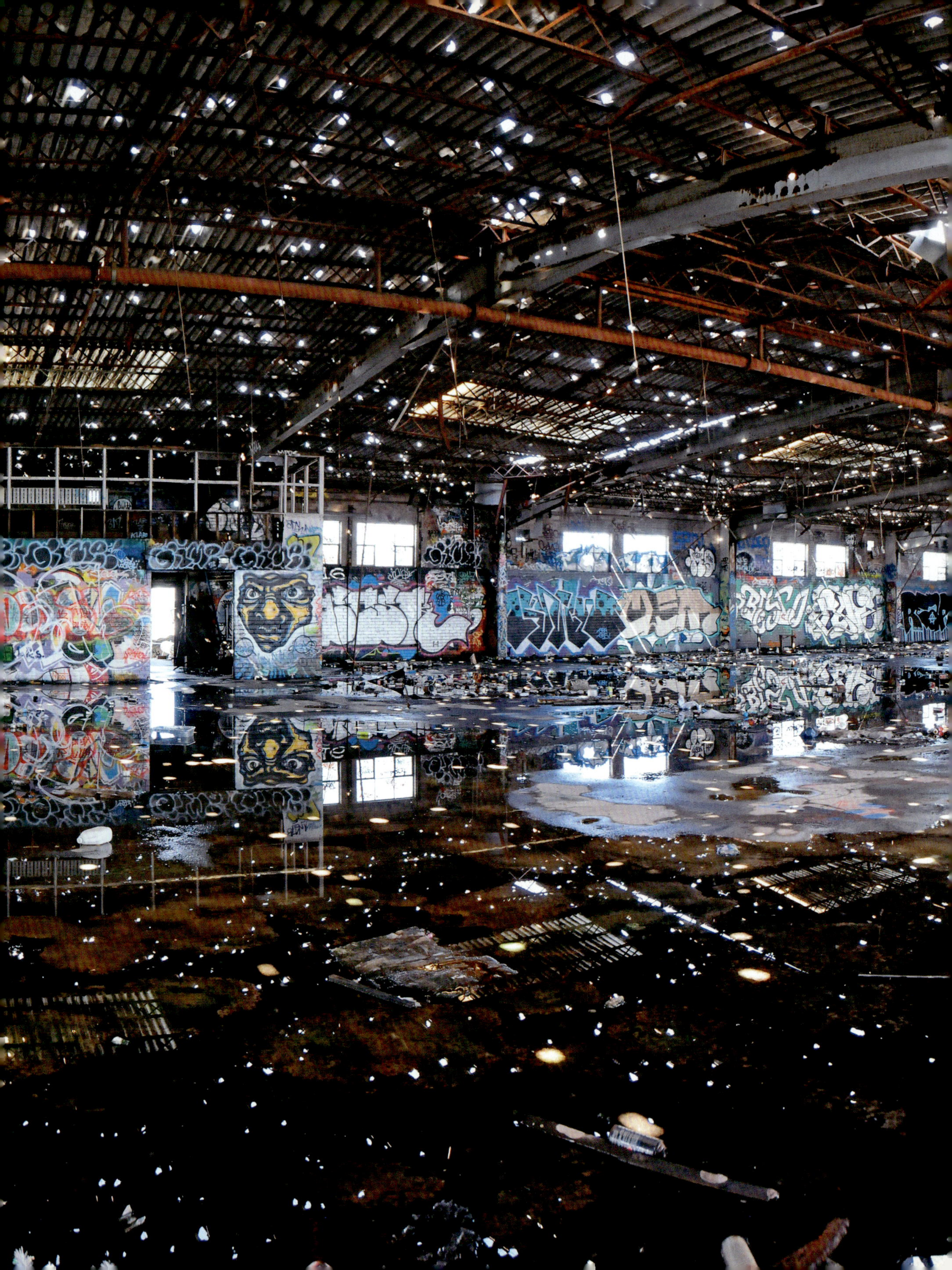

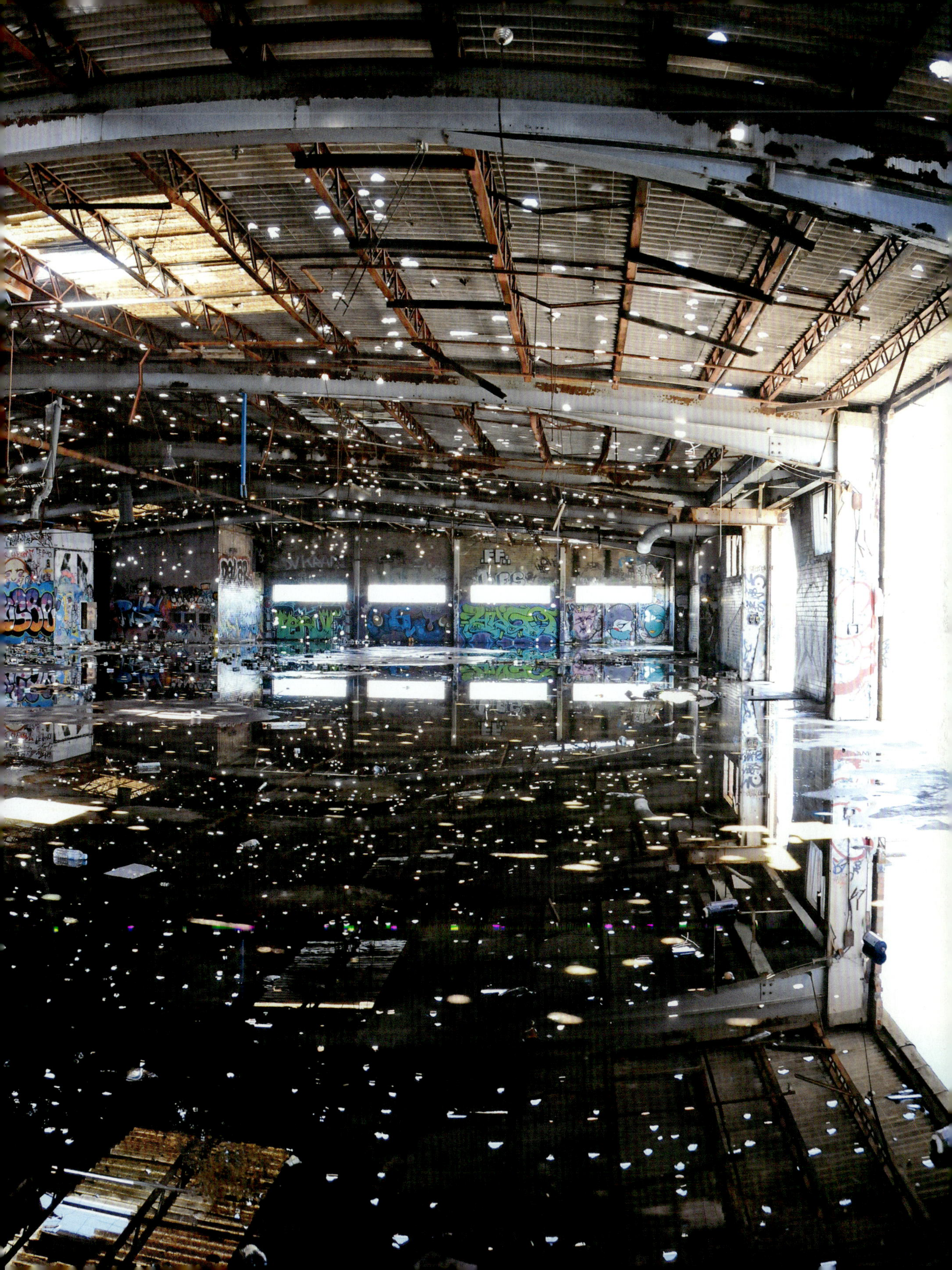

FROM LEFT:
Fintan Magee in Sydney/
Vexta in Melbourne.

PAGES 152-3,
CLOCKWISE FROM TOP
LEFT:
Makatron/Guido
Van Helten/Rone/
Collaboration between
Meggs and Rone in
Melbourne.

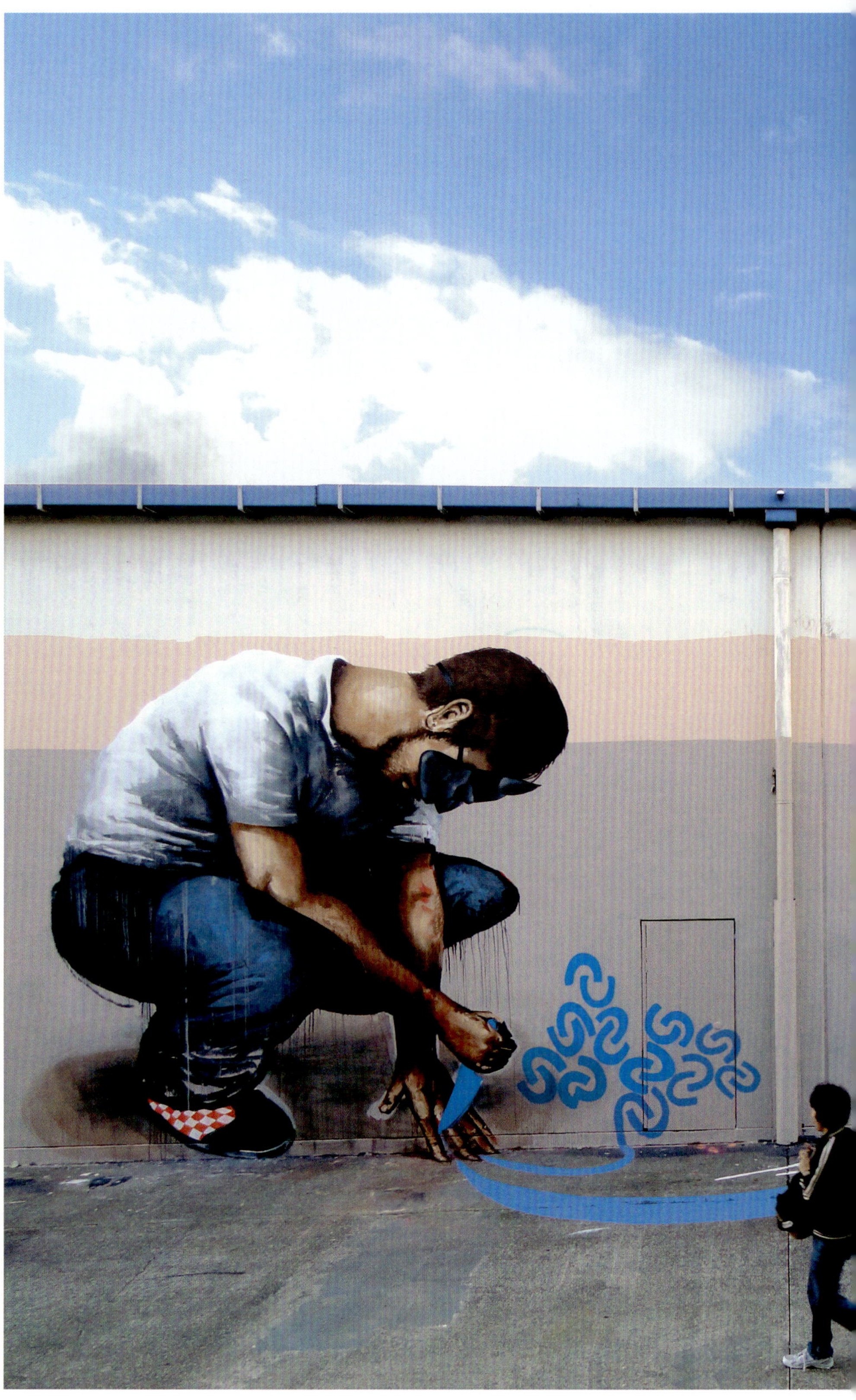

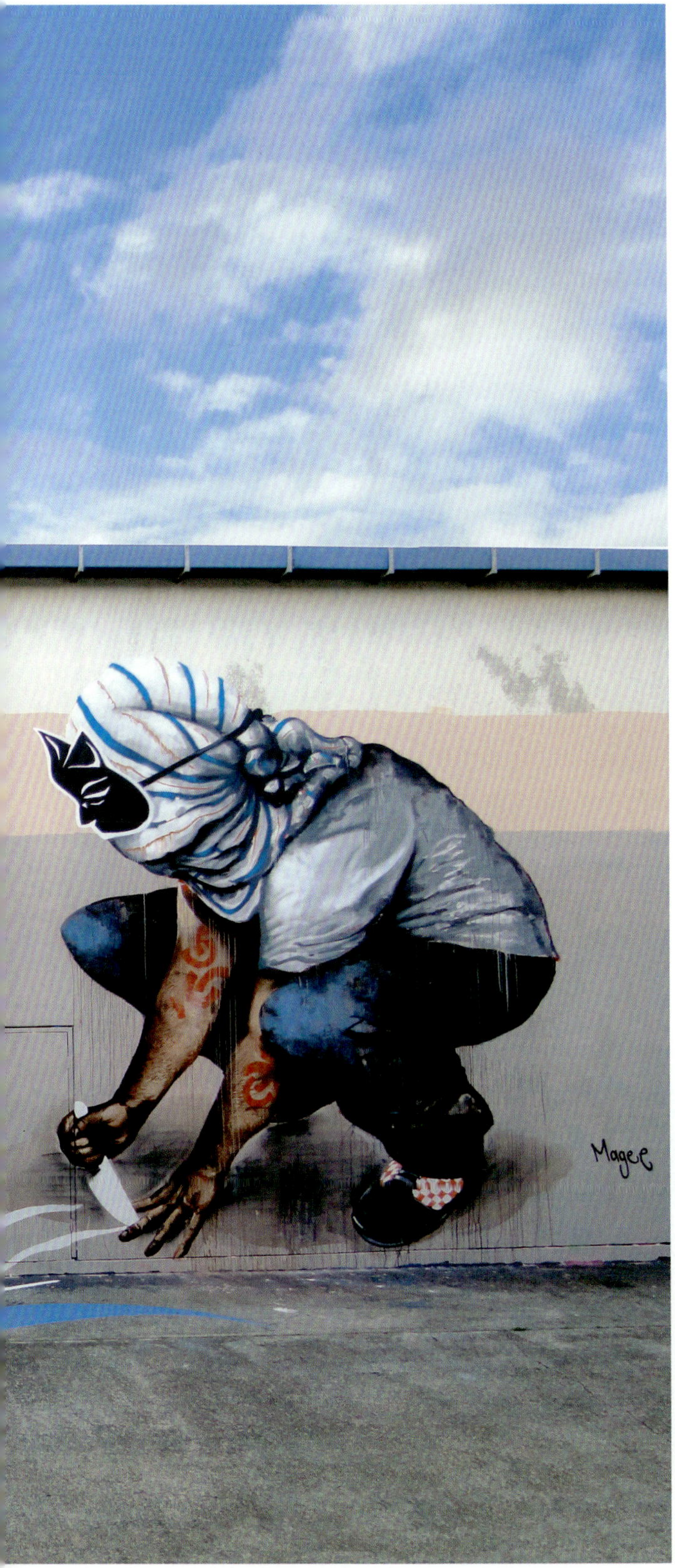

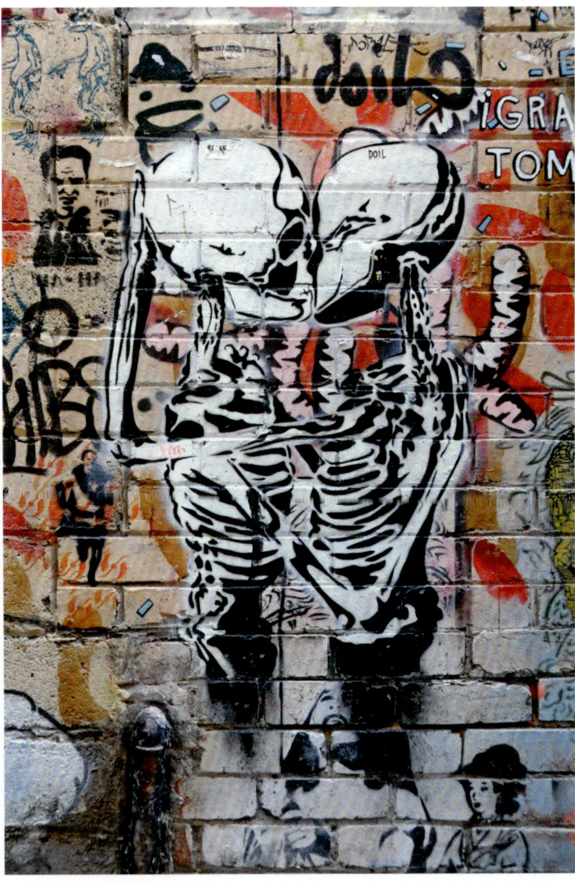

Magee

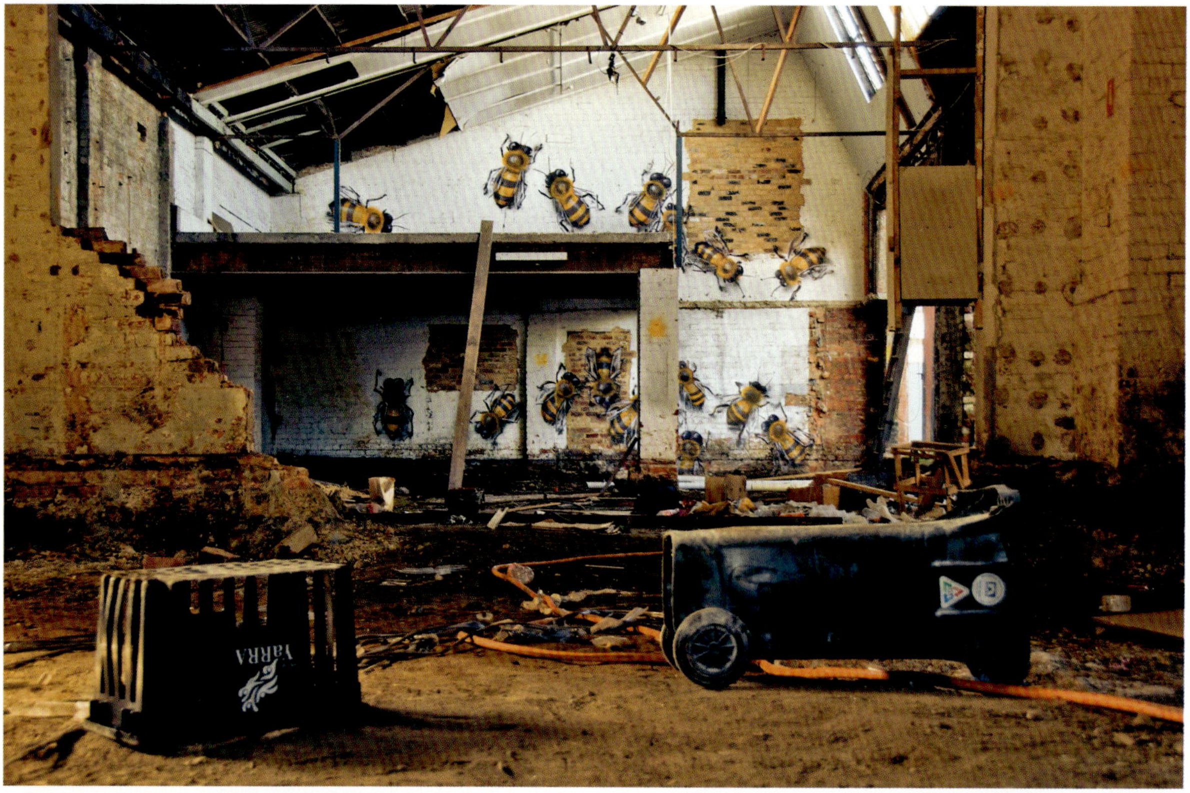

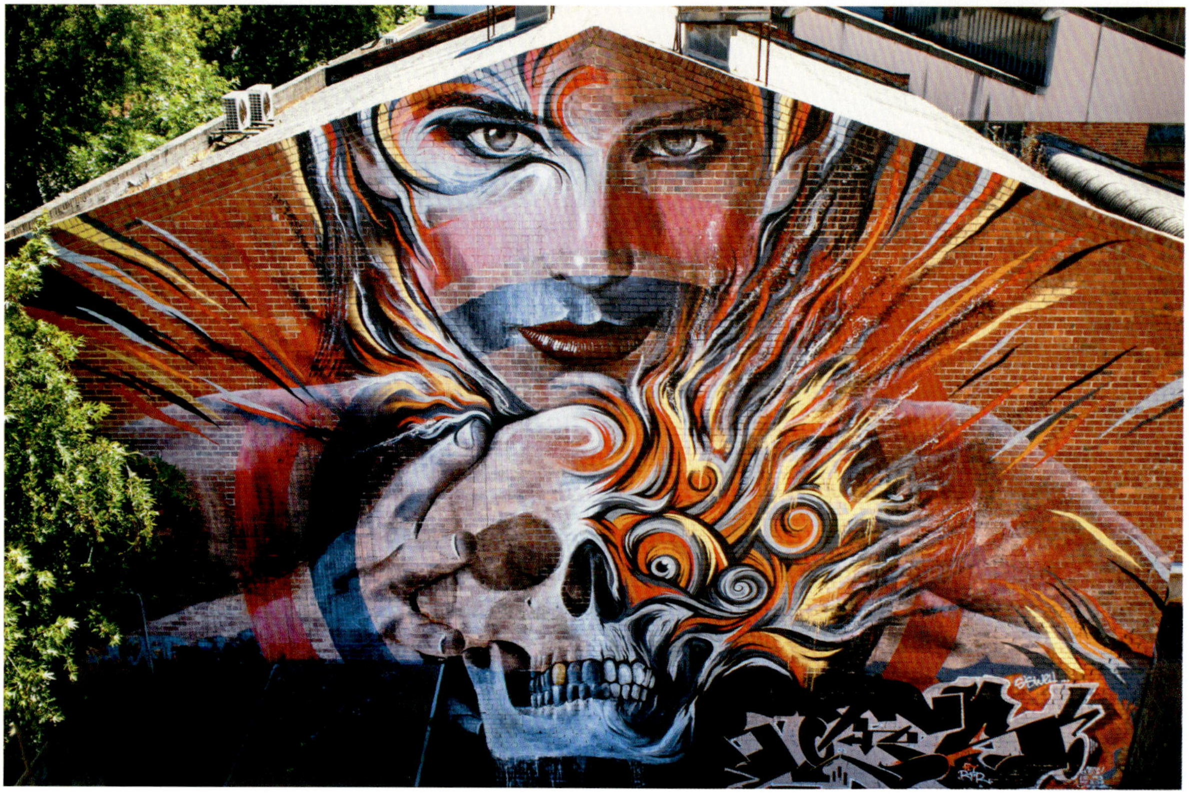

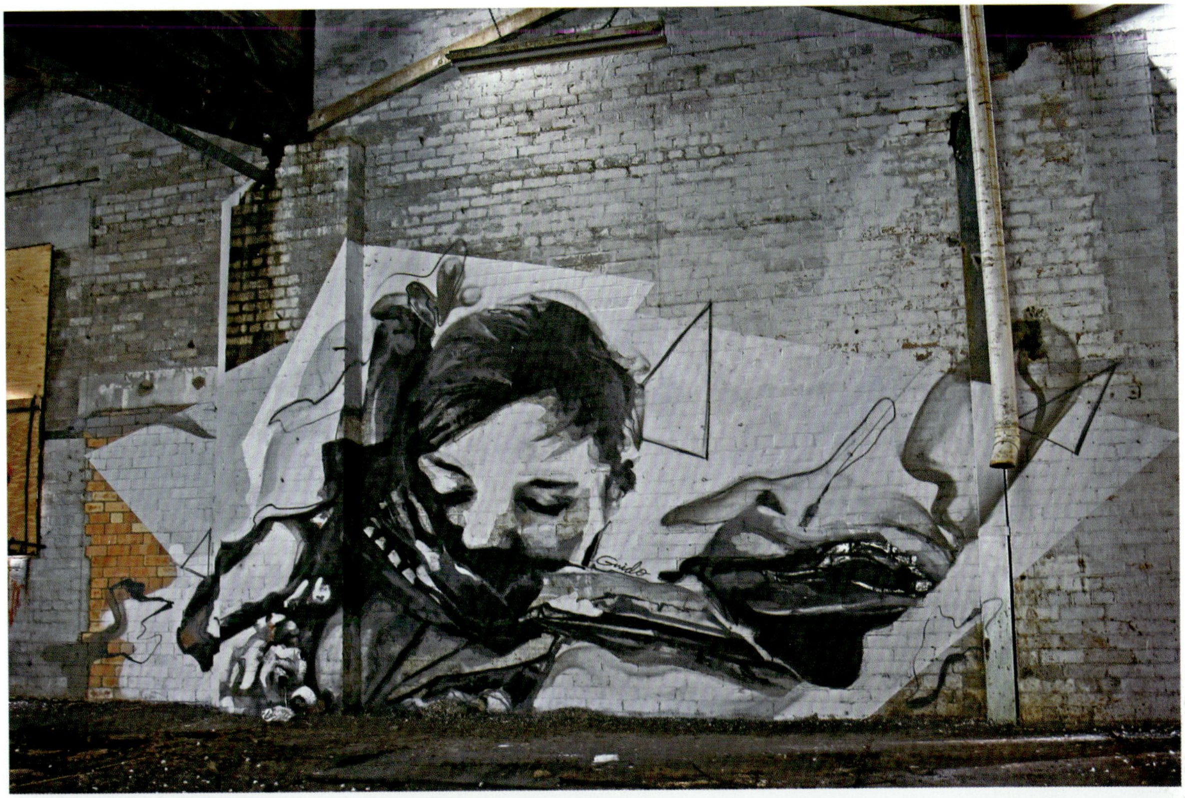

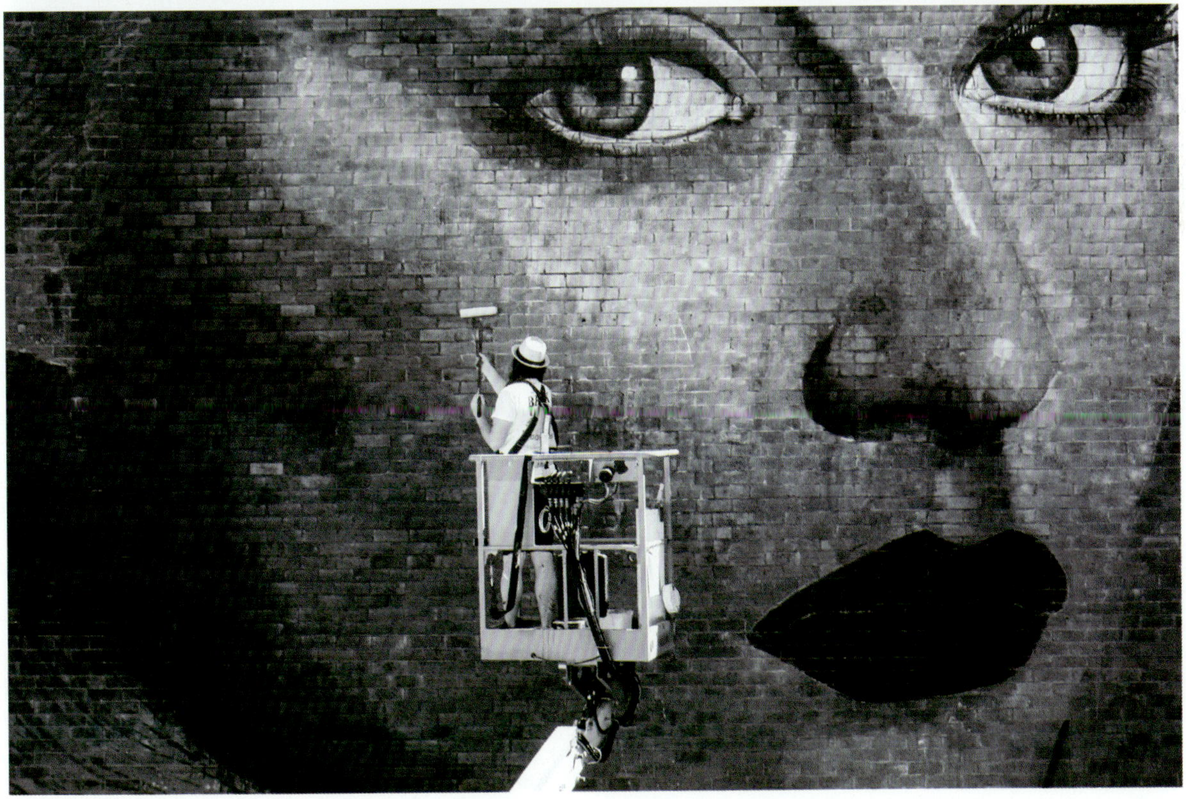

CLOCKWISE FROM
BELOW:
South African artist
Faith 47 in China/JNJ
Crew in South Korea/
Ima-One and Suiko
in Japan.

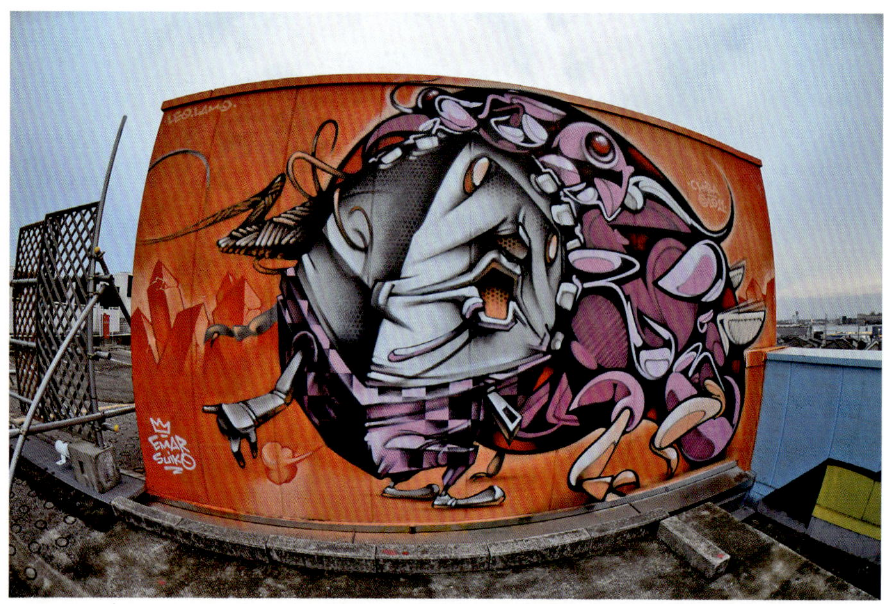

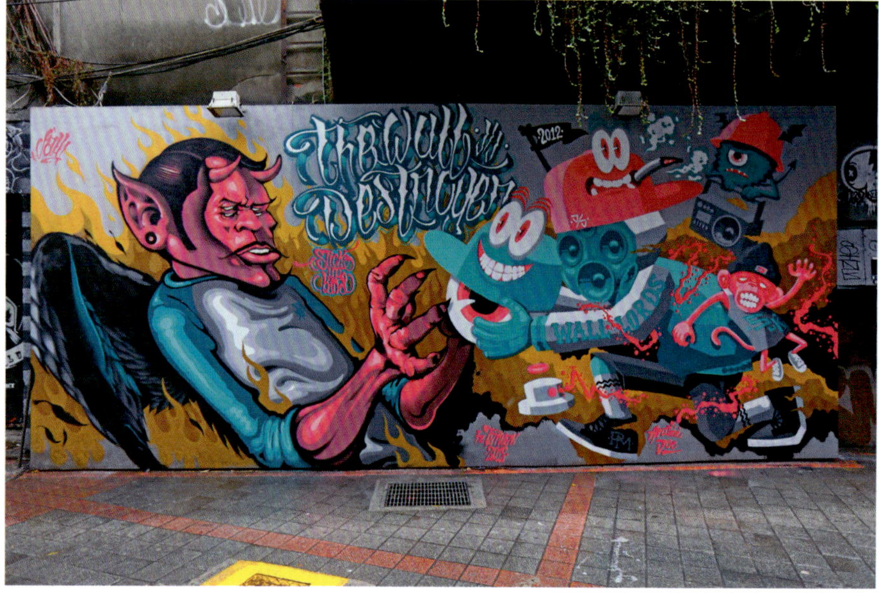

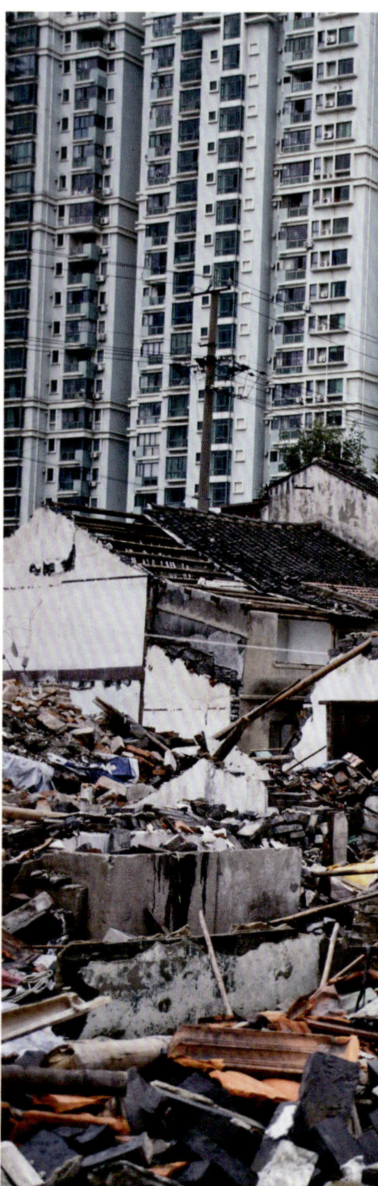

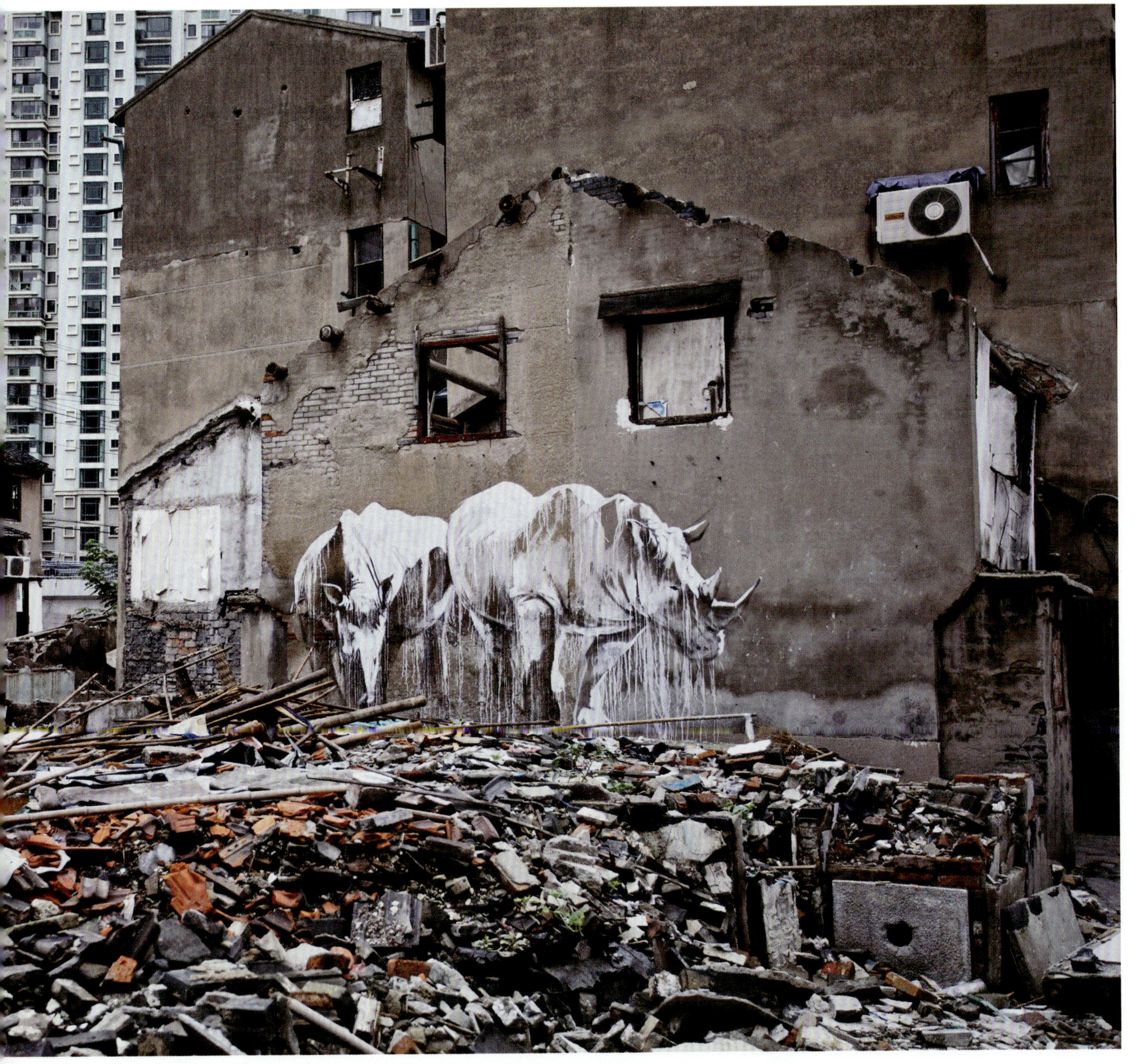

CLOCKWISE FROM
RIGHT:
South Africa's Faith
47/Australia's Makatron
in Cape Town.

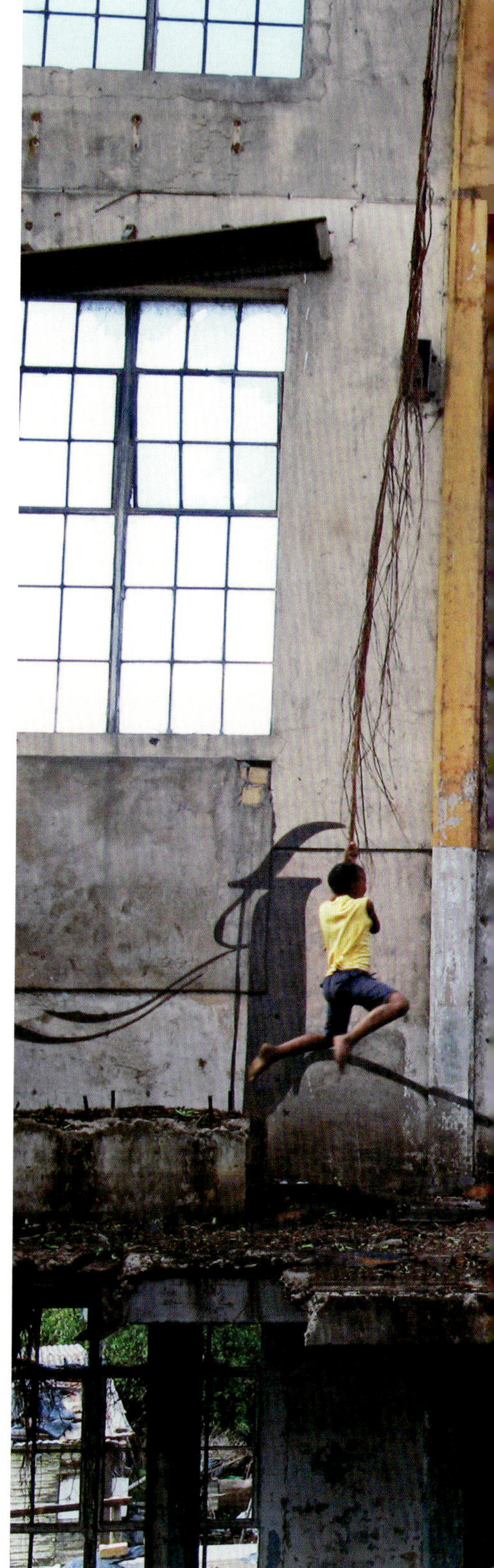

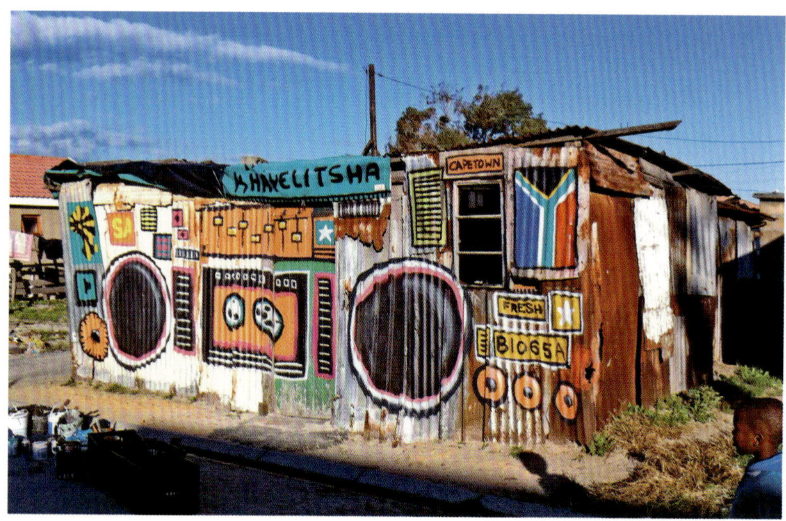

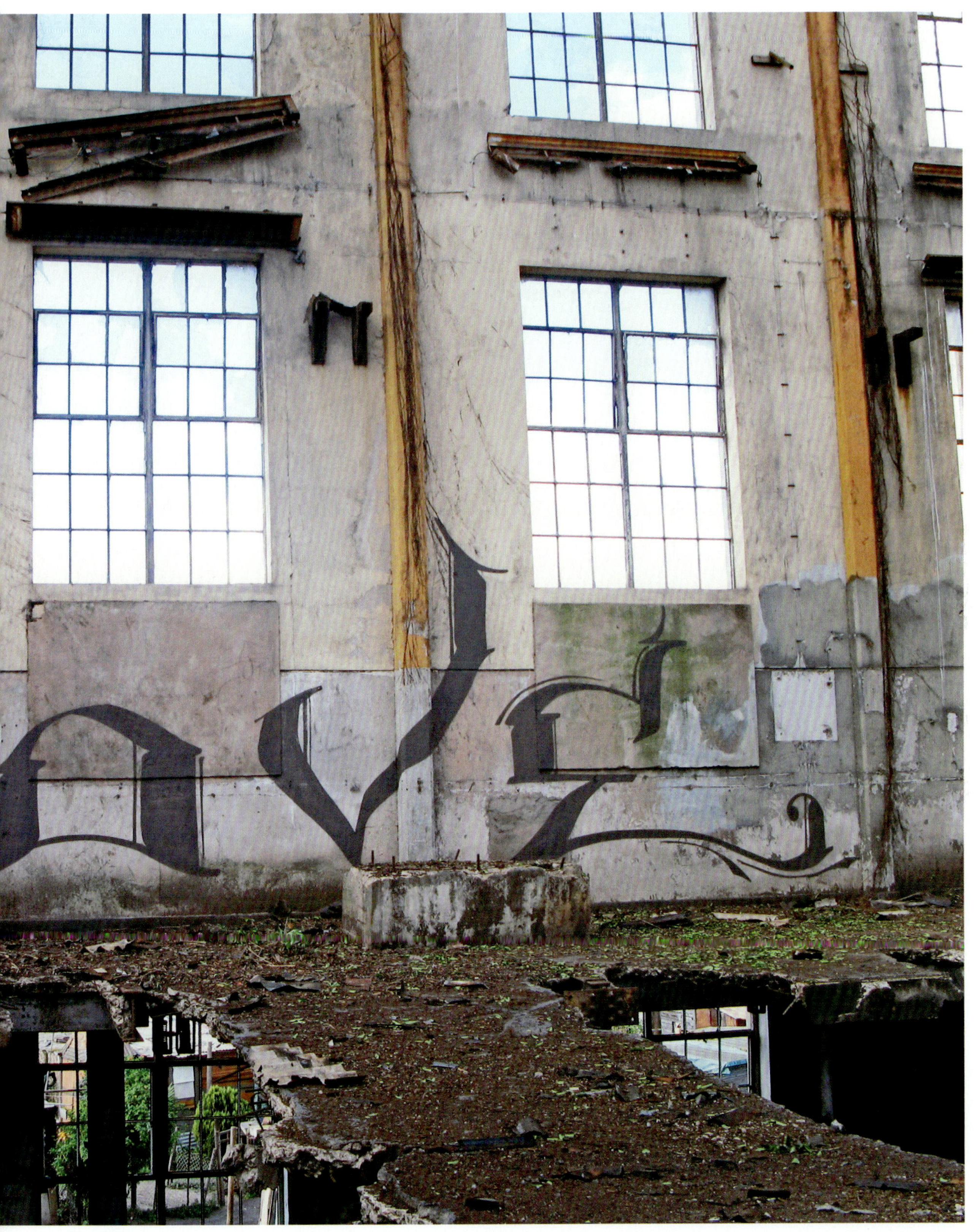

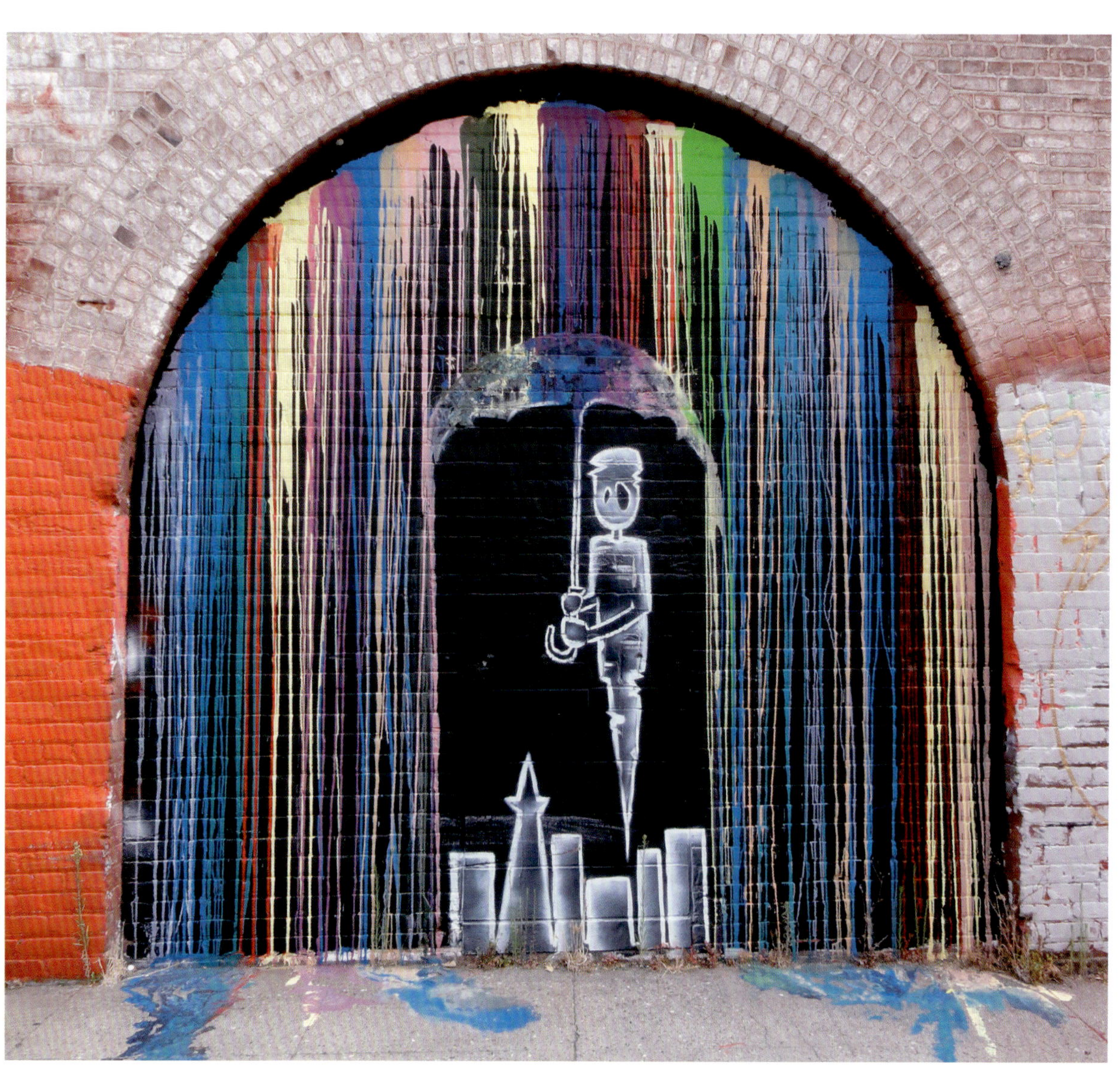

TECHNIQUES

US artist John Fekner described street art as 'all the art on the street that's not graffiti'. So unsurprisingly the term covers a number of separate practices and techniques that have different geographic and cultural origins. The boundaries of street art and graffiti are somewhat vague and will differ depending on who is setting them. In addition, many artists are taking elements from street art and incorporating them into their graffiti and vice versa. While it may not be possible to set rigid limits to the definitions of street art and graffiti, it may help the reader to extract some general features as a basic reference point. It is worth remembering that there are often exceptions, however. The typical notion that graffiti is created to be seen by other graffiti writers and that street art is made to be seen by the public is not entirely true; even in the earliest days of graffiti, writers were accompanying their pieces with messages for a broader audience than their own community, some of which were political (such as anti-nuclear proliferation statements).

Where once there was a clear dichotomy between graffiti and street art, their boundaries are now much less clear. The historical differentiation between the two focused on graffiti as 'writing' and particularly writing a chosen name repeatedly in order to gain prestige from other writers. This element of competition and risk lies at the heart of graffiti culture right back to its 1960s origins on the USA's East Coast. While all graffiti isn't illegal (unless you take a very narrow definition of the term based on the crime alone but not the art form or the subculture) the elements of competition and peer recognition mean that similar pieces will often 'count' more if painted illegally. Street art also gains something in illegality but is often, inaccurately and increasingly, portrayed as a legal alternative to graffiti. It is certainly true that street art is less insular and often directed more to the public than a narrow peer group. Consequently, street art has received wider media attention, and typically depicts a broader subject matter than graffiti. If one defines street art through its distinctions from graffiti then you will invariably notice a much wider range of techniques and materials being employed. Similarly, because of the vague boundaries inherent in the definition, many local cultures and aesthetic traditions that pre-existed the modern term of 'street art' have now been classified as such. We find it useful to distinguish between the crime, the art form and the subculture when talking about either street art or graffiti.

The development of street art, influenced by graffiti, has been the focus of much discussion. The press, and arguably those outside of graffiti culture, have not focused on (and perhaps are unaware of) how much development has happened within the graffiti art form itself. The following pages show how far graffiti artists have pushed their skills. It's not simply the case that graffiti is alive and well; artists are actively pushing new limits and developing the art form.

PAGE 158:
Unknown artist in San Francisco.

RIGHT:
The Netherlands's Does (not to be confused with Brazil's Does who shares the same name) in Bologna, Italy.

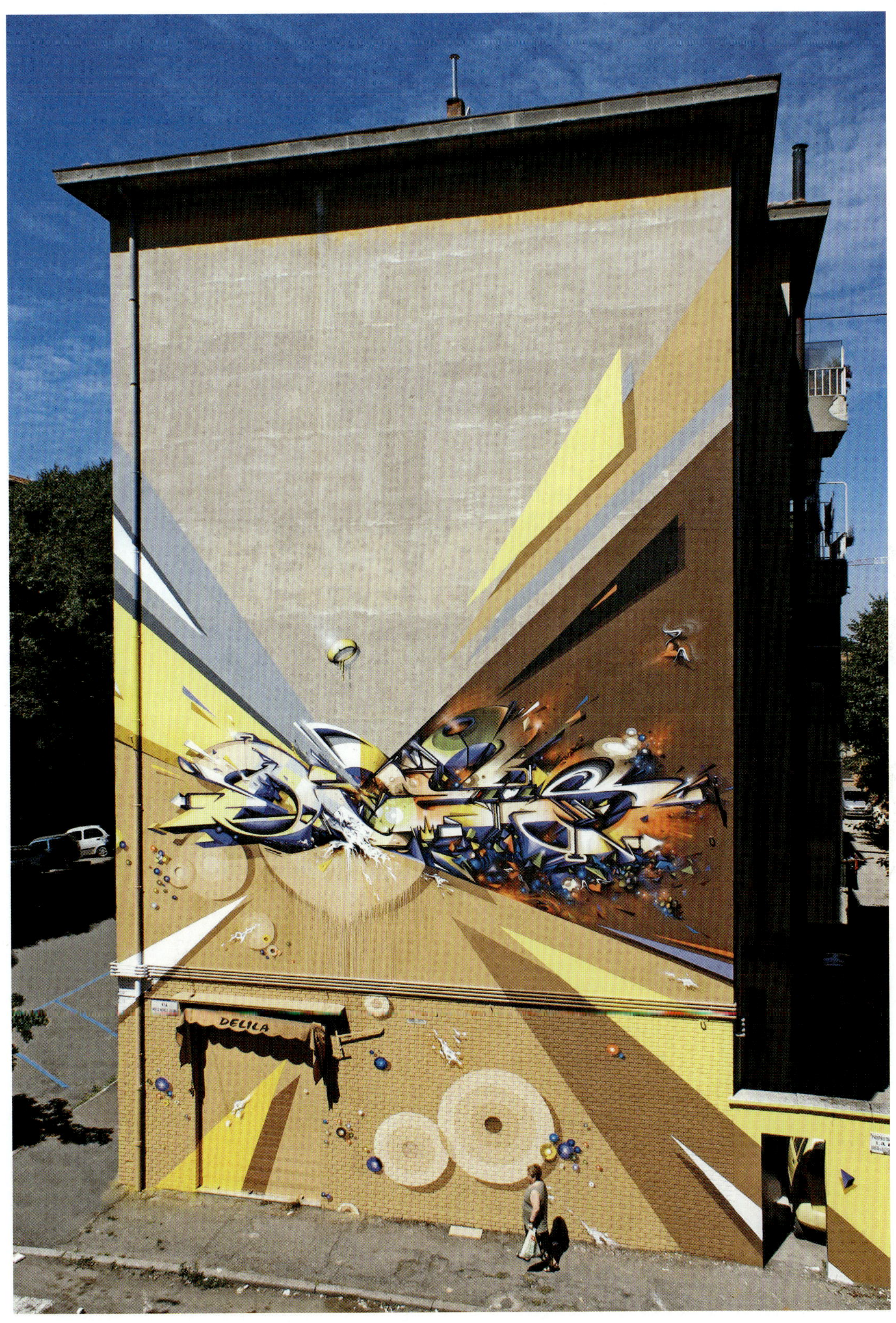
DELILA

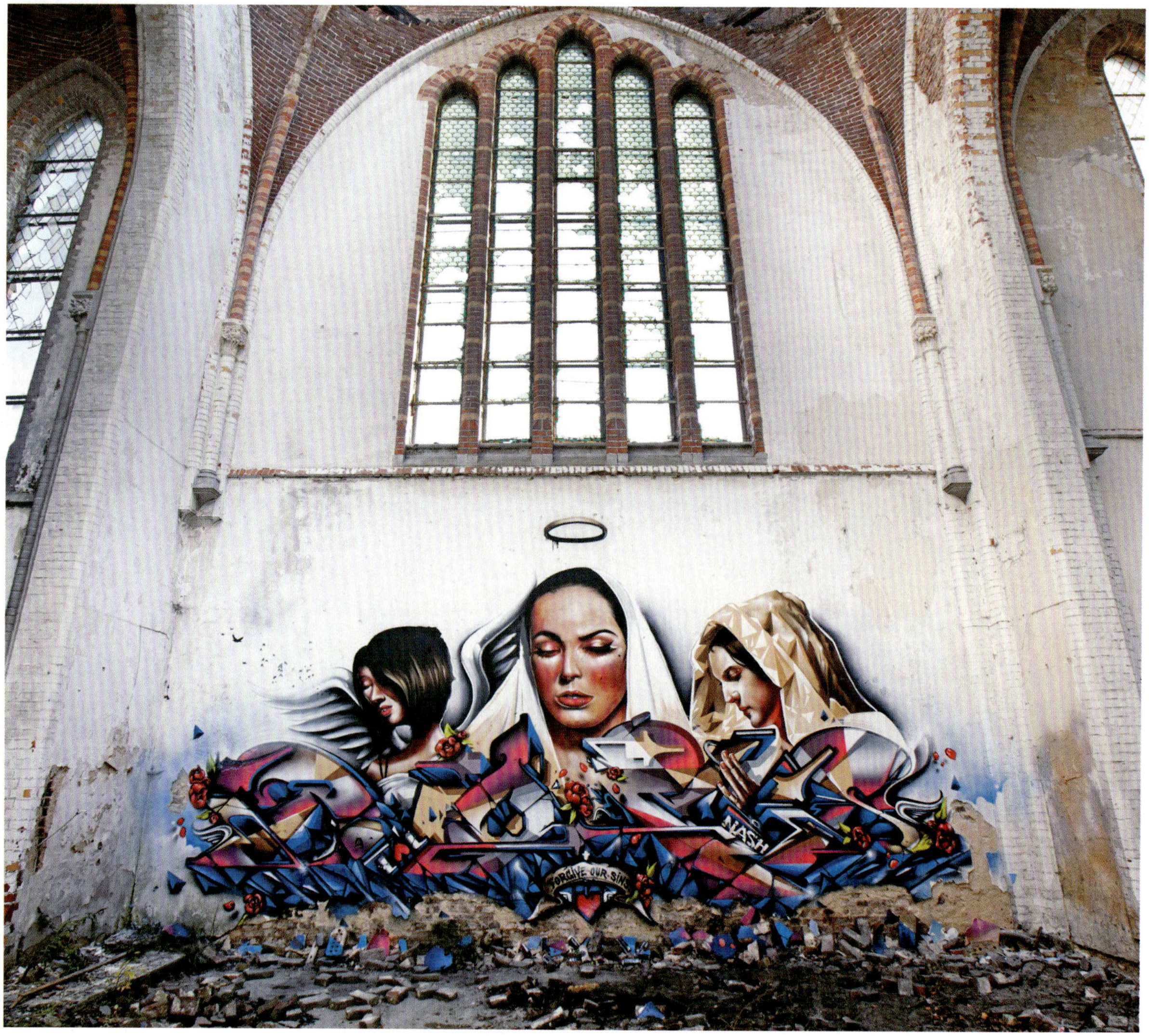

CLOCKWISE FROM
ABOVE:
Does and Nash in Sitard,
The Netherlands/Wais in
Russia/Wais in Russia/
Pariz-One in Lisbon.

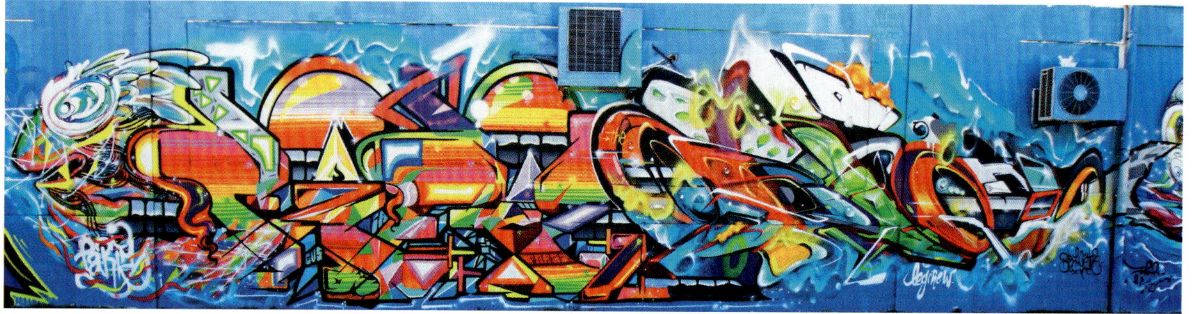

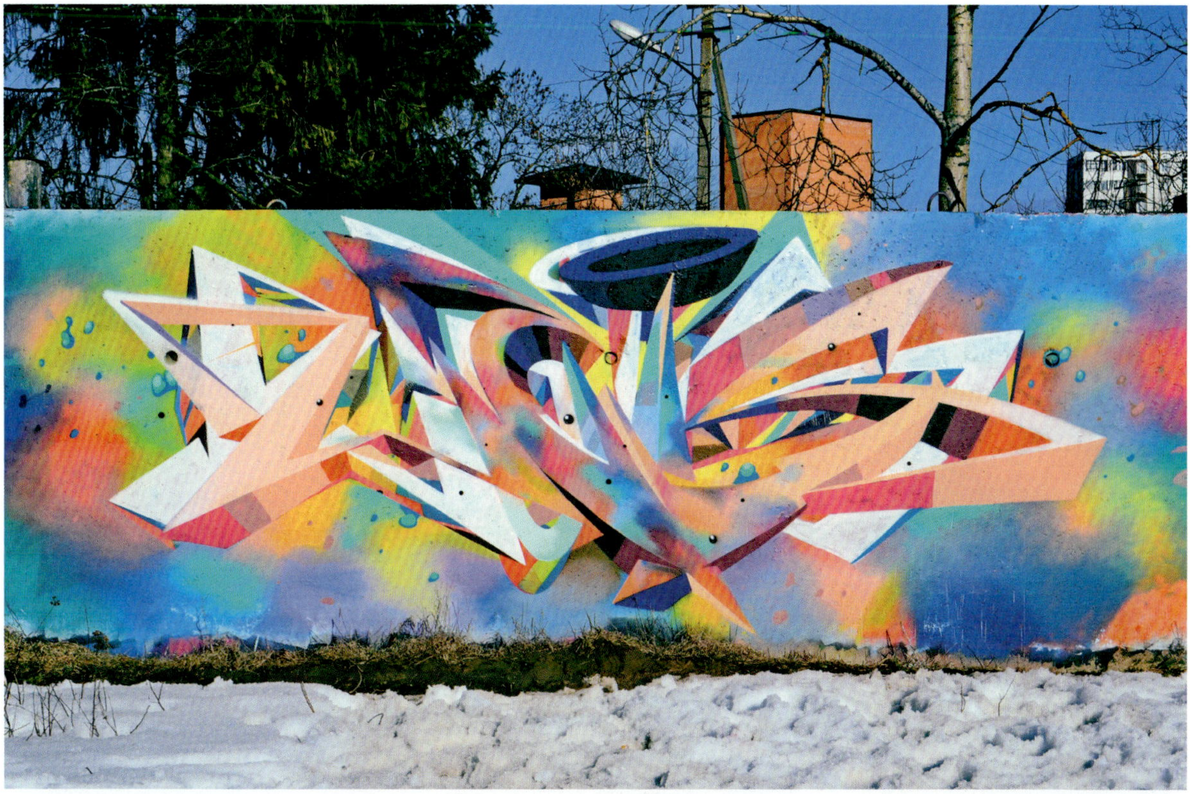

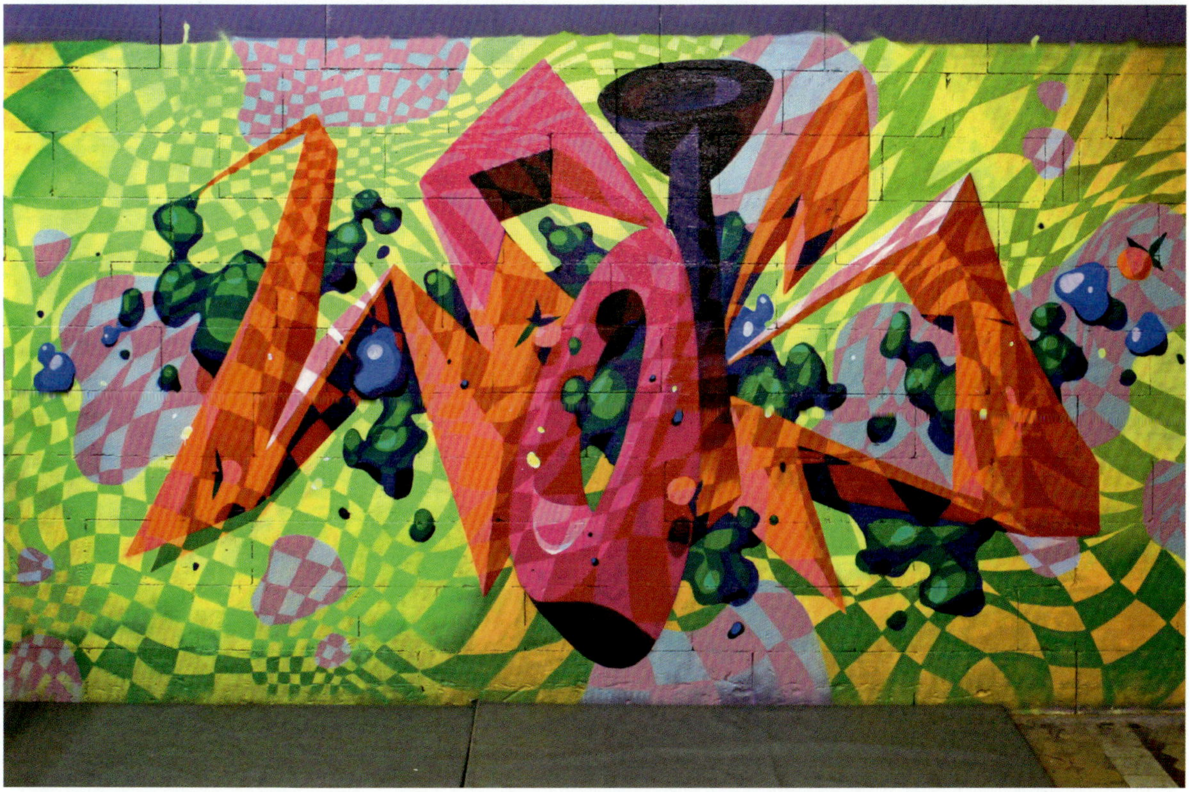

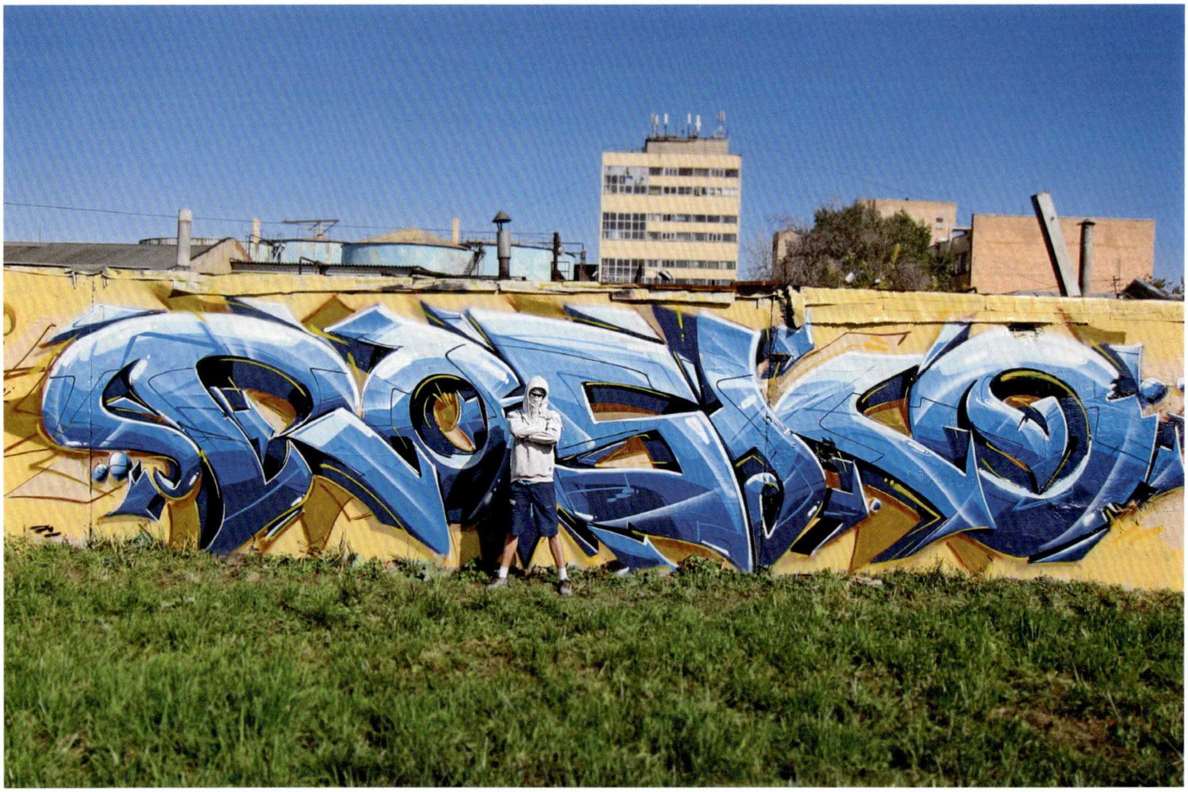

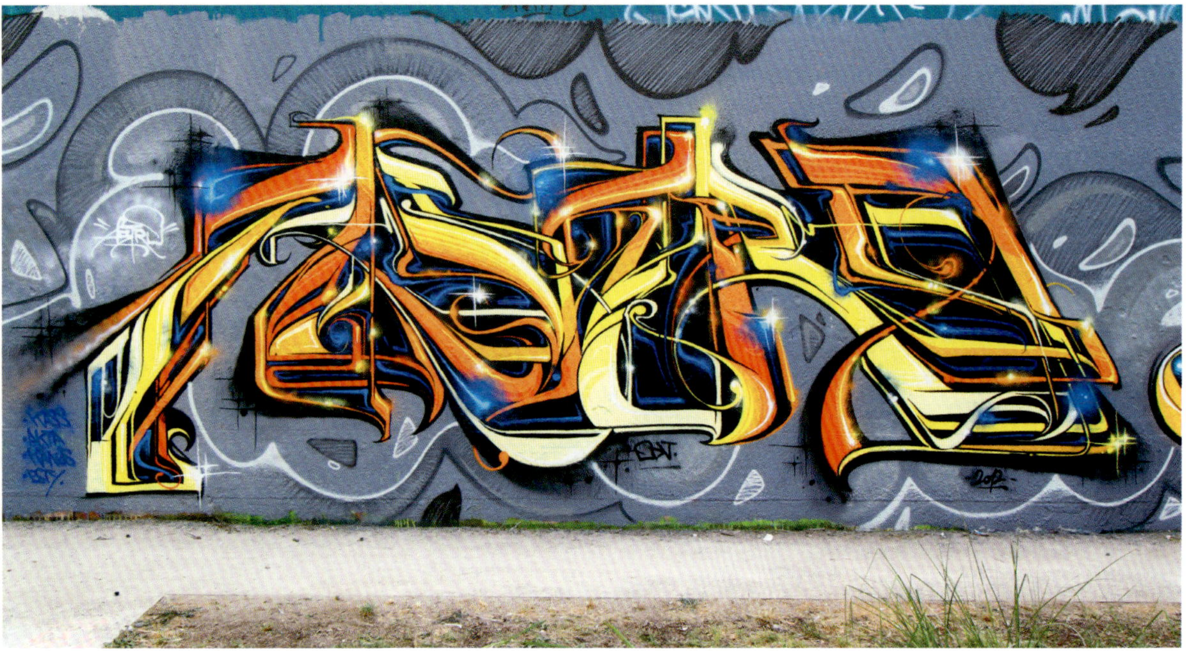

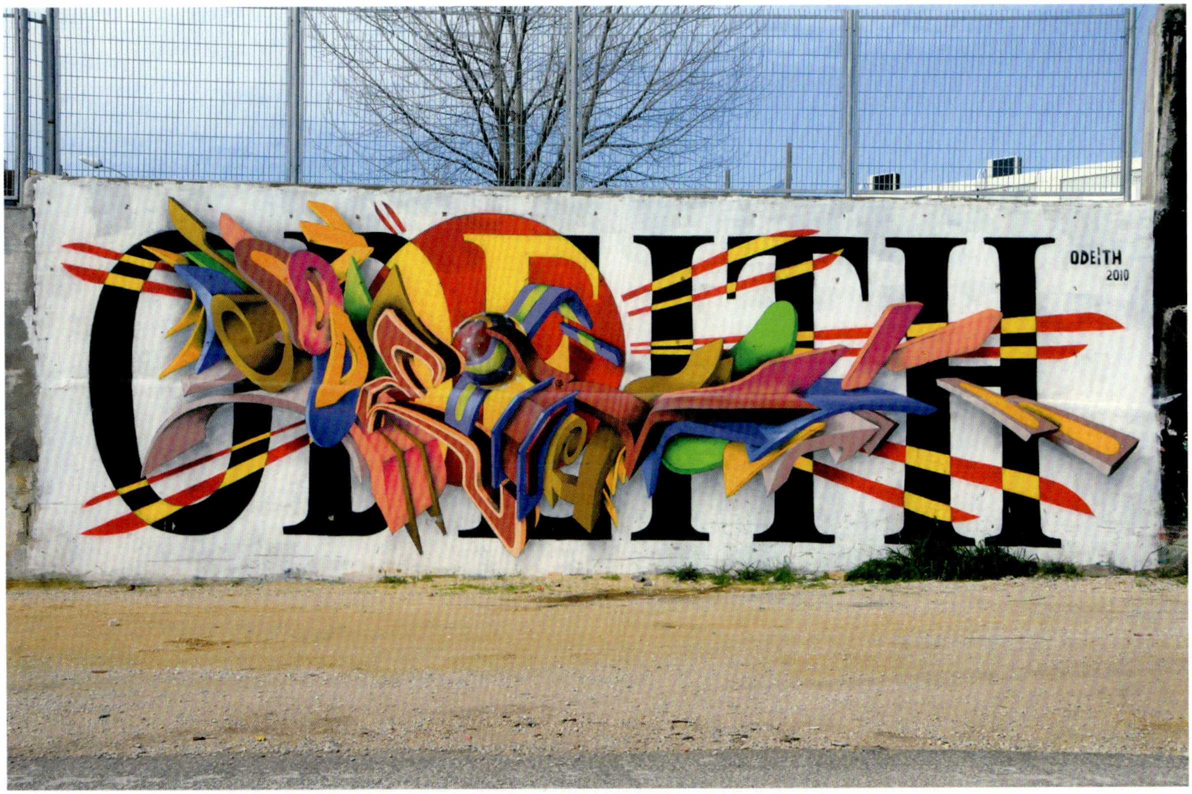

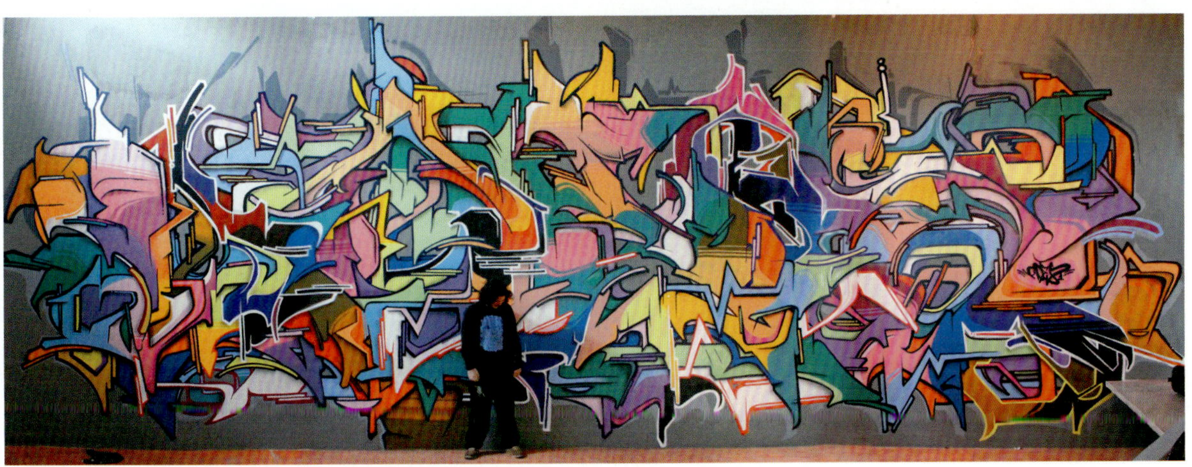

ODEITH
2010

CLOCKWISE FROM TOP
LEFT:
Rasko in Moscow/Odeith
in Lisbon/Brazil's
Does/Astro in Paris.

These images demonstrate how painting freehand with spraypaint is being combined with other techniques to produce new effects. Zed1 from Italy has pasted paper 'clothes' over his character; the poster layer has degraded and peeled away from the piece over time. Zoer CSX, in contrast, has truly pushed what is possible with stencil caps, which are made by cutting the back away from the lid of a spraypaint can, and punching a hole in the front. A stencil cap 'fires' the normal jet of spraypaint through a small hole, so that the spray comes out very fine. Stencil caps allow the artist to create works with very fine detail.

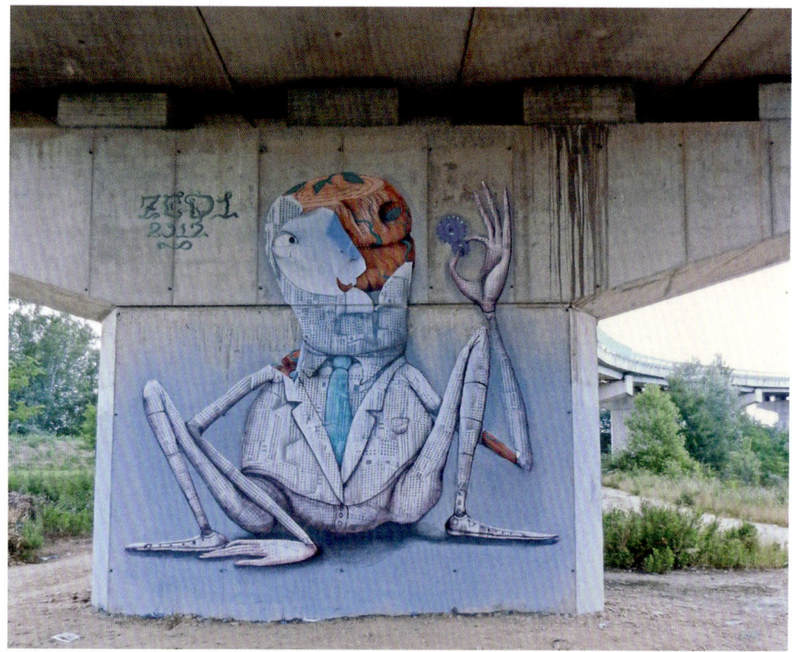

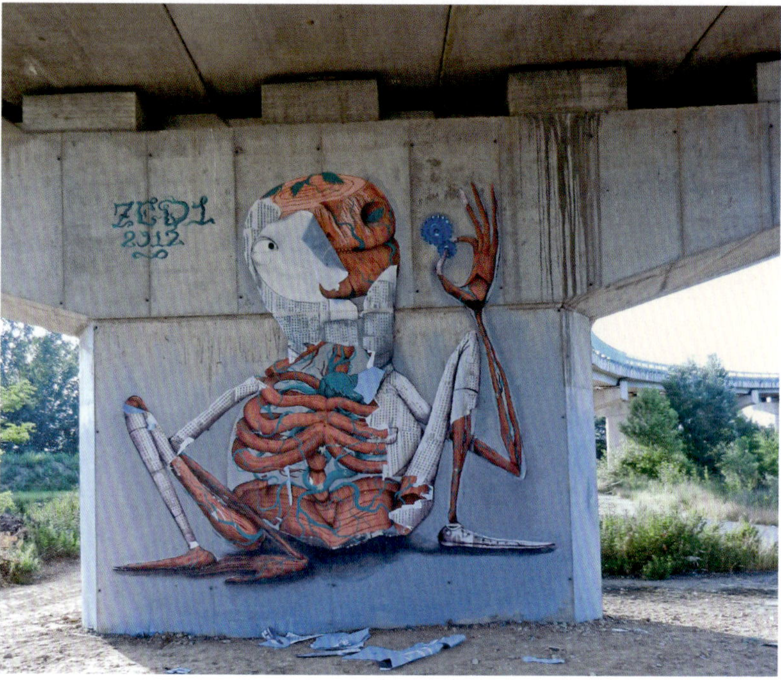

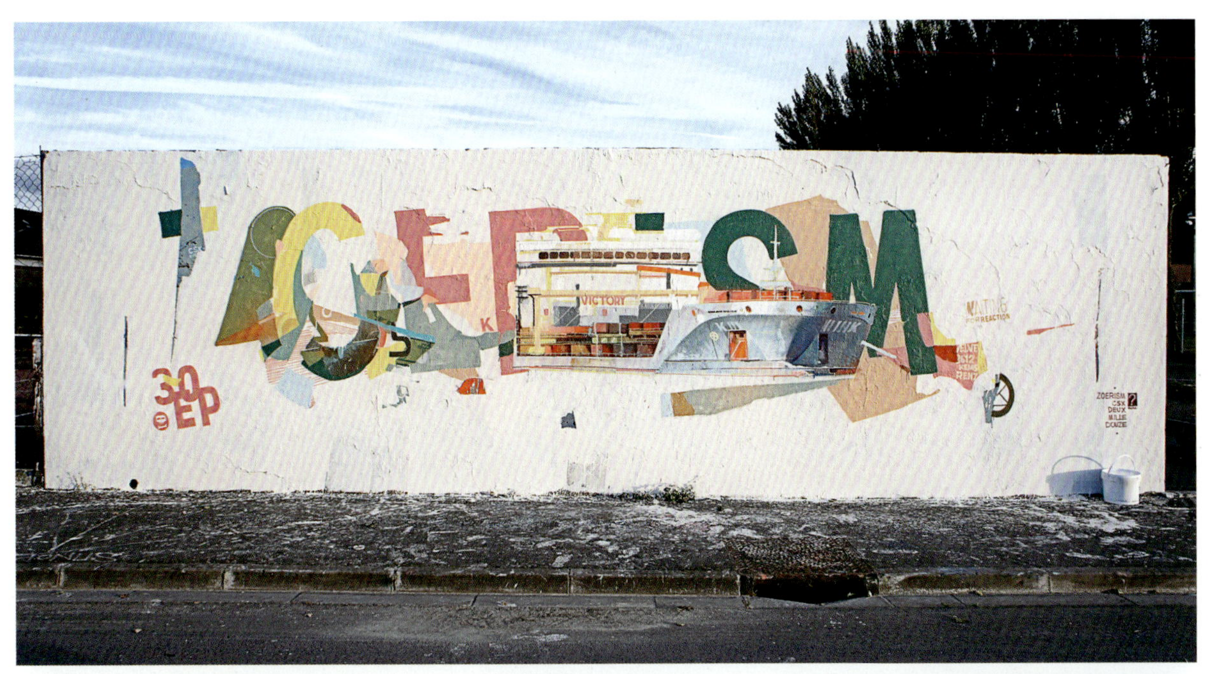
VICTORY
30
EP

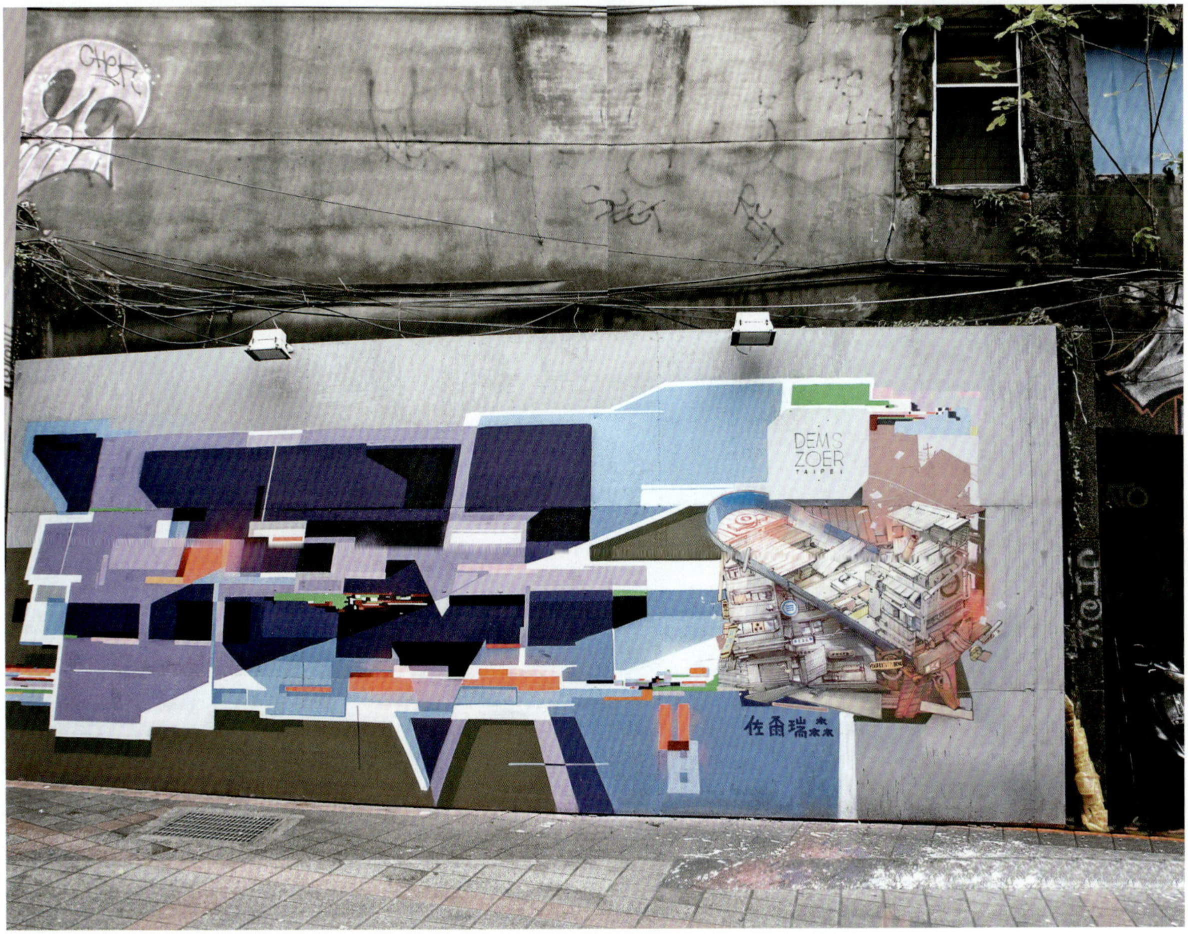

DEMS
ZOER
TAIPEI
佐雨瑞

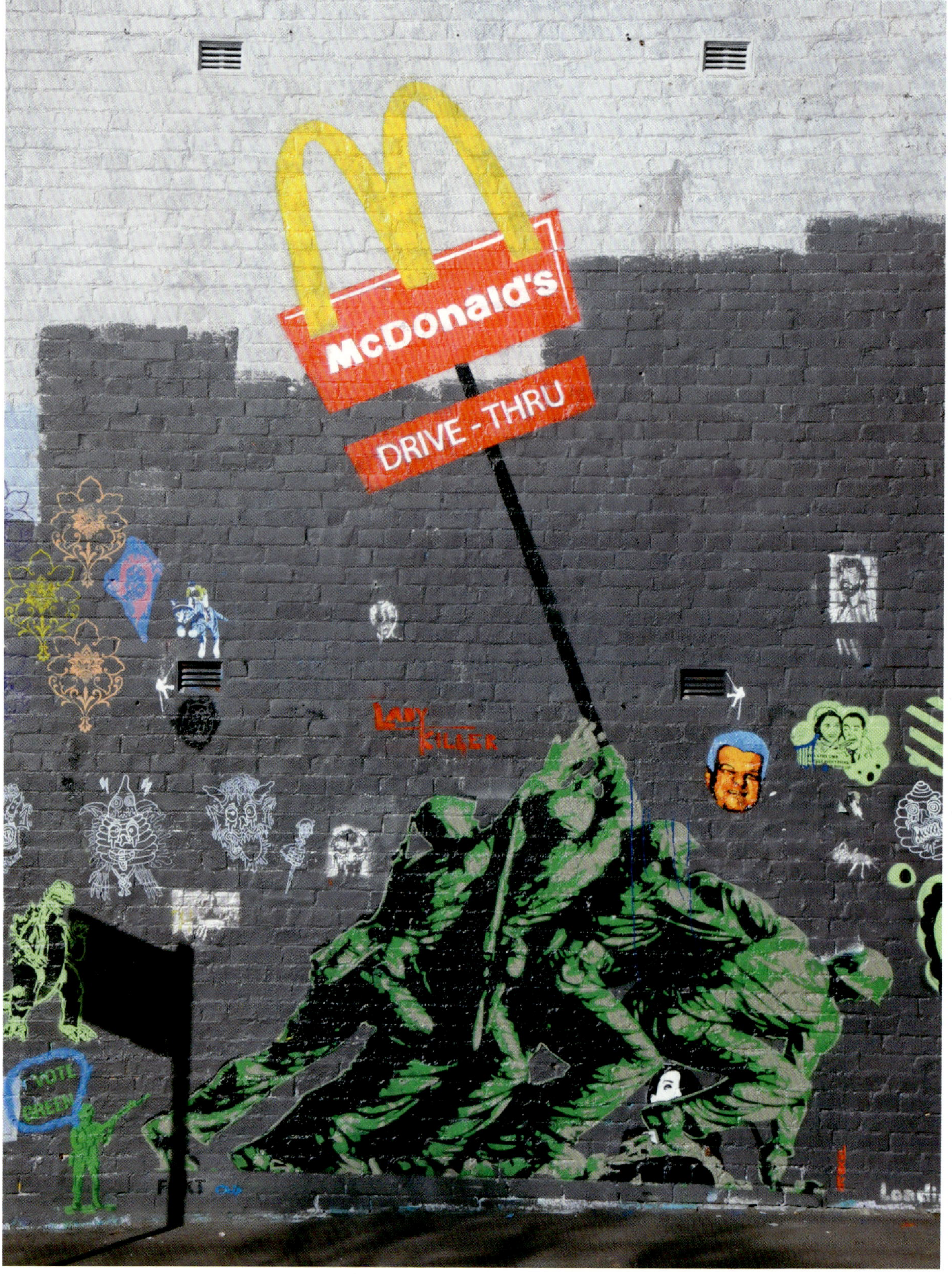

McDonald's
DRIVE - THRU
LADY KILLER
I VOTE GREEN

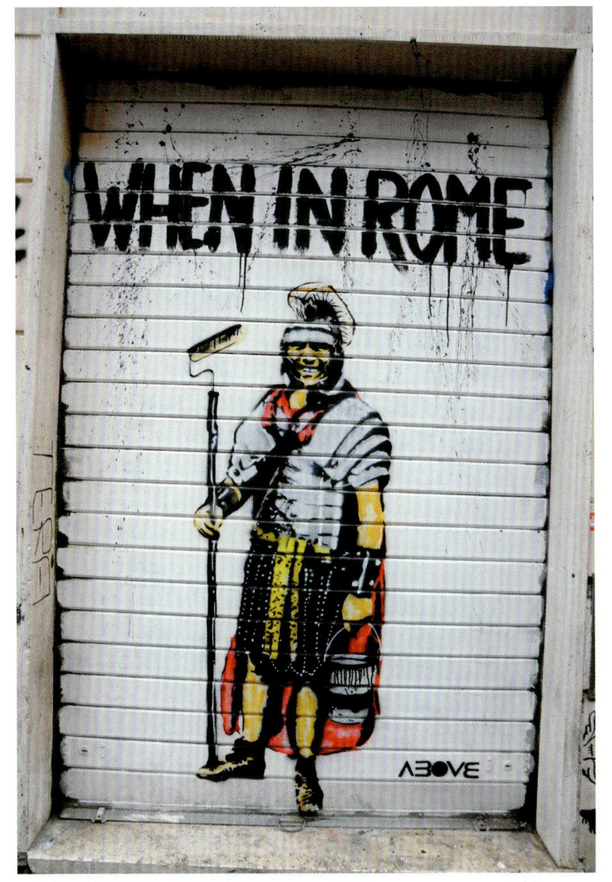

WHEN IN ROME
ABOVE

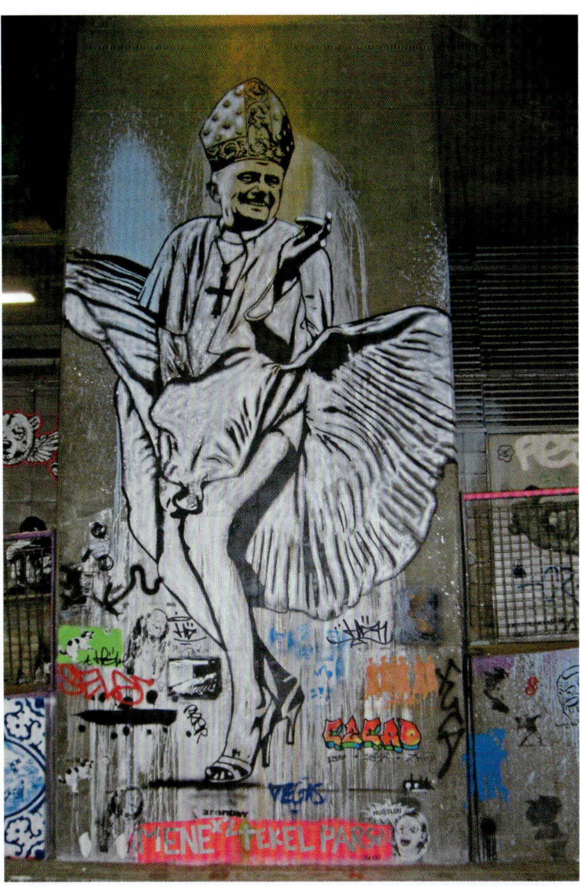

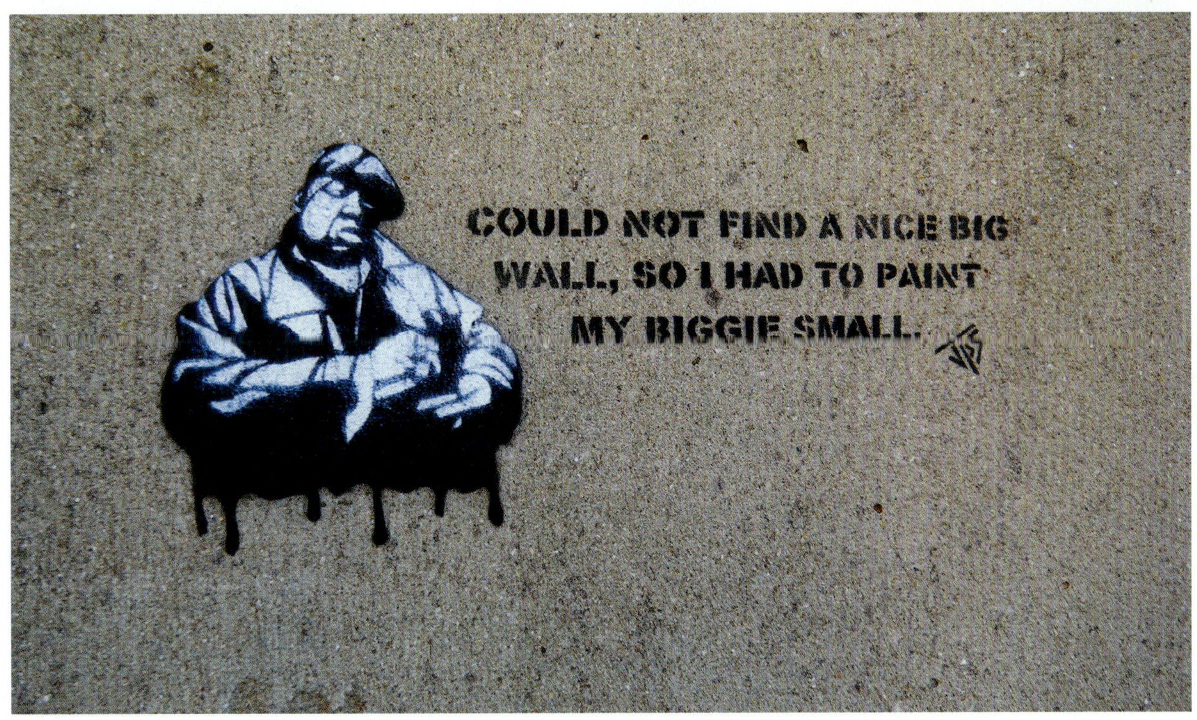

COULD NOT FIND A NICE BIG
WALL, SO I HAD TO PAINT
MY BIGGIE SMALL.

CLOCKWISE FROM BELOW:
Flix Robotico in
Venezuela/Be Free in
Melbourne/Be Free in
Melbourne/France's Clet
Abraham in Seville.

PAGE 172, CLOCKWISE
FROM TOP LEFT:
QTP, Pnub and Yerp/
Glitch. Tool, QTP, Pnub
and Yerp/Kerm/Tool, 100
Percent, Pnub and Yerp.

PAGE 173, CLOCKWISE
FROM TOP LEFT:
Yerp and 100 Percent/
Lamont, Nerd, Yerp,
Glitch, 100 Percent
and Radius/QTP/Many
artists.

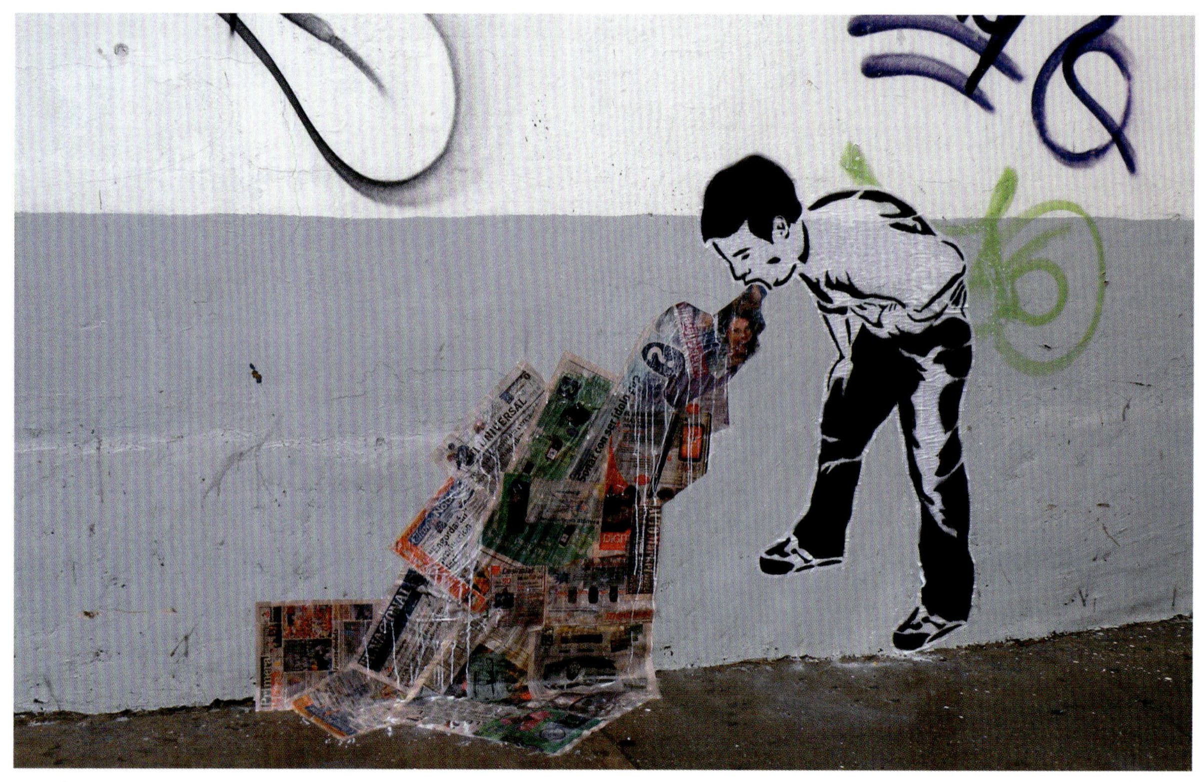

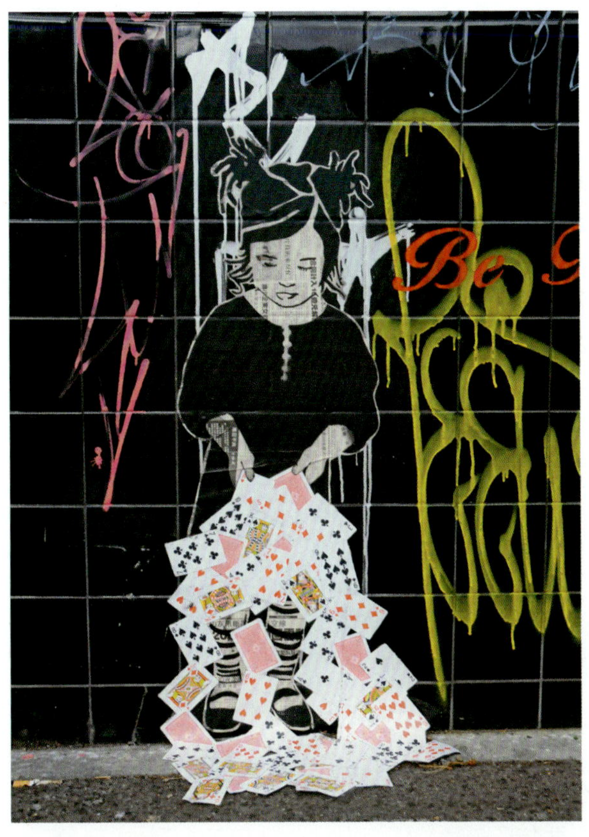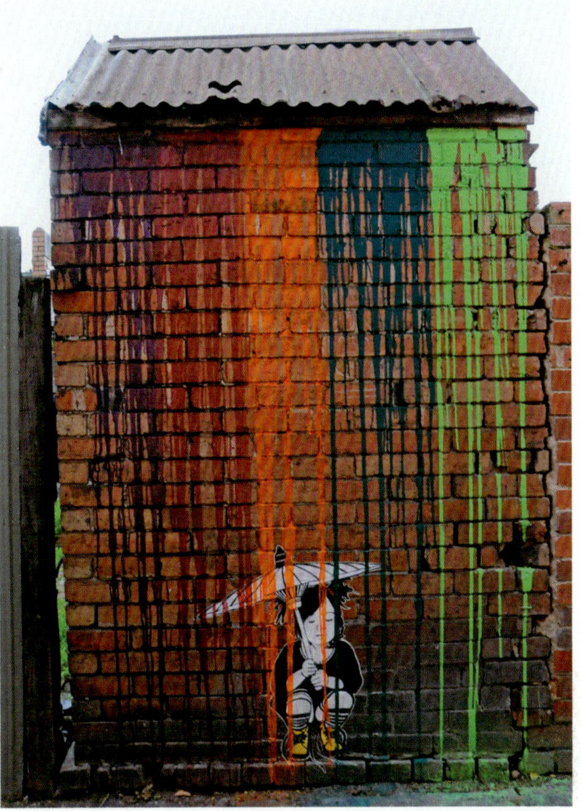

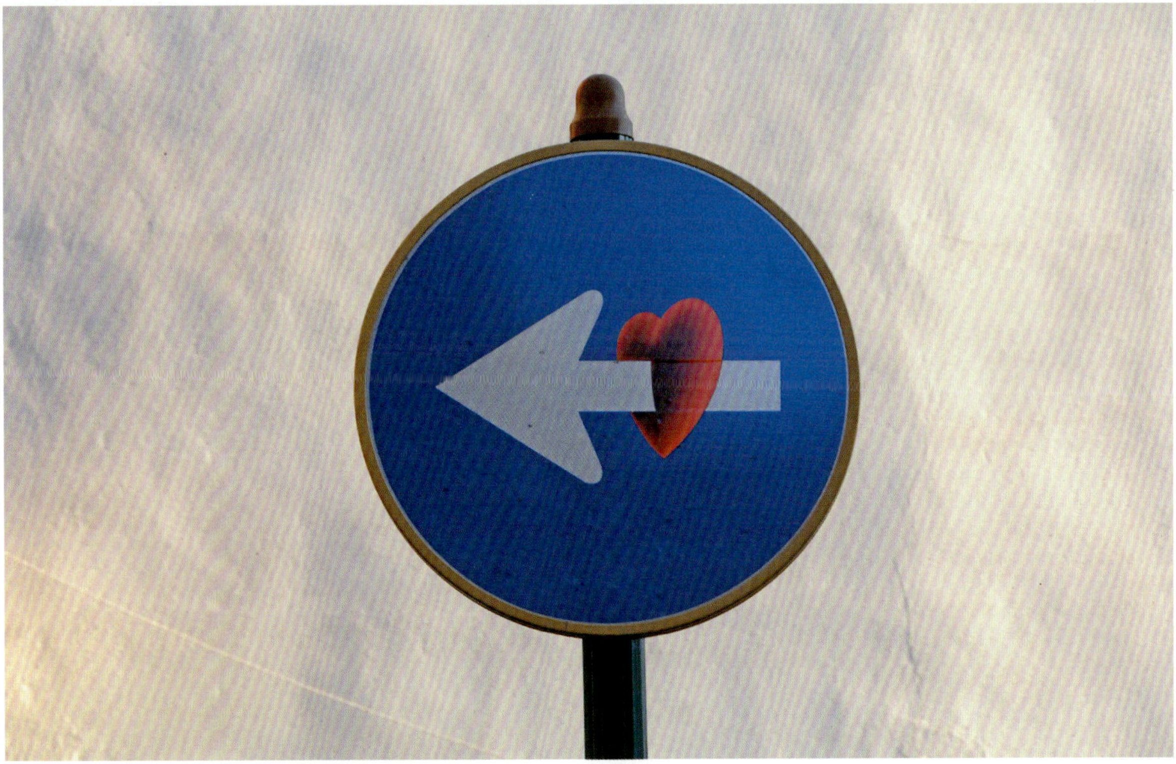

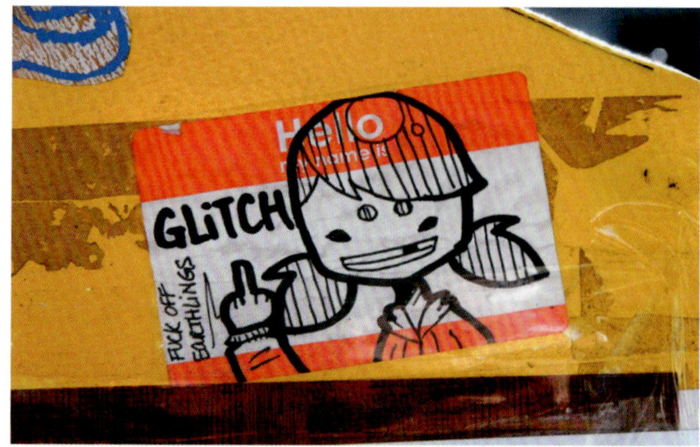

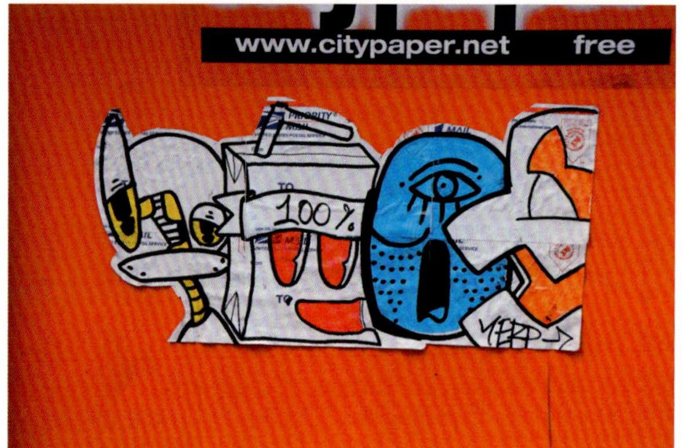

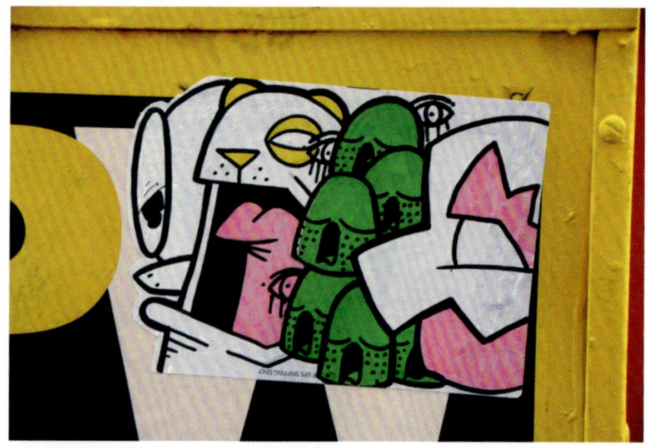

I discovered Philly's sticker culture accidentally, walking around the city when I was visiting a friend. I started noticing hand-drawn stickers on the dispenser boxes for the free newspapers and real-estate bulletins in the centre of the city. I began recognizing a number of more prolific artists and realized there was a culture here; there were even collaborative stickers featuring four or five different artists at a time. Philly sticker culture is, from what I have seen, different from most other sticker cultures in that the stickers are almost all hand-drawn on postal address label stickers. The second time I went to Philly I found new work by some of the old artists, work by new artists, and some of the artists I saw the first time were conspicuous in their absence. A new generation was emerging! What I love most about Philly's sticker culture is that it is invisible in plain sight, right under the noses of – but ignored by – most Philly residents. It's a self-contained and organic local art culture. Awesome!

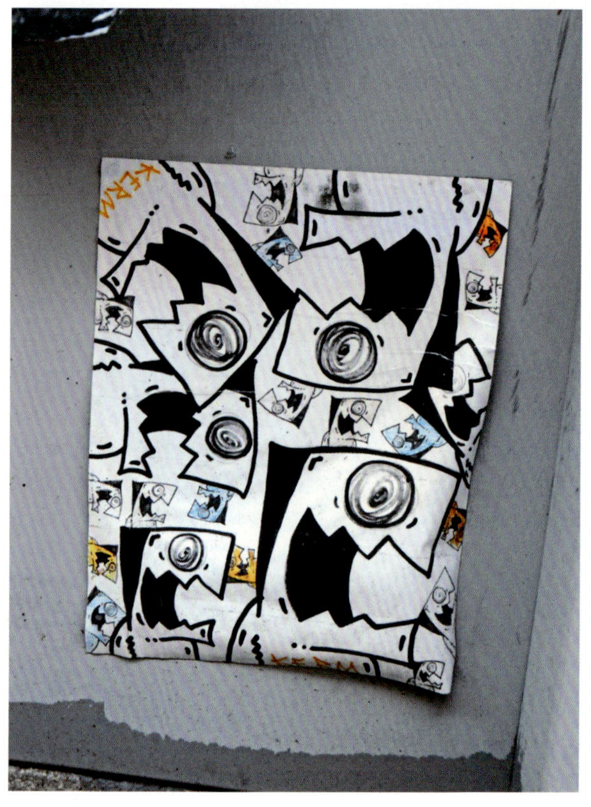

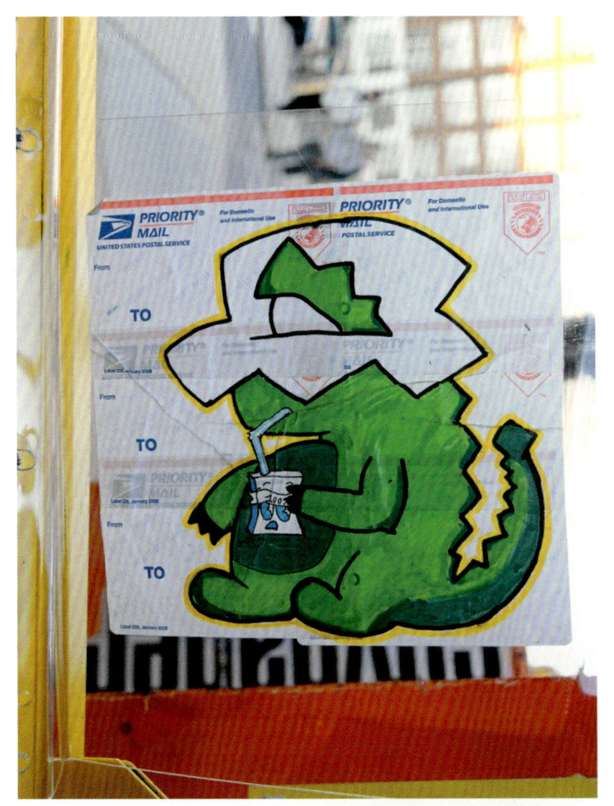

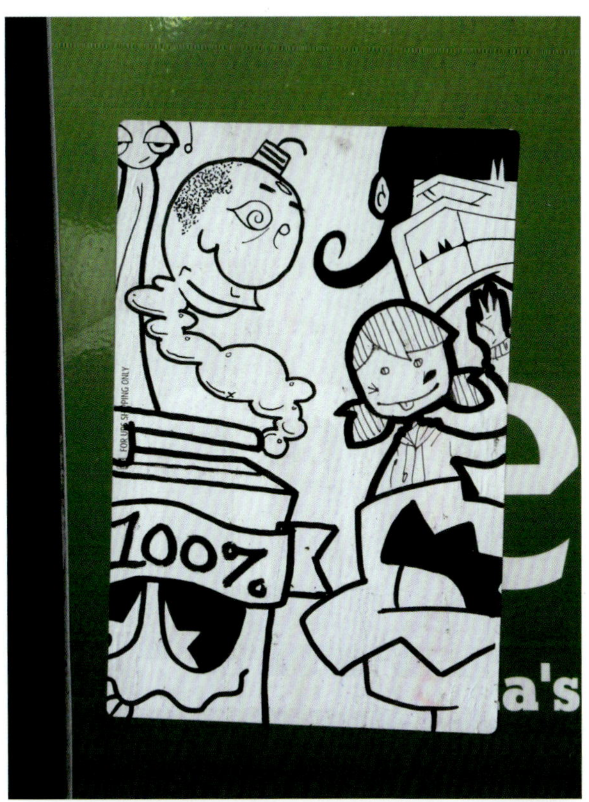
100%
a's

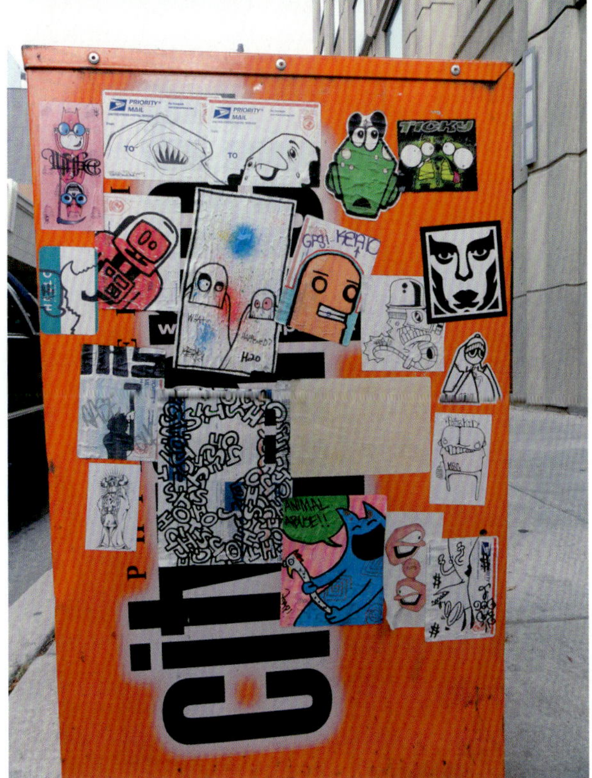

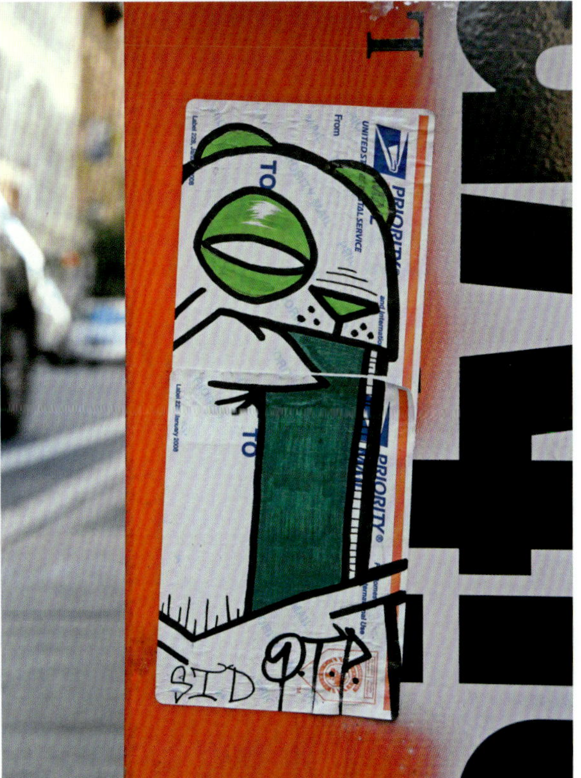
SID

Although street art is thought of as ephemeral, some artists have restricted or exaggarated this notion by producing work that may last many years or only days. Yarn, tape and cellophane are materials that are short-lived within the urban environment, while tiles and metals last longer. Beyond this, some artists work on urban interventions, which may include elements of performance. These artistic acts are not meant to last beyond their execution. However, the ubiquity of cameras and video recorders means that making a permanent record of these pieces is now both simple and possible, as shown on the following few pages.

CLOCKWISE FROM BELOW:
Sum Times by New York's Aakash Nihalani/London-based artist Isaac Cordal/Isaac Cordal.

PAGES 176-7, CLOCKWISE FROM TOP LEFT:
France's Invader in São Paulo/Portugal's Vhils in London/USA's Dan Witz in Norway/Austria's China Girl in London.

PAGES 178-9, CLOCKWISE FROM TOP LEFT:
Nicky Nahafahik in The Netherlands/USA's Hot Tea in New York/Hot Tea in New York/Poland's Olek in London.

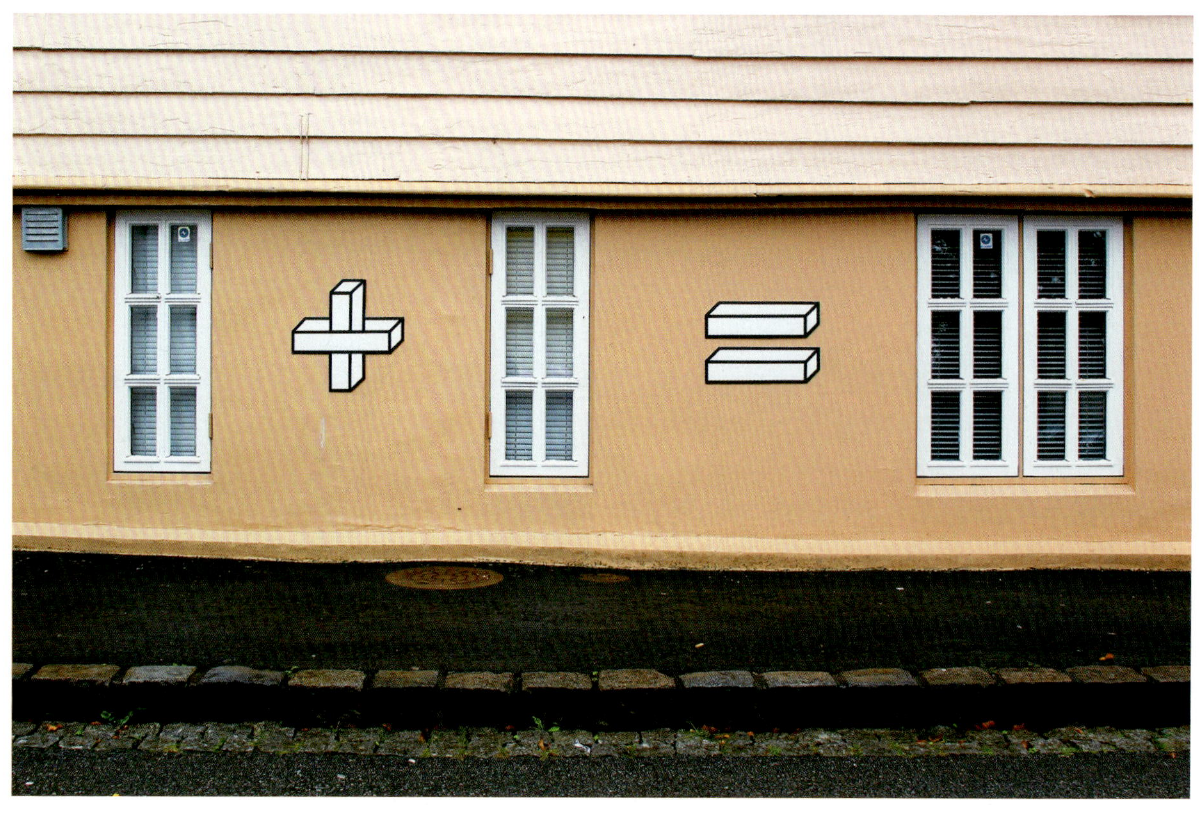

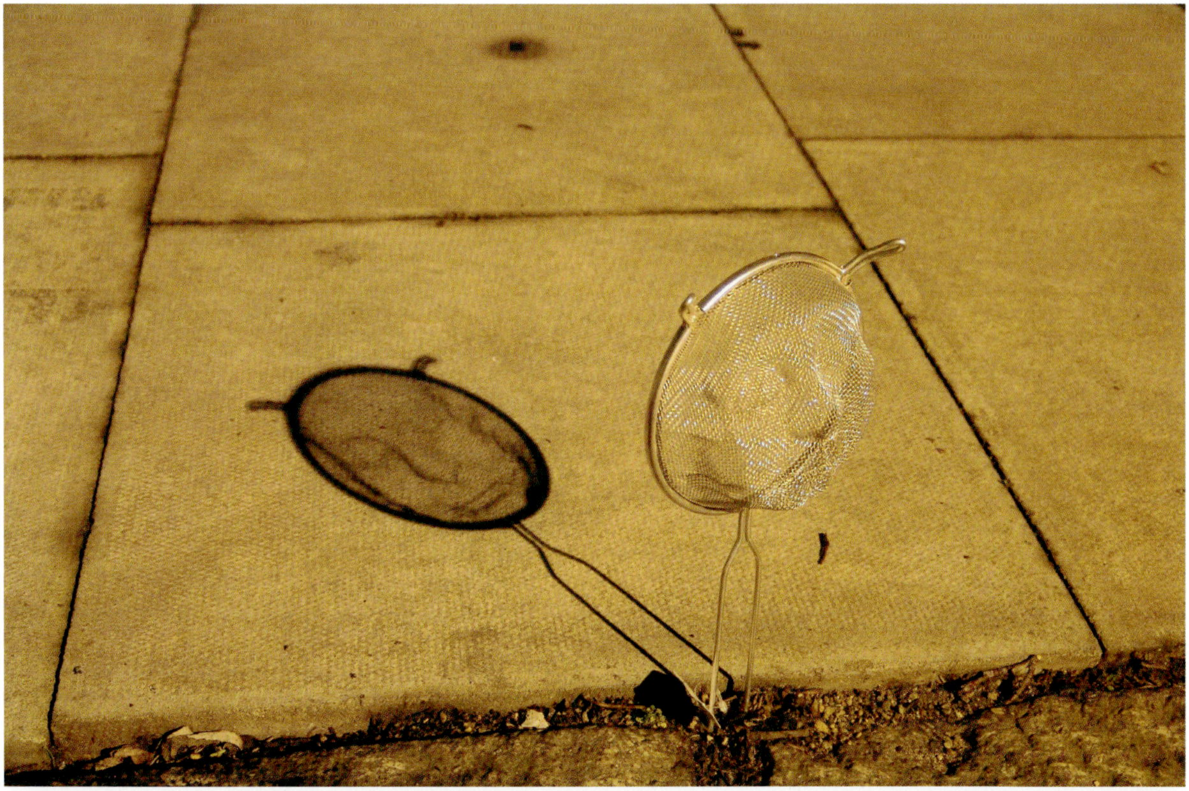

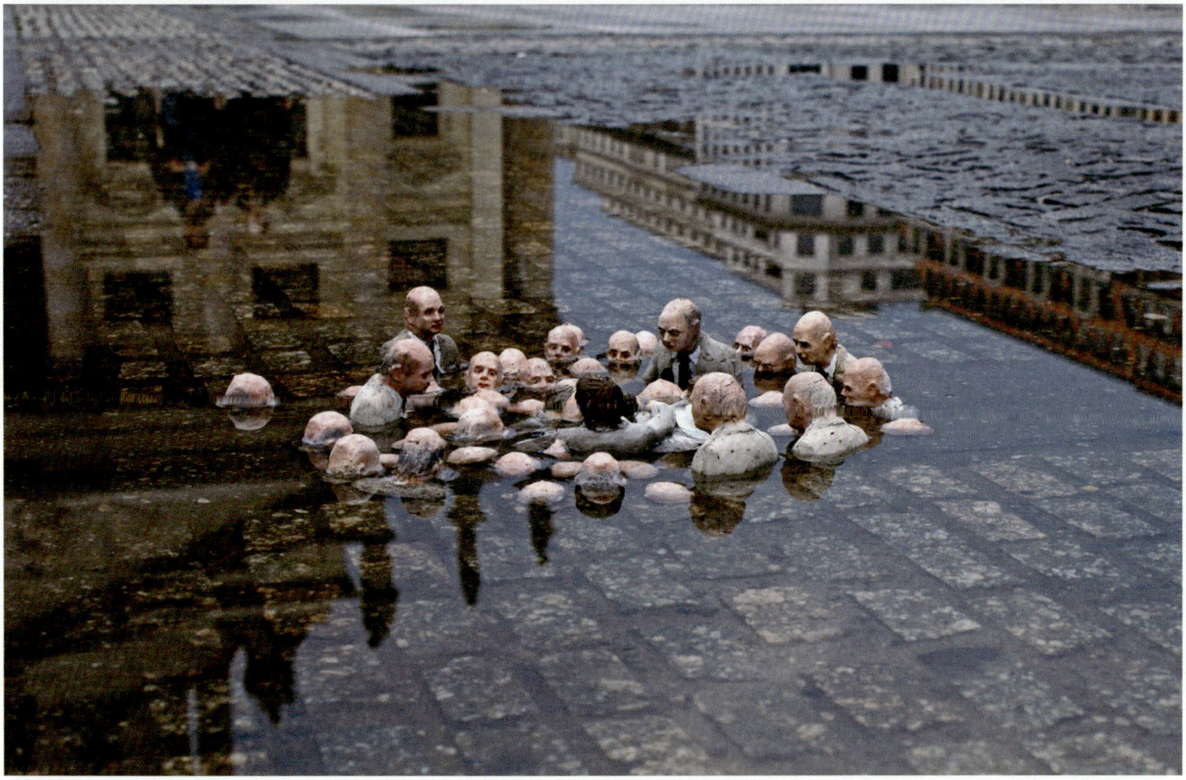

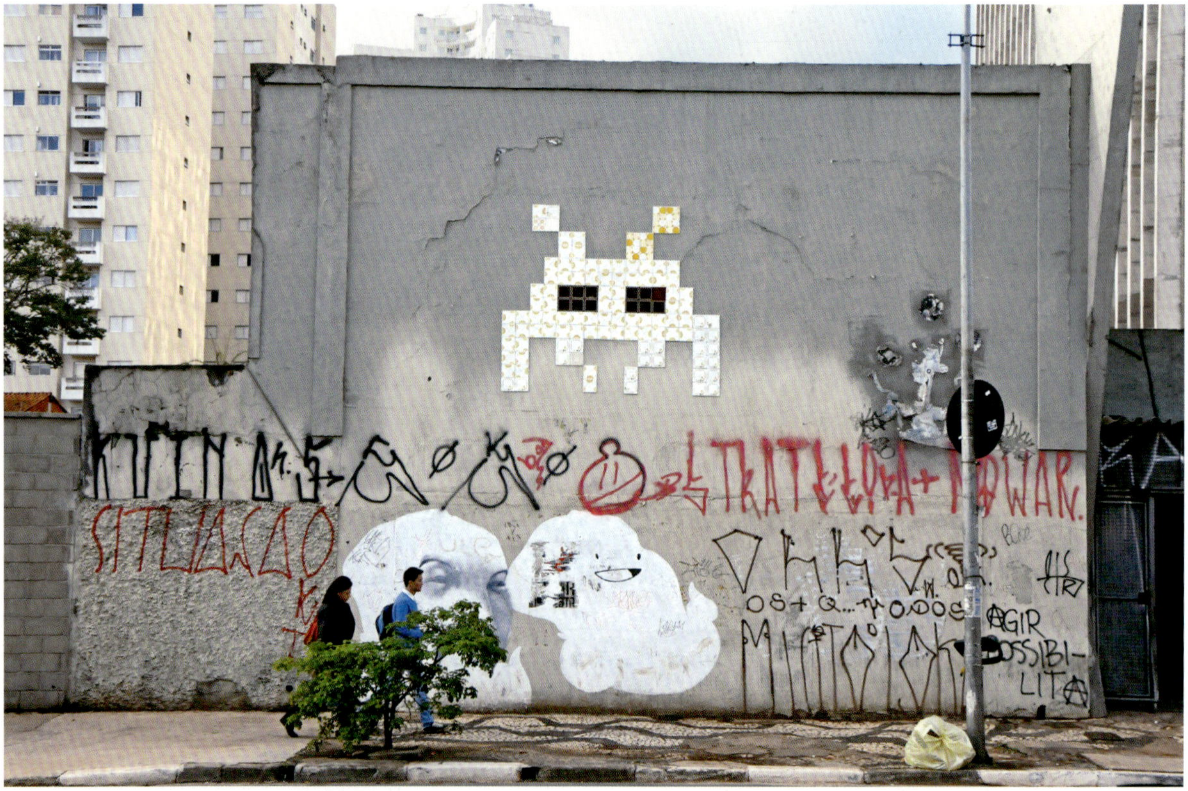

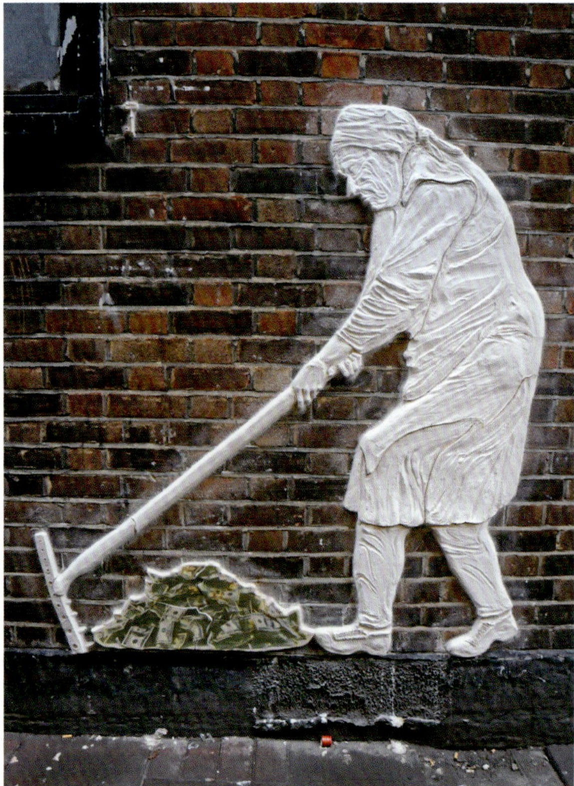

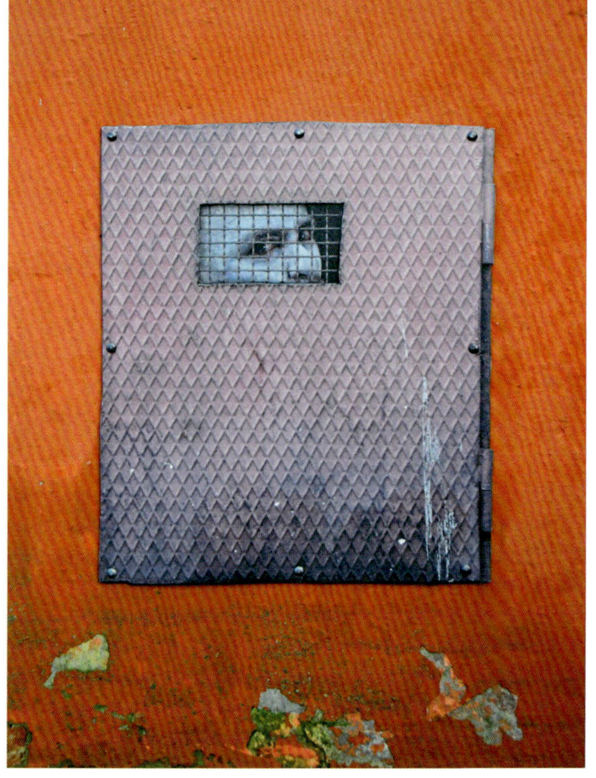

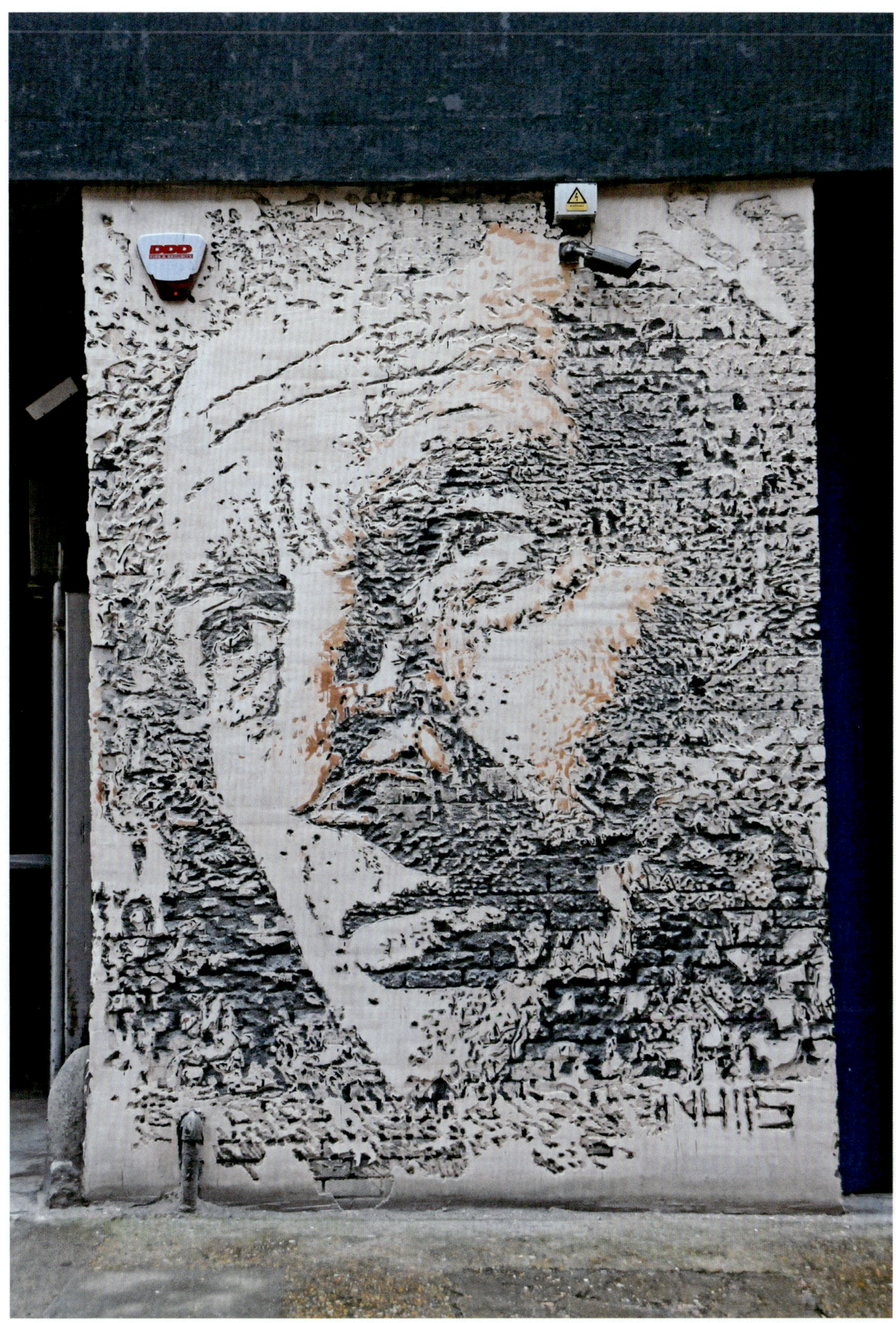

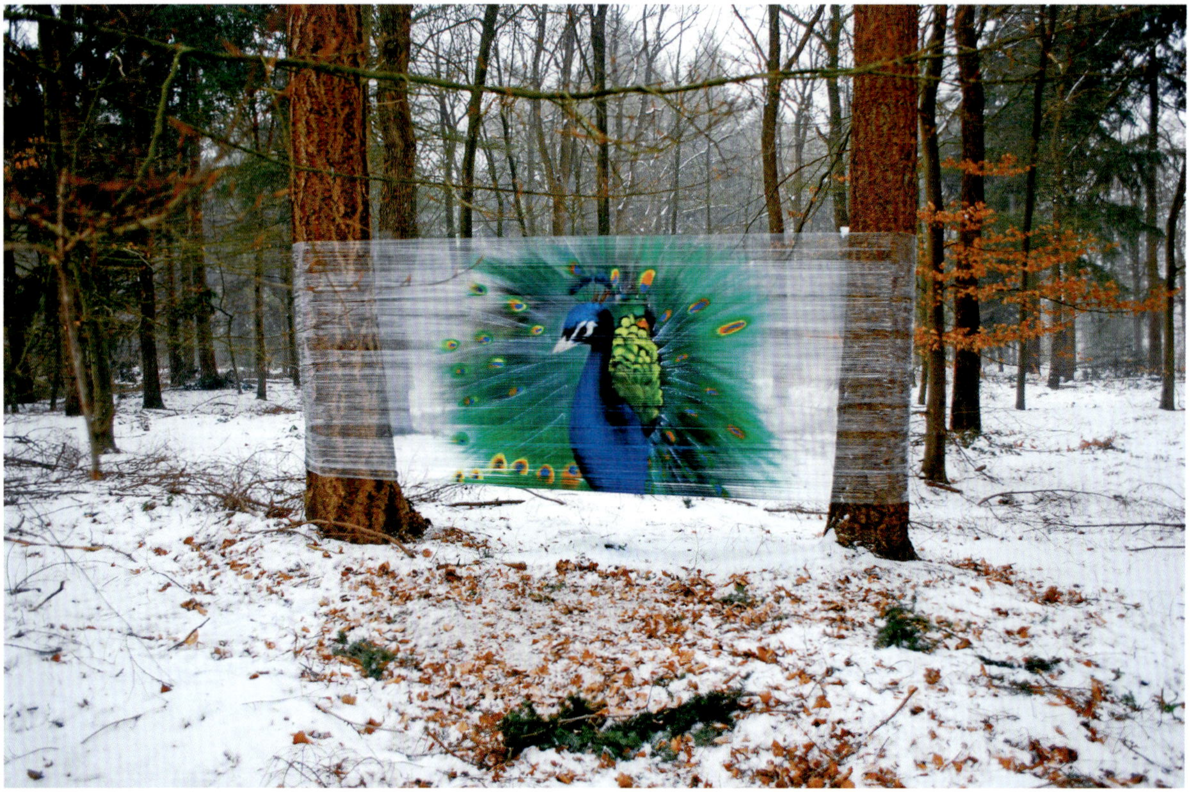

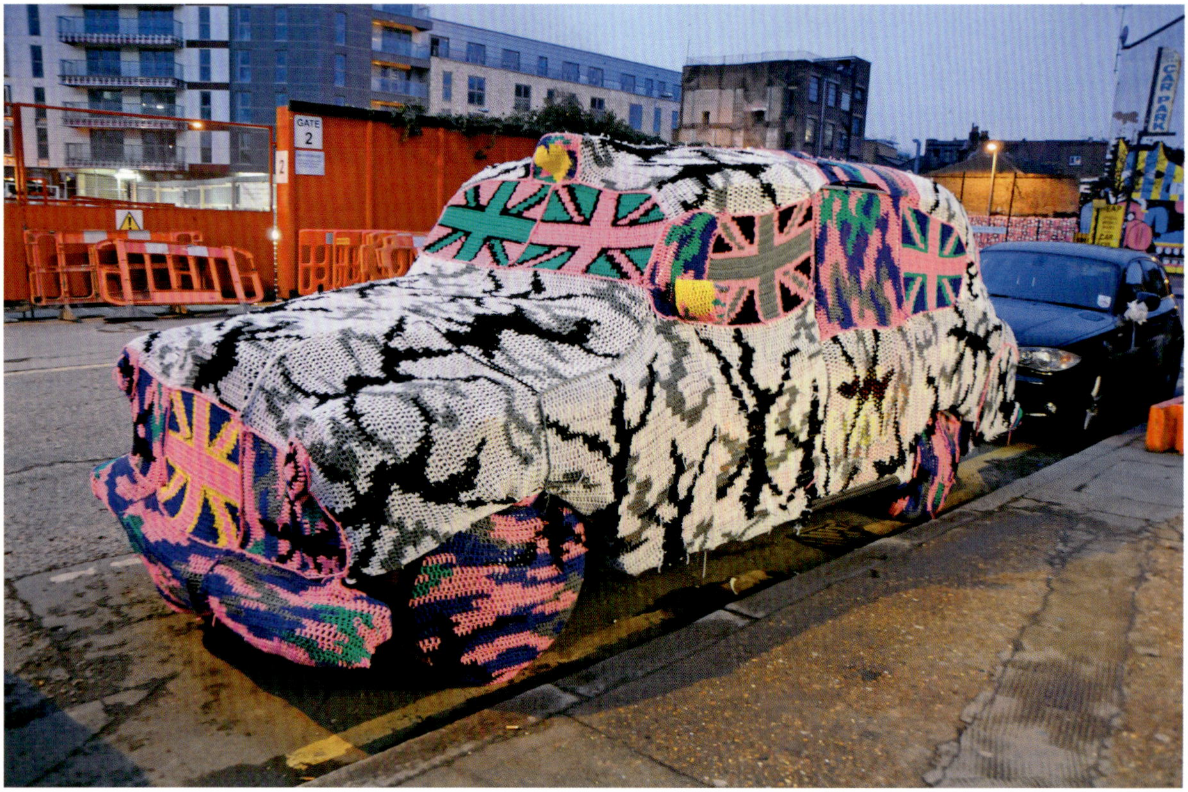

GATE
2
CAR PARK

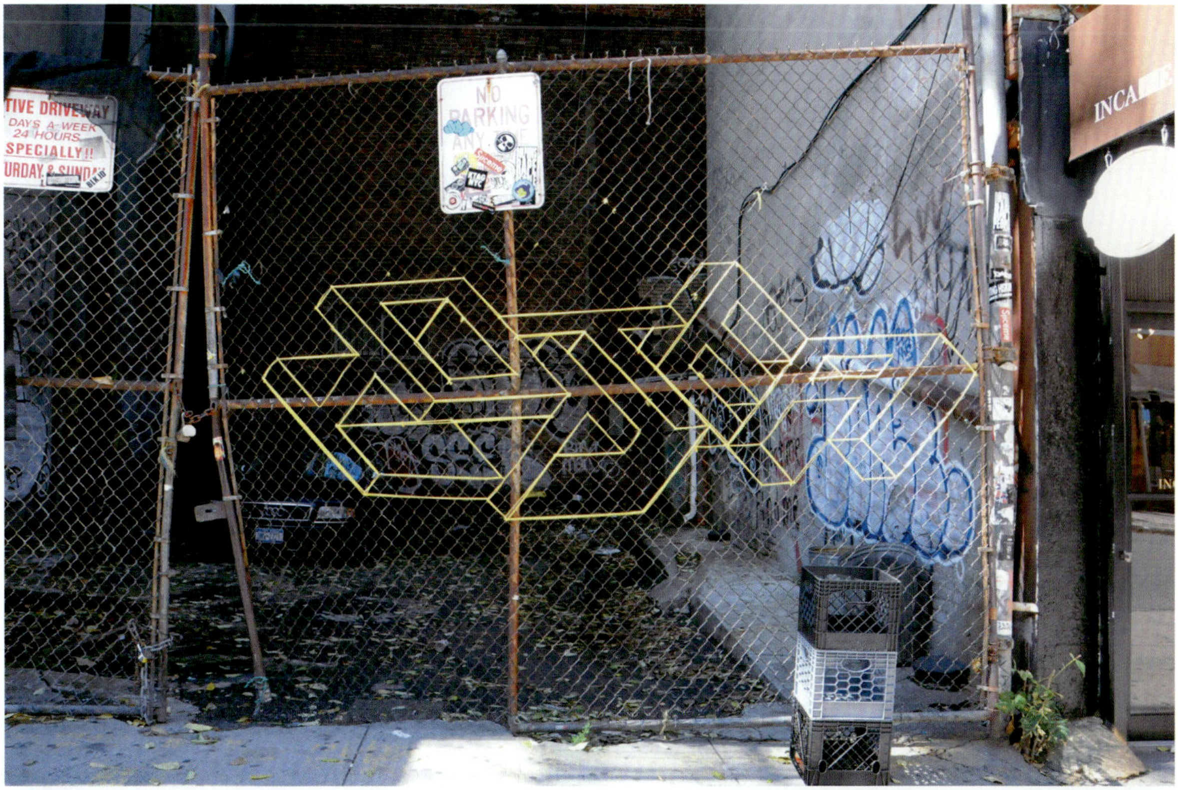
DAYS A WEEK
24 HOURS
NO PARKING

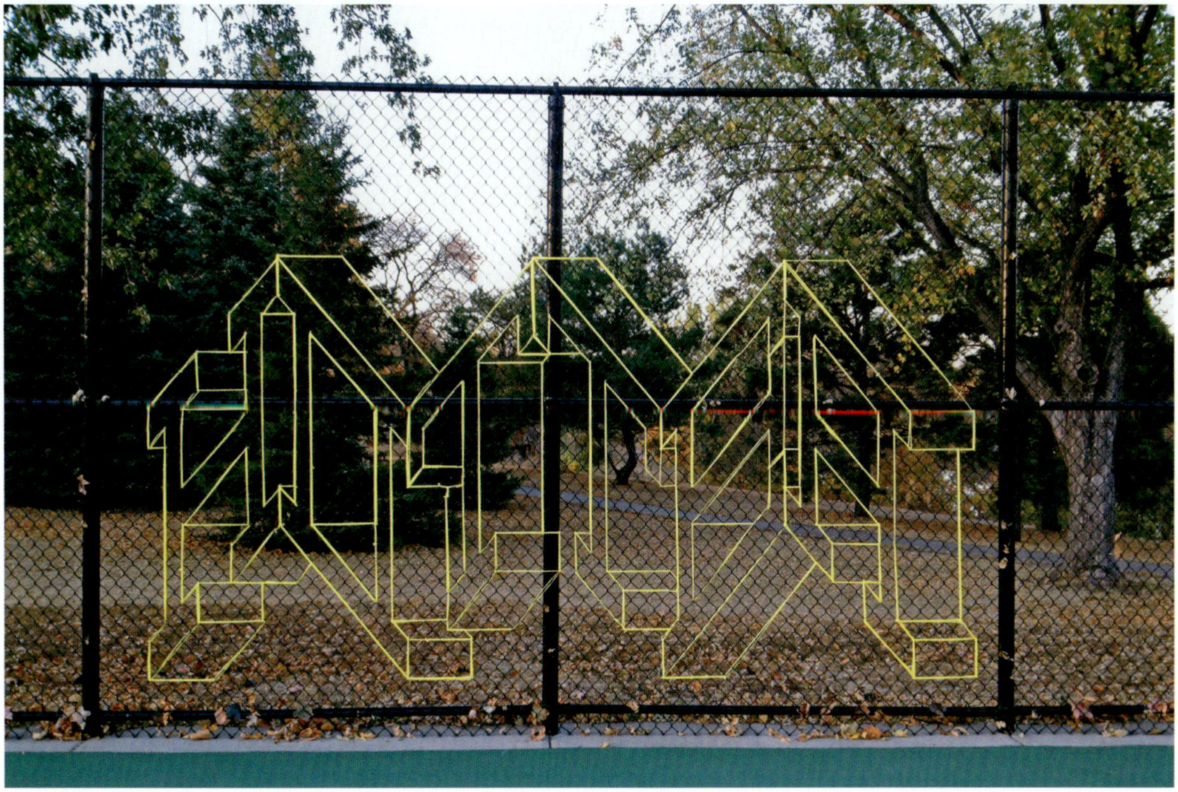

Information Innovation

During the pre-internet era, graffiti images were shared nationally and internationally by networks of artists who traded photographs (reproductions and photocopies) by post. Magazines and books were, of course, also an important mode of disseminating images, ramping up largely from the early 1990s. One of the most famous international graffiti magazines, *Graphotism*, started off as a black-and-white publication and ran from 1992 until 2012.

The internet has facilitated a lot of changes in graffiti culture, for better and for worse. From the mid-1990s, when internet use spread across the USA and Europe, graffiti writers have wrestled with photographs of their work being put online both with and without their consent.

One of the first graffiti-sharing websites, indeed one of the very first websites at all, was *Art Crimes*, founded by Susan Farrell, which went public in September 1994 and continues to this day. Early websites like Art Crimes were largely about publishing photographs and articles by individuals from the writer community who wanted to reach other writers.

As the internet developed and became more interactive, with the advent of forums and then more sophisticated social media tools, the notion of the 'writers' bench' has somewhat moved online. Artists can maintain some anonymity in online communities, which allows them to share images with their online peers with a (perhaps misplaced) sense of impunity. Pieces can now be seen instantly by an enthusiastic fan community around the world and not just other writers in one's own city.

Digital cameras have also had a significant impact on graffiti and street art communities; photo quality has increased while camera prices have fallen. Indeed, because of the ephemeral nature of street art and graffiti, which are exposed to the elements, the 'buff' (being cleaned by authorities) and the actions of other writers (who may spoil writers' pieces), the photograph is the only permanent record of the art.

Most of the earliest documentation of street art and graffiti came about thanks to a limited number of professional – or at least very dedicated – photographers (film was expensive and the young writers could not afford it). Since then, free image sharing on the internet, together with cheaper cameras and camera phones, has supported the growth of the street art fanbase – including well-equipped photographers who document street art. Advances in GPS technology have made mapping street art simpler too, giving rise to location-centric street art websites and apps.

To some extent the greater affordability of digital camera technology has also impacted on the art itself. There are a number of artists who work specifically with the photographs of the art in mind, as opposed to what it looks like *in situ*. Competition among artists today does not need to be about having the largest or the highest number of pieces; new avenues of competition have opened up and some artists focus on producing and recording very small or subtle pieces of art.

The ubiquity of cameras and forums also has drawbacks. Older writers sometimes note that the virtual world gives inexperienced artists more of an outlet for their opinions than in the pre-internet age. Furthermore, artists today have little to no control over who sees their work, which can pose additional legal risks.

The internet has had a different type of impact on stylistic innovation. Undoubtedly, some local styles have been lost as younger artists have absorbed influences from different parts of the world. However, the greater pool of visual cues and global network may have led to faster innovation, since artists are now competing for attention with others the world over.

The progressive expansion of the commercial realm into shared public space and increased internet access has made our current generation the most visually literate in history. Whether or not we can name different artists or artistic movements, we have become increasingly aware of their work as we are constantly bombarded by images.

Visual literacy increased dramatically even before the advent of the internet. Contributing factors may include: increased TV ownership and the increasing amount of leisure time spent in front of a screen; the proliferation of magazines and other publications; and increased penetration of advertisements in shared public spaces.

Innovation in Materials

In addition, through the internet artists can draw more easily on influences from different time periods, not just different cities and countries. Many of the most innovative street artists and writers today are taking their lead from disparate sources, including futurism, constructivism, art nouveau, etc.

Other social innovations and developments have also impacted upon artists, including: increased higher education over the past 30 years, and an expansion in the number of design-related courses and the software that underpins these courses; the proliferation in well-organized street art festivals (discussed later); increasing commercial opportunities for artists; and low-cost flights allowing graffiti tourism to more permissive countries.

Technology has always played an important role in graffiti. The spraypaint originally used by graffiti writers was not designed for graffiti but for other household and industrial purposes. Writers have always played with their materials; fat caps (wide-spraying spray nozzles from other consumer products) enabled writers to paint faster as long ago as the early 1970s.

The first paints designed specifically for graffiti writers were created in 1994 by the Spanish company Montana. The advent of dedicated graffiti paint companies greatly accelerated innovations in paint formulation, as well as the availability of spraypaint caps that produce different effects, and the range of available paint colours. Today there are companies developing high-tech polymers that can protect street art murals against the elements for decades, allowing street art projects to take on greater relevance to architectural and city planning.

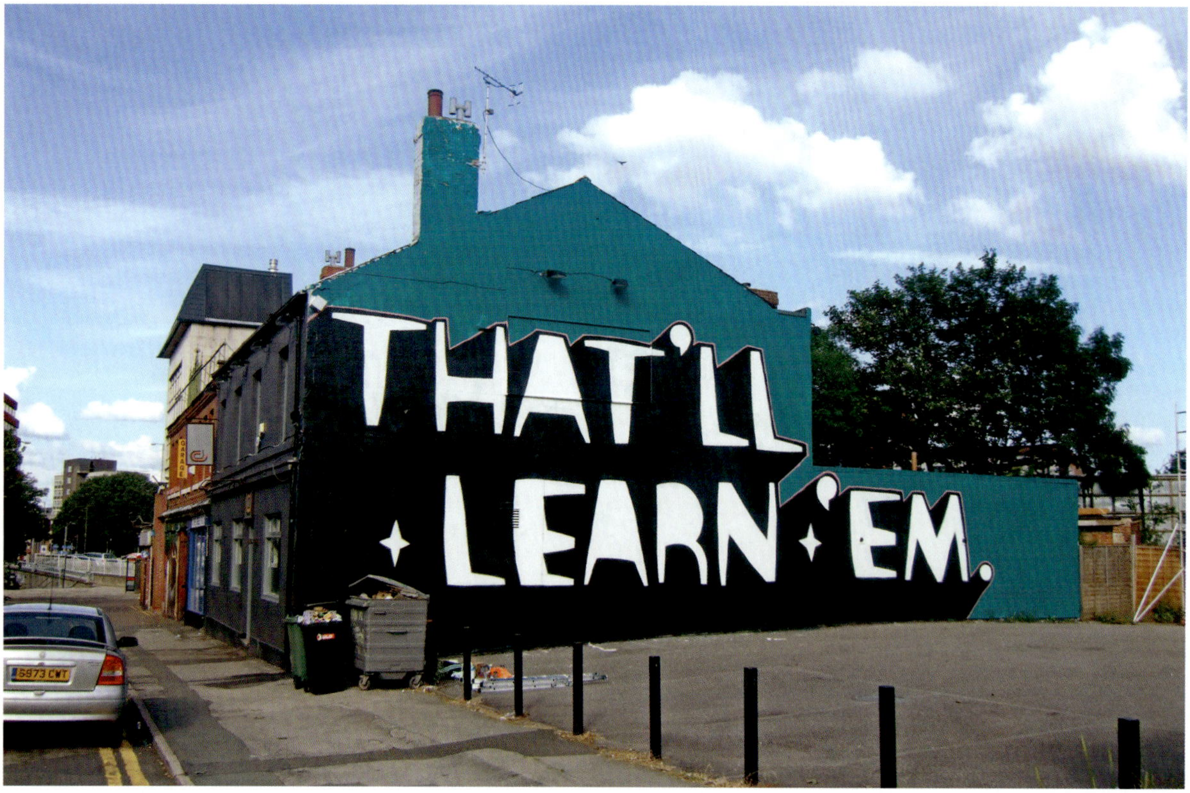

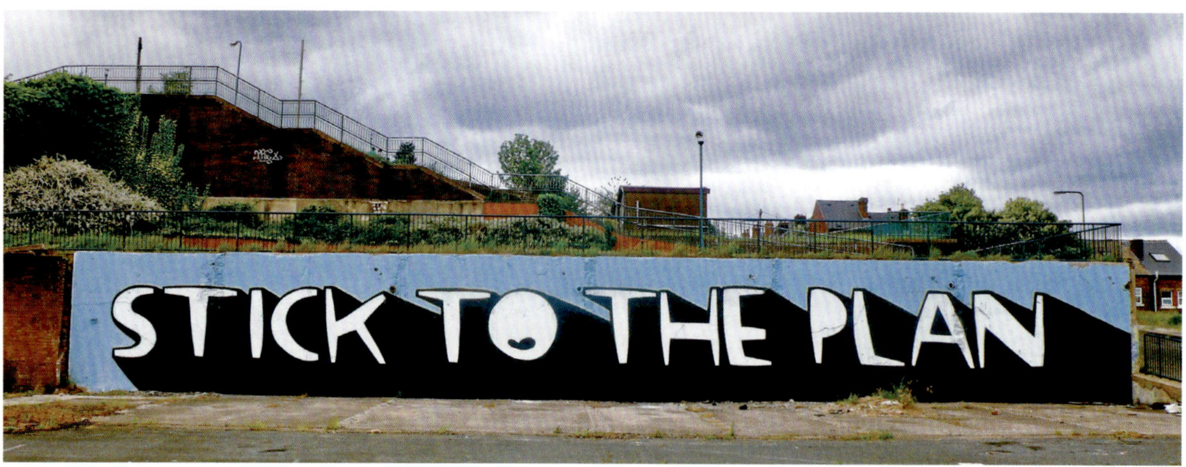
THAT'LL LEARN 'EM.
STICK TO THE PLAN

MOVEMENTS & THEMES

The following photographs show some of the visual trends in street art and graffiti. The first key trend comes squarely from a graffiti background: alluding to shapes in three dimensions. Through years of refinement and careful study of form and light, graffiti artists have developed ever more realistic interpretations of 3D shapes on walls. One result of this trend has been that some artists have moved into sculpture. Other developments we look at are: anamorphic street art and graffiti, photorealism and abstracted photorealism, font work, calligraphy and forms of abstraction.

Modern street artists sometimes choose past artistic movements as their influences and not their social peers. The photographs on these pages show how contemporary street artists have used past masters as raw materials for their own art.

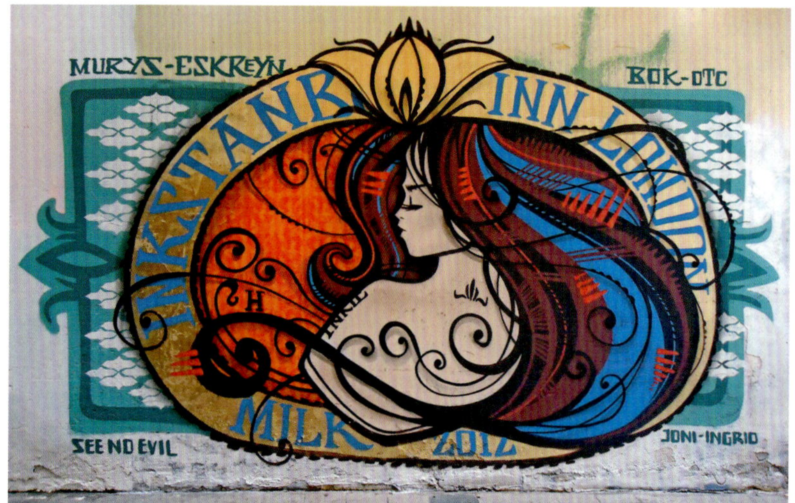

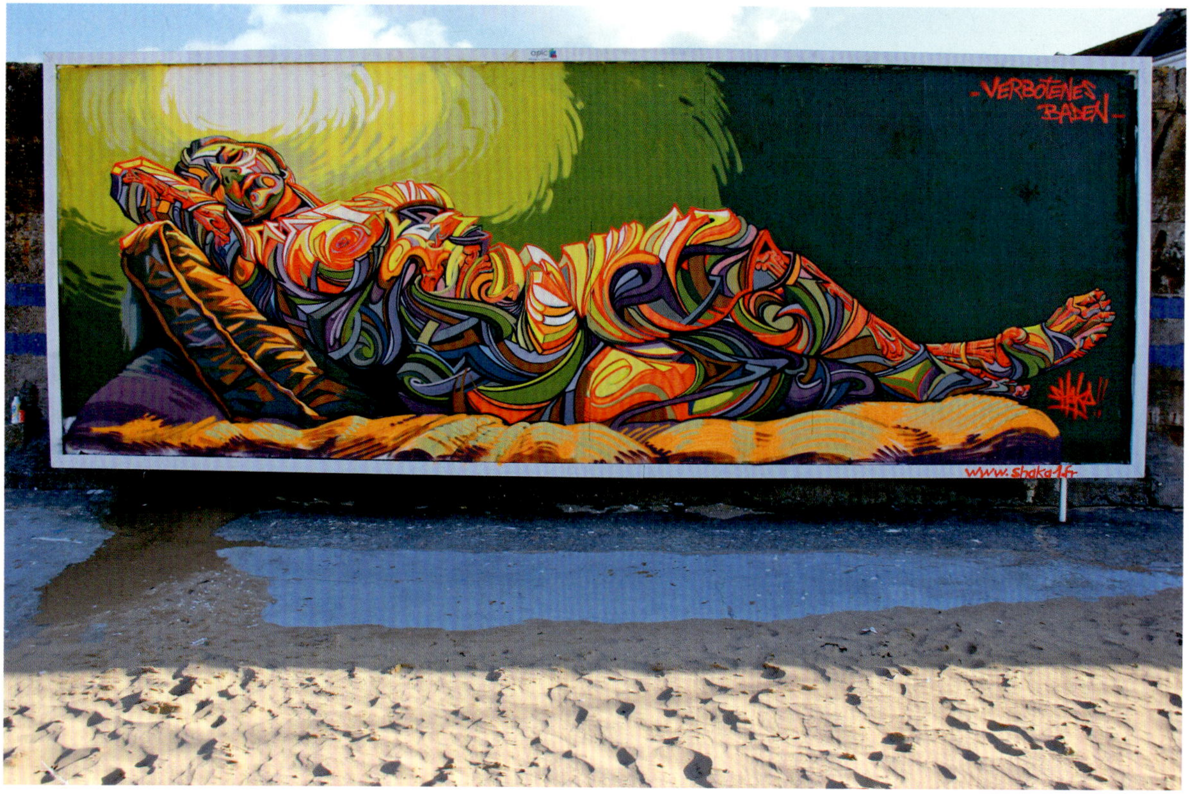

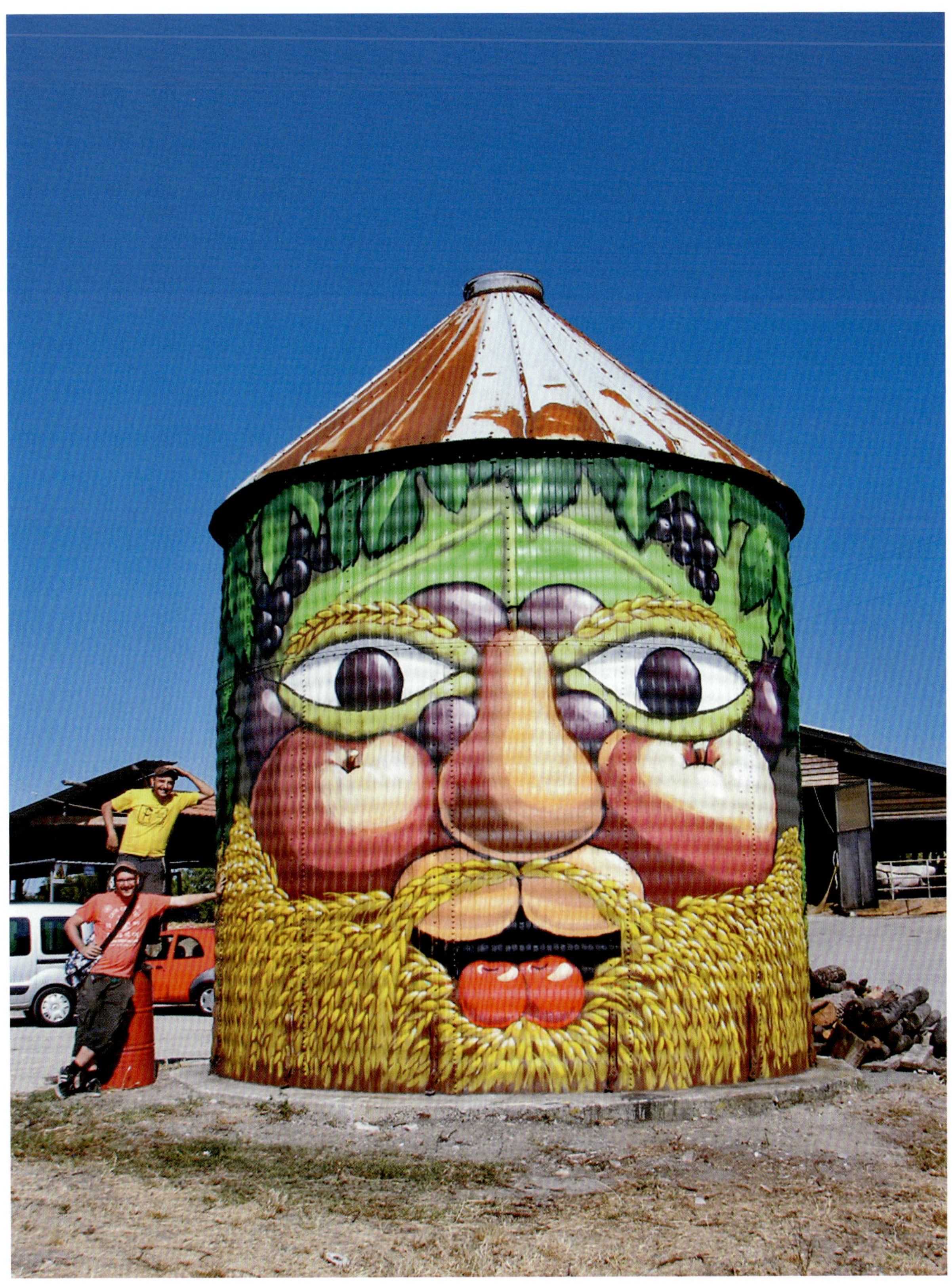

Graffiti has always alluded to a physical form – a presence in three-dimensional space. From a very early point in the history of graffiti, not long after artists were making full pieces, effects were added to give the impression that pieces were coming out of the wall (or train). Artists added shadows under their pieces and 3D blocks behind the letters, and they have continued to develop the concepts of 3D in two ways: making their pieces look more 3D by better approximating how incumbent light would reflect off of their piece, and through anamorphic work and tromp l'oeil.

The following pages show how today's artists are capable of producing realistic 3D forms on walls and reveal examples of artists moving beyond walls to produce sculptures. Also covered is the rediscovery of anamorphic painting (where the painting looks like it exists in three-dimensional space when viewed from a specific angle).

Artists working on pavements with chalk have long used anamorphic work, but it has only become popular in the last few years among those with a more graffiti-orientated background. Some artists, such as Replete from the UK, are combining anamorphism with other techniques, such as painting on cellophane. This development makes it look as if the object the artist is painting really exists in space, and is not connected to the ground in any way.

PAGE 182:
Kid Acne in Sheffield.

PAGES 184-5,
CLOCKWISE FROM TOP
LEFT:
UK's Inkie in
Istanbul, influenced
by Alphonse Mucha/
Italy's Pao, influenced
by Arcimboldo/France's
Shaka, influenced by Van
Gogh.

CLOCKWISE FROM
BELOW:
Germany's Daim and
Loomit (this is a
section of a larger
mural)/Mies and Urok
in Potsdam, Germany/
Mies and Urok in
Potsdam, Germany.

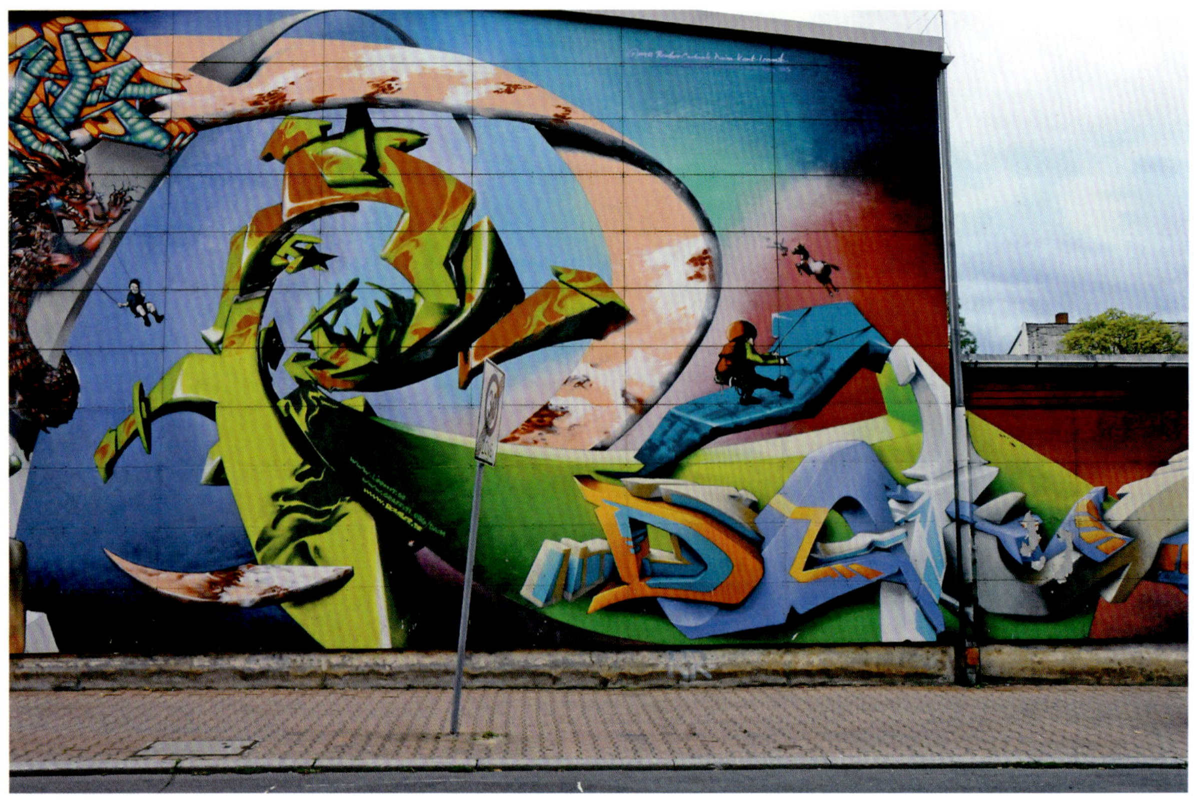

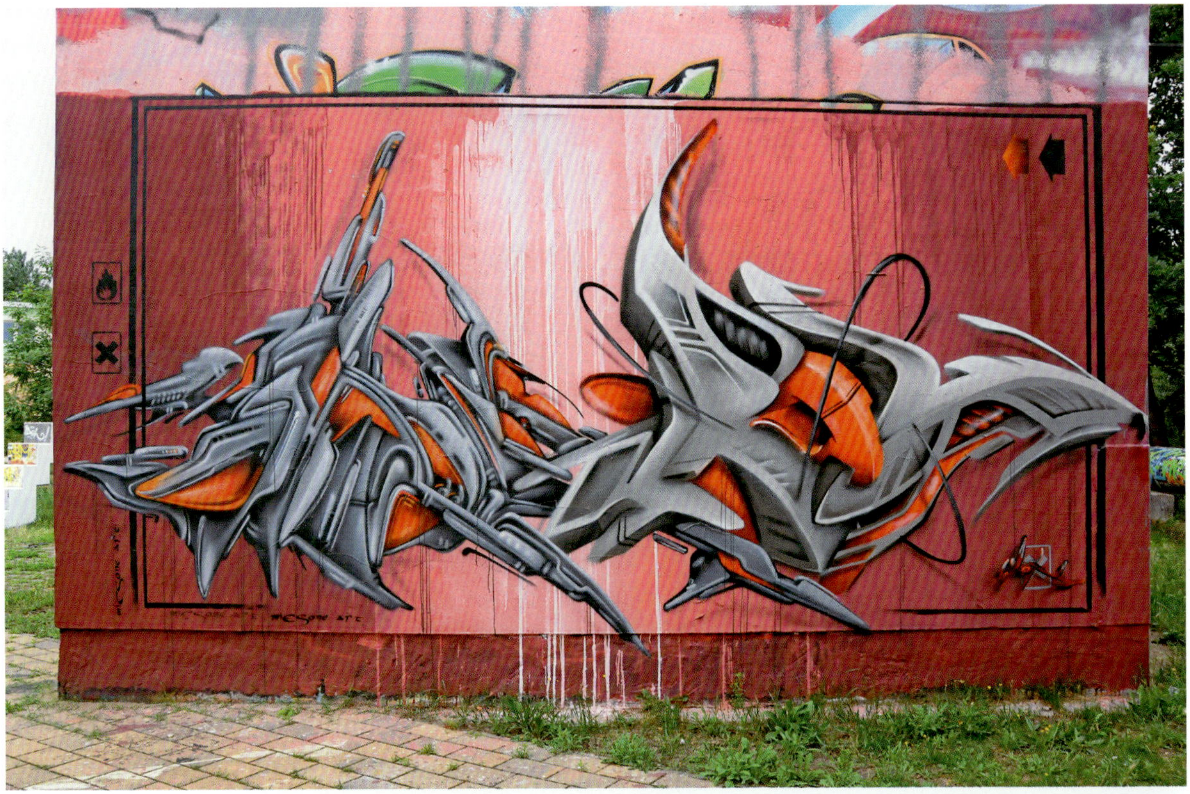

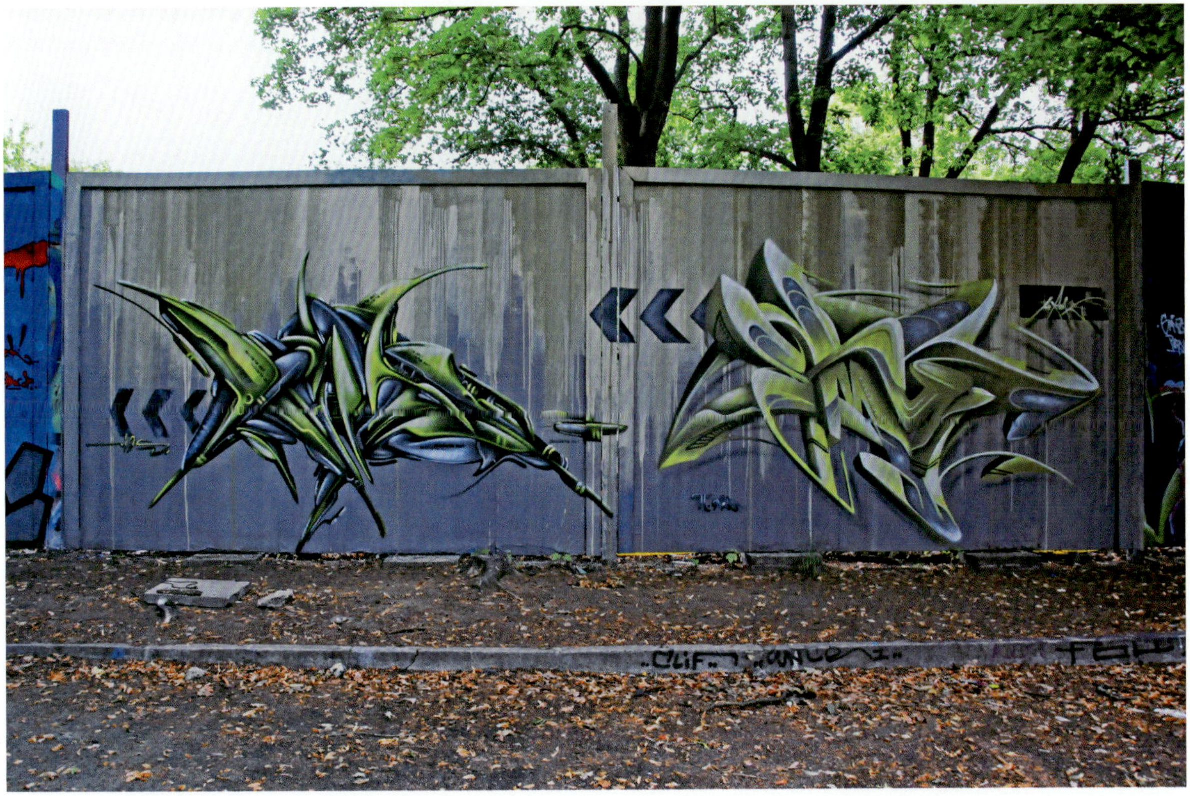

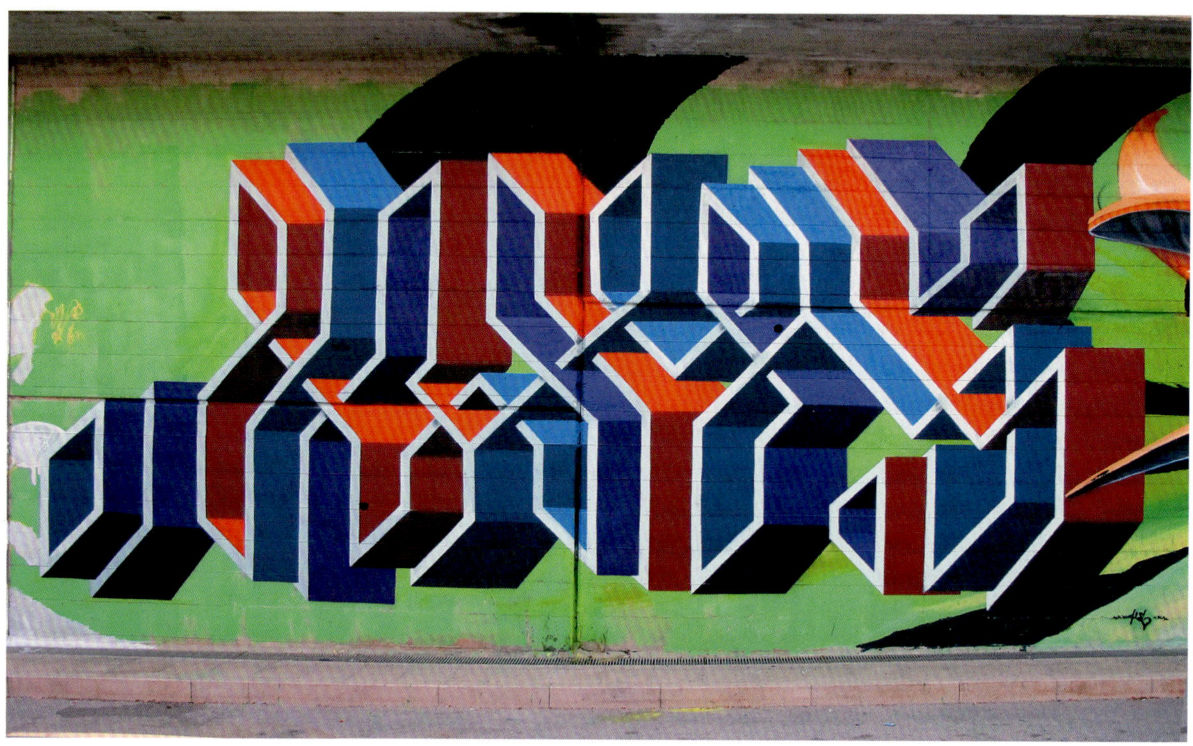

CLOCKWISE FROM
ABOVE:
Joys in Italy/Made 154
in Italy/Made 154 in
Italy.

PAGES 190-1,
CLOCKWISE FROM TOP
LEFT:
Daim in Munich,
Germany/Dado in New
York/Dado in Italy/
Etnik in Pisa, Italy.

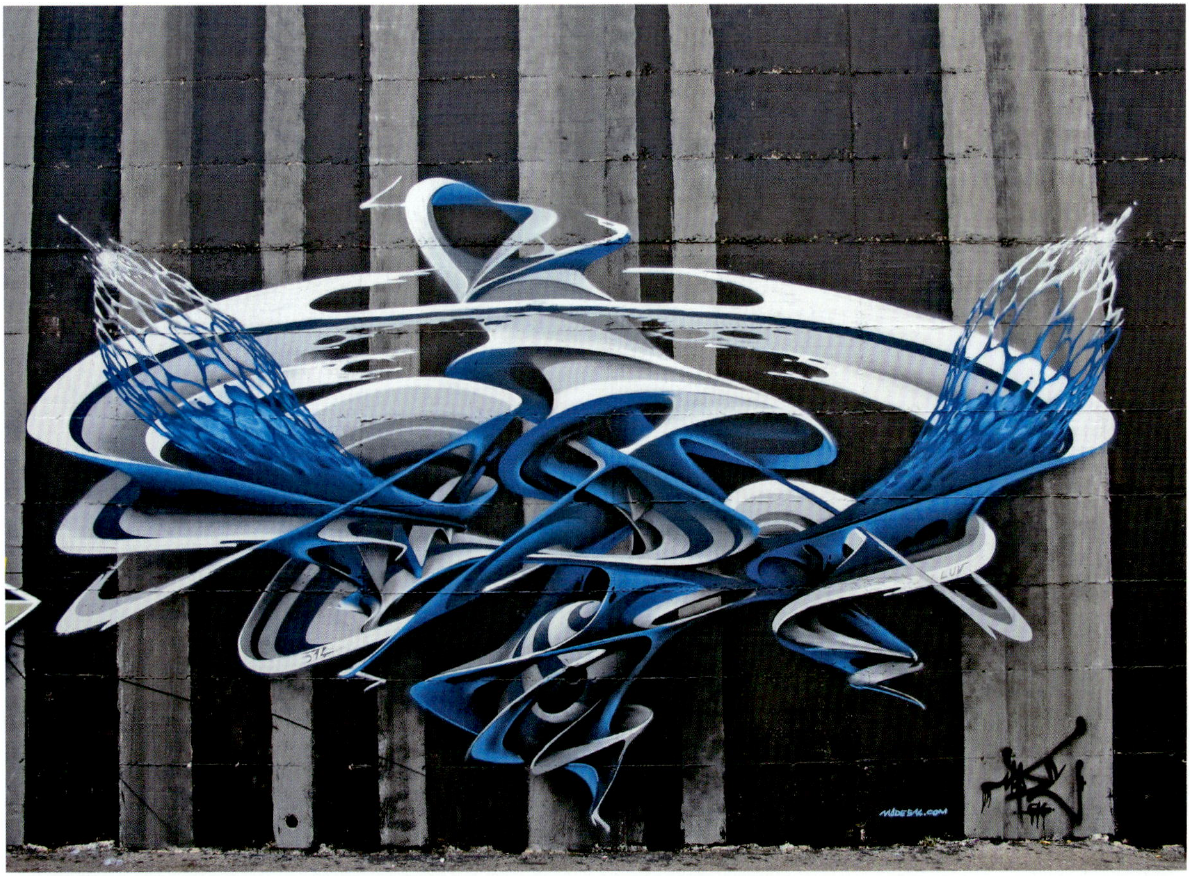

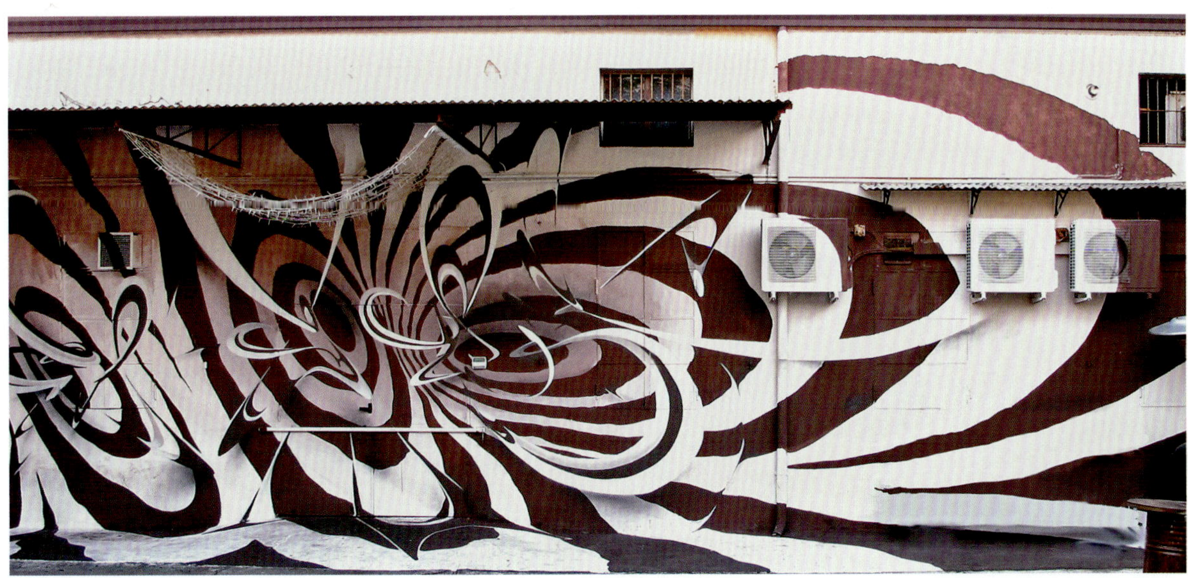

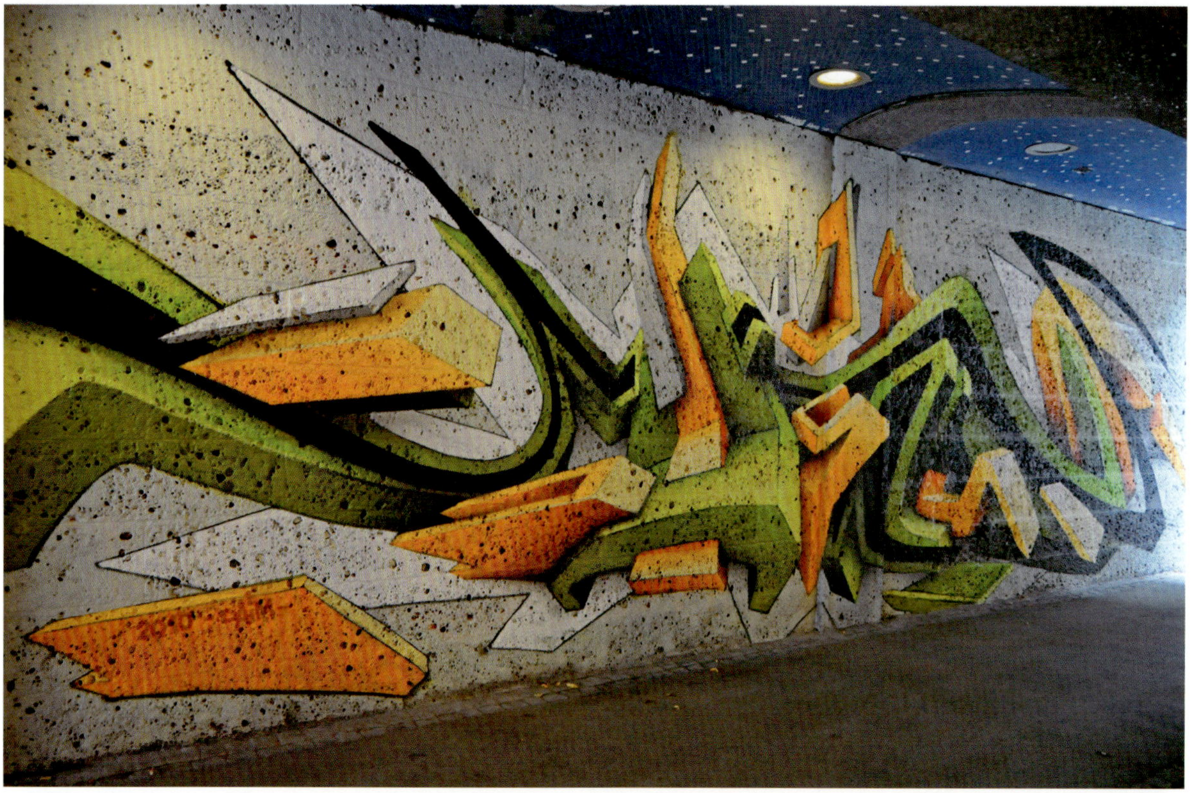

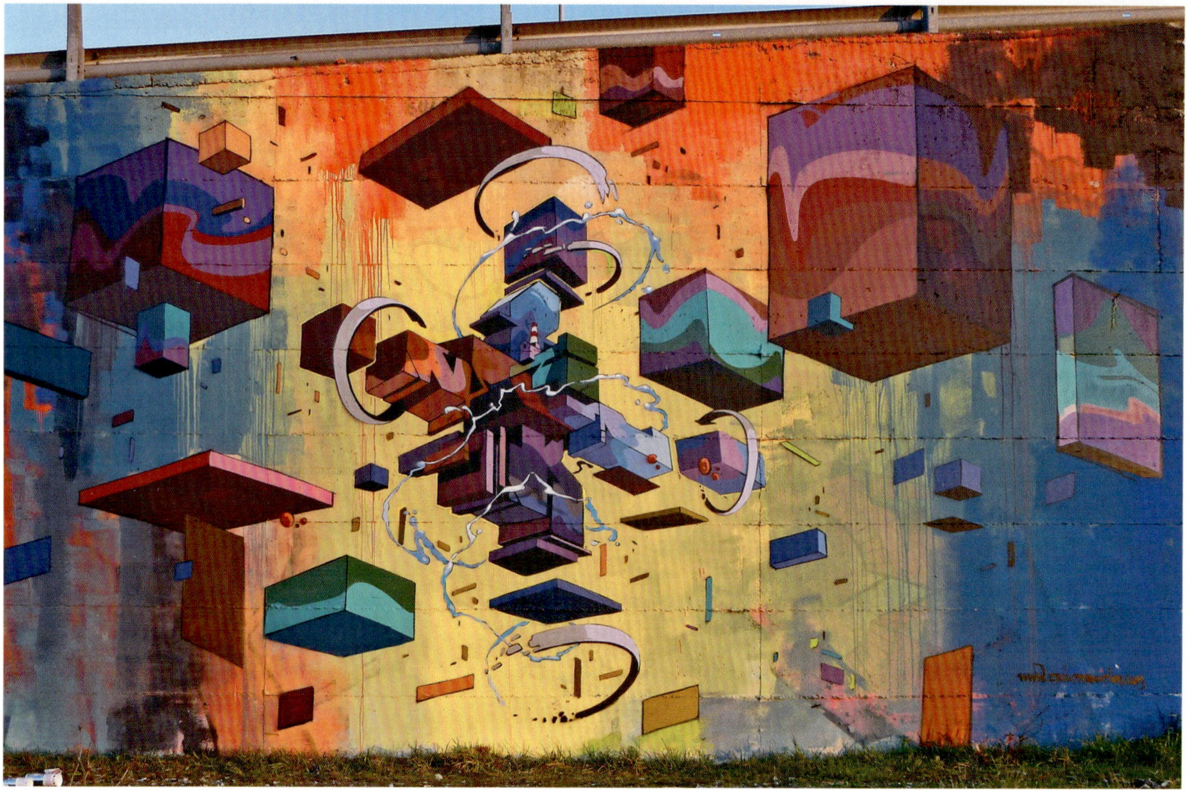

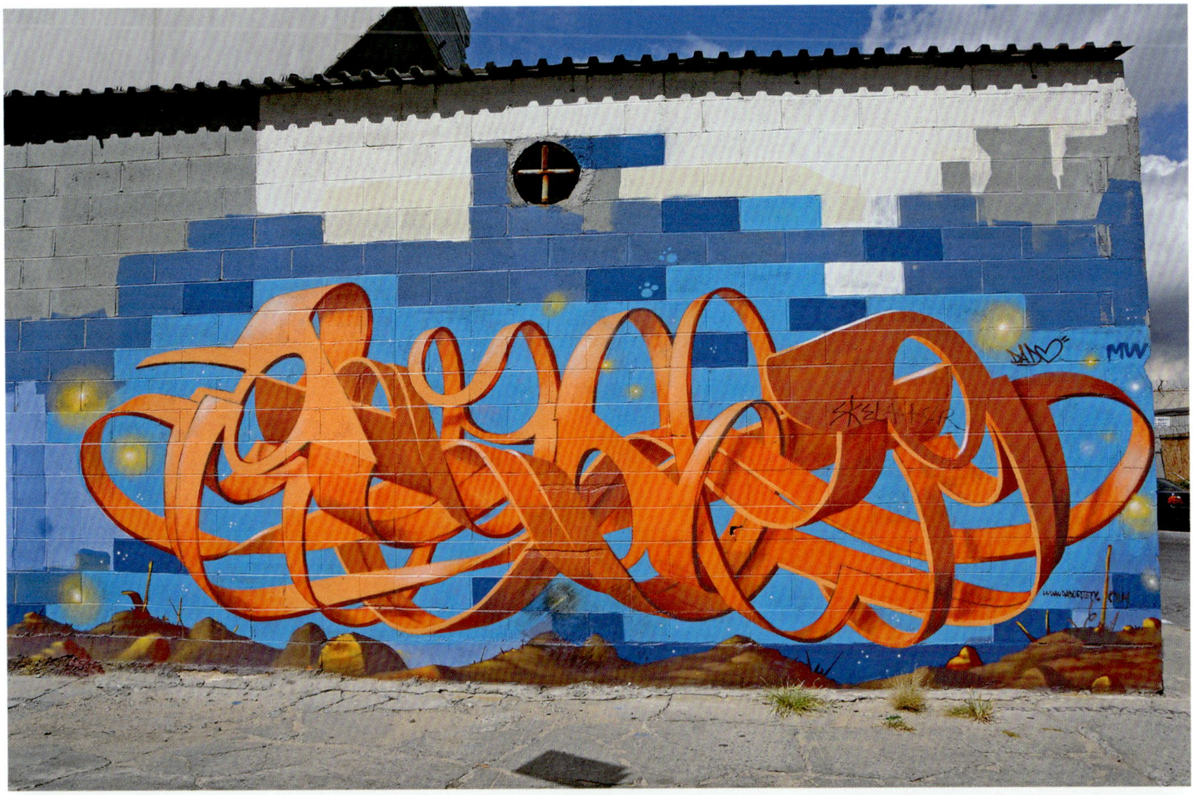

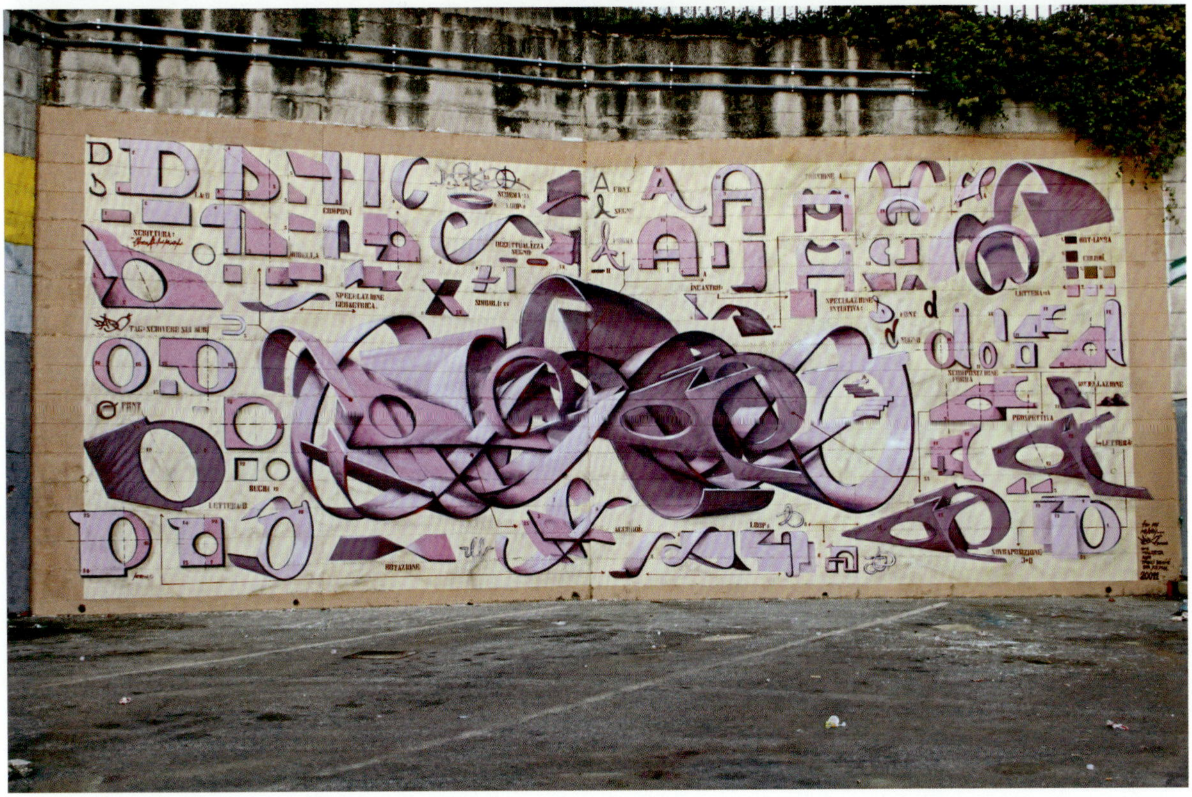

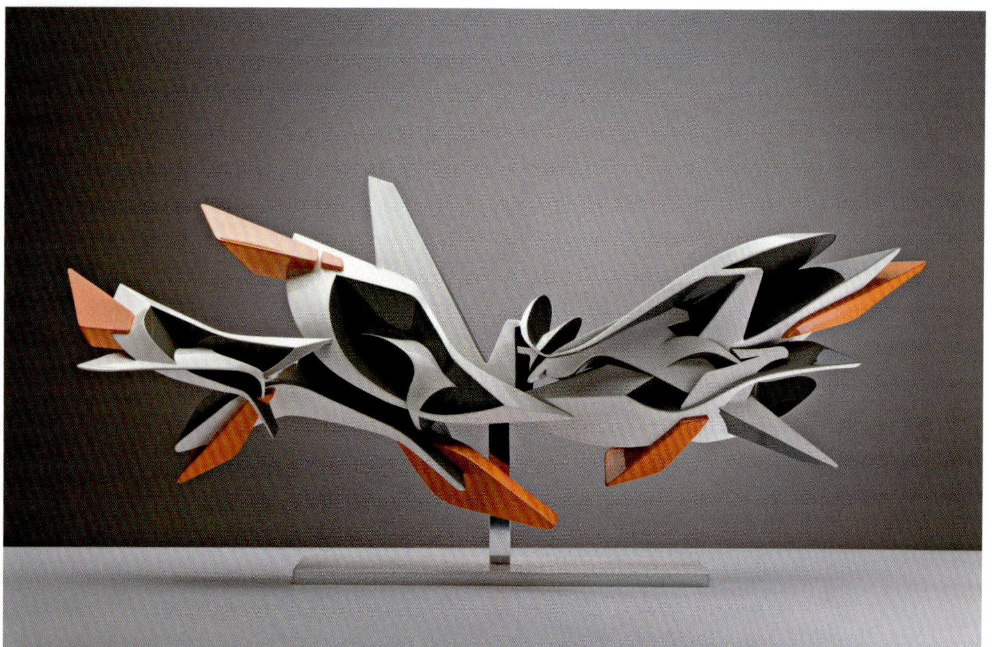

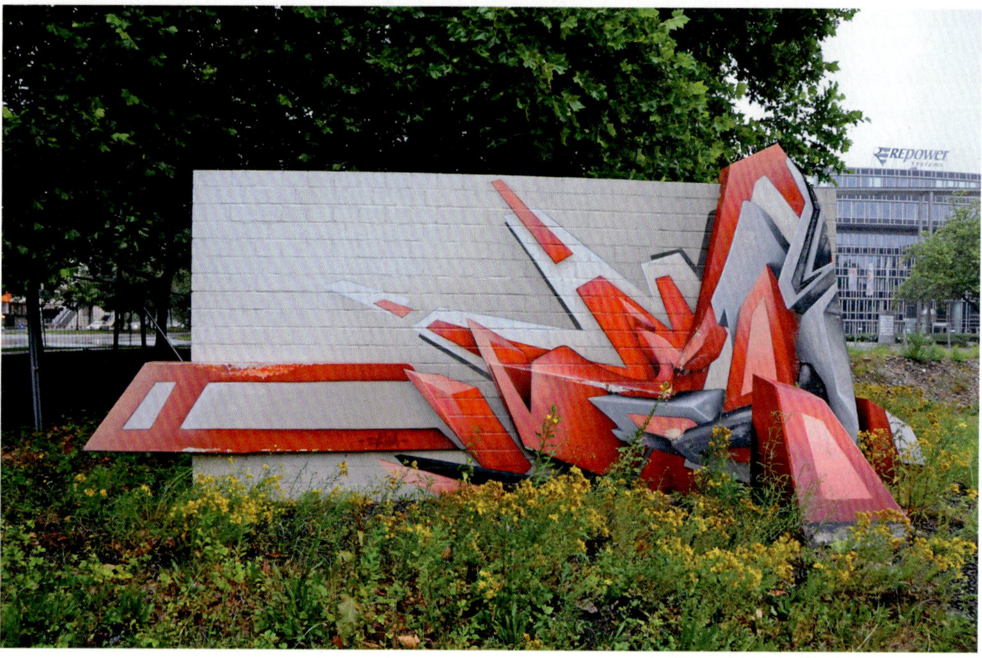

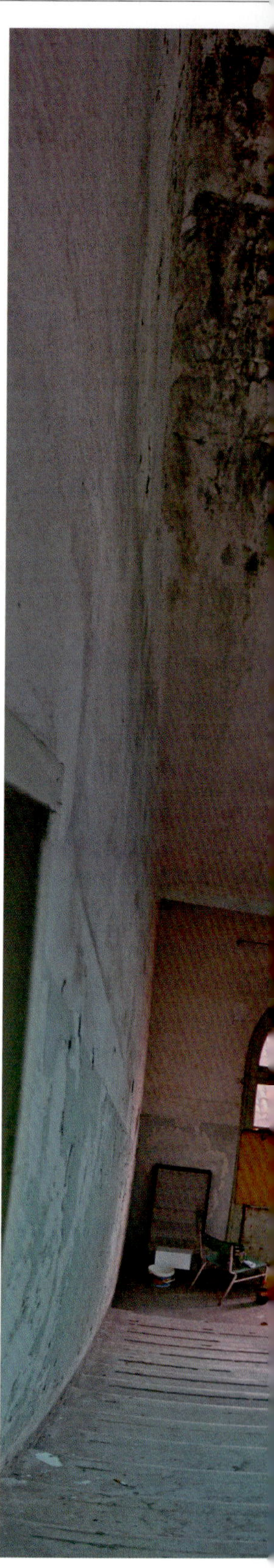

CLOCKWISE FROM
RIGHT:
Peeta in Venice/
Sculpture by Daim in
Hamburg/Sculpture by
Peeta.

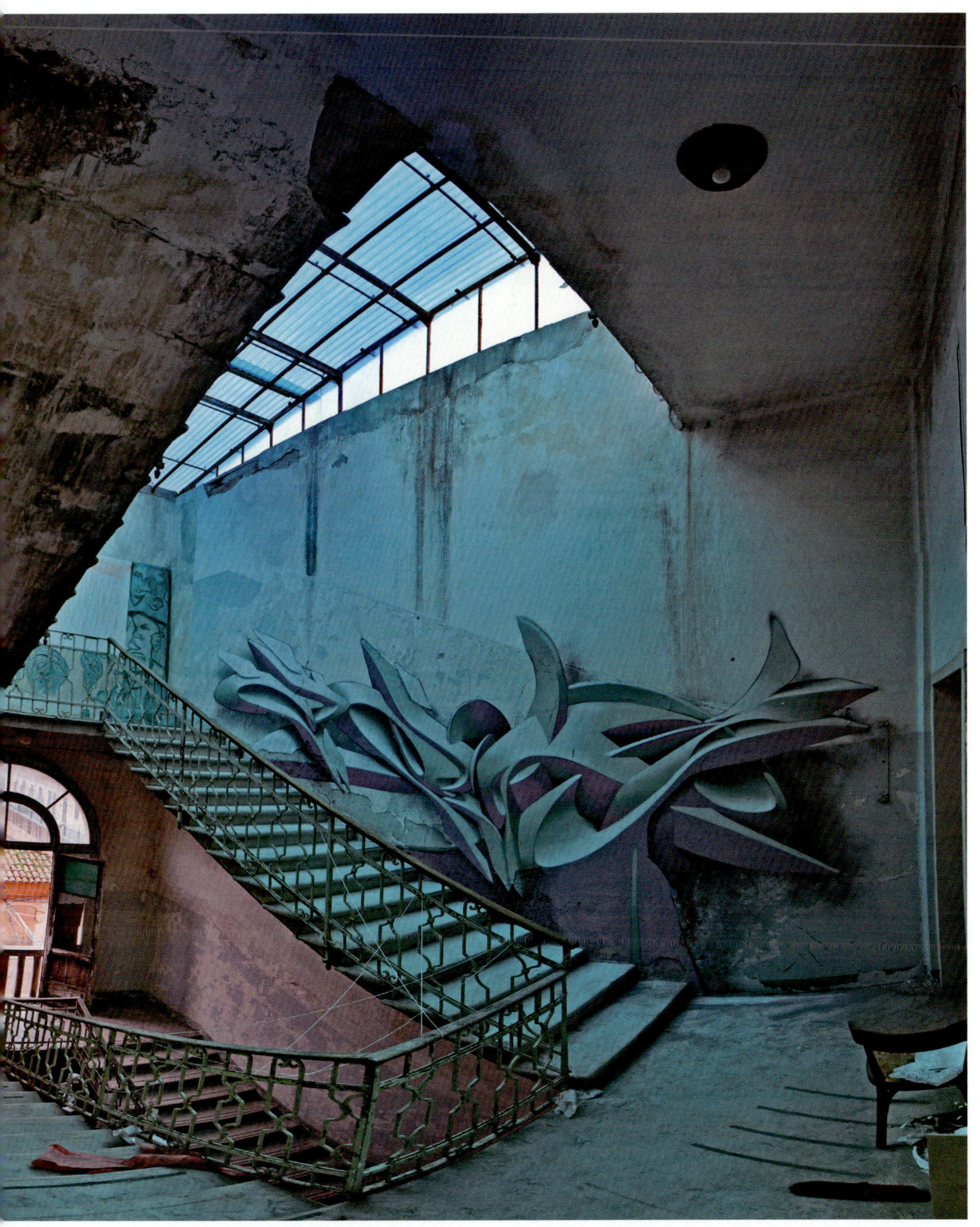

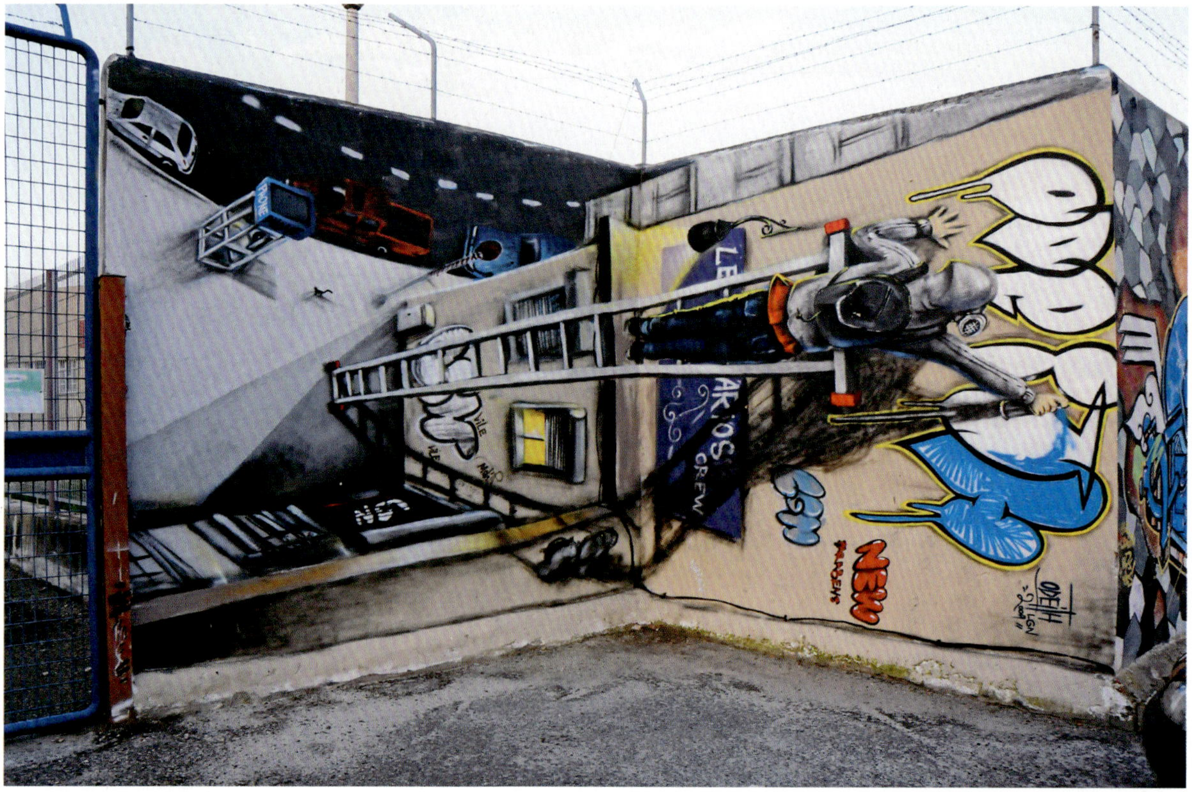

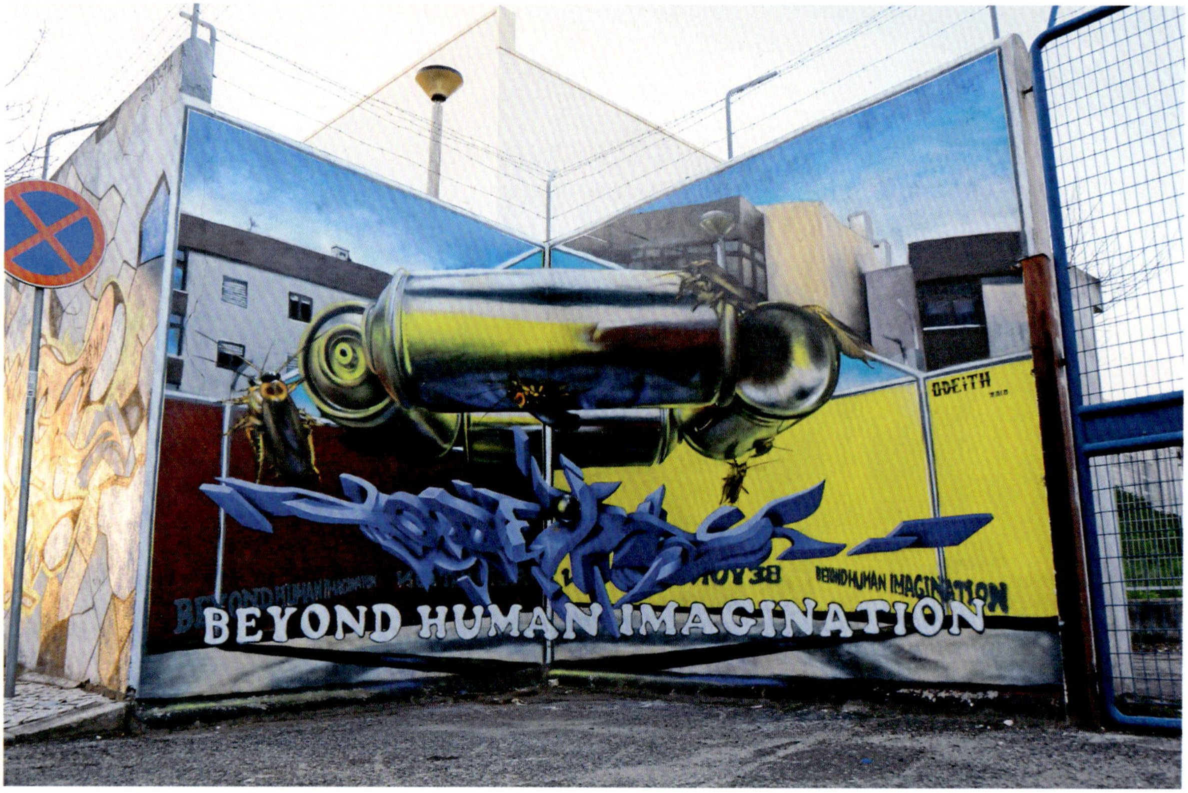

ODEITH

ODEITH
BEYOND HUMAN IMAGINATION
BEYOND HUMAN IMAGINATION

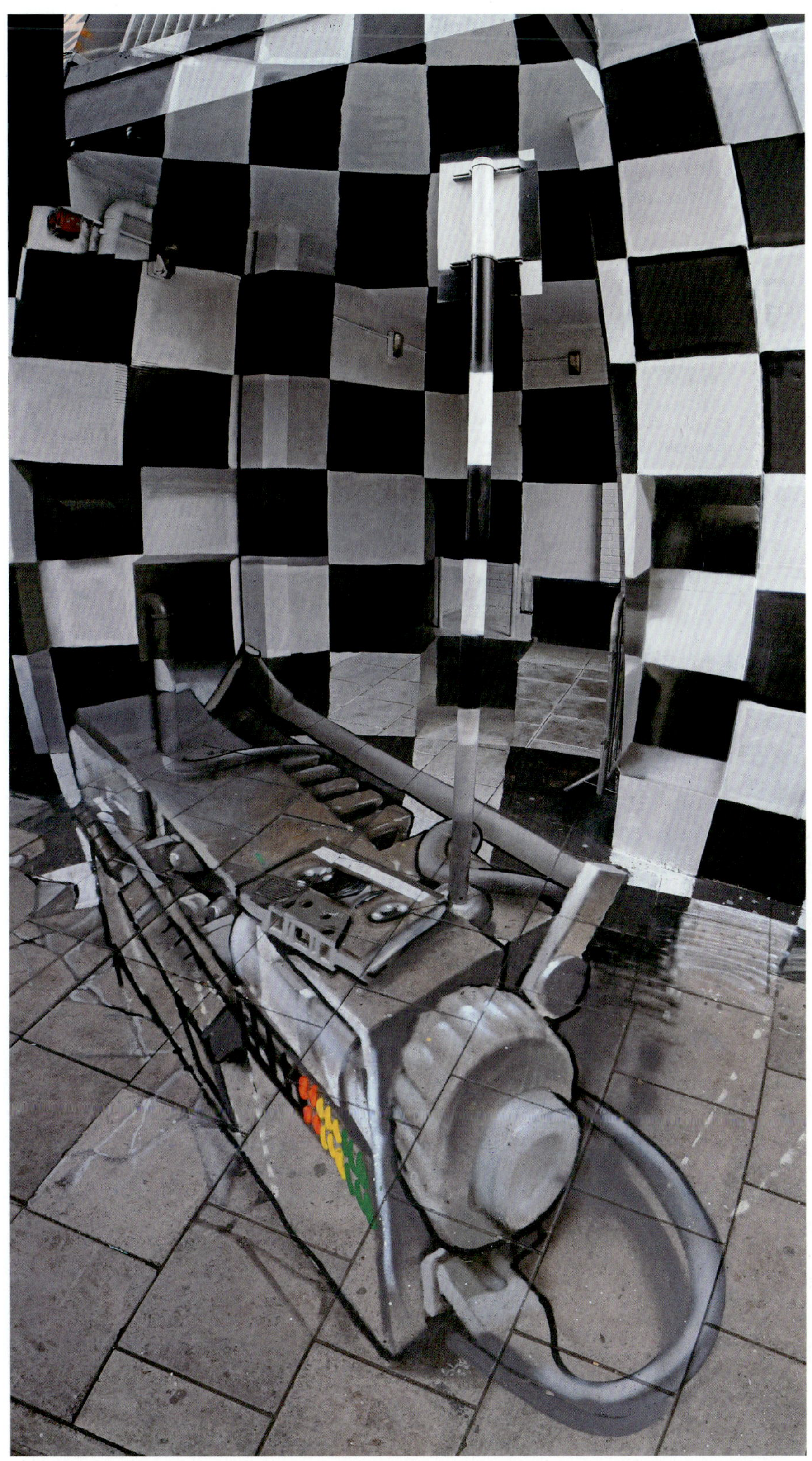

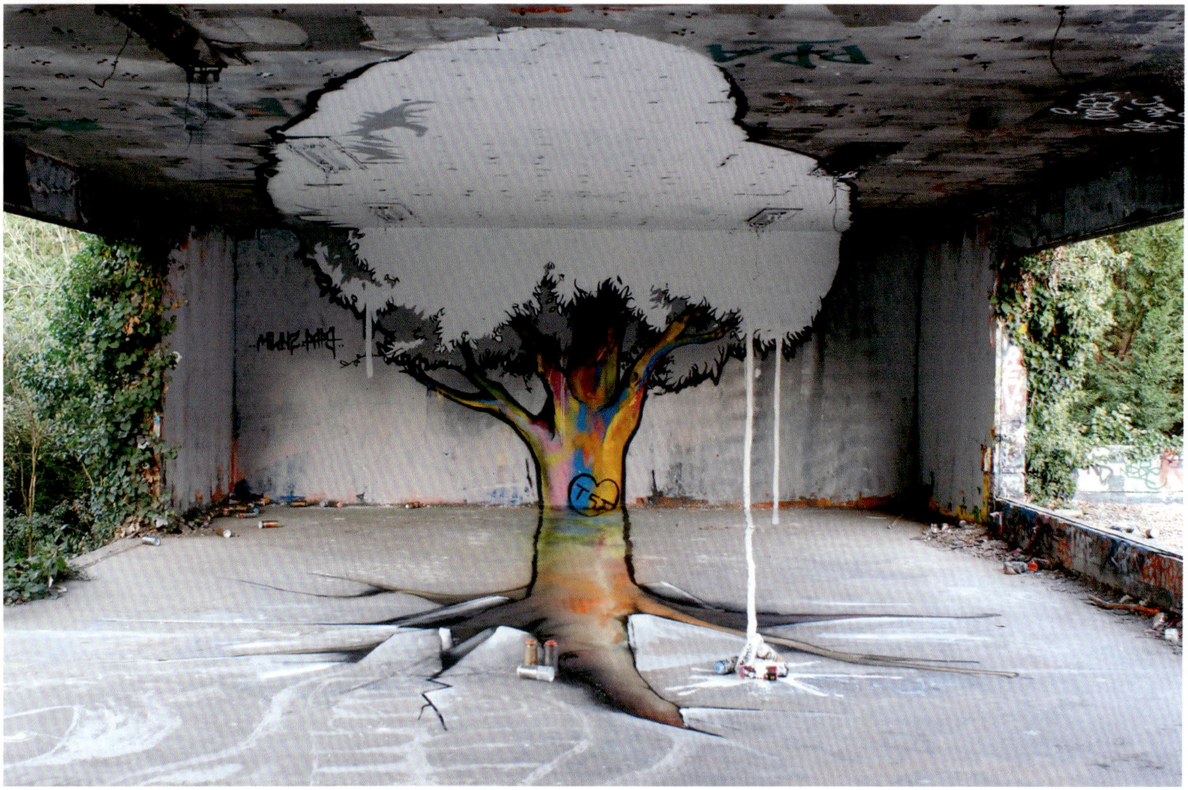

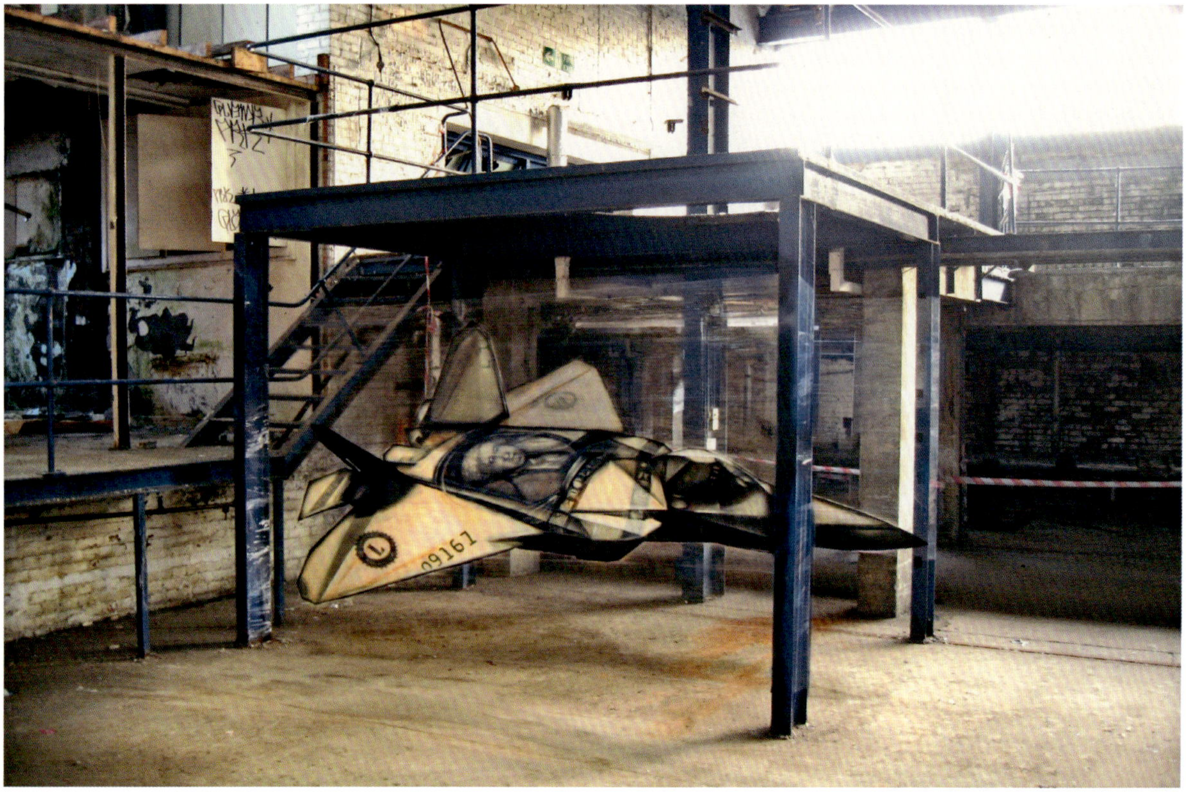

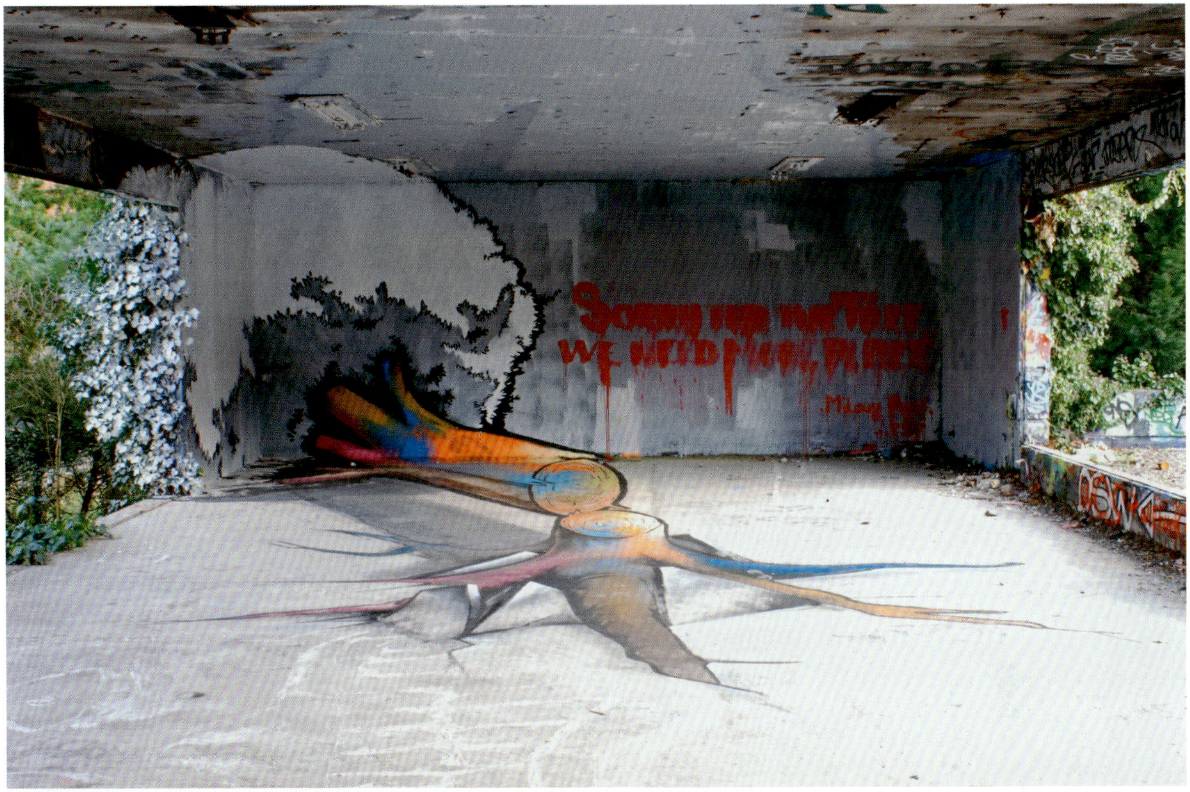

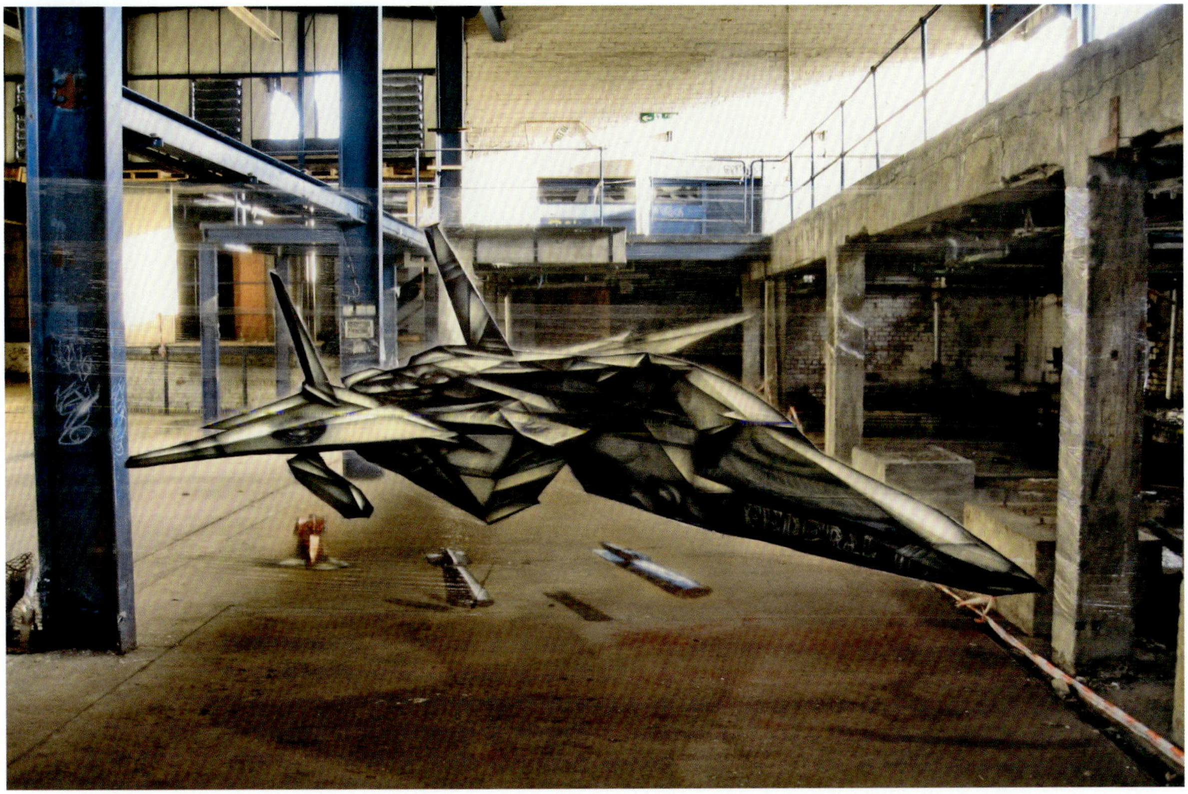

Artists approximating increasing levels of reality are something we have already seen. However, with the increasing popularity of figurative street art and graffiti artists working on ever-more realistic characters, there have been major strides in producing photorealistic artwork on the streets. Furthermore, there are also artists who have taken their capabilities to produce photorealistic characters and have twisted them, producing fantasy characters that look highly realistic.

CLOCKWISE FROM
BELOW:
Trans-One in Essex,
UK/Mateo Lara in
Barcelona/Cry
in Essex, UK.

PAGES 200-1,
CLOCKWISE FROM TOP
LEFT:
Spain's Belin in
Eindhoven, The
Netherlands/Gaser
in Spain/Belin.

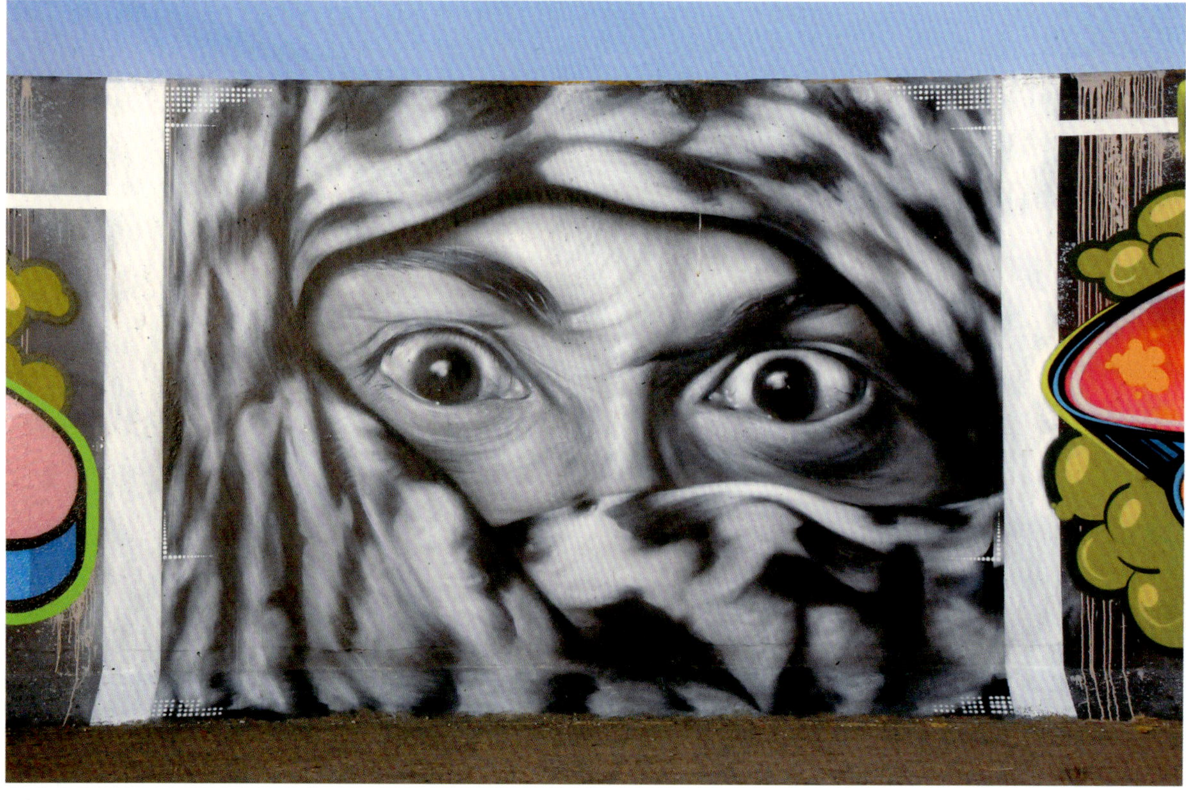

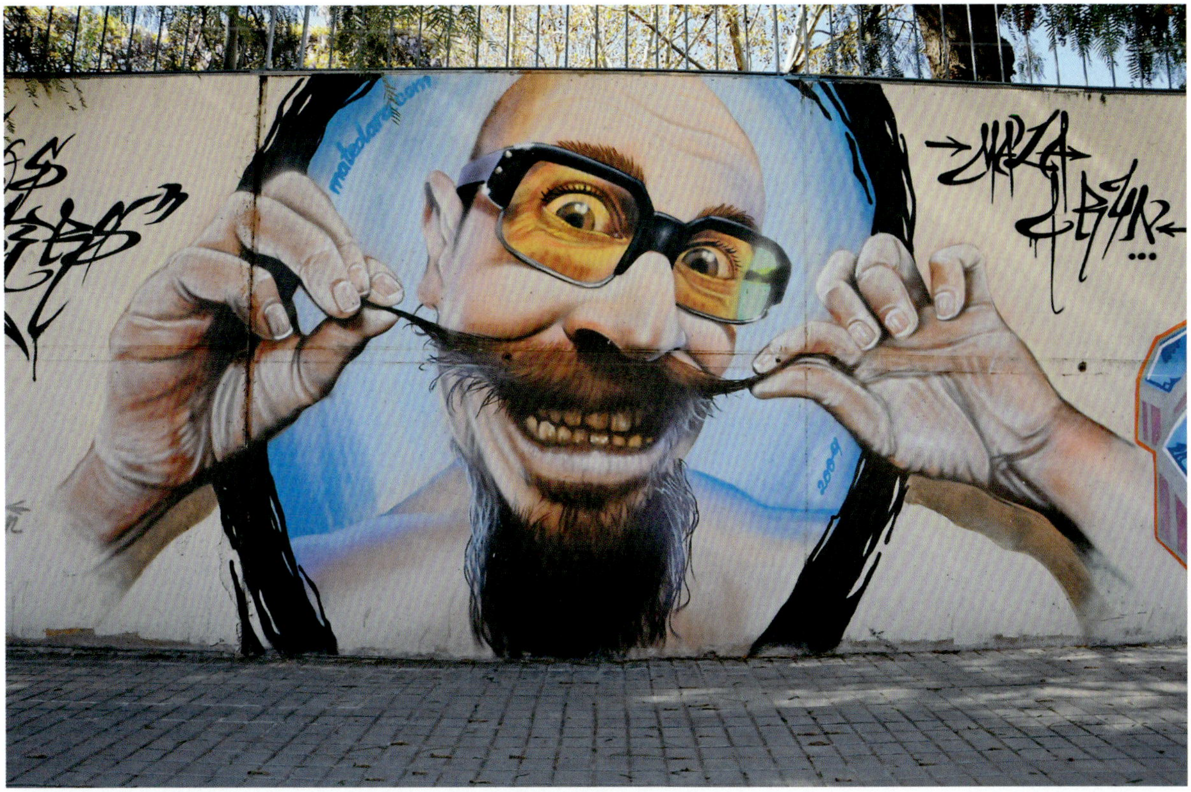

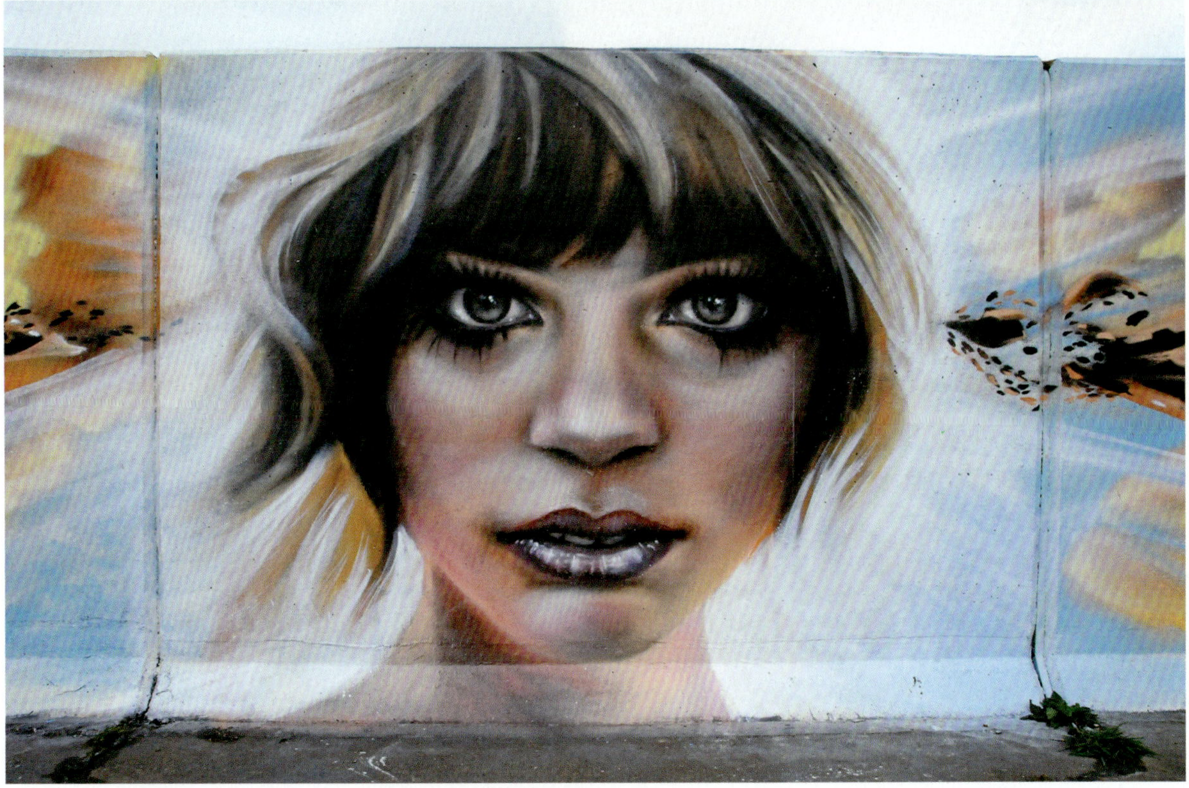

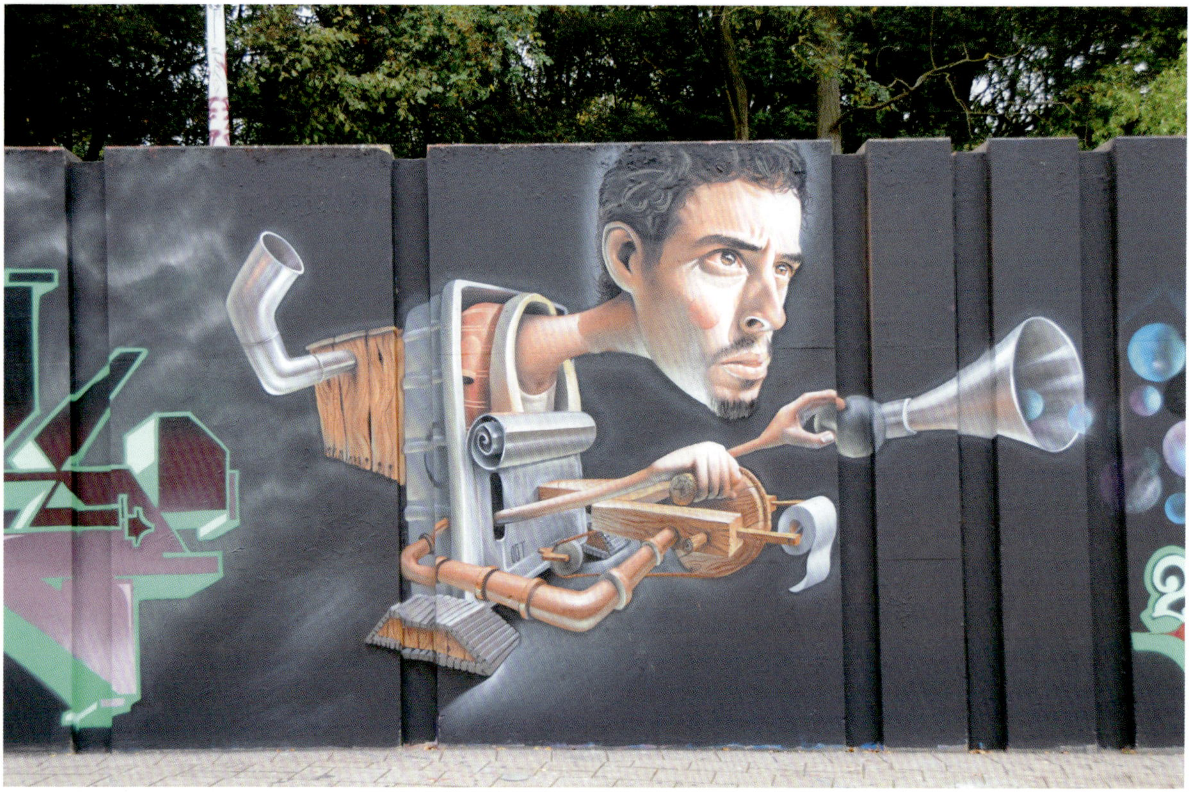

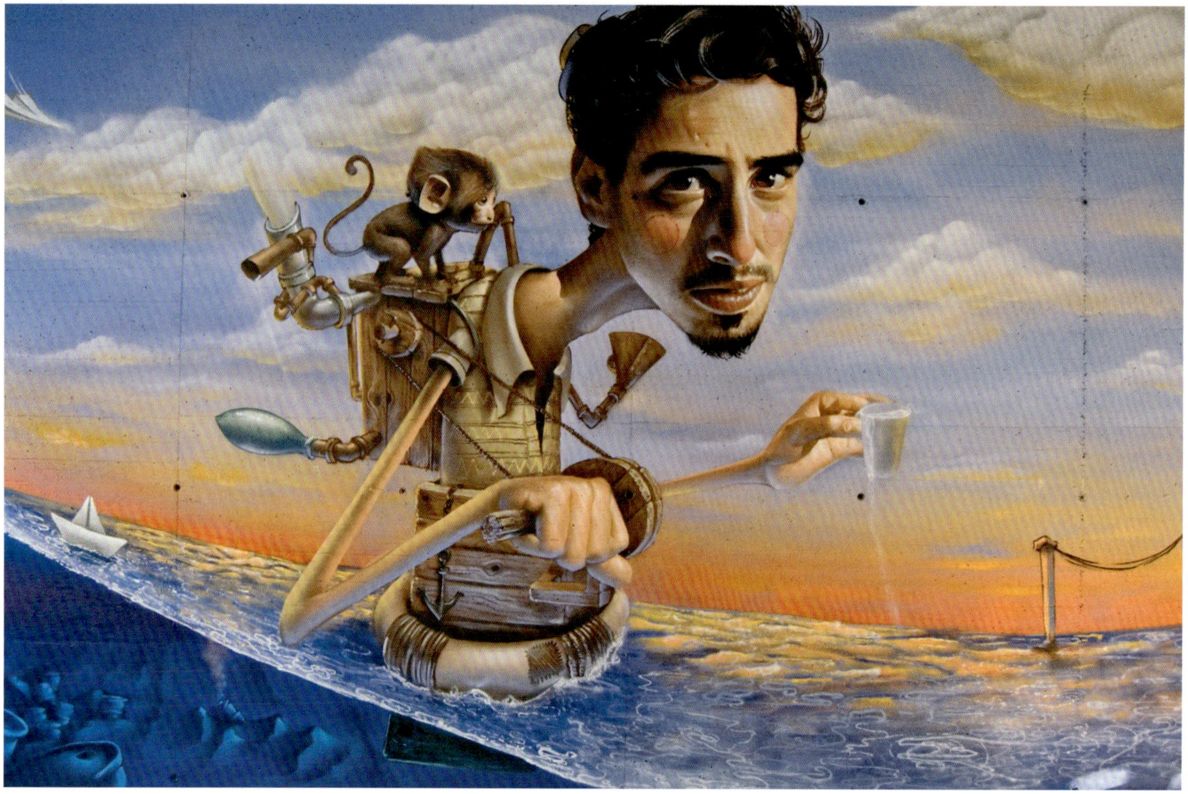

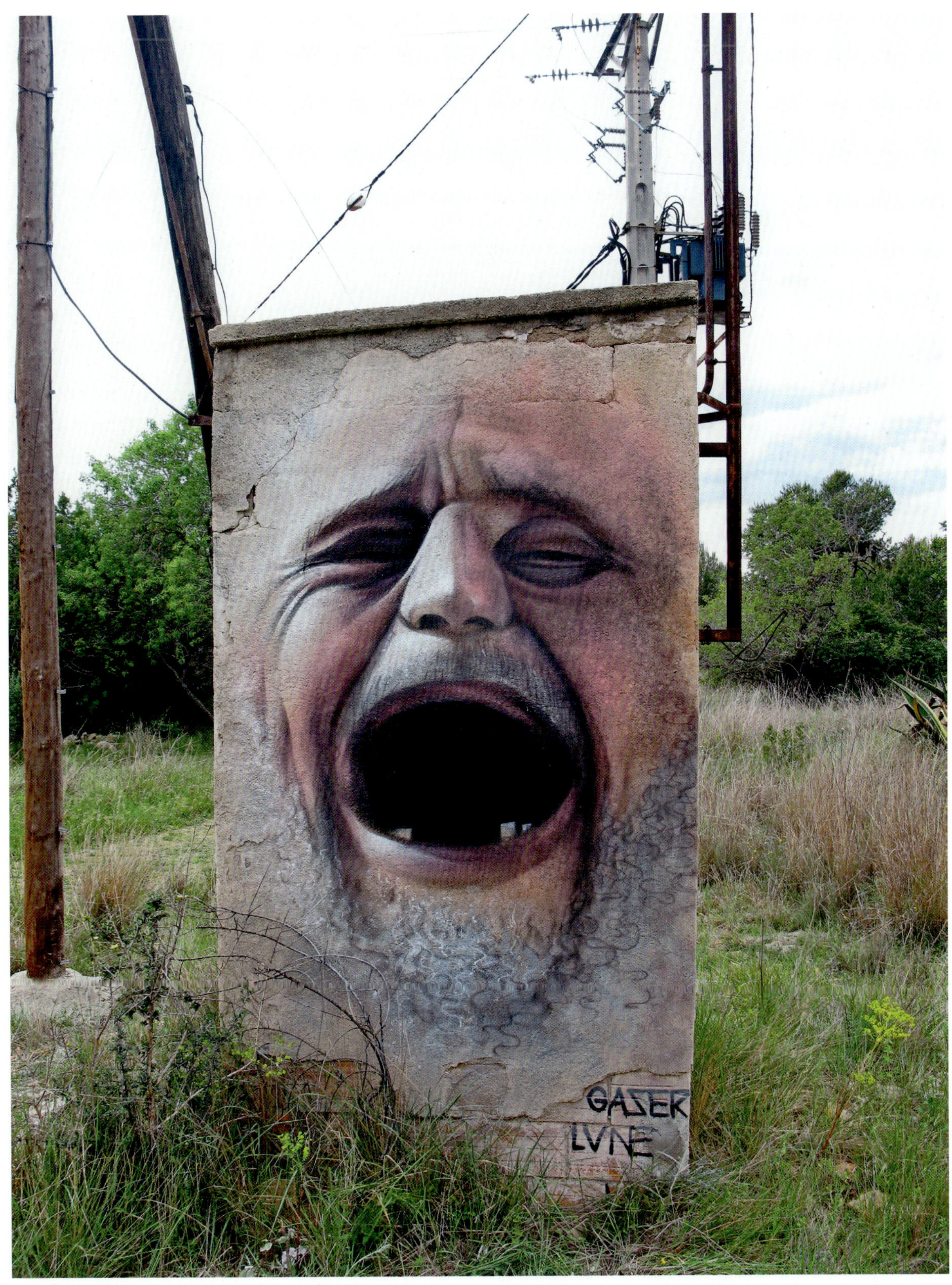
GASER
LVNE

Even within photorealism there are discernable topics and sub-trends that artists focus on. One example is honing in on the eyes, as shown here.

CLOCKWISE FROM
BELOW:
Just Cobe in Germany/
Smug in Bristol/Eoin in
Ireland/Ino in Athens/
Ireland's Eoin in
Hawaii/Ino in Athens.

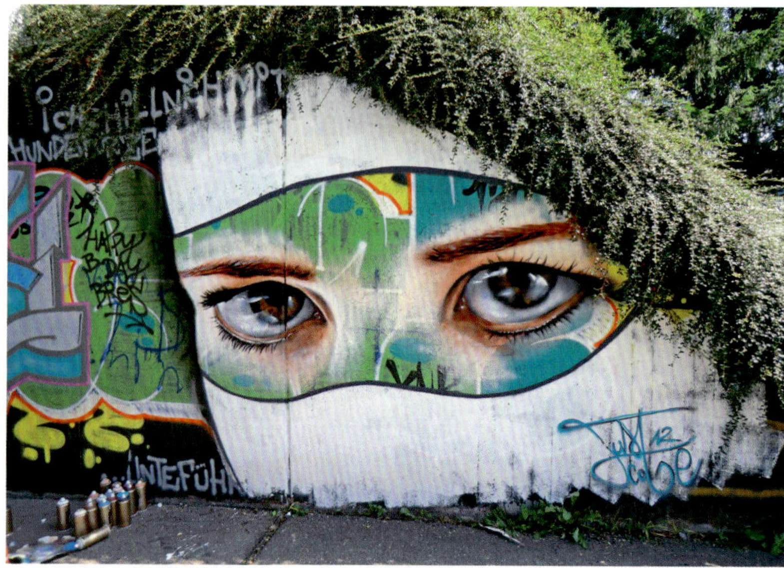

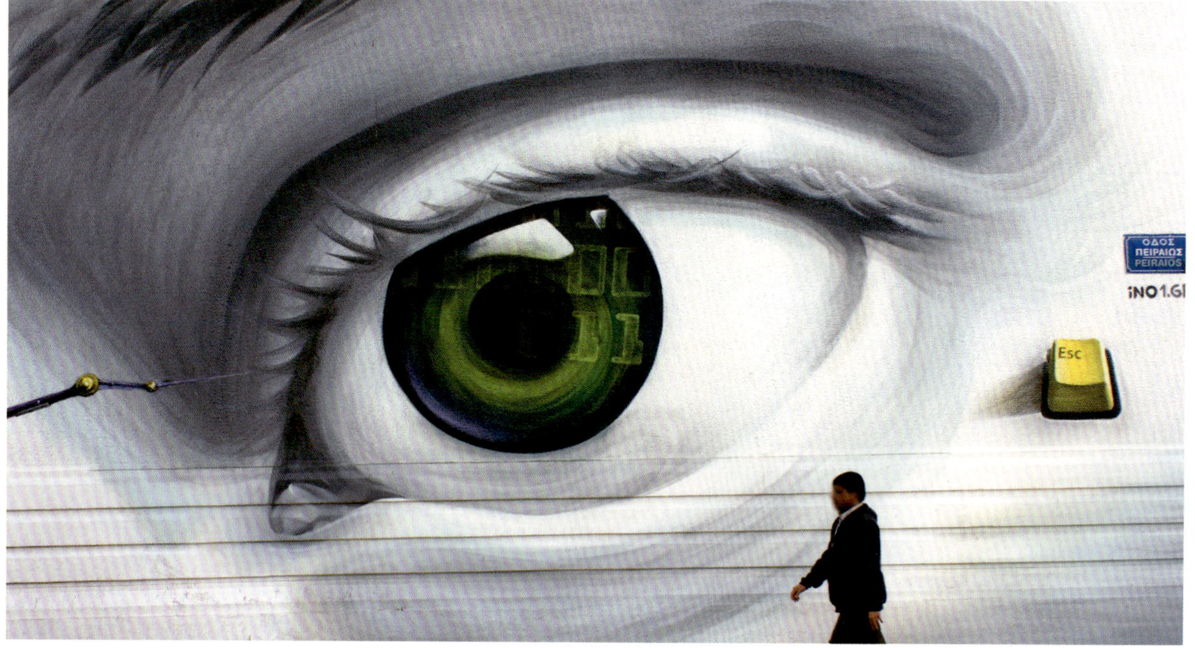

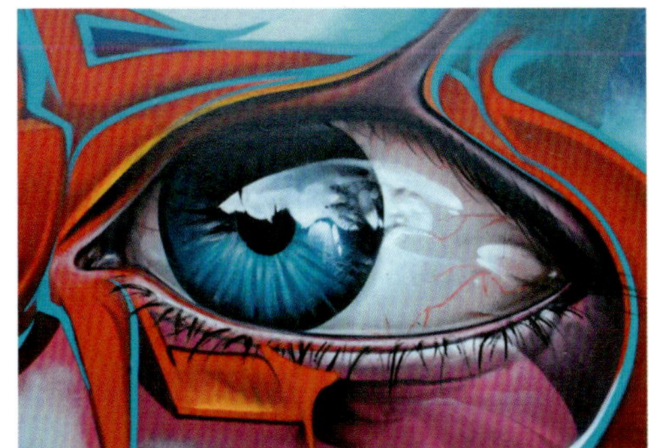

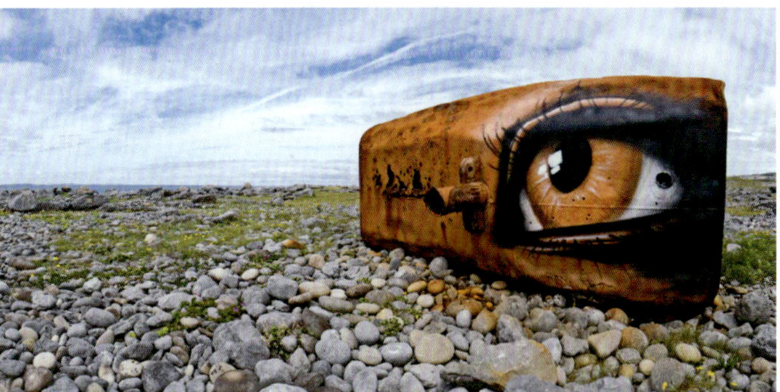

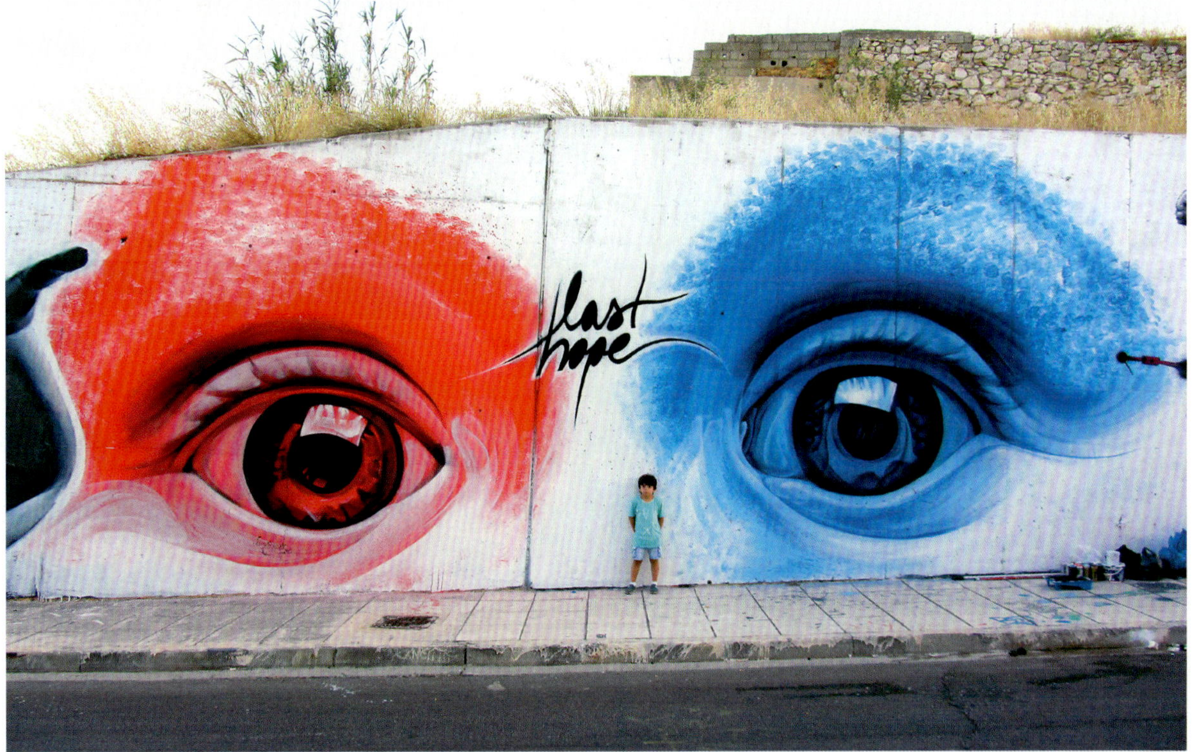
last
hope

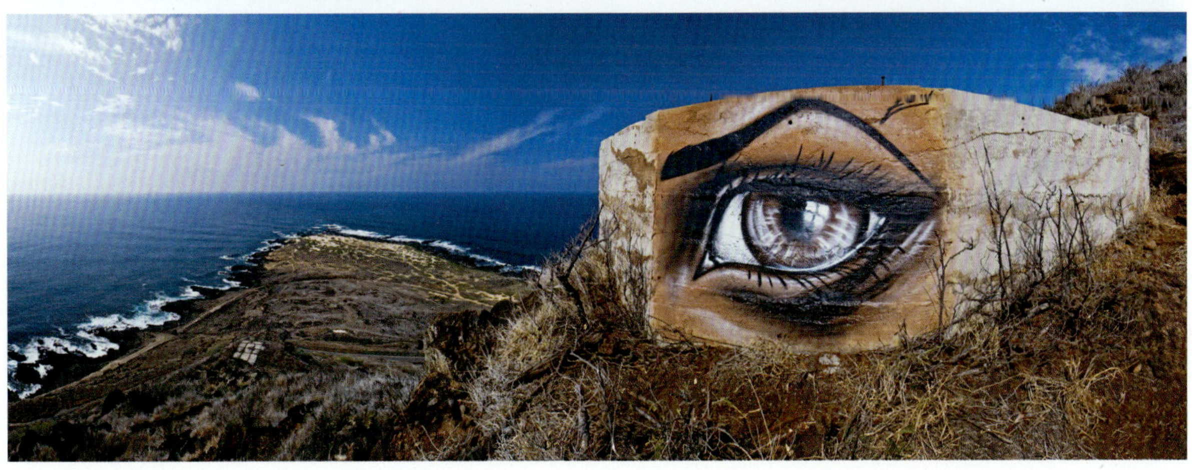

Although graffiti has pushed lettering towards complexity and away from legibility, the artists featured in the following pages have returned to the notion of carefully crafted fonts, which is a significant trend within street art and harks back to a golden age of sign-writing.

CLOCKWISE FROM RIGHT:
USA's Above in Cape Town/Eine in London/ Eine in London.

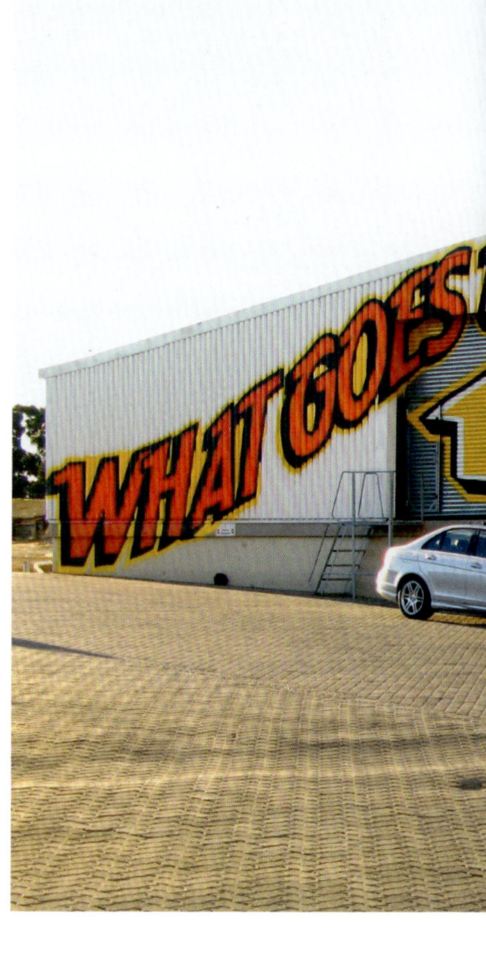

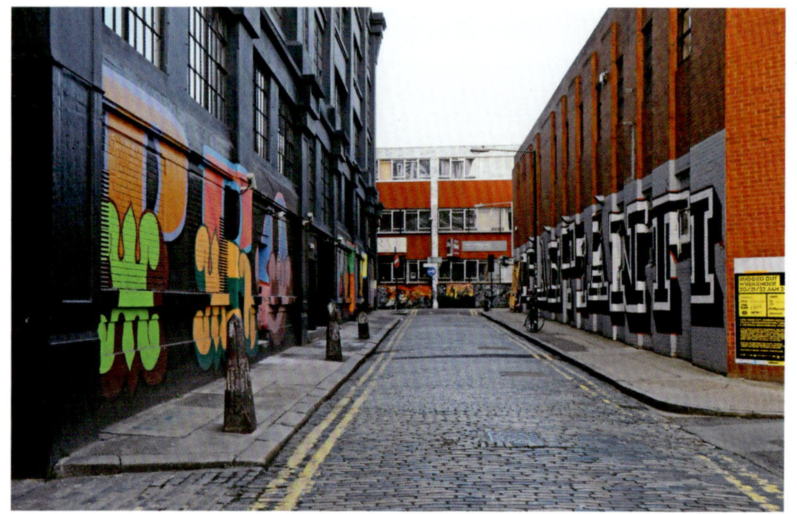

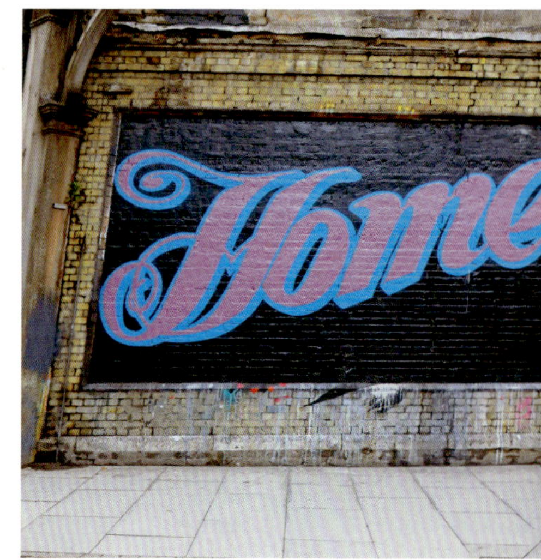

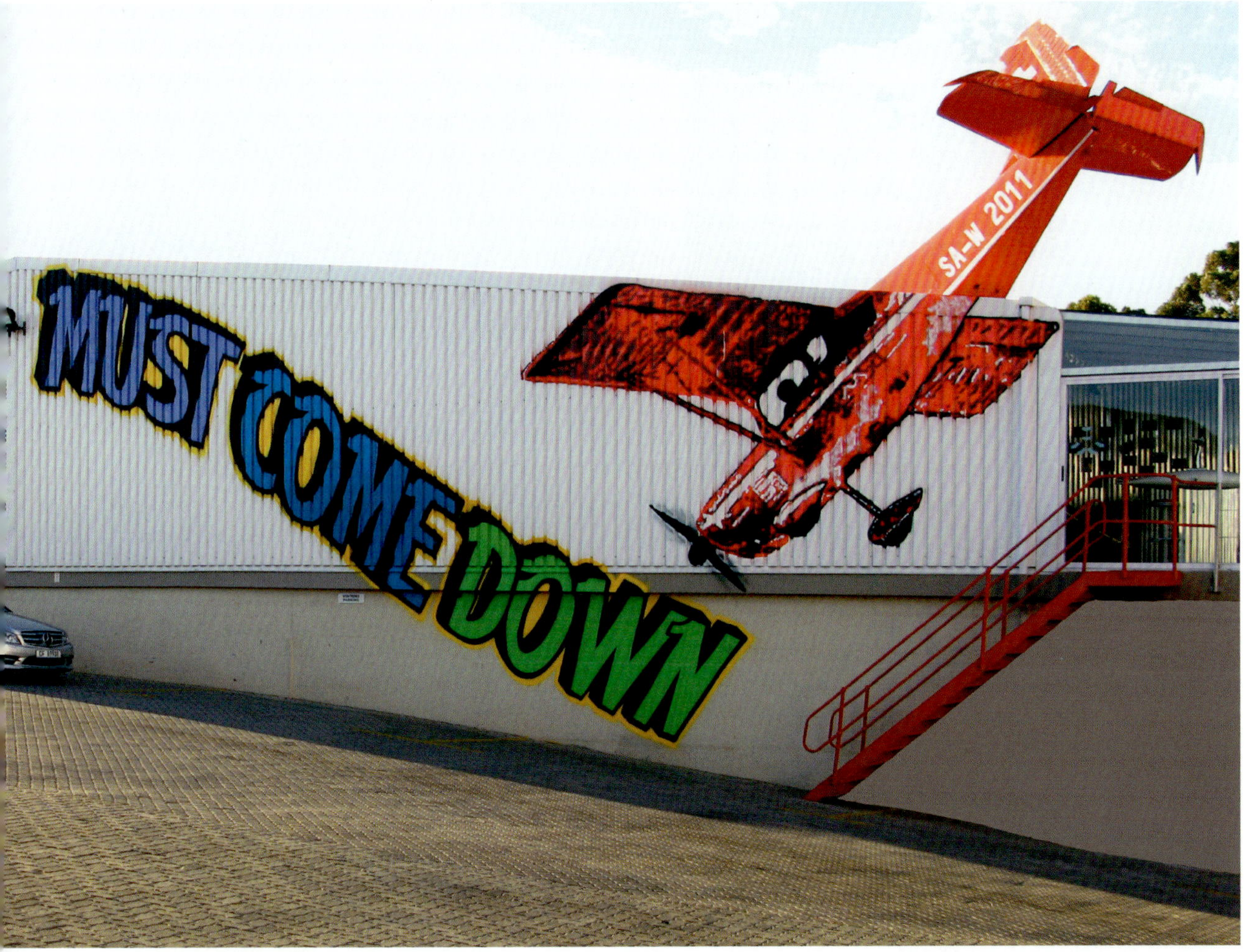

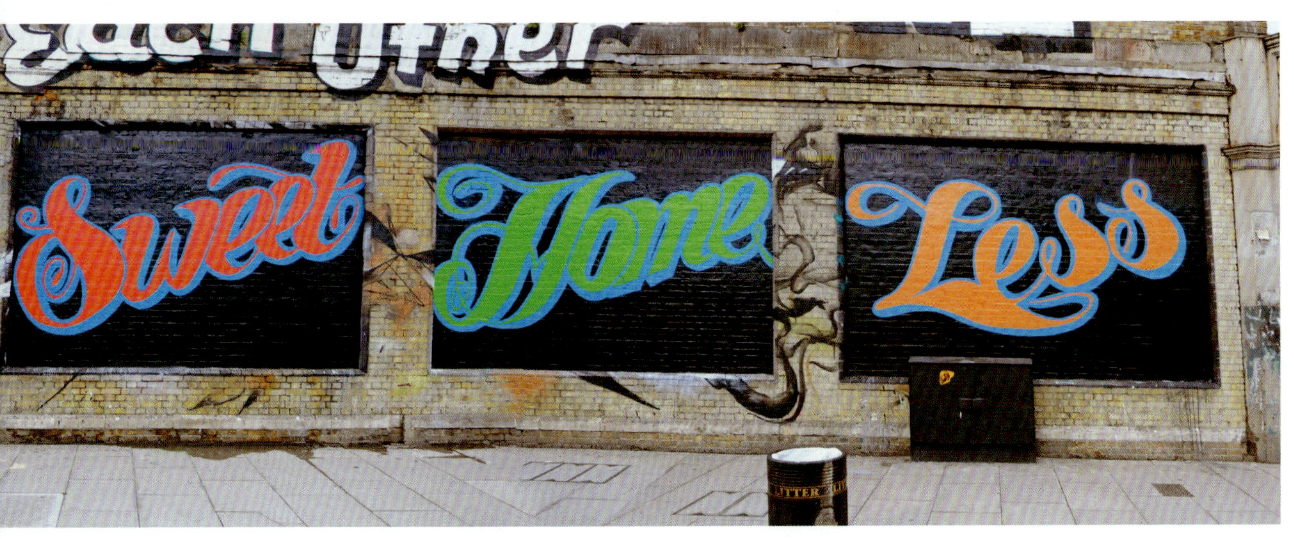
MUST COME DOWN
SA-W 2011
Sweet Home Less
each other

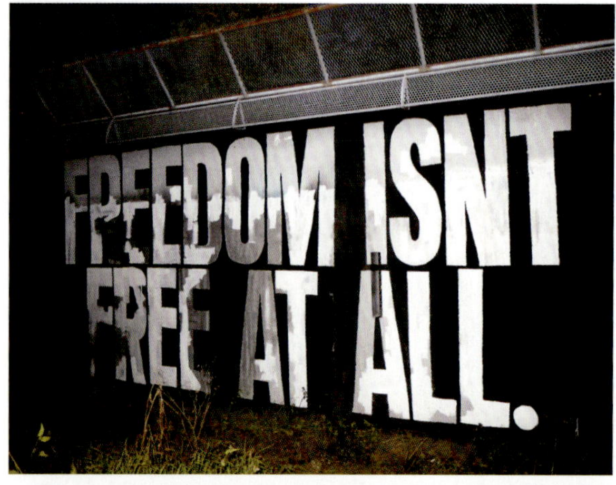

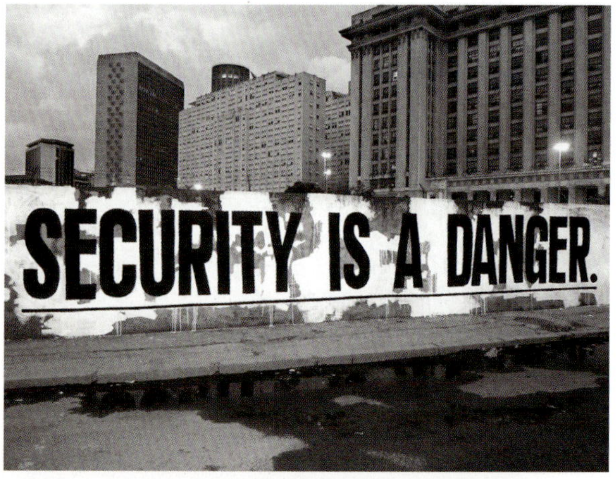

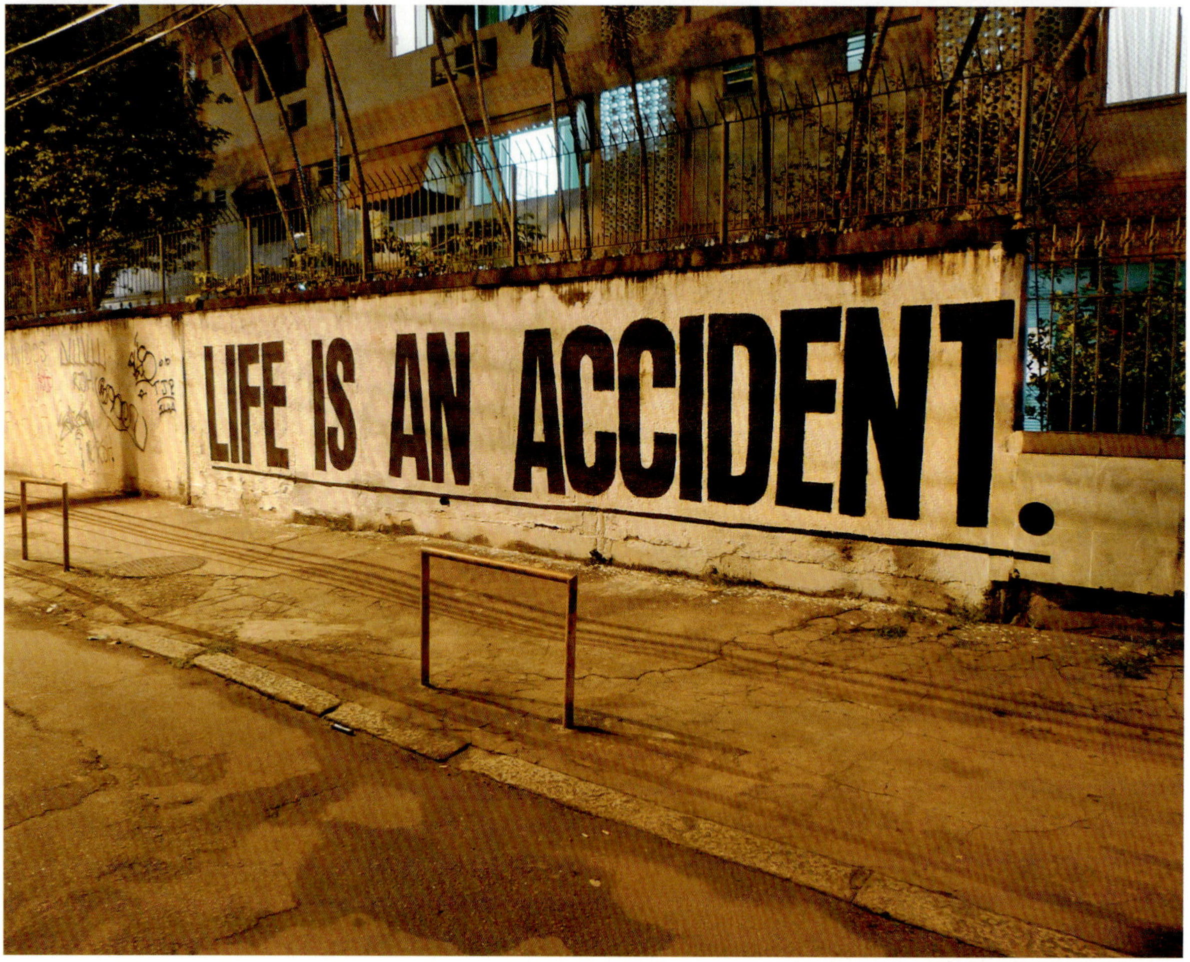

THIS PAGE:
France's Sean Hart
in Rio.

PAGE 207:
Spain's Eme.

PAGES 208-9:
UK's Pref from ID Crew
in London (note the
overlaying of words in
his works, which read
'Don't Read This',
'Colour Greys', 'Light
Shade' and 'White Fade
Dots'.

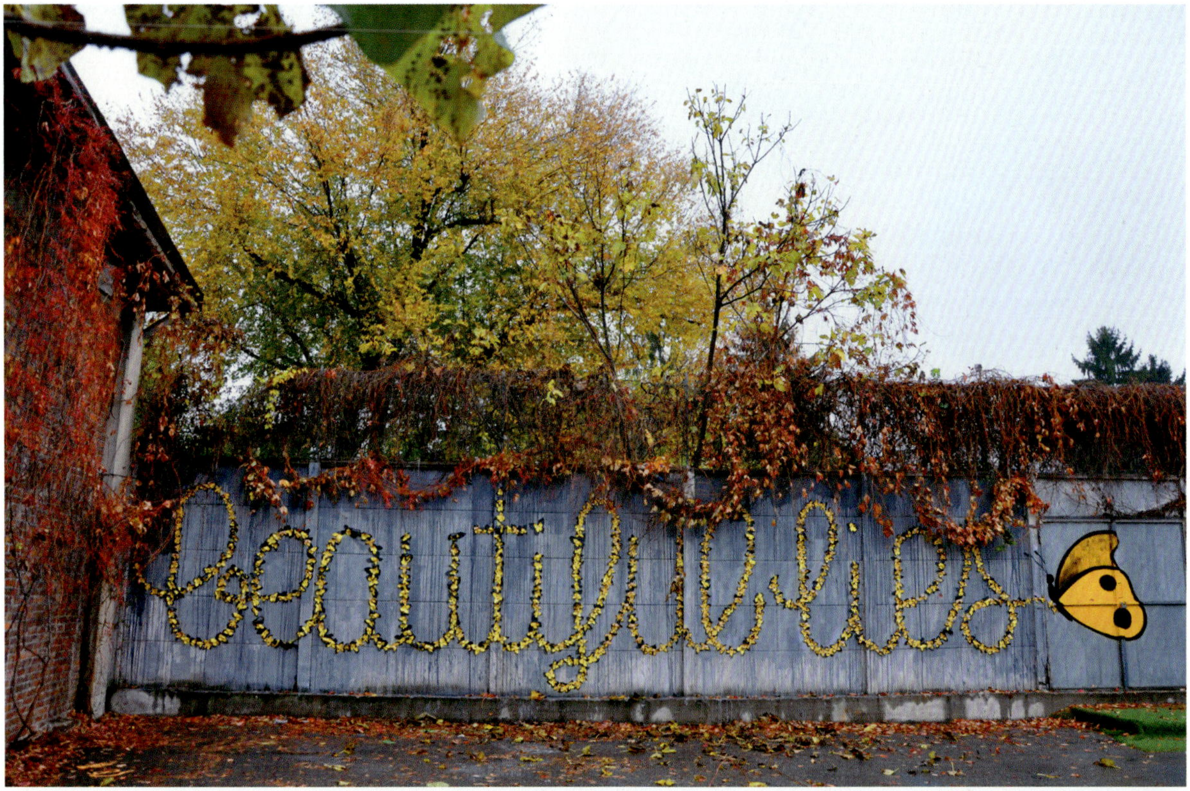

beautylies

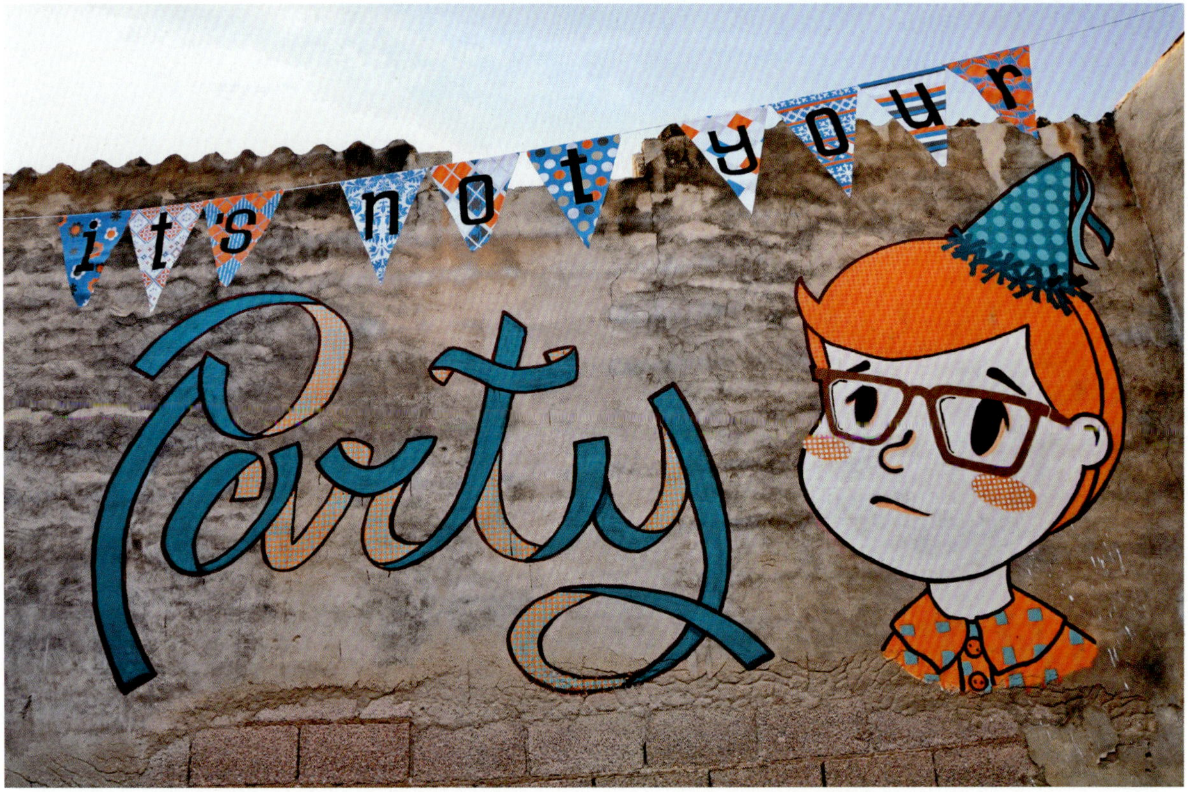

it s n o t y o u r
Party

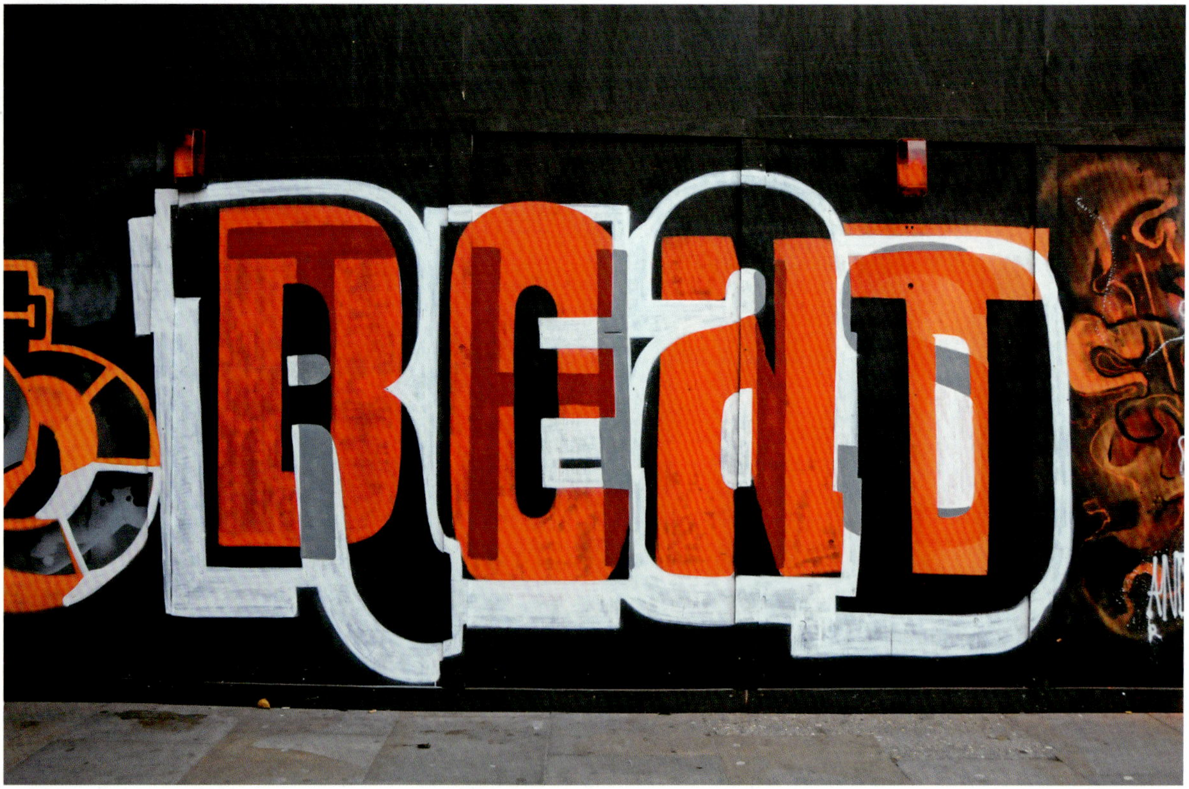

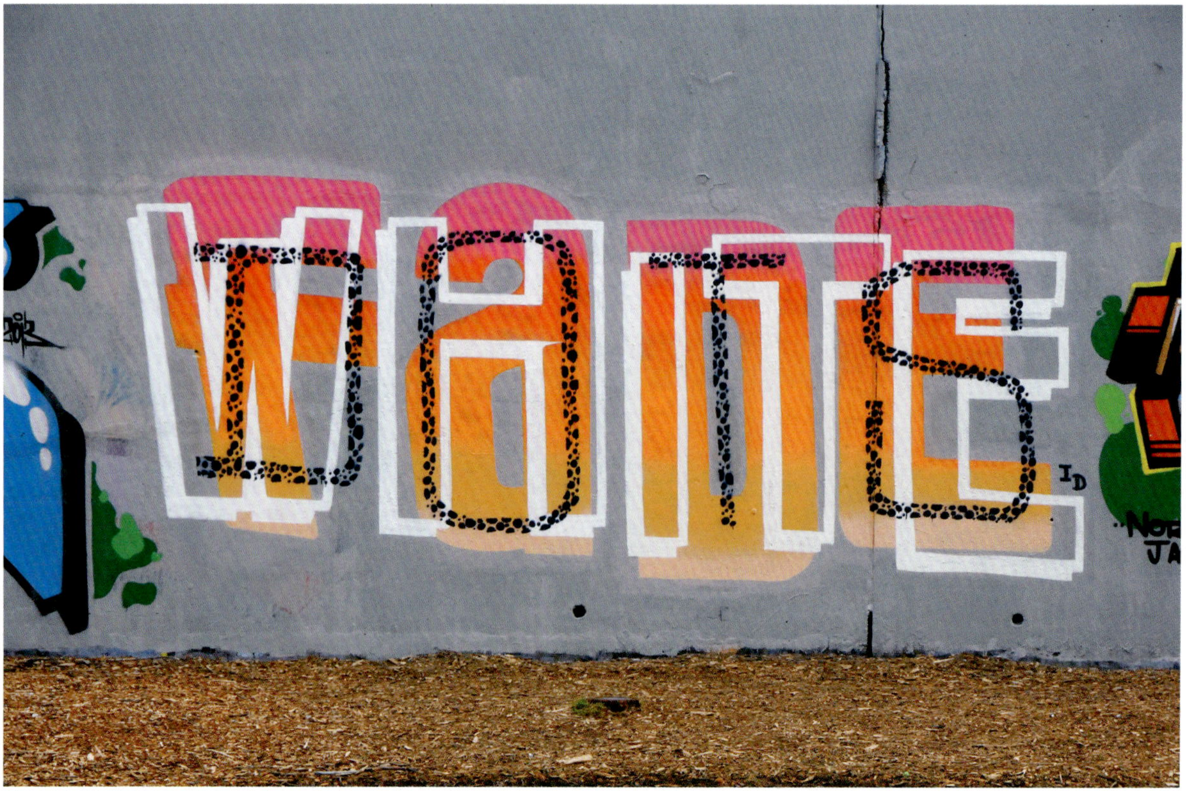

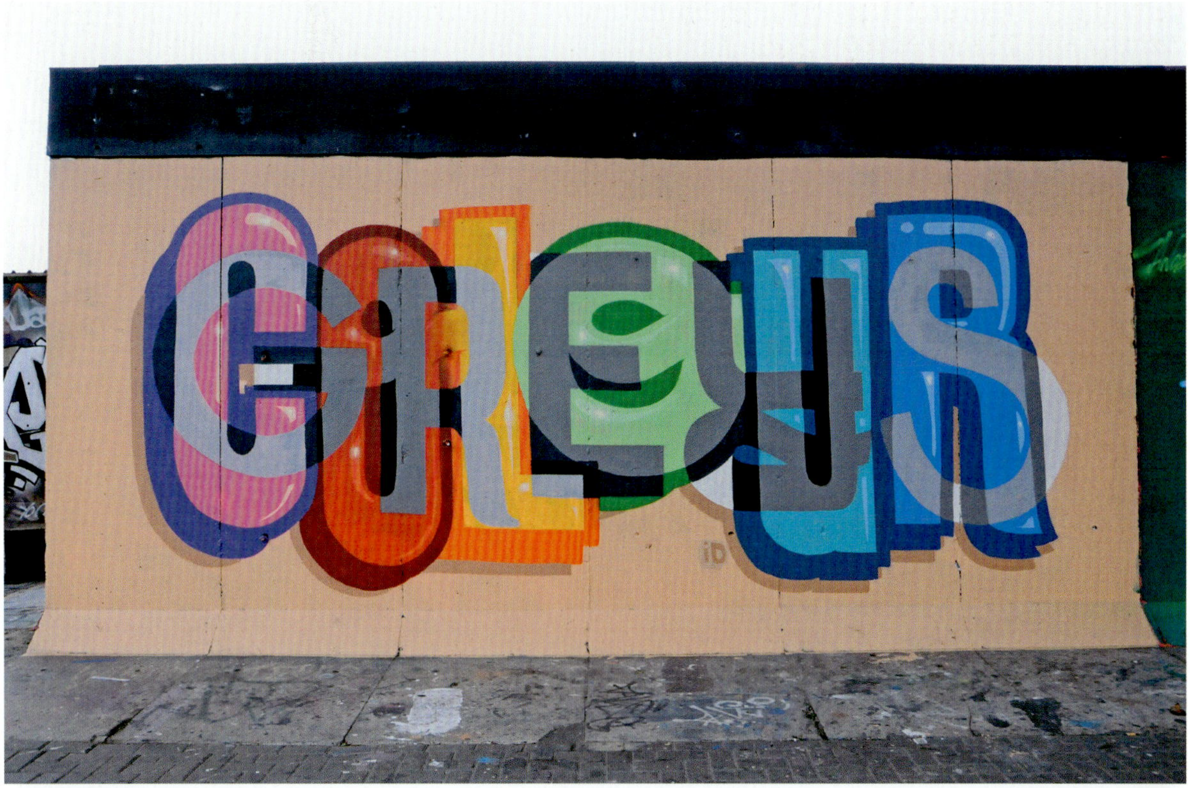

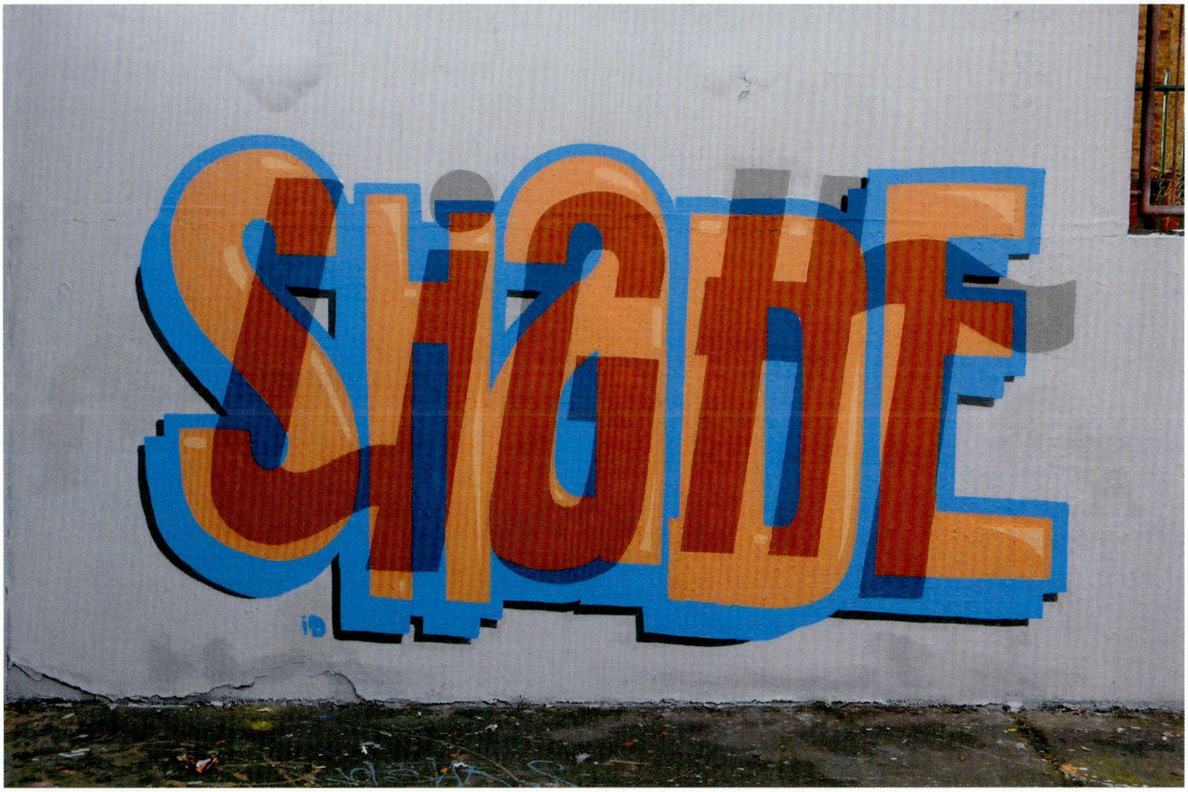

In a similar fashion to fontwork, a number of artists are also pushing calligraphy to new levels, working over large scales and with new materials. Amsterdam's Shoe is one artist who has pushed calligraphic graffiti, or 'calligraffiti', in particular.

Of course, graffiti doesn't have to be based on Latin alphabets. It could be based on any alphabet or written language. Arabic is particularly appropriate for graffiti because of the flowing nature of the text. The following pieces by Tunisian artist eL Seed are strong examples of how beautiful Arabic graffiti can be.

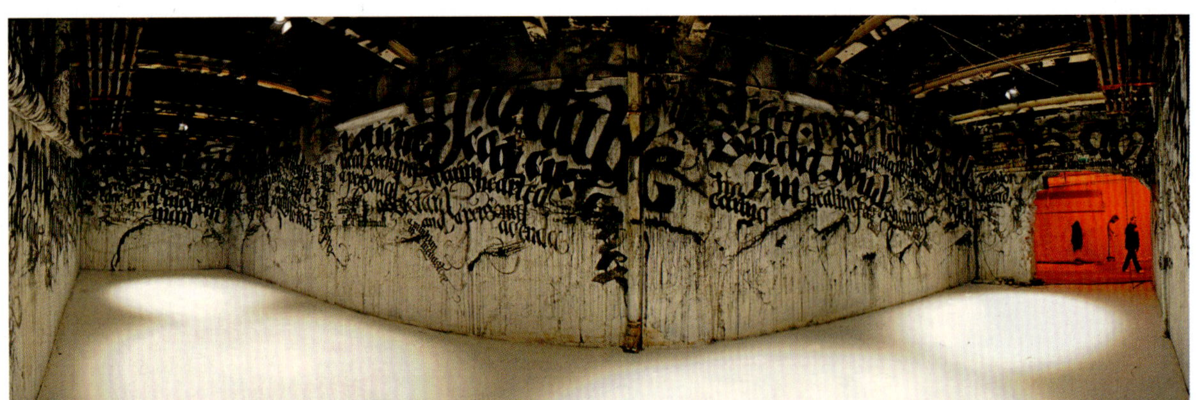

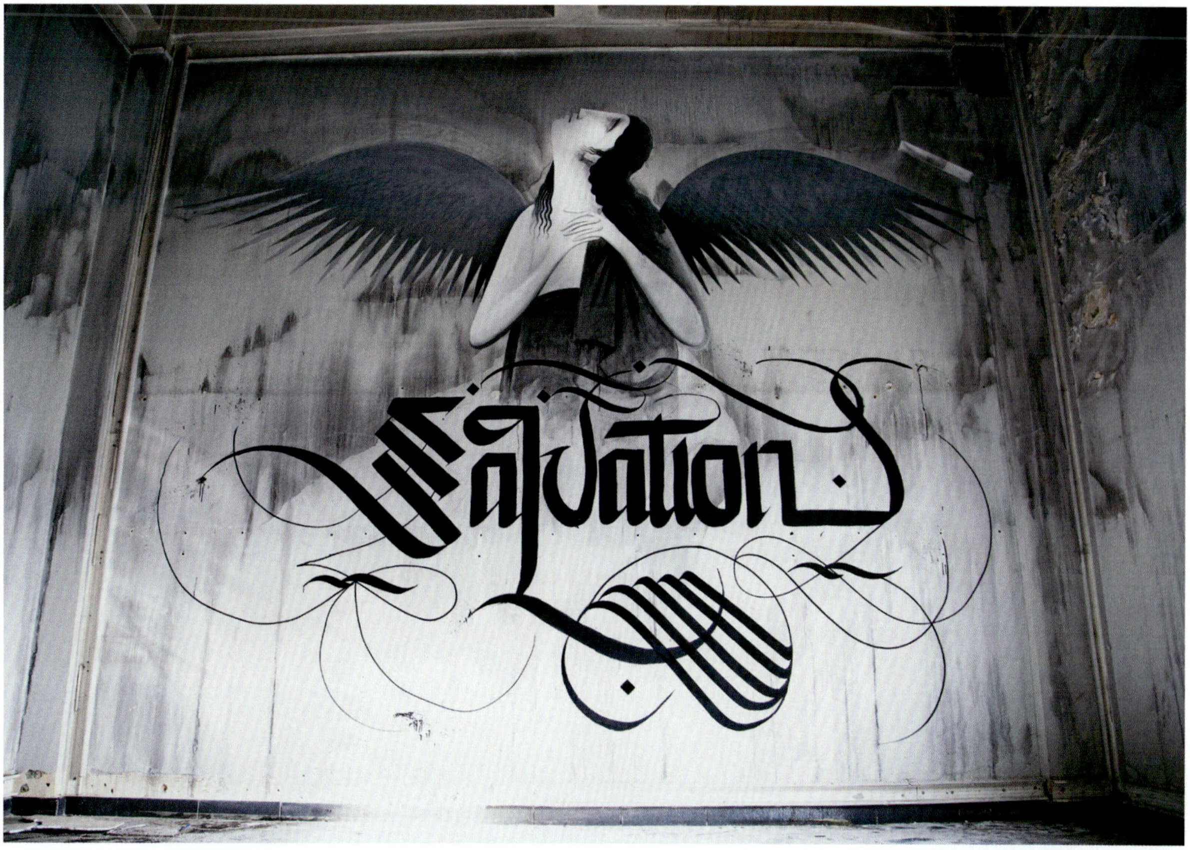

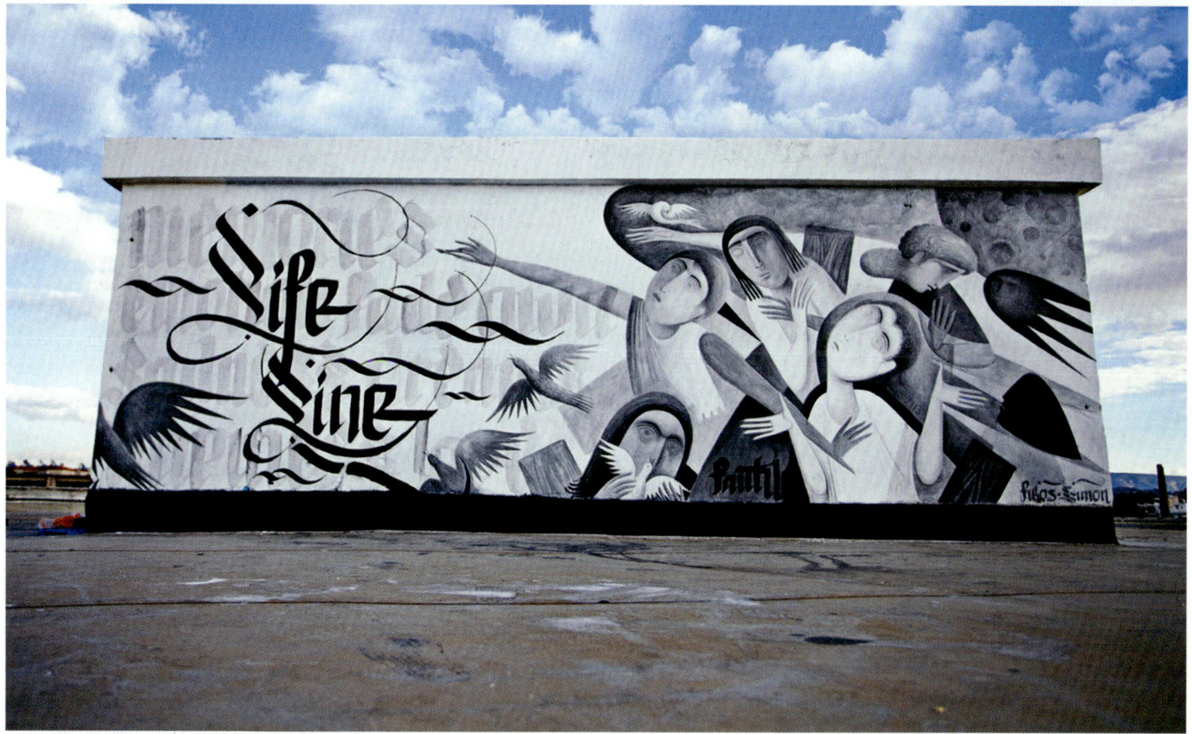

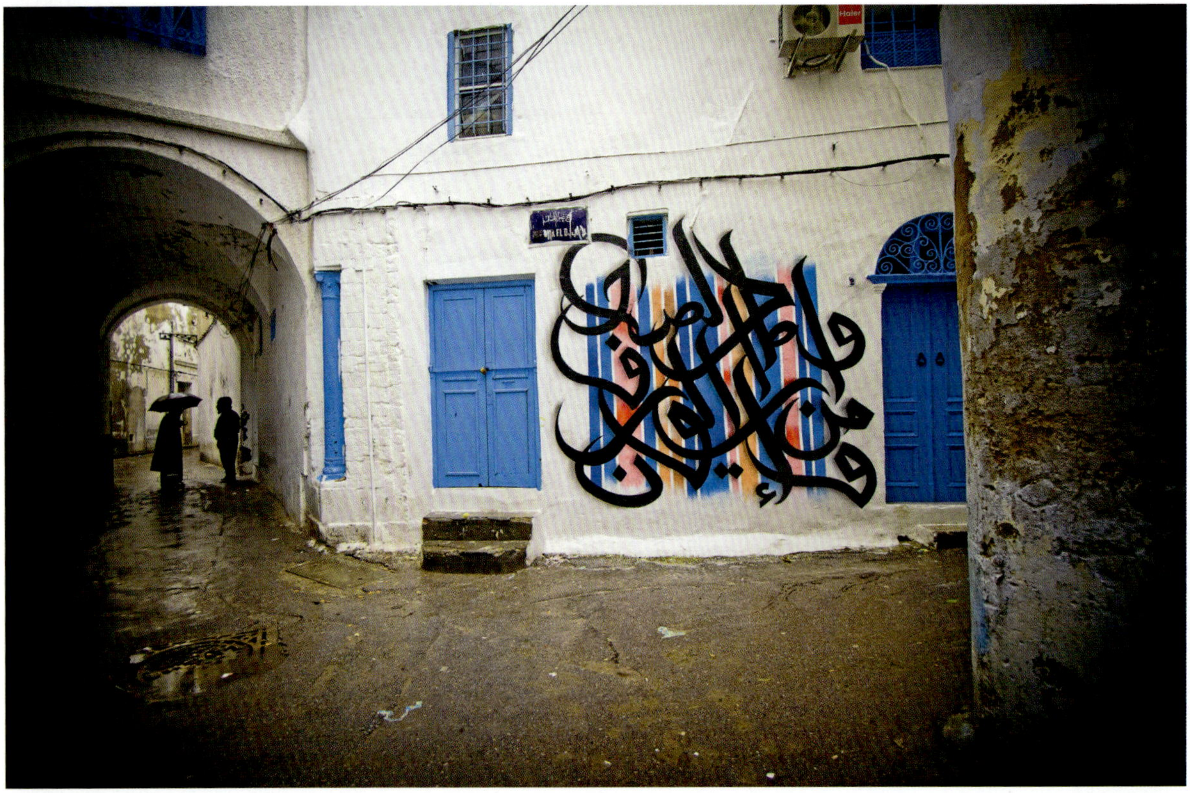

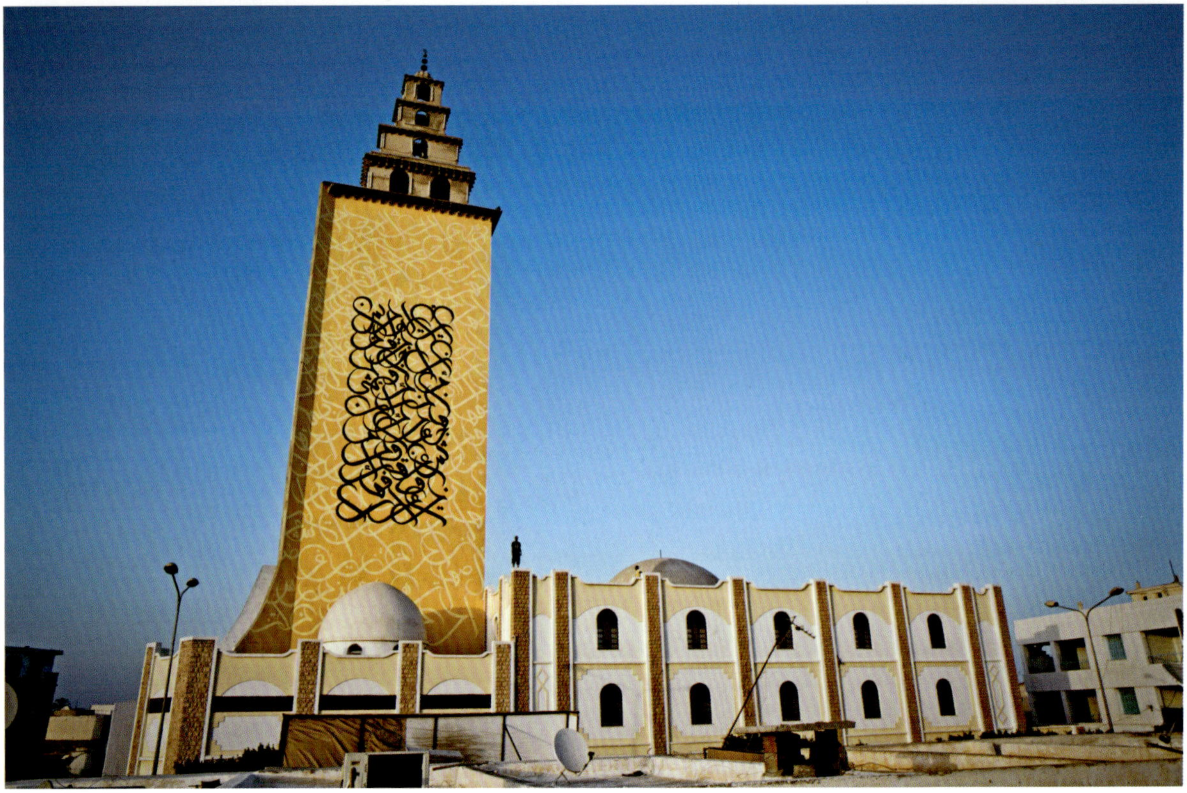

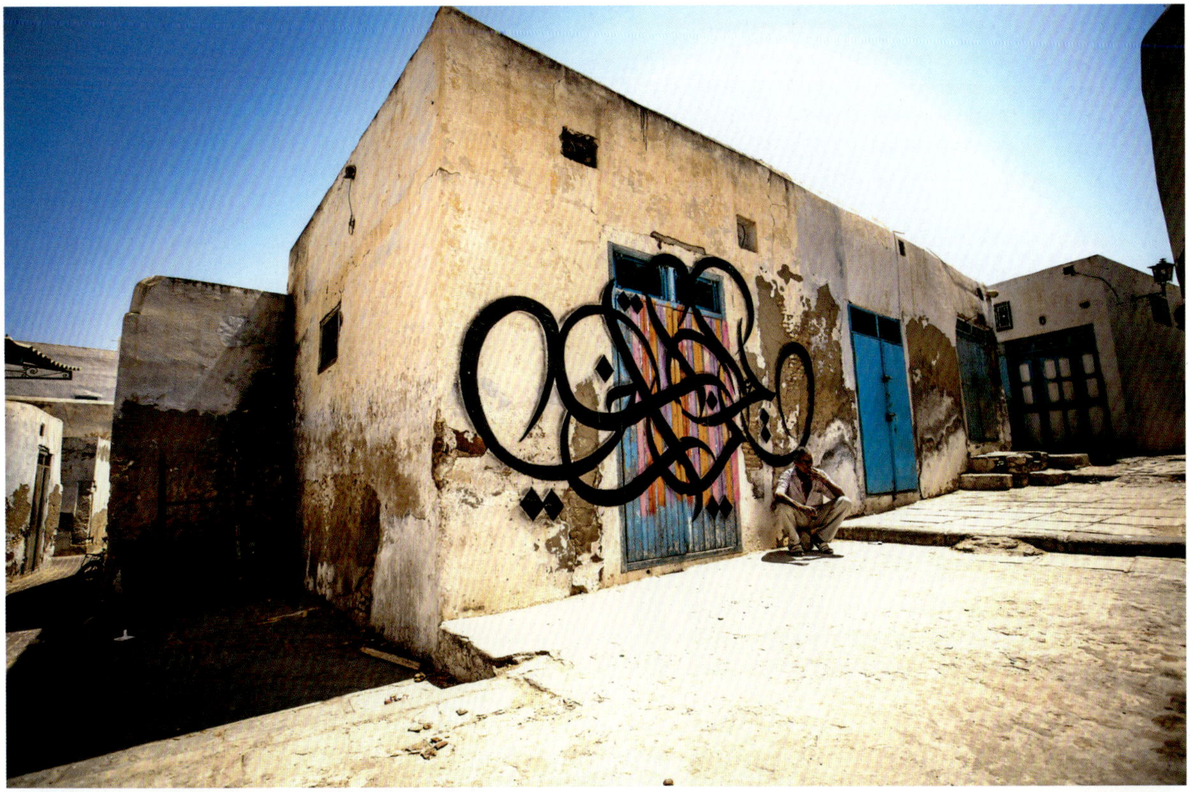

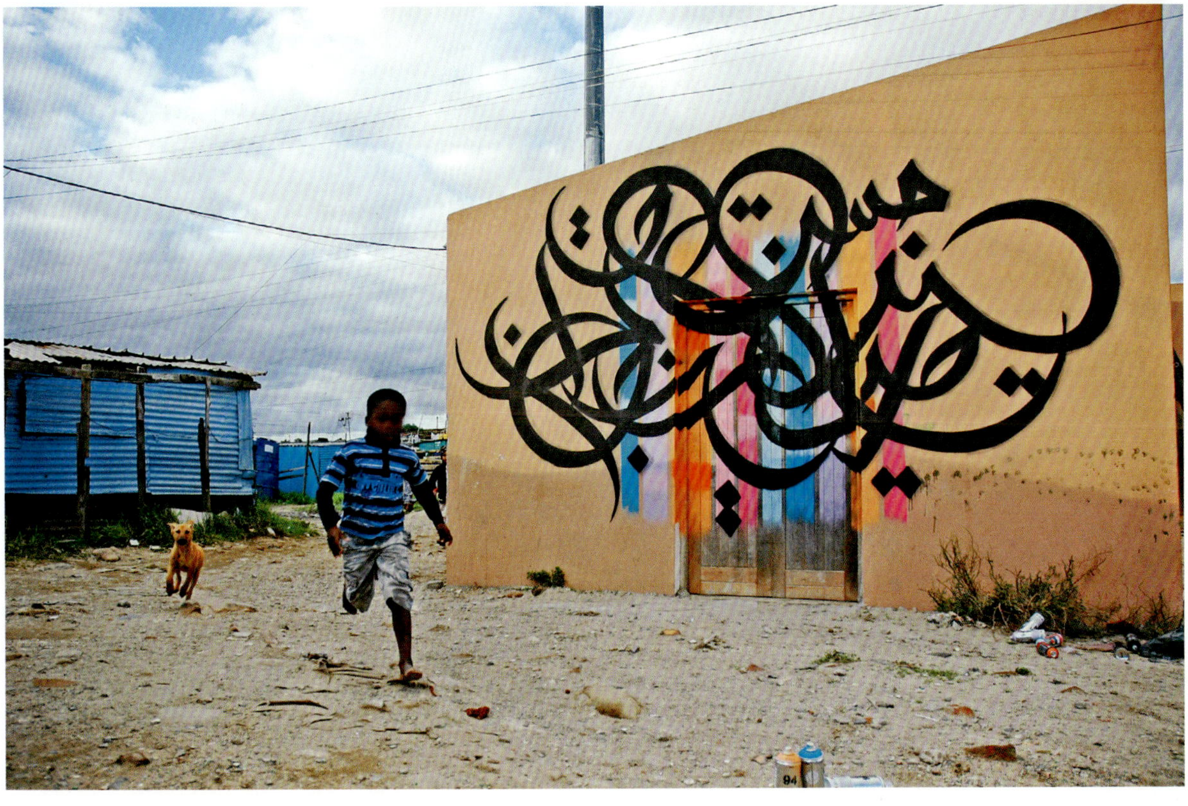

In recent years (and in contrast to the photorealism explored earlier) there have been increasing movements towards abstraction in street art. The number of artists around the world painting abstract pieces, often rooted in geometric forms, is staggering. The following photographs highlight some abstract work but abstraction in street art could take up whole books in itself (and indeed has).

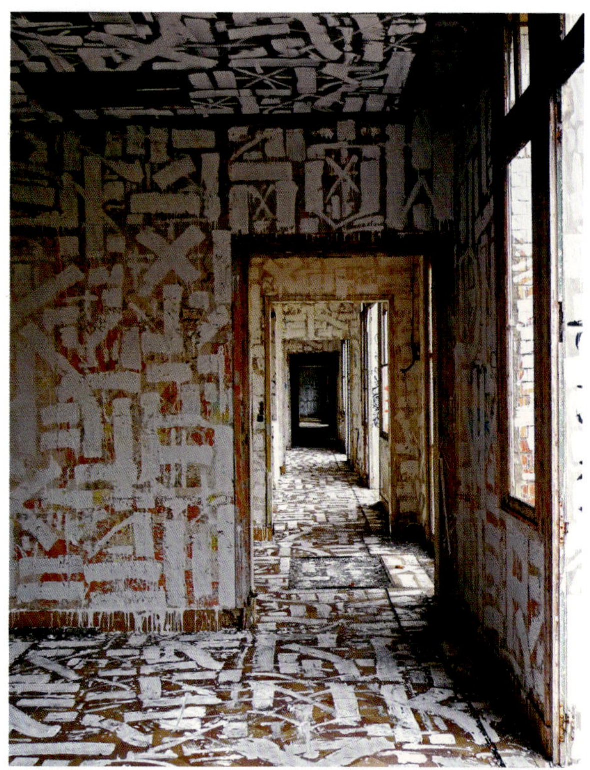

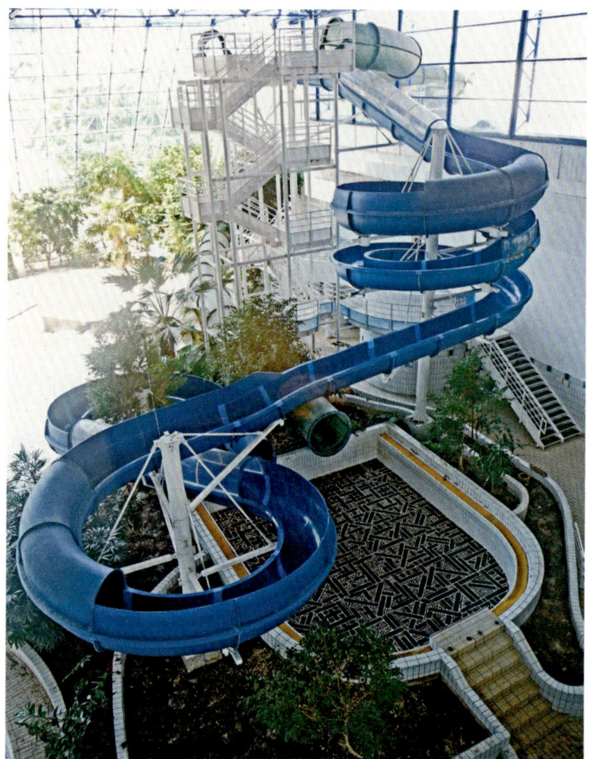

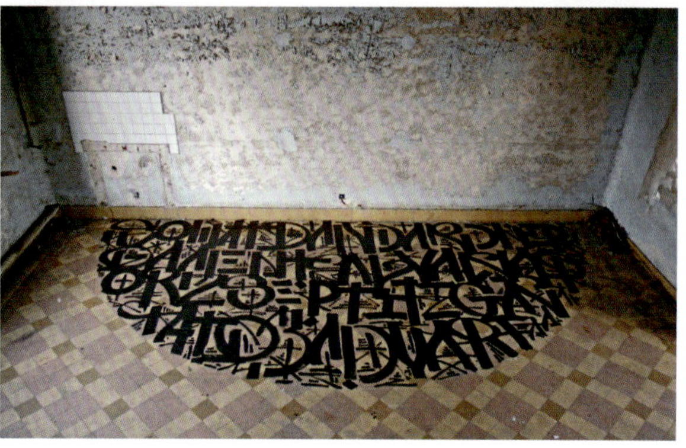

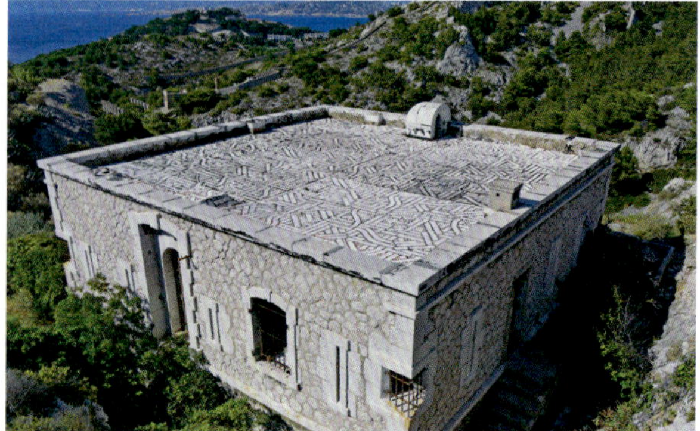

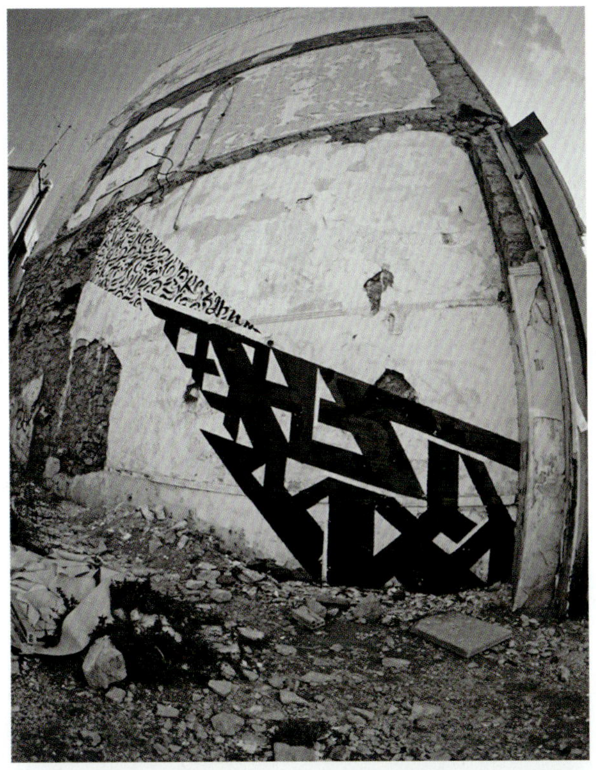

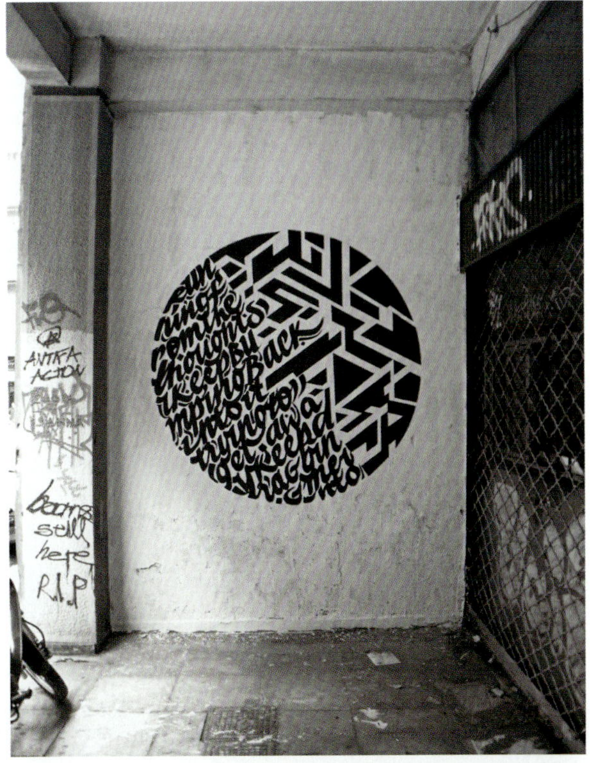

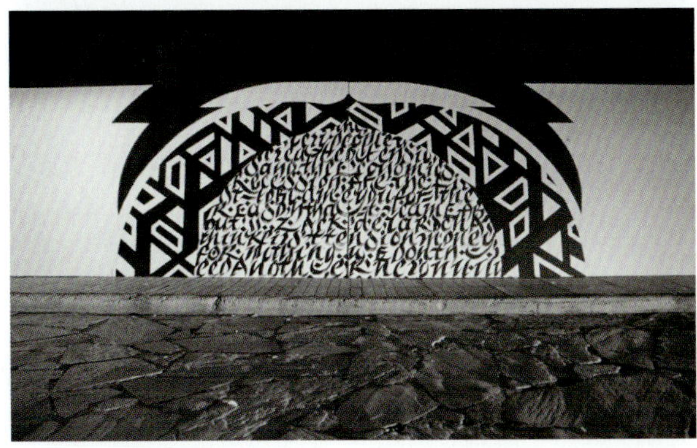

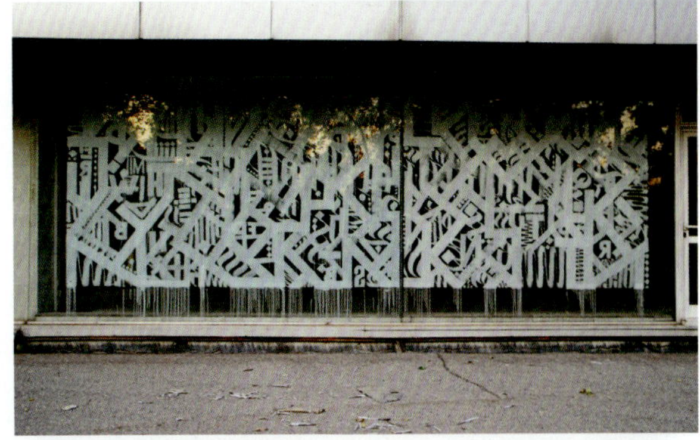

PAGE 214:
France's Sowat
(all works).

THIS PAGE:
Blaqk (Greg
Papagrigoriou and
Simek) in Athens
(all works).

PAGE 216:
USA's Kofie in Melbourne
(both works).

PAGE 217:
Reab in Brussels.

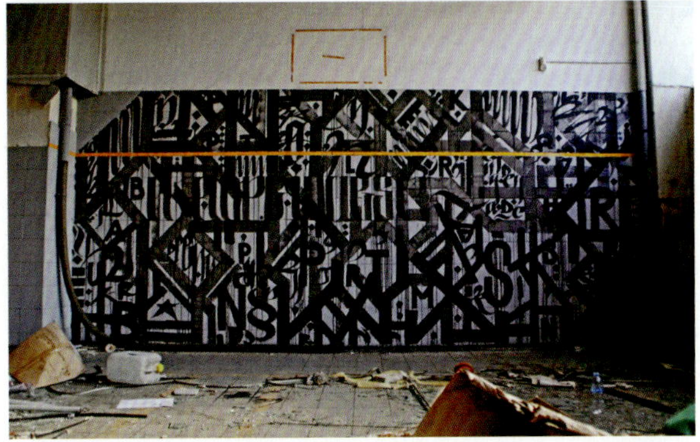

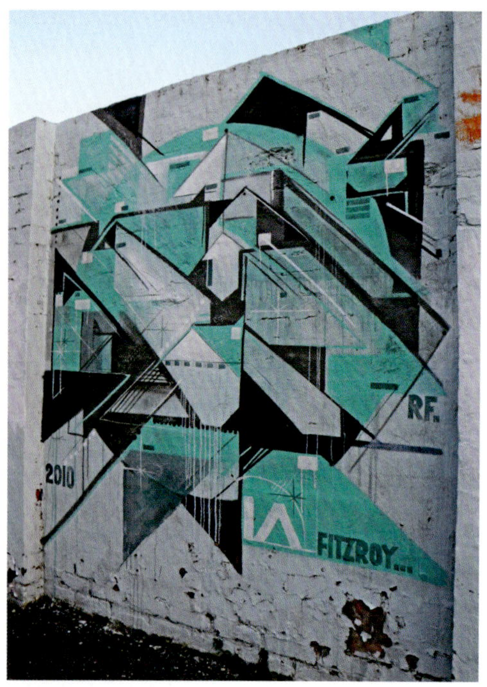

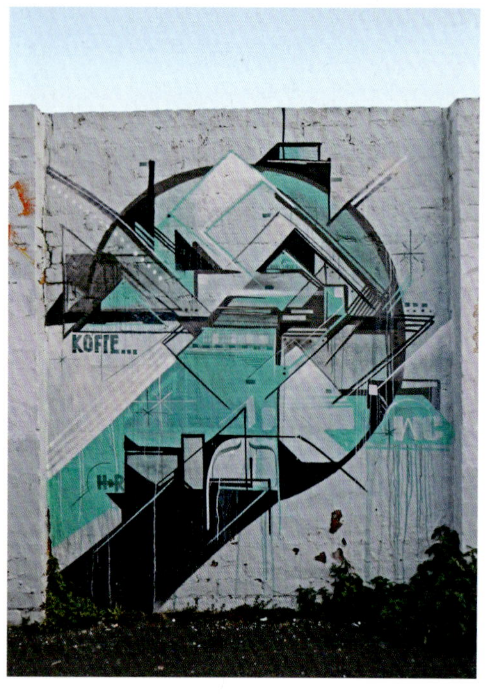

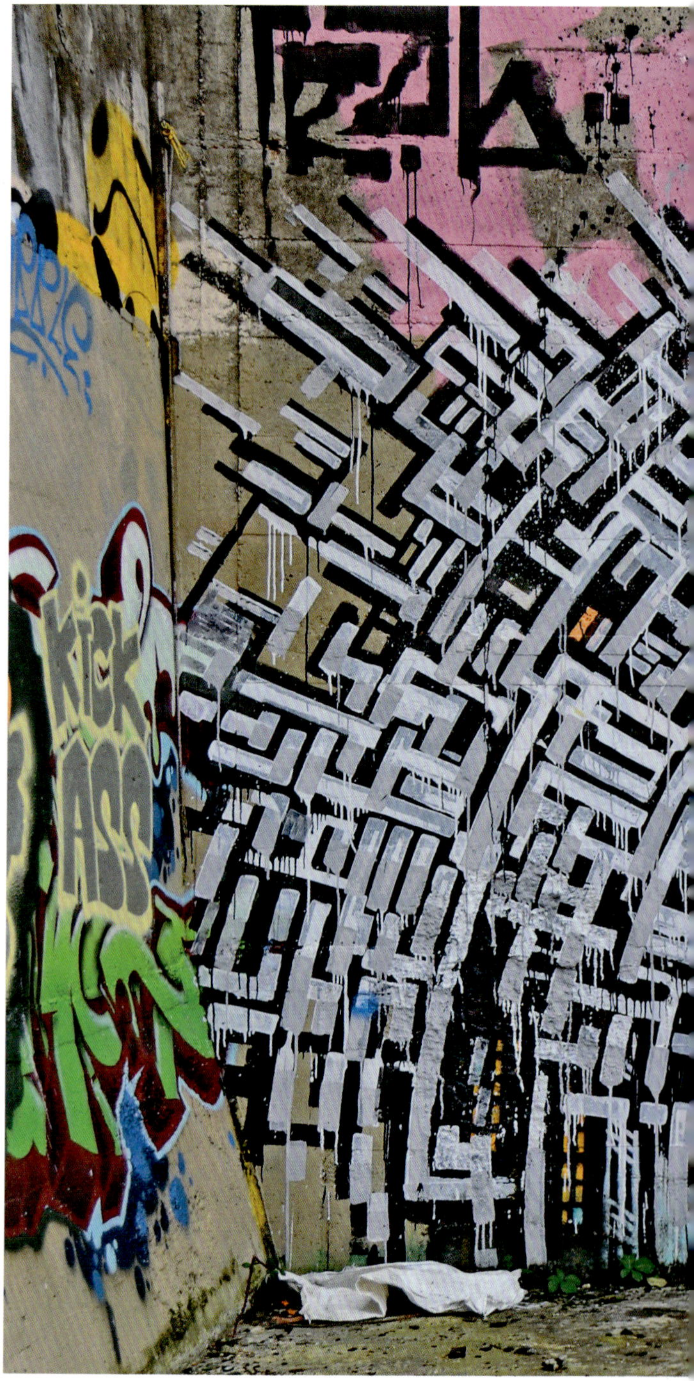

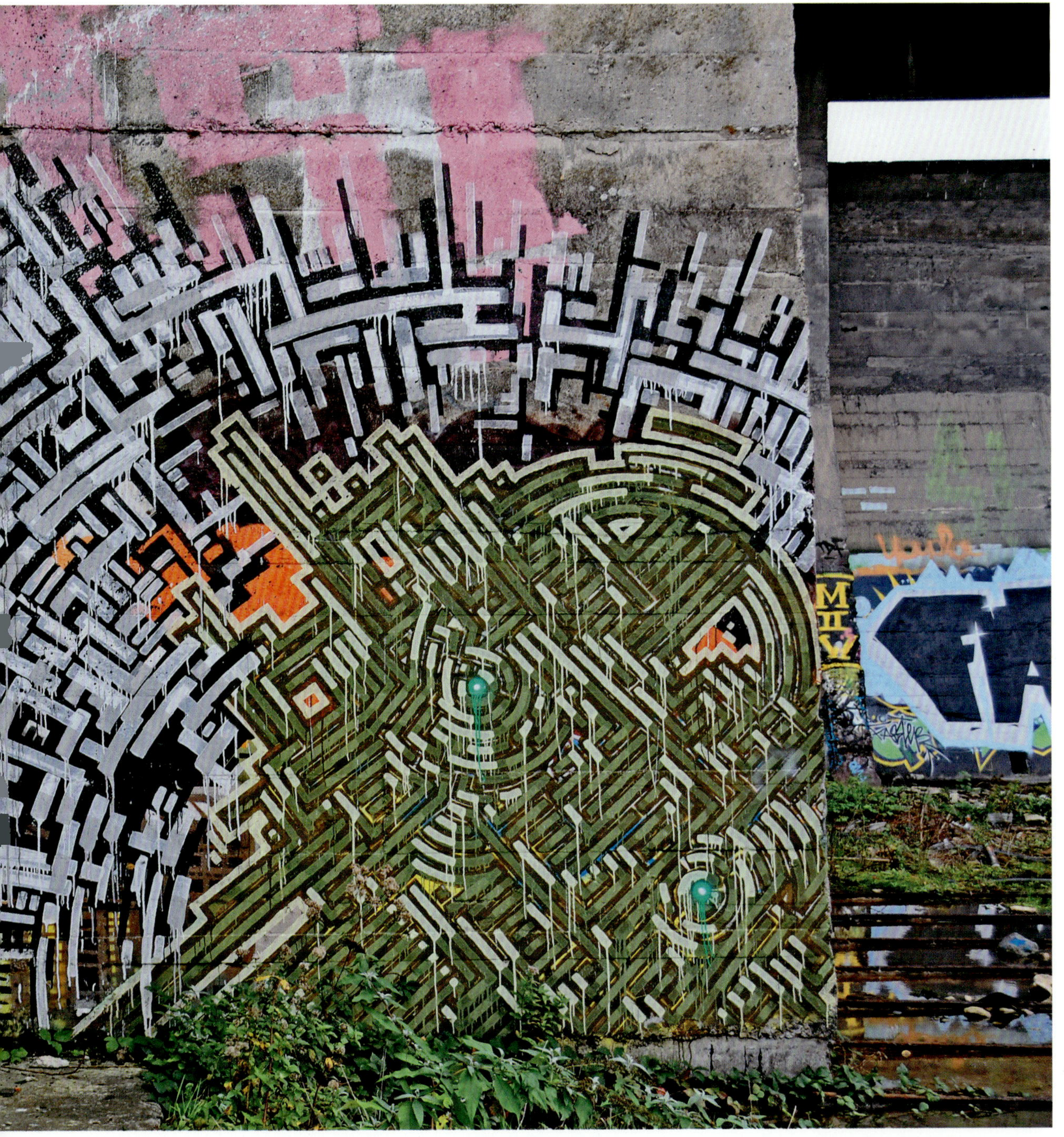

Across graffiti and street art, all around the world, it's possible to identify recurring themes to which artists keep returning, as explored in the following pages.

CLOCKWISE FROM
BELOW:
Nicky Nahafahik in
Basel/Sipros in São
Paulo/Jean Linnhoff
in Amsterdam.

PAGES 220-1,
CLOCKWISE FROM LEFT:
Smates in Belgium/
Binho in São Paulo/
Kolja Reuter in Kassel,
Germany (note the pole
at the front!).

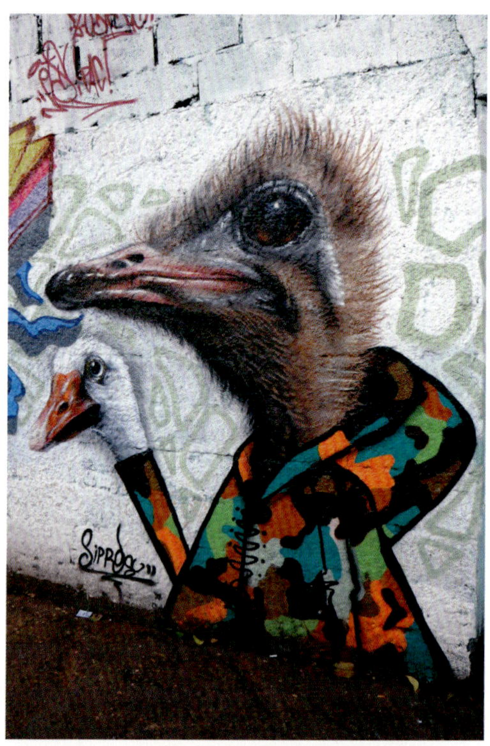

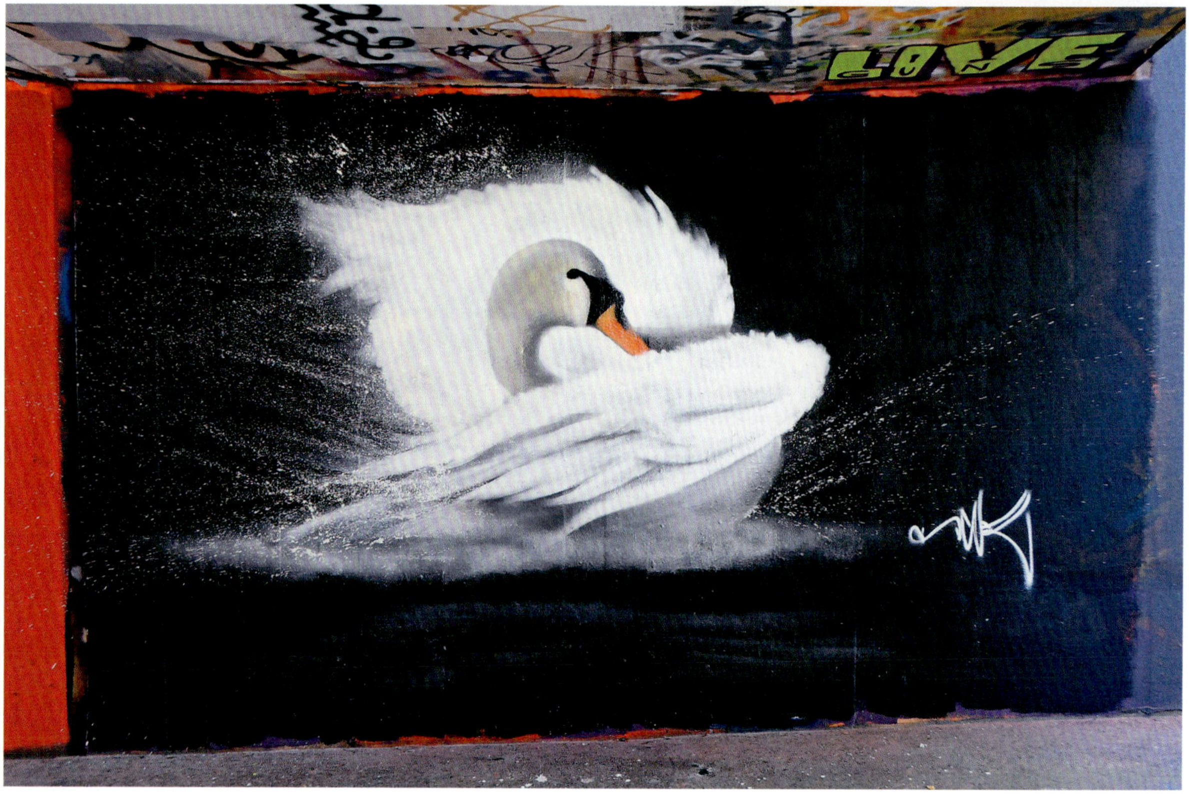

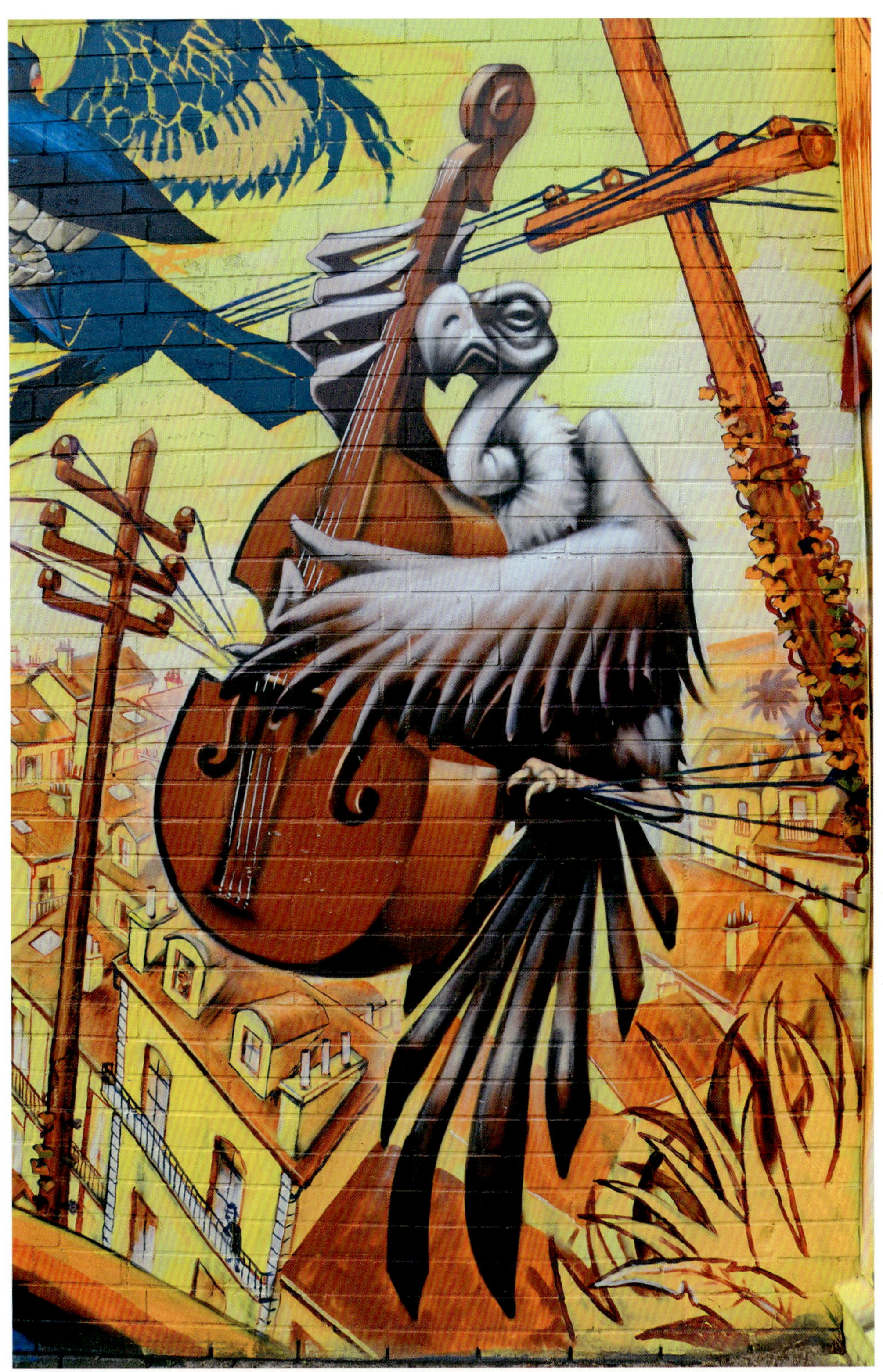

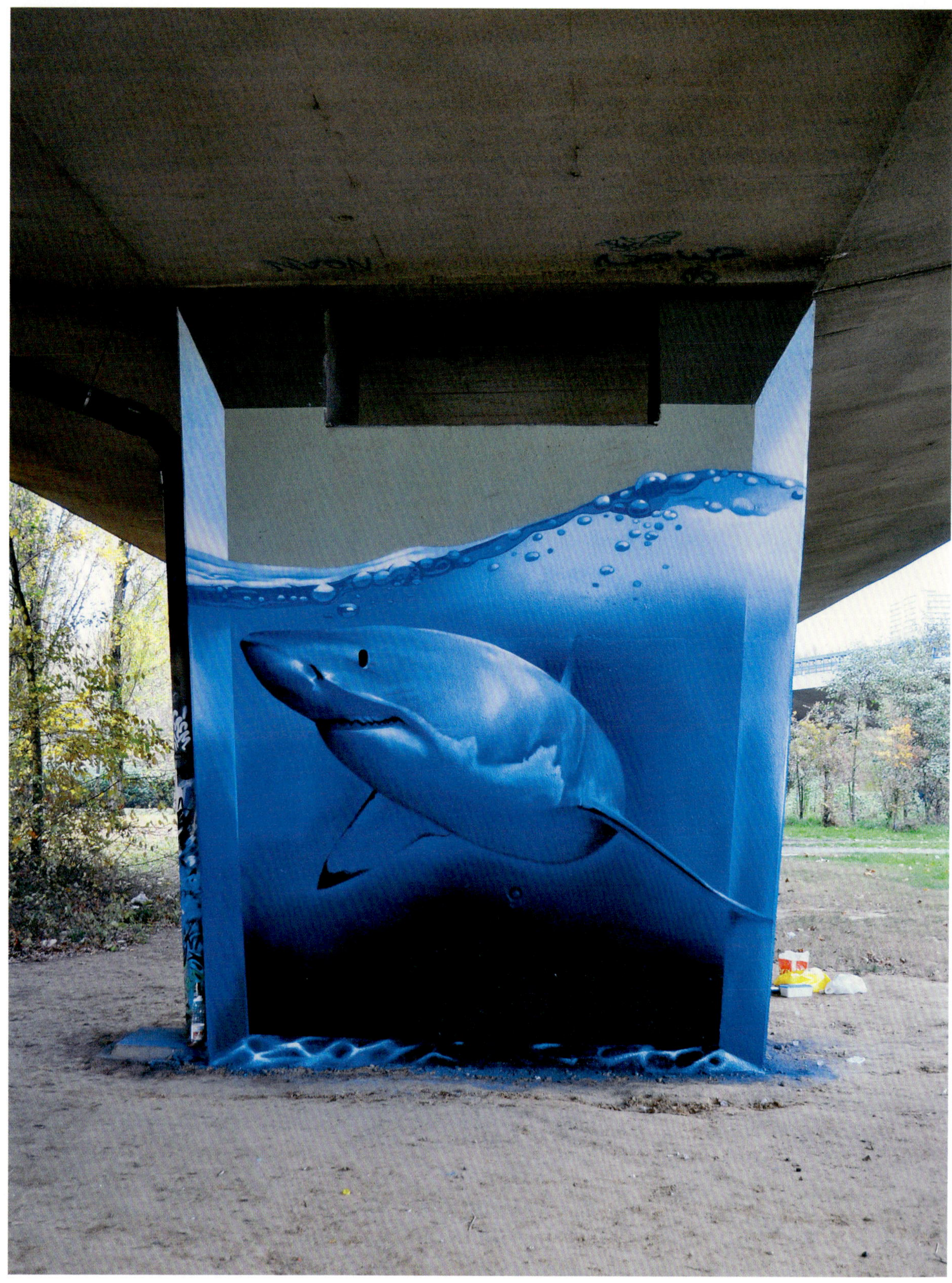

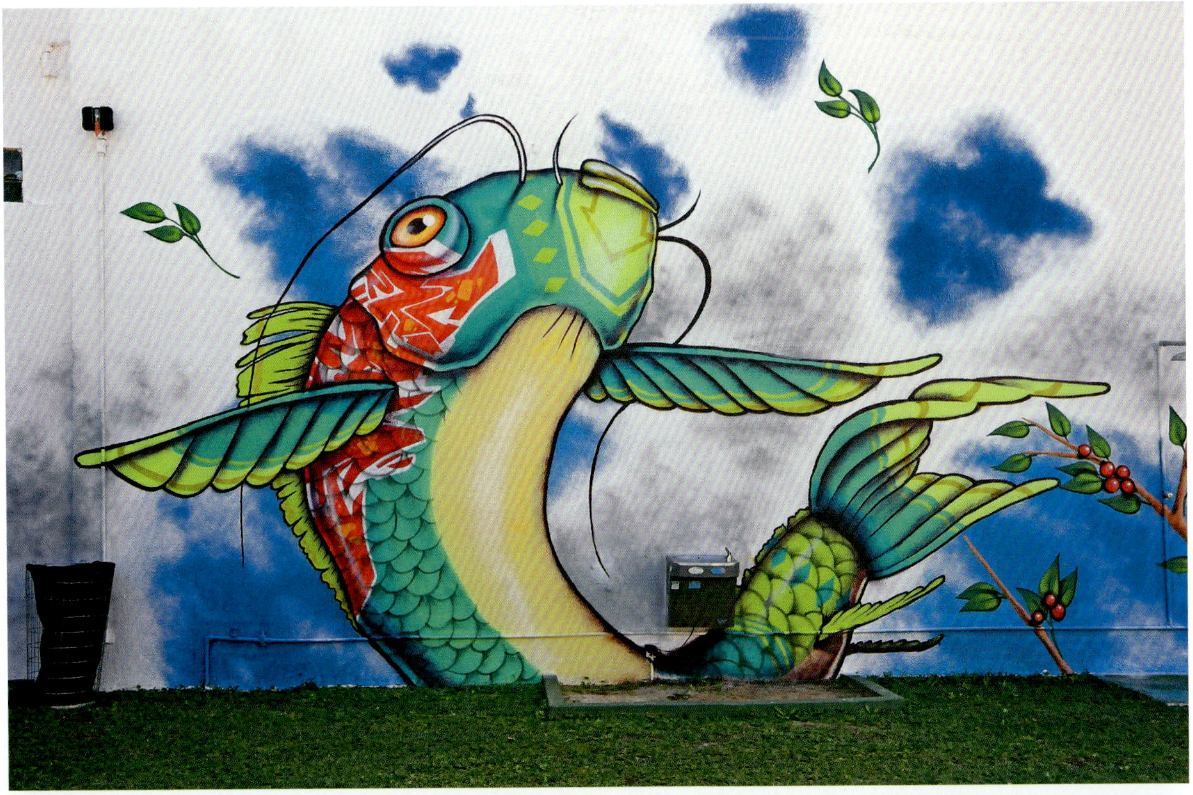

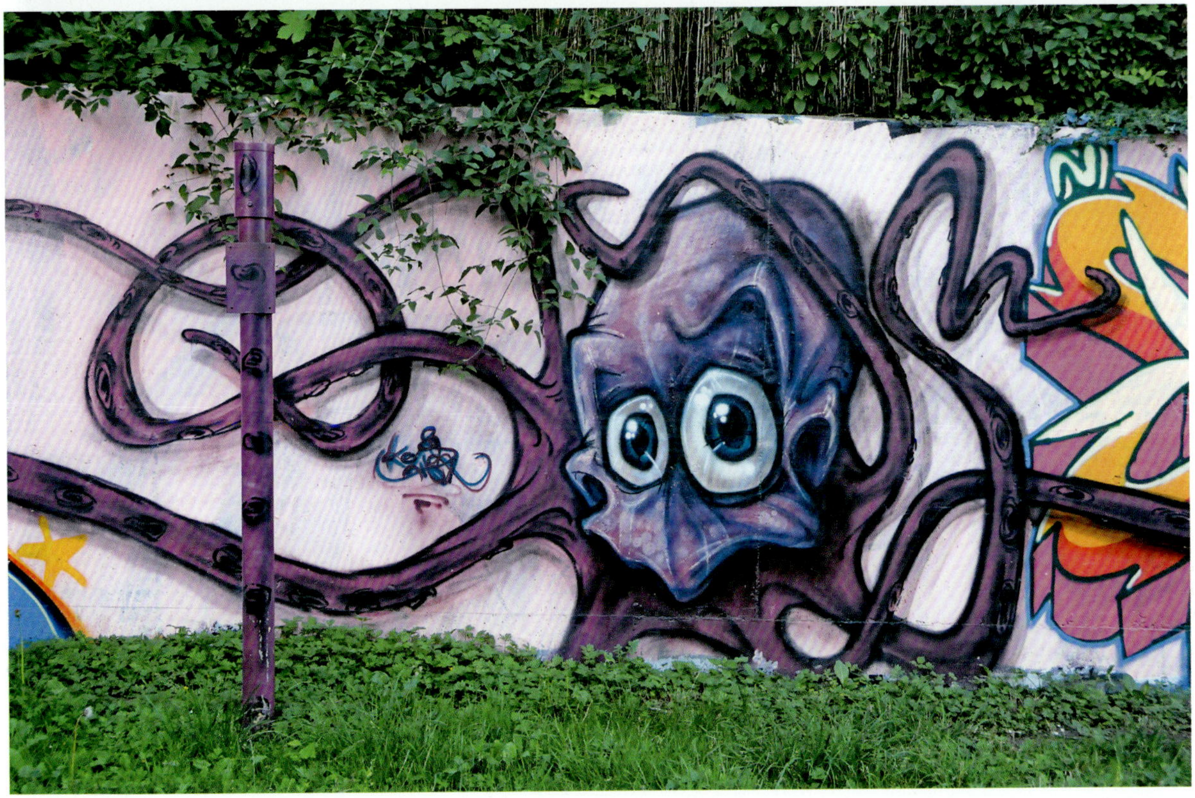

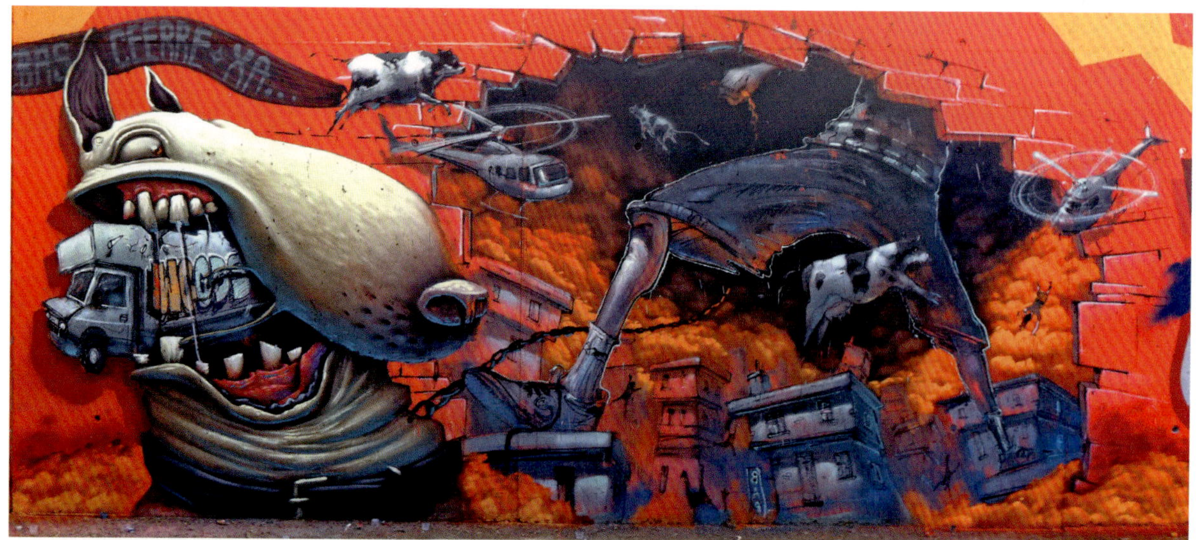

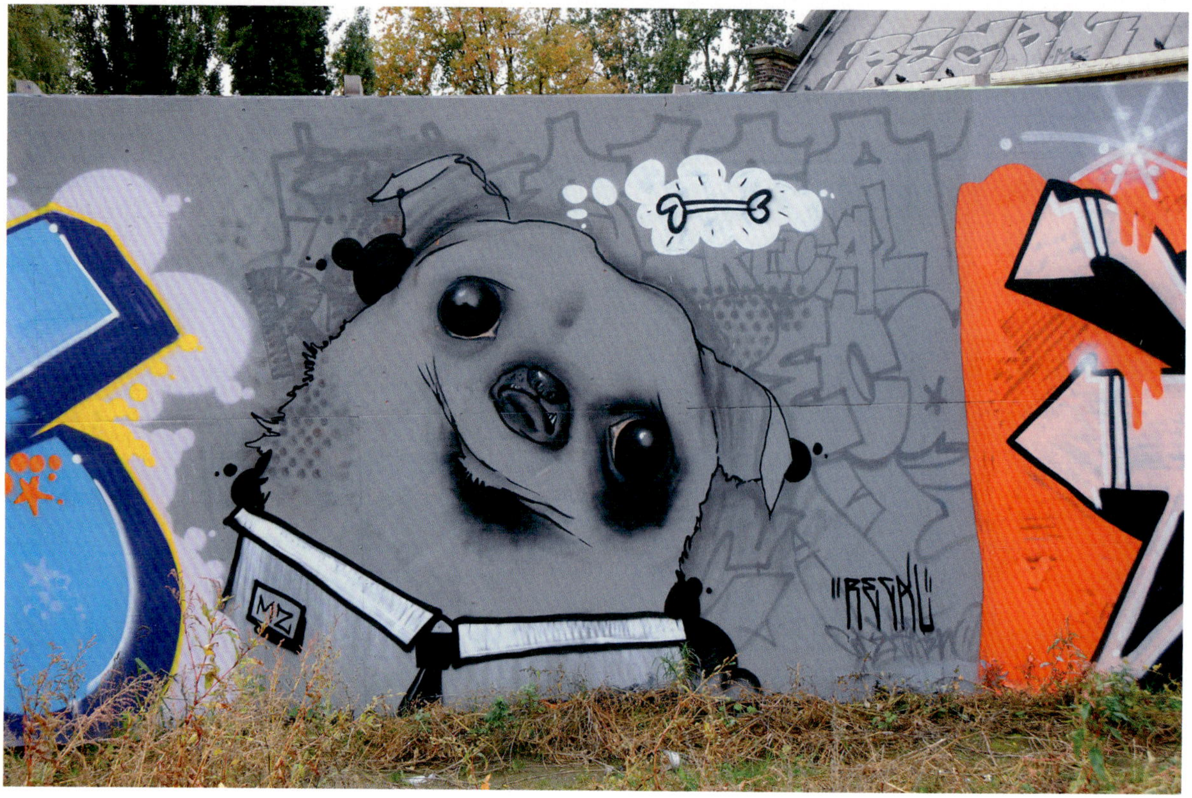

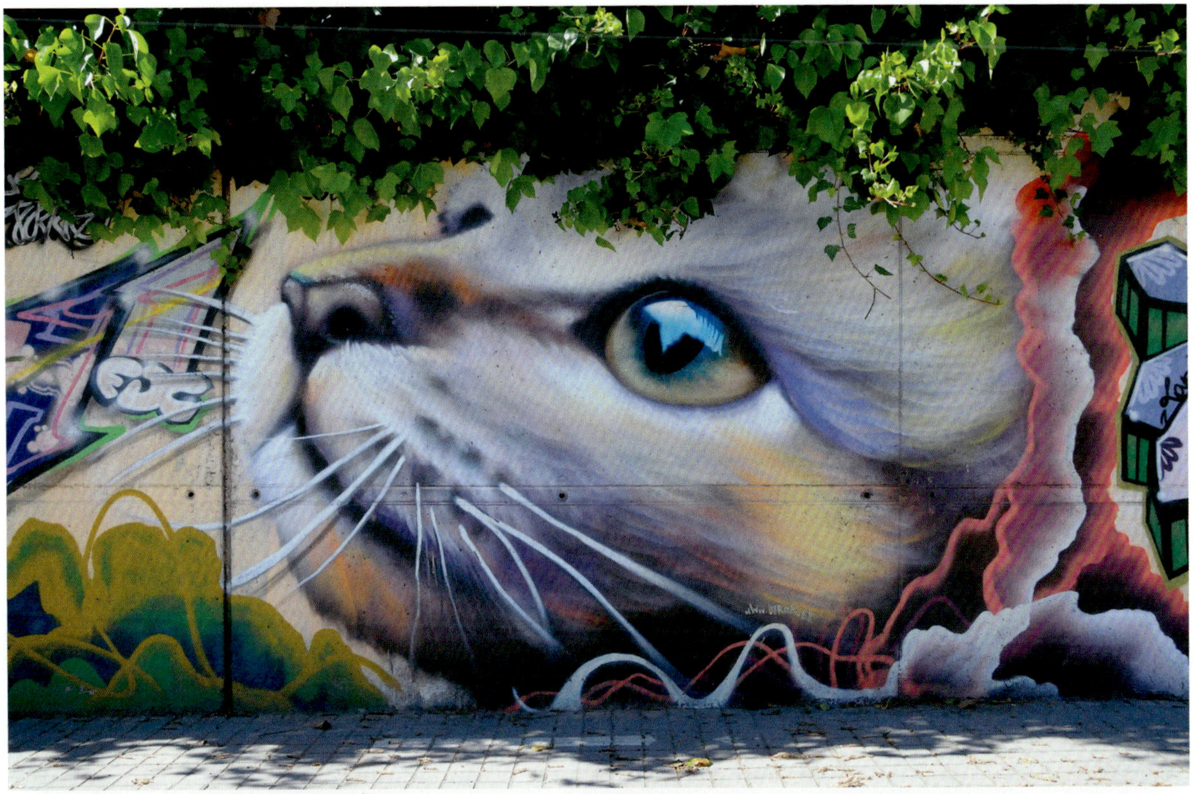

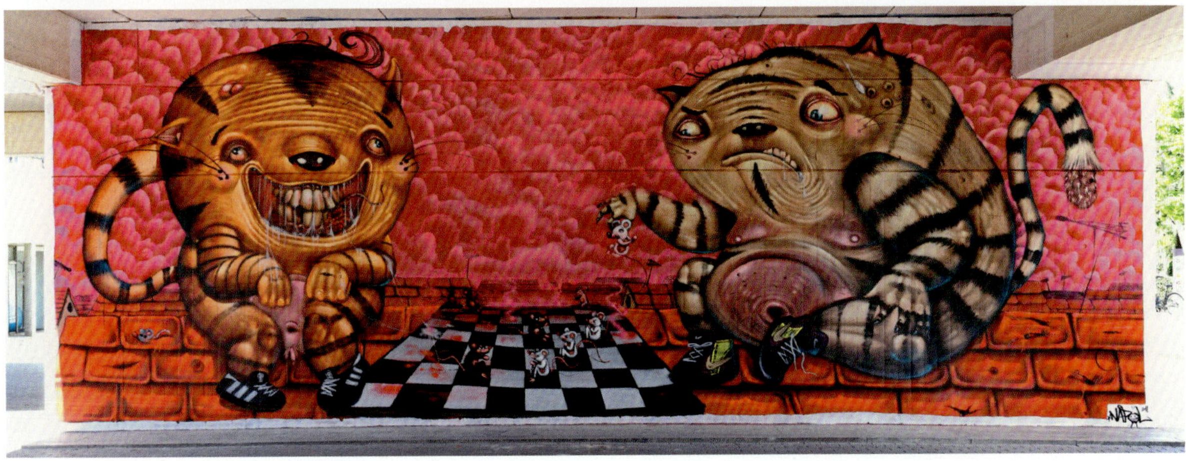

CLOCKWISE FROM TOP
LEFT:
Spain's Dulk/Berok
in Spain/Napol in
Spain/Recal in The
Netherlands.

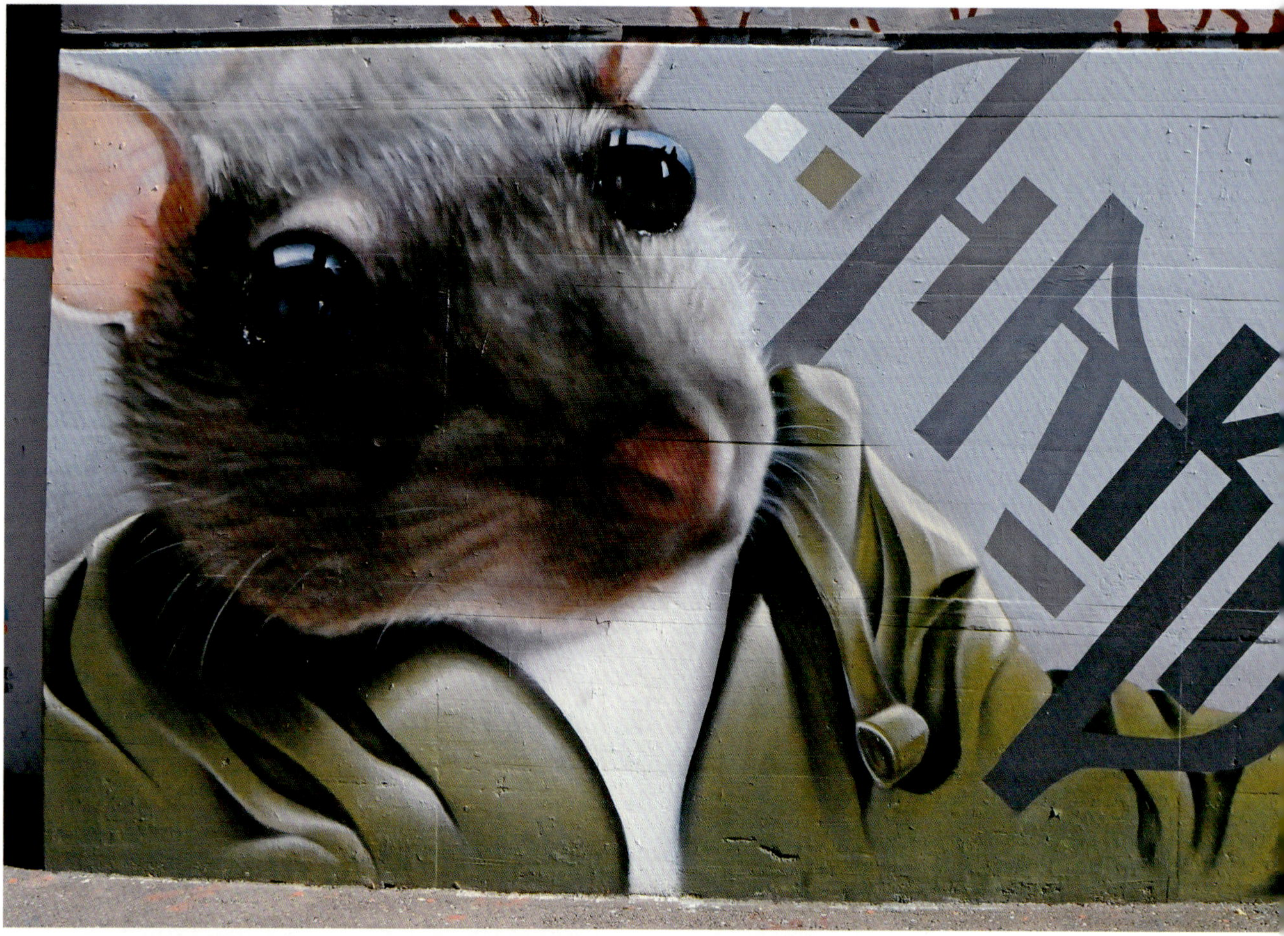

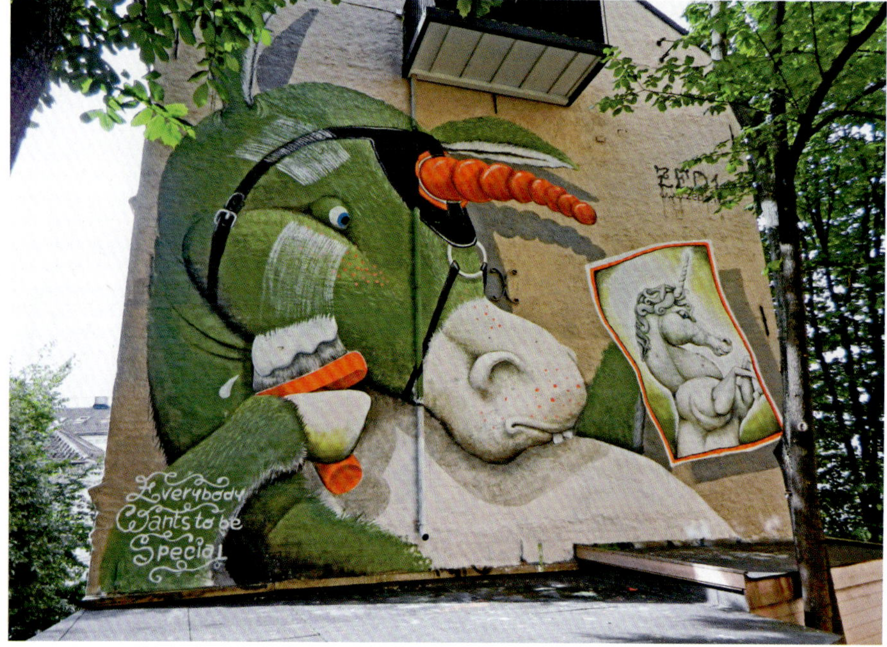

CLOCKWISE FROM LEFT:
Italy's Zed1 in
Norway/Disk in Baden,
Switzerland/USA's Never
Crew in Switzerland.

PAGES 226-7,
CLOCKWISE FROM TOP
LEFT:
Phlegm in Norway/BCP
Crew in Brussels/Estria
in Oakland, California/
El Chico Iwana in
Spain.

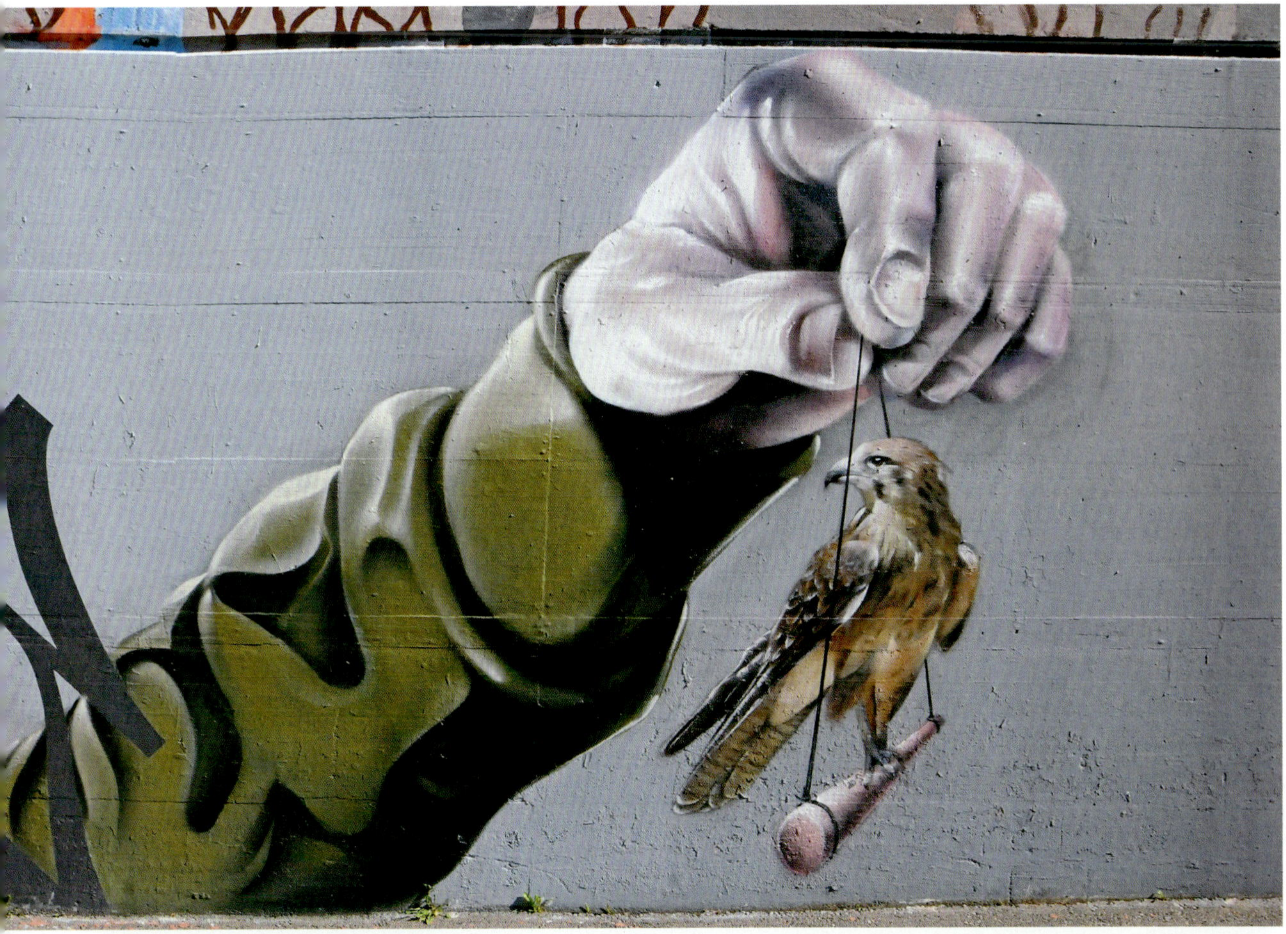

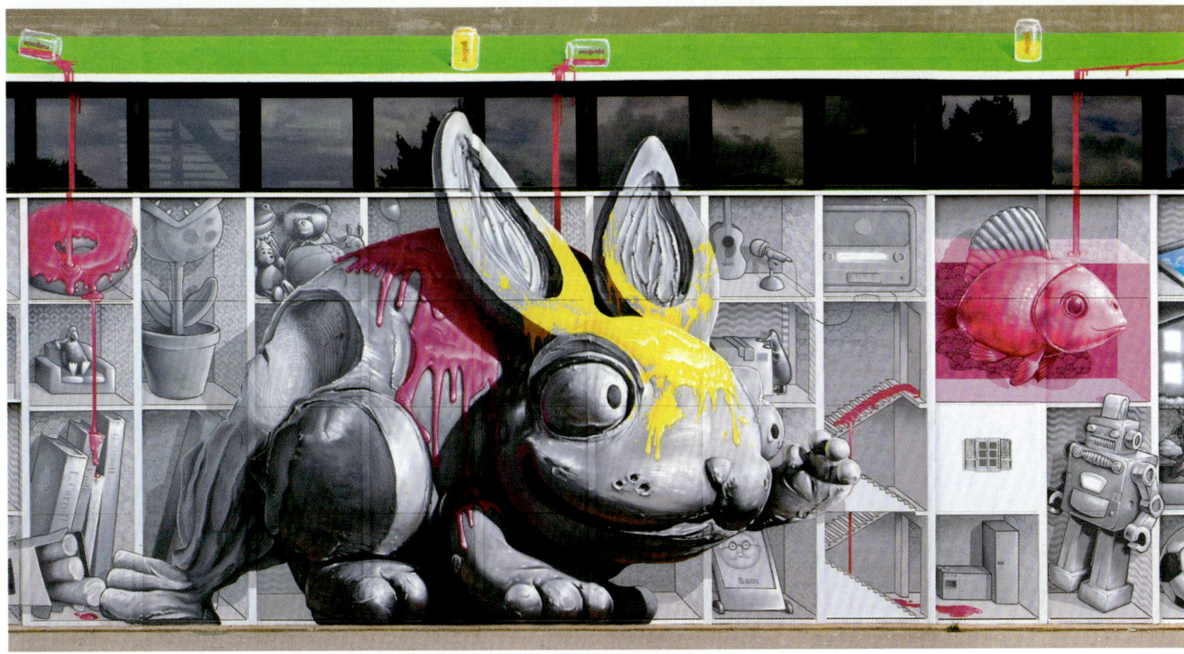

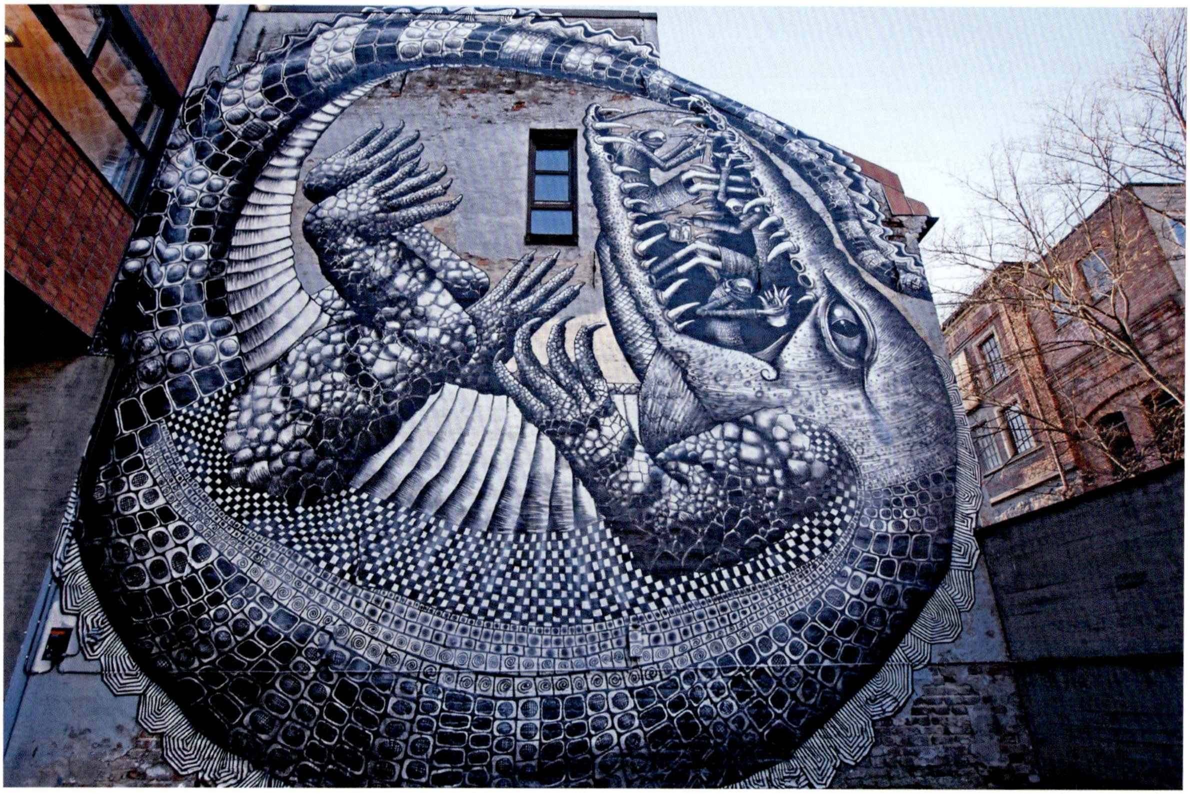

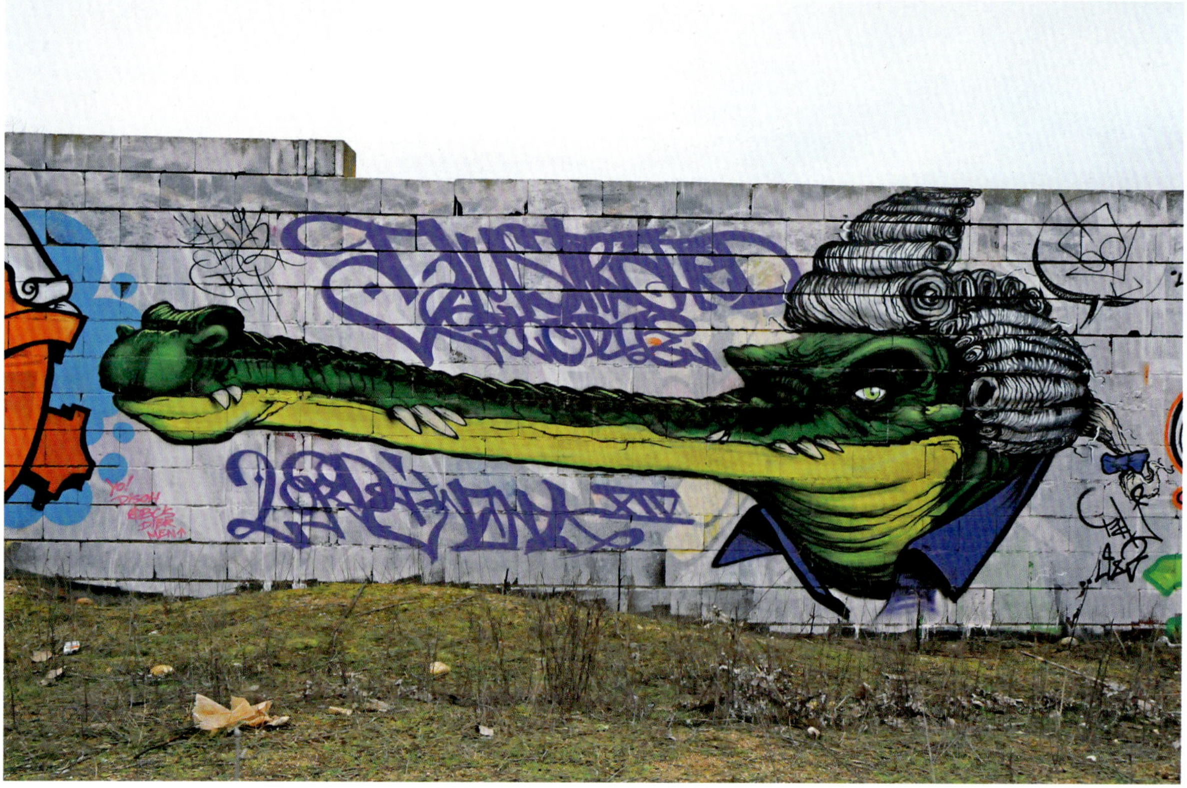

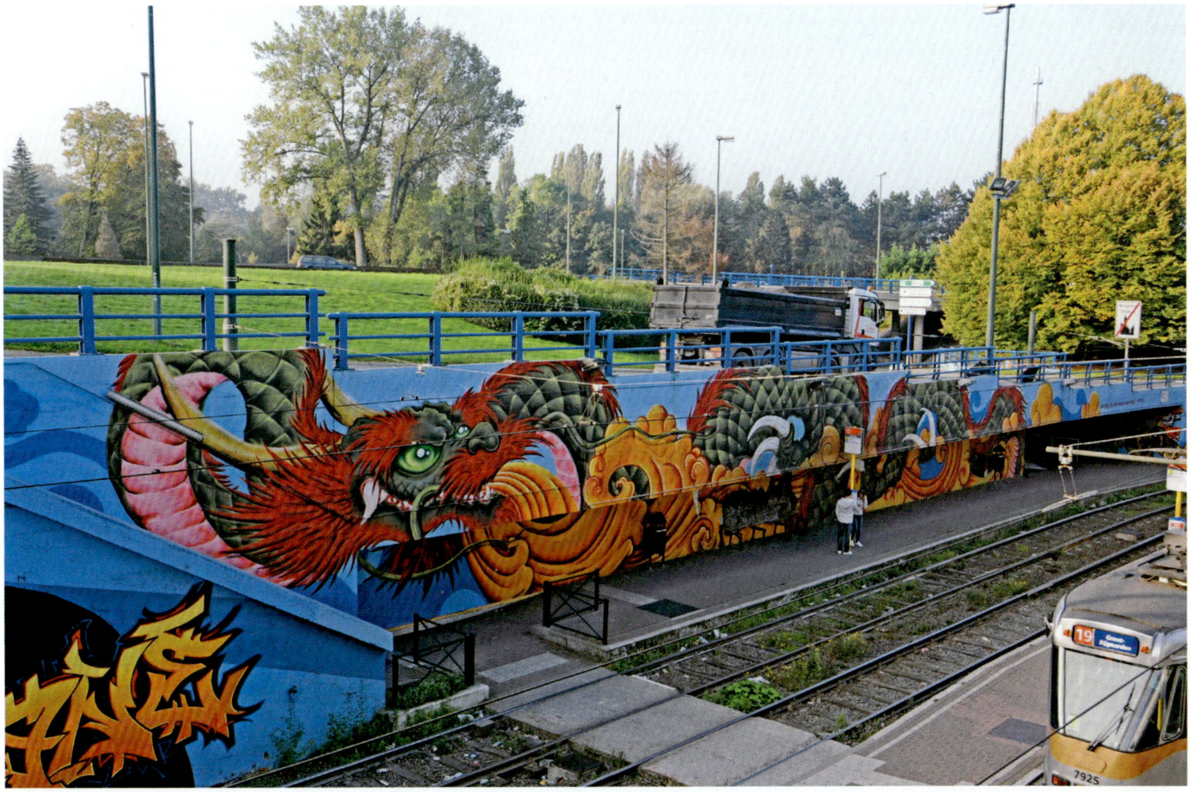

19
7925

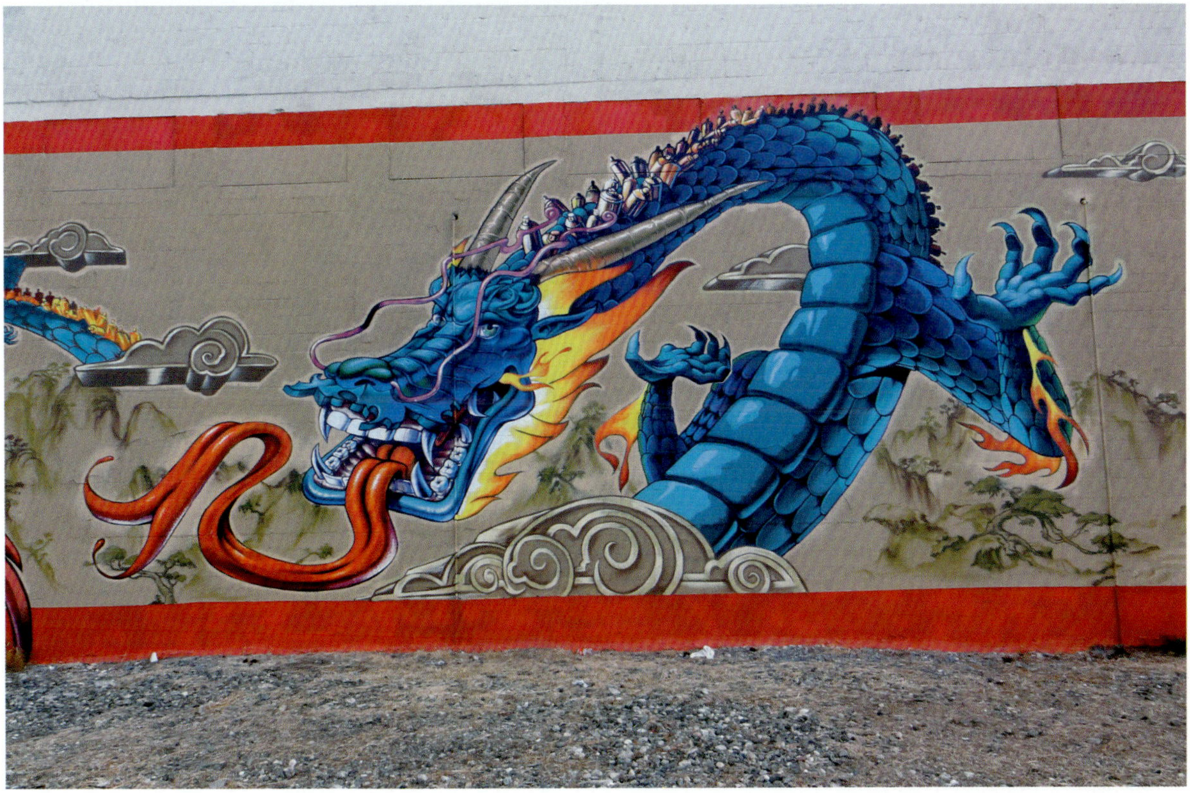

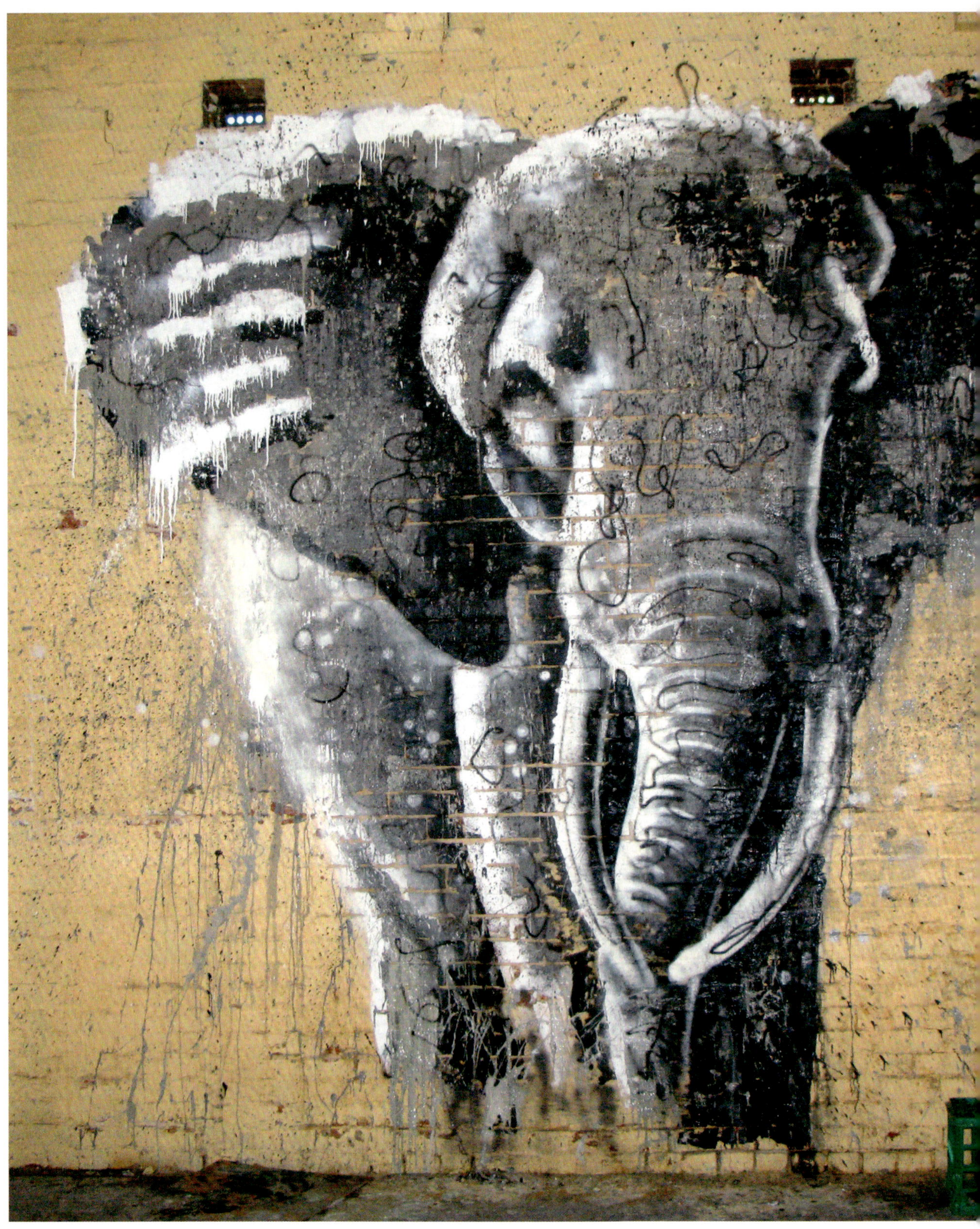

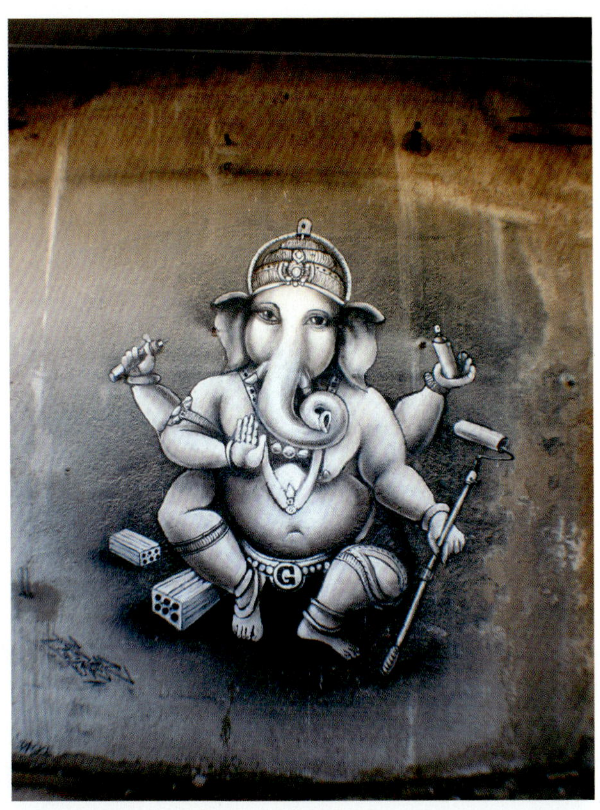

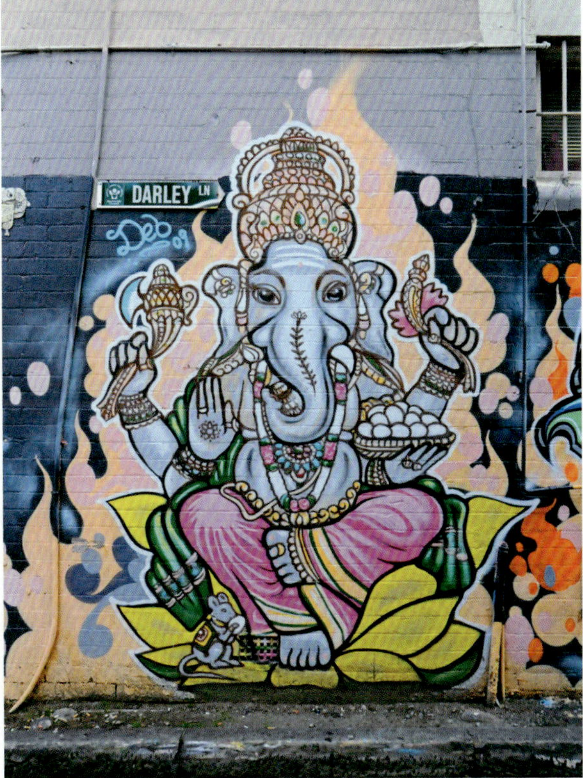

DARLEY LN
Deb

CLOCKWISE FROM FAR
LEFT:
Makatron in Northcote,
Melbourne/Gaser in
Spain/Deb in Melbourne.

PAGES 230-1,
CLOCKWISE FROM TOP
LEFT:
Spain's Drew in
Granada/Tats Cru's
Nicer in New York/
Dutch artist Zedz
in Amsterdam/ Juan
Carlos Muñoz Hernandez
in Madrid/Seyo Crew
in Biel-Bienne,
Switzerland/France's
Bom'k in London.

229

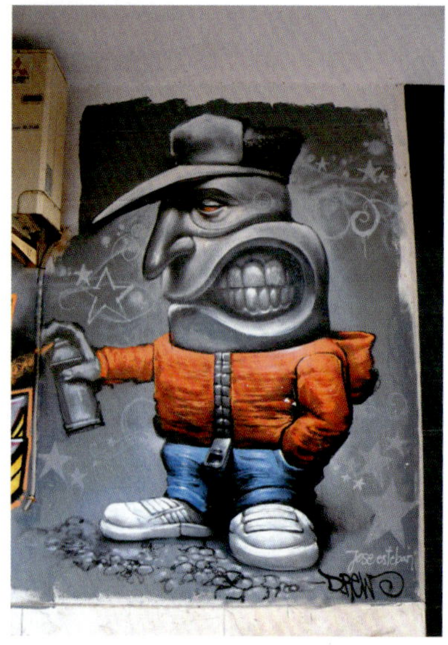

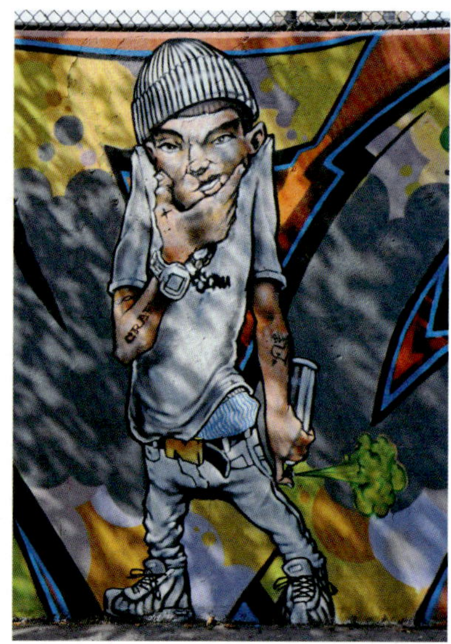

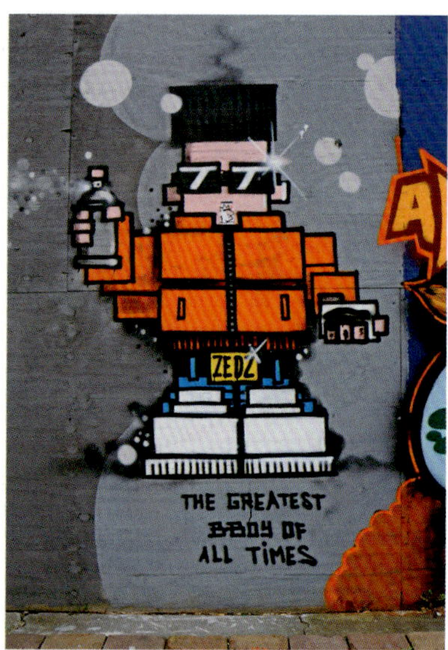

Hip-hop characters (b-boys, DJs, MCs and writers) are still a staple of graffiti. Graffiti subculture often references itself in the art, so these characters usually reflect stylized ideals of what it means to be a part of the subculture. Hip-hop aficionados have paid careful attention to how their icons dress, move and talk. At its essence, hip-hop has always been about taking something from your environment and adding a refined style: MCing stylized speaking, b-boying (breakdancing) stylized movement and graffiti stylized writing – while DJing stylized wrecking your parents' record collection.

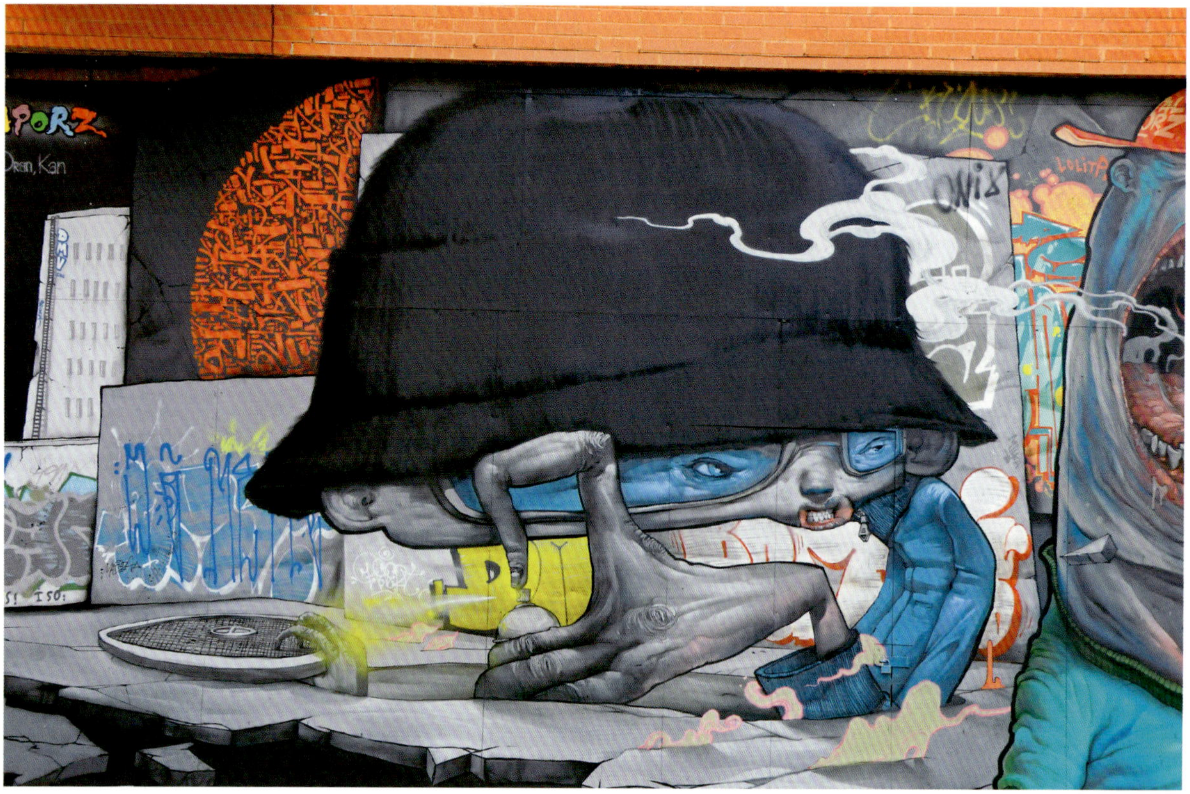

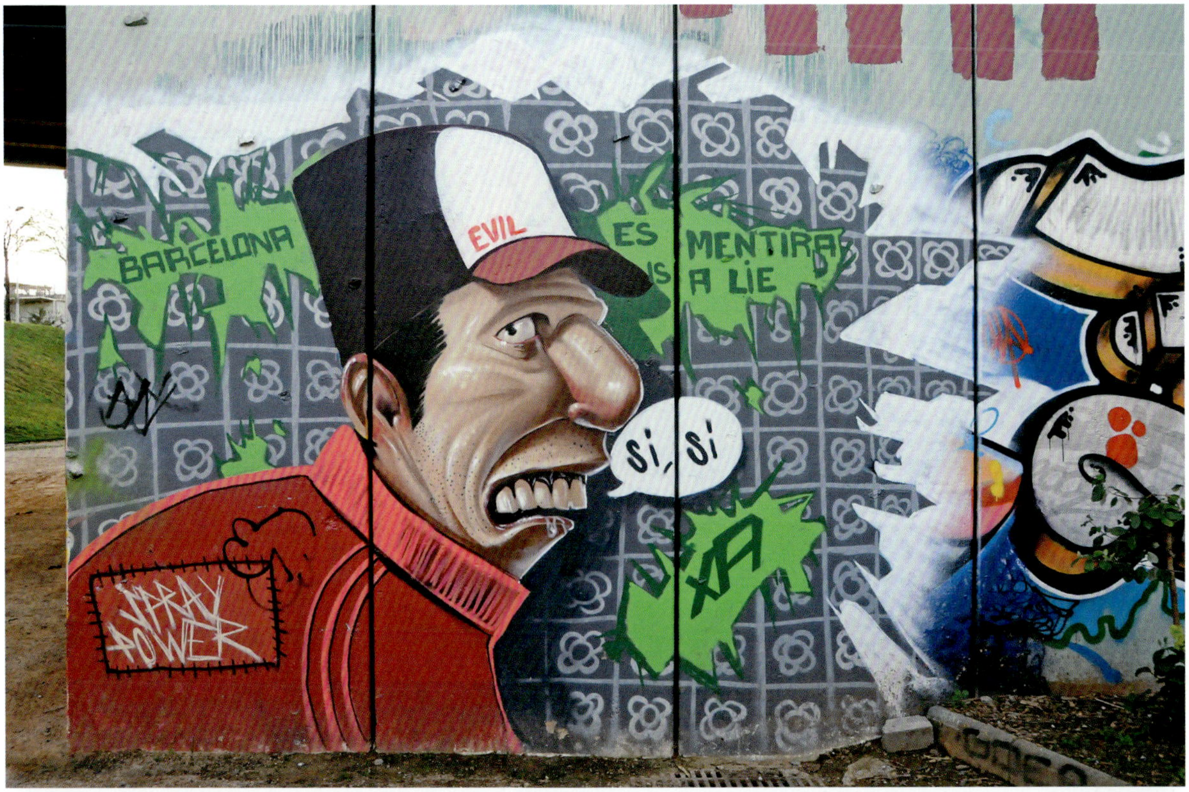

BARCELONA
EVIL
ES MENTIRA
IS A LIE
Si, si
SPRAY POWER

www.scyo.ch
J-ROC
JE 415 198

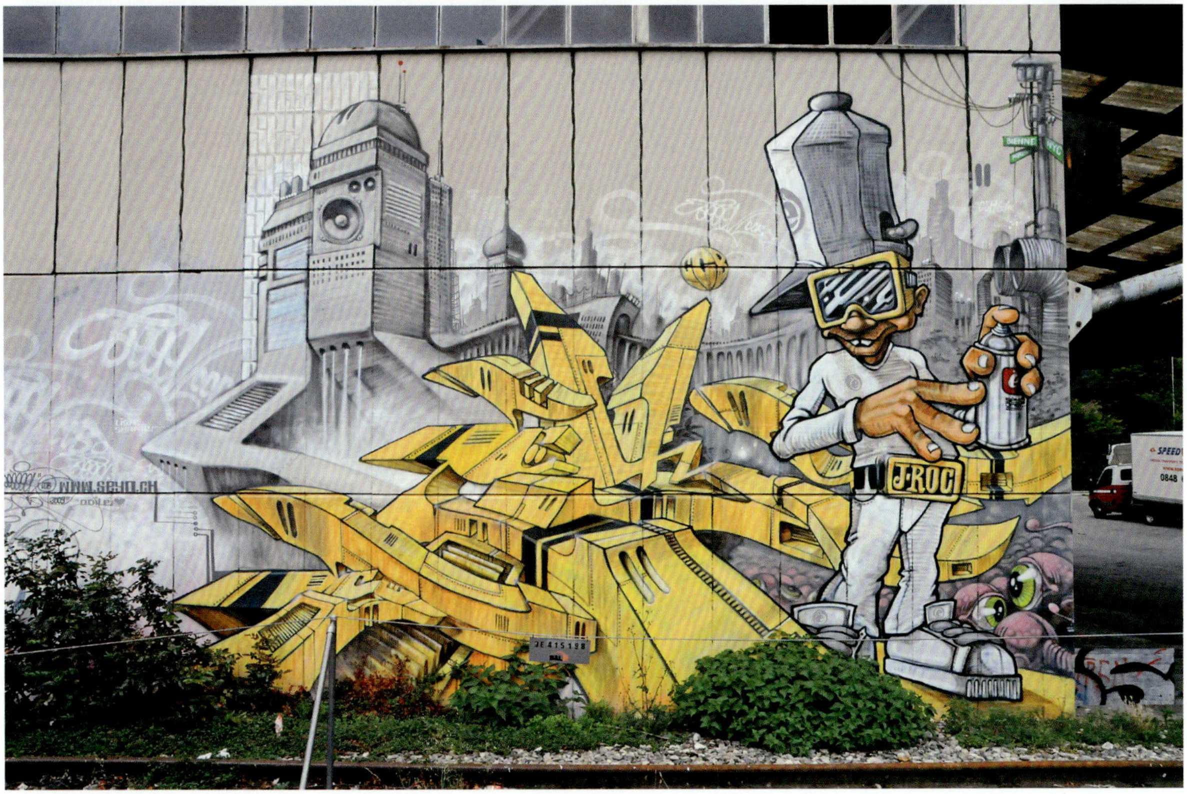

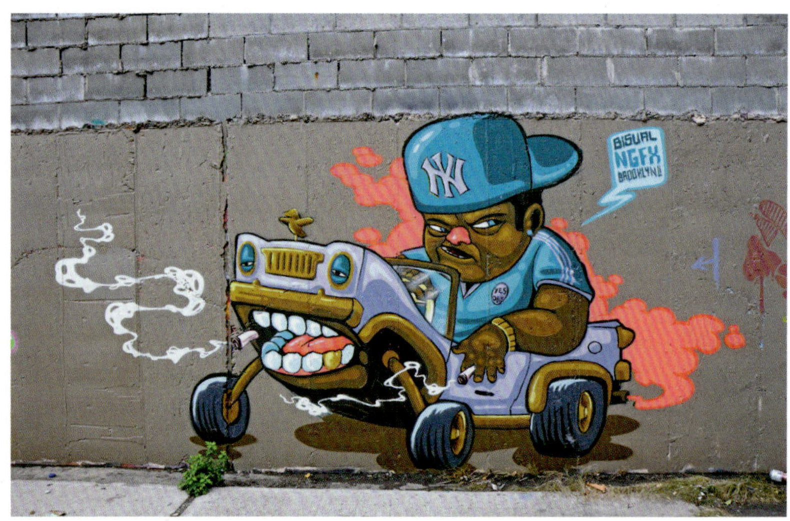

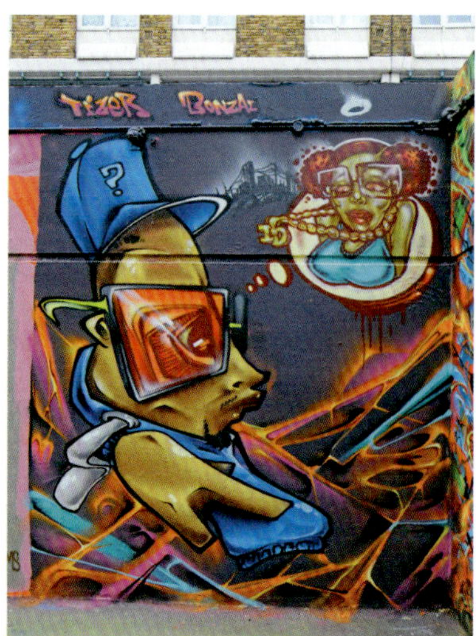

CLOCKWISE FROM
ABOVE:
Spain's Bisual in New
York/Bonzai and Tizer
One in London/Bonzai in
London/Cheo in Bristol/
Anus-1 in Münster,
Germany/Dutch artist
Nash.

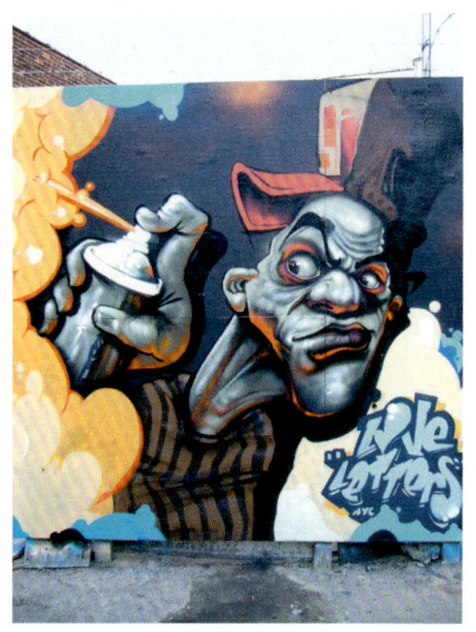

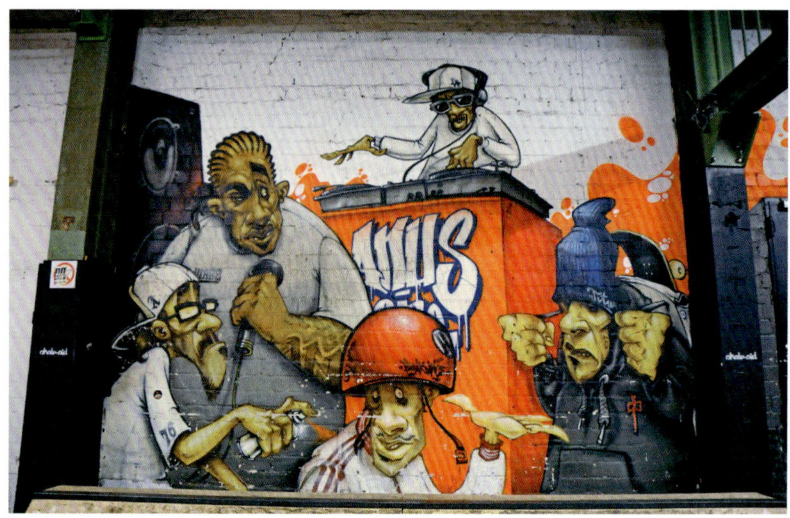

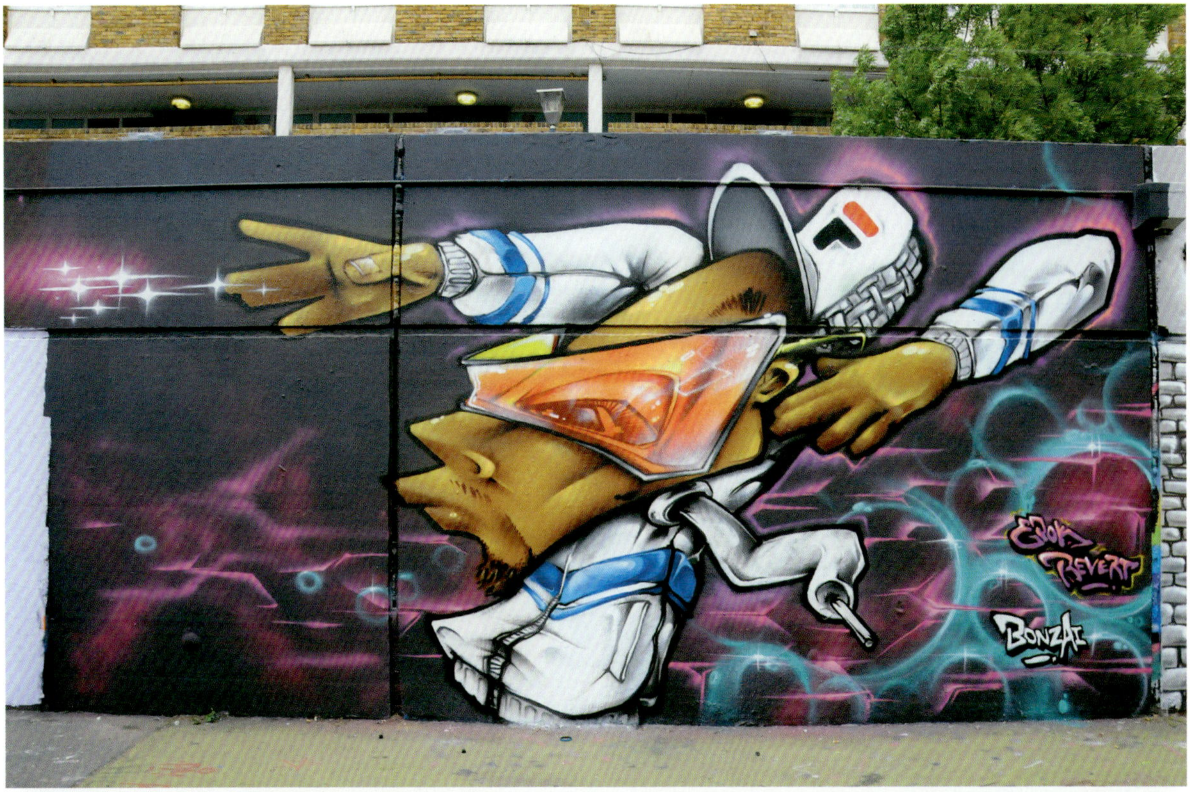

EWOK
REVERT
BONZAI

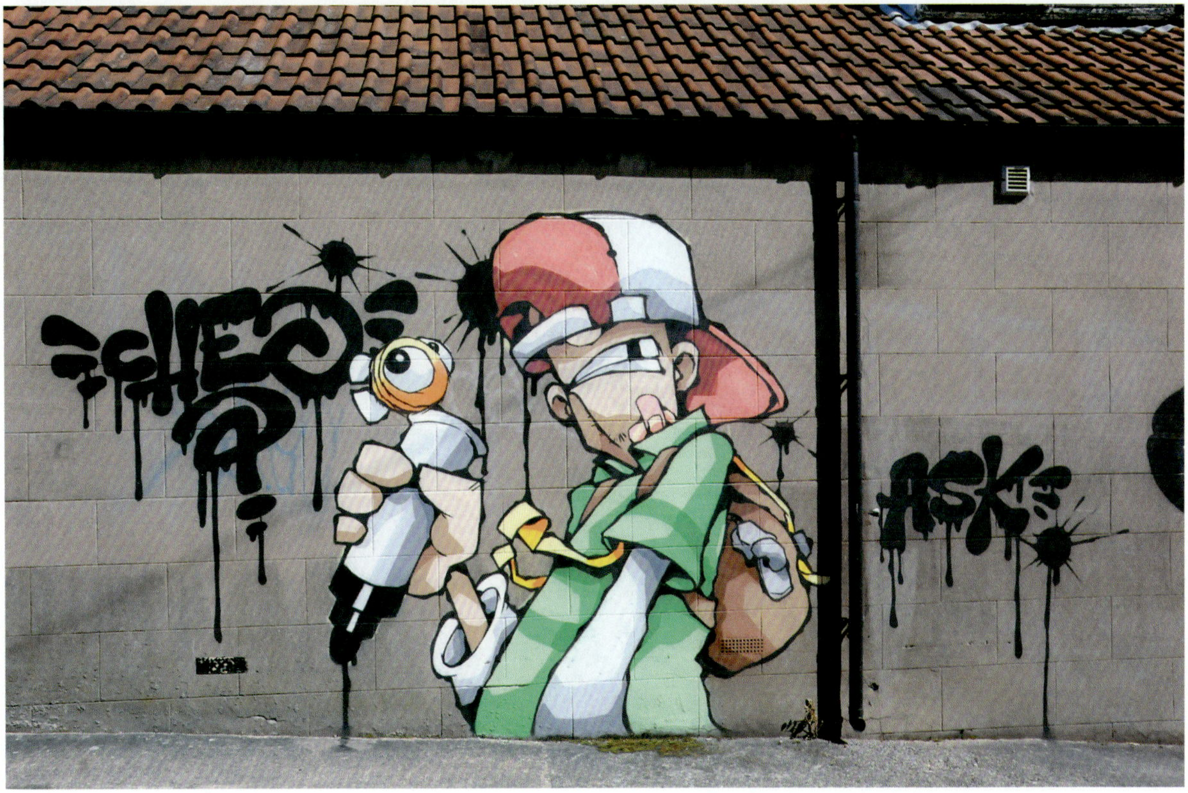

CHE
ASK

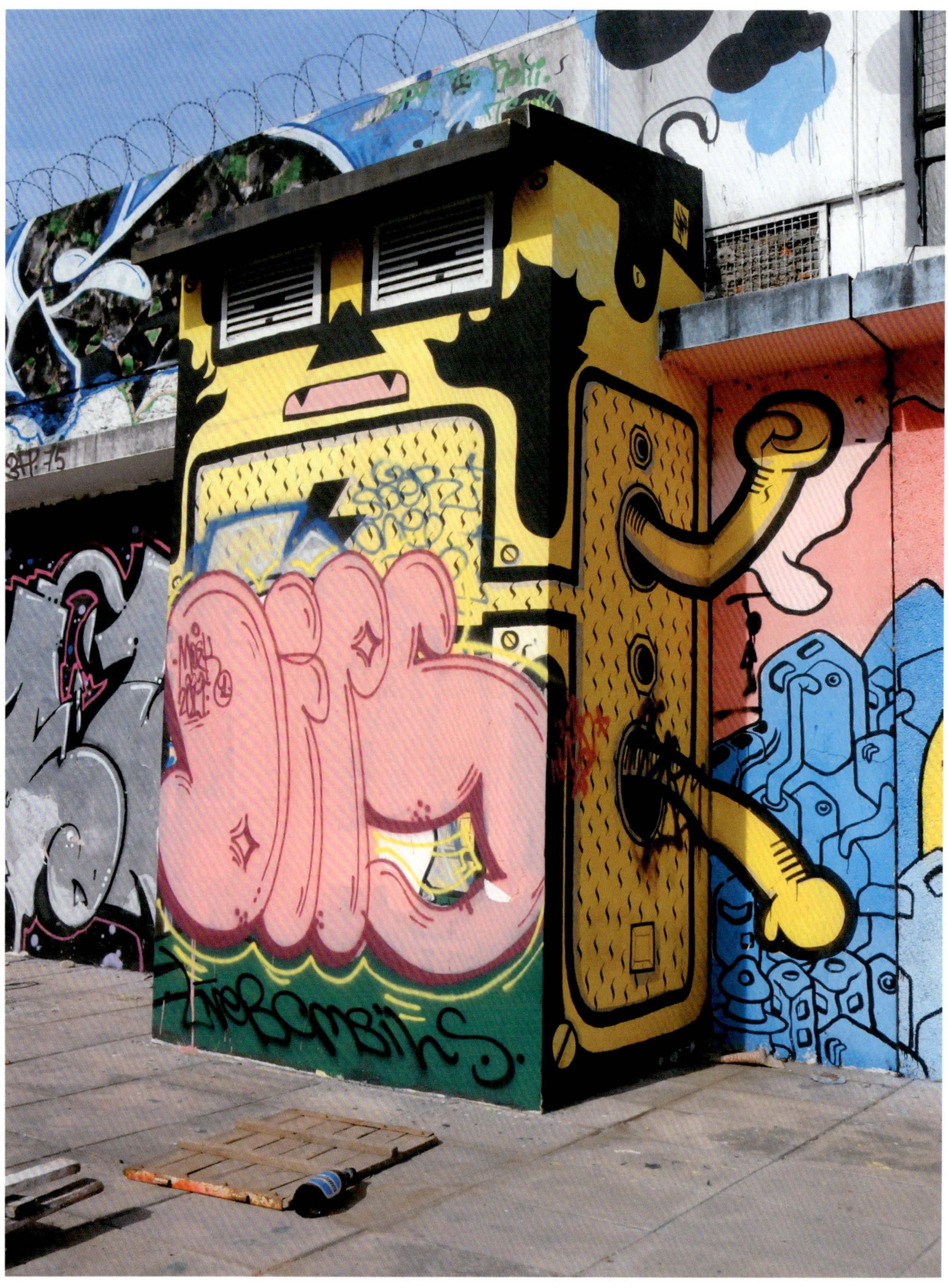

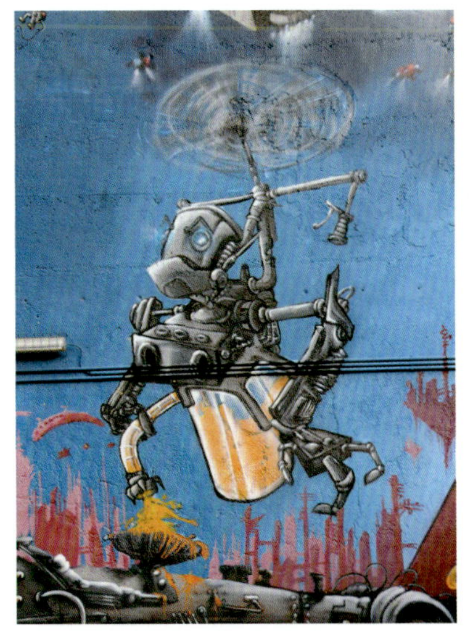 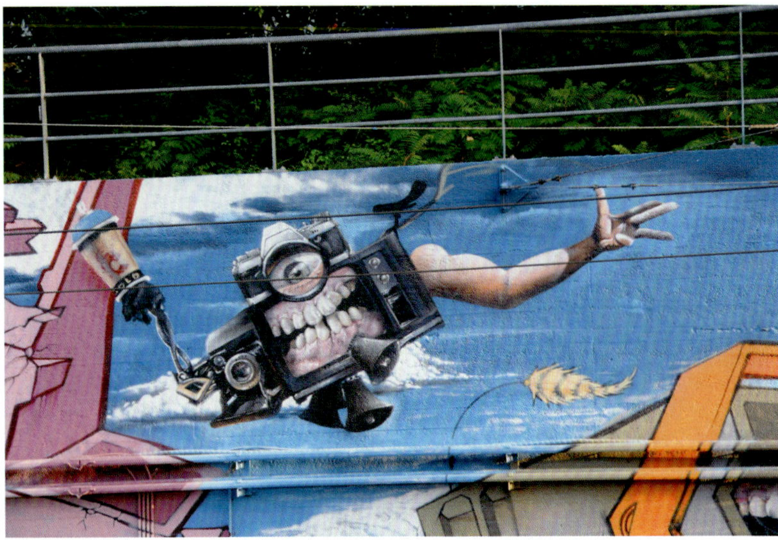

CLOCKWISE FROM LEFT:
P3dro Perelman in Buenos
Aires/Members of D2F
Crew, including artist
Kent, in Brussels/D2F
Crew in Brussels/Shé in
Lleida, Spain.

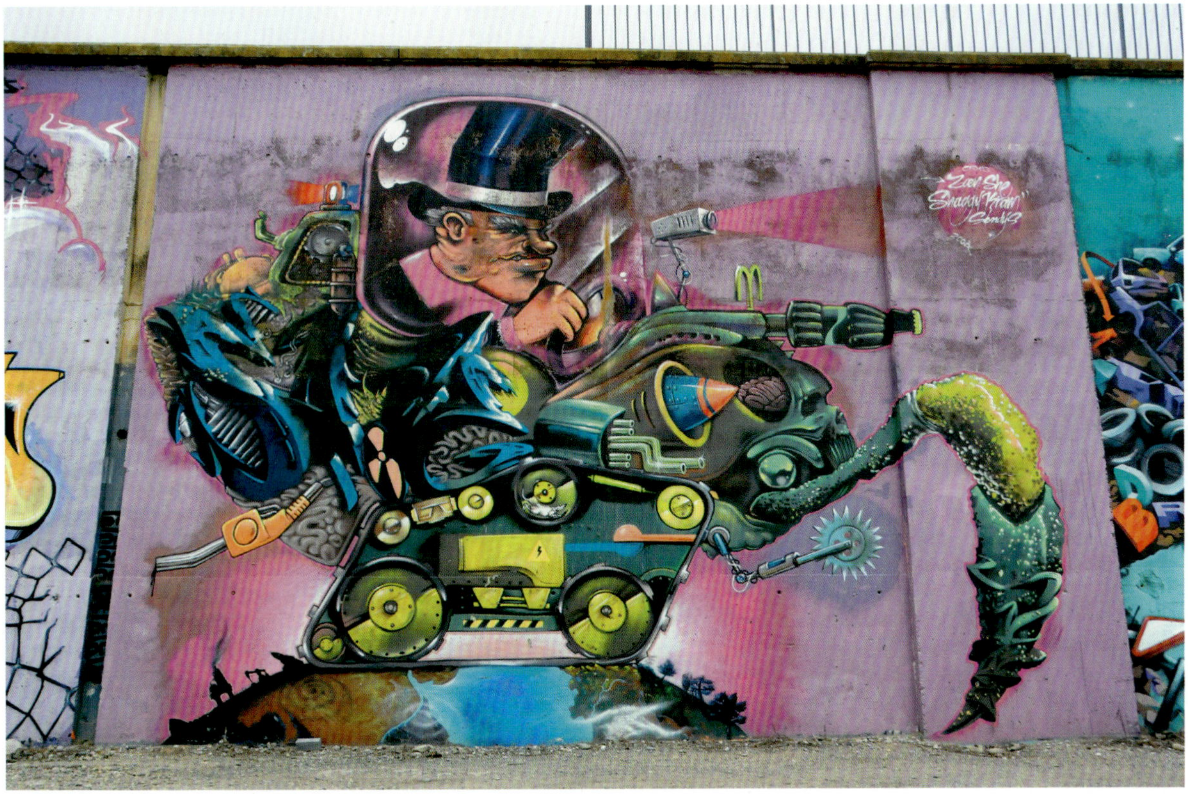

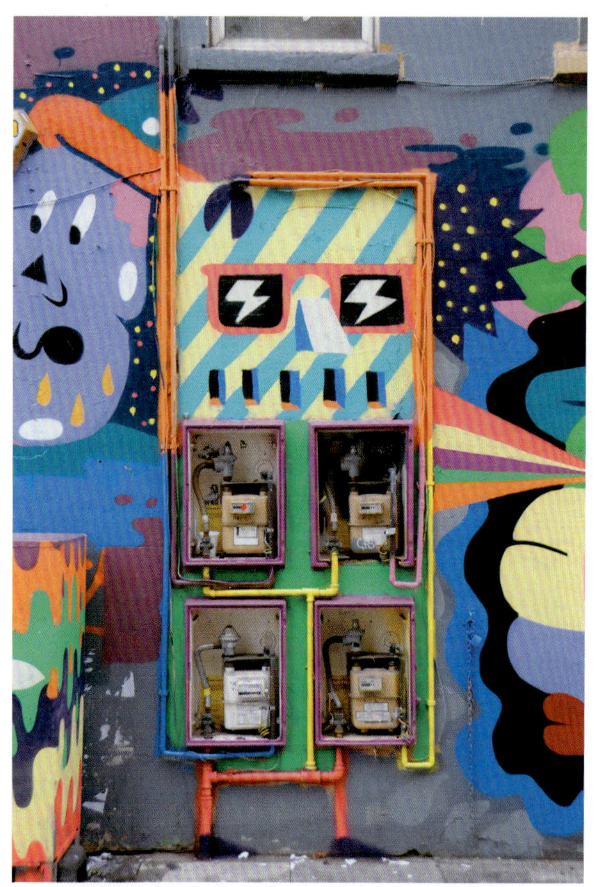
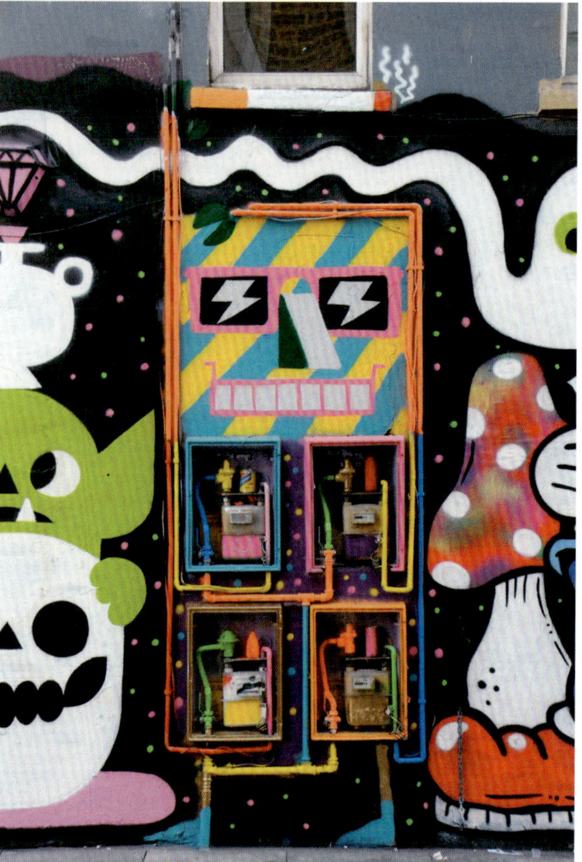
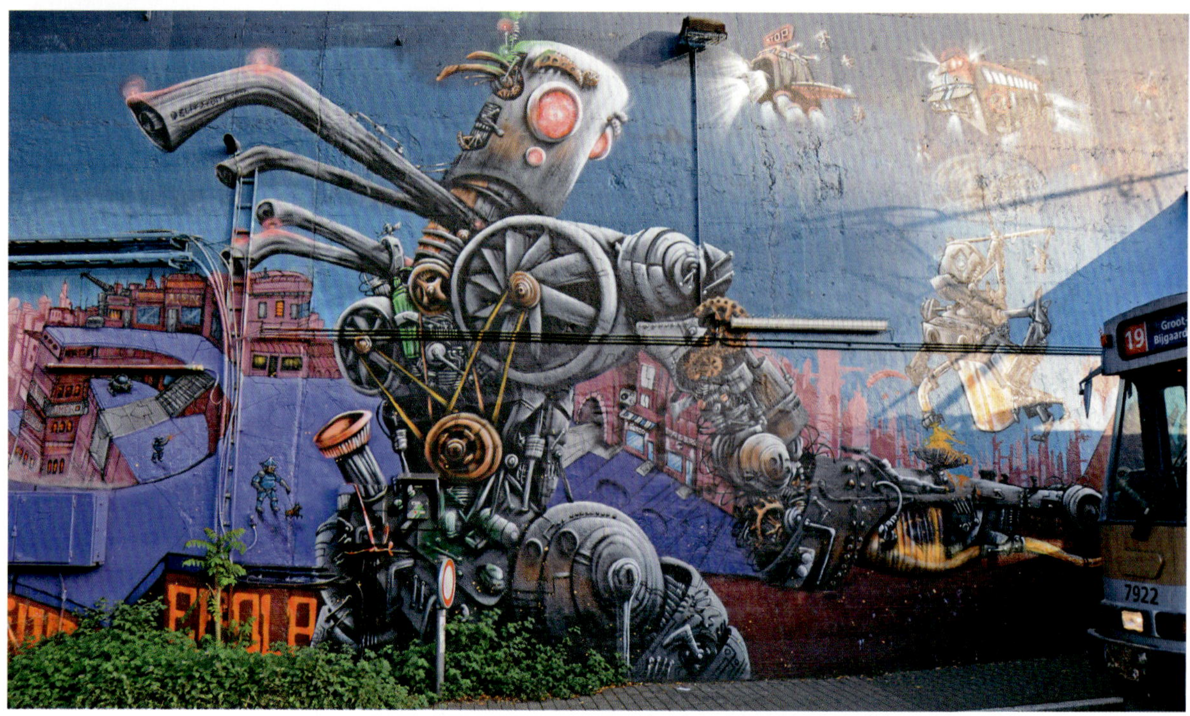
19
Groot-
Bijgaard
7922

SPACES & SURFACES

Spaces influence the art created for them. Much of the context for contemporary art is the neutral 'white cube' of the commercial gallery system, and artists have to produce objects because they are moved once they are sold. Our cities provide a different set of constraints: while they do not encourage the production of saleable objects, their surfaces are often uneven, impacting on the art and working in conjunction with other constraints, including time. The following photographs look at how graffiti and street artists work with features of urban spaces to which gallery-based artists do not have access, and how the art differs when it is framed by trucks or trains, or is painted on the road. There is also a special section to show how the uneven surfaces on which street artists paint influence and are often integrated into their work.

PAGE 236, CLOCKWISE FROM TOP LEFT:
UK's Malarky in London/
Malarky in London/
Ebola from D2F Crew in
Brussels.

CLOCKWISE FROM
RIGHT:
Italy's Cristian Sonda/
Italy's Mr Thoms/*Nature*
by France's Vinie/*Man
vs Wild* by France's
Shaka.

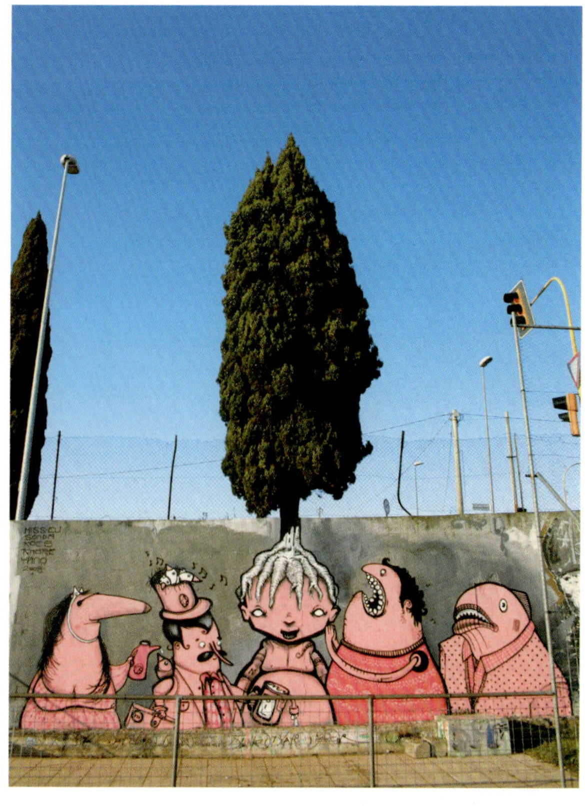

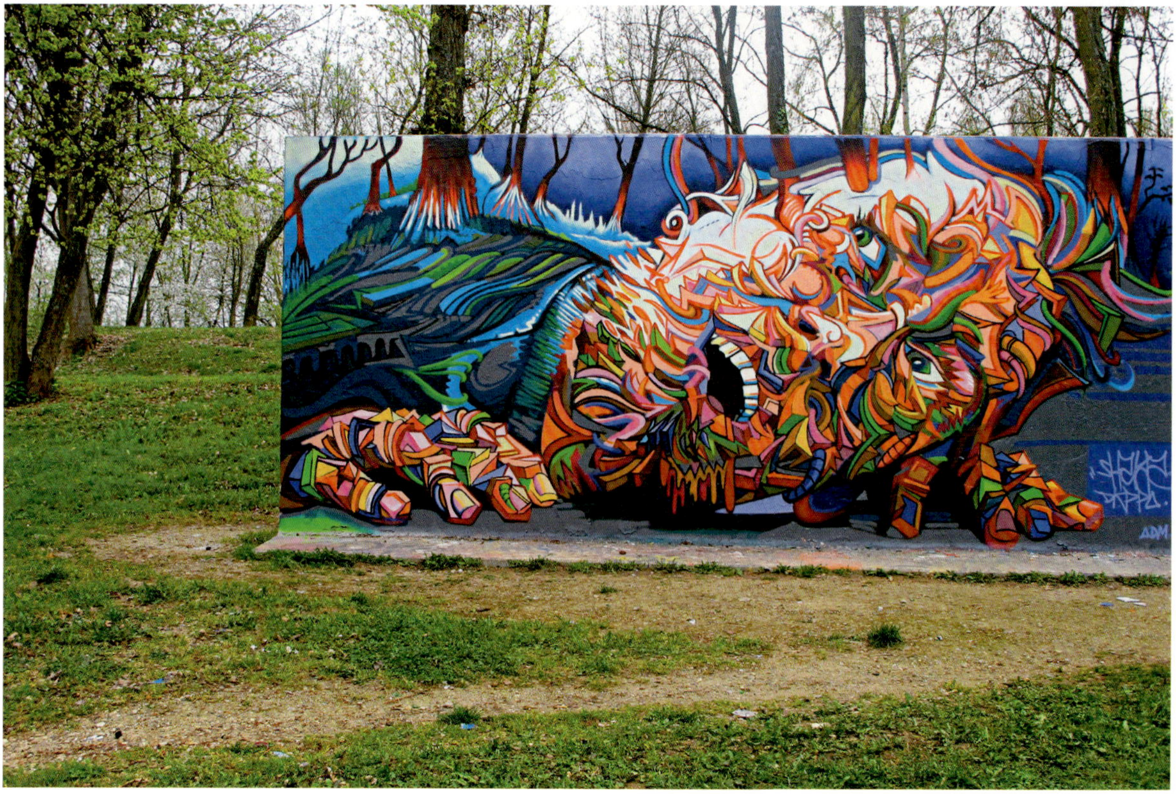

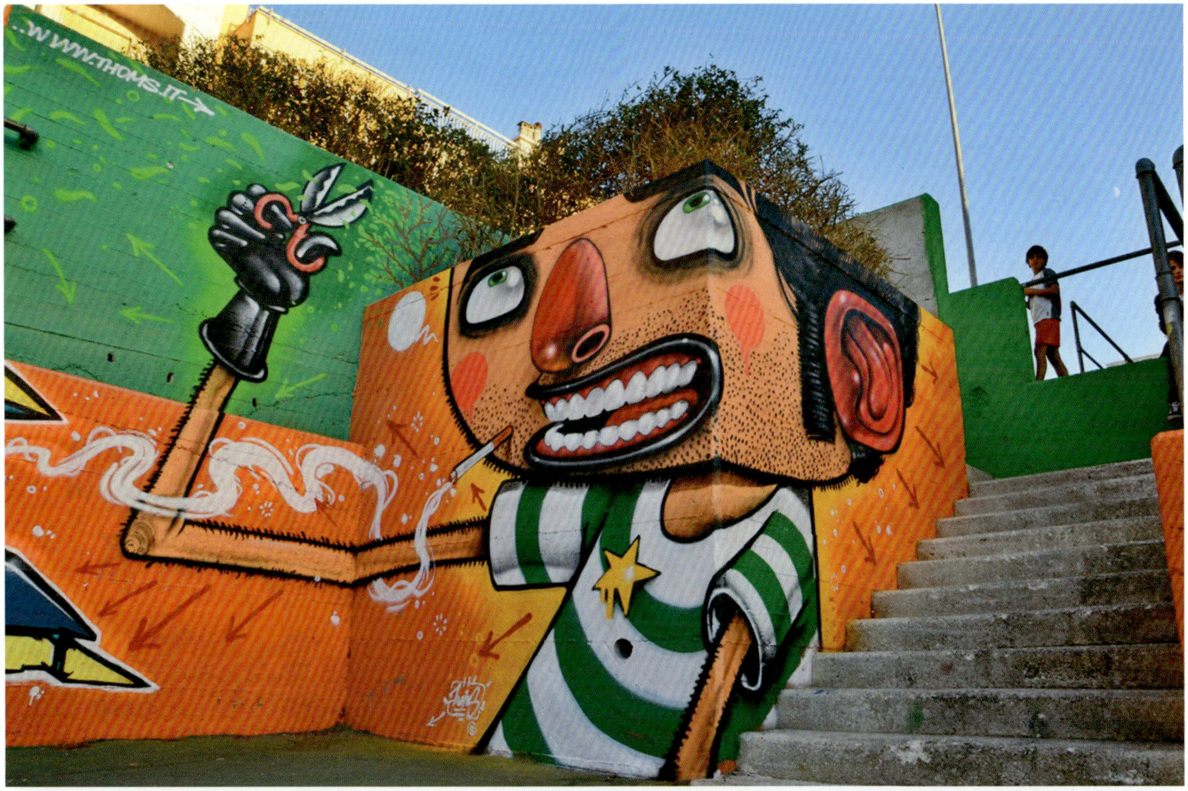

W.WW.THOMS.IT

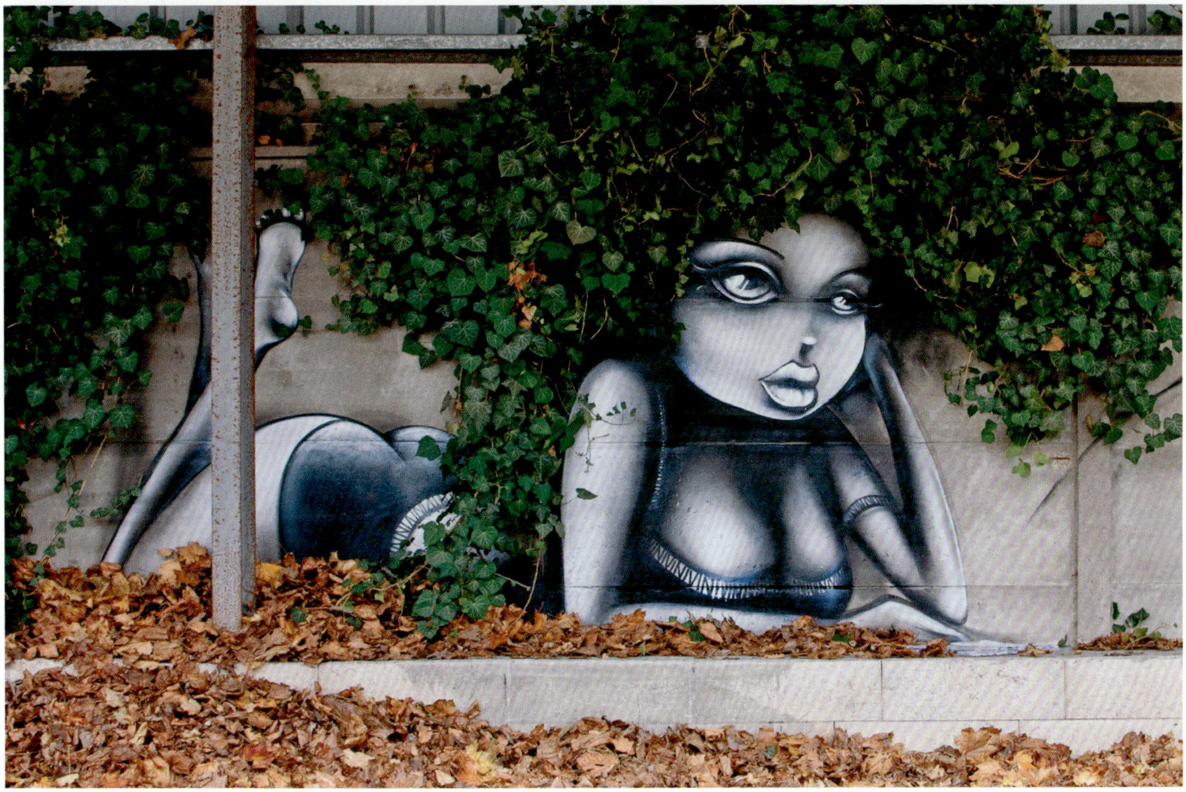

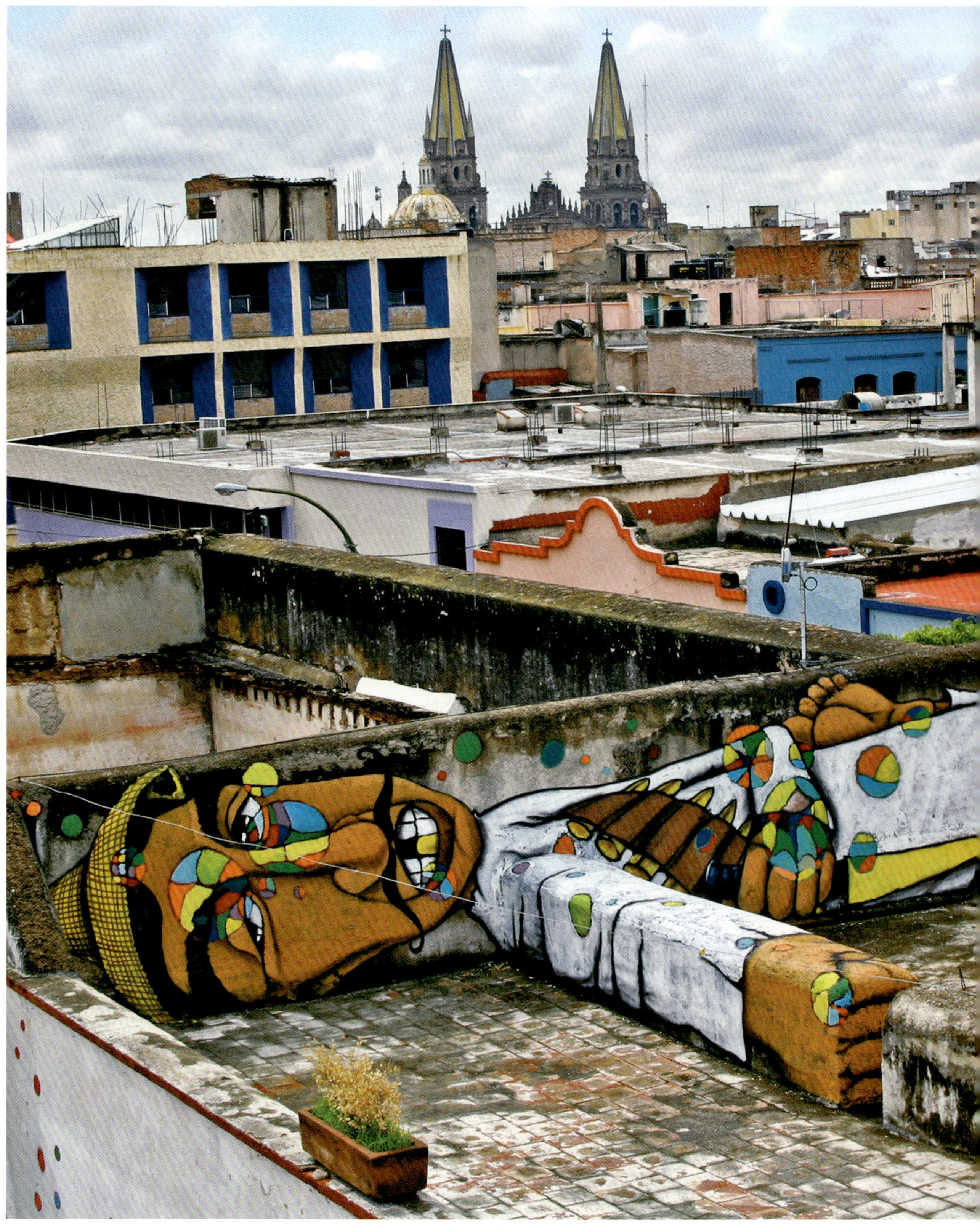

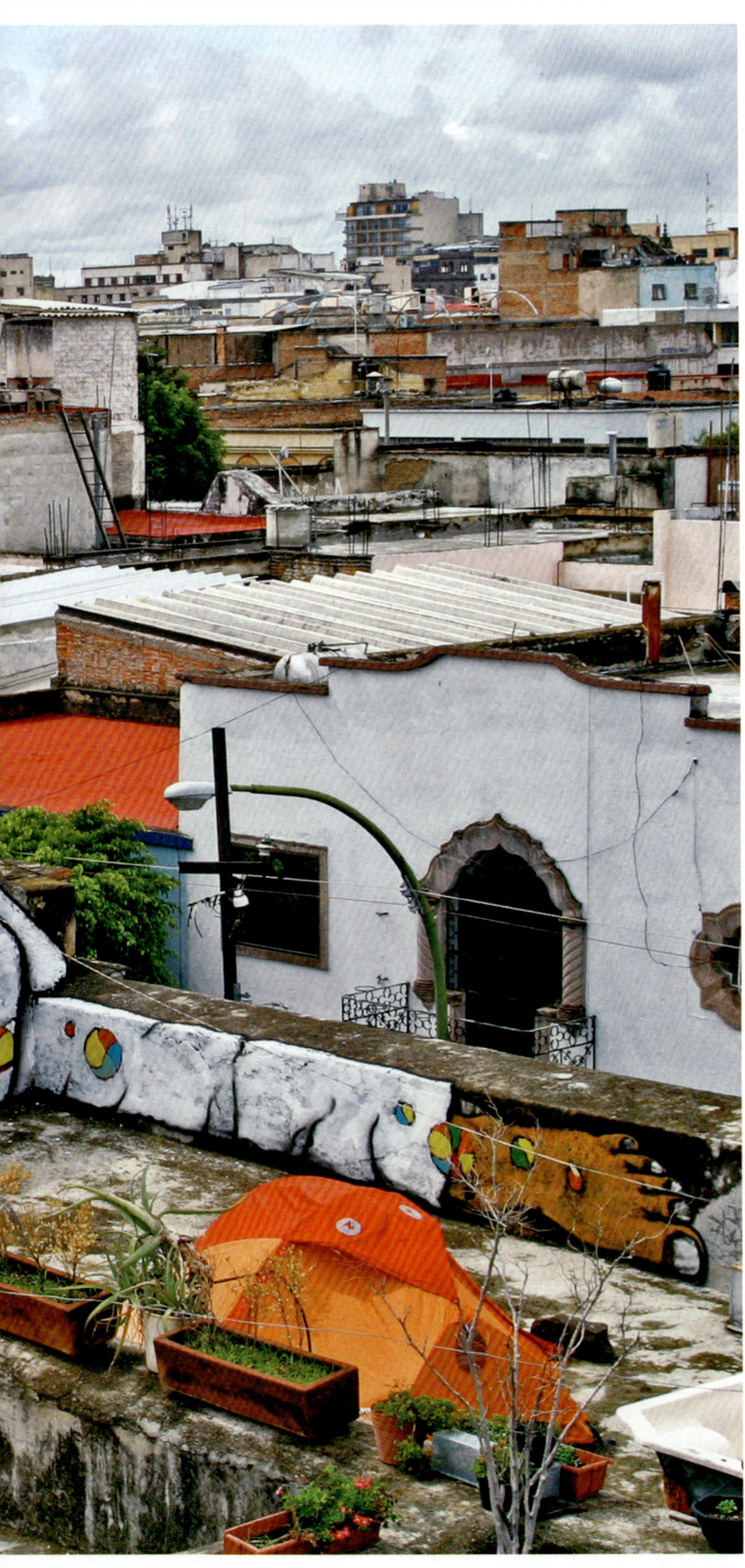

THESE PAGES:
German artist Lake in
Guadalajara, Mexico.

CLOCKWISE FROM BELOW:
Switzerland's Never Crew/Italy's Mr Thoms in honour of his dog/*Sweet Tongue* by Poland's Natalia Rak.

PAGES 244-5, CLOCKWISE FROM TOP LEFT:
Spain's Saiko in Lleida (note how the edge of the bridge has been turned into a spraycan)/*Holding Hand* by Germany's Dome/Argentinia's Gualicho in San José.

PAGES 246-7, CLOCKWISE FROM TOP LEFT:
Germany's Tasso in Lisbon/Spain's Saiko/Russia's Nomerz/Nomerz.

PAGES 248-9, CLOCKWISE FROM LEFT:
Dr Frankenstein by France's Jeaze Oner (note how the artist's presence in the photograph is a key part of the art itself)/France's Vinie/*White Tiger* by Canada's Roadsworth.

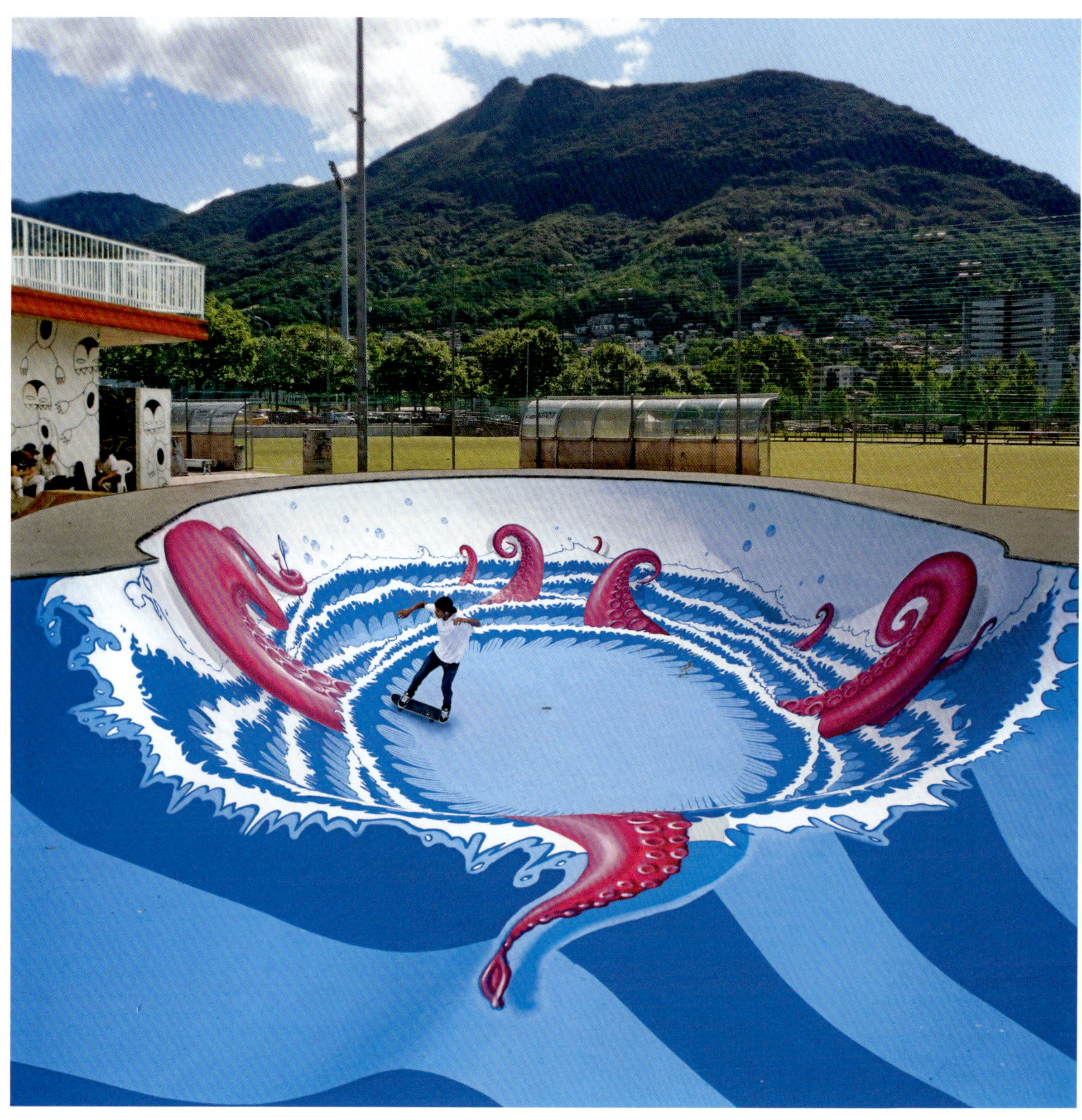

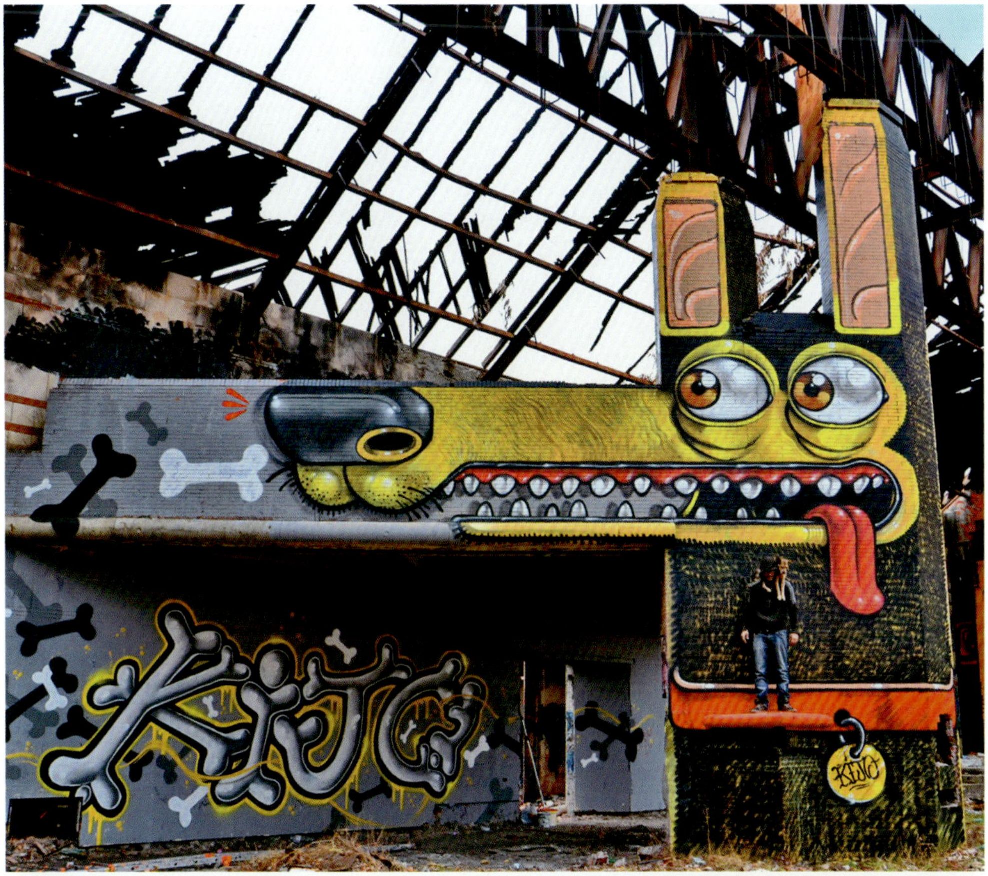

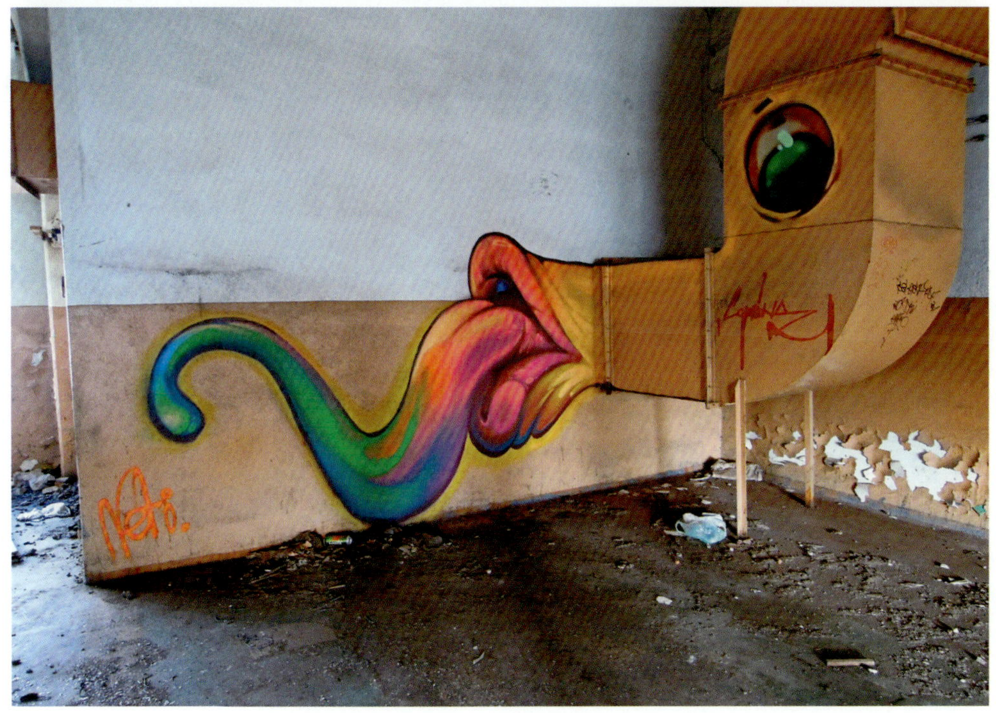

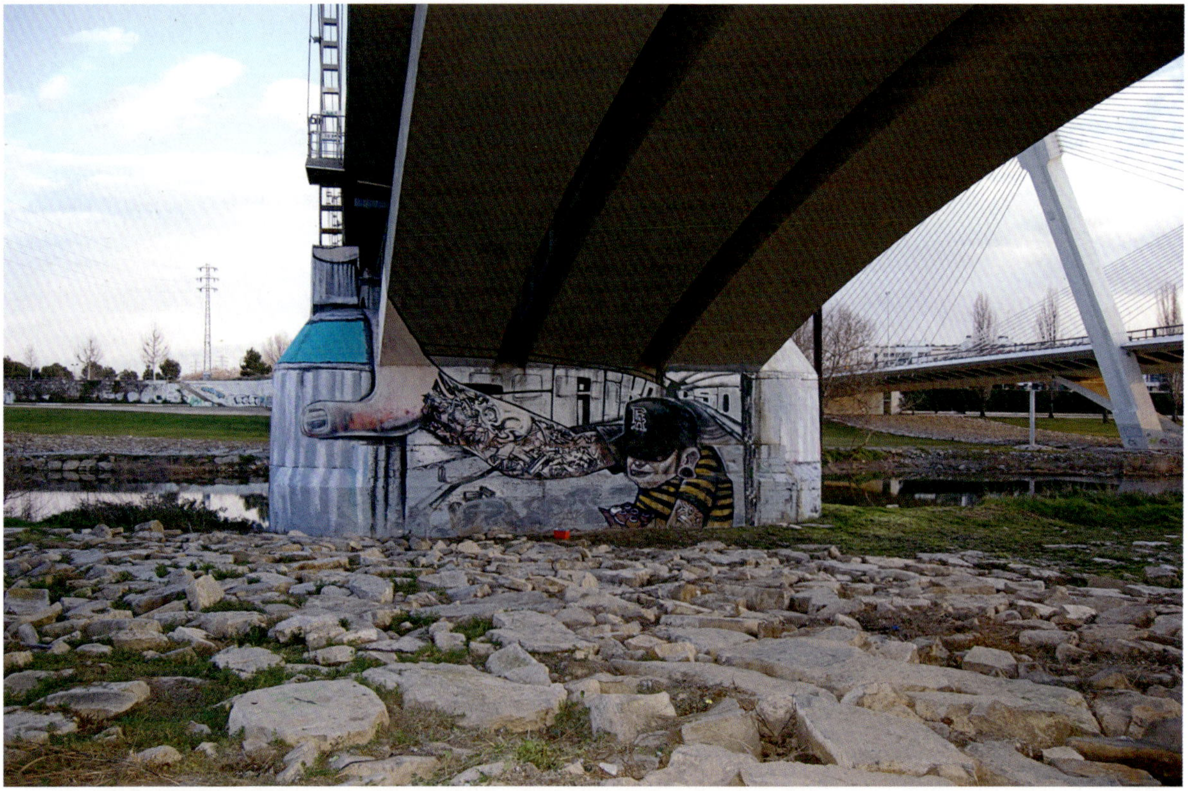

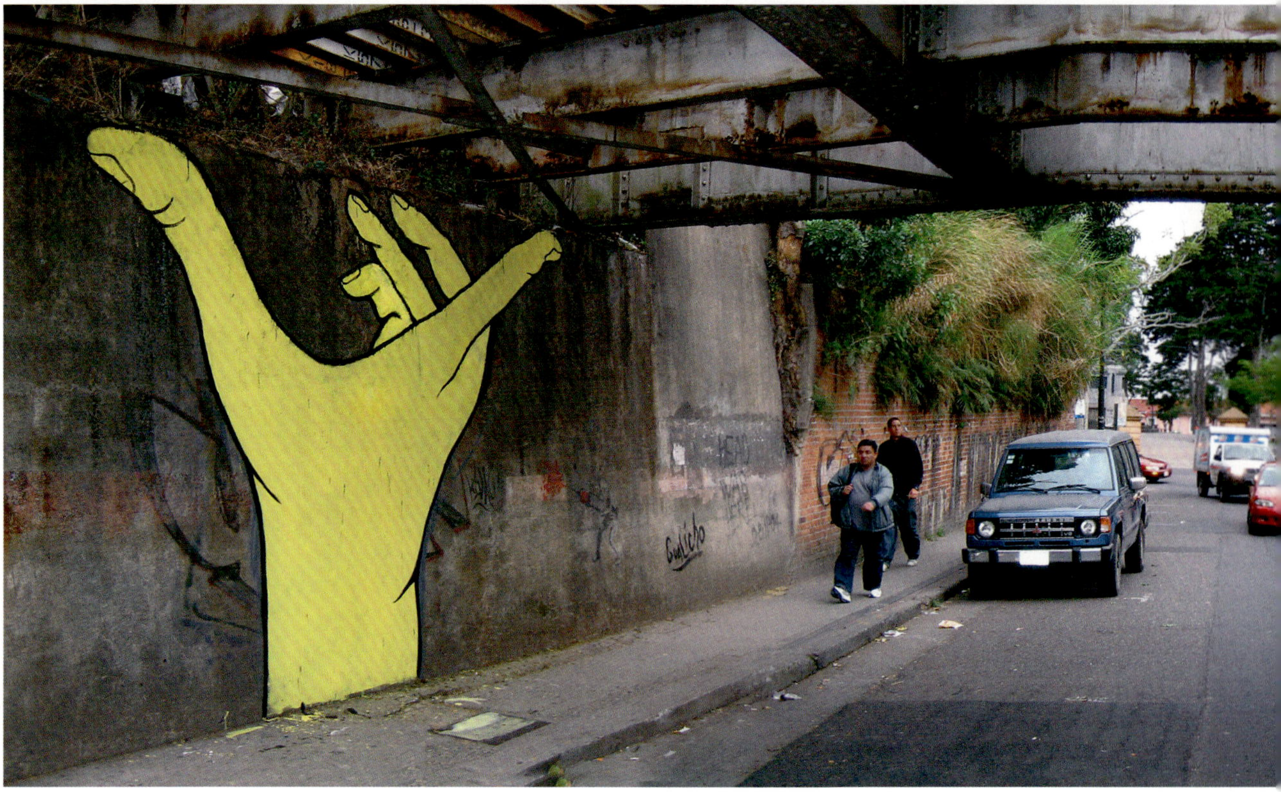

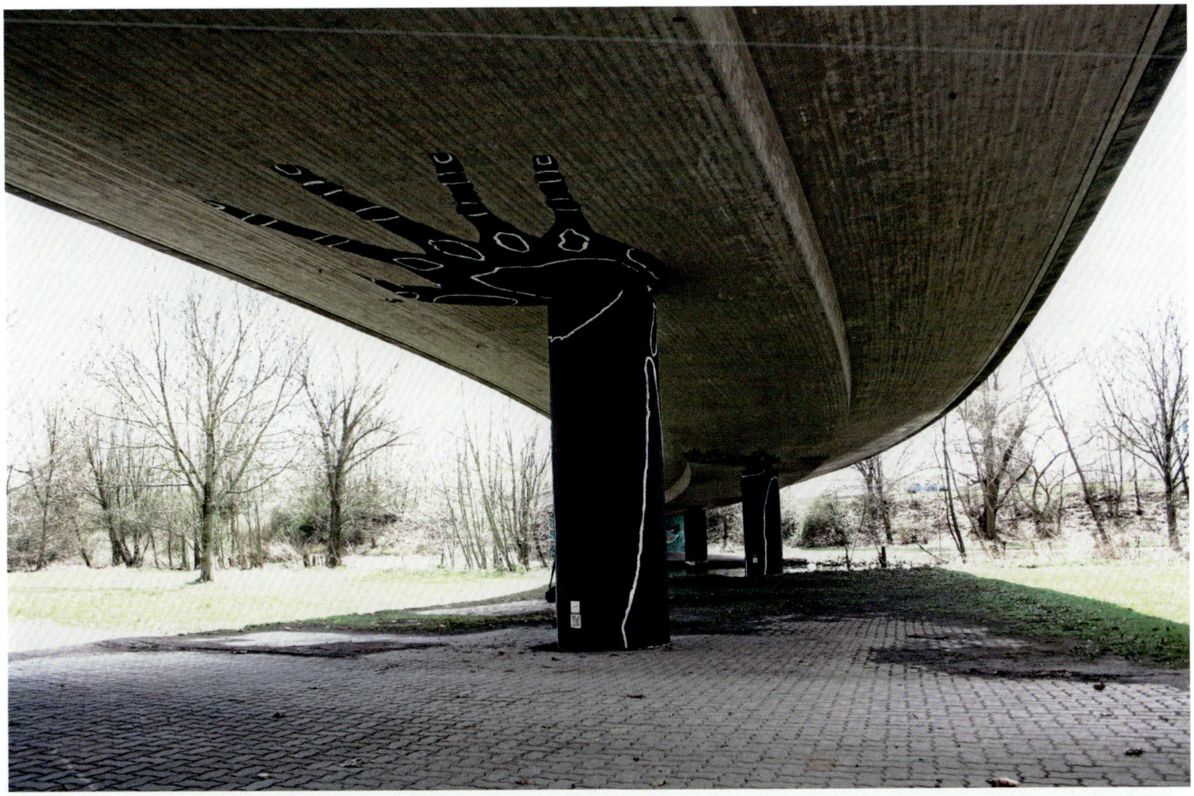

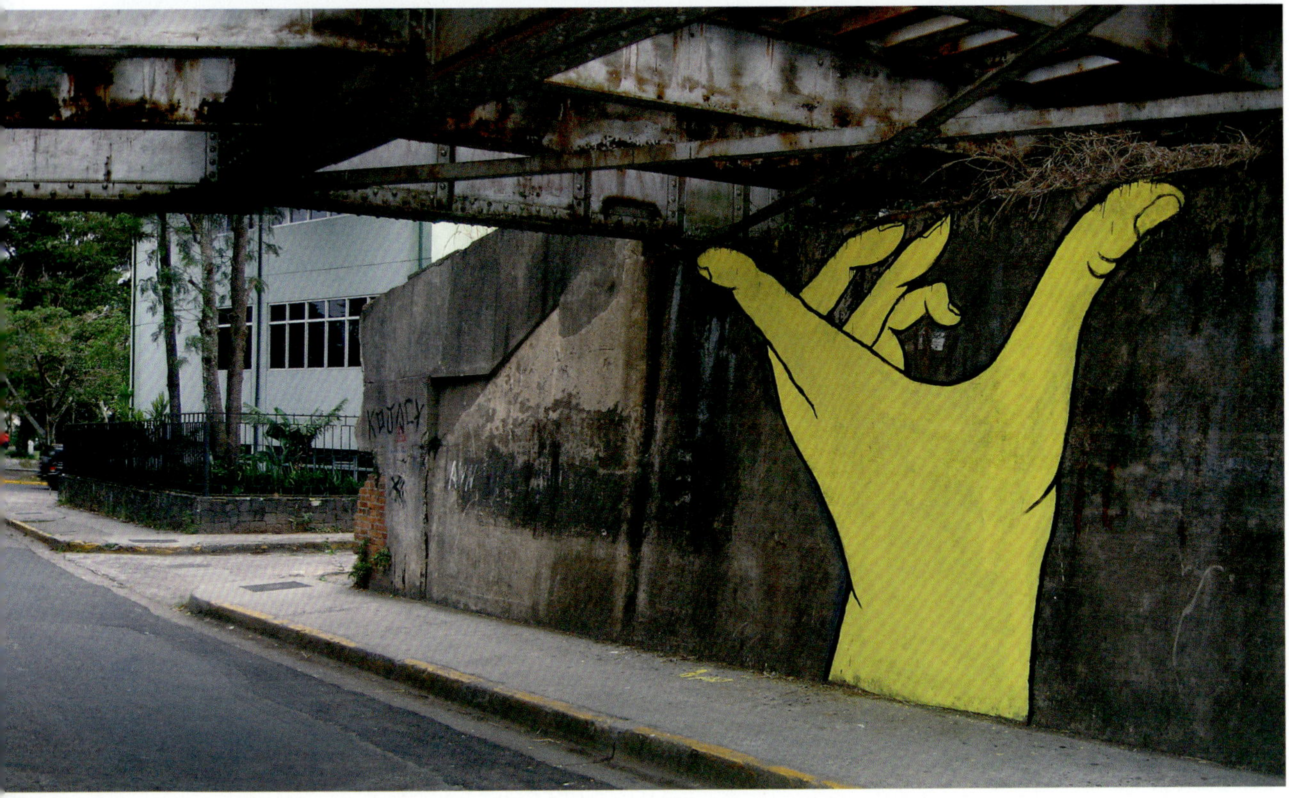

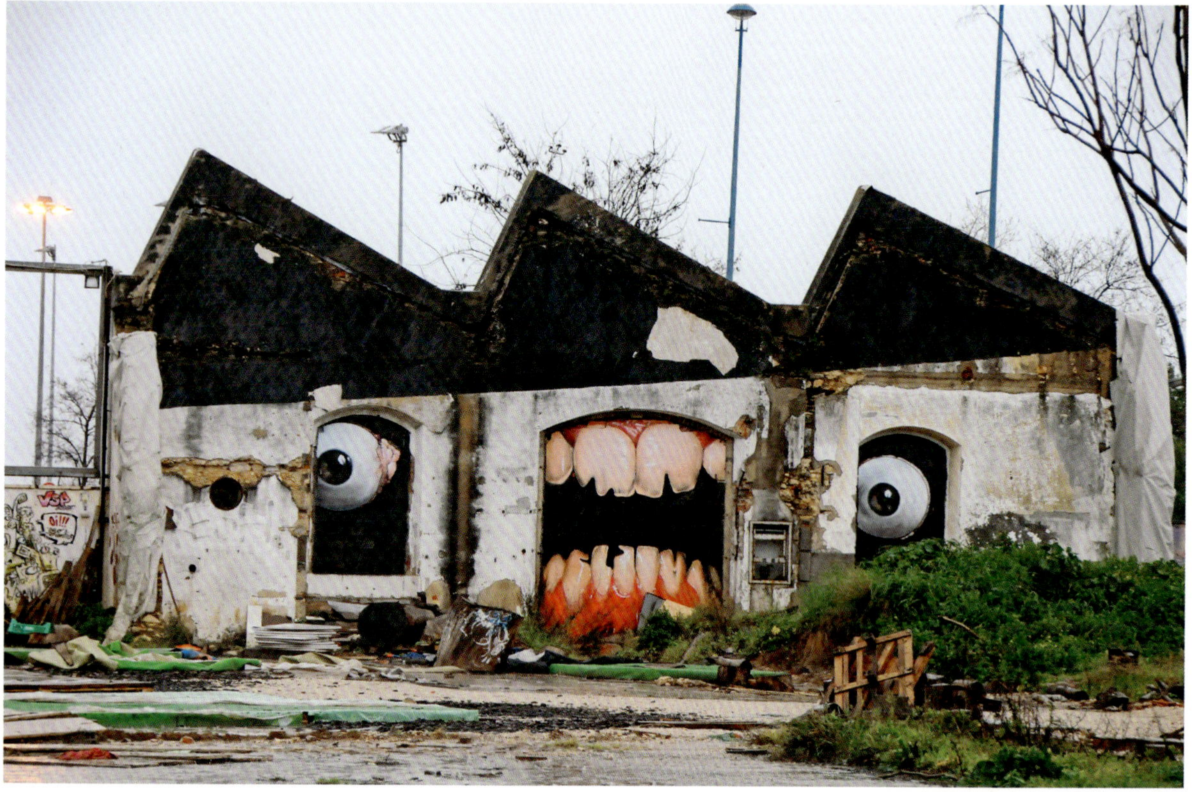

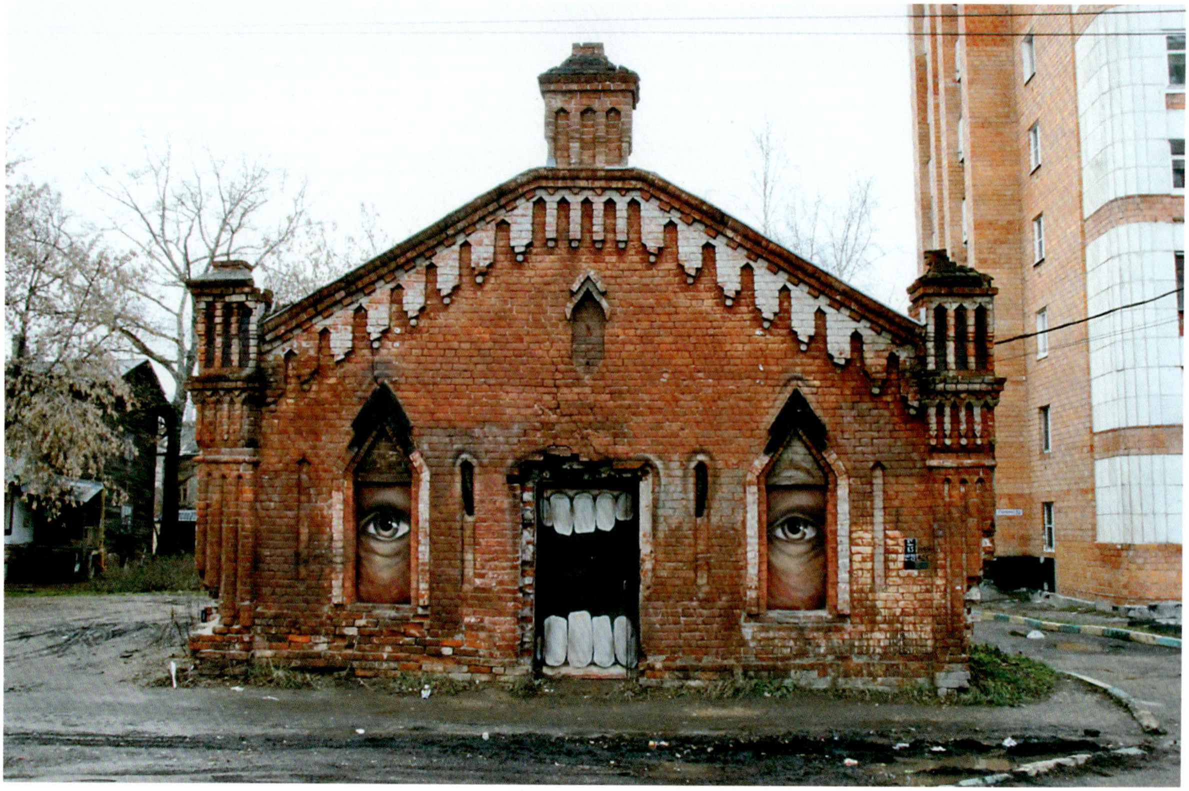

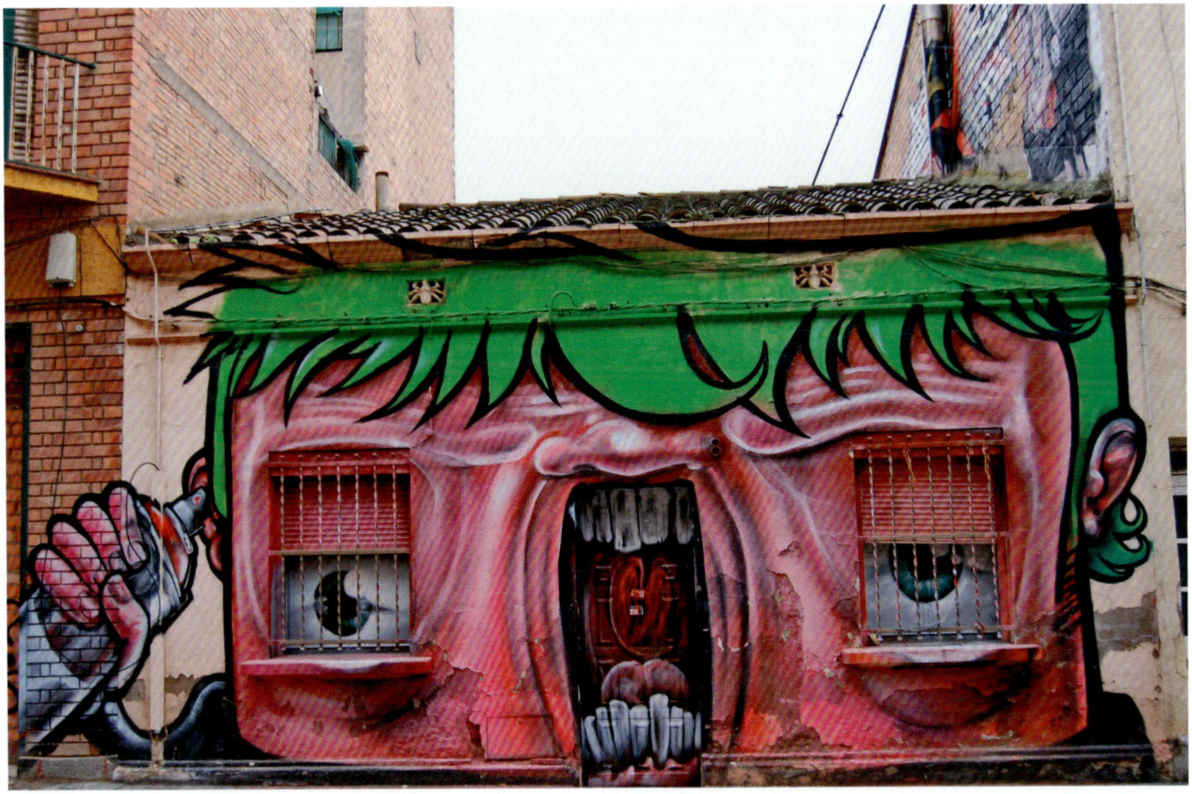

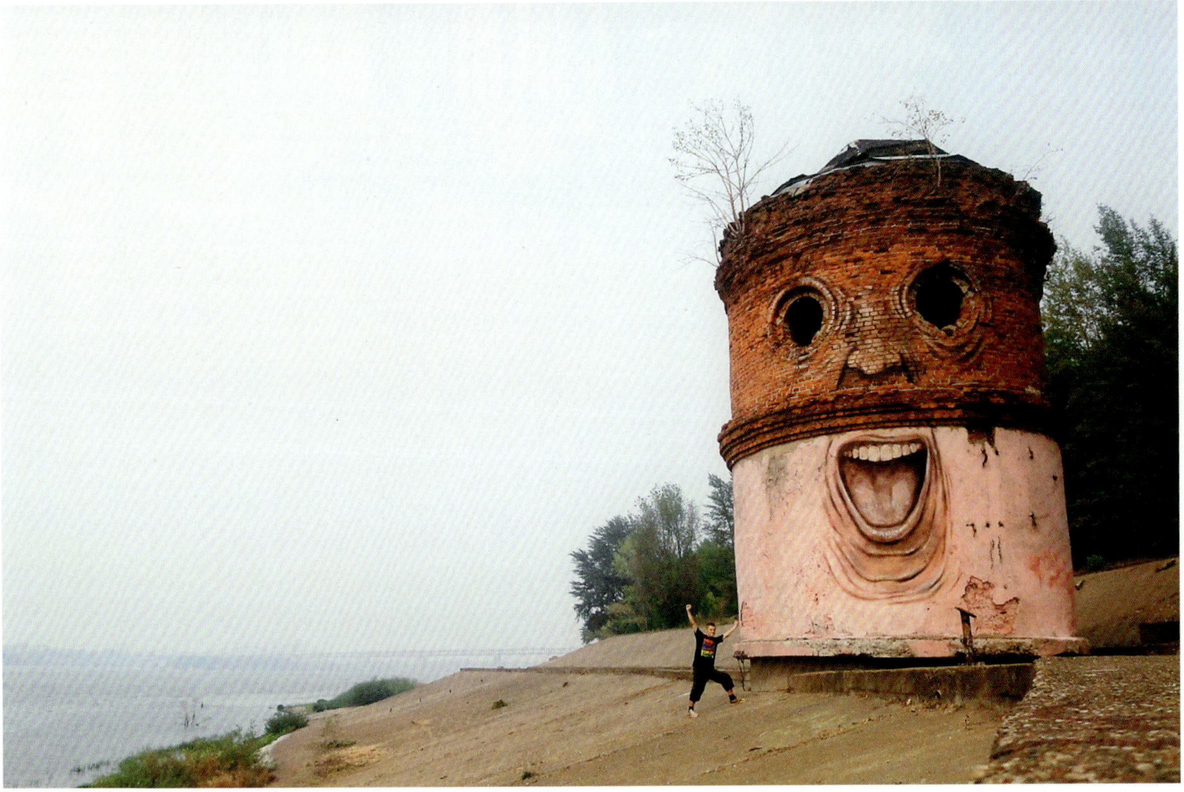

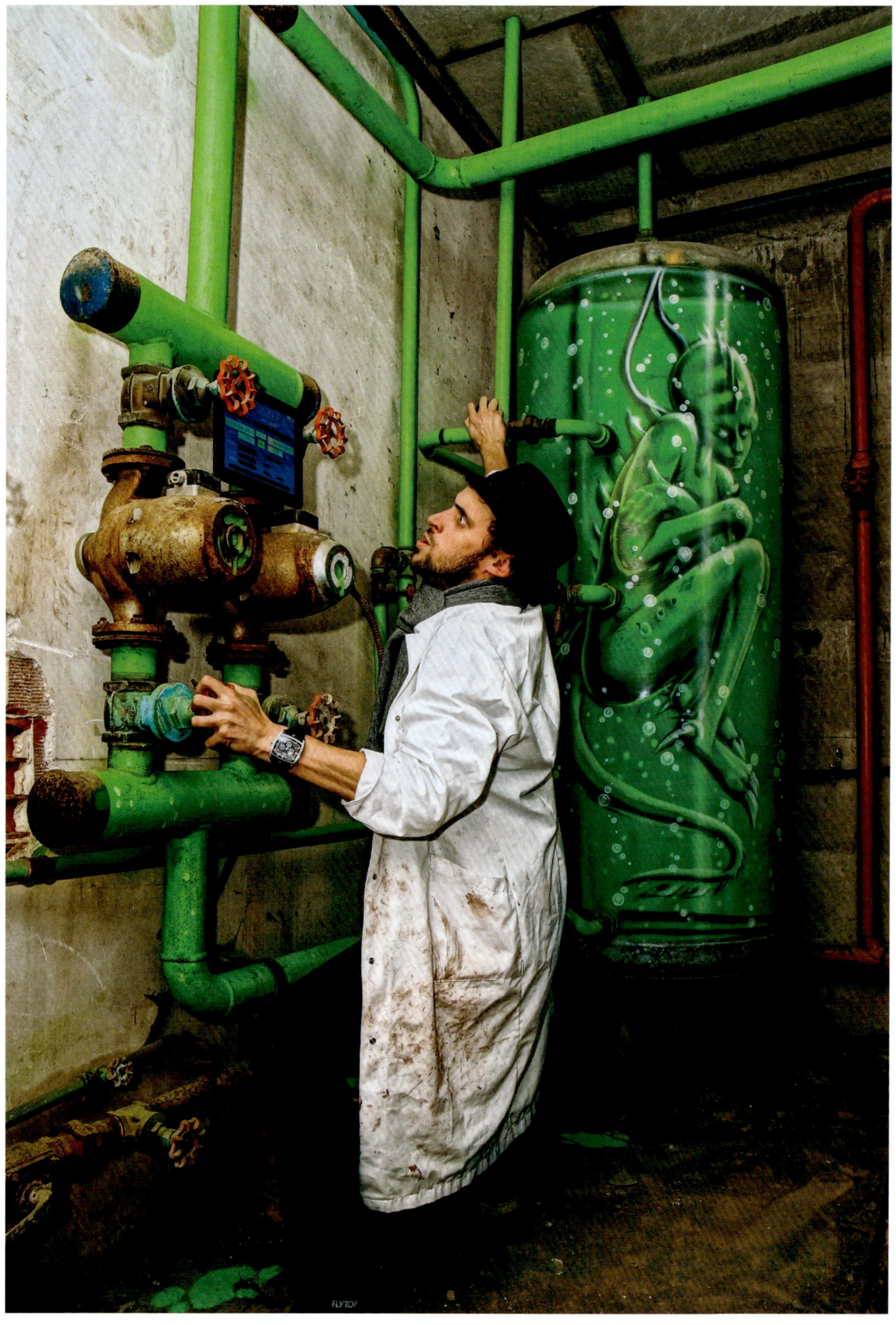

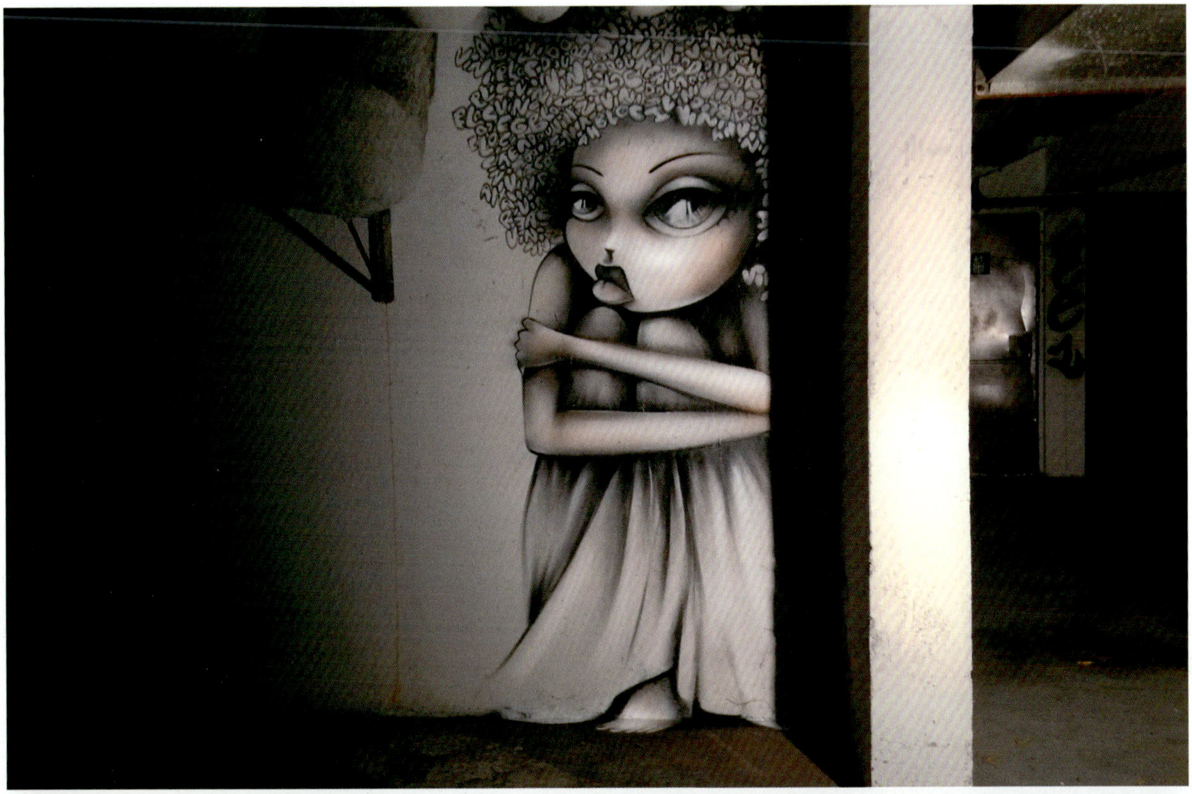

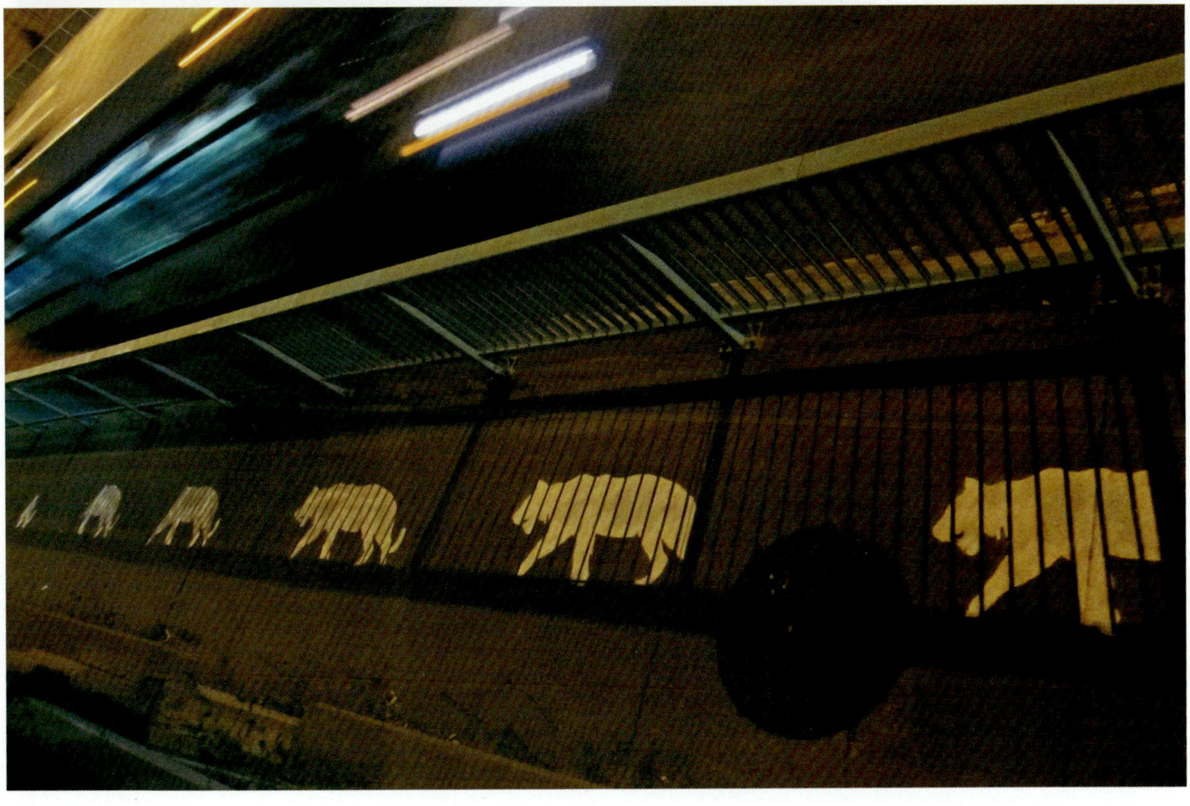

CLOCKWISE FROM RIGHT:
Last Ride by Mr Dheo
in Portugal/Various
artists in San
Francisco.

PAGES 252-3, CLOCKWISE
FROM TOP LEFT:
Days One in Sydney/DV8
in Melbourne/Spain's
Pez in Colombia.

PAGES 254-55, CLOCKWISE
FROM LEFT:
Argentina's Tec in
São Paulo/Canada's
Roadsworth/Roadsworth.

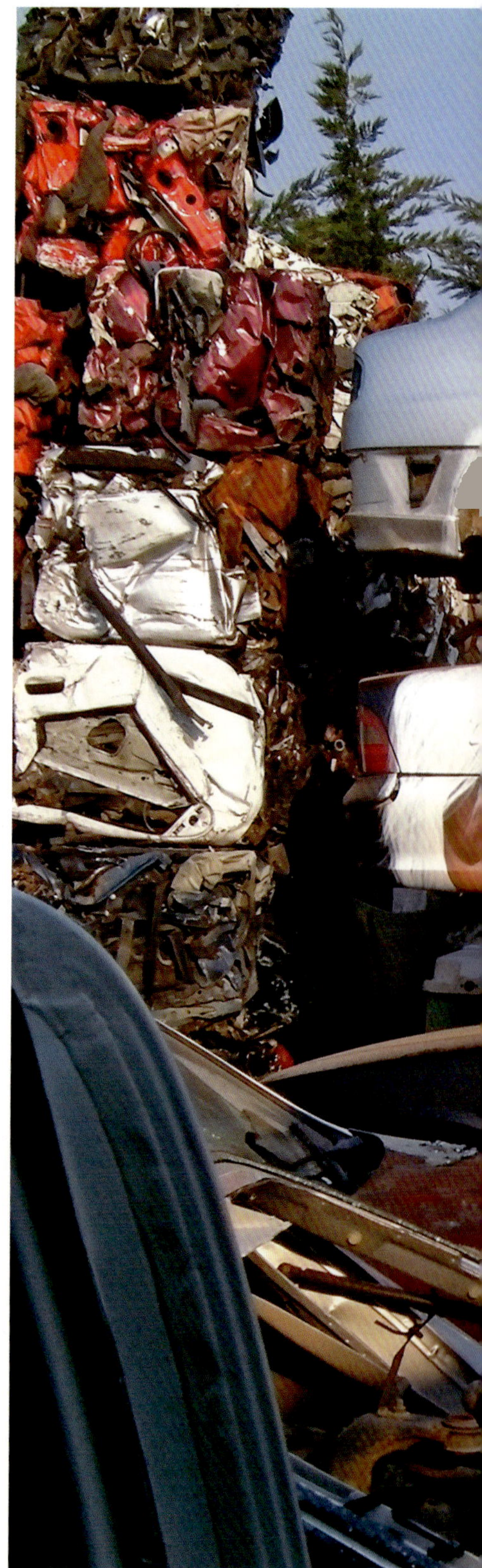

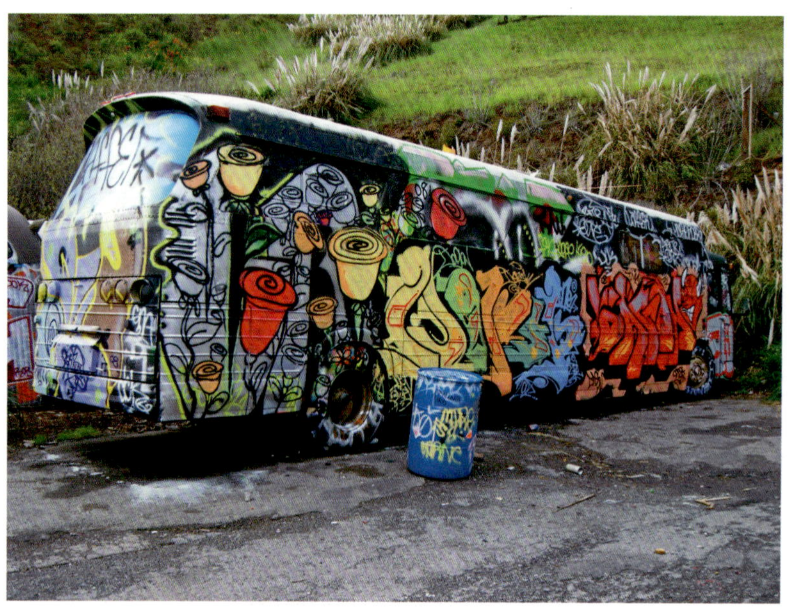

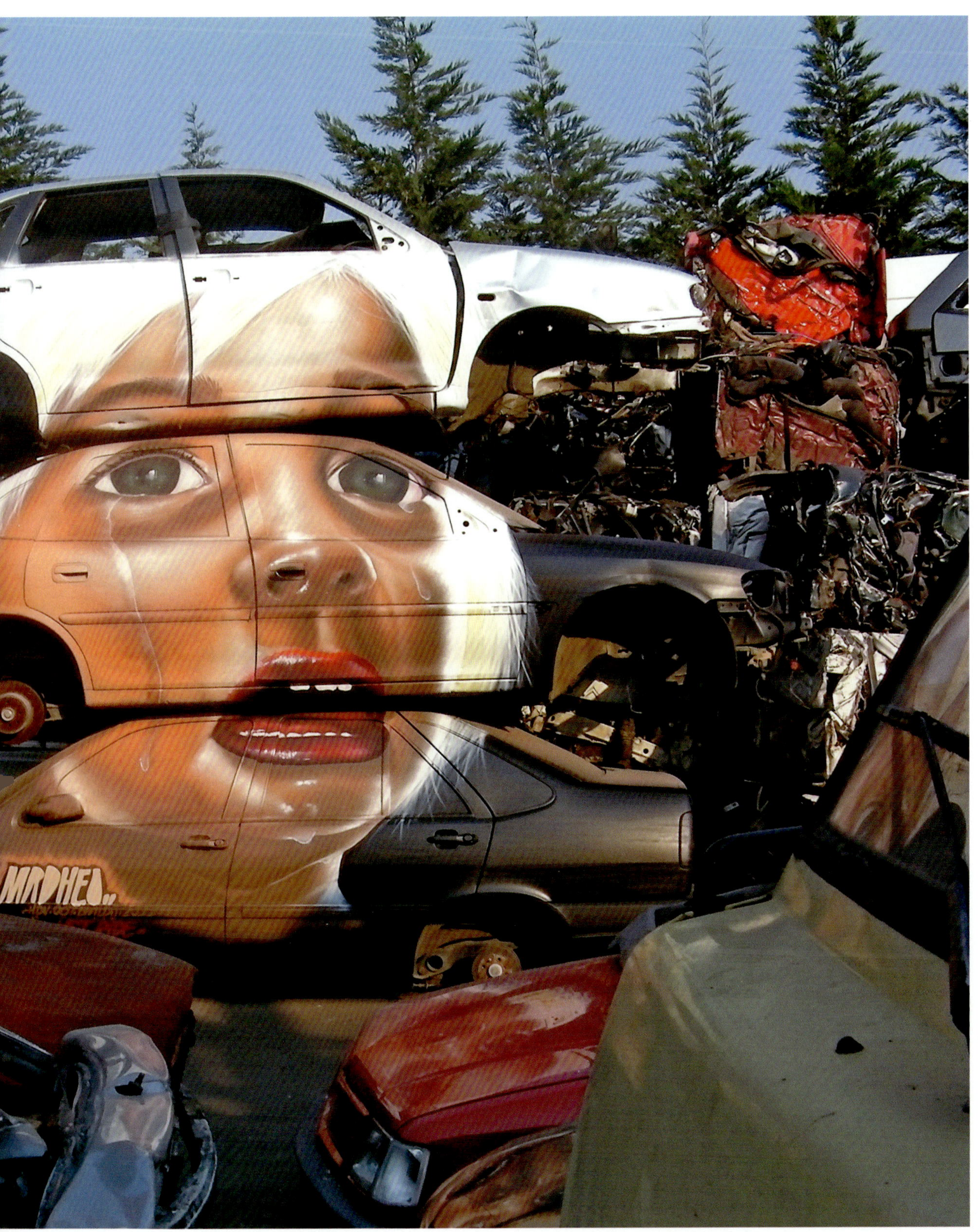

MADHED..

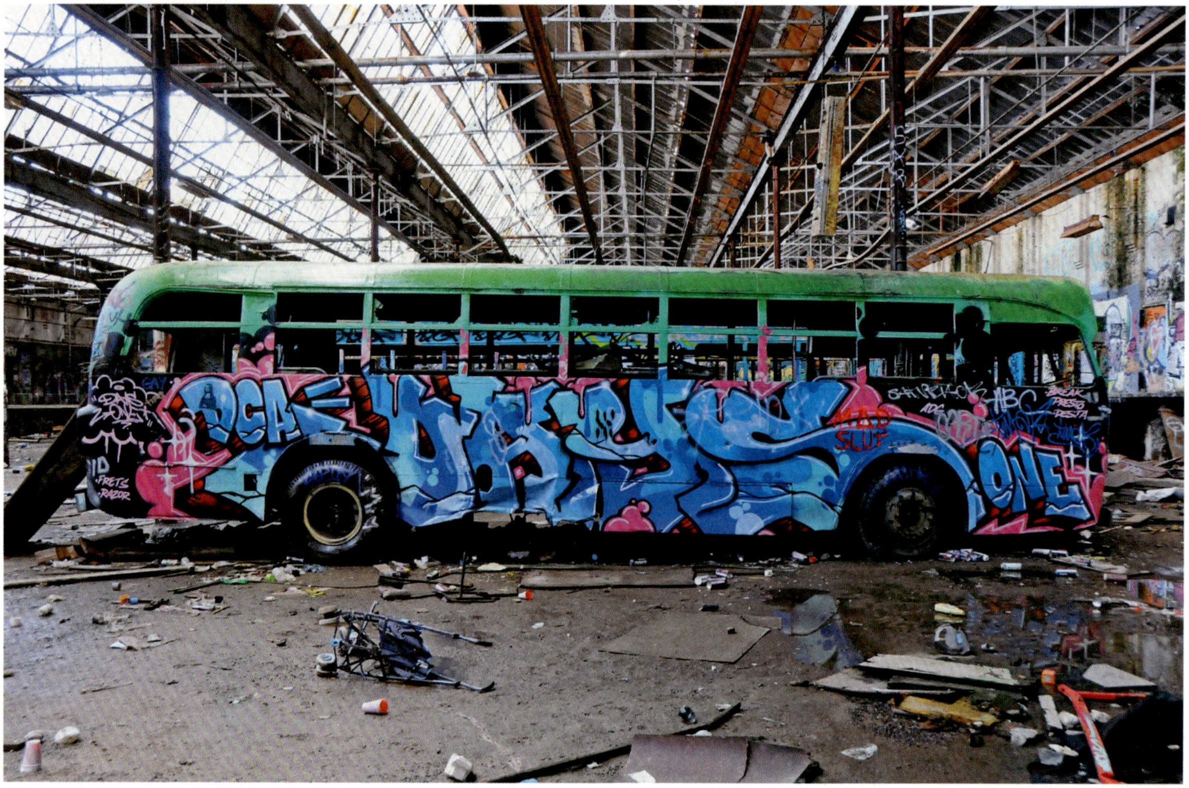

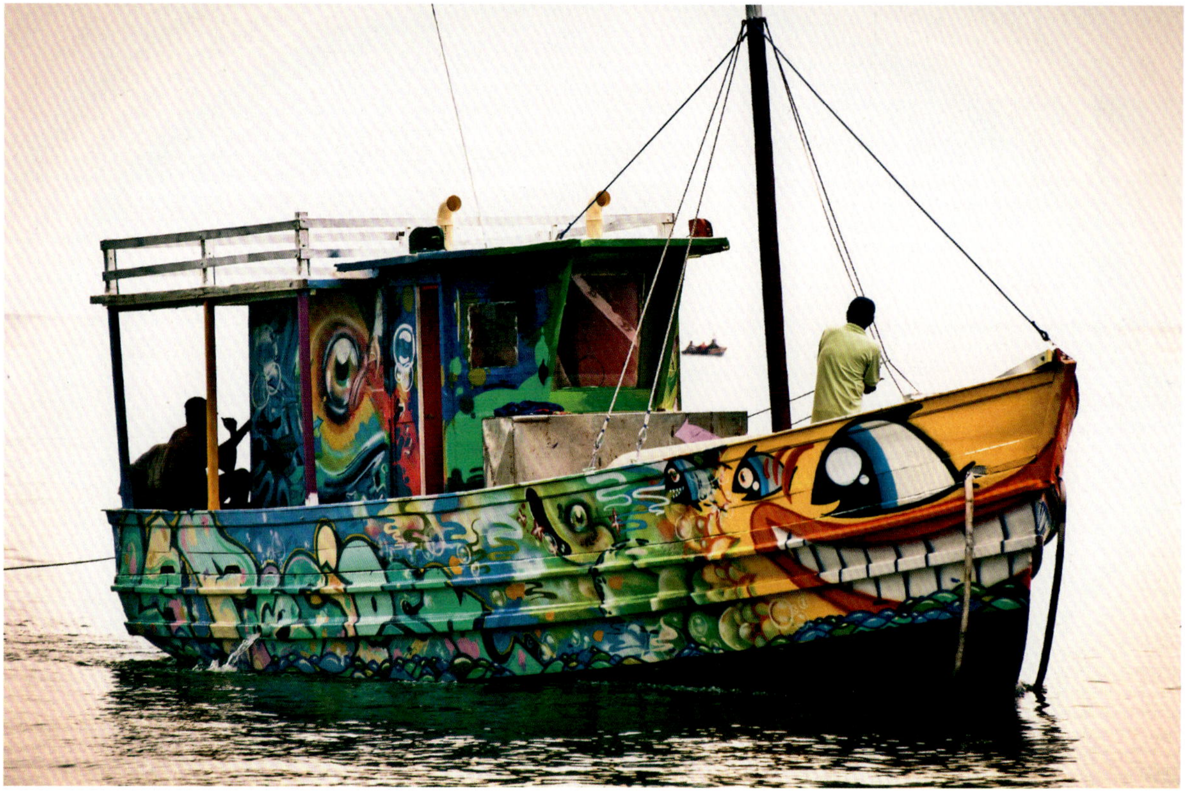

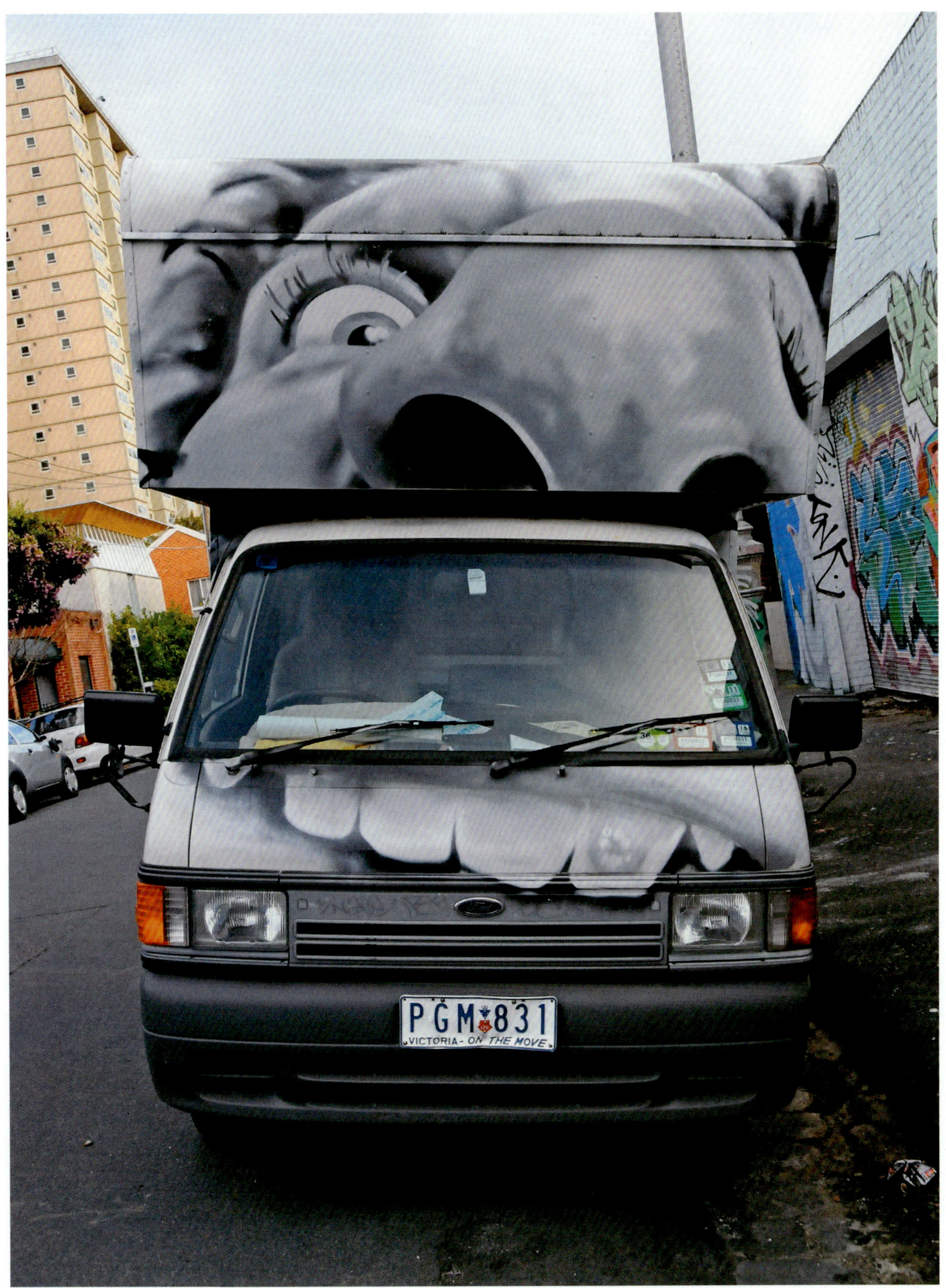

PGM·831
VICTORIA · ON THE MOVE

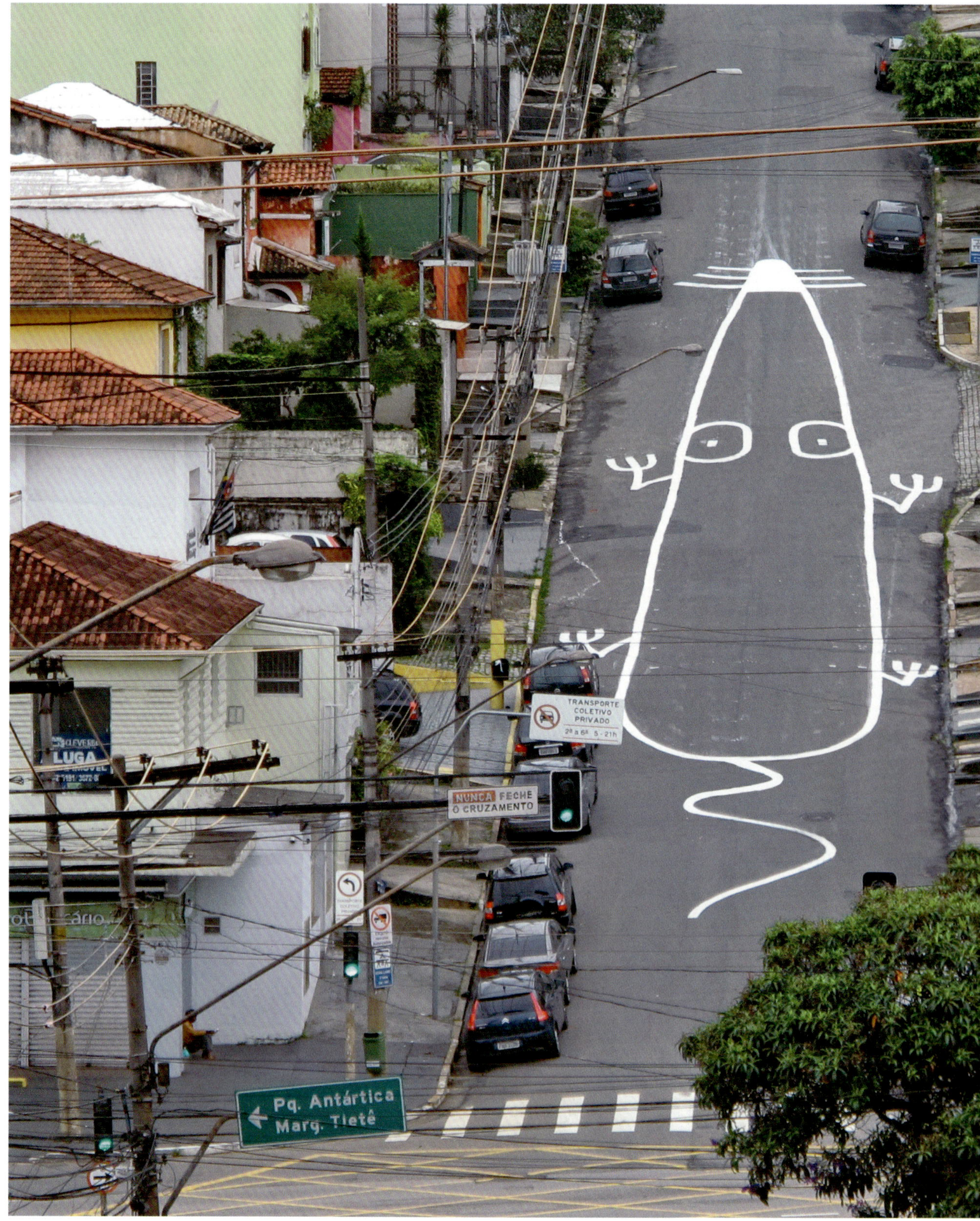
TRANSPORTE
COLETIVO
PRIVADO
2ª a 6ª 5 - 21h
NUNCA FECHE
O CRUZAMENTO
Pq. Antártica
Marg. Tietê

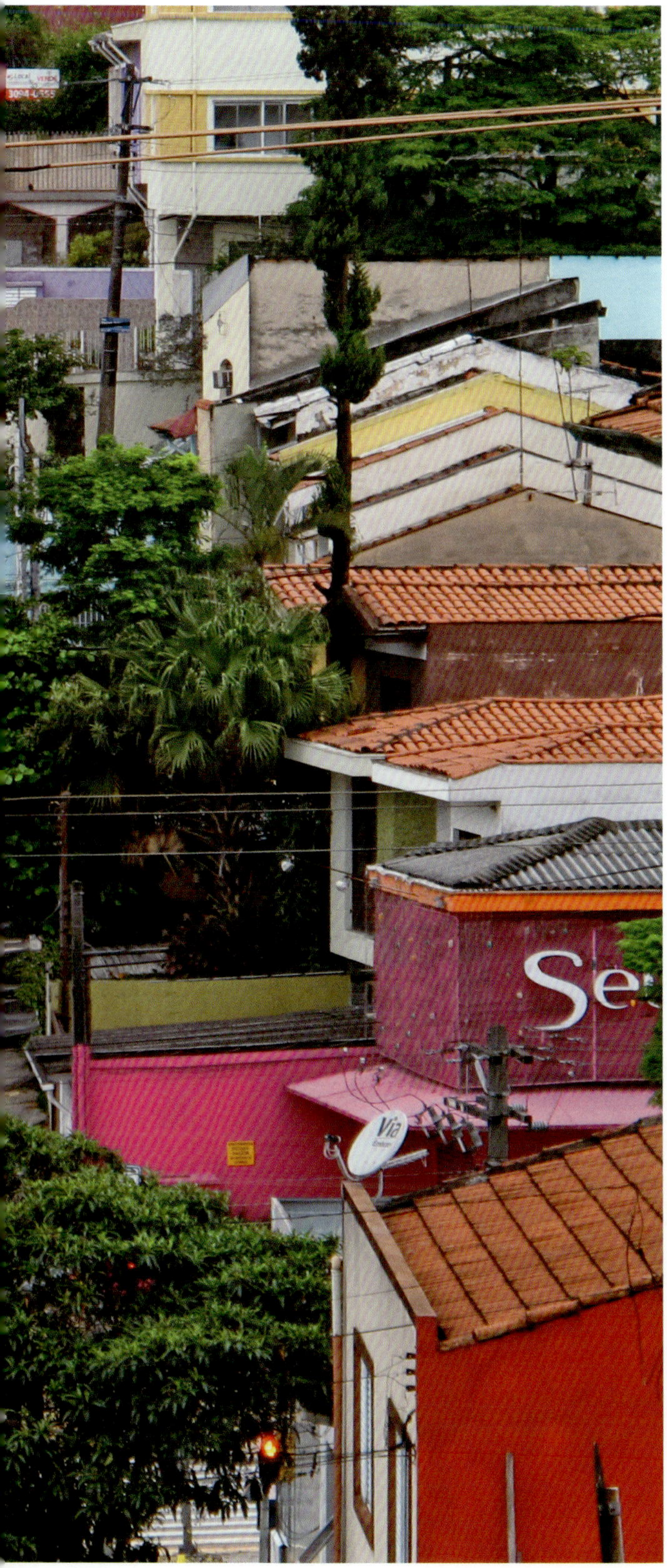

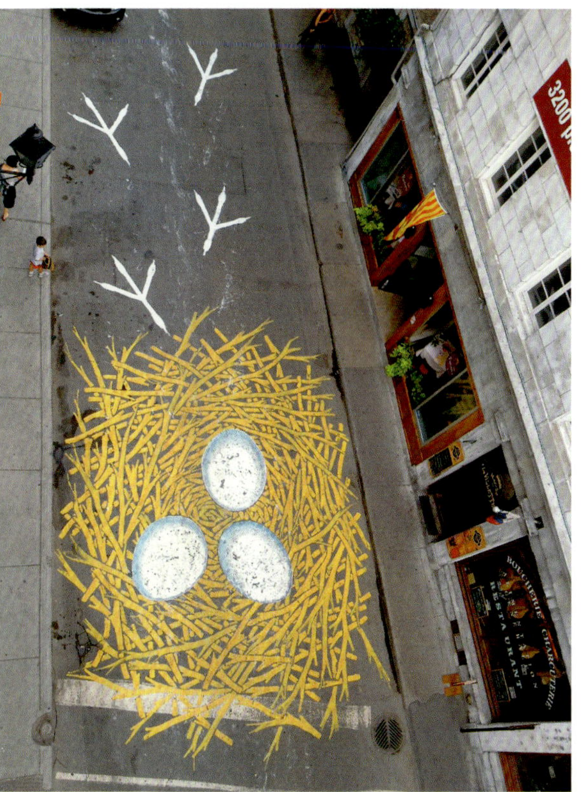

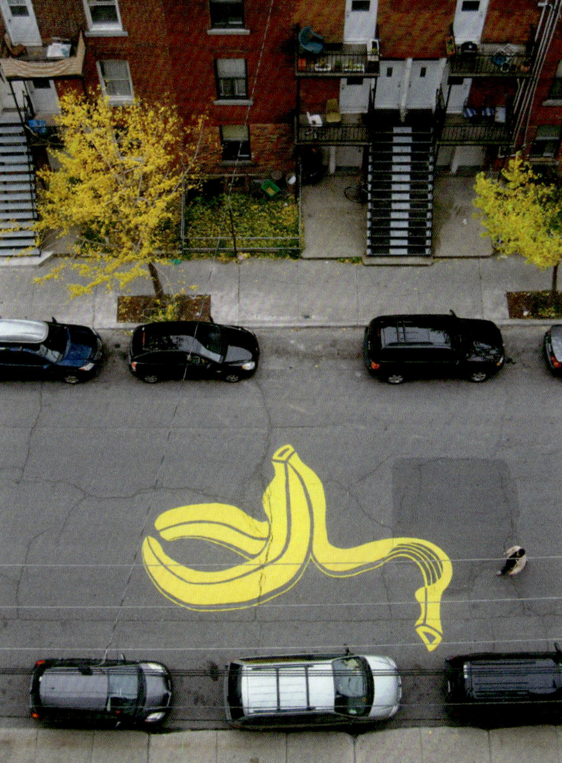

For a graffiti photographer, trains are the holy grail. Maybe because trains are the most challenging surfaces to paint; maybe because the works embody the spirit in which they were made: the audacity and the risk. Getting good photographs of train graffiti is no trivial task – there often isn't enough space in the station to take pictures and I've had my camera almost confiscated on a number of occasions.

RIGHT:
Copenhagen. Danish train drivers often lean out of the windows as the trains pull in!

PAGES 258-9, CLOCKWISE FROM TOP LEFT:
Passenger train in Buenos Aires/Freight train in Portland, Oregon, USA/A trash train in the UK.

PAGE 260
All you need is a steep hill! This shot was taken from Overlook Park, which (as the name suggests) overlooks the Albina rail yard in Portland, Oregon. I recommend the diner nearby!

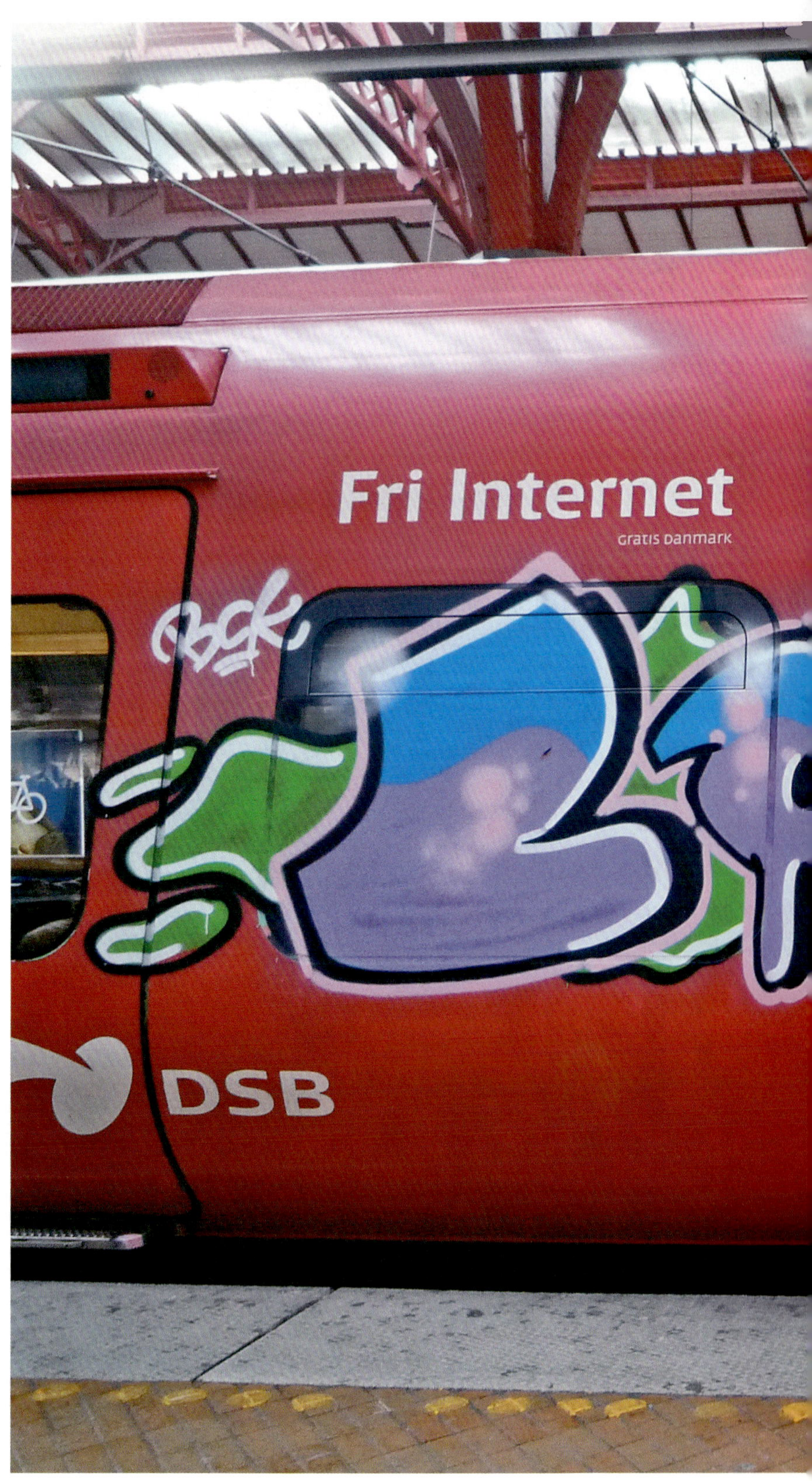

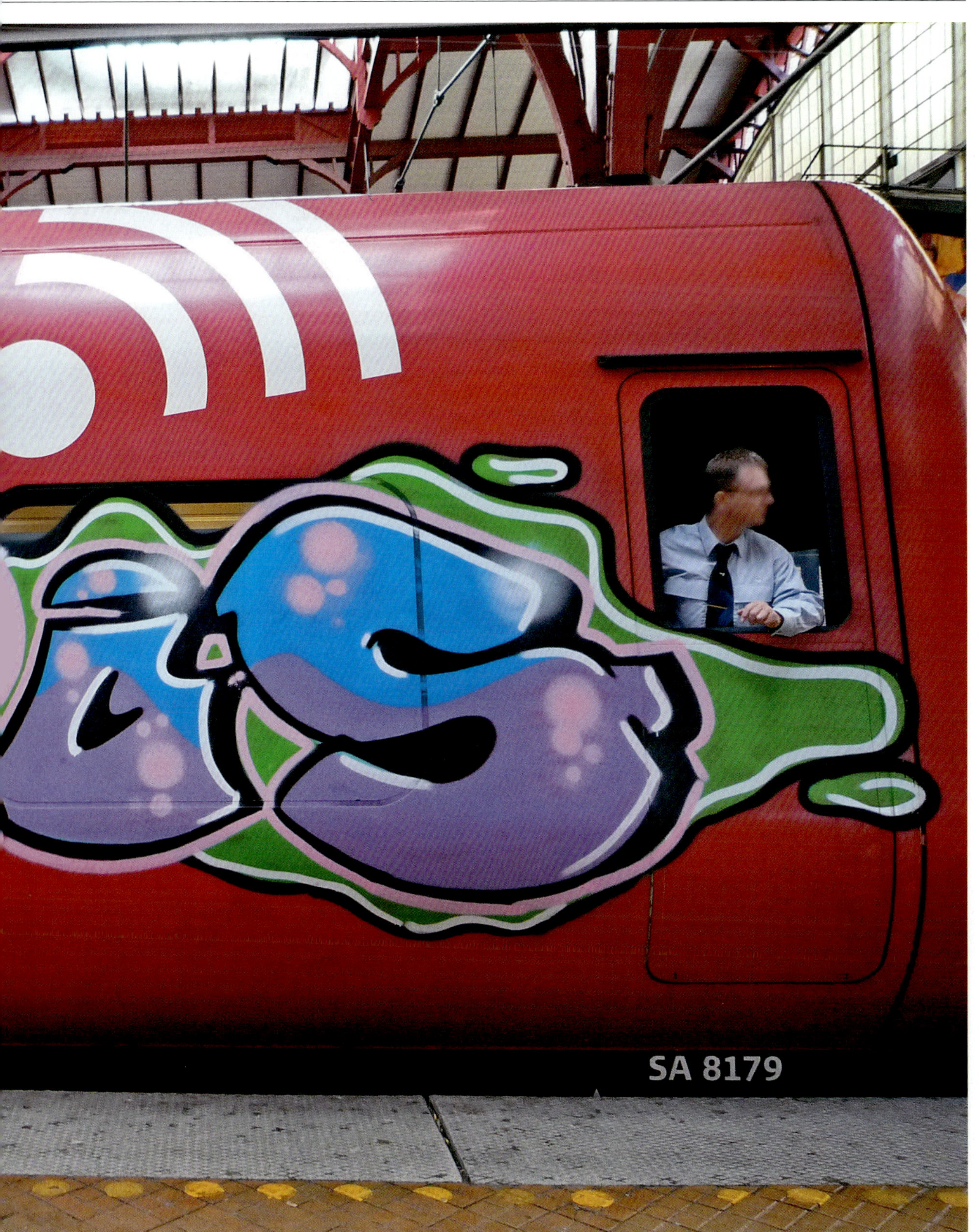

SA 8179

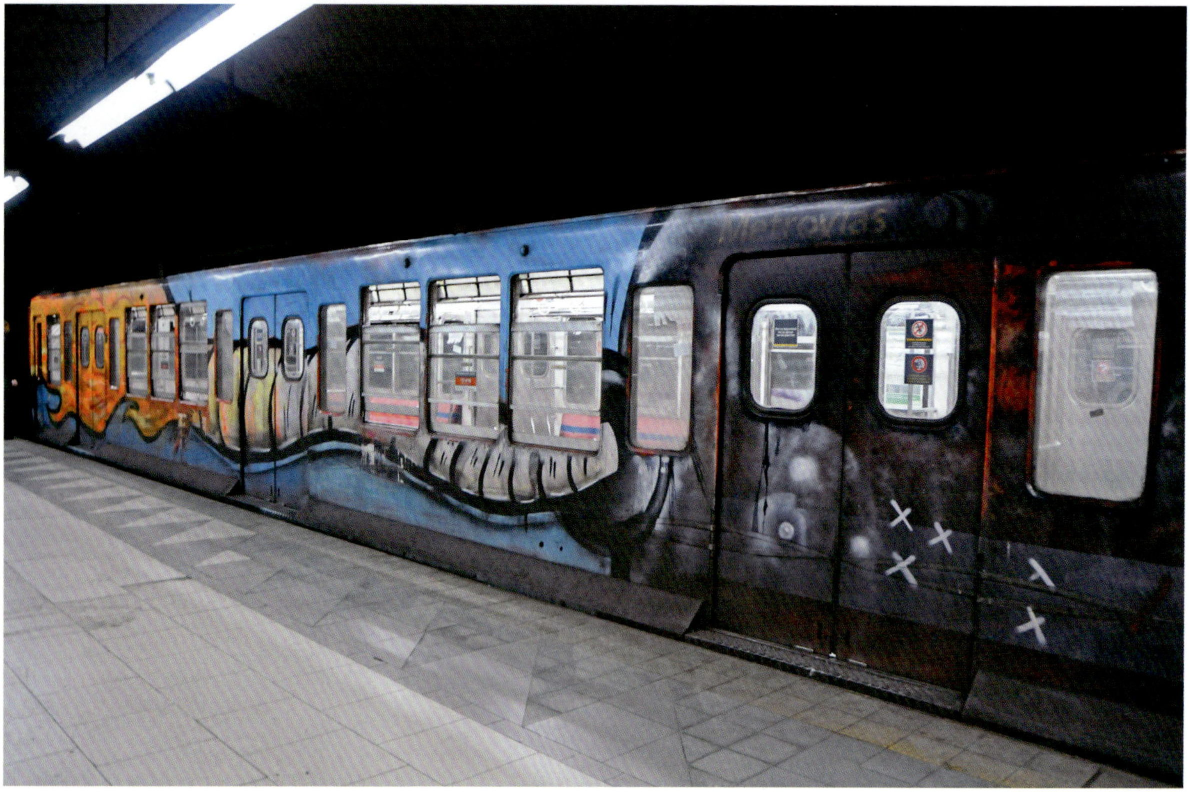

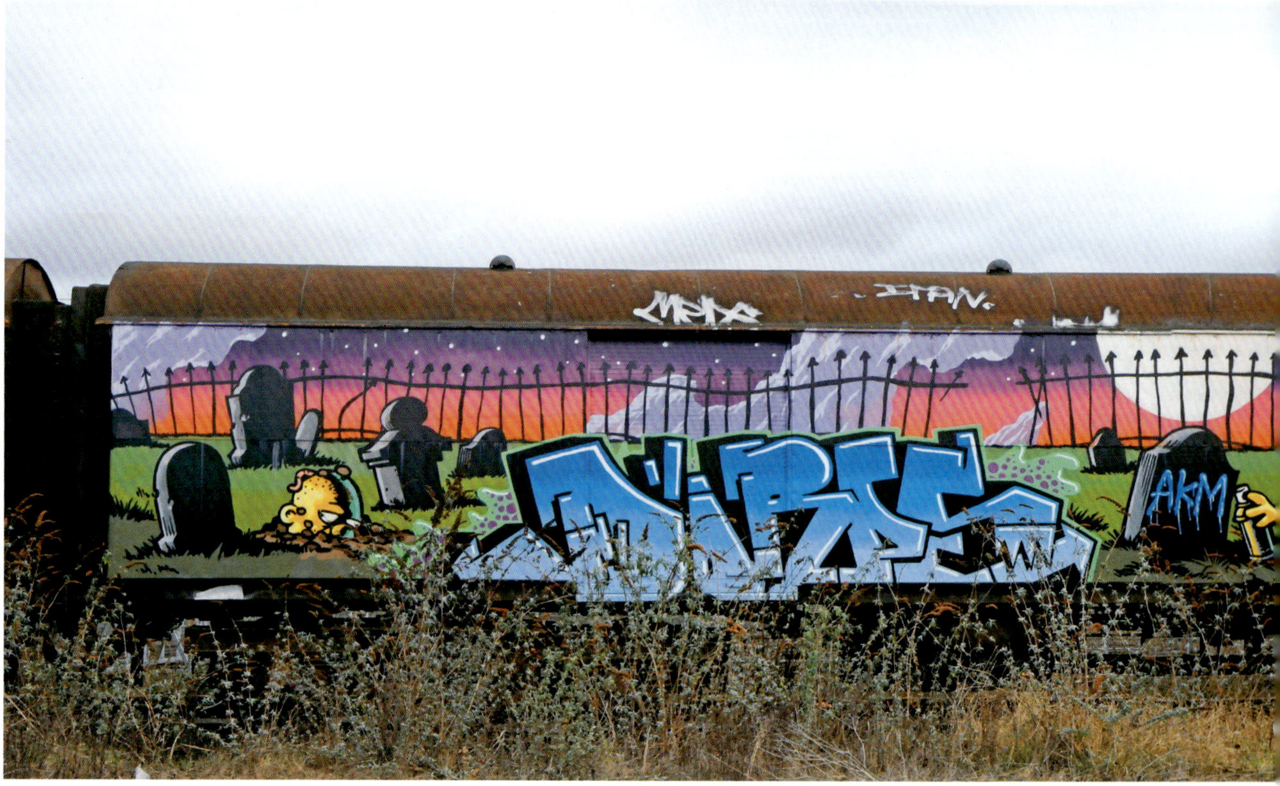

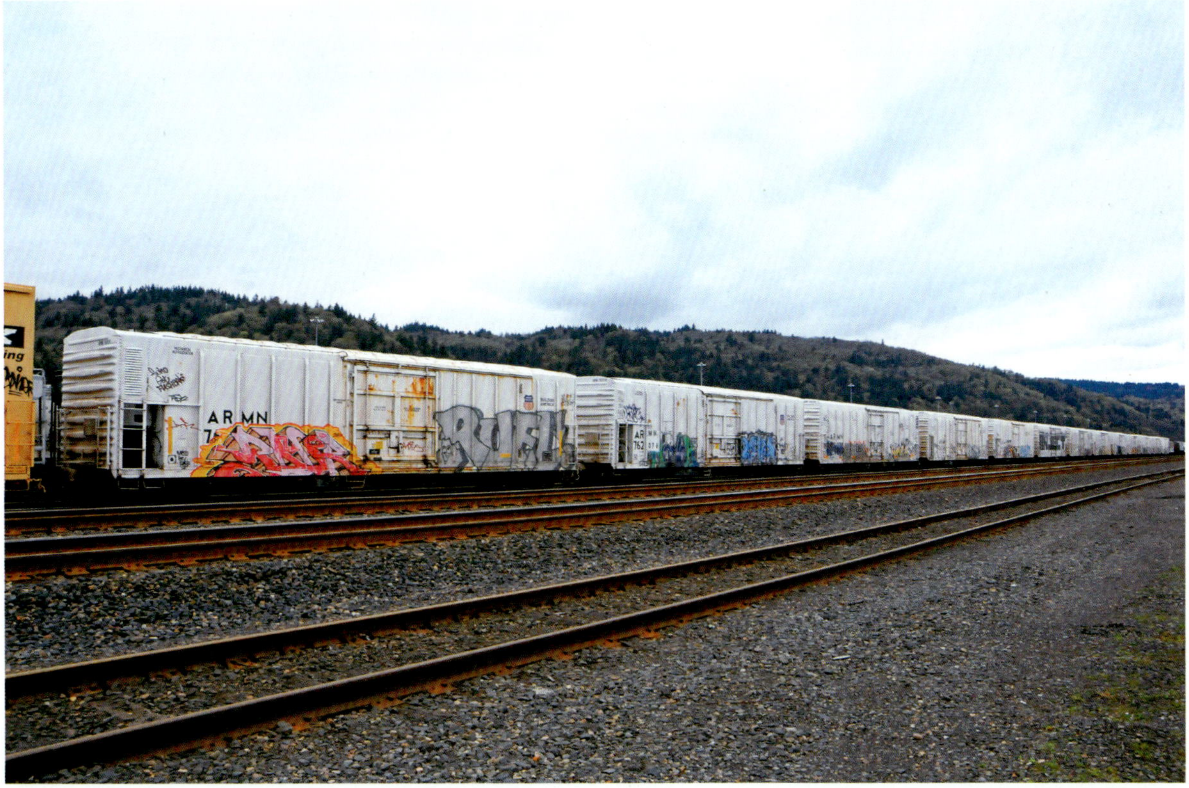

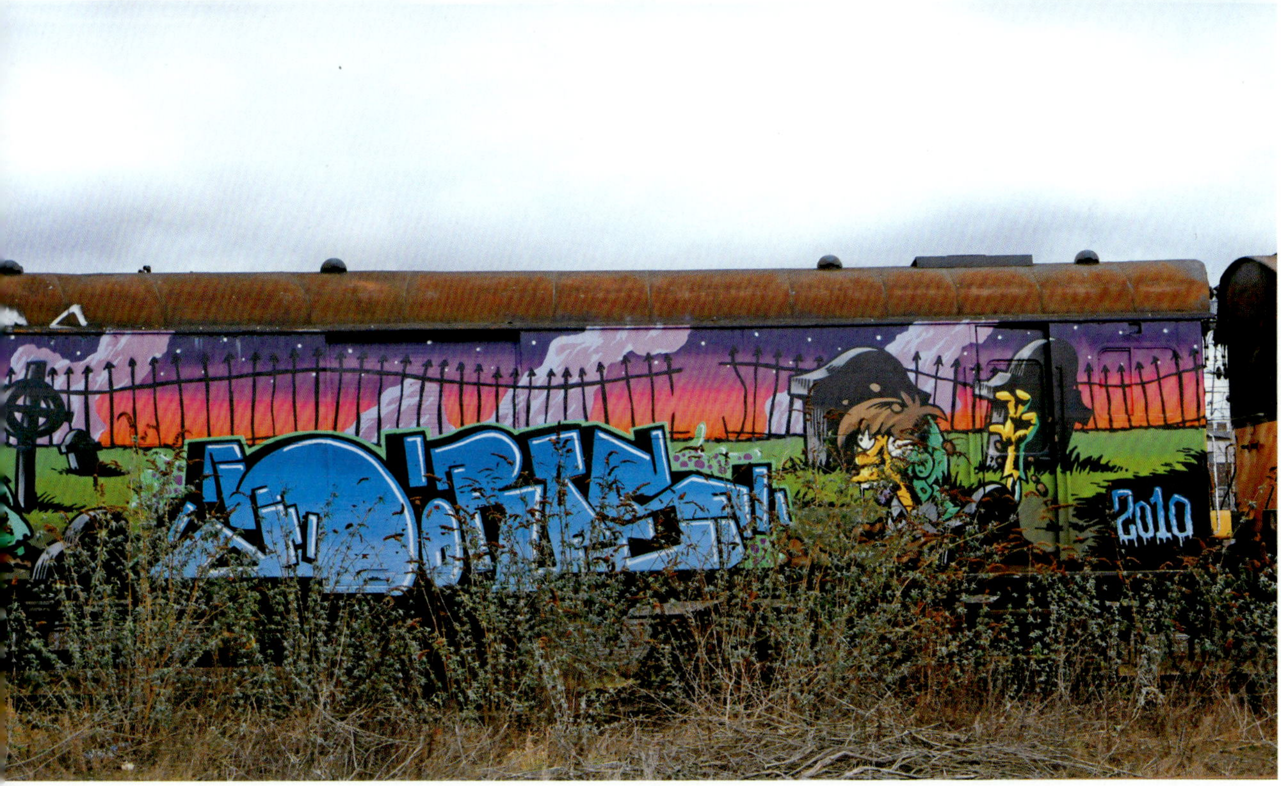

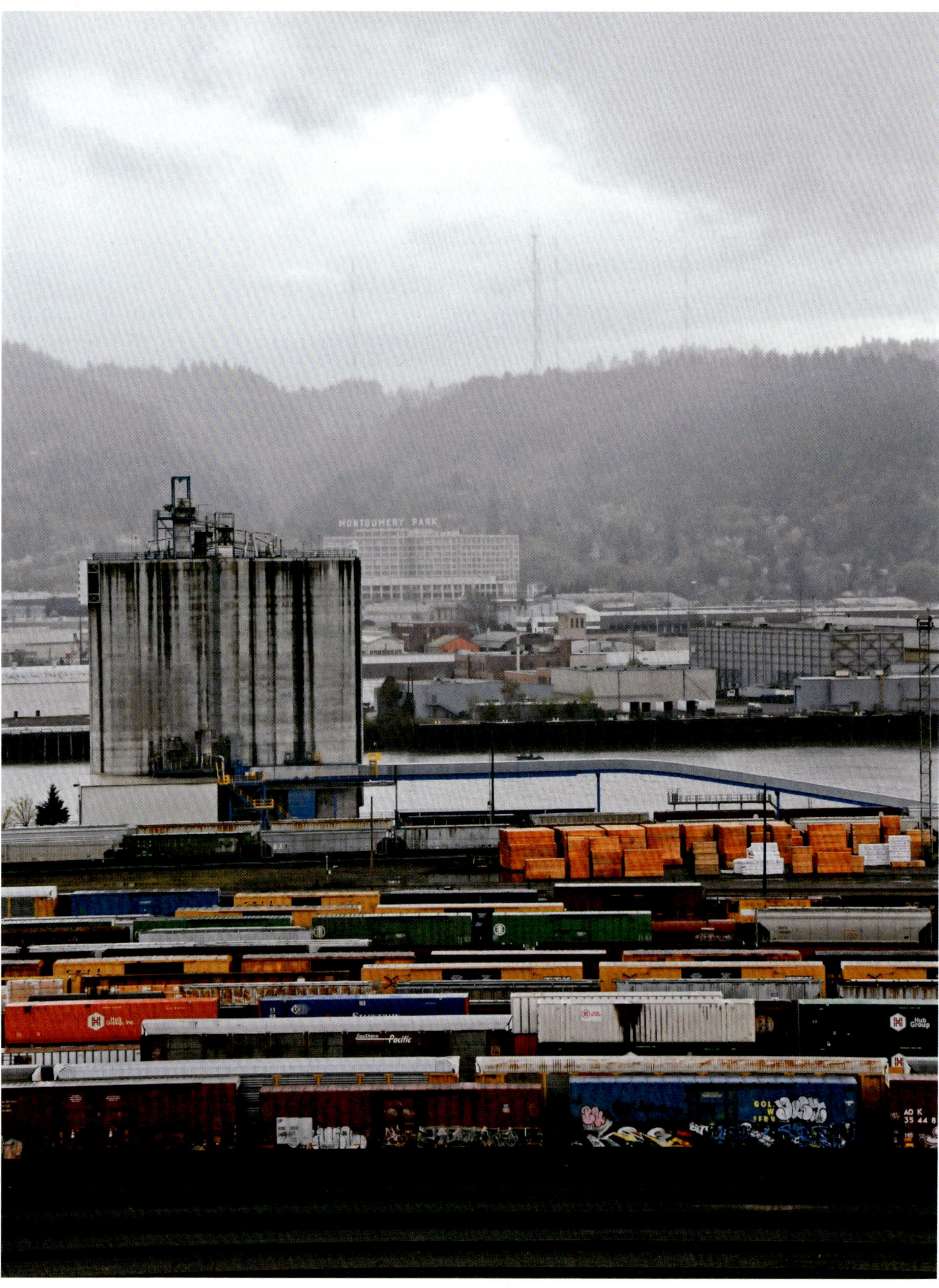
MONTGOMERY PARK

CONCRETE CANVAS

In the past four decades, graffiti has developed into a celebrated international art form and street art has emerged with an awareness of the graffiti movement. Public perceptions have seen a seismic shift: pieces of street art (including graffiti) have moved from often being perceived as a nuisance and a menace to being much more widely viewed as a cultural asset within cities. From a public perspective, whether or not street art or graffiti is actually 'good' probably depends on how the art makes people feel about being in a given space: do they feel the space is cared for or neglected? Sadly, these discussions often lack any acknowledgment of other aspects of the spaces, including lighting, litter and density of people. Nevertheless, the notion of how art makes people feel about a space will likely continue to impact how we view street art and graffiti in the future.

The Illegal: Move Along, Nothing to See Here

The outlook for illegal graffiti is mixed for the next decade, varying wildly from country to country and indeed from city to city. While the artistic institutional acceptance of street art and graffiti has increased, penalties for practitioners have also increased in developed economies since the days of the inception of the graffiti movement, especially post 9/11.

In cities with long histories of graffiti, such as New York and London, publicly visible train graffiti has been dramatically reduced. There is no shortage of active writers in these cities, although those that paint trains do not expect their pieces to reach the light of day. It doesn't matter: writers can record their actions more easily than ever before and they can then get up online. Often, the photograph is enough.

Tightening of security measures clearly moves the goalposts for writers. They may now get a similar amount of respect for choosing what were once considered softer targets or even more respect for overcoming tougher odds. In the US, for example, there are large numbers of writers who focus on freight trains and not passenger trains, in part because freight trains are so ubiquitous and the yards are less secure than those of passenger trains.

New, young writers will continue to emerge, and the appeal of writing on the outside of trains is unlikely to diminish – writers will continue to try, no matter how tight the security. Graffiti is not something authorities can 'kill'. They merely encourage the culture to manifest itself in different ways.

Graffiti serves a purpose for young men with few financial resources (and others), allowing them to gain status in a meritocratic culture that respects boldness and dedication. As these young men grow older they typically write less illegal graffiti. Many give up painting altogether, often because they have more to lose. The skills that these men learn while writing illegal graffiti can actively help them in legal ways in later life.

The Legal: A Curated World

The amount of street art produced legally has increased around the world, creating opportunities for artists and fans. Indeed, the industry associated with street art and graffiti has grown in general, and now includes publishers, street art tour companies, mural painting companies, fashion and merchandise companies and street/urban art specialist galleries.

These trends probably reflect changing public attitudes towards graffiti and street art.

There are three key forms of legally produced street art (including graffiti): well-organized street art festivals, special projects and legal walls. The outlook is very positive for street art festivals and increasingly positive for the number of 'fixers' but the trends for legal walls are mixed.

Street Art & Galleries

Is it possible to show street art in a gallery and is this worthwhile? These questions are culturally relevant, affecting how institutions might work with street art, and financially relevant, as the commercial gallery system struggles to monetize street art.

The answers depend on how you define both 'street art' and 'gallery'. For example, if street art only exists on the street and a gallery must be an indoor space, then one can't put street art into a gallery unless you put the street into a gallery. This implies that by cutting a Banksy off a wall and then moving it into a gallery it is no longer street art. However, there are other art forms, such as architecture, that cannot be put into galleries but are still exhibited. Like architecture, the closest you can get to putting street art in a gallery is to display representations of the art (e.g. photographs, pieces of wall, canvases by street artists, etc.).

The difficulty in defining street art has led many galleries to use the term 'urban art' to describe art that has some of the feel or techniques of street art, or is produced by artists that are commonly known as street artists. It would be odd to assume that an artist who produced high-quality work outside was incapable of producing equally good work for commercial galleries, although there would likely be significant differences between the art produced indoors and that produced outdoors.

Street art is rarely displayed in museums or established galleries – much like many other successful visual cultures such as animation, comic book illustration or graphic design. Should we move street art into indoor galleries? In the few cases where relatively large or established art galleries have held street art exhibitions, the public interest has been very high. Both Art in the Streets (2011) at MOCA and the Banksy exhibition (2009) at Bristol Museum were the most visited exhibitions to date at their respective institutions. If public engagement is an important factor for art institutions, then there is a strong case for working with street artists.

Displaying work by street artists inside a gallery has interesting effects. Most people do not go out to the streets to see art, so they rarely stop to appreciate it when it's there – unlike in a gallery, where the art itself is the destination. I would argue that taking street art into galleries (or art by artists who also work outside) focuses the viewer's attention on the art.

Perhaps, however, we might wish to revisit our definition of a gallery. Galleries are often commercial entities, insofar as they may sell or acquire art for their collections. If we think of street art as site-specific work, produced in situ, then this poses another problem: you can't move most street art because it doesn't produce objects (things you can readily move and therefore buy or sell). On top of that, street art gets defaced, cleaned away and worn by the elements; it is by its very nature ephemeral. However, if we remove the notion that galleries must be indoors, then street art can be displayed in galleries – we just have to move the gallery outside. This is a feeling that underpins street art festivals, which are a powerful tool to re-imagine how we think of public spaces.

One of the great beauties of street art is that it is free and readily available to the public. Given that there are minimal barriers to entry for putting work out on the streets, artists have direct contact with a viewing public and can circumvent the commercial gallery system. It also means that artists can display their work regardless of quality. The commercial gallery system, especially at the higher end, has tended not to look too kindly on street art as a genre in the past. It is perhaps for these reasons that many mature artists who have backgrounds painting outside shun being labelled as 'street artists'.

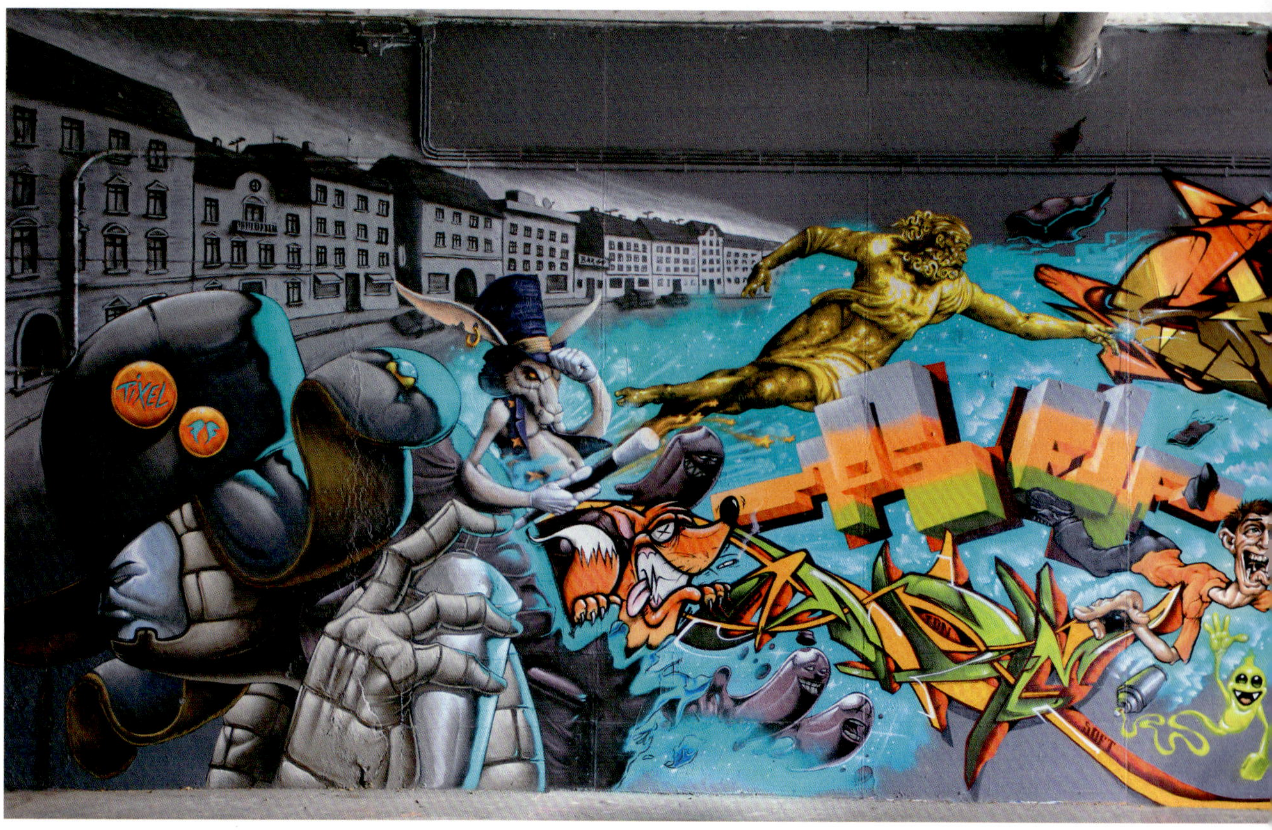

Festivals

I n the past five years there has been a massive upsurge in the number of street art festivals across the globe. Last summer Global Street Art was contacted by a lot of new festivals, including many in Eastern Europe and South America. These festivals tend to support the production of large-scale works by well-known artists, as well as lesser-known – typically local – artists. The ongoing trend in well-organized street art festivals is likely to continue internationally as they can leave a lasting positive impact on the visual landscape of the city, boosting local esteem and tourism.

Hopefully festivals will continue to involve developing artists, despite the temptation to favour ever-larger murals by 'headlining' international artists. Furthermore, with increasing relationships between independent organizers and municipalities, street art festivals must ensure that they support the production of art that is not banal, sanitized or expected.

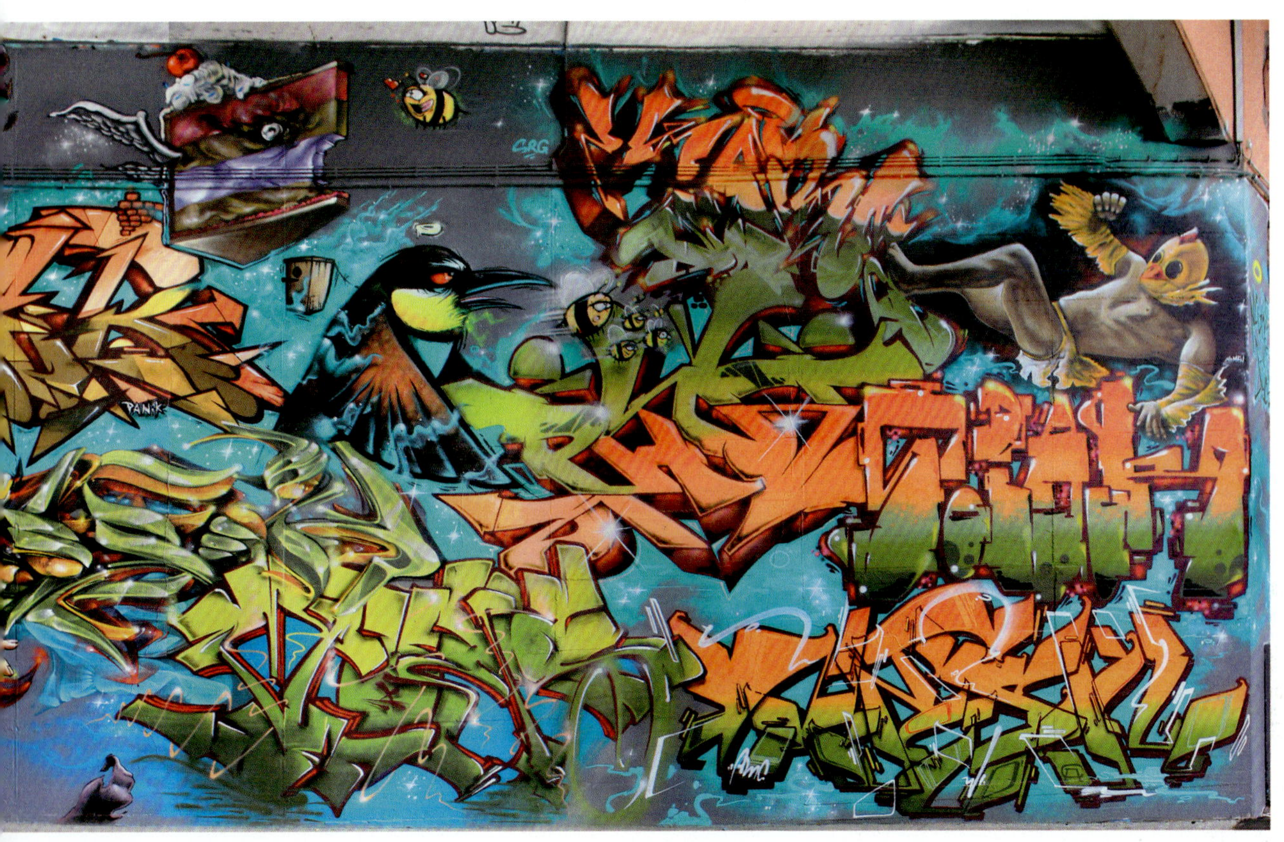

Meeting of Styles is an international graffiti festival that traces its roots to the mid-1990s, when it emerged as a way of delaying the demolition of an abandoned slaughterhouse in Wiesbaden, Germany. Today it is a graffiti Hall of Fame. MOS was officially founded in 2002 in the wake of the increasing criminalization of graffiti that happened throughout Europe post 9/11. In its first year, MOS took place in eight different European cities, providing a forum for artists to exchange ideas as well as allowing a broader audience to realize the potential of graffiti and urban art. Today MOS appears in roughly 12 cities a year (in countries as diverse as Argentina, America, Russia and China); over 140 events have taken place in total since its inception.

Funding differs from place to place and the MOS team tries to find paint, infrastructure and financial support on an international and national level.

Manuel Gerullis works as a volunteer at the core of MOS, coordinating the international festivals and maintaining the website. In Manuel's own words: '*To me, graffiti is an expression of my desire to make the world a better place. It's a colorful revolution. The Meetings are my contribution to help build a better society, in which creativity rules and is considered more valuable than materialism and senseless consumption.*'

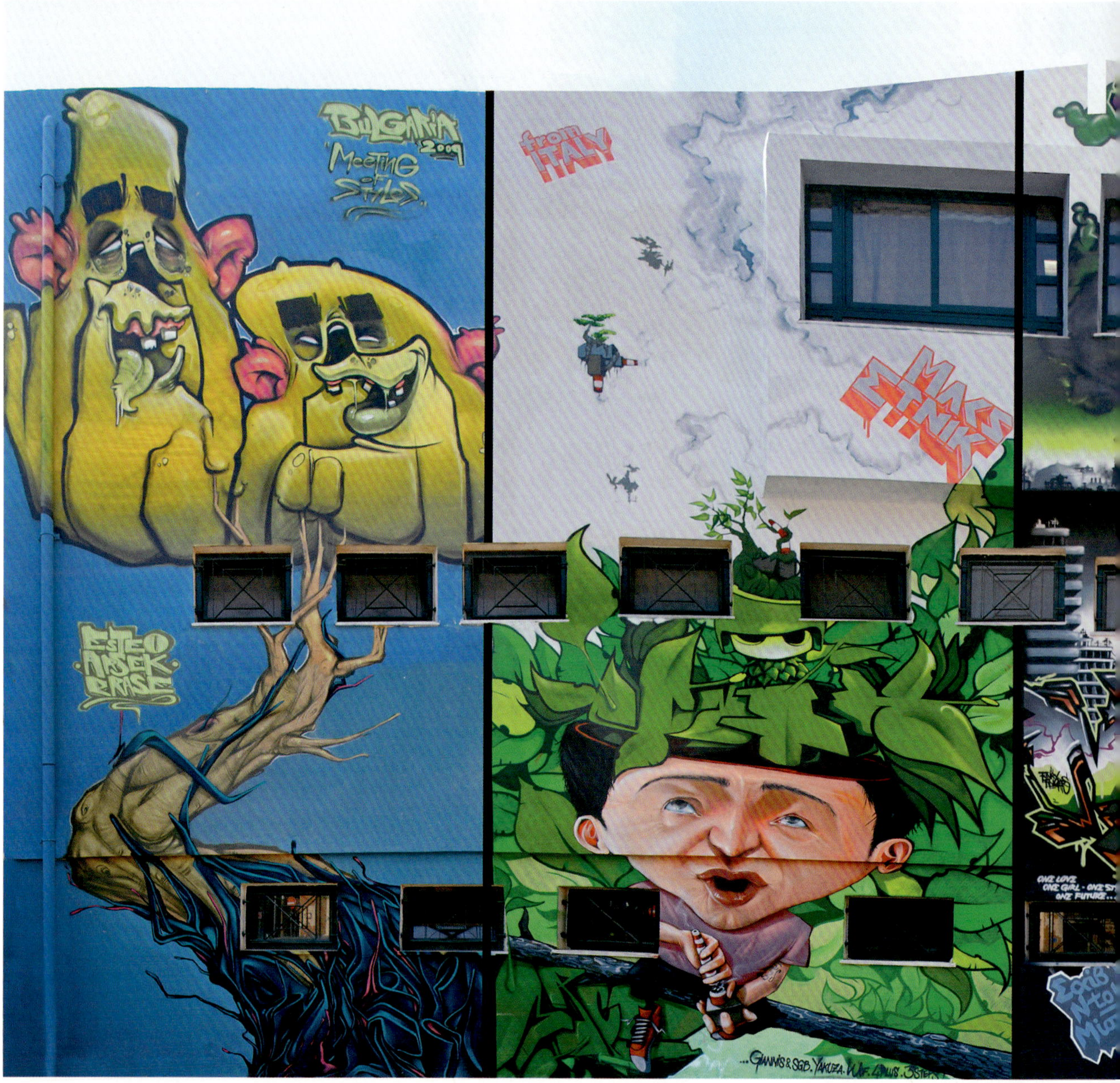

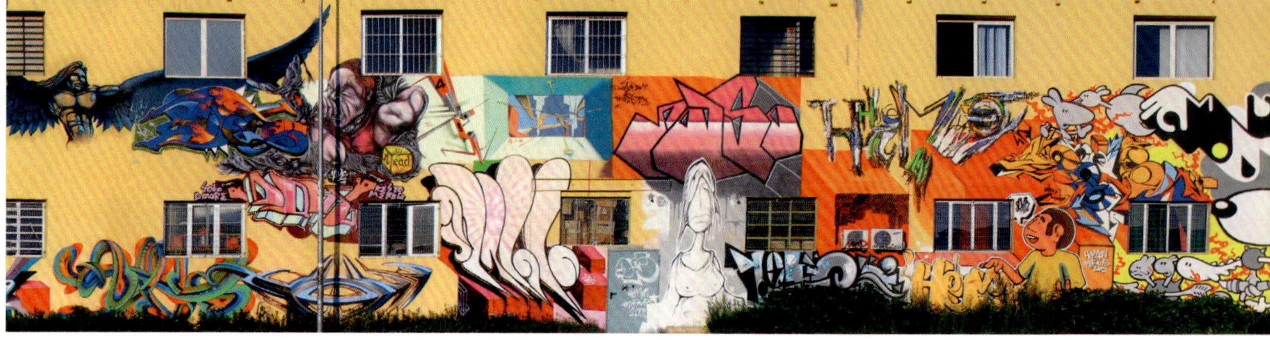

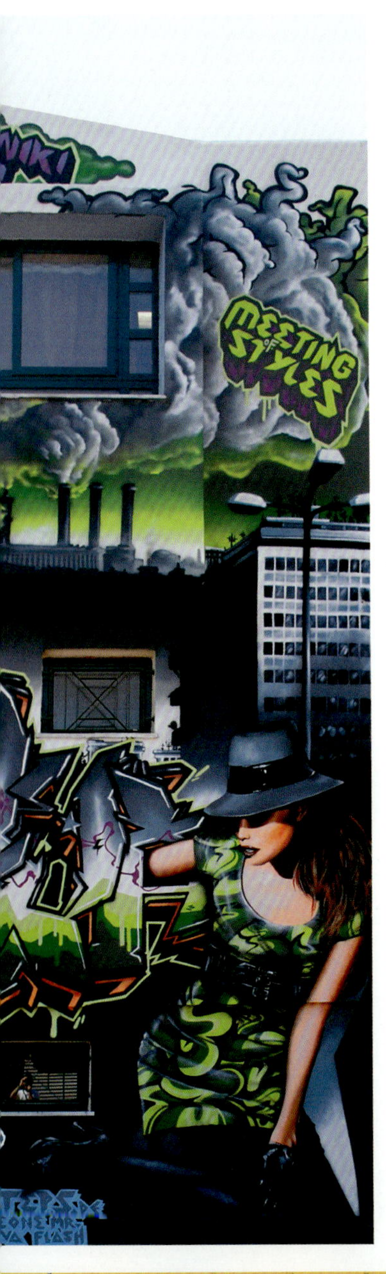

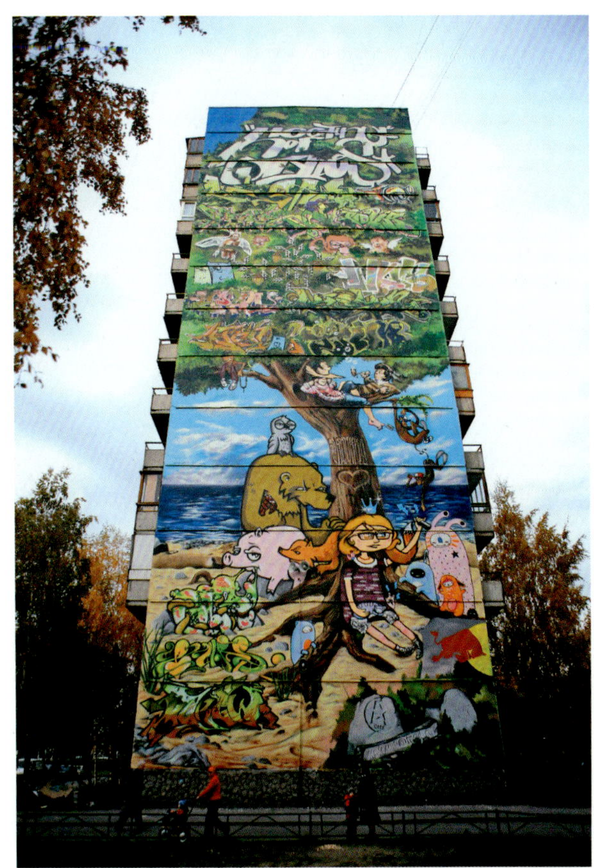

From various cities,
all courtesy of Meeting
of Styles.

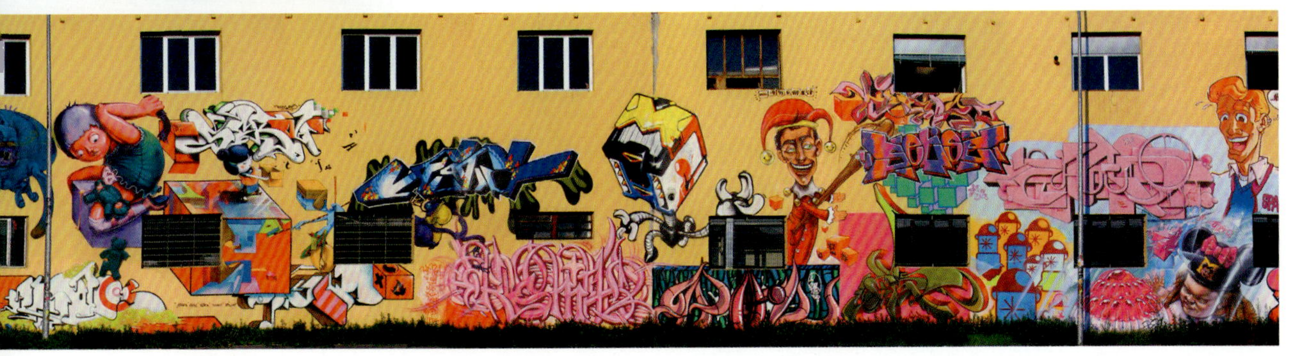

Bristol's See No Evil festival, founded in 2011, is the largest street art festival in Europe, judging by the number of attendees and the amount of surface painted. See No Evil is curated by Bristol-born artist Inkie, who originally proposed the idea of an 'art street' to Bristol City Council; the idea evolved into a block party. SNE is produced by Team Love, the Bristol-based arts collective behind Glastonbury's Wow Stage, and is fully supported by Bristol City Council, which helps by granting building permissions and closing the street for the party. SNE was mostly funded through the Arts Council last year and over 50 artists were involved.

See No Evil has become part of the fabric of Bristol, regenerating Nelson Street where it takes place, and encouraging other areas of the city to open up to street art. SNE is part of the local arts curriculum and local schools now visit the street with pupils. Public feedback has been overwhelmingly positive and the city's tourist industry has benefited.

Respected artists and the public are consulted over which artists should be brought in for the festival, while Inkie ensures that the festival also brings in relatively unheard-of artists from different parts of the world. Finally, the festival also has an outreach program, sending artists into the wider community to paint in youth centres and run workshops.

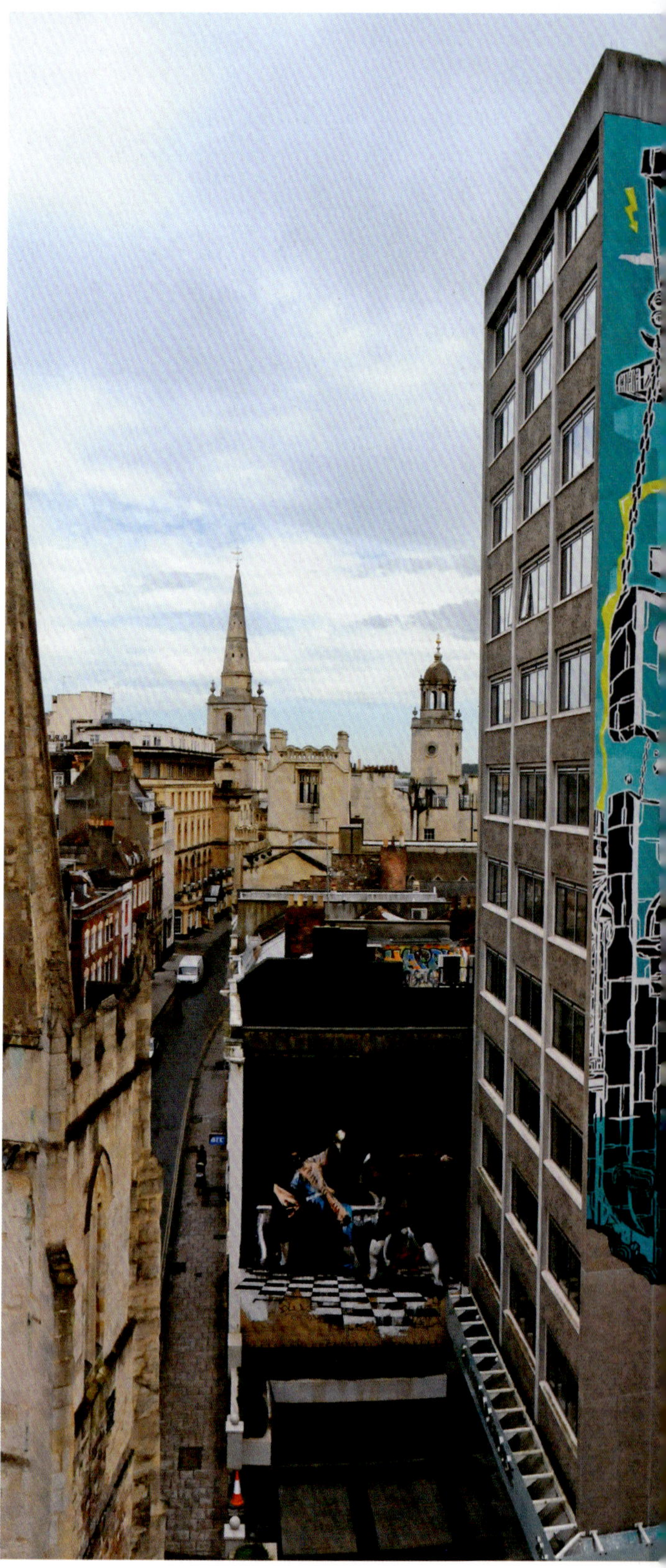

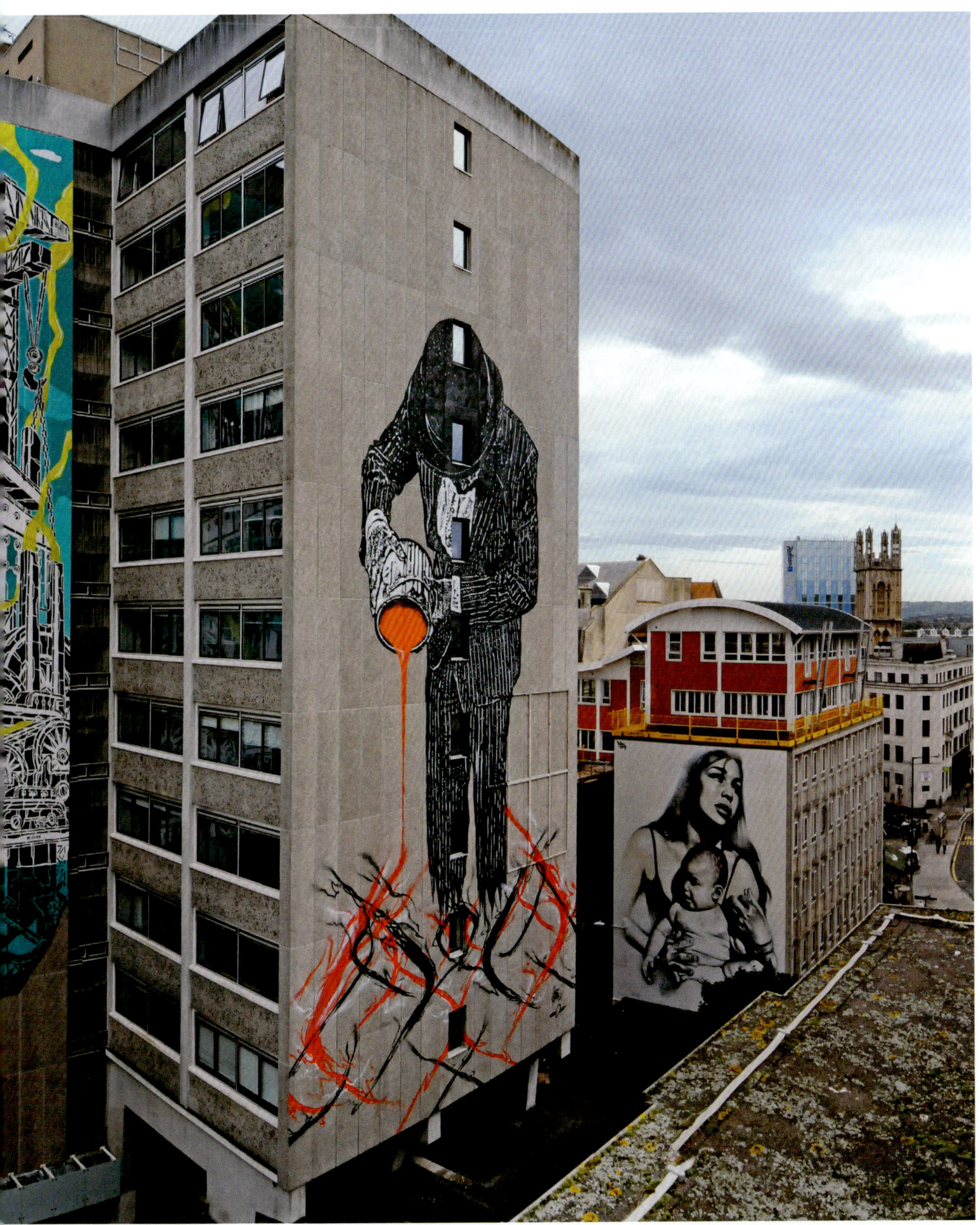

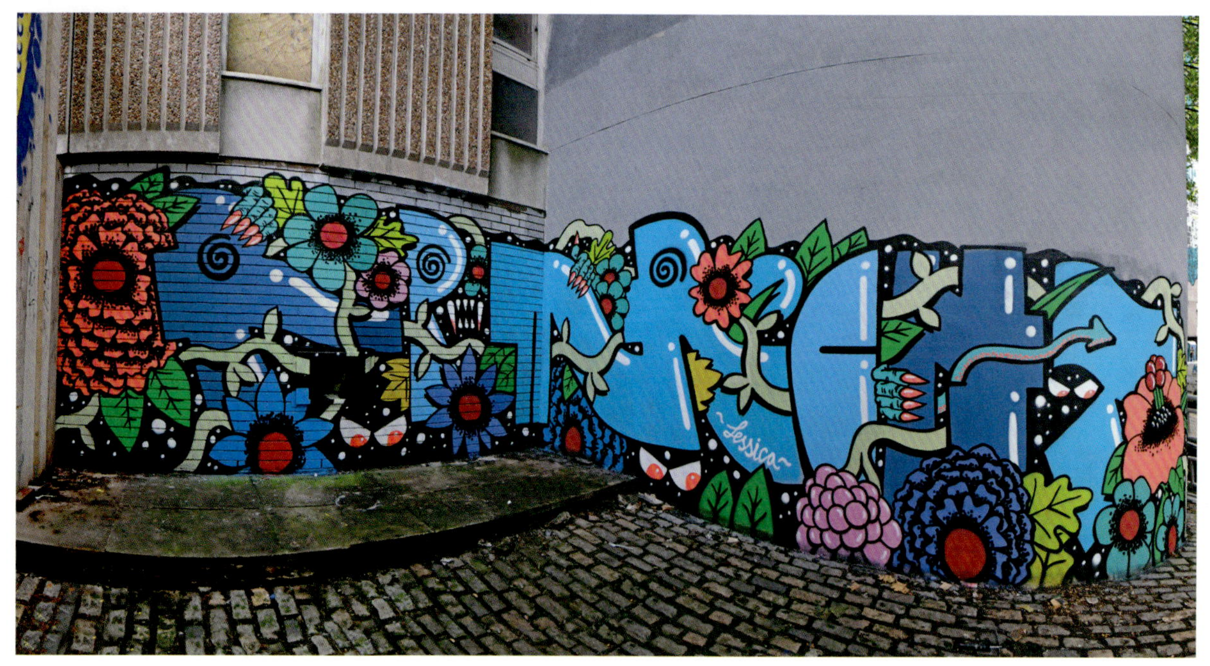

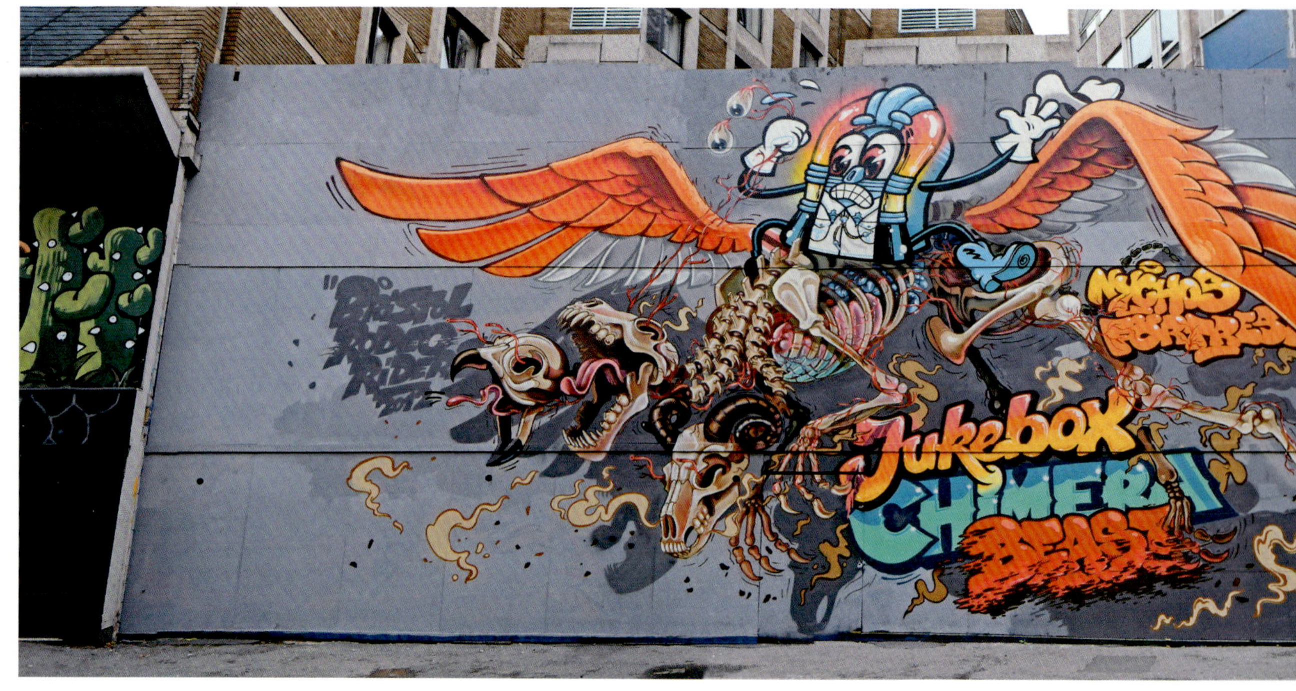
Nychos
Rumpus
Jukebox
CHIMERA
BEAST

CLOCKWISE FROM LEFT:
Bristol's 45 RPM/
France's Seize aka
Happy Wallmaker/
Bristol's Inkie, who
also curates See No
Evil/Nychos and Flying
Fortress (from Austria
and Germany).

PAGES 272-3:
UK's Mobstr.

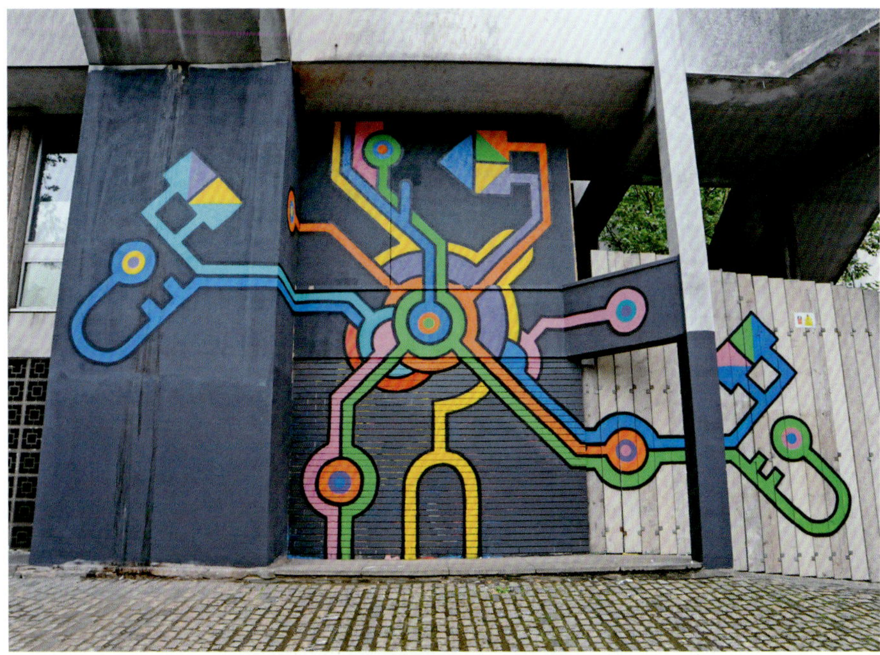

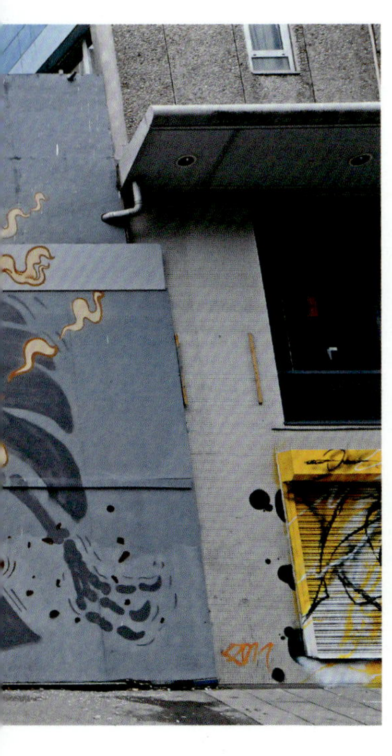

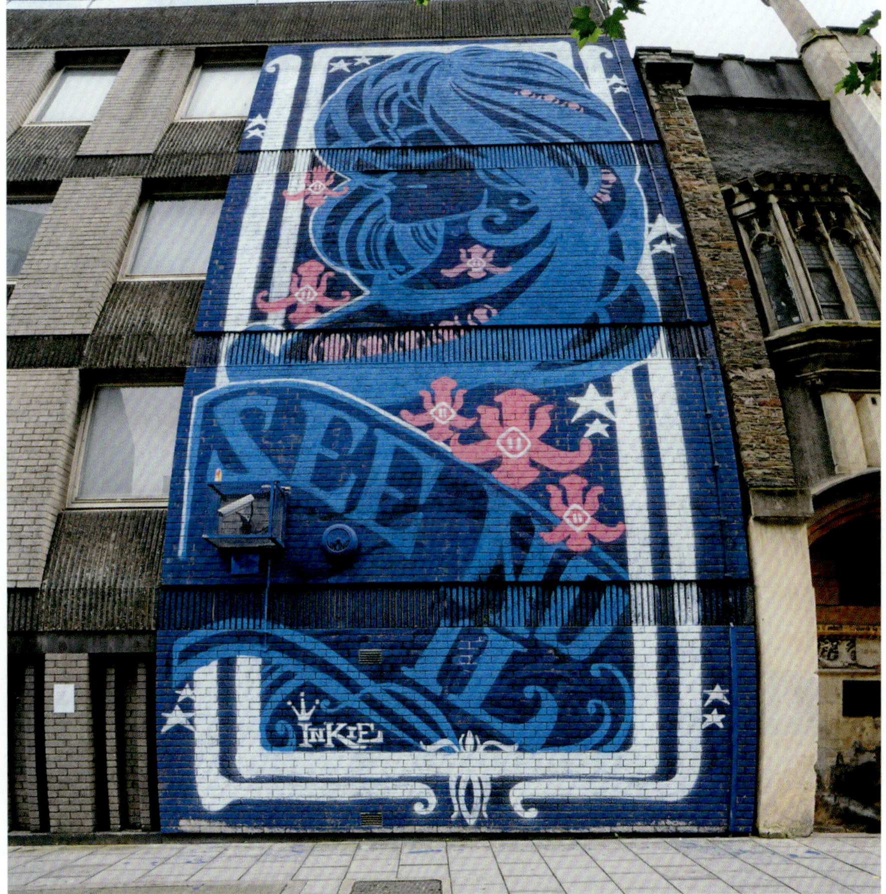

Nuart is an annual international street art festival established in 2001 with a focus exclusively on street art since 2005. The festival is based in the small city of Stavanger on the west coast of Norway. Each September, an international team of street artists is invited to leave their mark on the city's walls, both indoors and out. What surprised me most about Nuart was the long-lasting and positive impact the murals had on a city where the colours were otherwise muted.

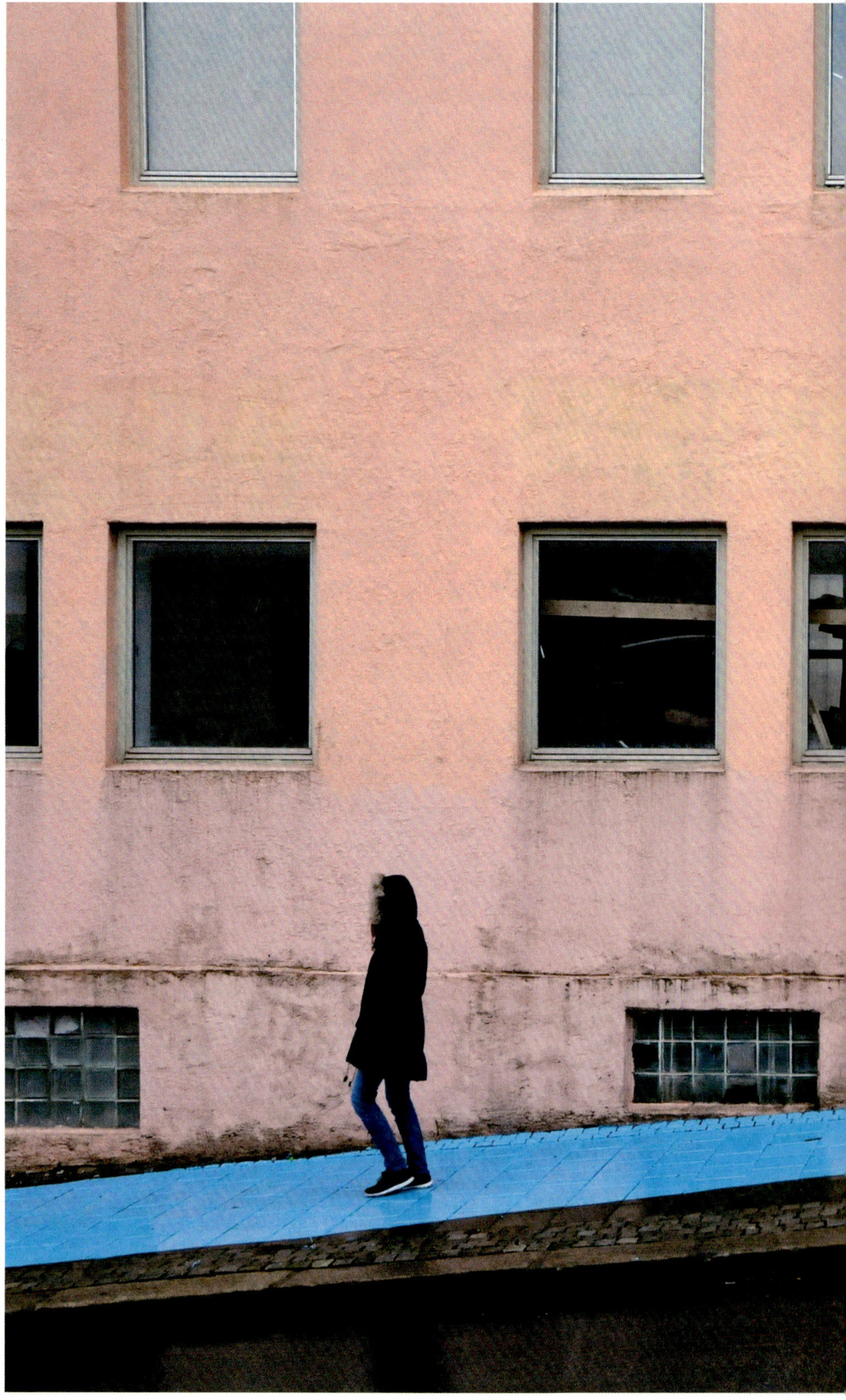

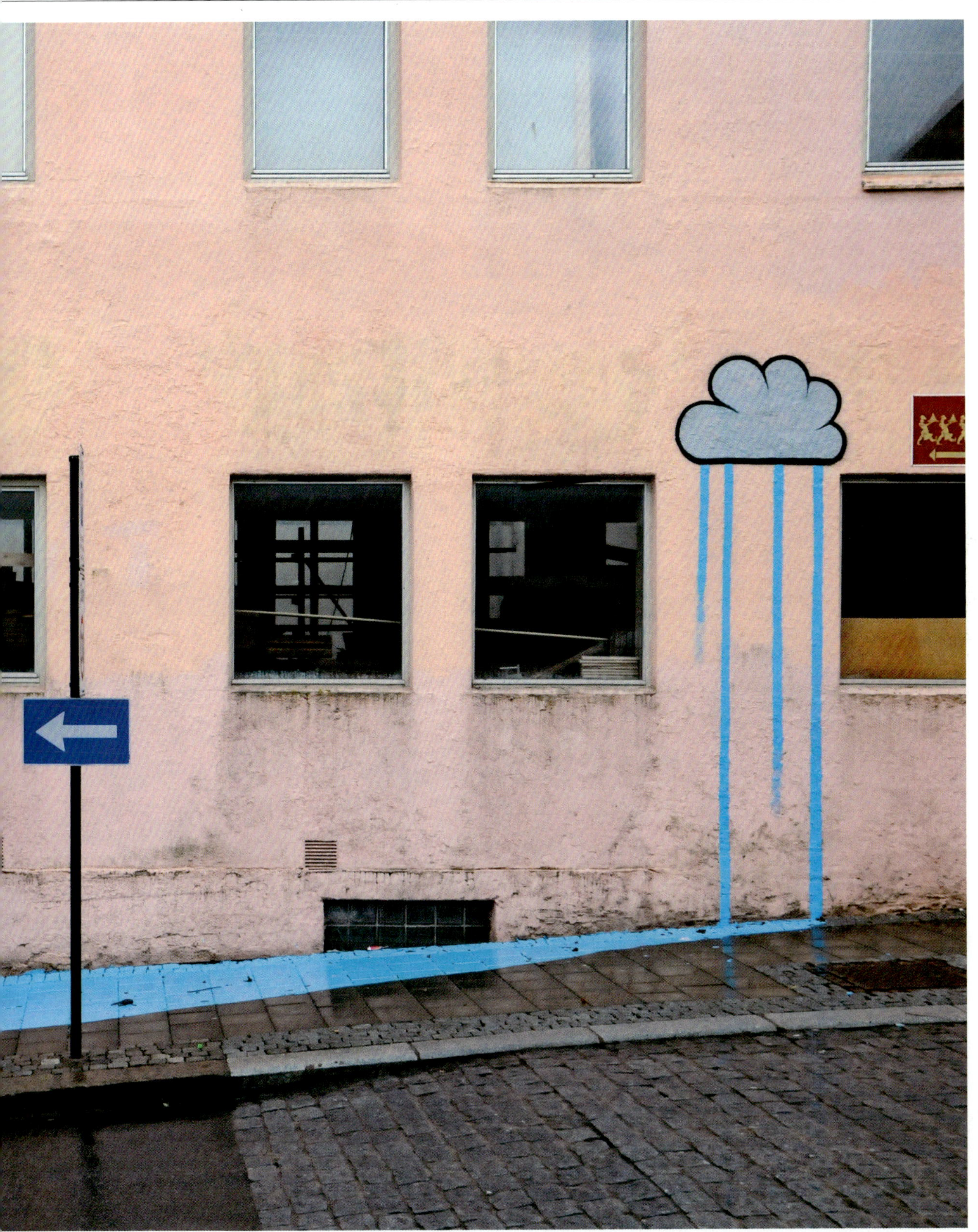

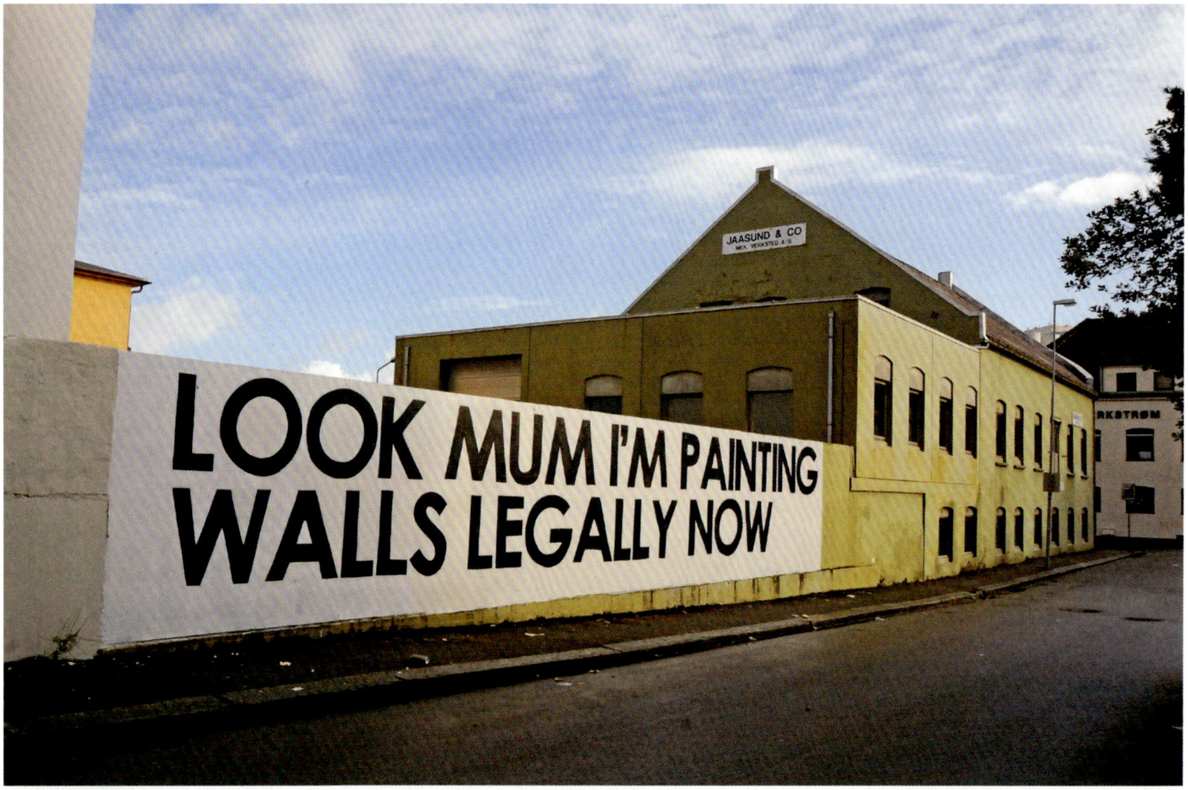

JAASUND & CO
LOOK MUM I'M PAINTING WALLS LEGALLY NOW

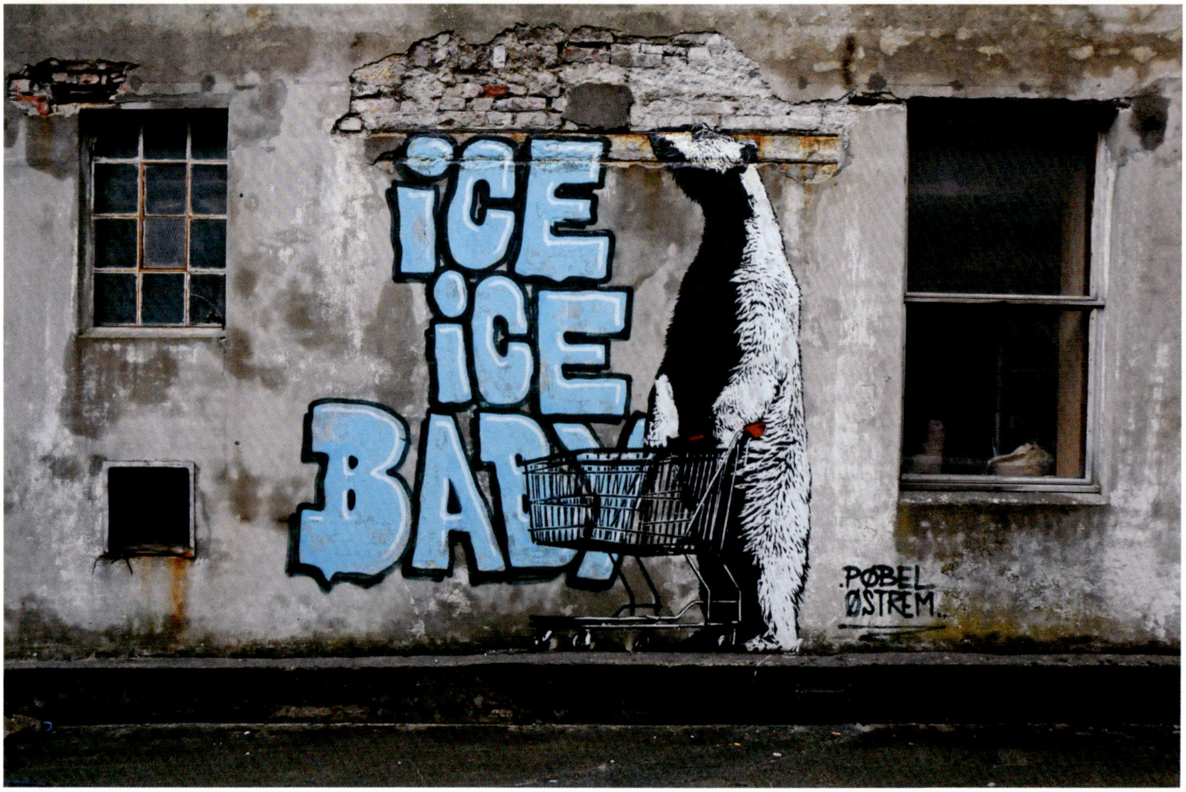

ICE
ICE
BABY
PØBEL
ØSTREM

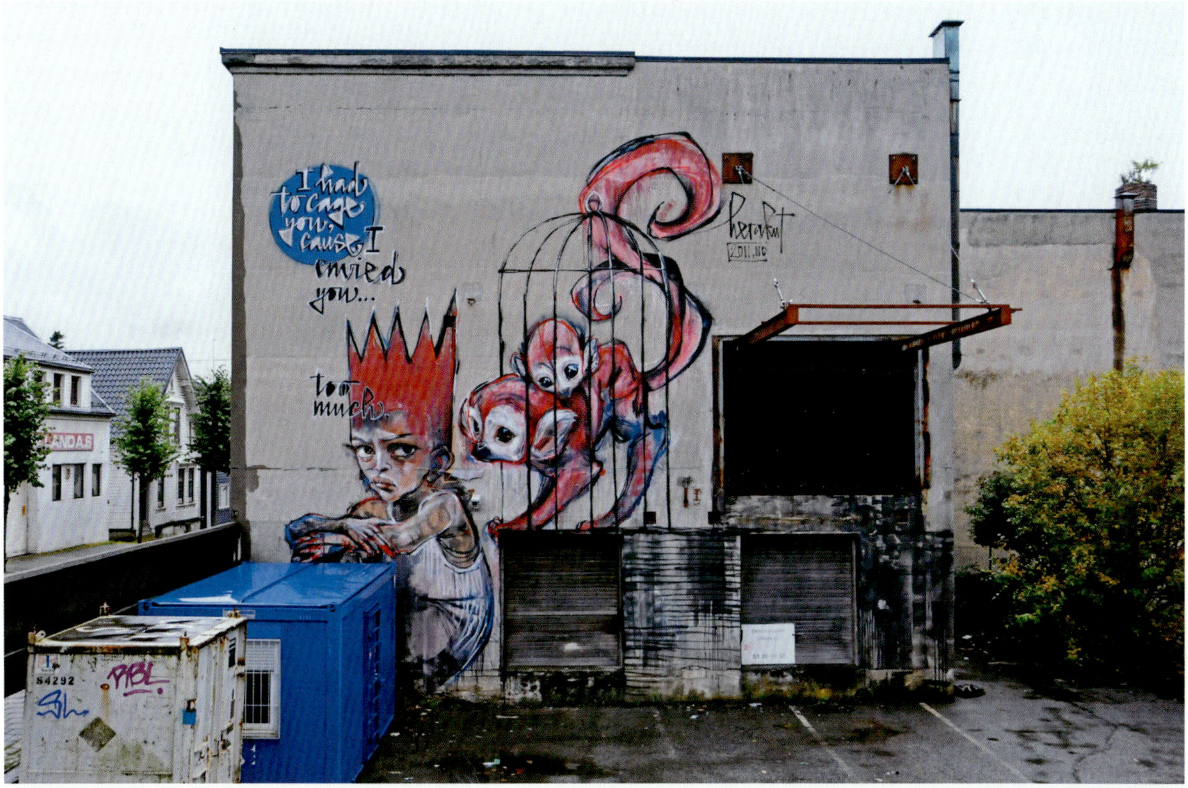

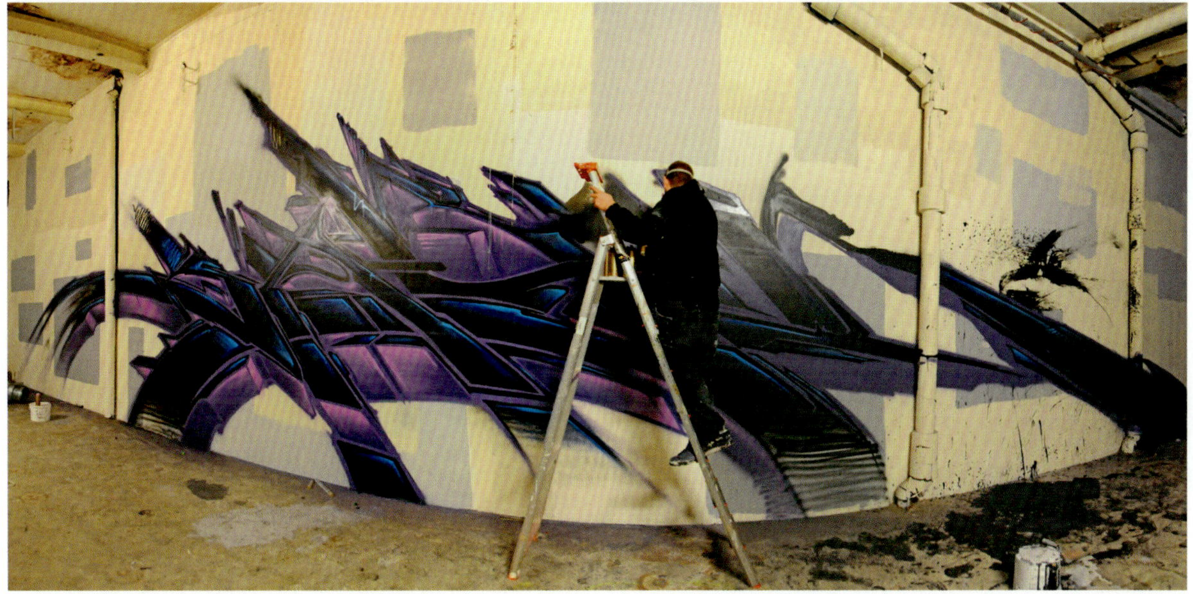

CLOCKWISE FROM TOP
LEFT:
UK's Mobstr/German duo
Herakut/LA's Saber from
MSK Crew/Norway's Pøbel
and Ostrem.

Most of us see more street art online than we do on the street. The art we see online has already been filtered through a decision to post, repost or share, so I would argue that the average quality of online street art is higher than much of what we encounter in the real world. The improvement in the average quality of art we see has most likely galvanized more people into paying attention to it, and taking and sharing photos. As the fanbase has grown, so has the number of people willing to help artists find new spaces to paint. This section explores just a handful of those projects, including Global Street Art's own Walls Project.

The Walls Project started in early 2012 and has now found space for more than 500 new pieces of street art in London. We speak with wall owners and arrange permission for artists to paint. It's nothing glamorous – in practice it's often me jumping on and off my bike on the way to and from the office!

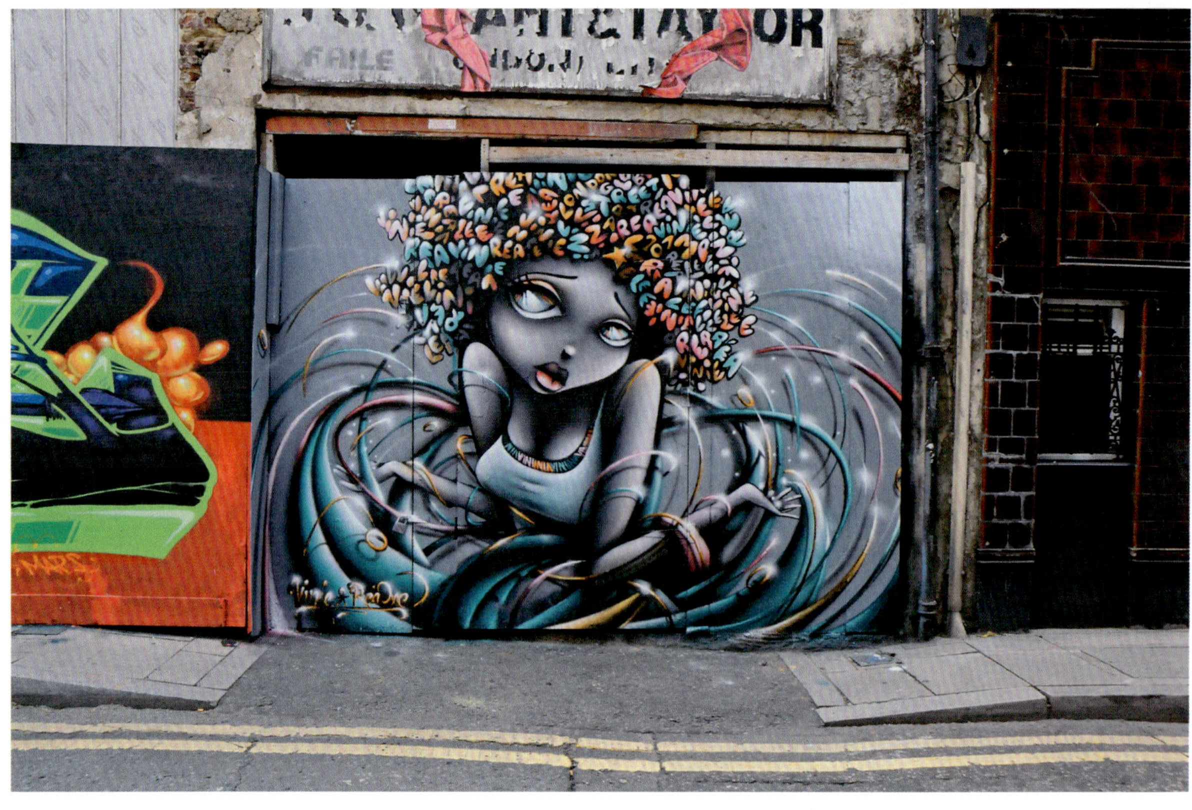

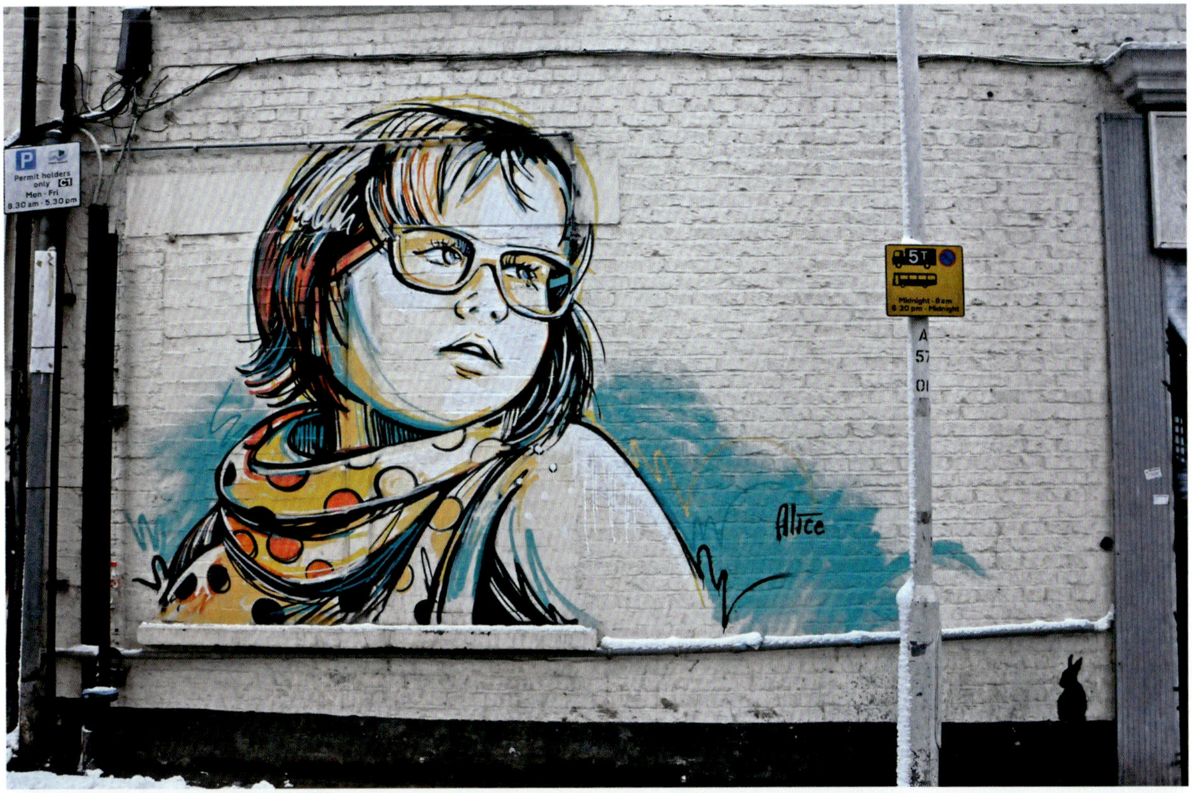

Alice

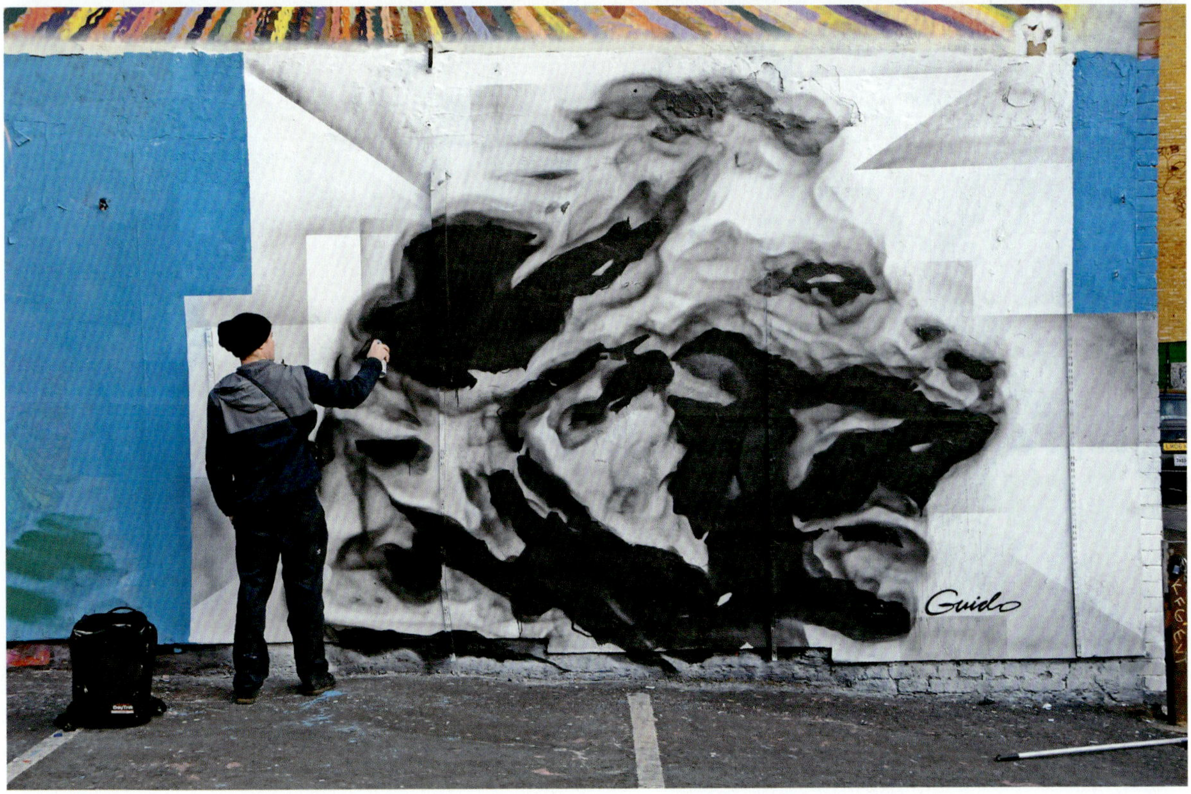

Guido

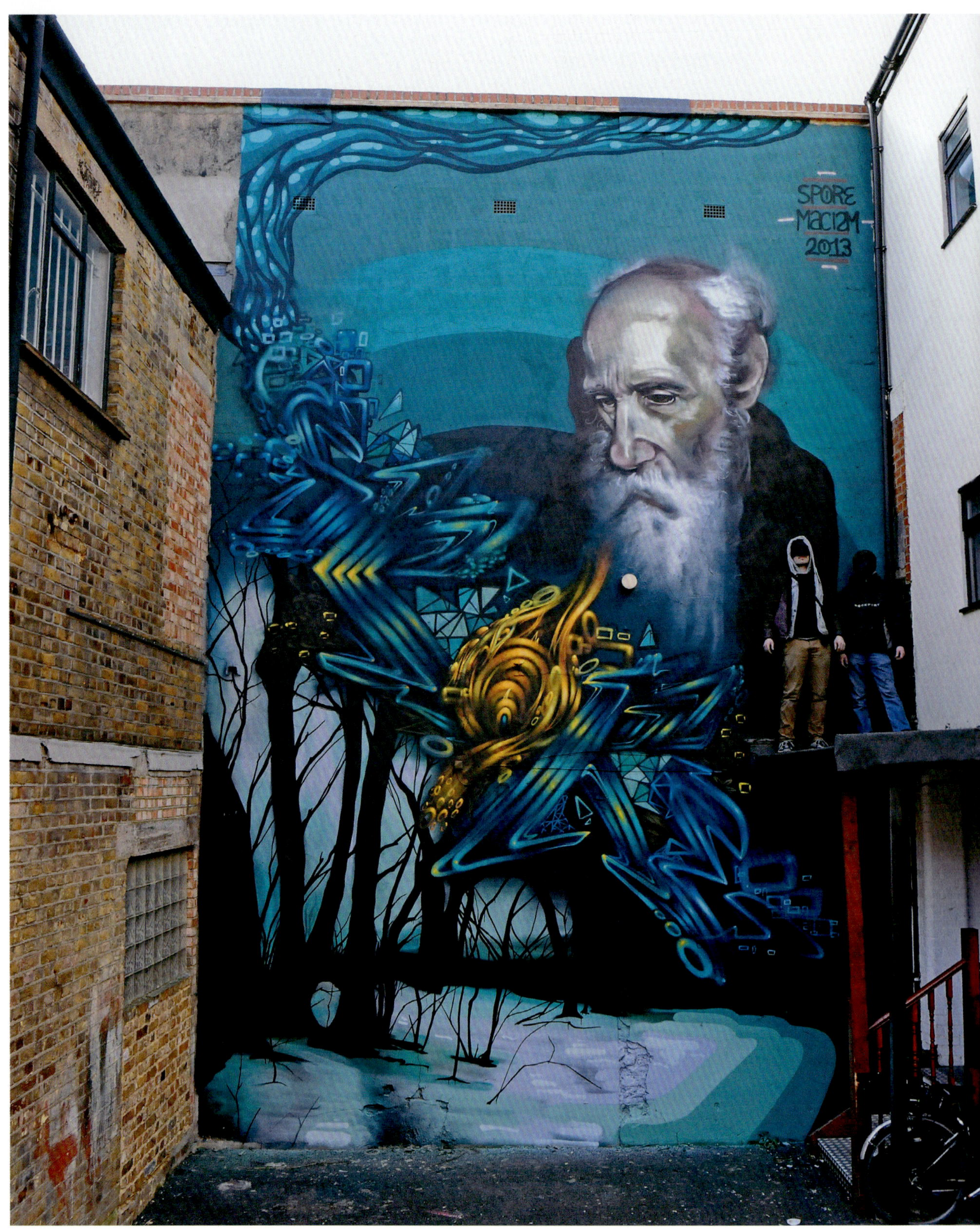
SPORE
MACI2M
2013

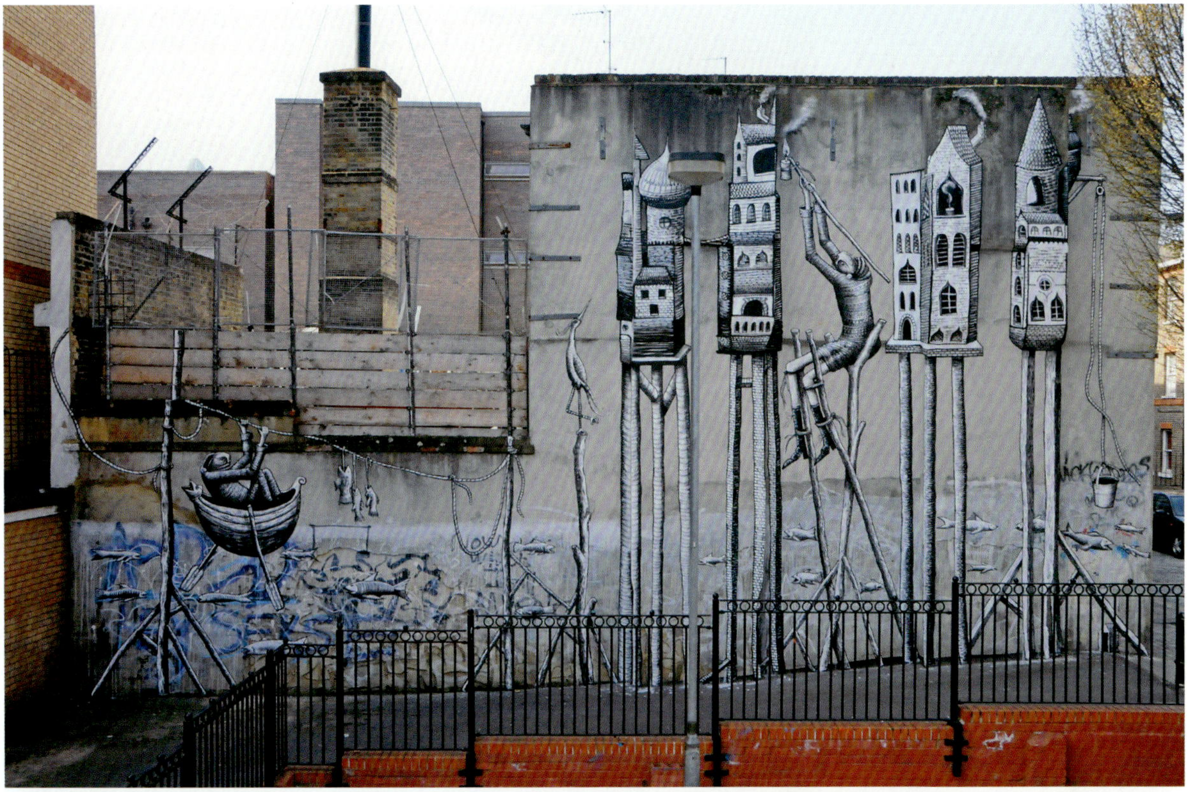

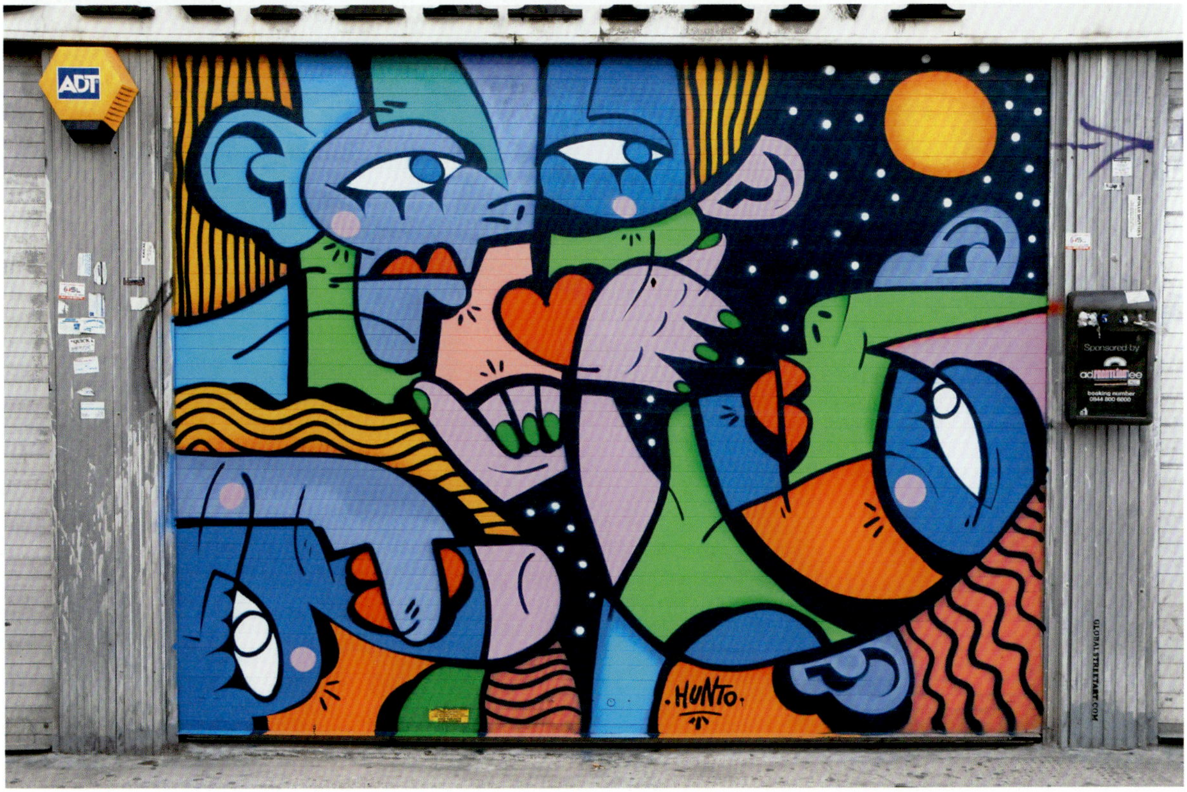

HUNTO

CLOCKWISE FROM NEAR RIGHT:
UK's Gnasher/Italy's Krio/UK's Zadok as part of a longer mural featuring many other artists.

PAGES 282-3:
From left to right, *Reign* by Cyrcle, a collaboration between Italian artists Run and Never 2501; *London, You Beast* by South Africa's Faith 47; a giant Frank by UK's Mysterious Al; a piece by Australia's Rone; and (partly obscured) a work in progress by Greece's Woozy, all organized as part of the Walls Project.

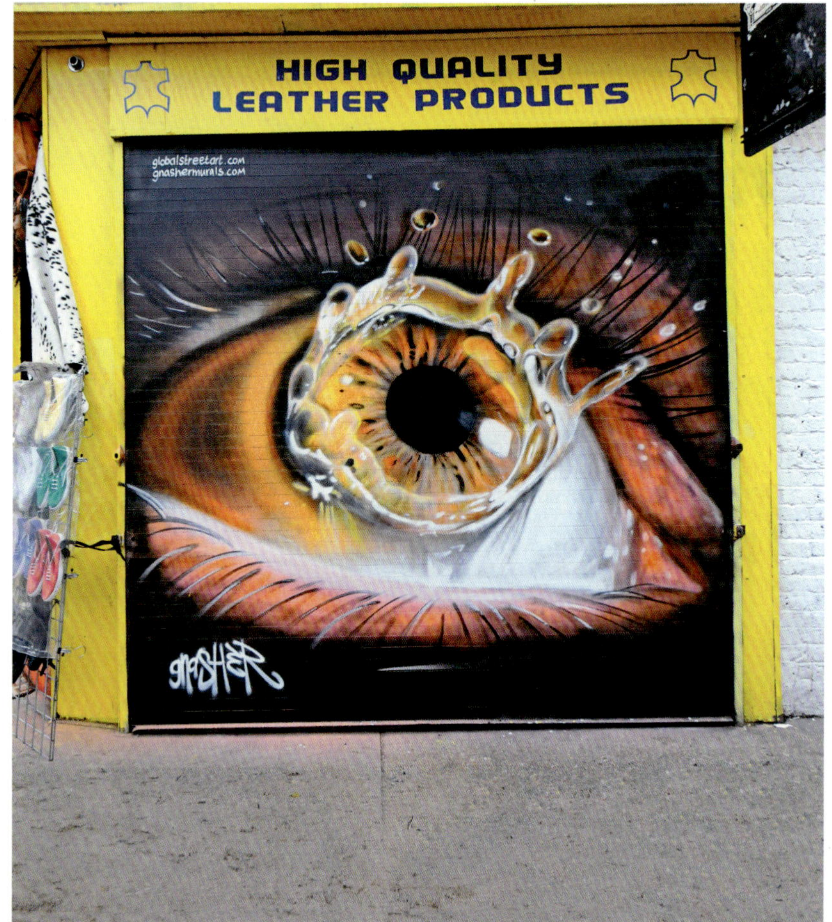

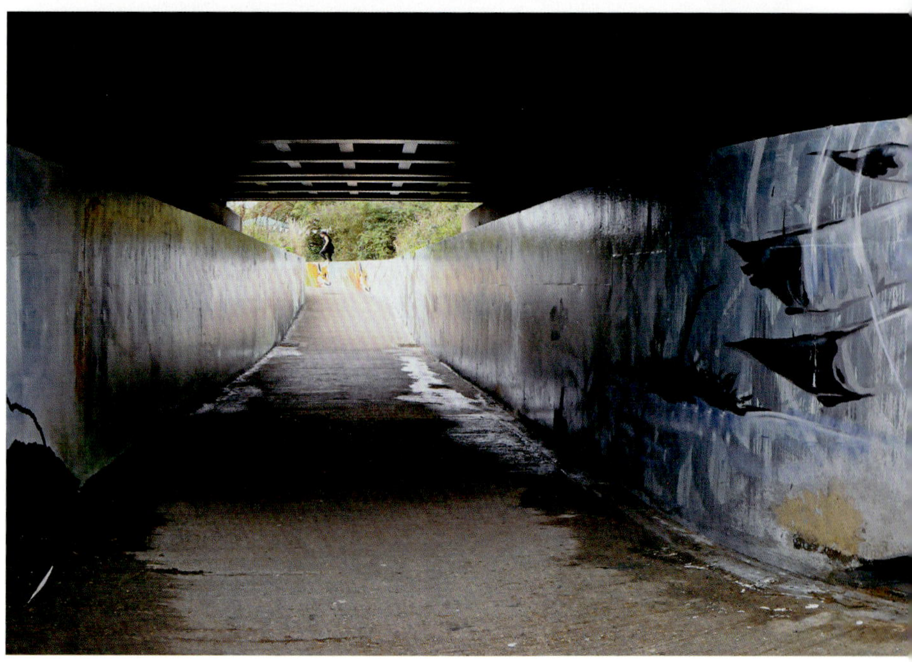

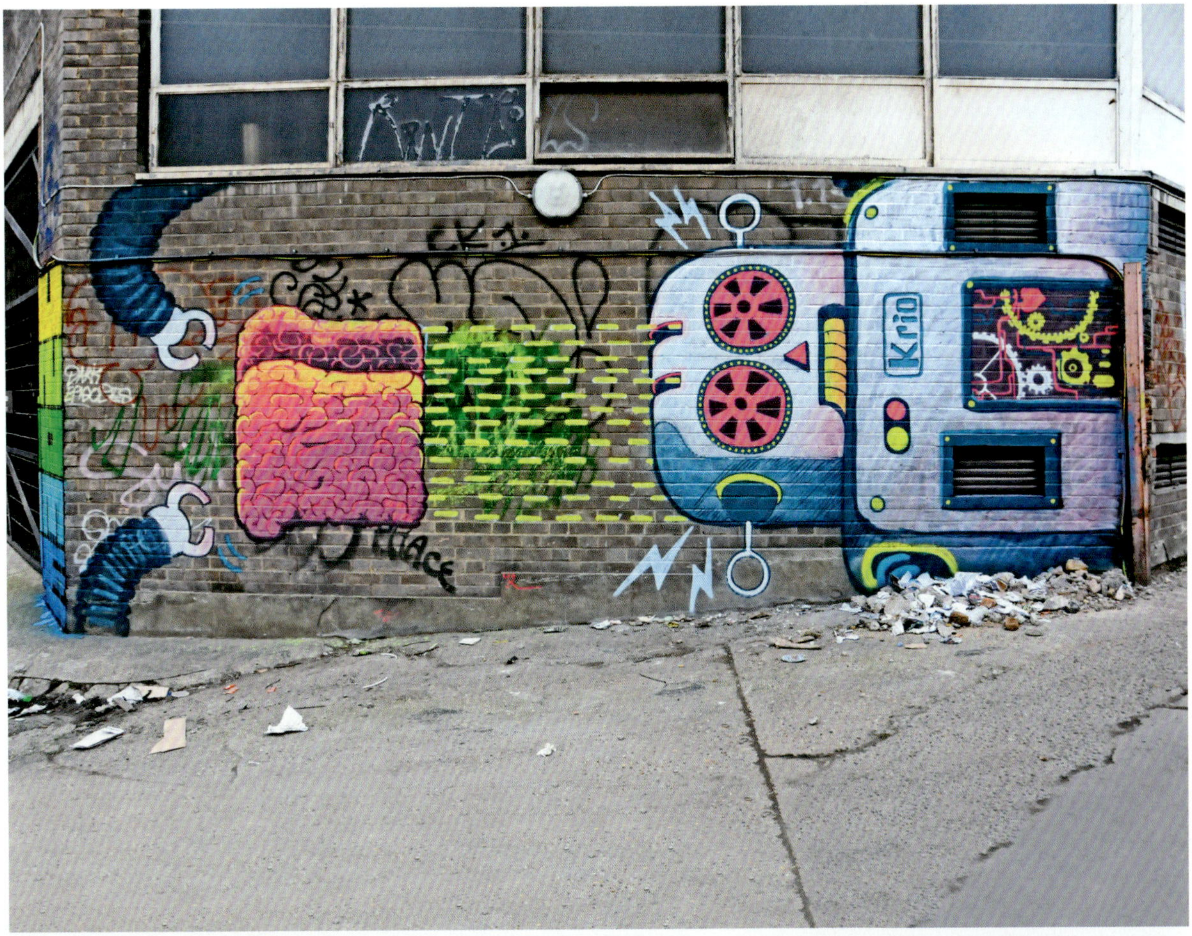

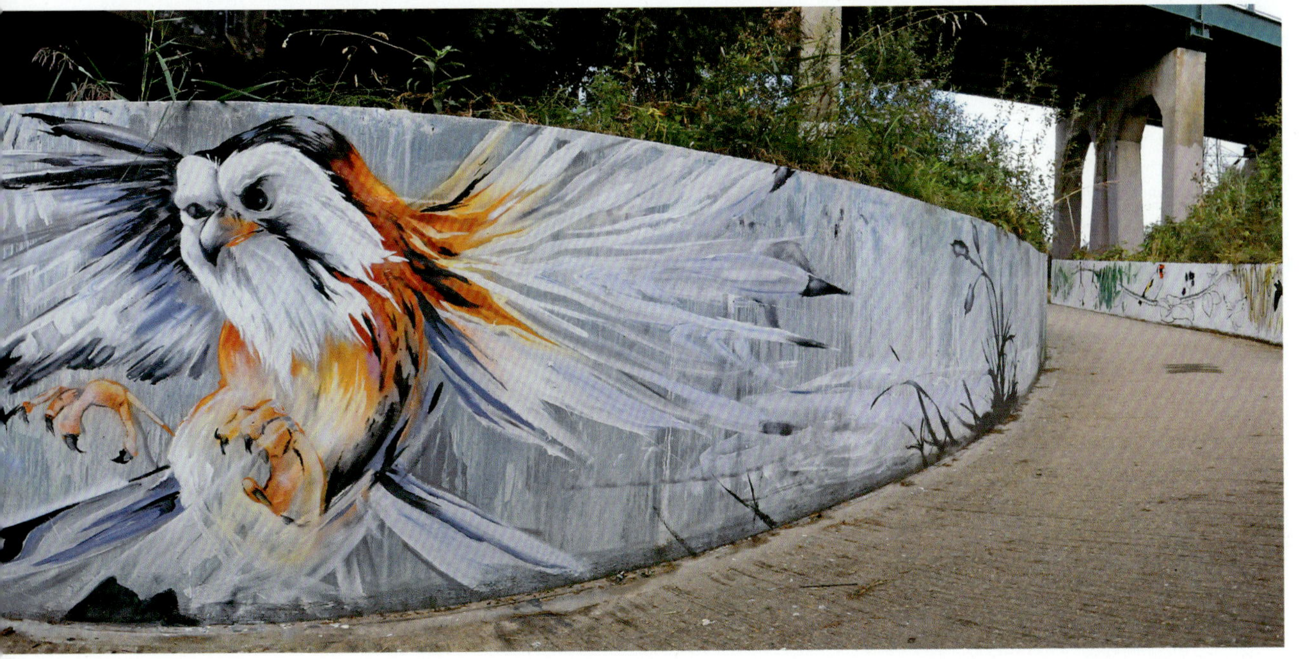

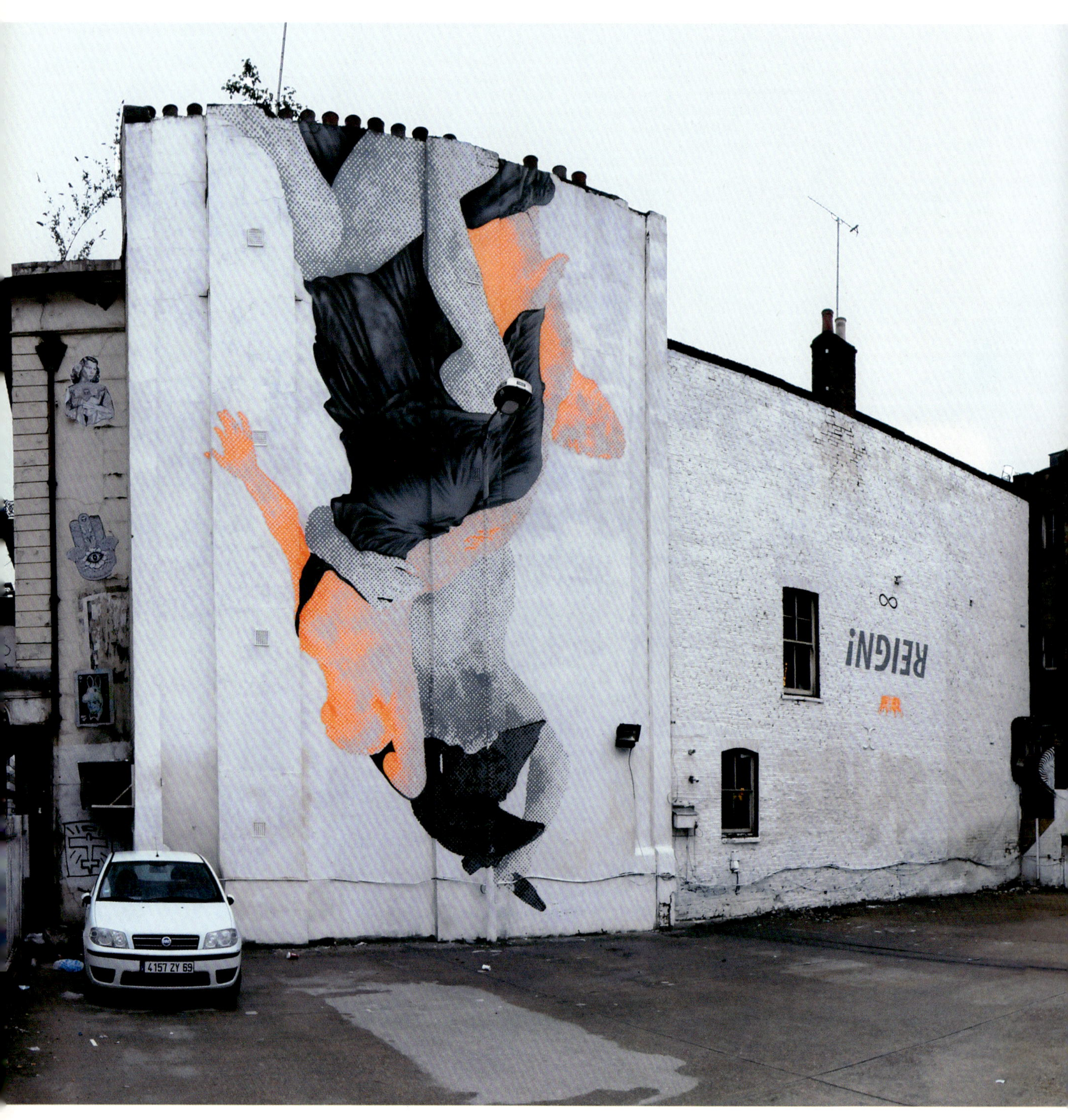

REIGN!

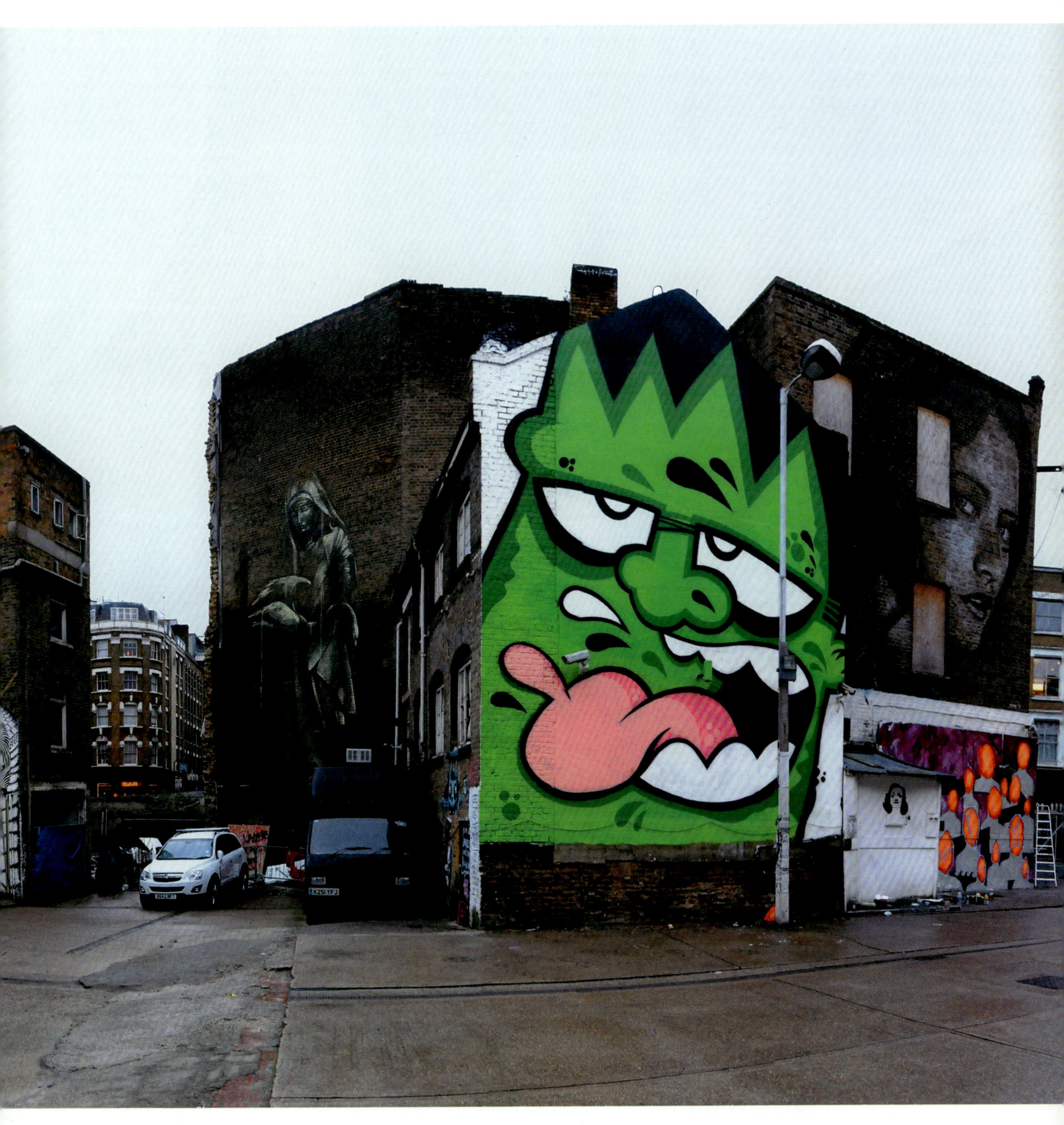

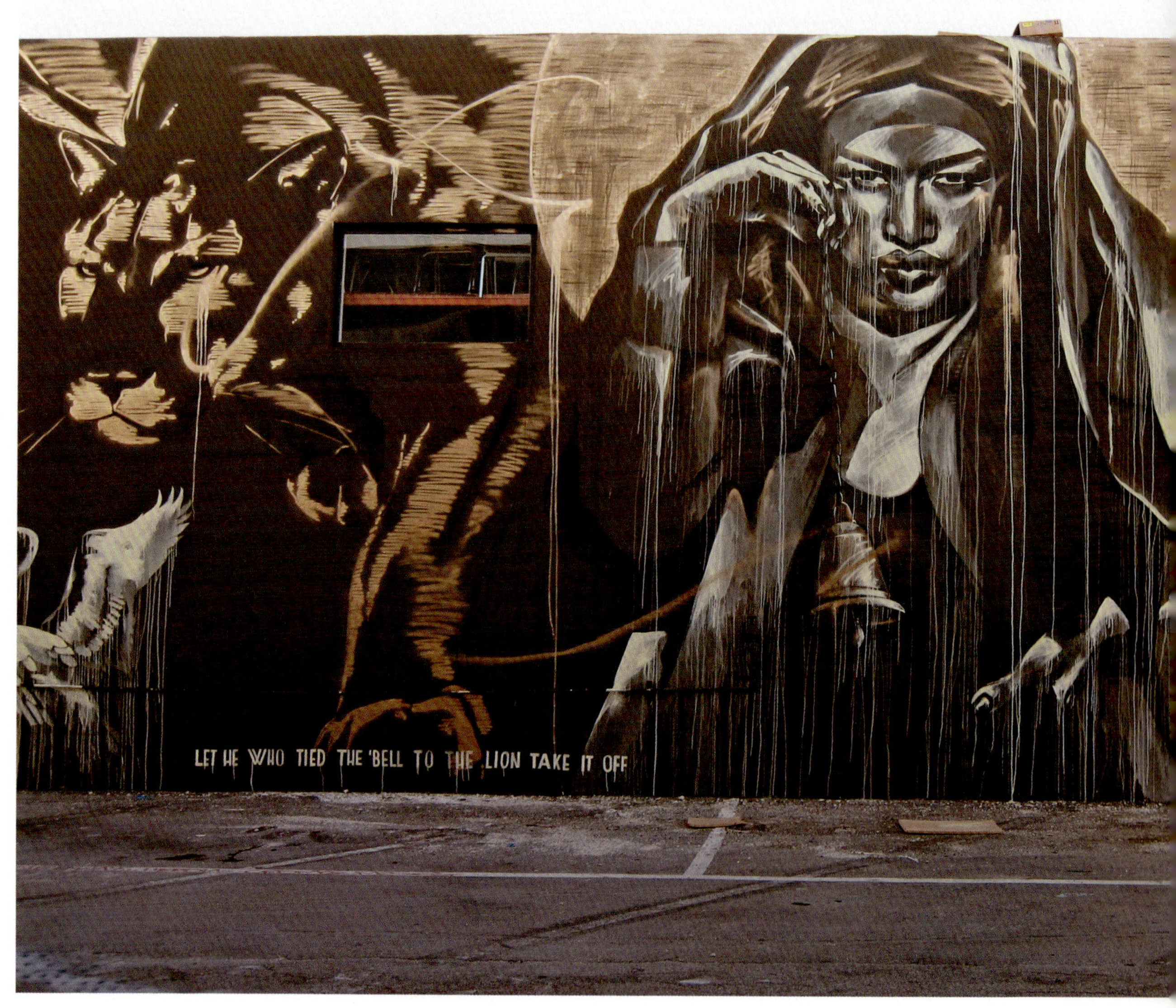

LET HE WHO TIED THE 'BELL TO THE LION TAKE IT OFF

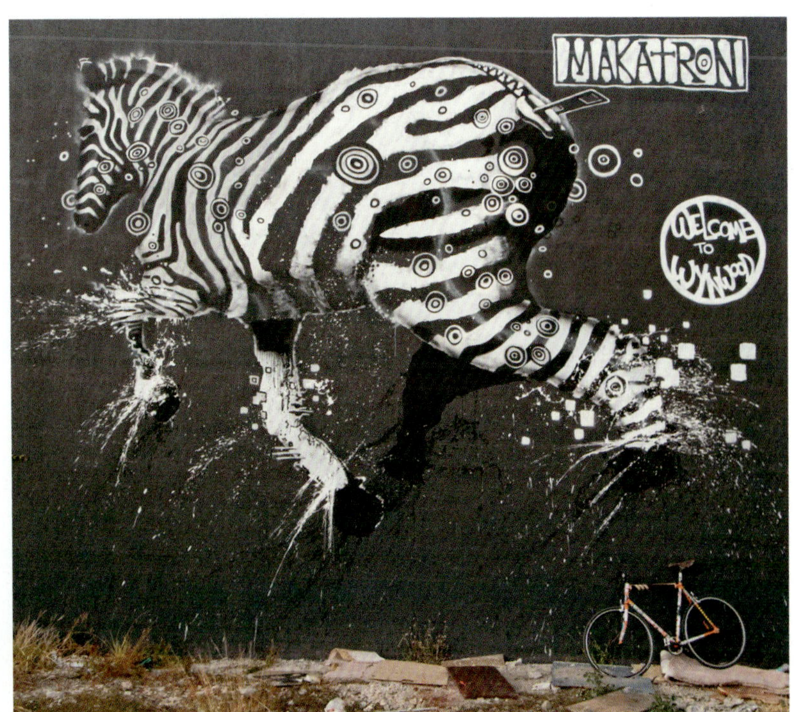

MAKATRON
WELCOME TO WYNWOOD

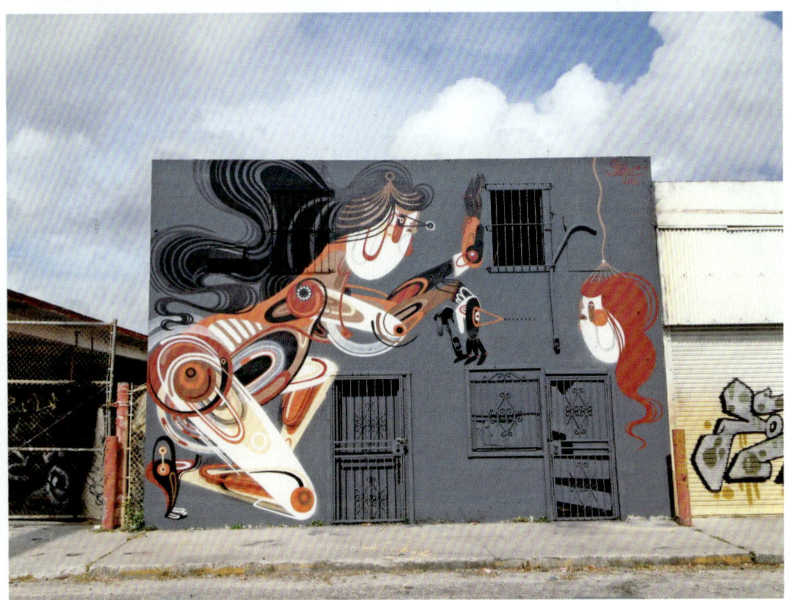

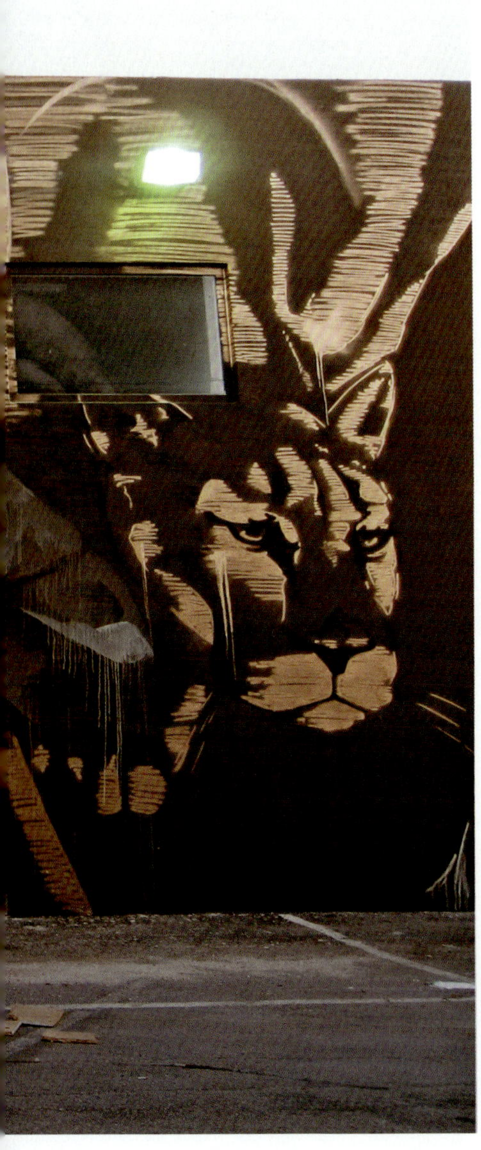

CLOCKWISE FROM TOP:
Australia's Makatron/
Australia's Reka/*Let
he who tied the bell
to the lion take it
off* by Faith 47.

The Black Duke is a 380-foot, disused passenger ship moored in Wales, on the banks of the River Dee. The Black Duke Project has so far brought more than ten artists to paint huge pieces along the ship with more artists planned for the future. The project has the full support of the ship's owners and is independent of local council involvement. Coordinators and photographers are volunteers, and the project is self-funded through merchandise sales in the online shop. The project has been covered extensively in the press.

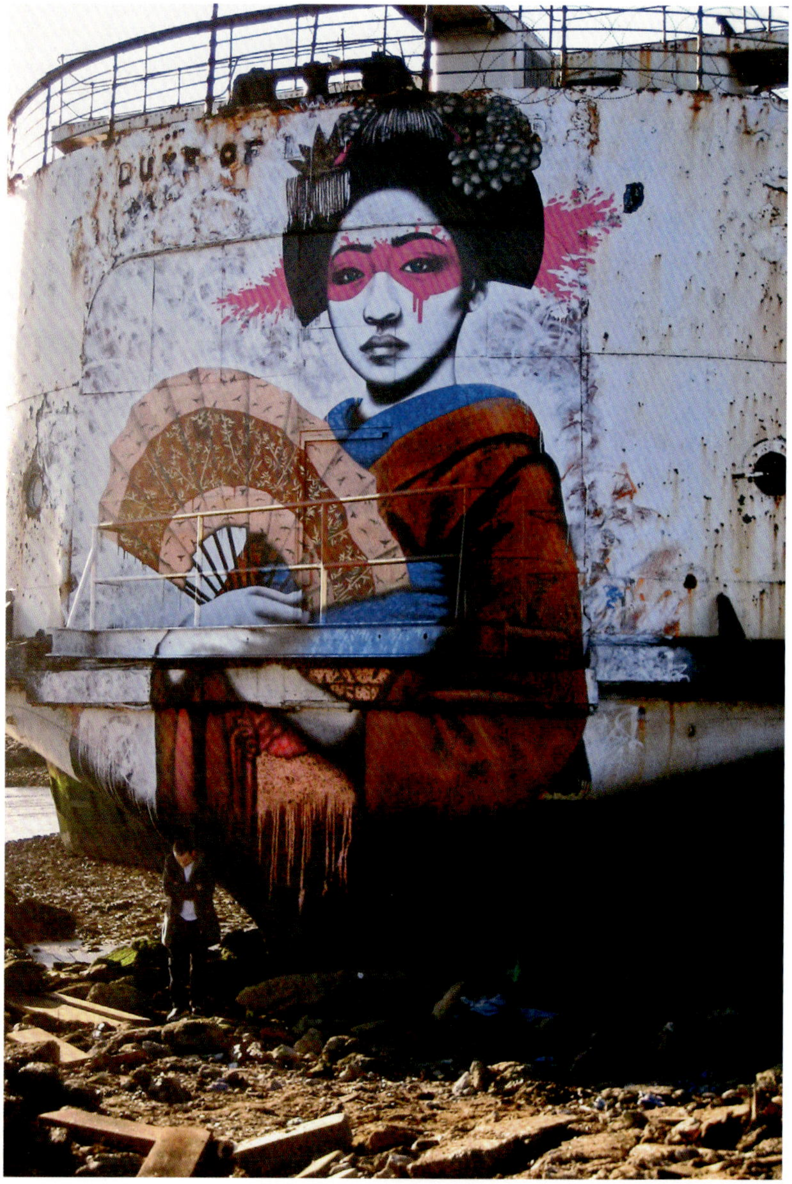

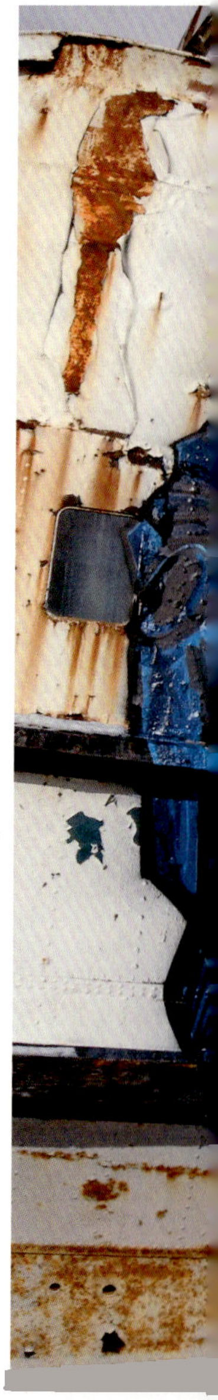

FROM LEFT TO RIGHT:
Fin DAC/Snub 23.

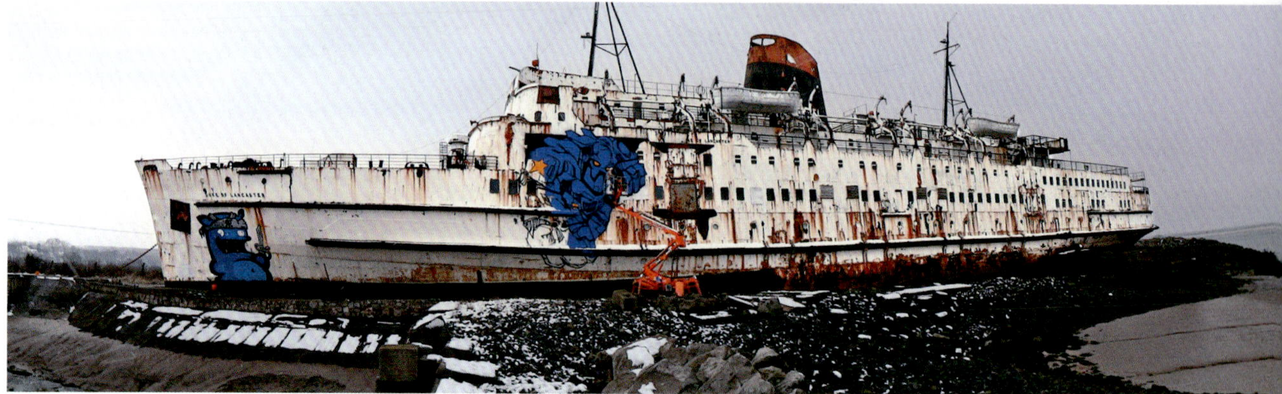

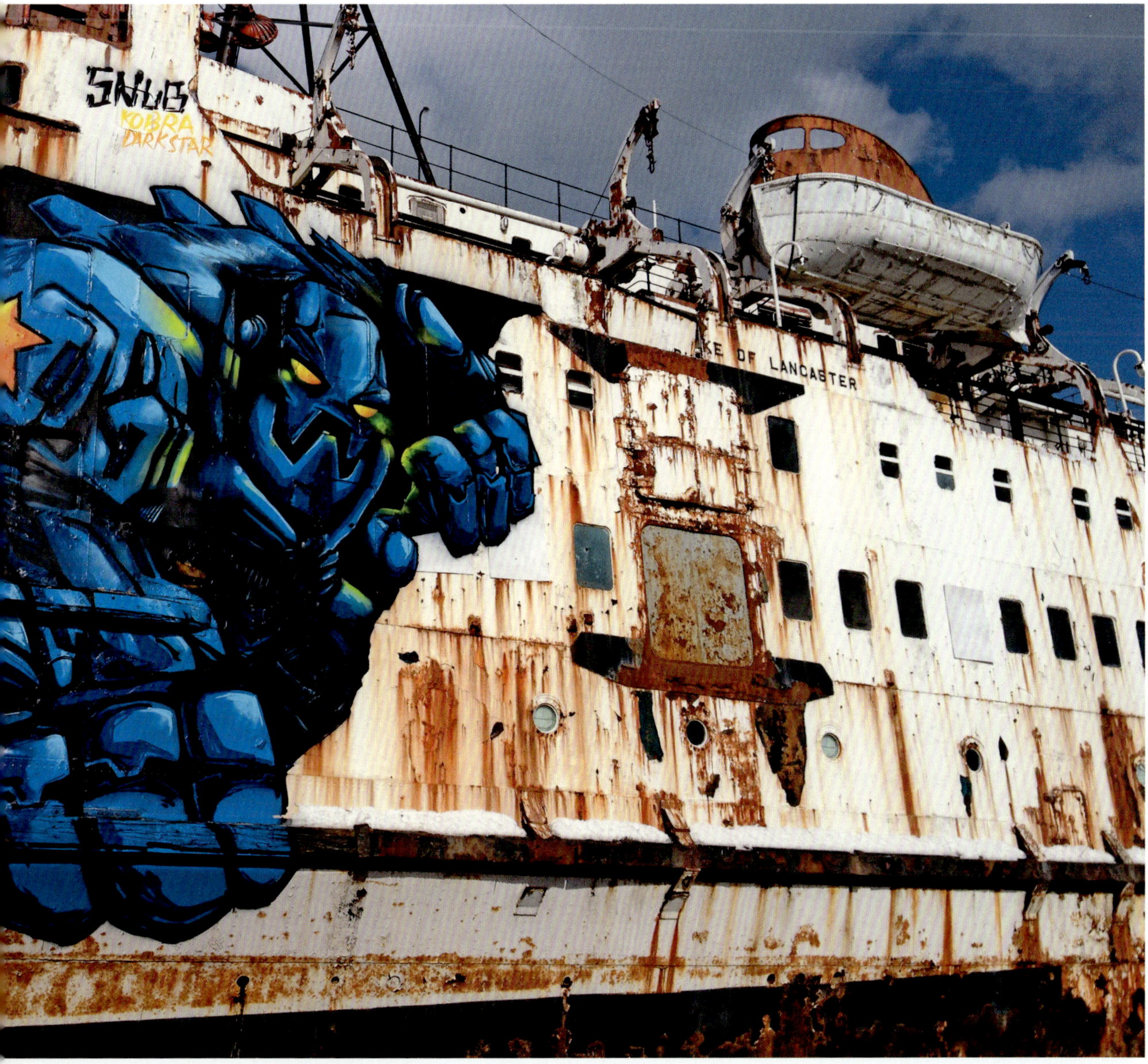

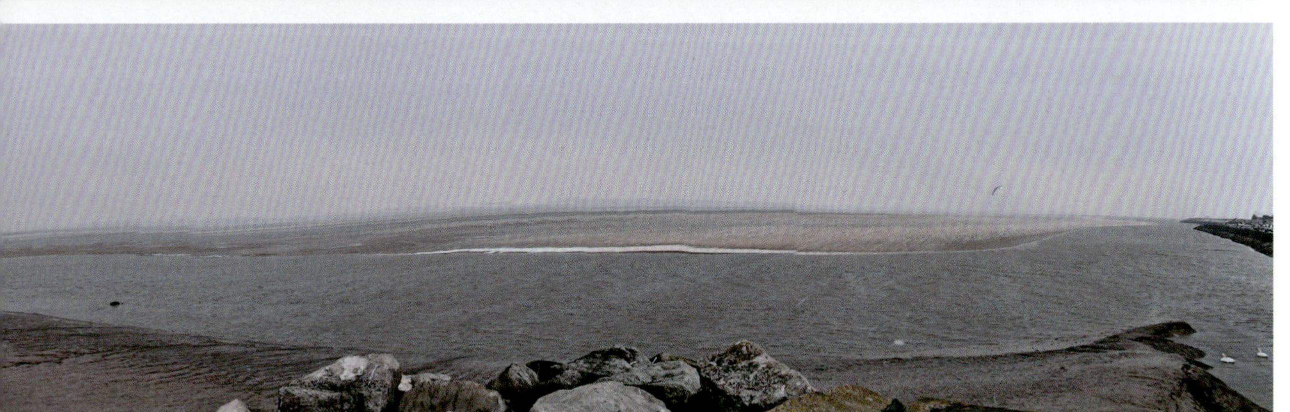

Legal Walls

Legal walls are spaces where local authorities have granted explicit permission for artists to paint graffiti and street art (unlike spaces that are simply ignored or out of the way), often including skateparks and ball courts. Areas are typically quite well contained, which helps prevent the surrounding areas from being painted or tagged. Legal walls – at least in Europe and the USA – are not that numerous and so their life cycle depends on neighbourhood development. The artists that paint in legal spaces are often not local residents; they travel from other parts of the city or beyond. This means that their opinions are typically not taken into account when changes to the space are proposed.

Globally, the trend in the number of legal walls is unclear. The concept of a legal wall doesn't exist in cities, like São Paulo, where authorities usually turn a blind eye to graffiti. In other places, such as the Fitzroy neighbourhood of Melbourne, it appears that most of the walls have been provided by private landowners and are not under the jurisdiction of the local authorities. In other countries, such as Spain, the embankments of the municipal rivers that often run dry in the summer act as huge graffiti galleries, and there is consequently an abundance of places to paint.

In cities where private landowners do not support street art, and if trends are towards the removal of legal walls, this presents a problem because there are no alternative legal options for this kind of public expression. If the numbers of legal walls are diminished, artists can only stop painting, travel further or break the law to paint.

Gentrification in Western cities happens when artists move into neighbourhoods where the rents are cheap; during this time street art is most likely to have the opportunity to increase. As the area develops an artistic reputation, more affluent young professionals move to the area. Over time the rents increase and artists start moving away. As more expensive shops establish in the area the profile begins to change and street art risks being run out of town. Street art is culturally atypical in up-market areas for most cities around the world. Changes in mindset and in the perceived value of street art are required if we are to live in truly painted cities.

What is missing from the discussion around legal walls is how features of the space and its management affect the quality of the art there: accessibility, foot traffic, lighting, etc, affect whether the local artists visit the space and consequently how much responsibility certain artists take for looking after the space. Other factors aside, the quality of art is highest in spaces that are curated by a community of artists, who choose to paint over weaker art and leave the more powerful work up for longer. I believe lessons can be taken from different legal walls and can be applied to new places.

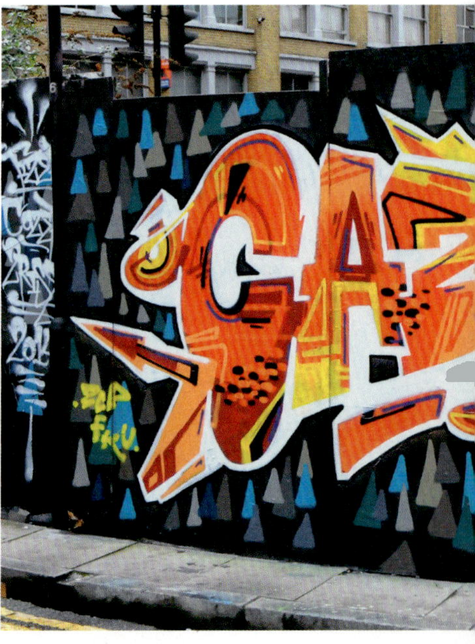

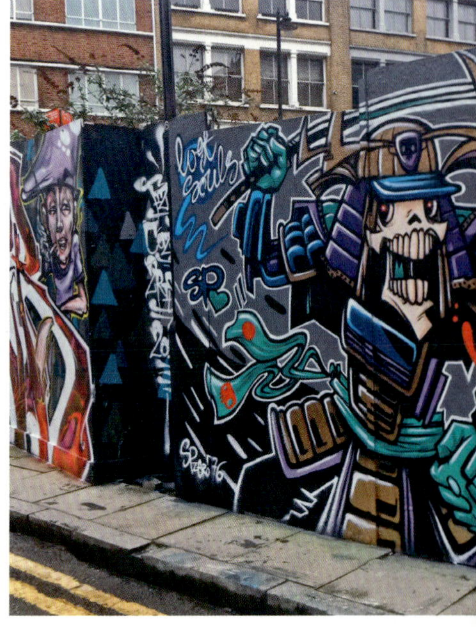

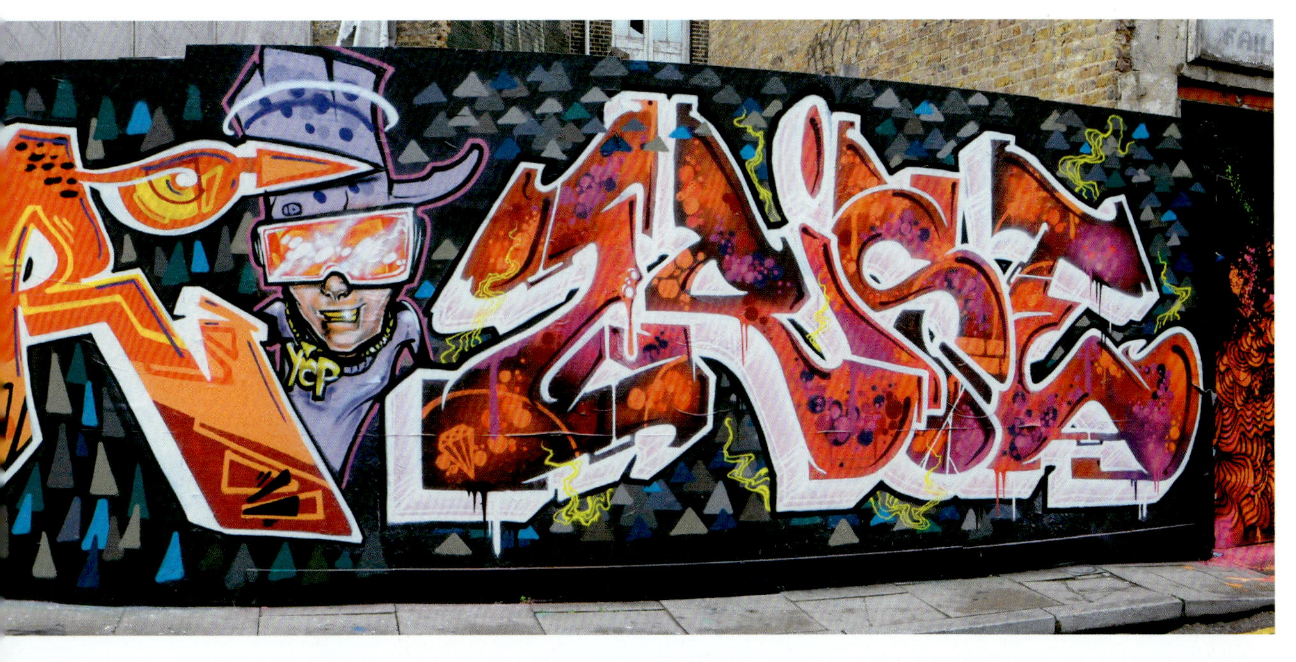

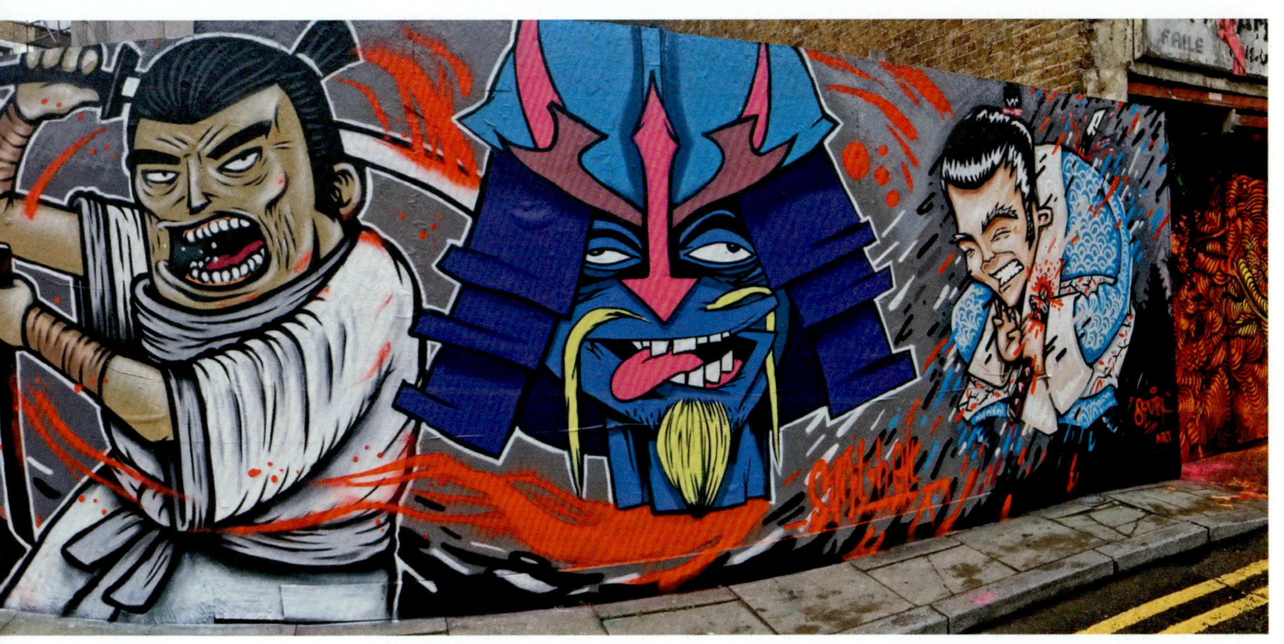

Stockwell Park Estate in South London is a great legal space where a small number of talented artists paint regularly, together with other less regular attendees. There is a virtuous cycle in Stockwell whereby great art is photographed and shared online; this encourages other artists to bring their best work too. Stockwell is not a place for weak pieces! In a 2012 survey by Community Trust Housing, a body that serves local residents in the Stockwell Park Estate, most residents stated they actively liked the graffiti and wanted it to remain. In other words: residents chose to keep graffiti on their estate. This is a powerful statement, because it shows that the negative connotations of the word graffiti are sometimes misplaced.

Stockwell contrasts with Leake Street in London, which is very close to Waterloo, the major train station. Great work is put up in Leake Street, but it tends not to last – the very high foot traffic and accessibility make it difficult to maintain the space; there is not the same investment of effort from the artist community and so the average quality of work is lower. This is not necessarily a bad thing; Leake Street has a reputation whereby anyone can go along and paint, and it's important that such places exist, otherwise less experienced artists would not have spaces where they can practise legally. Leake Street is not visible from any residences, only by pedestrians going to or from the station, so the average quality is probably less important from a neighbour's point of view.

PAGES 288-9, FROM TOP:
Cazer, Tizer One and Two
Rise/UK's The Lost Souls
Crew (from left to right:
SPzero76, Captain Kris,
Si Mitchell and Squirl).

CLOCKWISE FROM RIGHT:
UK's Bonzai/Bonzai/UK's
Solo-One.

PAGES 292-3:
The full wall features
Solo One, Lovepusher and
Bonzai. The detailed
pieces are both by UK's
Lovepusher.

PAGES 294-5:
A huge production in
Trellick Tower, West
London, featuring work
by Vibes, Monster, Roids,
Zoer CSX, Rela, Ders,
Towns and more. The
pieces shown in detail
are by Roids MSK and
France's Zoer CSX.

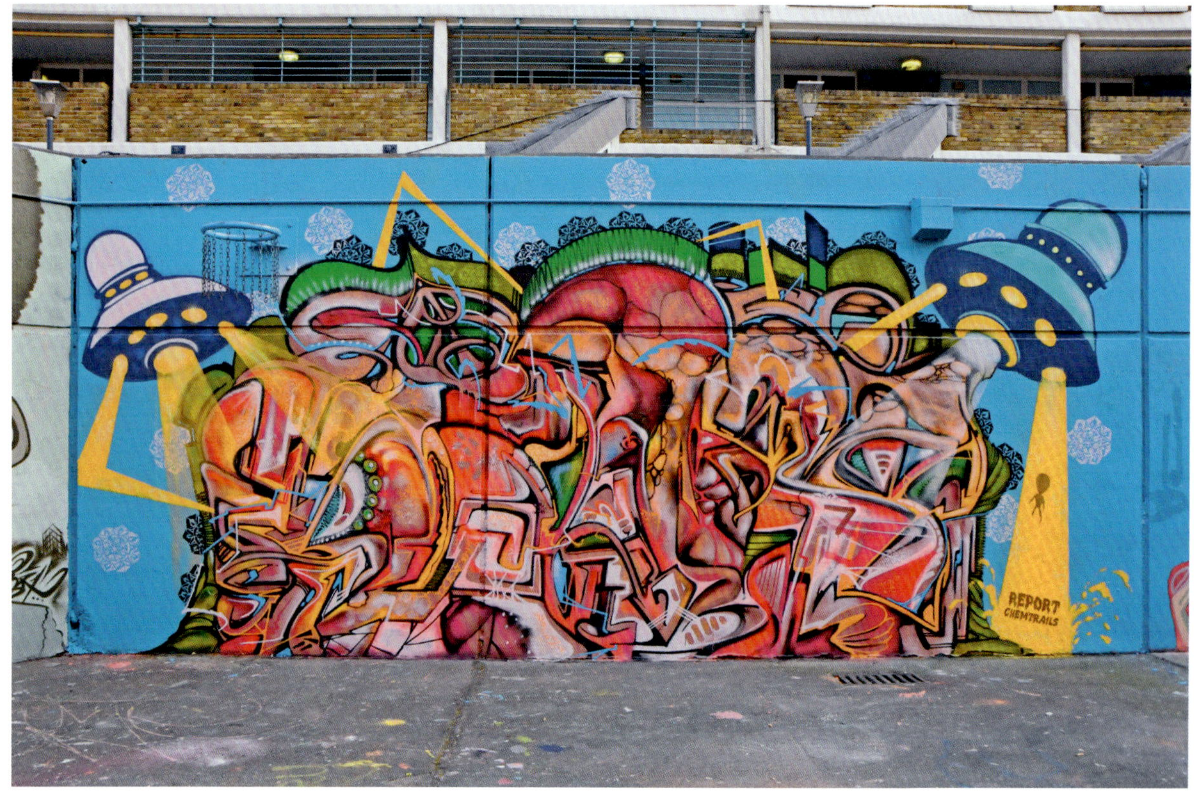

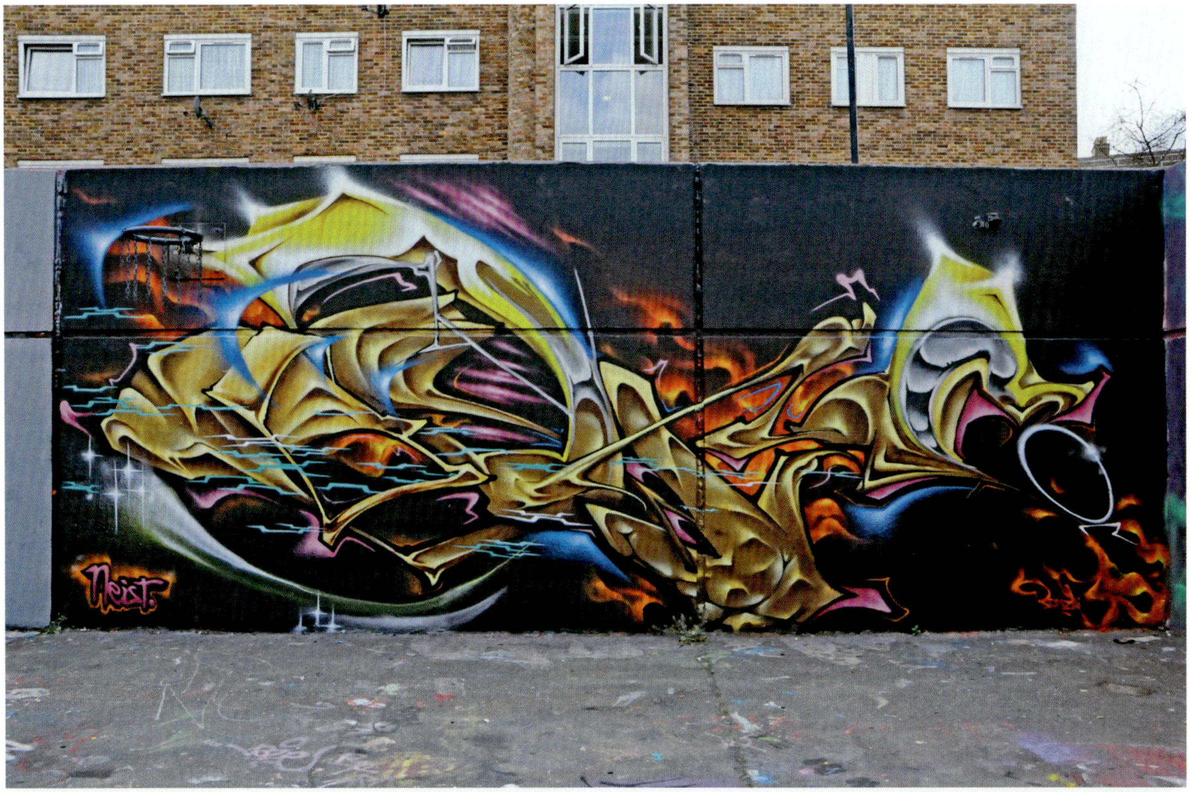

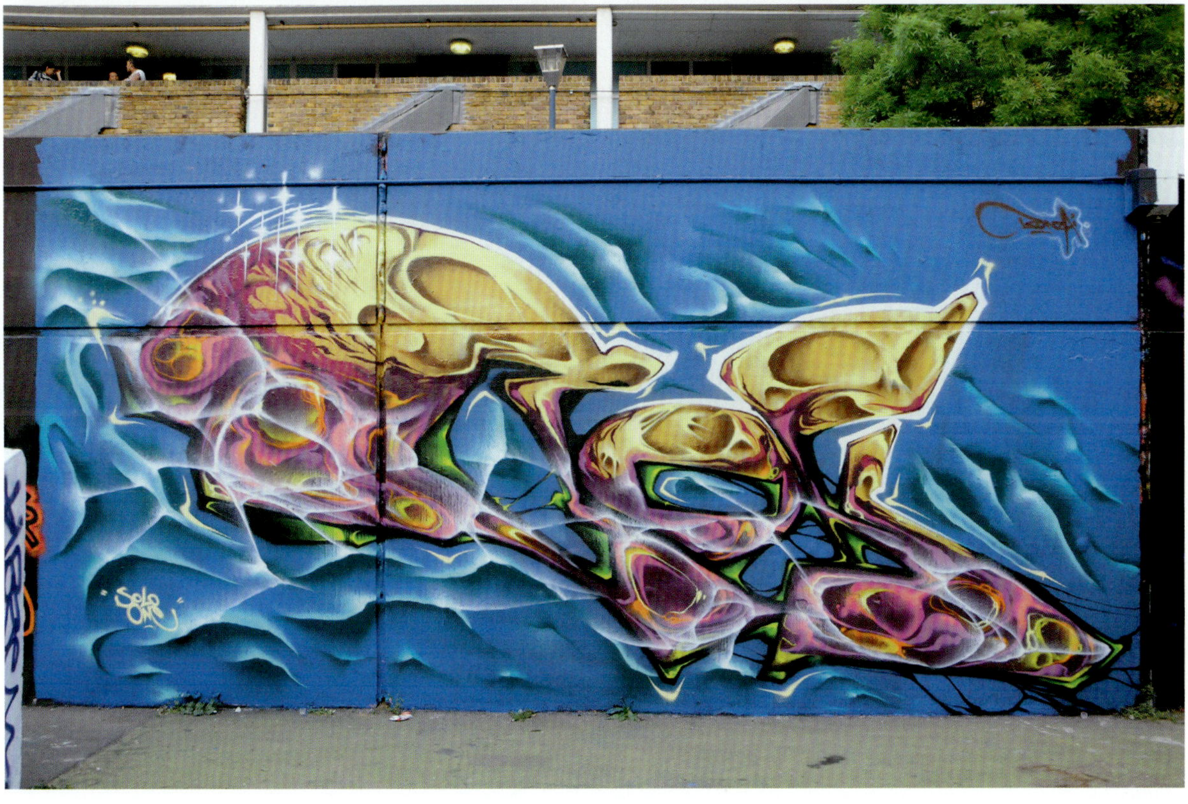

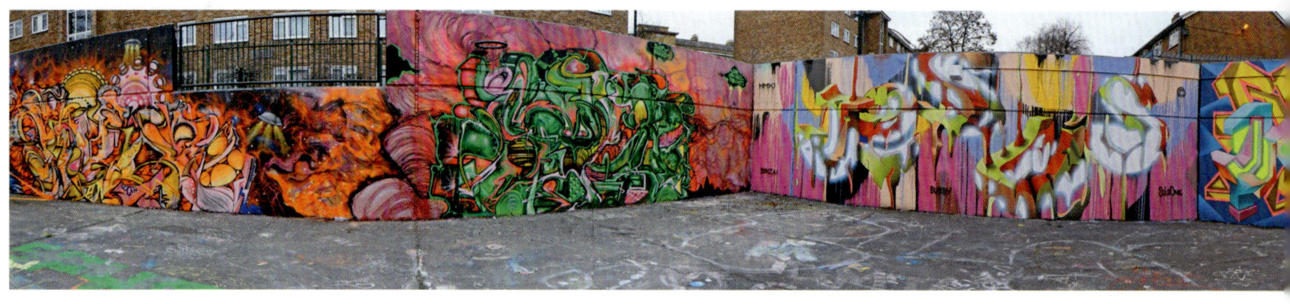

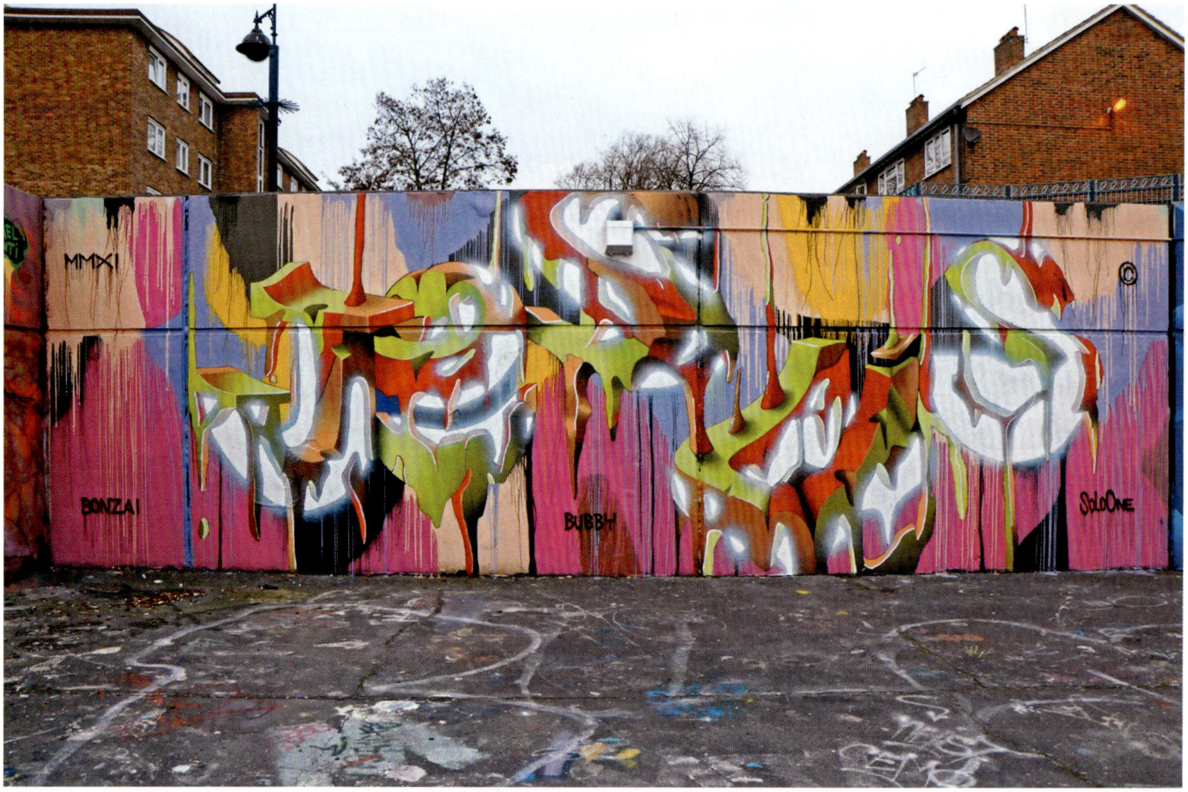

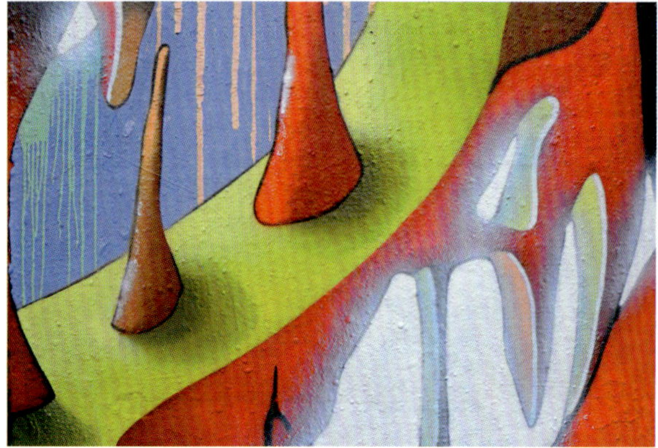

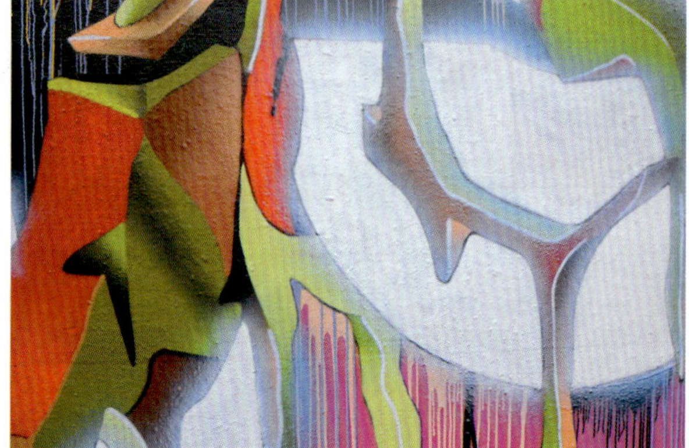

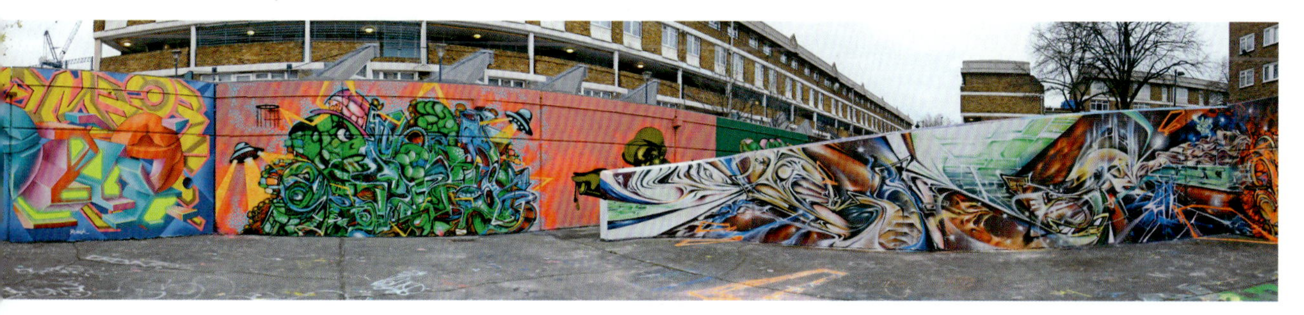

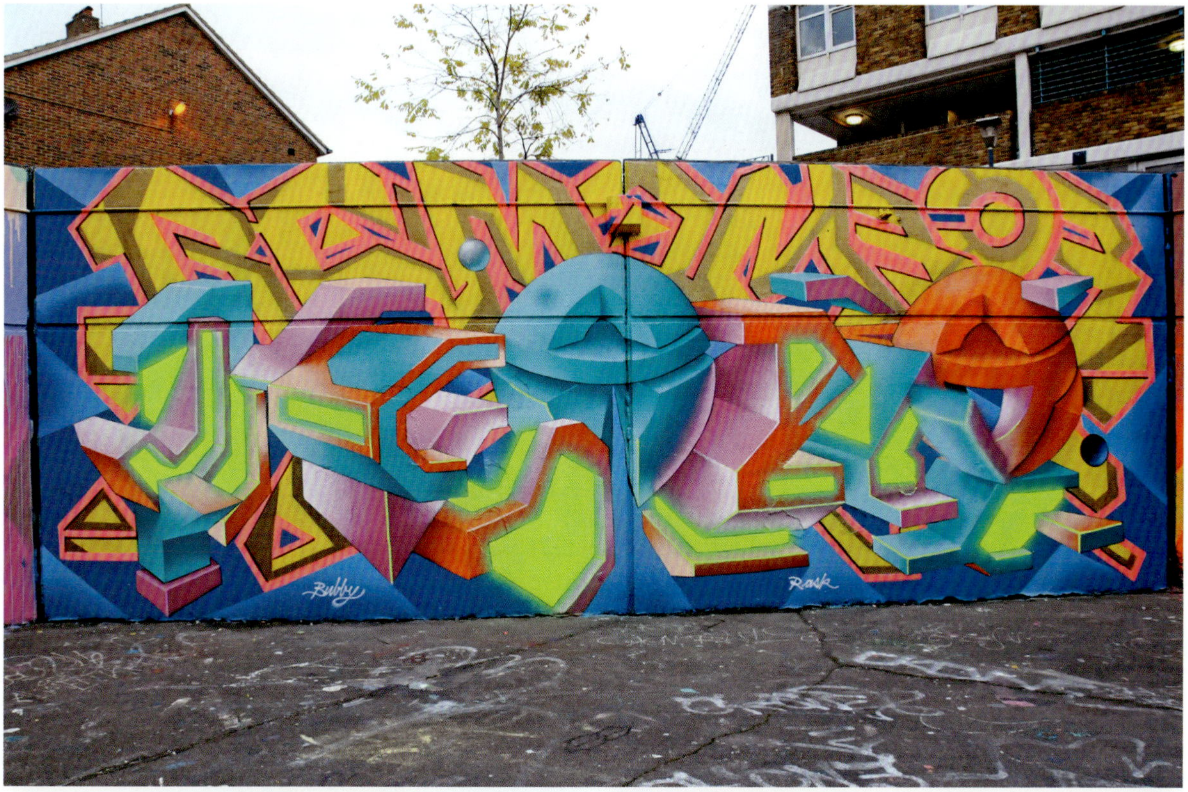

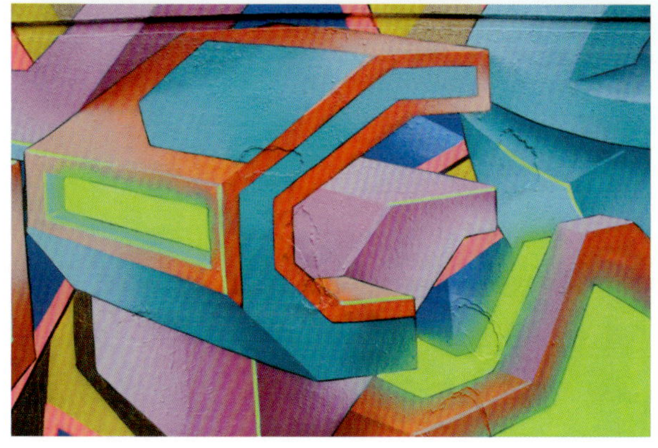

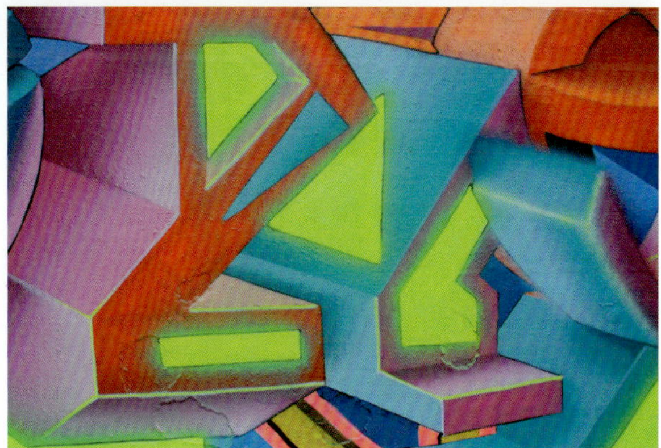

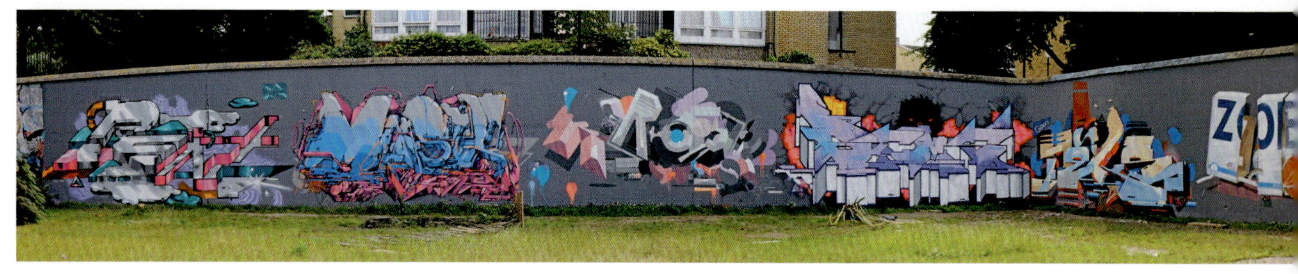

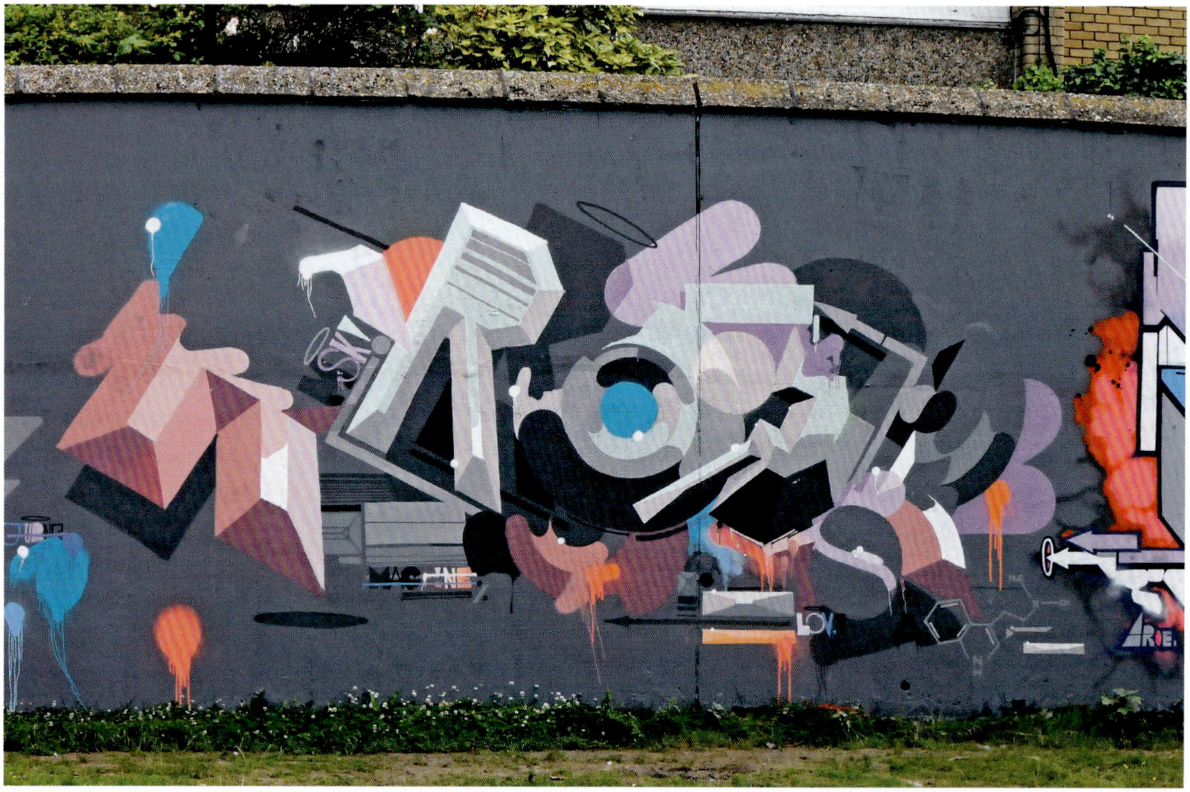

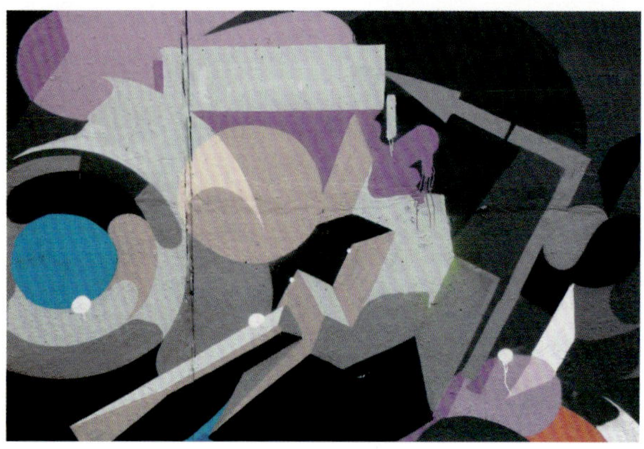

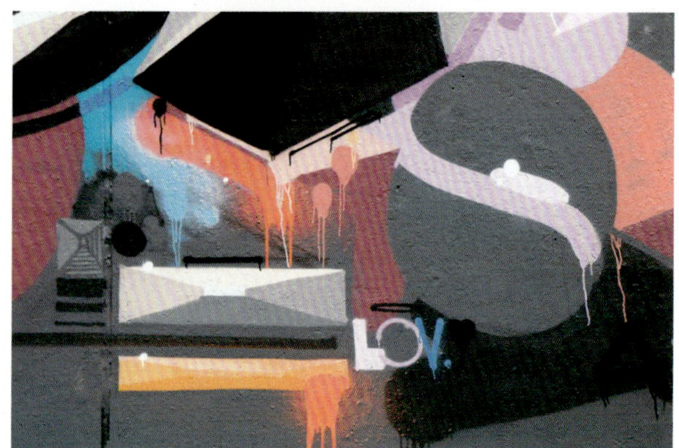

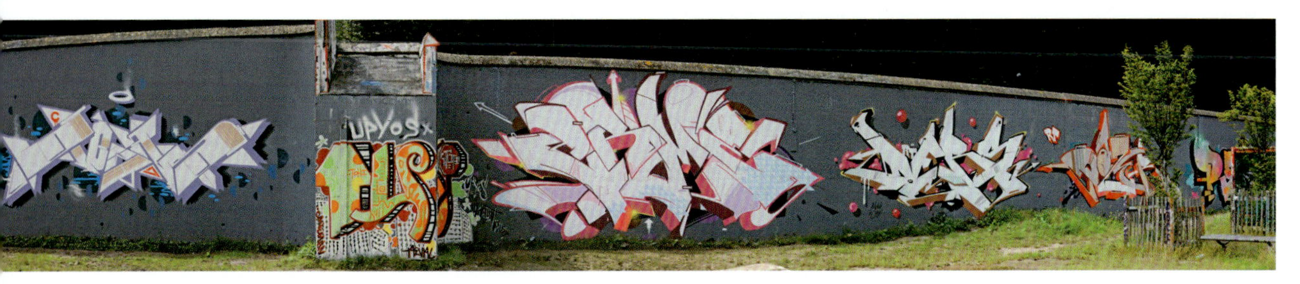

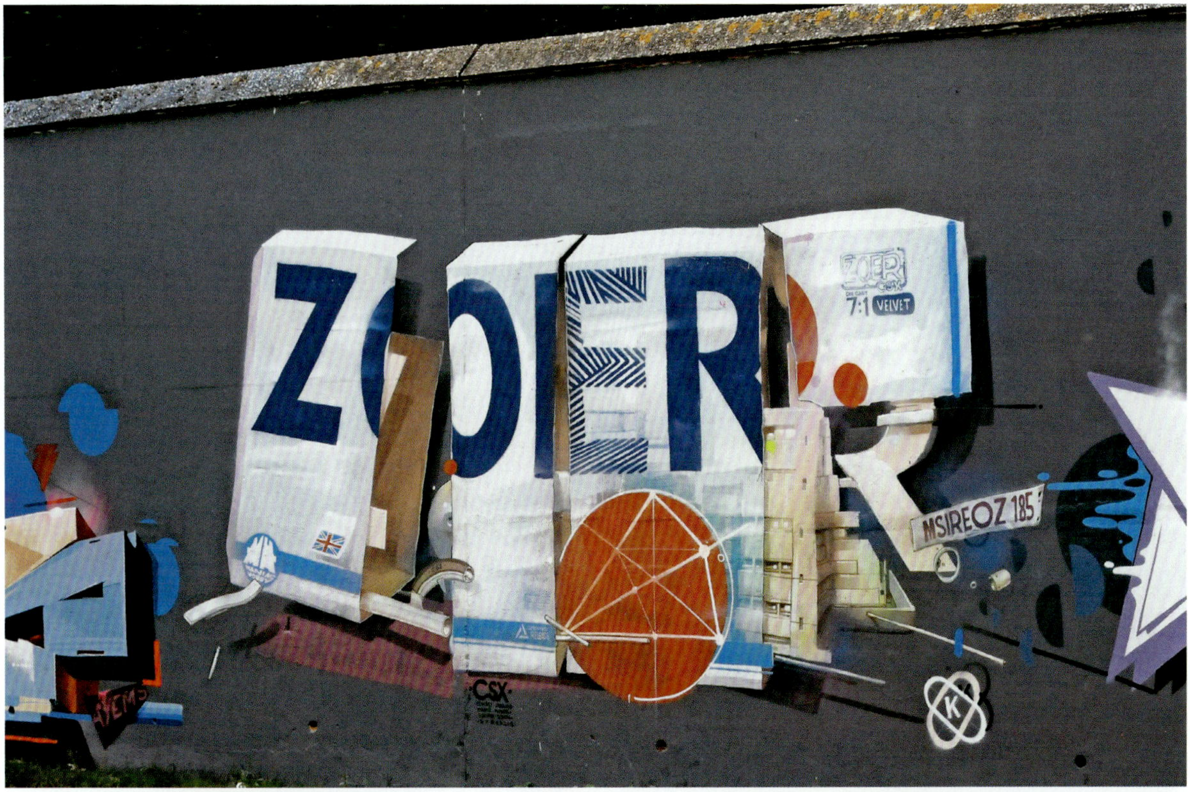

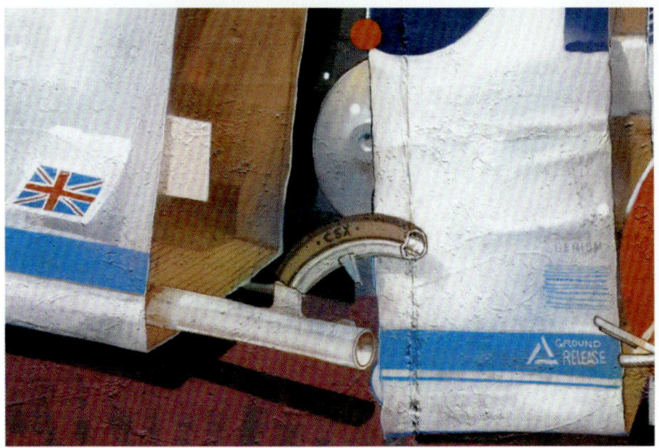

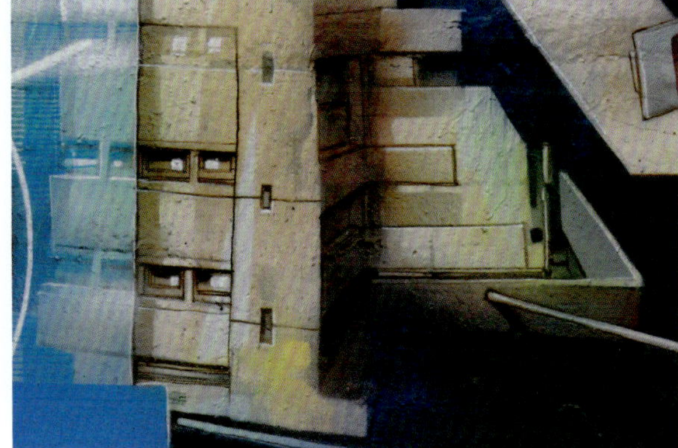

The public nature of street art makes it a great tool for artist-activists. There are many successful and lauded artists producing work on the streets that expresses their political and social spirit.

Mundano, from São Paulo, uses his art to support the working poor: the Cartadores, who collect trash in São Paulo to sell for recycling. They are not homeless, they support themselves and they help to address an environmental problem. By painting their carts, Mundano is highlighting their value to society – they deserve recognition when they are often dismissed.

American artist Ron English, on the other hand, has a different focus, satirizing various aspects of American life from brands to politics. The social and political commentary of artists like Mundano and Ron English ensure that at least some street work will keep its relevance and impact beyond mere technical prowess.

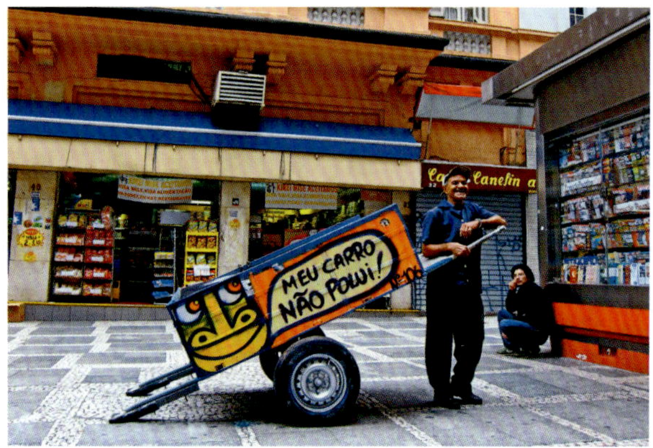

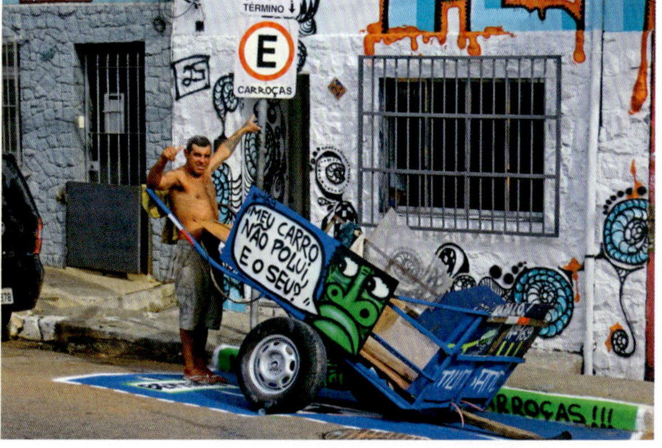

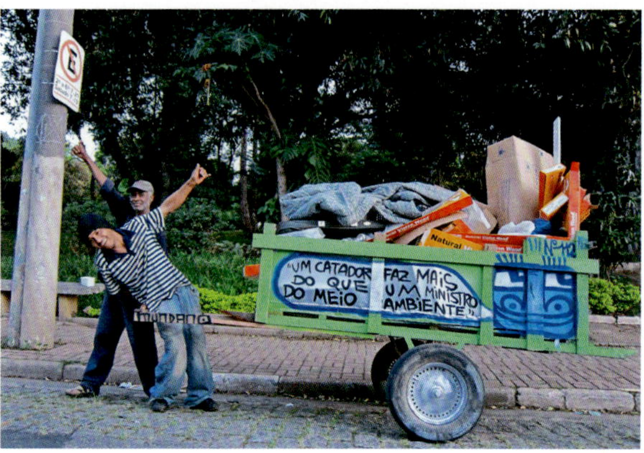

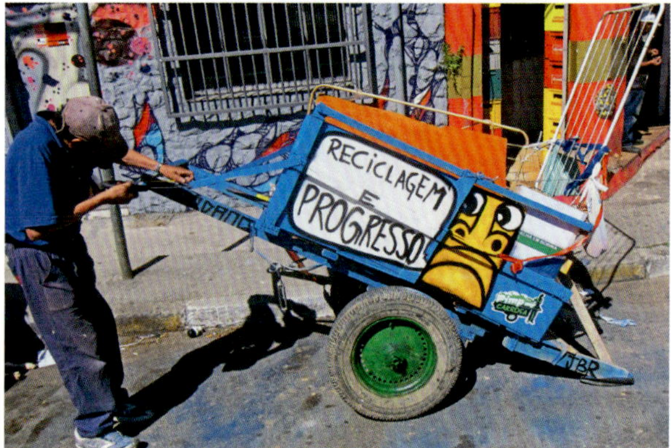

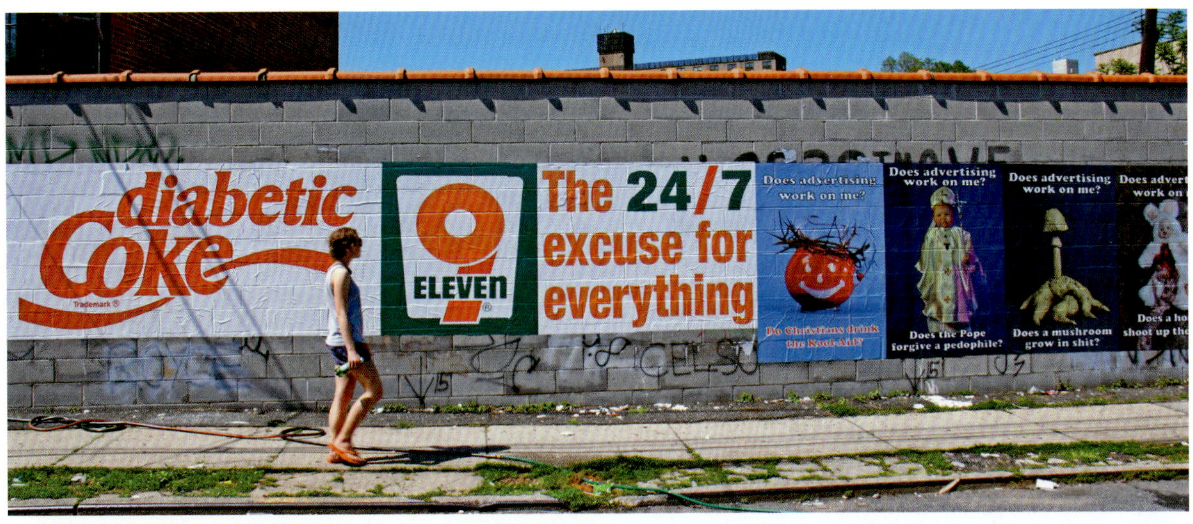

diabetic Coke
Trademark ®
9 ELEVEN
The 24/7 excuse for everything
Does advertising work on me?
Do Christians drink the Kool-Aid?
Does advertising work on me?
Does the Pope forgive a pedophile?
Does advertising work on me?
Does a mushroom grow in shit?
Does advertising work on me?
Does a ho shoot up the

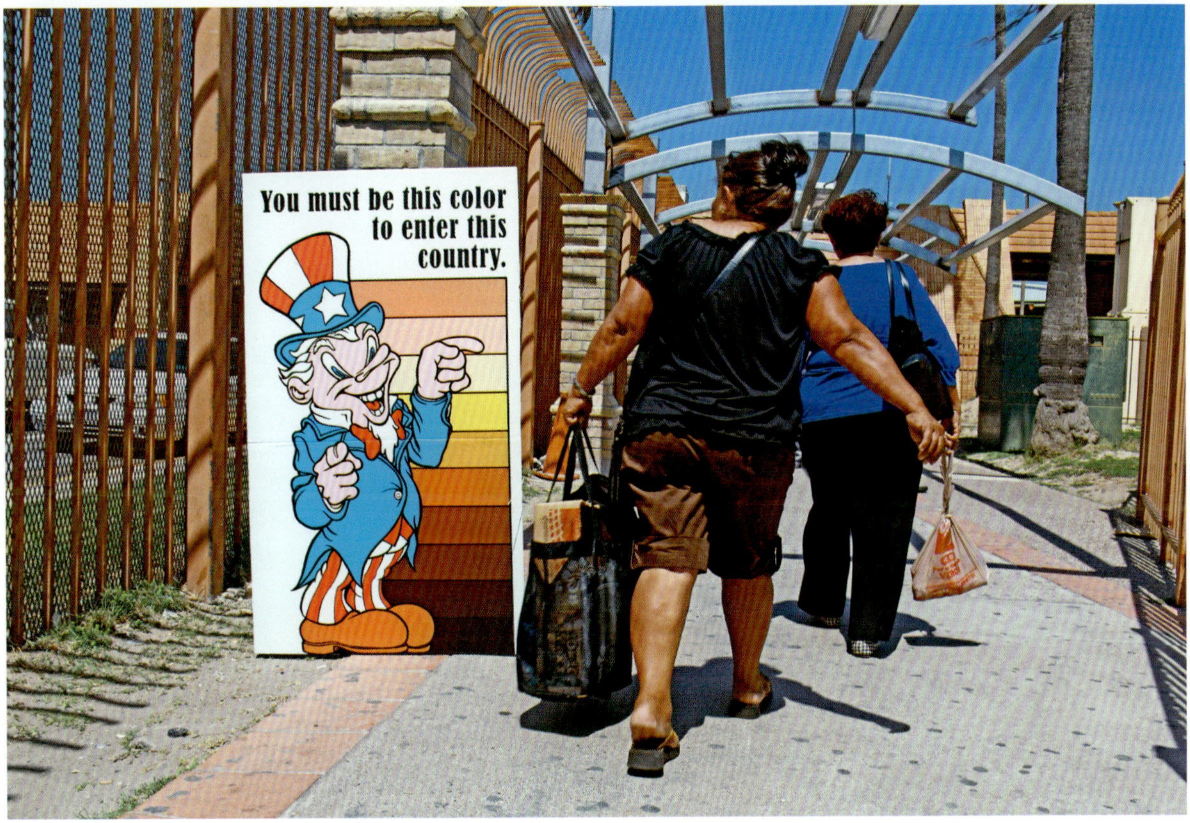

You must be this color to enter this country.

Conclusion

This shows how early we are in the development of street art and our understanding of it: the directions this book has highlighted within street art show wildly different art forms that have little in common other than that they are expressed on city walls. We already know that these art forms are different from traditional gallery-based art and we're only just discovering new possibilities for calligraphy, font work, photorealism, etc.

As street art and graffiti continue to spread around the world, mixing with local norms and materials, we can look forward to our ideas of what street art is being shattered again and again. Art from the fringes of established culture will then feed back and influence countries that have a longer history of street art traditions.

Graffiti made illegally will remain as long as the appeal of being a rebel remains. Improvements in security only set the bar higher and add to the appeal of writing on trains for the dedicated hardcore. The inwardly focused graffiti culture is persistent and resourceful, and whatever the constraints, there will always be some manifestation of graffiti that remains.

On the legal side of street art and graffiti, there is an increasing number of opportunities for the production of larger-scale and more refined work. There is little sign of this trend abating, despite the tendency for media attention to dip in and out as fashion dictates.

Global Street Art exists to celebrate and support street art and artists internationally, as well as the positive impact they can have on public space. Photography is the only permanent record of street art, and photographs of the best pieces make a strong case for painted cities. Looking forward, it is inevitable that a street art museum will exist one day and that is how we see ourselves. We want to build a permanent physical museum dedicated to supporting street artists, challenging the notion that museums are strictly indoor entities.

This is a book about public space and the cities in which we choose to live. By showing beautiful international examples of street art and graffiti we ask you to imagine a more painted world. If another visual order is possible, so is another way of experiencing our cities and another way of living: the writing is on the wall.

Index of artists

3Dom www.facebook.com/3dom22
www.globalstreetart.com/3dom
45 RPM www.thebearded45.co.uk

Aakash Nihalani www.aakashnihalani.com
Above www.goabove.com
Acme www.facebook.com/AcmeOficial
Ador www.ador.book.fr
www.globalstreetart.com/ador
Agotok
Aislap www.aislap.com
Alice Pasquini www.alicepasquini.com
www.globalstreetart.com/alice-pasquini
Anus-1
Apex-One www.theapexer.com
Aroe www.aroemsk.com
Askew www.askew1.com
Astro www.astrograff.com
Ayer

Bastardilla www.bastardilla.org
Be Free
Belin www.belin.es
Berok www.berokart.com
Bier en Brood Collective www.bierenbrood.nl
Big Bruno www.brunobig.com
Binho www.binhoribeiro.com.br
Bio www.tatscru.net
Bisual

Blaqk www.blaqk2.tumblr.com
Bom'k www.damentalvaporz.com
Bonzai www.facebook.com/thedavebonzai
Boortorrie www.lastplak.com
Brigada Neotropica
Broken Fingaz Crew www.brokenfingaz.com

C215 www.c215.com
Carlos Muñoz www.carlosmunyoz.blogspot.co.uk
Cere www.globalstreetart.com/cere
Cern www.cernesto.com
Chapu
Chase www.theartofchase.com
Cheo www.cheo.co.uk
China Girl www.chinagirltile.com
Chor Boogie www.chorboogie.com
Chu www.schudio.co.uk
Claudio Ethos www.twitter.com/EthosSP
www.globalstreetart.com/ethos
Clet Abraham www.twitter.com/CletAbraham
Conor Harrington
www.conorsaysboom.wordpress.com
Cranio www.cranioartes.com
Cristian Blanxer www.cristianblanxer.com
Cristian Sonda www.cristiansonda.com
www.globalstreetart.com/cristian-sonda
Cry www.flickr.com/photos/cryola
Cuellimangui www.flickr.com/photos/cuellimangui

D2F Crew (includes Ebola)
Dabs & Myla www.dabsmyla.com
Dado www.imdado.com
Daim www.daim.org
Dan Kitchener www.dankitchener.co.uk
  www.globalstreetart.com/dank
Dan Witz www.danwitz.com
David Walker www.artofdavidwalker.com
Days One www.daysone.com
Deb www.deb.net.au
Ders www.globalstreetart.com/ders
Disk www.facebook.com/monllordavid
Does www.digitaldoes.com
Dolk www.dolk.no
Dome www.domeone.de
Drew
Dulk www.dulk.es
  www.globalstreetart.com/dulk
Dust www.davidstegmann.de
DV8 www.graffixcreative.com
DXTR www.flickr.com/dxtrs

Eco www.marceloeco.com
Eine www.einesigns.co.uk
El Chico Iwana www.chicoiwana.blogspot.co.uk
el Marian www.facebook.com/elmariantedomenico
  www.globalstreetart.com/elmarian
El Niño de las Pinturas aka Sex
  www.elninodelaspinturas.es
eL Seed www.elseed-art.com
EMA www.florenceblanchard.com
Eme www.emedemati.com
Eoin www.artbyeoin.com
  www.globalstreetart.com/eoin
Estria www.estria.com
ETAM Cru www.etamcru.com
Etnik www.etnikproduction.com
  www.globalstreetart.com/etnik
Ever www.eversiempre.com
Ezra-One www.ezraone.com

Faif www.pausampera.com
Faith 47 www.faith47.com
Faunagraphic www.faunagraphic.com
  www.globalstreetart.com/faunagraphic
Feik www.feikfrasao.tumblr.com
  www.globalstreetart.com/feik
Fikos www.fikos.gr
  www.globalstreetart.com/fikos
Fin DAC www.findac.tumblr.com
Finok www.finok.com.br

Fintan Magee www.fintanmagee.com
  www.globalstreetart.com/fintan-magee
Flesh Beck Crew www.instagram.com/brfbc
  www.instagram.com/marcioswk
Flix Robotico www.globalstreetart.com/flix
Flying Fortress www.teddytroops.net
Fukt www.fukt.com.au

Gaser www.facebook.com/6aser
Gnasher www.gnashermurals.com
  www.globalstreetart.com/gnasher
Gr170 www.gr170.com
Graphis www.instagram.com/graphis_ar
Gris-One www.grisone.tumblr.com
  www.globalstreetart.com/grisone
Guido van Helten www.guidovanhelten.com
  www.globalstreetart.com/guido-van-helten

Hamilton Yokota aka Titifreak www.tfreak.com
Hendrik Beikirch aka ECB
  www.hendrikbeikirch.com
Herakut www.herakut.de
Hot Tea www.flickr.com/hotandtea

Ima-One www.imaone.com
Indigo www.indigosadventures.wordpress.com
Inkie www.inkie.co.uk
Ino www.ino.net
  www.globalstreetart.com/ino
Inti www.inti.cl
Invader www.space-invaders.com
Isaac Cordal www.cementeclipses.com

Jack (TML) www.instagram.com/jack_tml
  www.globalstreetart.com/jack-tml
Jaz www.francofasoli.com.ar
Jean Linnhoff www.jeanlinnhoff.com
Jeaze www.jeaze-resa.com
  www.globalstreetart.com/jeaze-oner
JNJ Crew www.facebook.com/jnjcrew
John Fekner www.johnfekner.com
Joys www.joys.it
JPS www.twitter.com/JPSArtist1
  www.globalstreetart.com/jps
Just Cobe www.justcobe.blogspot.de

Kaja Man www.kajaman471.blogspot.com.br
Kalama
Kashink www.kashink.com
Kem & Mef www.kemefinc.co.uk
Kislow www.flickr.com/photos/kislow

Kobra www.eduardokobra.com
Kofie www.keepdrafting.com
Kolja Reuter
Kram www.kram.es
Krio www.flickr.com/krio_special-k

Labrona www.labrona.net
Lake www.lake-oner.de
Lango Oliveira www.langooliveira.com
Law-One
Lelo www.flickr.com/people/joaolelo
Loomit www.loomit.de
Lovepusher www.flickr.com/lovepusher

Macism
Macs www.aboutmacs.it
   www.globalstreetart.com/macs
Made 154 www.made514.com
   www.globalstreetart.com/made514
Madruga & Nitcho
Makatron www.makatron.com
Malakkai www.malakkai.es
Malarky www.malarko.com
Maniaks Crew www.facebook.com/mnksworks
Marcelo Ment www.marceloment.com.br
Martin Ron www.martinron.com.ar
Mate
Mateo Lara www.twitter.com/MateoLara
Mear-One www.mearone.com
Meggs www.houseofmeggs.com
Mies www.facebook.com/miesoneart
Mobstr www.mobstr.org
Mone e Celo www.facebook.com/MoneCelo
   www.globalstreetart.com/mone-e-celo
Mr Dheo www.mrdheo.com
Mr Thoms www.thoms.it
   www.globalstreetart.com/misterthoms
MTO www.facebook.com/mto.page
MüCke32 www.muecke32.com
Mundano www.flickr.com/artetude
Myla www.dabsmyla.com
Mysterious Al www.mysteriousal.com
   www.globalstreetart.com/mysteriousal

Napol www.napoleone.es
   www.globalstreetart.com/napol
Nash www.iam-nash.com
Natalia Rak www.nataliarak.blogspot.co.uk
Nemos www.whoisnemos.com
   www.globalstreetart.com/nemos
Never www.noentrydesign.com

Never 2501 www.2501.org.uk
Never Crew www.nevercrew.com
   www.globalstreetart.com/nevercrew
Nicer www.tatscru.net
Nicky Nahafahik www.ninakleurt.nl
Nicolina www.nicolinaart.com
Ninguem Dormi
Nomerz www.nomerz.com
Nychos www.rabbiteyemovement.at

Oco Sapiens www.flickr.com/ocosapiens
Odeith www.odeith.com
   www.globalstreetart.com/odeith
Olek www.oleknyc.com
Ostrem www.atleostrem.com

P3dro Perelman www.pedro-perelman.com
Pao www.paopao.it
   www.globalstreetart.com/pao
Paris www.paris1974.com
Pariz-One www.pariz-one.com
Peeta www.peeta.net
Peque www.pequevrs.blogspot.com.au
Pez www.el-pez.com
   www.globalstreetart.com/pezbarcelona
Phibs www.phibs.com
Phlegm www.phlegmcomics.com
Piguan www.flickr.com/photos/piguan
Pøbel www.pobel.no
Pref www.instagram.com/pref_id
Prozak www.facebook.com/mazuprozak

Rallito X www.rallitox.org
Rasko www.facebook.com/rasko187
Raspazjan www.raspazjan.com
Rea One
Reab www.vincentdubos.be
Recal www.recalone.com
Reka www.rekaone.com
Rela
Renato Hunto www.huntoland.com
   www.globalstreetart.com/renato-hunto
Rens-One www.rensone.com
Replete www.repletes.net
   www.globalstreetart.com/replete
Revok www.revok1.com
Risk www.riskrock.com
Roadsworth www.roadsworth.com
Rocket01 www.rocket01.co.uk
   www.globalstreetart.com/rocket01
Roids www.twitter.com/ROIDSMSK

Ron English www.popaganda.com
Rone www.r-o-n-e.com
   www.globalstreetart.com/rone
Run www.runabc.org
   www.globalstreetart.com/run

Saber www.saberone.com
Saiko
Sat-One www.satone.de
Scene-One
Sdkaroe www.sdkaroe.de
Sean Hart www.seanhart.org
Seher-One www.seherone.com
Seize aka Happy Wallmaker www.seizegraff.free.fr
   www.globalstreetart.com/happywallmaker
Seth Globepainter www.globepainter.com
Seyo Crew www.seyo.ch
Shai Dahan www.thevacantwall.com
Shaka www.shaka1.fr
Shé
Shepard Fairey www.obeygiant.com
Sheryo www.sheryoart.com
Shoe ww.nielsshoemeulman.com
Simon Silaidis www.urbancalligraphy.com
Sipros www.facebook.com/siprosgraffiti
Skount www.skountworks.com
   www.globalstreetart.com/skount
Smates www.smates.be
   www.globalstreetart.com/smates
Smug www.facebook.com/smuggraffiti
Snub 23 www.snub23.com
Sokram www.sokramutante.blogspot.ca
Solo-One www.soloone.blogspot.com
Sowat www.sowat1.com
Spaik www.facebook.com/spaik45
   www.globalstreetart.com/spaik
Spore www.flickr.com/sporegraffiti
   www.globalstreetart.com/spore
Stik www.stik.org.uk
Suiko www.suiko1.com

Tasso www.ta55o.de
Tec www.tecalbum.com
SPzero76 www.spzero76.com
   www.globalstreetart.com/spzero76
Captain Kris www.kristiandouglas.com
   www.globalstreetart.com/captainkris
Squirl www.squirl-art.com
   www.globalstreetart.com/squirlart
Si Mitchell www.simitchell.co.uk
   www.globalstreetart.com/simitchell

Tika www.tikathek.com
Tinho www.walternomura.blogspot.co.uk
Trans-One
TSF Crew www.tsfcrew.com

Urok www.facebook.com/pages/UROKone-PIEcrew/552359561453639

Veng www.robotswillkill.com
Vexta www.vexta.com.au
   www.globalstreetart.com/vexta
Vhils www.alexandrefarto.com
Vibes www.anysurface.co.uk
Vinie www.viniegraffiti.com
   www.globalstreetart.com/vinie
Vitae Viazi Crew www.facebook.com/vitaeviazi
Vitché www.vitche.com.br
Vyal www.vyalone.com

Wais www.wais1.tumblr.com
Won ABC www.wonabc.com

Yok www.theyok.com
Yosh www.yosh.mn

Zadok www.drzadok.com
Zed1 www.zed1.it
Zedz www.zedz.org
Zezao www.zezaoarts.com.br
Zoer CSX www.facebook.com/zoerism

Acknowledgments

For their ongoing support I would like to thank my family and my business partner, Global Street Art's co-founder, Koenraad. I would like to thank Dan for building an amazing platform and James for his boundless enthusiasm. I would also like to thank all of the artists, photographers, fans and friends for the time and help along the way. The world needs more people like Kevin and Mark Hat. Thank you too for buying this book and supporting the movement. A street art museum is inevitable; let's hope we get there sooner rather than later. We're moving forwards!

All photographs are from the collection of Global Street Art with the exception of those listed below. The author and Octopus Publishing would like to acknowledge and thank the following for providing additional photographs: **Aakash Nihalani** 174; **Above** 205a; **Ador** 89; **Askew** 45b; **Astro** 164b; **Belin** 200b; **Big Bruno** 118b; **The Black Duke Project** 286, 287; **Blaqk** 215; **Brian Albert** 27; **CBS Crew's Mear-One** 39a, 39b; **Chapu** 84al, 84ar; **Chor Boogie** 40; **Cristian Blanxer** 85a; **Cristian Sonda** 238a; **Cuellimangui** 84b, 85b; **Dado** 191b; **Dan** 55a; **Dank** 60a, 60b; **David Bushell** 139; **Disk & Dust** 98b; **Does** (from Brazil) 165b; **Does** (from The Netherlands) 161, **Does & Nash** 162a; **Dome** 71a, 244b; **Dulk** 83, 222a; **Dust** 65a; **El Marian** 127b; **eL Seed** 212a, 212b, 213a, 213b; **Eme** 207; **Eoin** 203ar, 203b; **Etnik** 115, 190b; **Ezra-One & Mate** 98a; **Faith 47** 154a, 157, 285b; **Fintan Magee** 150; **Flix Robotico** 142, 143, 170; **Gaser** 201, 229a; **Goulven Gonthier** 248; **Gris-One** 140b; **Gualicho** 128, 245a; **Guido Van Helten** 153a; **Hendrik Beikirch** 31a, 31b; **Hot Tea** 179a, 179b; **Ima-One & Suiko** 154b; **Ink Crew** 141b; **Inkie** 184a; **Ino** 202b, 203c; **Inti** 136; **Isaac Cordal** 175a, 175b; **Jack from TML** 145b; **JNJ Crew** 155; **John Fekner** 26a, 26b; **Joys** 188; **JPS** 169b; **Just Cobe** 202a; **Kashink** 93a, 93b; **Kislow** 103a; **Kislow & Seth Globepainter** 102b; **Labrona** 45ar; **Lake** 119a, 240; **Macs & Etnik** 100b; **Made 154** 189a, 189b; **Makatron** 156b, 228, 284; **Maniaks Crew** 86b; **Maniaks Crew & Draw** 86a; **Martin Ron** 126b; **Meeting of Styles** 264, 265; **Melissa Findley** 152a; **Mone & Celo** 124a; **Mr Dhe** 251; **Mr Thoms** 239a, 243a; **MSK Crew's Saber** 38; **MTO** 90; **Mundano** 296; **Napol** 76a, 76b, 77; **Nash** 232bl; **Natalia Rak** 243b; **Nemos** 100a, 101a; **Never** 30a, 30b; **Never Crew** 242; **Nicky Nahafahik** 178a; **Nomerz** 246b, 247b; **Pao** 185; **Pariz-One** 162b; **Peeta** 192a, 193; **Pez** 252b; **Phlegm** 226a; **Prozak** 118a; **Rallito X** 68; **Rasko** 164a; **Raspazjan** 102al, 102ar; **Reka** 285a; **Rensone** 94a, 94b; **Replete** 196b, 197b; **Roadsworth** 249b, 255a, 255b; **Rone** 152b, 153b; **Ron English** 297; **Saiko** 244a, 247a; **Sat-One** 64a; **Sean Hart** 206; **Seher-One** 141a; **Seize aka Happy Wallmaker** 92a; **Shai Dahan** 144; **Shaka** 184b; **Simon Silaidis & Fikos** 211a, 211b; **Skount** 69a; **Smates** 220; **Sokram** 82; **Sowat** 214; **Spaik** 140a; **Spore** 60c; **Suiko** 92b; **Tec** 254; **Tony Brown** 88; **TSF Crew** 196a, 197a; **Vinie** 239b, 249a; **Vitae Viazi Crew** 104a, 104b; **Vyal** 45al; **Wais** 163a, 163b; **Zed1** 166a, 166b, 223b, 224b.
(a: above, b: below, c: centre, l: left, r: right)